MODERN REAL ESTATE
PRACTICE IN
TEXAS

ELEVENTH EDITION

CHERYL PEAT NANCE, Ed.D., DREI, CREI

Dearborn™
Real Estate Education

This publication is designed to provide accurate and authoritative information in regard to the subject matter covered. It is sold with the understanding that the publisher is not engaged in rendering legal, accounting, or other professional service. If legal advice or other expert assistance is required, the services of a competent professional person should be sought.

Vice President: Roy Lipner
Publisher: Evan Butterfield
Development Editor: David Cirillo
Production Manager: Bryan Samolinski
Senior Typesetter: Janet Schroeder
Creative Director: Lucy Jenkins

Published by Dearborn™ Real Estate Education
a division of Dearborn Financial Publishing, Inc.®
155 N. Wacker Drive
Chicago, Illinois 60606-1719
(312) 836-4400
http://www.dearbornRE.com

Printed in the United States of America.

02   03   04   10   9   8   7   6   5   4   3   2

Library of Congress Cataloging-in-Publication Data

Nance, Cheryl Peat
    Modern real estate practice in Texas / Cheryl Peat Nance.—11th ed.
      p. cm.
    Includes index.
    ISBN 0-7931-3483-8
    1. Vendors and purchasers—Texas.   2. Real Estate Business—Law and legislation—Texas.   I. Title.

    KFT1326.M6   2001
    346.76404'37—dc21   2001047835

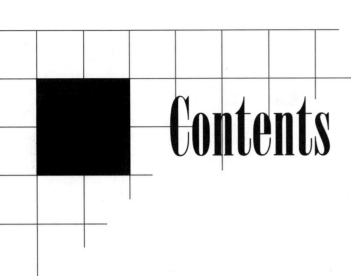

Contents

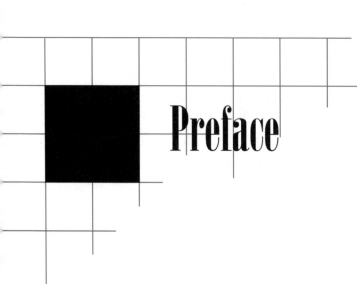

Preface

The new millennium has arrived—and with it, the promise of an ever-increasing pace for business. The use of computers and other advanced technologies is essential for success as a new agent in the real estate industry. The 11th Edition of *Modern Real Estate Practice in Texas* includes explanations of new and projected technologies affecting the real estate industry and Internet resources for both the agent and the consumer.

Although the new millennium is continuing to usher in technological changes, a basic knowledge of real estate laws, practices, and terminology is still essential for persons desiring to enter the industry. Whether you are preparing for a state licensing examination, fulfilling a college or university requirement, looking for specific guidance about buying a home or an investment property, or simply expanding your understanding of this fascinating field, you can rely on *Modern Real Estate Practice in Texas*, the recognized authority for accurate, comprehensive information in a format that is easy to use. Within the first 21 chapters, this text covers all of the topics required by the Texas Real Estate License Act in a principles core course. This text also provides a reference for persons employed in real estate-related positions within financial institutions, insurance companies, property management firms, or real estate departments of corporations.

In 1999 there were more than 5 million sales of existing homes in the United States alone, generating approximately $650 billion. More than 200,000 new real estate sales licenses are issued annually. Just as today's real estate market is challenging and complex, today's real estate students are increasingly sophisticated and demand a high level of expertise and efficiency. This 11th Edition of *Modern Real Estate Practice in Texas* meets those expectations. This edition contains revisions brought about by the 77th Legislative Session in 2001 as well as changes in governmental policy and industry practice and procedure. In addition, the book has been enhanced by

- Hot issues" such as real estate **technology** and the **environment.**
- *For Example* and **In Practice** paragraphs to illustrate key concepts, providing real-life explanations for further clarification of real estate principles.
- *Math Concepts* at relevant points in the chapters—where they would normally occur in a transaction—to help you understand the real-life

application of the mathematics of real estate. Chapter 19, Real Estate Mathematics, provides additional math applications for further study and review.

- ***Margin Notes*** to help direct your attention to important vocabulary terms, concepts, study tips, and related news.
- ***Exam Prep*** appendix information to assist in studying for the state licensing examinations.

In the new millennium as in the past, the fundamental goal of *Modern Real Estate Practice in Texas* is to help students understand the dynamics of the real estate industry and to assist students in preparing for the licensing exams. This text provides the tools necessary to develop a foundation for advanced study in the general practice of real estate or in any one of the real estate specialties. The questions at the end of each chapter provide the opportunity to apply the principles and tools presented in the text. To derive the maximum benefit from this textbook, become familiar with the key terms listed at the beginning of each chapter and the definitions included in the Glossary.

Modern Real Estate Practice in Texas was originally adapted from the classic text, *Modern Real Estate Practice* by Galaty, Allaway, and Kyle (1959), which has helped more than 3 million readers to obtain a critical edge as they enter the world of real estate. Permission to use the material in *Modern Real Estate Practice* has been granted to the author of this 11th edition of *Modern Real Estate Practice in Texas.* The 24 chapters herein cover the broad subject of real estate, together with real estate law and operating procedures that apply to the State of Texas.

Real estate practice in each state is controlled by federal laws and regulations as well as the respective state laws, regulations, and court decisions. Additionally, the practice of real estate in any specific location in Texas may be influenced by local agencies, bureaus, and organizations such as county and city governments or local real estate boards.

Statements of law in this book are general summaries that are not intended to substitute for an experienced legal counsel. Unique situations require specific application of the law. Therefore, this text should be used only as a general guideline and not as a final statement of the law on any given matter. The authors and editors assume no responsibility for any errors, omissions, or inadvertent misinterpretations of the law.

Acknowledgments

Thanks go to the members of the *Modern Real Estate Practice in Texas* Editorial Review Board, listed on the inside front cover, and to the following industry professionals in the Amarillo, Potter/Randall County area and in Austin who helped update the contents of this edition:

Carol Autry, Tax Assessor/Collector, Randall County
Patty Beard, Senior Underwriter
Dennis Cleaver, CPA, Accountant and Investment Counselor
Michele Fortunato, Attorney
Robert E. Keys, RPLS, Surveyor

Renil C. Linér, Commissioner, Texas Appraiser Licensing and
    Certification Board, Austin
Janette Litz, Associate Executive, Apartment Association of the Panhandle
Sara Messer, Escrow Officer
Oth Miller, Attorney, Title Company
Virginia Rhodes, SRA, Appraiser
Alan Stucky, Attorney
Texas Panhandle Builders' Association
Laurie Thomas, Chief Planner, City of Amarillo

Special credit is extended to the following groups for permission to use materials or forms: Texas Appraiser Licensing and Certification Board, Texas Association of REALTORS®, and Texas Real Estate Commission.

Special thanks goes to the late G. E. Irby, Texas series advisor to Real Estate Education Company® and author of the Fifth and Sixth Editions of this book.

Also, special thanks go to the 11th Edition reviewers whose hard work and attention to detail help keep this the best real estate principles book in Texas. This time around they were:

Peter C. Glover, Austin Community College
Rick Knowles, Capital Real Estate Training
Mary Milford, Collin County Community College

Cheryl Peat Nance, the author of the Seventh, Eighth, Ninth, Tenth, and Eleventh editions of *Modern Real Estate Practice in Texas* holds a BBA degree from Texas Tech University, an MBA degree from West Texas State University, and an EdD in Business Education from Texas Tech University. Nance has been a real estate practitioner in Amarillo, Texas, since 1978. She holds the Distinguished Real Estate Instructor (DREI) designation from the Real Estate Educators Association (REEA) and the Certified Real Estate Instructor (CREI) designation from the Texas Real Estate Teachers Association (TRETA). From 1994 to 1999, she served as the instructional coordinator for the CREI program in Texas. She is a past-president of TRETA (1992 conference year) and a senior instructor for the Real Estate Educators Association. Nance teaches real estate at Amarillo College. She is the owner-broker of Real Estate Investment Group in Amarillo, specializing in townhome sales, and CJ Investments, a property management company. She was the 1999 recipient of the Don Roose Award of Excellence given by the Texas Real Estate Teachers Association.

1 Introduction to Modern Real Estate Practice

Key Terms

agricultural real estate
commercial real estate
common law
industrial real estate
National Association of
REALTORS®

precedent
Realtist
REALTOR®
residential real estate
salesperson

seven sources of law
special-purpose real
 estate
Texas Real Estate
 License Act

OVERVIEW

The real estate business is "big" business; some type of real estate transaction occurs at every moment. A commercial leasing company rents space in a mall to an electronics store. The owner of a building rents an apartment to a retired couple. An appraiser gives an expert opinion of the value of 100 acres of farmland, which is now surrounded by residential subdivisions. A bank lends money to a professional corporation so it can purchase a medical office building. And, of course, the typical American family sells its old house and buys a bigger new home. All of this adds up to billions of dollars in revenue every year.

Real estate also is big business in terms of laws and regulations. Because real estate is a heavily regulated market, the real estate practitioner must be familiar with many sources of law on the federal, state, and local levels.

This chapter introduces students to the industry in general, as well as to many legal considerations that affect today's real estate professional.

REAL ESTATE—A BUSINESS OF MANY SPECIALIZATIONS

Despite the size and complexity of the real estate business, many people think of it as being made up of only brokers and salespersons. Actually, the real estate industry is much bigger than that. Appraisal, property management, financing, and property development are among the many separate businesses within the real estate field. To succeed in a complex industry, every real estate professional must have a basic knowledge of these specialties.

Brokerage. The business of bringing together people who are interested in making a real estate transaction is *brokerage.* Typically the *broker* acts as an *agent* of the buyer or seller (or both) in negotiating the sale, purchase, or rental of property. A **salesperson** is a licensee employed by or associated with a broker who conducts brokerage activities on behalf of the broker for a fee or commission. Brokerage is discussed further in Chapter 5.

Appraisal. The process of estimating the value of a parcel of real estate is *appraisal.* Although brokers must have some understanding of valuation as part of their training, qualified appraisers are employed when property is financed or sold by court order and large sums of money are involved. The appraiser must have sound judgment, experience, and a detailed knowledge of the methods of valuation. Appraisals for federally related loan transactions require a separate state license. Appraisal is covered in Chapter 14.

Property management. A real estate agent who operates a property for its owner is involved in *property management.* The property manager may be responsible for soliciting tenants, collecting rents, altering or constructing new space for tenants, monitoring insurance coverage, ordering repairs, and generally maintaining the property. The manager's basic responsibility is to protect the owner's investment and maximize the owner's return on the investment. Property management is discussed in Chapter 22.

Apartment locating. A *residential rental locator* matches landlords and tenants. Working as an independent contractor for several apartment complexes, the locator finds apartment units for prospective tenants, qualifies prospective tenants, and negotiates leases with the apartment complexes. A rental locator is generally paid by the owner of the apartments and must be licensed by the Texas Real Estate Commission (TREC).

Financing. The business of providing the funds necessary to complete real estate transactions is *financing.* Most transactions are financed by means of a mortgage loan, in which the property is pledged as security for the eventual repayment of the loan. Real estate financing is examined in Chapters 15 and 16.

Property inspection. A *real estate inspector* is generally hired by a prospective purchaser to inspect real property and to give an opinion as to the condition of the structural items, electrical items, mechanical systems, plumbing systems, or equipment. Property inspectors must be licensed by the Texas Real Estate Commission.

Property development. The profession of *property development* includes the work of land developers and subdividers, who purchase raw land, divide it into lots, build roads and install utilities; the work of builders and architects, who plan and construct the houses and other buildings; and the work of either the developer or the builder, who sells the improved real estate, either directly or through brokerage firms.

Counseling. A *real estate counselor* helps clients choose among the various alternatives involved in purchasing, using, or investing in property. A counselor's role is to furnish clients with the data needed to make informed decisions; a counselor must, therefore, have a broad range of real estate knowledge and experience.

Education. Both the real estate practitioner and the consumer can learn more about the complexities of the real estate business through *education.* Colleges, schools, real estate organizations, and continuing education programs conduct courses and seminars in all areas of the business. These courses often are taught by experienced real estate professionals.

Title and abstract. Ensuring good title to the buyer of real estate is the business of *title insurance and abstract* companies. No real estate license is required, but a broad knowledge of real estate title, conveyancing, and lien law and a good grasp of real estate math are very beneficial. Title records and closing transactions are discussed in Chapters 18 and 20.

Urban planning. One of the most rapidly expanding specializations among the real estate professions is *urban planning.* Urban planners work with local governments to make recommendations for new streets, sewer and water lines, schools, parks, and libraries.

Other careers. Many other real estate career options are available. Lawyers specializing in real estate are always in demand. Large corporations with extensive land holdings often have real estate and/or property tax departments. Licensees may be employed as assistants to individual salespeople to handle the paperwork of residential or commercial sales. Specialists in real estate finance can work for mortgage banking firms, government agencies and mortgage brokers as well as for banks and savings associations. Building managers and superintendents handle real estate belonging to industrial firms, banks, trust companies, insurance firms, and other businesses. Environmental professionals ascertain prior uses of land and assess the potential for environmental hazards for buyers, sellers, and lenders. Government opportunities include, among others, the U.S. Department of Agriculture, the U.S. Department of the Interior, the National Park Service, and the Department of Veterans Affairs. Local governments have staff personnel in appraisal, land use, inspections, and urban renewal. Additional career information can be obtained from the National Association of REALTORS® web site at www.nar.realtor.com.

Uses of Real Property Just as there are many areas of specialization within the real estate industry, there are many different types of property in which to specialize (see Figure 1.1). Real estate generally can be classified as

- **residential**—all property used for housing, from small city lots to acreage, both single-family and multifamily, in urban, suburban, and rural areas;
- **commercial**—business property, including offices, shopping centers, stores, theaters, hotels, and parking facilities;
- **industrial**—warehouses, factories, and land in industrial districts;
- **agricultural**—farms, timberland, pastureland, ranches, and orchards; or
- **special-purpose**—places of worship, schools, cemeteries, and government-held lands.

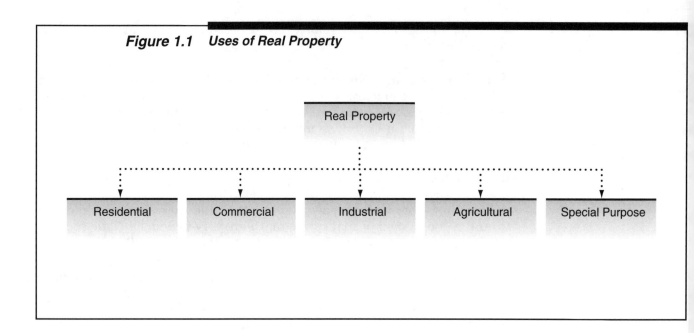

Figure 1.1   Uses of Real Property

The market for each of these types of properties can be further subdivided into (1) the sales market, which involves the transfer of title, and (2) the rental market, which involves the transfer of space on a lease basis.

In Practice   Although in theory a real estate person or firm can perform all these services and handle all five classes of property, this is rarely done except in small towns. Most real estate firms tend to specialize to some degree, especially in urban areas.

REAL ESTATE LAW

The purchase of real estate is an entirely different type of transaction from the purchase of personal property such as groceries, clothing, fuel, automobiles, or television sets. Although every type of sales transaction creates a change of ownership involving certain relatively simple legal problems, *even the simplest of real estate transactions brings into play a body of complex laws.*

Real estate brokers and salespeople must have a broad understanding of law and how various laws affect real estate activities. However, if legal questions or problems arise, the real estate practitioner *must* advise the parties to consult an attorney, preferably one who specializes in real estate law.

Sources of Real Estate Law   Generally, in the United States, **seven sources of law** affect the ownership and transfer of real estate (see Figure 1.2). These sources are *the Constitution of the United States; laws passed by Congress; federal regulations adopted by the various agencies and commissions created by Congress; state constitutions; laws passed by state legislatures; ordinances passed by cities, towns, and other local governments; and court decisions.* Texas has adopted

Figure 1.2   Sources of Real Estate Law

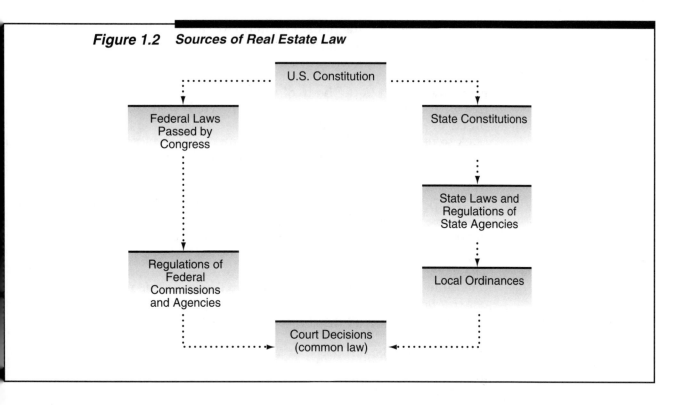

the English common law for certain rules and has drawn heavily on Spanish law for doctrines such as community property and separate property.

The primary purpose of the *U.S. Constitution* and the individual *state constitutions* is to establish the rights of citizens and delineate the limits of governmental authority. For example, the Fourteenth Amendment to the U.S. Constitution provides civil rights protections that serve as the basis for federal fair housing legislation; homestead and community property laws derive from the Texas constitution.

Laws passed by Congress and by *state and local legislative bodies* may establish specific provisions, or they simply may set broad standards of conduct and establish administrative enforcement agencies. Federal fair housing laws prohibiting discrimination are examples of laws passed by Congress; the Texas Real Estate License Act, which regulates the real estate industry, is a state statute.

Governmental agencies that enact rules and regulations range from the Federal Housing Administration to the Texas Real Estate Commission to local zoning boards. The regulations passed by these agencies are a means of implementing and enforcing legislative acts; they provide detailed information on legal and illegal actions and practices; they designate penalties and violations; and they expand on the law and have the effect of law.

Court decisions of federal, state, and municipal courts serve to clarify and interpret laws, regulations, and constitutional provisions. By applying and interpreting the laws in relation to a specific event, a court decision expands the meaning of the law, establishing a **precedent** for future decisions. However, the courts are not always bound by established precedent. Courts in one jurisdiction (area of authority) may not be bound by the decisions of courts in other jurisdictions. Furthermore, a court with superior authority in its jurisdiction may, at its discretion, reverse the ruling of a lower court.

Real estate ownership and transfer are affected by what is known as **common law,** which is the body of rules and principles founded on custom, usage, and decisions and opinions of the courts. It is derived mainly from practices developed in England and, as it applies to the United States, dates back to practices in effect during the American Revolution. Today common law includes not only custom but also previous court decisions.

In some situations, the court may feel that the strict application of common law would be too harsh. To solve this problem, *courts of equity* evolved. These are not separate courts and judges but rather the same court choosing to settle the case in an equitable or fair manner.

Laws Affecting Real Estate Practice

The general sources of law encompass a number of specific areas that are important to the real estate practitioner. These include the *law of contracts, general property law, landlord-tenant law,* the *law of agency* (which covers the obligations of a broker to the person who engages his or her services), the *real estate license law,* and *fraud and consumer protection laws.* All of these areas will be discussed in this text.

Real Estate Laws

- Contract law
- General property law
- Landlord-tenant law
- Agency law
- Real estate license law
- Consumer protection law

Real estate license law. Because real estate brokers and salespeople engage in the business of handling other people's real estate and money, the need to regulate their activities has long been recognized. In an effort to protect the public from fraud, dishonesty, or incompetence in the buying and selling of real estate, all states, the District of Columbia, and all Canadian provinces have passed laws that require real estate brokers and salespeople to be licensed. The first real estate license law was passed in California in 1919. The first law to regulate real estate brokerage in Texas, the *Texas Real Estate Dealers Act,* was passed in 1939. The law that currently regulates real estate in Texas is the **Texas Real Estate License Act,** passed in 1949. The act has been revised many times, most recently in 2001, and is administered by the Texas Real Estate Commission.

Persons who deal only with their own property are not required to hold a real estate license. However, any person who, for compensation or the promise of compensation, lists or offers to list; sells or offers to sell; buys or offers to buy; negotiates or offers to negotiate—either directly or indirectly—for the purpose of bringing about the listing, sale, exchange, purchase, option to purchase, auction, rental, or leasing of real estate is required to hold a valid real estate broker's license.

The applicant must possess certain stated personal and educational qualifications and must pass an examination to prove adequate knowledge of the business. In addition, to qualify for license renewal and continue in business, the licensee must follow certain prescribed standards of business conduct and meet continuing education requirements.

The Texas Real Estate License Act requires that the license examination "be of scope sufficient in the judgment of the commission to determine that a person is competent to act as a real estate broker or salesperson in a manner to protect the interest of the public." Chapter 7 describes more fully the License Act and the required education and sponsorship standards.

Table 1.1   **Professional Organizations**

American Institute of Architects	www.aiaonline.com
American Land Title Association	www.alta.org
American Planning Association	www.planning.org
Appraisal Institute	www.appraisalinstitute.org
Building Owners and Managers Association International	www.boma.org
International Council of Shopping Centers	www.icsc.org
Mortgage Bankers Association of America	www.mbaa.org
National Apartment Association	www.naahq.org
National Association of Exclusive Buyer's Agents	www.naeba.org
National Association of Home Builders	www.nahb.com
National Association of Real Estate Brokers	www.nareb.com
National Association of REALTORS®	www.realtor.com
Real Estate Educators Association	www.reea.org
Texas Association of REALTORS®	www.texasrealestate.com
Texas Land Title Association	www.tlta.org
Texas Real Estate Teachers Association	www.treta.org

PROFESSIONAL ORGANIZATIONS

Many trade organizations serve the real estate industry, as shown in Table 1.1. The largest is the **National Association of REALTORS® (NAR)**, founded in 1908. It serves members' interests by keeping them informed of developments in their field, publicizing the services of members, improving standards and practices, and recommending or taking positions on public legislation and regulations affecting the operations of members and member firms. NAR also sponsors various affiliated organizations that offer professional designations to brokers, salespersons, and others who complete required courses in areas of special interest. Some of the organizations and their designations are listed in Table 1.2.

NAR is composed of state, regional, and local associations. Members subscribe to a strict Code of Ethics and are entitled to be known as **REALTORS®** (a registered trademark). The Texas Association of REALTORS® (TAR) is affiliated with NAR and works closely with local associations of REALTORS® in developing the interests of individual REALTORS® and the buying and selling public. Some local associations have a separate REALTOR-Associate® membership category for salespersons who are affiliated with active REALTOR® members as employees or independent contractors. Membership in NAR and TAR is voluntary. The NAR Internet site at www.realtor.com™ has two parts: a public site with real property ads and other consumer information and a private, password-protected site (One REALTOR Place™) accessible only by NAR members.

Other professional associations include the Appraisal Institute, the Building Owners and Managers Association International, the Mortgage Bankers Association of America, the National Association of Real Estate Brokers, the

---

Table 1.2 *National Association of REALTORS® Institutes, Societies, and Professional Designations*

Institute	Designation
CIREI—Commercial and Investment Real Estate Institute	CCIM—Certified Commercial Investment Member
CRE—Counselors of Real Estate	CRE—Counselor of Real Estate
IREM—Institute of Real Estate Management	CPM—Certified Property Manager AMO—Accredited Management Organization ARM—Accredited Residential Manager
NAR—National Association of REALTORS®	GRI—Graduate, REALTORS® Institute CIPS—Certified International Property Specialist RAA—Residential Accredited Appraiser GAA—General Accredited Appraiser
REBAC—Real Estate Buyer's Agent Council	ABR—Accredited Buyer Representative ABRM—Accredited Buyer Representative Manager
RLI—REALTORS® Land Institute	ALC—Accredited Land Consultant
RNMI—REALTORS® National Marketing Institute 　Real Estate Brokerage Managers Council 　Residential Sales Council	CRB—Certified Real Estate Brokerage Manager CRS—Certified Residential Specialist
SOIR—Society of Industrial and Office REALTORS®	*
WCR—Women's Council of REALTORS®	LTG—Leadership Training Graduate RRC—Referral and Relocation Certification

*No specific designation offered.

Texas Land Title Association, the Real Estate Educators Association, and the Texas Real Estate Teachers Association. The members of the National Association of Real Estate Brokers (NAREB) are known as **Realtists.**

Summary

Although selling and leasing are the most widely recognized activities of the real estate business, the industry also involves many other services, such as appraisal, apartment locating, property inspection, property development, counseling, property financing, education, title work, and urban planning. Most real estate firms specialize in one or two of these areas. However, the highly complex and competitive nature of the real estate industry requires that a practitioner be competent in a number of fields.

Real property can be classified according to its general use as residential, commercial, industrial, agricultural, or special-purpose. Although many brokers deal with more than one type of real property, they usually specialize to some degree.

Even the simplest real estate transactions involve a complex body of laws. In the United States, the seven sources of law are the U.S. Constitution, laws passed by Congress, federal regulations, state constitutions, laws passed by state legislatures, local ordinances, and court decisions.

Much of real property law is based on common-law practices developed in England. Common law includes rules and principles founded on custom and prior court decisions. Spanish law also has influenced Texas real estate law.

The real estate business is a dynamic industry that employs hundreds of thousands of professionals. Every state, the District of Columbia, and every Canadian province has some type of licensing requirement for real estate brokers and salespeople. Students should become familiar with Texas licensing requirements.

Various professional organizations afford the licensee an opportunity to stay current on issues related to real estate. Some of these organizations are the National Association of REALTORS®, the Texas Association of REALTORS®, local associations of REALTORS®, and the National Association of Real Estate Brokers.

Questions

1. Professional associations of specialists in various fields of real estate activity were organized to serve the interests of their members. Which of the following is **NOT** generally a service expected of such organizations?
   a. Keeping members informed of developments in their field
   b. Improving standards and practices
   c. Providing a clearinghouse of information
   d. Passing laws to regulate brokers and salespeople

2. There are seven sources of law in the United States. Which of the following is **NOT** an example of one of them?
   a. Local zoning laws
   b. FHA/VA regulations
   c. Court decisions
   d. Precedent set by decisions of the city council

3. Laws passed by the Congress and various state legislatures may
   a. not designate penalties and violations.
   b. set precedents for future court decisions.
   c. empower administrative agencies to carry out the provisions of the law.
   d. clarify and interpret court decisions.

4. The legal concept of precedent
   a. applies only to state court decisions.
   b. always must be followed by judges when formulating court decisions.
   c. grew out of common law.
   d. binds courts in all jurisdictions, regardless of superior authority.

5. Constitutional provisions
   a. establish the rights of citizens and delineate government authority.
   b. set down specific provisions on every issue.
   c. can be waived by signing a release.
   d. designate penalties and violations.

6. Real estate license laws
   a. are consistent from state to state.
   b. apply only to licensed brokers.
   c. were passed to protect the public from the possible fraud, dishonesty, and incompetence of unscrupulous brokers and salespeople.
   d. apply to persons who sell their own property.

7. Common law
   a. is derived from practices developed in the Spanish Empire.
   b. has no effect on today's real estate practices.
   c. includes both custom and court decisions in its application today.
   d. establishes the limitations of municipal court decisions.

8. A REALTOR® is
   a. a specially licensed real estate professional who acts as a point of contact between two or more people in negotiating the sale, purchase, or rental of property.
   b. any real estate broker or salesperson who assists buyers, sellers, landlords, or tenants in any real estate transaction.
   c. a real estate licensee who is a member of the National Association of REALTORS®.
   d. a member of the National Association of Real Estate Brokers who specializes in residential properties.

9. Which of the following is an example of commercial real estate?
   a. Office buildings converted to low-income housing
   b. Apartments for rent
   c. Retail space for lease
   d. Factories

10. Peter Dickinson is a real estate broker in Dallas. Chances are his real estate firm
    a. performs most or all of the various real estate specializations.
    b. deals only in farm property.
    c. deals only in insurance.
    d. performs only one or two of the various real estate specializations for one or two types of property.

11. Which of the following is an example of special-purpose real estate?
    a. A public library
    b. A shopping center
    c. An industrial park
    d. An apartment complex

12. Brenda holds a real estate license and has several years of experience in the industry. However, she has "retired" from actively marketing properties and now helps clients choose among the various alternatives involved in purchasing, using, or investing in property. What is her profession?
    a. Real estate counselor
    b. Real estate appraiser
    c. Real estate educator
    d. REALTOR®

2 Real Property

Key Terms

air rights	land	reservation
attachment	personal property	severance
bundle of legal rights	personalty	subsurface rights
chattel	real estate	surface rights
fixture	real property	trade fixture
improvement		

OVERVIEW

Will Rogers often is quoted as having said, "Buy land—they ain't making any more of the stuff!" The preamble to the National Association of REALTORS® Code of Ethics begins with the words "Under all is the land. . . . " We see it, touch it, and refer to it every day, but what exactly is land? When we own it, do we own just the ground beneath our feet and, if so, how deep does this ownership go? What about the trees we sit under and the air we breathe—are these part of the land also?

This chapter discusses the nature and characteristics of real estate as well as the similarities and distinctions among land, real estate, and real property. In addition, the chapter illustrates the distinctions between real estate and personal property and shows how an item of personal property can be converted into real property, and vice versa.

LAND, REAL ESTATE, AND REAL PROPERTY

The words *land, real estate*, and *real property* commonly are used to describe the same commodity. In the broader sense, they appear to be interchangeable; however, their technical meanings have subtle but important differences.

Land   The term *land* refers to more than just the surface of the earth; it includes the underlying soil and things that are attached permanently to the land by nature, such as trees and water. From a legal standpoint, land ownership

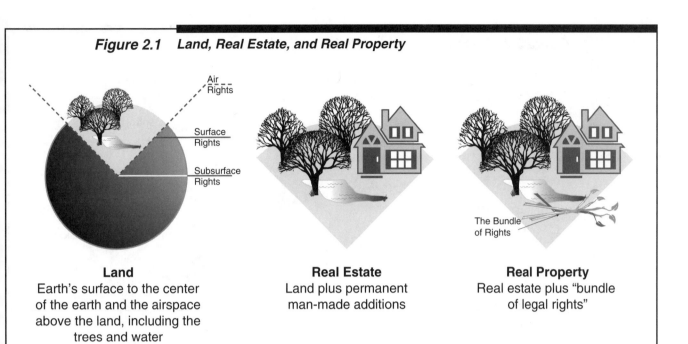

Figure 2.1 *Land, Real Estate, and Real Property*

Air Rights

Surface Rights

Subsurface Rights

Land
Earth's surface to the center of the earth and the airspace above the land, including the trees and water

Real Estate
Land plus permanent man-made additions

Real Property
Real estate plus "bundle of legal rights"

The Bundle of Rights

also includes possession and control of the minerals and substances below the earth's surface, together with the airspace above the land up to infinity.

Thus, **land** is defined as *the earth's surface extending downward to the center of the earth and upward to infinity, including things permanently attached by nature, such as trees and water* (see Figure 2.1).

Real Estate The term *real estate* is somewhat broader than the term *land* and includes not only the physical components of the land as provided by nature but also all man-made permanent improvements on and to the land. In actual practice, the word **improvement** applies to the buildings erected on the land as well as to streets, utilities, sewers, and other man-made additions to the property.

Real estate, therefore, is defined as *the earth's surface extending downward to the center of the earth and upward into space, including all things permanently attached to it by nature or by people* (see Figure 2.1).

Real Property The term *real property* is broader still; it refers to the physical surface of the land, what lies below it, what lies above it, and what is permanently attached to it, as well as to the *legal rights of real estate ownership,* often described as the **bundle of legal rights.** The *bundle of legal rights* (see Figure 2.2) includes the right to *control* of the property within the framework of the law, the right of *exclusion* (to keep others from entering or occupying the property), the right of *possession,* the right of *disposition* (to be able to sell or otherwise convey the property) and the right of *enjoyment* (to use the property in any legal manner). Within these ownership rights are included further rights: to mortgage or encumber, lease or license, cultivate or mine, will, dedicate or give away, share, trade, or exchange.

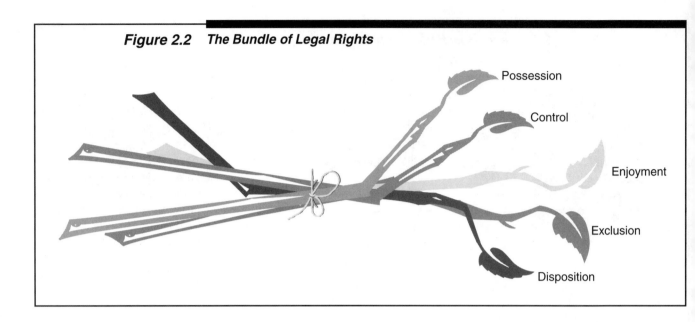

Figure 2.2   The Bundle of Legal Rights

Possession

Control

Enjoyment

Exclusion

Disposition

Thus, **real property** is defined as *the earth's surface extending downward to the center of the earth and upward into space, including all things permanently attached to it by nature or by people, as well as the interests, benefits, and rights inherent in the ownership of real estate* (see Figure 2.1).

In Practice   Although real estate and real property have different meanings as described above, they are used interchangeably in everyday use and generally are considered synonymous terms. People use the term *real estate* when referring to buying or selling homes, office buildings, or land. Thus, in casual usage, real estate generally includes the legal rights of ownership specified in the definition of real property. For simplicity, the term *real estate* will be used in this textbook.

Subsurface and air rights. Ownership of land can be *laterally severed* into **subsurface rights, surface rights,** and **air rights.** The owner of surface rights (the rights to use the surface of the earth) does not always control the subsurface or air rights to the property.

Lateral severance— separates subsurface, surface, and air rights

Subsurface rights are the rights to the natural resources below the earth's surface. Texas recognizes as separate estates oil and gas (as one right) and other mineral rights.

For example, a landowner may sell to an oil company his or her rights to any oil and gas found in the land. Later, the same landowner can sell the remaining interest to a purchaser but in the sale reserve the rights to all coal that may be found in the land. After these sales, three parties have ownership interests in this real estate: (1) the oil company owns all oil and gas, (2) the seller owns all coal, and (3) the purchaser owns the rights to all the rest of the real estate.

A Texas landowner does not own the water beneath the land. He or she owns the right to drill for and remove water that is found.

In Texas, when subsurface rights are sold separately from surface rights, the owner of mineral rights is legally entitled, unless otherwise specified, to reasonable entry onto the property of the surface owner to extract the minerals for which he or she holds subsurface rights. Typically, a general grant of mineral rights does not include any substance such as iron ore, strip-mined coal, limestone, or gravel, the removal of which would substantially spoil or deplete the surface lands. These substances would belong to the holder of the surface rights.

Air rights, the rights to use the air above the land, may also be sold or leased independently of the land. They can be an important part of real estate, particularly in large cities where air rights over railroads have been purchased or leased to construct office buildings such as the Met Life Building in New York City and the Merchandise Mart in Chicago. For the construction of such buildings, developers must acquire not only the air rights above the land but also numerous small portions of the land's surface for the building's foundation supports.

In Practice   Although a property owner has the rights to the air upward to infinity, the courts permit reasonable interference with these rights for aircraft, so long as the owner's right to use and occupy the land is not unduly lessened. Texas law has provided air easements over land near commercial airports for the benefit of the airports, including height restrictions for buildings to prevent interference with airborne operations. To enhance citizens' rights, city zoning ordinances restrict residential development in noise-impacted areas. However, if an airport is built near an existing residential area, the airport owner (a city, county or other entity) would be required to soundproof existing homes, to make a financial settlement with homeowners in the noise-impacted area, or to buy the homes and raze them to make room for possible commercial development.

REAL PROPERTY VERSUS PERSONAL PROPERTY

Property may be classified as either real or personal. As noted, real estate is defined as a part of the earth, including the permanent additions or growing things attached to it, the airspace above it, and the minerals below it. **Personal property,** sometimes referred to as **personalty,** is *all property that does not fit the definition of real estate.* Thus, personal property has the unique characteristic of being *movable.* Items of personal property, also referred to as **chattels,** include such tangibles as chairs, tables, clothing, money, bonds, and bank accounts (see Figure 2.3).

Personal property = personalty = chattel

Title to real estate passes by a recordable document such as a deed or will, whereas title to personal property usually passes by a bill of sale.

It is possible to change an item of real estate to personal property by **severance.** For example, a growing tree is real estate, but if the owner cuts down the tree and thereby severs it from the earth, the tree becomes personal property.

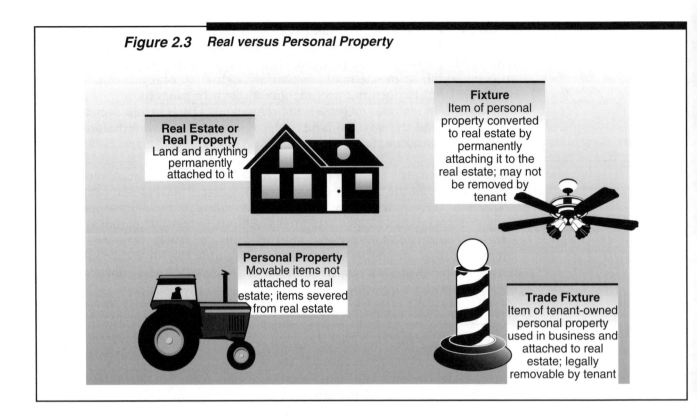

Figure 2.3 Real versus Personal Property

Real Estate or Real Property
Land and anything permanently attached to it

Fixture
Item of personal property converted to real estate by permanently attaching it to the real estate; may not be removed by tenant

Personal Property
Movable items not attached to real estate; items severed from real estate

Trade Fixture
Item of tenant-owned personal property used in business and attached to real estate; legally removable by tenant

The reverse situation, changing personal property into real estate, also is possible. If an owner buys cement, stones, and sand and constructs a concrete walk on his or her parcel of real estate, the component parts of the concrete, which were originally personal property, are converted into real estate by **attachment** because they have become a permanent improvement on the land.

Manufactured Housing

The distinction between real and personal property is not always obvious. A manufactured home (mobile home), for example, is generally considered to be personal property because it is movable. However, in Texas a manufactured home may be considered real estate *if* (a) it is placed on land that is titled in the name of the owner of the manufactured home (ownership of the land may be through a deed or a contract for sale), (b) it is permanently attached to the real property and connected to a utility, and (c) the document of title to the manufactured home has been canceled by the Texas Department of Housing and Community Affairs and a "certificate of attachment" issued and filed in the county deed records (Section 2.001 of the Texas Property Code, as amended by House Bill [H.B.] 1869, 2001).

For a lien on a manufactured home to have priority over previously existing liens, the Texas Certificate of Title Act requires that the lien must be listed on the document of title before the home is attached to a permanent foundation. Although the specific requirements for permanent attachment vary according to lender and insurance company requirements, Fannie Mae (a secondary market for mortgage loans) considers a permanent foundation to be concrete piers poured to ground level with a bolt, chain, or rebar in the concrete and welded or otherwise attached to the frame of the home.

A real estate broker or salesperson does not have to obtain a special license to sell manufactured homes (even when such homes are not classified as real property), as long as he or she conducts negotiations for a consumer while acting as the consumer's broker or salesperson (H.B. 2238, 1999). A mobile home *retailer* must provide consumers with a statutorily prescribed written statement listing items the purchaser should consider if planning to place a manufactured home on land he or she owns or plans to buy. Included in the items to consider are zoning and restrictive covenants, water access, sewer systems, homeowner association fees, real property taxes, road maintenance, property damage insurance, and mortgage insurance (H.B. 1869, 2001).

For more information, contact the Manufactured Housing Division of the Texas Department of Housing and Community Affairs at 1-800-500-7074 or search the web site at www.tdhca.state.tx.us. Additionally, a "Manufactured Housing Consumer's Guide" is available from the U.S. Department of Housing and Urban Development on its web site, www.hud.gov.

Plants and Minerals

Trees and crops generally fall into one of two classes. Trees, perennial shrubbery, and grasses that do not require annual cultivation are considered real estate. Annual plantings or crops of wheat, corn, vegetables, and fruit, known as *emblements,* are generally considered personal property. As long as an annual crop is growing, it will be transferred as part of the real property unless other provisions are made in the sales contract.

> The term used for plants that do not require annual cultivation (such as trees and shrubbery) is *fructus naturales* (fruits of nature); emblements are known as *fructus industriales* (fruits of industry).

As previously noted, ownership of real estate usually includes rights not only to the surface of the ground but also to the minerals and substances below the surface. When an owner drills into land, discovers oil, and stores the oil in tanks ready for transport, the oil is converted from real estate to personal property. In the case of minerals, it is customary to specify in a sales contract what is *not* included in the sale by providing for **reservations** in the deed to indicate what is being retained by the seller or a previous property owner.

Fixtures

An article that was once personal property but has been so affixed to land or to a building that the law construes it to be part of the real estate is a **fixture.** Examples of fixtures are heating units, elevator equipment in highrise buildings, kitchen cabinets, light fixtures, plumbing fixtures, and garage door openers. Almost any item that has been added as *a permanent part* of a building is considered a fixture and is automatically included with the real property when a sale occurs, unless other provisions are made in the sales contract. Paragraph 2 of the real estate sales contract shown on page 228 lists additional property considered to be fixtures in Texas.

Legal tests of a fixture. Courts apply four basic tests to determine whether an article is personal property or a fixture (and therefore part of the real estate). These tests are based on (1) the existence of an agreement, (2) the intention and relationship of the parties, (3) the adaptation of the article to the real estate, and (4) the permanence of the method by which the item is annexed.

A *written agreement* between parties to a contract is the one certain way to avoid a dispute between a buyer and seller or a landlord and tenant about whether a particular item should remain with the property as a part of the

Legal Tests of a Fixture

1. Agreement
2. Intent
3. Adaptation to real estate
4. Method of annexation

real estate. Although the Texas standard sales contract forms specify what normally constitutes a fixture, the real estate broker or salesperson should ensure that a sales contract includes a list of all articles included in the sale, particularly if any doubt exists as to whether they are permanently attached fixtures. Articles that might cause confusion include television antennas, garage door openers, carpeting that is not tacked down, ceiling fans, built-in appliances, built-in bookcases, and large breakfronts that seem to be affixed to the wall but are actually freestanding. Absence of a written agreement will necessitate the court's intervention and its use of the remaining three tests.

The *intent of the parties* at the time an article was attached is generally considered the most important factor in a court's deciding whether an article is a fixture. For example, a property owner who sets the post of a gas grill in concrete *appears to intend* for the grill to be permanent. However, if a short pipe with a larger diameter were set in concrete and the pipe for the gas grill simply set into the larger pipe, would the intent be permanence?

The *adaptation of an article* to use in a particular building is another test of a fixture: has it been customized for this home or is it a standard purchase item? For example, a fireplace screen custom built for an oval fireplace opening is considered a fixture, a portion of the real estate that should be included in the purchase of a home. A fireplace screen of a standard size that was purchased ready made is not automatically considered a fixture.

The *permanence of the manner of annexation,* or attachment, provides another basis for court decisions. An item attached to the land by permanent means such as cement, nails, or bolts becomes a fixture. For instance, a furnace, although removable, is usually attached in such a way that it cannot be taken out without causing extensive damage to the property.

Trade fixtures. An article owned by a tenant and attached to a rented space or building for use in conducting a business is a **trade fixture.** Examples of trade fixtures are bowling alleys, store shelves, bars, and restaurant equipment. Agricultural fixtures such as chicken coops and toolsheds are also included in this definition (see Figure 2.3). Trade fixtures are considered personal property of the tenant and, as such, must be removed on or before the expiration of the lease, without seriously damaging the building. Trade fixtures not removed become the real property of the landlord. Acquiring the property in this way is known as *accession.*

FOR EXAMPLE Paul's Pizza leases space in a small shopping center. Paul bolted a large iron oven to the floor of the unit. If Paul's Pizza relocates, Paul will be able to take his pizza oven with him if he can repair the bolt holes in the floor. On the other hand, if the pizza oven was set in concrete and welded to metal bracing on the wall, Paul might not be able to remove it without causing structural damage. In that case, the oven would become a fixture.

Trade fixtures are personal property *if* removed on or before the expiration of a lease.

Trade fixtures differ from other fixtures in the following three ways:

1. Fixtures belong to the owner of the real estate, but trade fixtures usually belong to, and are installed by, a tenant for his or her use.
2. Fixtures are considered a permanent part of a building, but trade fixtures are removable. Trade fixtures may be affixed to a building so as

to appear to be fixtures (real estate); however, due to the relationship of the parties (landlord and tenant), the law gives a tenant the right to remove trade fixtures if the removal is completed before the lease expires and if the rented space is restored to approximately its original condition. Leases usually require that upon expiration of a lease the tenant return the premises to the landlord in as good condition as they were at the beginning of the lease, except for reasonable wear and tear and damage by the elements.

3. Fixtures legally are construed to be real estate, but trade fixtures legally are construed to be personal property. Trade fixtures are not included in the sale or mortgage of real estate, except by special agreement.

Summary

Although most people think of land as the surface of the earth, this word really applies not only to the earth's surface but also to the mineral deposits under the earth and the air above it, including things permanently attached by nature. The term *real estate* expands this definition to include man-made improvements attached to the land. *Real property* is the term used to describe real estate plus the "bundle of legal rights" associated with its ownership.

The same parcel of real estate may be owned and controlled by different parties—one owning the surface rights, one owning the air rights, and another owning the subsurface rights.

All property that does not fit the definition of real estate is classified as personal property, or chattel. When articles of personal property are permanently affixed to land, they may become fixtures and as such are considered a part of the real estate. However, personal property attached to real estate by a tenant for the tenant's business is classified as a trade fixture and remains personal property.

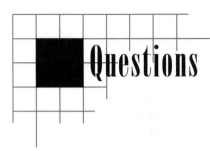

Questions

1. A construction firm builds an office center over a railroad right-of-way. This means that
   a. the developer must purchase from the railroad all land under the office center.
   b. trains no longer can operate on the tracks under the building during business hours if the noise disturbs the occupants of the office center.
   c. the construction firm has built the office center using the subsurface rights to the property.
   d. the developer must purchase or lease some land and air rights from the railroad.

2. The term *fructus naturales* refers to which of the following?
   a. Annual crops
   b. Real estate
   c. Fruits of industry
   d. Emblements

3. John Sexton purchases a parcel of land and sells the rights to any minerals located in the ground to an exploration company. This means that he owns all **EXCEPT** which of the following with regard to this property?
   a. Air rights
   b. Surface rights
   c. Subsurface rights
   d. Water rights

4. Manufactured housing
   a. is generally considered real property.
   b. may be considered real property if it is sold in conjunction with a parcel of land.
   c. may be considered real property even if it is not attached to a permanent foundation.
   d. may be considered real property without obtaining a certificate of attachment.

5. A store tenant firmly attaches appropriate appliances for his restaurant business on leased premises. Which of the following is true?
   a. The appliances are trade fixtures and will be sold if the building is sold during the lease term.
   b. The appliances are trade fixtures and must be removed before the lease expires.
   c. The appliances may not be removed without the landlord's permission.
   d. The appliances become the landlord's property on installation.

6. Real estate, by definition, includes many elements and parts. Which of the following items would be a part of real estate?
   a. Chattel   c. Farm equipment
   b. Patio furniture   d. Growing trees

7. Which of the following **BEST** defines real property?
   a. Land and air above it and subsurface below it
   b. Land and all that there is above or below the surface, including all things permanently attached to it and legal rights associated with it
   c. Land and the buildings permanently affixed to it
   d. Land and all the legal rights associated with it

8. A fixture is
   a. any item that is not a permanent part of the building.
   b. real estate that at one time was personal property.
   c. an item installed by a tenant for temporary use.
   d. not included in the sale or mortgage of real estate.

9. The definition of *land* includes all **EXCEPT** which of the following?
    a. Minerals in the earth
    b. The air above the ground up to infinity
    c. Buildings
    d. Trees

10. Fred and Celia Evers are adding an enclosed front porch to their home. The lumber dealer with whom they are contracting has just unloaded a truckload of lumber in front of their house that will be used to build the porch. At this point, the lumber is considered to be
    a. a fixture.
    b. real property.
    c. personal property.
    d. real estate.

11. When the new front porch, as described in question 10, is completed, the lumber that the dealer originally delivered will be considered to be
    a. personal property.   c. chattel.
    b. real estate.   d. emblements.

12. Suppose that halfway through the construction of the new front porch, as described in question 10, work is delayed indefinitely because of unforeseen difficulties. At this point, the lumber the dealer originally delivered would be considered to be
    a. personal property if it has been used in the construction of the porch.
    b. real estate if it has been used in the construction of the porch.
    c. real property of the contractor.
    d. real property of the dealer.

13. The definition of the term *real property* includes all **EXCEPT** which of the following?
    a. Items of personal property permanently affixed to the real estate
    b. Legal ownership rights
    c. Air and subsurface rights
    d. Chattels

14. Man-made, permanent additions to land are called
    a. chattels.
    b. emblements.
    c. improvements.
    d. fructus naturales.

15. Real estate may be converted into personal property by
    a. severance.   c. a bill of sale.
    b. accession.   d. inference.

16. Steve Jackson rents a detached, single-family home under a one-year lease. Two months into the rental period, Jackson installs permanent awnings over the building's front windows to keep the sun away from some delicate hanging plants. Which of the following is true?
    a. Because of their permanent nature, the awnings are considered to be personal property.
    b. The awnings are considered to be fixtures and may not be removed by the tenant.
    c. The awnings are now the personal property of the owner.
    d. Jackson may choose whether, on termination of the lease, the awnings remain.

17. Real estate is often referred to as a *bundle of legal rights.* Which of the following is **NOT** among these rights?
    a. Right of exclusion
    b. Right to use the property for illegal purposes
    c. Right of enjoyment
    d. Right to sell or otherwise convey the property

18. When a person purchases real estate from a seller,
    a. he or she actually is buying the legal rights to the property that were previously held by the seller.
    b. the seller legally cannot retain any rights of ownership.
    c. the mineral rights remain with the original owner of the property.
    d. he or she must buy subsurface, air, and surface rights.

3 The Real Estate Market

Key Terms

abatement	demographics	price
business cycle	market	subjective value
cost	objective value	supply
demand		

OVERVIEW

The real estate business is more than the neighborhood storefront with the "Realty" sign hanging in the window. Real estate is a national industry that has worldwide economic influence.

This chapter discusses the physical and economic characteristics of real estate and explains the concept of value, particularly how value is tested by the influences of supply and demand in the real estate market.

CHARACTERISTICS OF REAL ESTATE

Real estate possesses seven basic characteristics that determine its value and affect its use. These characteristics fall into two broad categories: economic and physical.

Economic Characteristics The economic characteristics of land affect its investment value. They are (1) relative scarcity, (2) improvements, (3) permanence of investment, and (4) area preference.

Relative scarcity. Although land as such is neither scarce nor rare, scarcity in an economic sense means that the total supply of land is fixed. Even though a considerable amount of land remains unused, land in a given location or of a particular quality is in short supply in some areas, such as downtown Houston.

Improvements. Construction of an improvement on one parcel of land can affect the value and use of a particular parcel of land as well as that of neighboring tracts and whole communities. For example, the construction of a steel plant or the building of an atomic reactor can directly influence a large area. An improvement can be new construction or a modification, and it can influence other parcels favorably or unfavorably.

Permanence of investment. The capital and labor used to build an improvement represent a large, fixed investment. Although older buildings can be razed to make way for newer buildings, improvements such as drainage, electricity, water, and sewerage remain. The return on such investments is long-term and relatively stable and usually extends over what is referred to as the *economic life* of the improvement. Consequently, real estate investment and land-use decisions must consider the usefulness of improvements 20 to 30 years into the future.

Area preference. This economic characteristic, sometimes called *situs*, does not refer to a particular geographic location but rather to people's choices and preferences for a given area. The unique quality of personal preference results in different values for similar units. Area preference is the reason that some residential purchasers pay more for a corner house lot than for a lot of the same size located in the middle of the block—and other purchasers might pay less. *Area preference is the most important economic characteristic of land.*

FOR EXAMPLE   A river runs through Bedford Falls, dividing the town more or less in half. On the north side of the river, known as North Town, houses sell for an average of $150,000. On the south side of the river, known as Southbank, identical houses sell for more than $200,000. The only difference is that homebuyers think that Southbank is a better neighborhood, even though no obvious difference exists between the two equally pleasant sides of town.

Physical Characteristics

Land has three basic physical characteristics: (1) immobility, (2) indestructibility, and (3) nonhomogeneity.

Immobility. Land, which is the earth's surface, is immobile. Some of the substances of land are removable, and its topography can be changed, but *the geographic location of any given parcel of land can never be changed. The location is fixed.*

Because land is immobile, real estate markets tend to be local in character. In addition, local governments are supported largely by property taxes on real estate. The fixed amount of land in a given area enables the local government to rely on a certain amount of annual revenue from property taxes, which in turn allows the government to make long-range plans based on the projected income.

Indestructibility. Land is also *indestructible.* This permanence of land, coupled with the long-term nature of improvements, tends to stabilize investments in real estate.

Of course, the fact that land is indestructible does not change the fact that the improvements on land depreciate and can become obsolete, which may

---

Economic Characteristics of Real Estate

1. Relative scarcity
2. Improvements
3. Permanence of investment
4. Area preference

Physical Characteristics of Real Estate

1. Immobility
2. Indestructibility
3. Nonhomogeneity

dramatically reduce the land's value. Because land is indestructible, it is not insurable.

Nonhomogeneity. No two parcels of land are ever exactly the same. Although they may be substantially similar, *all parcels differ geographically* because each parcel has its own location and, therefore, its singular legal address (enabling, among other things, a seller's transfer of property or a lender's placing a lien to ensure loan repayment). This characteristic may also be referred to as *heterogeneity.*

Characteristics Define Land Use

The various characteristics of a parcel of real estate affect its desirability for a specific use. Some specific physical and economic factors that affect land use include (1) contour and elevation of the parcel, known as *topography;* (2) prevailing winds; (3) transportation; (4) public improvements; and (5) availability of natural resources (such as water). For example, hilly or heavily wooded land would need considerable work before it could be used for industrial purposes but would be ideally suited for residential use. Likewise, flat land located along a major highway would be undesirable for residential use but would be well located for industrial, office, or commercial use.

REAL ESTATE—THE BUSINESS OF VALUE

The economic and physical characteristics of real estate form the underlying basis for the determination of value. *Value* can be defined as *the amount of goods or services offered in the marketplace in exchange for any given product.* It also has been described as *the present worth of future benefits arising from the ownership of real property.*

> *Subjective value:* A desk with an estimated cost of $30,000 reportedly sold for $1.3 million at the estate sale of Jacqueline Kennedy Onassis.

Value is based on objective and subjective factors. For example, a house fitted with a marble entrance hall and hardwood floors would have a greater **objective value** than would a house with only rough concrete floors. **Subjective value,** on the other hand, is affected by the relative worth an individual places on a specific item. Thus, a house may be beautifully designed and constructed with expensive materials and still be of no value to someone who does not want such a home.

A given parcel of real estate may have many different kinds of value at the same time, for example, market value (used to estimate selling price), appraised and taxable values (used for property taxes), insured value, mortgage value, and depreciated value.

Often, value is not the same as price, nor is it the same as cost. **Price** is the amount of money that is ultimately paid for a property; **cost** is the capital outlay for land, labor, materials, and profits necessary to bring a property into existence.

Supply and Demand

A **market** is a place where goods can be bought and sold. A market may be a specific place or it may be a worldwide economic system for moving goods and services around the globe. In either case, the function of a market is to provide a setting in which supply and demand can establish market value, making it advantageous for buyers and sellers to trade.

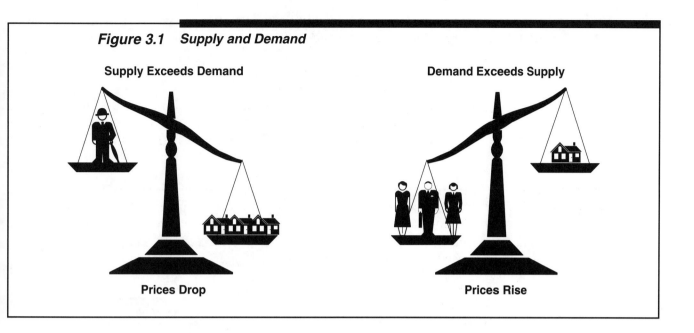

Figure 3.1 Supply and Demand

Supply Exceeds Demand

Demand Exceeds Supply

Prices Drop

Prices Rise

The economic forces of supply and demand continually interact in the market to establish and maintain price levels. Essentially, *when supply goes up, prices drop as more sellers compete for buyers; when demand increases, prices rise as more buyers compete for the product* (see Figure 3.1). When both supply and demand increase, real estate prices tend to remain stable. Although no one can accurately predict changes in real estate values, understanding what causes prices to go up and down can be helpful to the real estate practitioner.

Supply can be defined as *the amount of goods offered for sale within the market at a given price during a given time period.* To be a part of the available supply, land must be readily adaptable to the desired purpose at a price the market will bear. For example, very rocky land located near a city could be considered part of the supply of land available for residential housing only if the market prices of homes in the area were high enough to absorb the cost of removing the rocks before construction.

> Supply and price move in opposite directions.
>
> Demand and price move in the same direction.

Demand can be defined as *the amount of goods consumers are willing and able to buy at a given price during a given time period.* In real estate, demand is based on the benefits that can be derived from using land for a specific purpose. For example, an investor who buys a corner lot in a business district to construct an office building buys the land for the rental income it will generate.

Factors Affecting Supply

A number of factors affect supply in the real estate market. Some of the major ones include the labor force, construction costs, and government controls and financial policies (see Figure 3.2).

> **Supply Factors**
>
> Labor force
> Construction costs
> Government controls
> Financial policies

Labor force and construction costs. A shortage of skilled labor or building materials or a significant increase in the cost of labor or materials can decrease the amount of new construction. The impact of labor supply and price levels depends on the extent to which higher costs can be passed on to the buyer in the form of higher purchase prices. Technological advances

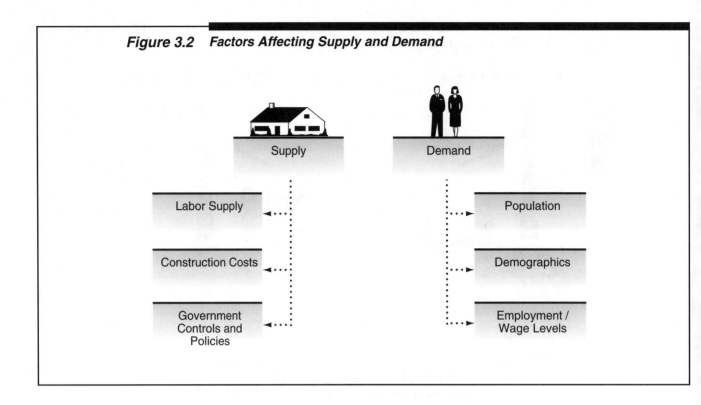

Figure 3.2   Factors Affecting Supply and Demand

that result in less expensive materials and more efficient means of construction may counteract some price increases.

Government controls and financial policies. Government monetary policy can have a substantial impact on the real estate market. The Federal Reserve Board establishes a *discount rate* of interest for the money it lends to commercial banks. That rate has a direct impact on the *interest rates* the banks charge to borrowers. Obviously, interest rates charged to builders, homebuyers, and commercial property developers play a significant part in determining the supply of real estate available. Government agencies such as the Federal Housing Administration (FHA) and Ginnie Mae (the Government National Mortgage Association) determine the terms and conditions under which money is available to lenders for mortgage loans (see Chapter 16).

Virtually any government action can have some effect on the real estate market. For instance, federal environmental regulations may increase or decrease the supply and value of land in a local market.

Local governments also influence supply. Land-use controls, building codes, zoning ordinances, and taxation policies help shape the character of a community and control the use of land. And they can have either positive or negative effects. High taxes may deter investors. On the other hand, tax incentives or tax **abatements** can attract new businesses and industries by reducing or eliminating their taxes. Of course, increased employment and expanded residential real estate markets should result from these new enterprises—encouraging developers to increase the supply of houses and commercial properties.

Factors Affecting Demand

Factors that tend to affect the demand for real estate include population, demographics, and employment and wage levels (see Figure 3.2).

Population. Shelter is a basic human need. The demand for housing grows with the population; and as housing needs grow, the demand for industrial and commercial areas also should increase. Although the total population of the country continues to rise, the demand for real estate increases faster in some areas than in others. In some locations, however, growth has ceased altogether or the population has declined. This may be due to economic changes (such as plant closings), social concerns (such as the quality of schools or a desire for more open space), or population changes (such as shifts from colder to warmer climates). The result can be a drop in demand for real estate in one area and an increased demand elsewhere.

Demographics. The study and description of a population is **demographics.** The characteristics of the population in a community are major factors in the quantity and type of housing in demand. Family size, the ratio of adults to children, the number of retirees, family income, lifestyle, and the growing number of single-parent and "empty nester" households are all demographic factors that contribute to the amount and type of housing needed.

Demand Factors

Population
Demographics
Employment levels
Wage levels

Employment and wage levels. Decisions about whether to buy or rent and how much to spend on housing are closely related to income. When job opportunities are plentiful, wages are competitive, and an employee feels secure in a job, demand for housing is likely to increase. When job opportunities are scarce or wage levels low, demand for real estate usually drops. The market might, in fact, be affected drastically by a single major employer's moving in or shutting down. Therefore, licensees must be aware of the business plans of local employers.

CYCLES

Over the years, business activity as measured by gross domestic product (GDP) has had its ups and downs. These irregular fluctuations in activity are called **business cycles.** They are caused by both internal forces (such as employment levels and consumer and investment spending) and external forces (such as wars, oil embargoes, and global economic forces). The business cycle generally can be characterized by four stages: *expansion, recession, depression,* and *revival.* Movements within the cycle generally are gradual but can be very sudden (see Figure 3.3).

To analyze the patterns of business cycles, a number of trends can be considered simultaneously. The long-term trend (referred to as the *secular trend*) tends to be smooth and continuous. It is most affected by basic influences such as population growth, technological advances, capital accumulation, and so on. Within this overall pattern are business cycles of varying lengths. Various segments or industries within the economy may have shorter cycles with different timing and different characteristics. Generally, residential real estate sales data reflect seasonal cycles with increases during spring and summer months—influenced by climatic conditions, vacation patterns, school schedules, and similar factors.

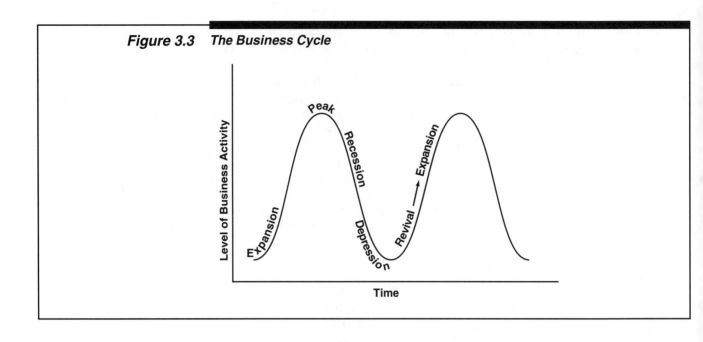

Figure 3.3   *The Business Cycle*

The real estate cycle. Because of the characteristics of nonhomogeneity and immobility, the real estate market generally is slow to adjust to sudden variations in supply and demand. The product cannot be transferred to another market, so an oversupply usually causes prices to drop. Because there is considerable lag time between the conception of real estate development and completion of construction, increases in demand may not be met immediately. Additionally, the number of "housing starts" can lead the economy either into a recession or out of a depression because the housing industry is very sensitive to changes in interest rates. A "tight" monetary policy during a period of expansion or inflation may drive the housing industry into a recession before affecting the rest of the economy. In contrast, an "easy" monetary policy, which results in lower interest rates, spurs consumer buying of residential real estate and may enable the home construction sector to lead the economy out of a recession.

> The real estate market is local in nature and generally slow to adjust to supply and demand.

Summary

The unique nature of land is apparent in both its economic and physical characteristics. The economic characteristics consist of scarcity, improvements, permanence of investment, and area preference. The physical characteristics are immobility, nonhomogeneity, and indestructibility.

The foundation of the real estate business is value, to which all real estate specializations relate directly or indirectly. A property's value is the present worth of its future benefits. Value is not the same as price, which is determined in the marketplace.

A market is a place where goods and services can be bought and sold and relatively stable price levels established. The ideal market allows for a continual balancing of the forces of supply and demand. Because of its unique characteristics, real estate is relatively slow to adjust to the forces of supply and demand.

Supply can be defined as the amount of goods available in the market for a given price. Demand is defined as the amount of goods that consumers are willing to buy at a given price.

The supply of and demand for real estate is affected by many factors, including population changes, demographics, wage and employment levels, construction costs and availability of labor, and government monetary policy and controls.

In the United States, fluctuations of business activity are observed in cycles. Business cycles generally have four stages: expansion, recession, depression, and revival. Stages of the real estate cycle are similar to—but do not necessarily coincide with—those in the overall business cycle.

Questions

1. *Value* is best defined as
    a. the highest price that a property will bring.
    b. capital outlay for land, labor, materials, and profits.
    c. a measure of the present worth of future benefits as perceived by each person.
    d. the amount a buyer agrees to pay and a seller agrees to accept.

2. The factors that influence the demand for real estate include
    a. wage levels and employment opportunities.
    b. local government ordinances.
    c. scarcity of building materials.
    d. labor supply.

3. Business cycles
    a. recur at regular intervals.
    b. cannot be regulated by government fiscal and monetary policy.
    c. involve periods of expansion, recession, depression, and revival.
    d. occur simultaneously throughout the state.

4. A factor that affects supply in the real estate market is
    a. construction costs.
    b. population.
    c. wage levels.
    d. demographics.

5. The real estate market is considered local in character because
    a. parcels of land are likely to be similar and confusion could occur concerning similar parcels in two different locations.
    b. each state has its own licensing requirements for real estate salespersons.
    c. land is fixed, or immobile.
    d. local taxation policies affect real estate values.

6. In general, when the supply of a certain commodity increases
    a. prices tend to rise.
    b. prices tend to remain level.
    c. prices tend to drop.
    d. demand tends to drop.

7. *Price* is best defined as
    a. the highest dollar amount a property will bring.
    b. the most likely amount a property will bring.
    c. the capital outlay for land, labor, materials, and profits.
    d. the amount a buyer agrees to pay and a seller agrees to accept.

8. Compared with typical markets, the real estate market
    a. is relatively quick to adapt to the forces of supply and demand.
    b. is national in scope.
    c. is relatively slow to adjust because of its nonhomogeneity and its immobile characteristics.
    d. does not have the problem of oversupply.

9. In general terms, a *market* refers to which of the following?
    a. A place where buyers and sellers come together to establish prices
    b. The amount of goods available at a given price
    c. An estimate of the selling price
    d. The amount of goods bought at a given price

10. Which of the following is an example of an economic characteristic of land?
    a. Immobility   c. Improvements
    b. Nonhomogeneity   d. Indestructibility

11. *Area preference* refers to
    a. a physical characteristic of land.
    b. nonhomogeneity.
    c. relative scarcity.
    d. an economic characteristic of land.

12. Which of the following physical and economic factors would **NOT** be a consideration for a land developer in determining the optimum use for a parcel of land for industrial purposes?
    a. Transportation
    b. Natural resources available
    c. Public improvements
    d. Indestructibility

13. The term *nonhomogeneity* refers to
    a. land's durability and indestructibility.
    b. capital expenditures represented by a fixed investment.
    c. the fact that no two parcels of land are exactly alike.
    d. the fact that the geographic location of land cannot be changed.

14. Relative scarcity implies that
    a. land available for development is scarce throughout Texas.
    b. land available for development may be in short supply in some areas.
    c. families may place different values on similar properties.
    d. families may prefer one area of a city over another.

4   Concepts of Home Ownership

Key Terms

capital gains	endorsement	homeowner's
coinsurance clause	equity	insurance policy
deductible clause	investment	

OVERVIEW

To rephrase an old quotation, a home is not a house—not necessarily, any-way. Although the term *home ownership* once referred mainly to detached single-family dwellings, today's homebuyer can choose among many different types of housing designed to satisfy individual needs, tastes, and financial capabilities.

This chapter discusses the various types of housing available as well as the factors a potential homeowner must consider in deciding what, where, and how much to buy. The chapter also covers the many tax benefits available to homeowners and the forms of property insurance designed to protect one of the biggest investments of a lifetime. Note that this chapter is devoted to the ownership of a *residence;* the ownership of income-producing property will be discussed in Chapter 24.

HOME OWNERSHIP

People buy their own homes for psychological as well as financial reasons. To many, home ownership is a sign of financial stability. It is an investment that can appreciate in value and provide federal income tax deductions. Home ownership also offers benefits that may be less tangible but are no less valuable: pride, security, and a sense of belonging to the community.

In the past, most homes were single-family dwellings bought by married couples with small children. Today, however, social demographic and economic changes have altered the residential real estate market considerably. Many of today's real estate buyers are *single* men and women; many are *empty-nesters,* married couples whose children have moved away from home. Others are married couples who choose not to have children and unmarried couples. Still others are friends or relatives who plan to co-own a home rather than share an apartment lease.

Types of Housing   As our society evolves, the needs of its homebuyers become more specialized. In addition to the traditional single-family dwelling, the homebuyer can select from the housing types listed in the following paragraphs.

A *condominium* is a popular form of residential ownership, particularly for people who want the security of owning property but do not want the responsibilities of caring for and maintaining a house. Ownership of a condominium—which shares party walls with other units—involves individual ownership of the airspace within the unit itself, plus shared ownership of common facilities such as halls, elevators, and surrounding grounds as undivided interests.

A *cooperative* is similar to a condominium in that it involves units within a larger building with common walls and facilities. An owner of a cooperative unit, however, owns not the unit itself but shares of stock in the cooperative (a type of corporation) that holds title to the building. In return for stock in the cooperative, the owner receives a proprietary lease, which entitles him or her to occupancy of a particular unit in the building.

Town houses, similar to single-family houses, are constructed on lots that are owned by the individual homeowners. They may be connected by a common wall (usually a fire wall), or they may be freestanding homes separated by airspace and attached to each other by exterior shingles and brick or siding. The names of some condominium projects indicate that they are town houses when in reality, if the land is not owned by the individual homeowners, they are condominiums. An examination of the legal description will reveal whether the property is a town home or a condominium (see Chapter 10).

A *planned unit development* (PUD) is a project or subdivision that consists of common property and improvements that are owned and maintained by an owners' association for the benefit and use of the individual housing units within the project. For a project to qualify as a PUD, the owners' association must require automatic, nonseverable membership for each unit owner and provide for mandatory assessments to maintain the common areas.

Converted-use properties are existing structures, such as factories, office buildings, hotels, schools, and churches, that have been converted to residential use as either rental or condominium units. Rather than demolish old structures to make way for new ones, developers often find it aesthetically and economically appealing to renovate the existing buildings into affordable housing. In this manner, an abandoned factory may be transformed into luxury loft condominium units and old warehouses converted to restaurants and shopping areas.

Retirement communities are widely accepted in Texas. They lend themselves particularly well to areas with mild weather conditions. In addition to residential units, retirement communities often provide shopping and recreational opportunities and, in some cases, health care facilities.

Highrise developments that combine office space, stores, theaters, and apartment units are popular across the country, especially in metropolitan areas close to a central city. These complexes usually are self-contained and include laundry facilities, restaurants, food stores, valet shops, beauty parlors, barbershops, swimming pools, and other attractive and convenient features.

Manufactured housing (or *mobile homes*) accounts for approximately one third of the new housing in Texas, according to the Texas Manufactured Housing Association. Relatively low cost, coupled with increased living space in the newer models, has made manufactured housing an attractive alternative to the conventionally constructed residence. Increased sales have resulted in growing numbers of "housing parks" in some communities. These parks offer complete residential environments with permanent community facilities as well as semipermanent foundations and hookups for gas, water, and electricity.

Modular homes, prefabricated structures that arrive at a building location in units preassembled at the factory, are gaining popularity as the price of on-site construction rises. Each preassembled section is set into place on the building site; later, workers finish the structure and install plumbing, wiring, and amenities. In this manner, entire developments can be built at a fraction of the time and cost for conventional construction.

Through *time-shares,* multiple purchasers share ownership of a single property, usually a vacation home. Each owner is entitled to use the property for a certain period of time each year, but many time-share trade agreements exist among developers of this type of property, allowing owners to vacation at various sites. In addition to the purchase price, each owner pays an annual maintenance fee.

Location

Once a buyer has determined the type of housing desired, the physical appearance of a house and its location are probably the most important factors in selecting a home. The elements that contribute to the desirability of a community go beyond geographic area. Five major factors influence the choice of location.

1. *Employment opportunities:* Industrial and commercial development offering vocational opportunities is essential if a community is to grow.
2. *Cultural advantages:* Schools, colleges, places of worship, libraries, theaters, museums, zoos, sports attractions, and parks all constitute a powerful sociological attraction to a given community.
3. *Governmental structure:* Police and fire protection, sanitation, water, and the many public utilities (gas, power, and telephone service, for instance) add to an area's desirability, as do various quasi-municipal authorities such as ports, public transportation, antipollution practices, and forest preserves. Real estate tax rates and a city's plan for and attitude toward growth may affect an area either positively or negatively.
4. *Social services:* The availability and quality of hospitals, clinics, community centers, and similar facilities also attract buyers to a community.

5. *Transportation:* A community's accessibility to people and goods depends on available air, rail, and highway systems. In recent decades, the automobile and truck dominated the transportation industry and made it possible to open new areas for commercial and residential development. Higher energy costs and increased pollution, however, have made the development of better mass transit facilities a greater priority, especially in urban areas. When gasoline prices rose sharply, the railroad attracted renewed interest as an economical means of moving people and freight.

The Real Estate Center at Texas A&M University maintains a web site that contains housing and economic information for each area of Texas. The web site address is http://recenter.tamu.edu.

HOUSING AFFORDABILITY

Certainly not everyone wants to own a home. Home ownership involves substantial commitment and responsibility, and the flexibility of renting suits some individuals' needs. People whose work requires frequent moves or whose financial position is uncertain benefit particularly from renting. Renting also provides more leisure time by freeing tenants from management and maintenance responsibilities.

Those who choose to take on the responsibilities of home ownership must evaluate many factors before they decide to purchase a particular property: mortgage terms, ownership expenses, ability to pay, and other investment considerations. It is often the responsibility of the real estate broker or salesperson to guide prospective homeowners in this process and to help them arrive at acceptable choices.

Mortgage Terms

Liberalized mortgage terms and payment plans offer many people the option of purchasing a home. Low-down-payment mortgage loans are available under programs sponsored by Fannie Mae, the Federal Housing Administration (FHA), and the Department of Veterans Affairs (VA).

In 2000, the home ownership rate reached a record high—66.8%.

An increasing number of creative mortgage loan programs are being offered by various government agencies and local lenders. Adjustable-rate loans, whose lower initial interest rates make it possible for many buyers to qualify for a mortgage loan, are common. Specific programs may offer lower closing costs or deferred interest or principal payments for low-income purchasers or for first-time buyers. Many innovative loans are tailored to suit the young buyer, who may need a low interest rate to qualify but whose income is expected to increase in the coming years.

Ownership Expenses and Ability To Pay

Home ownership involves many expenses, including utilities (such as electricity, natural gas, and water), trash removal, sewer charges, and maintenance and repairs. Owners also must pay real estate taxes, buy property insurance, and repay the mortgage loan with interest. Income lost because money invested in a home is not available for income-producing investments is also a cost of home ownership.

To determine whether a prospective buyer can afford a certain purchase, lenders have traditionally used a rule-of-thumb formula: the monthly cost of buying and maintaining a home (mortgage principal plus interest on the remaining balance plus one-twelfth of annual taxes and insurance) should not exceed 25 to 28 percent of a borrower's gross (pretax) monthly income. The payments on *all* debts should not exceed 33 to 36 percent of gross monthly income. Which qualifying ratio is used and how strictly those formulas are applied, however, depend on such factors as the type of loan, amount of down payment, potential future earnings, number of dependents, credit history, and general economic conditions.

> The basic costs of owning a home are mortgage *P*rincipal and *I*nterest, *T*axes and *I*nsurance, easily remembered by the acronym **PITI.**

FOR EXAMPLE A prospective homebuyer wants to know how much house he or she can afford to buy. The buyer has a gross monthly income of $3,000. The buyer's maximum PITI payment may be calculated as follows:

$3,000 gross monthly income × 28% = $840 maximum PITI payment

$3,000 gross monthly income × 36% = $1,080 total debt allowed (including PITI payment and other debt expense)

Investment Considerations

Building a new home to personal specifications versus buying a preowned home is an investment consideration. A new home may be considerably more expensive if the preowned market is oversupplied. In addition, the new-construction buyer must evaluate the ability to recoup the added costs of special custom features when the property is resold.

Investing in a home also offers several financial advantages. First, the mortgaged property represents an **investment.** If the property's value increases, a sale could bring in more money than the owner paid—resulting in a long-term gain. Second, as the total mortgage debt is reduced through monthly payments, the owner's actual ownership interest in the property increases. This increasing ownership interest is called **equity** and represents the current market value of the property minus any loans. Equity builds even faster when the property's value rises. The third financial advantage of home ownership is the tax deductions available to homeowners.

In Practice

As with other types of investments, real estate can be subject to negative market forces (similar to those that affect stocks and bonds). The market value of an investment can decrease as well as increase, even to the point that the loan balance exceeds the market value. This is a serious concern to lenders, mortgage loan insurers, and investors and should be considered by prospective owners.

Research Sources

Buyers, sellers, and real estate agents can access a wealth of information through the Internet. Consumer-oriented sites may contain "homes for sale," "neighborhood information," "finding a real estate agent," "financing options," "offer and closing," "moving," and "owning." Most sites include question-and-answer segments and worksheets to determine how much money a buyer could borrow. One site even includes a "virtual home tour with panoramic views." A few of these sites are www.homeadvisor.com, www.realtor.com, www.homepath.com, www.mbaa.org/consumer, and http://realestate.yahoo.com.

TAX BENEFITS FOR HOMEOWNERS

To encourage and enhance the viability of home ownership, the federal government allows homeowners certain income tax advantages. Besides mortgage interest, a homeowner may deduct real estate taxes and certain other expenses from gross income. Under certain circumstances, he or she may reduce or eliminate a tax liability on the profits received from the sale of a home. (These benefits are summarized in Table 4.1.)

Income Tax Deductions

For income tax purposes, homeowners are entitled to four deductions from their gross income:

1. Mortgage interest payments on first and second homes.
2. Real estate taxes.
3. Certain loan origination fees.
4. Certain loan discount points—*if* the mortgage is secured by the taxpayer's *principal* residence, *if* the points are paid in cash at closing, and *if* they are a charge for the use of money (interest, *not* fees), all loan discount points can be deducted in the year of the purchase. Otherwise, they are prorated over the term of the loan. For income tax purposes, discount points paid by the seller to the lender for the buyer's financing are deductible by the buyer.

Capital Gains

Capital gains are the *profits* realized from the sale or exchange of an asset, including real property. To stimulate investment in the economy, Congress at various times has allowed part of a taxpayer's capital gains to be free from income tax.

With the passage of the Taxpayer Relief Act of 1997 and its implementation for sales made on or after May 7, 1997, married homeowners who file jointly are able to exclude up to $500,000 of capital gains realized on the sale or exchange of a principal residence. For single homeowners, the maximum exclusion is $250,000. The exclusion is allowed each time a homeowner sells or exchanges a principal residence but generally no more frequently than once every two years.

> Married homeowners filing jointly may exclude up to $500,000 of capital gains on the sale of a principal residenceowner-occupied at least 2 of the 5 years preceding the sale.

To be eligible for the exclusion, a homeowner must have owned the residence and occupied it as a principal residence for at least two of the five years prior to the sale or exchange. A homeowner who fails to meet these requirements because of a change of place of employment, health, or other unforeseen circumstances is able to exclude the fraction of the $500,000 ($250,000 for a single taxpayer) that is equal to the fraction of two years that these residency requirements are met. In the case of persons filing jointly but not sharing a principal residence, an exclusion of $250,000 is available on a qualifying sale or exchange of the principal residence of one of the spouses. Similarly, if a single person who is otherwise eligible for an exclusion marries someone who has used the exclusion within the two years prior to the marriage, the newly married homeowner will be allowed a maximum exclusion of $250,000. Once both spouses satisfy the eligibility rules and two years have passed since the last exclusion was allowed to either of them, the taxpayers may exclude $500,000 of gain on their joint return.

For most homeowners, the net result of the Taxpayer Relief Act of 1997 is that *they will never pay capital gains tax on the sale of their homes.* Con-

Table 4.1 **Homeowner's Tax Benefits**

Capital Gains

- Up to $500,000 exclusion of profit on the sale of a home owned and occupied as principal residence for at least two of the five years before the sale ($250,000 for a single taxpayer)
- Exclusion of profit allowed on each sale of a principal residence but not more often than every two years
- Capital gains tax rates limited to 20% (in the 28% bracket) or 10% (in the 15% bracket)

Income Tax Deductions

- Loan interest on first and second homes, subject to limitation
- Real estate taxes
- Loan origination fees
- Some loan discount points

First-Time Homebuyers

- Penalty-free withdrawals up to $10,000 from an IRA for first-time homebuyers

Estate Tax Exemption

- For owners of family farms and small businesses, $1.3 million until 2004
- For other Americans, up to $1 million until 2004

cerns about the capital gains consequences of a sale are effectively eliminated for the majority of homeowners. Sellers of higher-bracket homes who have accumulated profits that exceed $500,000 will continue to face federal capital gains taxation for the gains over $500,000. However, the Taxpayer Relief Act of 1997 limits the tax rate to 20% on long-term capital gains (10% for individuals in the 15% tax bracket). Under certain circumstances for purchases closed after December 31, 2000, a lower rate of 18% (8% for taxpayers in the 15% tax bracket) applies to transactions in which the asset was held more than five years.

First-Time Homebuyers

To meet down payment requirements, first-time homebuyers may make penalty-free withdrawals from their tax-deferred individual retirement accounts (IRAs). The limit on such withdrawals for a first-time down payment is $10,000.

Estate Tax Exemption

For owners of family farms and small businesses, the death tax exemption was increased to $1.3 million on January 1, 1998. For most Americans, the federal estate tax exemption was raised to $1 million in assets for the years 2002-2003, up from $675,000 for 2000-2001. The exemption will increase for all Americans to $1.5 million in 2004, $2.0 million in 2006, and $3.5 million in 2009. The estate tax is scheduled to be eliminated in 2010.

In Practice

Consult the Internal Revenue Service, a certified public accountant, or a tax lawyer for further information on, and precise applications of, these and other income tax issues. IRS regulations are subject to frequent revision and official interpretation. **It is illegal for a real estate licensee to give tax or legal advice to clients or customers, unless the licensee is also a tax specialist or licensed attorney.**

HOMEOWNER'S INSURANCE

Home ownership represents a significant financial investment, and home buyers usually *want* to insure their property to protect this investment. If the property is used to secure a loan, lenders usually *require* that a homeowner obtain insurance.

Although it is possible for a homeowner to obtain individual policies for fire or windstorm, injury to others, and theft of personal property, most buy a package **homeowner's insurance policy** to cover all these risks on owner-occupied property.

Characteristics of Homeowner's Packages

Although coverage may vary among policies, all homeowner's policies have three common characteristics: (1) fixed ratios of coverage, (2) indivisible premium, and (3) first-party and third-party insurance.

Fixed ratios of coverage require that each type of coverage be maintained at a certain level. This means that the amount of coverage on household contents and other items must be a fixed percentage of the amount of insurance on the building itself. Although the amount of contents coverage may be increased, it cannot be reduced below the standard percentage, which is 60 percent on an *HO–B* policy. In addition, theft coverage may be contingent on the full amount of the contents coverage.

An *indivisible premium* combines the rates for covering each peril into a single amount. For the single rate, the insured receives coverage for all perils included in the policy (see the lists that follow); the insured may not pick and choose the perils to be included.

First-party and third-party insurance provides coverage for damage or loss to the insured's property or its contents. It also covers the insured's legal liability for losses or damages to another's property or injuries suffered while on the owner's property.

The basic form of homeowner's coverage in Texas, known as *HO-A*, provides property coverage against the following perils:

- Fire or lightning
- Glass breakage
- Windstorm or hail
- Explosion
- Riot or civil commotion
- Damage by aircraft
- Damage from vehicles
- Damage from smoke
- Vandalism
- Theft
- Loss of property removed from the premises when endangered by fire or other perils

Most Texas homeowners purchase *HO-B* policies.

Increased coverage is provided under the most commonly issued Texas homeowner's policy, *HO-B,* which covers the following additional perils and provides for replacement-cost coverage:

- Falling objects
- Weight of ice, snow, or sleet
- Collapse of the building or any part of it
- Bursting, cracking, burning, or bulging of a steam or hot water heating system or of appliances used to heat water*
- Accidental discharge, leakage, or overflow of water or steam from within a plumbing, heating, or air-conditioning system*
- Freezing of plumbing, heating, and air-conditioning systems and domestic appliances
- Injury to electrical appliances, devices, fixtures, and wiring from short circuits or other accidentally generated currents.

Further coverage may be provided by adding other comprehensive forms known as **endorsements** or *riders.* These policies allow increased contents or liability coverage and can cover all possible perils except flood, earthquake, war, and nuclear attack. The most common endorsements cover glass breakage; replacement cost on personal property; increased liability coverage; and increased limits on jewelry, watches, and furs. The homeowner's insurance policy provides very broad coverage that goes far beyond the minimum coverage requirements of lenders. Mortgage lenders generally require only fire and extended coverage (hail, windstorm, and such) in an amount at least equal to the loan balance. This type of insurance applies only to the structure and not to its contents. Real estate agents also should be aware that insurance companies may require that properties purchased below replacement cost (as might be the case in foreclosure or other distress sale situations) be insured at market value rather than at purchase price.

Claims   Most homeowner's insurance policies contain a **coinsurance clause.** The State Board of Insurance requires that the insured maintain property fire insurance in an amount equal to *at least* 80 percent of the *replacement cost* of the dwelling (not including the price of the land); however, some insurance companies require 90 to 100 percent coverage on certain policies. If the owner carries such a policy, a claim may be made for the cost of the repair or replacement of the damaged property without deduction for underinsurance.

For example, a homeowner's dwelling that has been damaged by fire has a replacement cost of $100,000 and a repair estimate for $71,000 damage. If the homeowner carries at least $80,000 insurance on the dwelling ($100,000 × .80), the claim against the insurance company can be for the full $71,000.

If the homeowner carries coverage of less than 80 percent of the full replacement cost of the dwelling, the loss will be settled either for the actual cash value (cost of repairs less depreciation) or for a prorated amount calculated by dividing the percentage of replacement cost actually covered by the policy by the minimum coverage requirement (usually 80 percent), whichever is greater. For example, if the building is insured for only 60 percent of its value and there is a $71,000 loss, the insurance company will pay only $53,250 (60 percent ÷ 80 percent, or 75 percent of $71,000 = $53,250).

---

* Covers water damage only, not plumbing repairs.

In any event, *the total settlement cannot exceed the face value of the policy.* Because of coinsurance clauses, homeowners periodically should review all policies to be certain that the coverage is equal to at least 80 percent of the current replacement cost of their homes unless the policy contains an "inflation clause," which automatically adjusts the amount of coverage.

To discourage the filing of a large number of small claims, which would take a significant amount of paperwork and expense to handle, **deductible clauses** are included in insurance policies. In general, the larger the deductible, the lower the premium.

National Flood Insurance Program

The *National Flood Insurance Act of 1968* was enacted by Congress to help owners of property in floodplain areas by subsidizing flood insurance and by requiring communitywide land management and flood control programs. The Federal Insurance Administration (FIA) conducts a detailed study of a community and issues a detailed Flood Insurance Rate Map, establishing zones and rates for the entire area. Federal law requires that owners of properties on which a "structure" is located in a floodplain area obtain flood insurance if properties are financed by loans provided, regulated, or insured by the federal government or purchased by Fannie Mae or Freddie Mac secondary mortgage market agencies. As a condition for making a loan, an individual lender may require flood insurance if *any part* of the property is in a flood zone. All types of buildings—residential, commercial, industrial, and agricultural—are required to maintain this coverage for either the value of the improvement or the amount of the mortgage loan, subject to the maximum limits available.

The Federal Emergency Management Agency (FEMA) sets program standards; the FIA sets rates, coverage limits, and eligibility requirements for flood insurance. Annual policies can be written directly with the National Flood Insurance Program (NFIP) or any licensed property insurance carrier. In participating communities, the NFIP also offers a Preferred Risk Policy for any one- to four-unit dwelling not existing in a floodplain area and not having more than one previous flood loss in excess of $1,000.

The NFIP defines flooding as a general and temporary condition during which the surface of normally dry land is partially or completely inundated by water. Covered losses include

- an overflow of inland or tidal waters,
- an unusual and rapid accumulation or runoff of surface waters,
- mudslides or mudflows on the surface of normally dry land areas, and
- the collapse of land along the shore of a body of water (under certain circumstances).

Flood policies exclude coverage for many of the same types of property as those that are not covered by fire insurance. The list includes such items as money, lawns, livestock, motorized vehicles, fences, swimming pools, and underground structures and equipment. More information about the National Flood Insurance Program can be obtained from the Houston regional office at 1-713-531-5990 or from the FEMA home page at www.fema.gov.

Summary

Current trends in home ownership include traditional single-family homes, condominiums, cooperatives, town houses, planned unit developments, converted-use properties, retirement communities, high-rise developments, manufactured housing, modular homes, and time-shared occupancy of vacation homes. A prospective homebuyer should note a house's specific characteristics and evaluate the desirability of the community based on its cultural activities, employment opportunities, recreational and social facilities, and transportation (among others).

Prospective buyers should be aware of both the advantages and disadvantages of home ownership. Although a homeowner gains financial security and pride of ownership, the costs of ownership—both the initial price and the continuing expenses—must be considered.

An income tax benefit available to homeowners is deduction of mortgage interest payments and property taxes from their federal income taxes. Married homeowners who file jointly are able to exclude up to $500,000 of capital gains on the sale or exchange of a principal residence. A homeowner must have owned the residence and occupied it as a principal residence for at least two of the five years prior to the sale or exchange. For gains exceeding $500,000, the tax rate is capped at 20 percent.

To protect their real estate investment, most homeowners purchase a standard homeowner's insurance policy that covers fire, theft, and liability and can be extended to cover other risks. Most homeowner's policies contain a coinsurance clause that requires that the policyholder maintain fire insurance in an amount equal to 80 percent of the replacement cost of the home. If this percentage is not met, the policyholder may not be reimbursed for full repair costs if a loss occurs. In addition to homeowner's insurance, the federal government makes flood insurance mandatory for people who wish to obtain federally regulated or federally insured mortgage loans on properties in flood-prone areas.

Questions

1. The real cost of owning a home includes expenses that many people tend to overlook. Which of the following is **NOT** a cost or an expense of owning a home?
   a. Interest paid on borrowed capital
   b. Homeowner's insurance
   c. Maintenance and repairs
   d. Taxes on personal property

2. If a single person who is eligible for a tax exclusion marries someone who has used the exclusion within the two years prior to the marriage, what is the maximum exclusion he or she may claim?
   a. $500,000
   b. $125,000
   c. $175,000
   d. $250,000

3. In buying a house using a mortgage loan, the difference between the amount owed on the property and its current market value represents the homeowner's
   a. tax basis.
   b. equity.
   c. replacement cost.
   d. capital gain.

4. When choosing a location in which to live, a homebuyer is **LEAST** likely to be influenced by the area's
   a. transportation facilities.
   b. employment opportunities.
   c. availability of medical facilities.
   d. street signage.

5. A homeowner's insurance policy excludes
   a. the cost of medical expenses for a person injured in the policyholder's home.
   b. riot and civil commotion.
   c. accidental overflow of water from within a plumbing system.
   d. flood damage.

6. A building that is remodeled into residential units and no longer is used for its original purpose is a
   a. converted-use property.
   b. cooperative.
   c. planned unit development.
   d. modular home.

7. In a homeowner's insurance policy, the term *coinsurance* refers to
   a. the specific form of policy purchased by the owner.
   b. the stipulation that the homeowner must purchase fire insurance coverage equal to at least 80 percent (in some cases 90 to 100 percent) of the replacement cost of the structure to be able to collect the full insured amount in the event of a loss.
   c. the stipulation that the homeowner must purchase fire insurance coverage equal to at least 70 percent of the replacement cost of the structure to be able to collect the full insured amount in the event of a loss.
   d. additional insurance held by the homeowner other than the homeowner's policy.

8. Federal flood insurance is
   a. required in certain areas to insure against flood damage for 100-year floodplain properties financed by federally related mortgage loans.
   b. a common part of a homeowner's insurance policy.
   c. an option available to the homeowner on properties financed by FHA or VA mortgage loans.
   d. optional for most homes in flood-prone areas.

9. Under the provisions for liability coverage in a homeowner's insurance policy, the insurance company may settle a claim for
   a. physical damage to the insured's property.
   b. funeral expenses for the insured's child.
   c. personal injury to a delivery person who is injured on the insured's property.
   d. flood damage.

10. A town house is most closely associated with which of the following types of housing?
    a. Highrise development
    b Cooperative
    c. Urban homestead
    d. Single-family residence

11. As a rule of thumb, today's mortgage lenders will not make a loan in which each monthly payment exceeds what percentage of a borrower's monthly income?
    a. 25 to 28 percent   c. 20 percent
    b. 33 to 36 percent   d. 30 percent

12. Under the Taxpayer Relief Act of 1997, the profit a homeowner receives from the sale of his or her residence
    a. is never taxable.
    b. is always considered "taxable gain" for tax purposes.
    c. can be excluded from taxation if a couple has occupied the residence for at least two years prior to the sale.
    d. cannot be excluded from taxation for a couple if one spouse has previously taken the exclusion.

13. A homeowner sold his house for $127,500. The house had been purchased new three years earlier for $75,000. What is the homeowner's gain on this transaction?
    a. $53,250   c. $51,750
    b. $52,500   d. $75,000

14. In question 13, how much of the gain will be subject to income tax?
    a. All of it   c. $21,300
    b. $20,700   d. None

15. Brendon and Sara Wilson, ages 36 and 38, sell their home and realize a gain from the sale. If certain conditions are met, the tax levied on the profit from the sale may be
    a. excluded up to $250,000 if one spouse has used the exclusion in the last 2 years.
    b. excluded up to $500,000 if the couple occupied it as a residence for one year prior to the sale.
    c. excluded up to $500,000 if both spouses have used the exclusion within two years prior to their marriage.
    d. excluded up to $500,000 if one year has passed since the last exclusion.

16. A development that includes office space, stores, theaters, and apartment units is an example of which of the following?
    a. A planned unit development
    b. A highrise development
    c. A converted-use property
    d. A cooperative

5 Real Estate Brokerage and the Law of Agency

OVERVIEW

The business of bringing buyers and sellers together in the marketplace is **brokerage.** In the real estate business, a **broker** is defined broadly as a person who is licensed to buy, sell, exchange, or lease real property *for others* and to *charge a fee* for his or her services.

This chapter discusses the complex legal relationships among buyers, sellers and brokers in real estate. The chapter also examines the nature of the real estate brokerage business.

THE LAW OF AGENCY

The **law of agency** defines the rights and duties of the parties in a real estate transaction—the principal, the agent, and the customer. The **principal,** or **client**—the person who employs the broker—may be a seller, a prospective buyer, an owner who wishes to lease his or her property, or a person seeking property to rent. The real estate broker acts as the **agent** of

> An agent is a person authorized to act on behalf of another.

the principal, and may use other licensed brokers to assist as **subagents.** The principal usually compensates the broker with a **commission** or fee. This compensation is contingent on the broker's performing successfully the service for which he or she was employed, which generally is negotiating a transaction with a third party or **customer**—a prospective purchaser, seller, lessor, or lessee—who is ready, willing, and able to complete the contract.

> An agent works *for* the *client* and *with* the *customer.*

In the traditional real estate sales transaction, the broker is hired by a seller to market his or her real estate. In this situation the broker is an *agent* of the seller; the seller is the broker's *client.* Unless otherwise agreed on, a buyer who contacts the broker to review properties listed with the broker's firm is merely the broker's *customer.* Though obligated to deal honestly and fairly with all parties to a transaction [TREC Rule 22 TAC 535.156(b)], the broker is strictly accountable *only to the principal*—in this case, the seller. The broker must never mislead the buyer into thinking the buyer is being represented by the broker. To clarify the role of the broker or salesperson, the Texas legislature requires that the licensee make clear to all parties which party he or she is acting for [TRELA 15(a)(6)(D)]. It is becoming increasingly common for a broker to represent a buyer for a fee, and in this situation the statute requires that the broker disclose the buyer agency to the seller and the seller's agent, if the seller has one.

Types of Agencies

The authorized activity of an agent is as simple or as complex as the principal dictates and the agent consents to. An agent may be classified as a general agent or a special agent, based on the authority delegated.

A **general agent** is empowered to represent the principal in a *broad range of matters* and may bind the principal to any contracts within the scope of the agent's authority. The real estate broker typically does *not* have this scope of authority as an agent in a real estate transaction. However, the relationship between a broker (as a principal) and the broker's salesperson (as an agent) is usually a general agency relationship. The relationship of a property owner to a property manager is also an example of general agency.

> A general agent represents the principal *generally;* a special agent represents the principal only for *special occasions*, such as the sale of a house.

A **special agent** is authorized to represent the principal in *one specific act or business transaction, under detailed instructions.* A real estate broker is usually a special agent. If hired by a seller, the broker is limited to finding a "ready, willing, and able" buyer for the property. A special agent for a buyer has the limited responsibility of finding a property that meets the buyer's criteria. As a special agent, the broker may not bind or obligate the principal (client).

Creation of Agency

Agency is created at the broker level, not the salesperson level. The real estate broker-seller relationship generally is created by an employment contract, commonly referred to as a **listing agreement** (see Chapter 13). A broker-buyer agency relationship is created by a **buyer representation agreement.**

Written listing agreements and buyer representation agreements are examples of **express agency,** in which the parties state the contract's terms and express their intentions. On the other hand, a broker's actions may create an **implied agency** relationship. Buyers can easily assume that when they contact a salesperson to show them property, the salesperson becomes "their agent." An implied agency with the buyer can result if the words and conduct of the salesperson do not dispel this assumption.

Agency by ratification is an agency "after the fact." For instance, an agent who obtains a purchase contract for a property that has not been listed might be considered an agent by ratification if the seller subsequently ratified, or agreed to, the contract.

Although a written express agency listing agreement usually is preferred, having a written contract is not a requirement for creating an agency relationship. The primary ingredients in creation of agency are (1) delegation of authority by the principal, (2) acceptance of such by the agent, (3) reliance on the agent by the principal, and (4) control of the agent by the principal. Notice that compensation of the agent is not required; at best, it merely *indicates* an agency relationship. This means that the agent can work for nothing or be paid by anyone. In fact, the agent can be paid by either party, so long as the legally required disclosures are made.

A prudent real estate broker will not rely on an oral agreement from his or her principal but will require that all agreements be in writing and signed by the principal because oral agreements are unenforceable in court.

Termination of Agency

Generally, an agency relationship may be terminated at any time. An agency may be terminated by the acts of the parties or by operation of law for any of the following reasons:

- Death or incapacity of either party (notice of death is not necessary)
- Destruction or condemnation of the property
- Expiration of the term of the agency
- Mutual agreement to terminate the agency (must be written)
- Renunciation by the broker or revocation by the owner
- Bankruptcy of the owner if title transferred to receiver
- Completion or fulfillment of the purpose for which the agency was created

Agency cannot be assigned without the consent of the principal, because agency creates a personal obligation. Agency cannot be terminated wrongfully to avoid paying a fee.

Agent's Responsibilities to Principal

The role of a broker as the agent of the principal is a **fiduciary relationship**—one in which the agent is placed in a position of trust and confidence and normally is responsible for the money and/or property of another. As an agent, the broker owes the principal certain duties. They are not simply moral or ethical; they are the law—the *law of agency.* The agent owes the principal the duties of *care, obedience, accounting, loyalty* and *disclosure.*

Care. As an agent, the broker must exercise a reasonable degree of care while transacting business entrusted to the broker by the principal, and the broker is liable to the principal for any loss resulting from the broker's negligence or carelessness. If the agent represents the seller, care includes helping the seller arrive at an appropriate and realistic listing price, making reasonable efforts to market the property (such as advertising and holding open houses), and helping the seller evaluate the terms and conditions of offers to purchase. If the agent represents the buyer, care includes helping the buyer locate a suitable property; evaluate property values, neighborhood, and property conditions; and weigh financing alternatives, offers, and counteroffers—with the buyer's interests in mind.

Obedience. The broker is obligated to act in good faith at all times, obeying the principal's instructions. The broker, however, is not required to obey unlawful or unethical instructions because illegal acts do not serve the principal's best interest.

FOR EXAMPLE *A seller tells a broker that he or she will not sell to a member of a particular minority group. Because refusing to show a property to someone on the basis of race is illegal, the agent cannot follow the seller's instructions.*

Accounting. The broker must be able to report the status of all funds received from or on behalf of the principal. The Texas license law requires that brokers give accurate copies of all documents to all parties affected. In addition, the license law and related rules require that the broker deposit all funds entrusted to him or her in a special trust, or escrow, account "by the close of business of the second working day after execution of the contract by the principals." The law also makes it illegal for the broker to **commingle,** or mix, such monies with personal funds.

Loyalty. The broker owes the principal the utmost loyalty. An agent always must place a principal's interests above those of the agent and above those of others with whom the agent deals. Thus an agent cannot disclose information such as the principal's financial condition, the fact that the principal (if the seller) will accept a price lower than the listing price for his or her real estate, or any similar confidential facts that might harm the principal's bargaining position. On the other hand, loyalty dictates that the broker (if representing the seller as agent or subagent) must disclose to the seller any statements made by a buyer that reflect willingness to raise the offer if an initial offer is not accepted.

The Texas law forbids brokers or salespeople to buy property listed with them for their own accounts, or for accounts in which they have a personal interest, without first notifying the principal of such interest and receiving his or her consent. Likewise, by law neither brokers nor salespeople may sell property in which they have a personal interest without so informing the purchaser.

Disclosure. It is the broker's duty to keep the principal fully informed at all times of all facts or information the broker obtains that could affect the principal's decisions. The broker may be held liable for damages for failure to disclose such information. For example, an *agent for the seller* has a duty to disclose

- the agent's opinion of the market value of the property;
- all offers received (unless the seller has a binding contract on the property or has specifically instructed the listing broker not to bring offers below a certain price);
- the identity of prospective purchasers, including any relationship the agent has with them;
- the ability of a purchaser to complete the sale or offer a higher price;
- any interest the broker has in the buyer (such as the buyer's asking the broker to manage the property after it is purchased); or
- the buyer's intention to resell the property for a profit.

An *agent for a buyer* must inform the buyer of deficiencies of a property as well as sales contract provisions and financing that do not suit the buyer's

> The five fiduciary duties may be remembered by the acronym **COALD:** *C*are, *O*bedience, *A*ccounting, *L*oyalty, and *D*isclosure.

needs. The broker would suggest the lowest price that the buyer should pay based on comparable values, regardless of the listing price. The agent would disclose information about how long a property has been listed or why the seller is selling if it would affect the buyer's ability to negotiate the lowest purchase price. Note that this information, if the agent were representing the seller, would violate the agent's fiduciary duty to the seller.

In Practice

Because fiduciary obligations cannot be taken lightly, it is crucial that a broker exercise the right to reject any proposed agency relationship that in his or her judgment violates legal or ethical standards.

Principal's Responsibilities to Agent

The principal also owes certain duties to the agent or broker. Among these are compensation, information, indemnification, and availability.

The common-law duties of a principal (client) to an agent may be remembered by the acronym *CIIA*: *Compensation, Information, Indemnification* and *Availability*.

Compensation. The principal is liable for compensating the broker by paying the specified fee on completion of the broker's duties. This means that the principal must pay a commission or fee when the broker has performed the broker's portion of the listing agreement and produced a buyer who is ready, willing, and able to purchase.

Information. The principal must furnish accurate information requested by the broker. The broker is entitled to rely on such information, unless he or she has reason to know of its falsity.

Indemnification. The principal agrees to indemnify or reimburse the broker if the broker suffers financial injury while performing his or her duties as broker. This means the broker is "held harmless" during the agency relationship.

Availability. The principal must be available at reasonable times to consider offers, to accept notices, or to permit the showing of the property. If the principal will not be available, arrangements must be made to ensure accessibility for the broker.

Agent's Responsibilities to Customers

Even though an agent's primary responsibility is to the principal, the agent also has duties to third parties, or customers. For example, brokers must carefully monitor statements they or their staff members make about a parcel of real estate. Statements of opinion are permissible so long as they are offered as opinions and without any intention to deceive. Making exaggerated or unsubstantiated statements of value when selling real estate is called **puffing.** Although permissible under agency law, statements of opinion and puffing should be avoided because of possible claims under the *Deceptive Trade Practices Act* that they misled the consumer.

Puffing = opinion

Misrepresentation = unintentional untruth

Fraud = intentional untruth or nondisclosure

Brokers and salespeople must secure accurate information to avoid **misrepresentation,** the *unintentional* misstatement of a fact. Additionally, they must ensure that none of their statements can be interpreted in any way as involving fraud. **Fraud** is the *intentional* misstatement of a material fact for the purpose of harming or taking advantage of another person. In addition to false statements about a property, the concept of fraud covers intentional concealment or nondisclosure of important facts. If a contract to purchase real estate is obtained as a result of fraudulent misstatements made by a broker or his or her salespeople, the contract may be disaffirmed or rescinded by the purchaser. In such a case, the broker will lose a commission. If either party suffers loss because of a broker's misrepresentations, the broker also can be held liable for damages. If the broker's misstatements are based on the owner's inaccurate statements to the broker, however, the broker may be entitled to a commission even if the buyer rescinds the sales contract.

Parties to and licensees in a transaction are protected from liability for the misrepresentation or concealment of material facts by each other or by a subagent unless the party or licensee knew of the falsity of the misrepresentation or concealment and failed to disclose that knowledge. Brokers, however, are still responsible for the acts or omissions of their salespeople.

> An agent owes a customer the duties of *reasonable care and skill; honest and fair dealing,* and *disclosure of known material facts about the property.*

Brokers and salespeople should know that the courts have ruled that a seller is responsible for revealing to a buyer any *hidden,* or *latent, defects* in a building. *A latent defect is one that is known to the seller but not to the buyer and that is not discoverable by ordinary inspection.* As an agent of the seller, a broker is likewise responsible for disclosing known latent defects. Buyers have been able to either rescind the sales contract or receive damages in such instances. Examples of such circumstances are cases in which a buried drain tile caused water to accumulate, a driveway was built partly on adjoining property, or a house was built over a ditch that was covered with decaying timber. Section 15(E)(2) of the *Texas Real Estate License Act* releases a seller or seller's agent from the duty to disclose information related to whether a death by natural causes, suicide, or accident unrelated to the condition of the property occurred on the property. Presumably other conditions related to any stigma attached to the property (e.g., murder or molestation on the property or a reputation for being haunted) would have to be disclosed. Further discussion of the *Texas Deceptive Trade Practices-Consumer Protection Act* and the *Fraud in Real Estate and Stock Transactions Statute* is included at the end of this chapter.

FOR EXAMPLE   *Case 1:* While showing a potential buyer a very average-looking house, a broker described even its plainest features as "charming" and "beautiful." Because the statements were obviously the broker's personal opinions, designed to encourage a positive feeling about the property (or puff it up), their truth or falsity probably would not be an issue.

Case 2: A broker was asked by a potential buyer if a particular neighborhood was safe. Although the broker knew that the area was experiencing a skyrocketing rate of violent crime, he assured the buyer that no problem existed. He also neglected to inform the buyer that the lot next to the house the buyer was considering had been sold to a waste disposal company for use as a toxic dump. Both the statement and the omission are examples of fraud.

In Practice   Because of the enormous exposure to liability that real estate licensees have under the law, some brokers purchase errors and omissions insurance policies for their firms. Similar to medical malpractice insurance, such policies generally cover liabilities for errors, mistakes, and negligence in the usual listing and selling activities of a real estate office. They do not cover intentional acts or trebling or multiplication of damages under the Texas Deceptive Trade Practices Act.

AGENCY POSITIONS AND DISCLOSURE

The Real Estate License Act defines four positions a broker might take when doing business with a seller, buyer, landlord, or tenant. The law requires that "a licensee shall furnish to a party in a real estate transaction at the time of the first face-to-face meeting with the party" a "written statement" that sets forth generalized information relative to seller representation, subagency, buyer representation, and the intermediary position (see Figure 5.1, Information About Brokerage Services). The statutorily prescribed written statement does not require signatures, dates, or licensee names and may be printed in any format that uses at least 10-point type. It is not required if

(1) the proposed transaction is for a *residential* lease for not more than one year and no sale is being considered (this exemption does not apply to commercial leases) or

(2) the licensee meets with a party who is represented by another licensee.

Furthermore, a face-to-face meeting requiring an agent to give a party the Information About Brokerage Services *form* does not include a meeting at an open house at which no substantive discussion occurs or a meeting that occurs after the parties have signed a contract. However, the Act does require that an agent *disclose* to persons visiting an open house (either orally or in writing) that he or she represents the seller [Section 15C(a)].

The following is a summary of broker agency positions:

- A broker who lists the property for sale or lease represents the owner as a *seller's agent,* usually through a written listing agreement (see Chapter 13).
- A broker who acts as a *subagent* represents the owner in cooperation with the listing broker; a subagent is not sponsored by or associated with the listing broker.
- A broker who acts as a *buyer's agent* represents the buyer, usually through a written buyer representation agreement (see Figure 5.2).
- A broker may act as an *intermediary* with the written consent of *each* party to the transaction. An **intermediary broker** may appoint a licensed associate **(appointed licensee)**, with the written consent of the parties, to communicate with and carry out instructions of each party. The written consent must state who will pay the broker and set forth the broker's obligations. The intermediary broker (or appointed licensee)

> **Four Statutory Agency Positions:**
>
> 1. Seller's agent
> 2. Subagent
> 3. Buyer's agent
> 4. Intermediary

(1) shall treat all parties honestly;

(2) may not disclose that the owner will accept a price less than the asking price;

(3) may not disclose that a buyer will pay a price greater than submitted in a written offer;

(4) may not disclose any confidential information or any information a party specifically instructs the broker in writing not to disclose unless otherwise instructed or required to do so;

(5) must comply with the Texas Real Estate License Act.

The intermediary broker is *not* allowed to give advice or opinion. However, an appointed licensee may provide advice or opinions to the party to which the licensee has been appointed but may not disclose confidential information prohibited above.

Figure 5.1 *Statement of Broker's Duties*

Approved by the Texas Real Estate Commission for Voluntary Use

Texas law requires all real estate licensees to give the following information about brokerage services to prospective buyers, tenants, sellers and landlords.

Information About Brokerage Services

Before working with a real estate broker, you should know that the duties of a broker depend on whom the broker represents. If you are a prospective seller or landlord (owner) or a prospective buyer or tenant (buyer), you should know that the broker who lists the property for sale or lease is the owner's agent. A broker who acts as a subagent represents the owner in cooperation with the listing broker. A broker who acts as a buyer's agent represents the buyer. A broker may act as an intermediary between the parties if the parties consent in writing. A broker can assist you in locating a property, preparing a contract or lease, or obtaining financing without representing you. A broker is obligated by law to treat you honestly.

IF THE BROKER REPRESENTS THE OWNER:
The broker becomes the owner's agent by entering into an agreement with the owner, usually through a written listing agreement, or by agreeing to act as a subagent by accepting an offer of subagency from the listing broker. A subagent may work in a different real estate office. A listing broker or subagent can assist the buyer but does not represent the buyer and must place the interests of the owner first. The buyer should not tell the owner's agent anything the buyer would not want the owner to know because an owner's agent must disclose to the owner any material information known to the agent.

IF THE BROKER REPRESENTS THE BUYER:
The broker becomes the buyer's agent by entering into an agreement to represent the buyer, usually through a written buyer representation agreement. A buyer's agent can assist the owner but does not represent the owner and must place the interests of the buyer first. The owner should not tell a buyer's agent anything the owner would not want the buyer to know because a buyer's agent must disclose to the buyer any material information known to the agent.

IF THE BROKER ACTS AS AN INTERMEDIARY:
A broker may act as an intermediary between the parties if the broker complies with The Texas Real Estate License Act.

The broker must obtain the written consent of each party to the transaction to act as an intermediary. The written consent must state who will pay the broker and, in conspicuous bold or underlined print, set forth the broker's obligations as an intermediary. The broker is required to treat each party honestly and fairly and to comply with The Texas Real Estate License Act. A broker who acts as an intermediary in a transaction:

    (1) shall treat all parties honestly;

    (2) may not disclose that the owner will accept a price less than the asking price unless authorized in writing to do so by the owner;

    (3) may not disclose that the buyer will pay a price greater than the price submitted in a written offer unless authorized in writing to do so by the buyer; and

    (4) may not disclose any confidential information or any information that a party specifically instructs the broker in writing not to disclose unless authorized in writing to disclose the information or required to do so by The Texas Real Estate License Act or a court order or if the information materially relates to the condition of the property.

With the parties' consent, a broker acting as an intermediary between the parties may appoint a person who is licensed under The Texas Real Estate License Act and associated with the broker to communicate with and carry out instructions of one party and another person who is licensed under that Act and associated with the broker to communicate with and carry out instructions of the other party.

If you choose to have a broker represent you, you should enter into a written agreement with the broker that clearly establishes the broker's obligations and your obligations. The agreement should state how and by whom the broker will be paid. You have the right to choose the type of representation, if any, you wish to receive. Your payment of a fee to a broker does not necessarily establish that the broker represents you. If you have any questions regarding the duties and responsibilities of the broker, you should resolve those questions before proceeding.

Real estate licensee asks that you acknowledge receipt of this information about brokerage services for the licensee's records.

_____   _____

Buyer, Seller, Landlord or Tenant   Date

Texas Real Estate Brokers and Salesmen are licensed and regulated by the Texas Real Estate Commission (TREC). If you have a question or complaint regarding a real estate licensee, you should contact TREC at P.O. Box 12188, Austin, Texas 78711-2188 or 512-465-3960.

FOR EXAMPLE A broker obtains a listing agreement with a seller and becomes the seller's agent. A salesperson in the broker's office has a client who expresses an interest in the property. If that buyer has signed a buyer representation agreement with the broker's firm, there is a potential for a conflict of interest because the broker has an agency relationship with both parties. Unless the broker refers either the buyer or the seller to another real estate firm, the broker will enter into an intermediary relationship with both parties. The broker must immediately obtain the written consent of both parties and explain how the intermediary relationship alters the original relationship with the clients. The broker *may* appoint another salesperson to work with the seller and continue the transaction through *appointed licensees;* however, the broker himself or herself may not serve as one of the appointed licensees.

A licensee who has an established agency relationship with one party in a proposed transaction must disclose that representation either orally or in writing at the time of the licensee's first contact with

(1) another party to the transaction or
(2) another licensee who represents another party to the transaction.

In Practice   The "Information About Brokerage Services" statement is intended to inform sellers, buyers, landlords, and tenants about the statutorily-created alternative methods for doing business with a real estate broker. It must state, "You have the right to choose the type of representation, if any, you wish to receive." This means that the consumer who feels competent to function without representation may elect to have no representation. The Texas Real Estate License Act provides for the suspension or revocation of a license for "failing to make clear, to all parties to a transaction, which party he is acting for . . ." Although S.B. 489 permits disclosure to "another party" or "another licensee" to be made orally or in writing, a broker may want licensed associates to make the agency disclosure in writing as an affirmative defense against a charge of fraud or deceptive trade practice.

Single agency exists when the agent represents only one party to the transaction—the buyer *or* the seller. *Dual agency,* a common-law agency representation, exists when the agent represents *both* parties in the transaction—the buyer *and* the seller. Dual agency can only exist with the informed consent of all parties. The agent's challenge is to fulfill the fiduciary duties— COALD—to both parties without creating a conflict of interest or compromising the interests of either party. In practice, most dual agency situations arise as a result of an express agreement with the seller and an implied agreement with the buyer. If both parties are not aware of and do not consent to the dual agency, an *undisclosed dual agency* relationship is created, which is always illegal—violating the requirement for informed consent of all parties and the common-law duties of loyalty and disclosure. Dual agency should be avoided by agents in favor of intermediary representation under Section 15C of the Texas Real Estate License Act.

Figure 5.2　*Buyer Representation Agreement*

TEXAS ASSOCIATION OF REALTORS®

BUYER/TENANT REPRESENTATION AGREEMENT - RESIDENTIAL

USE OF THIS FORM BY PERSONS WHO ARE NOT MEMBERS OF THE TEXAS ASSOCIATION OF REALTORS® IS NOT AUTHORIZED.
©Texas Association of REALTORS®, Inc. 2001

1. **PARTIES:** The parties to this agreement and the parties' contact information are as follows:

   Client: _____　Broker: _____

   Address: _____　Address: _____

   City, State, Zip: _____　City State, Zip: _____

   Phone: _____　Phone: _____

   Fax: _____　Fax: _____

   E-mail: _____　E-mail: _____

2. **APPOINTMENT:** Client grants to Broker the exclusive right to act as Client's real estate agent for the purpose of acquiring property in the market area.

3. **DEFINITIONS:**

   A. "Acquire" means to purchase or lease.

   B. "Closing" in a sale transaction means the date legal title to a property is conveyed to a purchaser of property under a contract to buy. "Closing" in a lease transaction means the date a landlord and tenant enter into a binding lease of a property.

   C. "Market area" means that area in the State of Texas within the perimeter boundaries of the following areas: _____
   _____
   _____.

   D. "Property" means any interest in real estate including but not limited to properties listed in a multiple listing service or Internet listing services, properties for sale by owners, and properties for sale by builders. Client intends to acquire _____ properties in the market area. If Client intends to acquire more than one property, the terms "property", "price", "purchase", and "lease" will be read to include the plural.

4. **TERM:** This agreement commences on _____ and ends at the earlier of:
   A. 11:59 p.m. on _____; or
   B. the closing of the transaction of the last property that Client intends to acquire.

5. **BROKER'S OBLIGATIONS:** Broker will:
   A. use Broker's best efforts to assist Client in acquiring property in the market area;
   B. assist Client in negotiating the acquisition of property in the market area; and
   C. comply with other provisions of this agreement.

6. **CLIENT'S OBLIGATIONS:** Client will:
   A. work exclusively through Broker in acquiring property in the market area and negotiate the acquisition of property in the market area only through Broker;
   B. inform other brokers, salespersons, sellers, and landlords with whom Client may have contact that Broker exclusively represents Client for the purpose of acquiring property in the market area and refer all such persons to Broker; and
   C. comply with other provisions of this agreement.

7. **REPRESENTATIONS:**
   A. Each person signing this agreement represents that the person has the legal capacity and authority to bind the respective party to this agreement.
   B. Client represents that Client is not now a party to another buyer or tenant representation agreement with another broker for the acquisition of property in the market area.
   C. Client represents that all information relating to Client's ability to acquire property in the market area Client gives to Broker is true and correct.
   D. Name any employer, relocation company, or other entity that will provide benefits to Client when acquiring property in the market area: _____.
   E. Client learned of Broker's firm by: _____.

Figure 5.2 ***Buyer Representation Agreement (Continued)***

Buyer/Tenant Representation Agreement between _____

8. **AGENCY RELATIONSHIPS:** Broker will exclusively represent Client in all transactions contemplated by this agreement except for the acquisition of property listed by Broker. For properties listed by Broker, Client consents to the following agency relationship with Broker. *(Check A or B only.)*

☐ A. Intermediary Status: Client desires to see Broker's listings. If Client wishes to acquire one of Broker's listings, Client authorizes Broker to act as an intermediary as follows. *(Check (1) or (2) only.)*

    ☐ (1) With the Possibility of Appointments:
        (a) If Client wishes to acquire one of Broker's listings that is serviced by an associate other than the associate servicing Client under this agreement, Broker will appoint the licensed associate then servicing Client under this agreement to communicate with, carry out instructions of, and provide opinions and advice during negotiations to Client. Broker will appoint the licensed associate then servicing the owner under the listing agreement to the owner for the same purpose.
        (b) If Client wishes to acquire one of Broker's listings that is serviced by the same associate that is servicing Client under this agreement Broker will notify Client that:
            (1) Broker will assign another licensed associate to communicate with, carry out instructions of, and provide opinions and advice during negotiations to Client and will appoint the licensed associate servicing the owner under the listing agreement to the owner for the same purpose; or
            (2) Broker will make no appointments to either party and the associate servicing the parties will act solely as Broker's intermediary representative. The associate may facilitate the transaction but will not render opinions or advice during negotiations to either party.

    ☐ (2) With No Appointments: Broker will not appoint specific associates to either Client or the owner. Any associate(s) servicing the parties will act solely as Broker's intermediary representative(s). The associate(s) may facilitate the transaction for the parties but will not render opinions or advice during negotiations to either party.

☐ B. No Intermediary Status:

    ☐ (1) Client does not wish to be shown or to acquire any of Broker's listings.

    ☐ (2) Broker exclusively represents buyers or tenants and does not represent sellers or landlords.

Notice: If Broker acts as an intermediary under Paragraph 8A, Broker and any of Broker's associates:
- **may not disclose to Client that the seller or landlord will accept a price less than the asking price unless otherwise instructed in a separate writing by the seller or landlord;**
- **may not disclose to the seller or landlord that Client will pay a price greater than the price submitted in a written offer to the seller or landlord unless otherwise instructed in a separate writing by Client;**
- **may not disclose any confidential information or any information a seller or landlord or Client specifically instructs Broker in writing not to disclose unless otherwise instructed in a separate writing by the respective party or required to disclose the information by the Real Estate License Act or a court order or if the information materially relates to the condition of the property;**
- **shall treat all parties to the transaction honestly; and**
- **shall comply with the Real Estate License Act.**

9. **COMPETING CLIENTS:** Client acknowledges that Broker may represent other prospective buyers or tenants who may seek to acquire properties that may be of interest to Client. Client agrees that Broker may, during the term of this agreement and after it ends, represent such other prospects, show the other prospects the same properties that Broker shows to Client, and act as a real estate broker for such other prospects in negotiating the acquisition of properties that Client may seek to acquire.

10. **CONFIDENTIAL INFORMATION:** During the term of this agreement or after its termination, Broker may not knowingly disclose information obtained in confidence from Client except as authorized by Client or required by law. Broker may not disclose to Client any information obtained in confidence regarding any other person Broker represents or may have represented except as required by law.

11. **BROKER'S FEES:** **(Notice: Section 15(a)(6)(D) of the Real Estate License Act prohibits a broker from receiving compensation from more than one party except with the full knowledge and consent of all parties.)**

    A. Broker's fees under this agreement are as follows: *(Check all that apply.)*

    ☐ (1) Commission: Broker will receive a commission calculated as follows:

        if Client agrees to purchase property in the market area: _____% of the gross sales price; or
        _____; and

        if Client agrees to lease property in the market area: _____% of one month's rent; or
        _____
        _____

Figure 5.2 Buyer Representation Agreement (Continued)

Buyer/Tenant Representation Agreement between _____

   (a) <u>Source of Commission Payment</u>:

   ❏ (1) Broker will seek to obtain payment of the commission specified in Paragraph 11A(1) first from the seller, landlord, or their agents. If such persons refuse or fail to pay Broker the amount specified, Client will pay Broker the amount specified less any amounts Broker receives from such persons.

   ❏ (2) Client will pay Broker the commission specified in Paragraph 11A(1).

   (b) <u>Earned and Payable</u>: A person is not obligated to pay Broker a commission until such time as Broker's commission is *earned and payable*.
       (1) Broker's commission is *earned* when Client enters into a binding written contract for the purchase or lease of property in the market area.
       (2) Broker's commission is *payable*, either during the term of this agreement or after it ends, upon the earlier of:
          (A) the closing of the transaction to acquire the property;
          (B) Client's breach of a written contract to purchase or lease a property in the market area; or
          (C) Client's breach of this agreement.
       (3) If Client acquires more than one property under this agreement, Broker's commissions for each property acquired are earned as each property is acquired and are payable at each closing of the properties acquired.

   (c) <u>Additional Compensation</u>: If a seller, landlord, or their agents offer compensation in excess of the amount stated in Paragraph 11A(1) (for example, marketing incentives or bonuses to cooperating brokers) Broker may retain the additional compensation in addition to the fees specified above. Client is not obligated to pay any such additional compensation to Broker.

   (d) <u>Acquisition of Broker's Listing</u>: Notwithstanding any provision to the contrary, if Client acquires a property listed by Broker, Broker will be paid in accordance with the terms of Broker's listing agreement with the owner and Client will have no obligation to pay Broker.

❏ (2) <u>Hourly Fees</u>: Client will pay Broker fees at the rate of $_____ per hour. If Broker also receives fees under Paragraph 11A(1) or if Client acquires one of Broker's listings, Broker will refund the hourly fees upon receipt of the fees under Paragraph 11A(1) or the listing. Broker's hourly fees are earned when Broker's services are rendered and are payable when billed.

❏ (3) <u>Retainer</u>: Upon execution of this agreement, Client will pay Broker a retainer of $_____. The retainer is earned at the time it is paid. Broker will refund the retainer to Client <u>only</u> upon Broker's receipt of all other fees under this agreement.

B. In addition to the fees under Paragraph 11A, Broker is entitled to the following fees.

   (1) <u>Construction</u>: If Client uses Broker's services to procure or negotiate the construction of improvements to property that Client owns or may acquire, Client will pay Broker at the time the construction is substantially complete a fee equal to: ___ _____. This Paragraph 11B(1) does not apply if the contractor pays Broker the amount specified in this paragraph under a separate agreement.

   (2) <u>Service Providers</u>: If Broker refers Client or any party to a transaction contemplated by this agreement to a service provider (for example, mover, cable company, telecommunications provider, utility, or contractor) Broker may receive a fee from the service provider for the referral.

   (3) <u>Other</u>: _____
       _____
       _____.

C. <u>Protection Period</u>:
   (1) "Protection period" means that time starting the day after this agreement ends and continuing for _____ days.
   (2) If, within the protection period, Client or a related party enters into a contract to acquire property in the market area that was called to Client's attention during the term of this agreement, Client will pay Broker, upon closing, an amount equal to the fees Broker would have been entitled to receive had Client entered into a contract to acquire the property during the term of this agreement, if Broker, not later than 10 days after this agreement ends, sends Client written notice identifying the properties called to Client's attention.
   (3) This Paragraph 11C survives termination of this agreement. This Paragraph 11C will not apply if Client is, during the protection period, bound under a representation agreement with another Texas-licensed real estate broker at the time the acquisition is negotiated and the other broker is paid a fee for negotiating the transaction.

D. <u>County</u>: All amounts payable to Broker are to be paid in cash in _____ County, Texas.

E. <u>Escrow Authorization</u>: Client authorizes, and Broker may so instruct, any escrow or closing agent authorized to close a transaction for the acquisition of property contemplated by this agreement to collect and disburse to Broker all amounts payable to Broker.

(TAR-1501) 7-6-01   Initialed for Identification by Broker/Associate _____ and Client _____, _____   Page 3 of 4

Figure 5.2 Buyer Representation Agreement (Continued)

Buyer/Tenant Representation Agreement between _____

12. **MEDIATION**: The parties agree to negotiate in good faith in an effort to resolve any dispute that may arise related to this agreement or any transaction related to or contemplated by this agreement. If the dispute cannot be resolved by negotiation, the parties will submit the dispute to mediation before resorting to arbitration or litigation and will equally share the costs of a mutually acceptable mediator.

13. **DEFAULT**: If either party fails to comply with this agreement or makes a false representation in this agreement, the non-complying party is in default. If Client is in default, Client will be liable for the amount of compensation that Broker would have received under this agreement if Client was not in default. If Broker is in default, Client may exercise any remedy at law.

14. **ATTORNEY'S FEES**: If Client or Broker is a prevailing party in any legal proceeding brought as a result of a dispute under this agreement or any transaction related to or contemplated by this agreement, such party will be entitled to recover from the non-prevailing party all costs of such proceeding and reasonable attorney's fees.

15. **LIMITATION OF LIABILITY**: Neither Broker, any other broker, or their associates is responsible or liable for Client's personal injuries or for any loss or damage to Client's property. Client will indemnify and hold Broker, any other broker, and their associates harmless from : (1) any personal injury; (2) loss or damage to Client's property; or (3) any injury or damage that Client may cause to others or their property.

16. **ADDENDA**: Addenda and other related documents which are part of this agreement are: **Information about Brokerage Services** and _____

_____.
This agreement will be automatically amended to include the legal description of any properties Client acquires or attempts to acquire under this agreement.

17. **SPECIAL PROVISIONS**:

18. **ADDITIONAL NOTICES**:

   A. **Broker's fees and the sharing of fees between brokers are not fixed, controlled, recommended, suggested, or maintained by the Association of REALTORS® or any listing service.**

   B. **Broker's services are provided without regard to race, color, religion, national origin, sex, disability or familial status. Local ordinances may provide for additional protected classes (e.g., status as a student, marital status, sexual orientation, or age).**

   C. **Broker is not a property inspector, surveyor, engineer, environmental assessor, or compliance inspector. Client should seek experts to render such services for any property Client seeks to acquire.**

   D. **If Client purchases property, Client should have an abstract covering the property examined by an attorney of Client's selection, or Client should be furnished with or obtain a title policy.**

   E. **Broker cannot give legal advice. READ THIS AGREEMENT CAREFULLY. If you do not understand the effect of this agreement, consult your attorney BEFORE signing.**

_____   _____   _____   _____
Broker's Printed Name   License No.   Client's Signature   Date

By: _____   _____   _____   _____
Broker's or Associate's Signature   Date   Client's Signature   Date

(TAR-1501) 7-6-01   Page 4 of 4

Nature of the Brokerage Business

Texas real estate license law regulates many of the day-to-day business operations of a real estate brokerage. Such matters include location of a definite, regular place of business for the firm; use of business signs; requirements for establishing and maintaining branch brokerage offices; proper accounting procedures; correct handling of client trust fund accounts; and the specific manner of execution and retention of documents involved in the real estate transaction. However, it is up to the broker to set effective written policies for every aspect of the brokerage operation: hiring of employees and salespeople, determination of compensation, and direction of staff and sales activities as well as procedures to follow in carrying out agency duties.

Broker-Salesperson Relationship

Although brokerage firms vary widely in size, few brokers perform their duties without the assistance of salespersons. Consequently, much of the business's success hinges on the broker-salesperson relationship.

A real estate salesperson is any person licensed to perform real estate activities on behalf of a licensed real estate broker. All of a salesperson's activities must be performed in the name of the supervising broker. In turn, the broker is fully responsible for the actions performed in the course of the real estate business by all persons licensed under the broker. The salesperson can carry out only those responsibilities assigned by the broker with whom he or she is licensed.

> If a broker intends to receive a commission, fee, or rebate from someone other than the broker's client, the broker must first obtain the consent of his client.
>
> If an agent is to receive a fee for referring a service provider who is being paid by a party the agent does not represent, the agent must get permission from that party to receive the fee.

A broker is licensed to act as the principal's agent and thus can collect compensation for performing assigned duties. A salesperson, on the other hand, has no authority to make contracts or receive compensation directly from a principal. All compensation to the salesperson must be paid with the knowledge and consent of or through the sponsoring broker or through the broker under whom the salesperson was licensed at the time the right to compensation was earned. *Remember that agency with the principal is at the broker level.*

Employee versus independent contractor. Brokers engage salespeople as either employees or independent contractors. Whether a salesperson operates under the broker as an employee or as an independent contractor affects the structure of the salesperson's responsibilities and the broker's liability to pay and withhold taxes from the salesperson's earnings (see Table 5.1).

Table 5.1 *Employee versus Independent Contractor*	
Employee	**Independent Contractor**
Must have income tax and Social Security withheld from wages by broker.	Assumes responsibility for paying own income tax and Social Security.
May receive "employee benefits" from broker.	Cannot receive any "employee benefits" from broker.
	Must have a written contract.
	Must be compensated on production.

The nature of the employer-employee relationship allows a broker to exercise certain *controls* over salespeople who are employees. A person who is required to comply with instructions about when, where, and how he or she is to work is ordinarily an **employee.** The broker may require that an employee adhere to regulations concerning such matters as working hours, office routine, and dress or language standards. As an employer, a broker is required by the federal government to withhold Social Security tax and income tax from wages paid to employees. He or she also is required to pay unemployment compensation tax on wages paid to one or more employees, as defined by state and federal laws. In addition, a broker may be required to provide employees with such benefits as health insurance and profit-sharing plans.

A broker's relationship with an independent contractor is different. The **independent contractor** salesperson operates more freely than an employee, and the broker may not control his or her activities in the same way. Crucial elements of preserving independent contractor status are

- the independent contractor's services must be performed under the terms of a written contract between the broker and the associate;
- the broker may control *what* the independent contractor does, but not *how* it is done; and
- the contract must state that the independent contractor assumes responsibility for paying any required income and Social Security taxes and receives nothing from the broker that could be construed as an employee benefit.

In Practice   Independent contractors provide their own health insurance (if coverage is desired), pay their own travel expenses, and furnish most if not all of their own tools and equipment. The Internal Revenue Service often investigates the independent contractor/employee situation in brokers' offices. A broker should have a clearly drawn employee or independent contractor agreement to define obligations and responsibilities of each salesperson on the staff and should verify that such agreements are being followed explicitly. A signed agreement means little to an IRS auditor if the actions of the parties are contrary to the document's provisions. Therefore, independent contractors are urged to keep detailed records to demonstrate compliance for the IRS.

Compensation   **Broker's compensation.** The broker's compensation is specified in the listing agreement, the buyer representation agreement, the management agreement, or other contract with the principal. Compensation usually is in the form of a commission, professional service fee, or brokerage fee computed as a *percentage of the total amount of money involved.* Such commission typically is considered *earned* once the broker has accomplished the work for which he or she was hired, and payment is *due* at the closing or on the principal's default. When no time is specified in the sales or listing agreement for the payment of the broker's commission, it generally is earned when a completed sales contract has been signed by a ready, willing, and able buyer and accepted by the seller—when the broker *performs* under the terms of the listing contract or buyer representation agreement. Therefore, if the listing contract or buyer representation agreement expires prior to the closing date of the earnest money contract, the broker's commission still is vested; that is, it is not necessary for the listing contract or buyer representation agreement to be extended to include the closing date. Most sales commissions are payable when the sale is consummated by *delivery of the seller's deed* or immediately on *default by the seller.*

According to common law, to be entitled to a sales commission, a selling broker must be able to show that he or she was the **procuring cause** of a sale—that the broker had taken action to start or cause a chain of events that resulted in the sale. Section 20 of the Texas Real Estate License Act lists three *requirements* for compensation:

> To be *a procuring cause,* the broker must have started a chain of events that resulted in a sale.

1. The person held a valid real estate broker's license,
2. The agreement to pay was in writing and signed by the party to be charged,
3. The broker or salesperson advised the buyer in writing prior to closing that the buyer should obtain or be furnished with a title insurance policy or have the abstract covering the subject property examined by an attorney of the buyer's choice.

On accepting an offer from a ready, willing, and able buyer, the seller is technically liable for the broker's commission regardless of whether the seller completes the sale, unless the broker knew or should have known the buyer was not financially able to complete the purchase. A **"ready, willing, and able buyer"** is one who is prepared to buy on the seller's terms and ready to take positive steps toward consummation of the transaction. A broker who has produced such a buyer is usually still entitled to a commission if the transaction is not consummated for any of the following reasons:

> A broker may be due a commission if a transaction is not closed because of the principal's (client's) default.

- The owner has a change of mind and refuses to sell.
- The owner's spouse refuses to sign the deed.
- The owner's title is defective.
- The owner commits fraud with respect to the transaction.
- The owner is unable to deliver possession within a reasonable time.
- The owner insists on terms not in the listing (for example, the right to restrict the use of the property).
- The owner and the buyer agree to cancel the transaction.

There are, however, some situations in which a broker would not be entitled to a commission, including

- failure to give the required title notice to the buyer. The required title notice is a part of the Texas promulgated sales contracts; however, if a licensee uses any contract form other than one promulgated by TREC, the title notice must be given by the licensee either separately or in the contract to purchase. In addition to losing a commission, the agent's real estate license may be revoked or suspended.
- failure to state an amount or percentage rate of commission in a listing contract. The rate of a broker's commission is *negotiable in every case.* If the commission rate was not negotiated, the broker may be unable to collect any fee at all.
- failure (without fault) on the part of the seller to deliver title assurance (an abstract or title insurance policy) to the buyer.

The Texas Real Estate License Act prohibits a real estate licensee from paying a commission, fee, or other valuable consideration to a person who is not licensed as a salesperson or broker for services as a real estate agent. This includes a prohibition against sharing a sales commission with an attorney who is not licensed by TREC. An attorney who is not licensed by TREC but performs brokerage services in a transaction must negotiate for a commission or fee from the principal to the transaction. Valuable consideration includes the giving of certain items of personal property (for instance, a broker giving a new TV to "a friend" for providing a valuable lead) and other premiums (vacations, rent, bonuses, and discounts), as well as finders' fees. A *gift* is permissible as long as the retail value does not exceed $50. Under certain circumstances, it is legal for a broker to *rebate* a portion of the commission to the principal if the payment is strictly a rebate and is not made for a real estate service (such as a referral).

> If a person makes a referral with the expectation of receiving cash, discounts, or gifts valued over $50, that person must be licensed.

Under statutorily defined circumstances, a real estate broker or licensed or certified real estate appraiser can file a lien on commercial real estate for commissions earned but not yet paid. The commission must exceed $2,500, and the broker or appraiser must have disclosed the right to the lien in the fee agreement. The commercial transaction can involve either a sale or a lease, but the property cannot include a person's homestead.

Salesperson's compensation. A salesperson's compensation is set by mutual agreement between broker and salesperson. A broker may agree to pay a salary (generally to an employee) or a share of the commissions from transactions originated by a salesperson (generally to an independent contractor). If a salesperson has a drawing account against his or her earned share of commissions, the salesperson should sign a note for each draw to preserve the independent contractor status.

Usually, the higher the commission split to the agent, the more expenses the broker will require the agent to pay. In a *100 percent commission* firm, all salespeople who achieve a predetermined sales quota receive 100 percent of the commissions from the sales they negotiate and pay a monthly service charge to their broker (to cover the costs of office space, telephones, and other overhead expenses).

Antitrust Laws

The real estate industry is subject to federal and state **antitrust laws.** These laws prohibit monopolies and contracts, combinations, and conspiracies that unreasonably restrain trade. The most common antitrust violations that can occur in the real estate business are price-fixing, boycotting competitors, and allocating customers or markets.

Price-fixing is the practice of setting prices for products or services rather than letting competition in the open market establish those prices. In real estate it occurs when brokers agree to set sales commissions, fees, or management rates, and it is illegal. Brokers must independently determine commission rates or fees only for their own firms. These decisions must be based on the broker's business judgment and revenue requirements without input from other brokers.

Multiple-listing organizations, Boards of REALTORS®, and other professional organizations may not set fees or commission splits, nor are they allowed to deny membership to brokers based on the fees the brokers charge. Either practice could lead the public to believe that the industry sanctions not only the unethical practice of withholding cooperation from certain brokers but also the illegal practice of restricting open-market competition.

The broker's challenge is to avoid any impression of attempts at price-fixing as well as the actual practice. Hinting in any way to prospective clients that there is a "going rate" of commission or fee implies that rates are in fact standardized. A broker must clarify to clients that the rate stated is only what that firm charges. Likewise, discussions of rates among licensees from different firms could be construed as a price-fixing activity and should be avoided.

Antitrust violations include

- price-fixing
- boycotting a competitor
- allocation of customers or markets

Boycotting competitors results when brokers are unfairly excluded from real estate professional associations or when two or more businesses conspire against other businesses or agree to withhold their patronage to reduce competition. For example, an agreement among brokers not to work with "discount" brokers or buyer brokers would be illegal.

Allocation of customers or markets involves an agreement between brokers to divide their markets and refrain from competing against each other. Allocations may take place on a geographic basis, with brokers agreeing to specific territories within which they will operate exclusively. The division also may take place along other lines; for example, two brokers may agree that one will handle residential properties under $100,000 in value and another will handle residential properties over $100,000 in value.

The penalties for such acts are severe. Under the Sherman Antitrust Act, individuals found guilty of a violation may be charged with either a misdemeanor or a felony, depending on the severity of the violation, punishable by a maximum $100,000 fine and three years' imprisonment. For corporations, the penalty may be as high as $1 million. In a civil suit, a person who suffered a loss because of the antitrust activities of a guilty party may recover triple the value of actual damages plus attorney fees and costs.

TEXAS DECEPTIVE TRADE PRACTICES—CONSUMER PROTECTION ACT

At one time, real estate transactions were governed solely by the maxim **caveat emptor,** Latin for "let the buyer beware." Through this principle, the courts charged the buyer with the responsibilities of inspecting the property and searching the public records to ascertain interests of other persons, including the rights of parties in possession.

Because of growing concern about consumer protection in the United States, the courts have modified the caveat emptor principle by placing more responsibility on the seller. Sellers of residential property in Texas are required to deliver a Seller's Disclosure Notice to a buyer on or before the effective date of a contract (see Chapter 13). Among other things, the disclosure must contain the seller's knowledge of the property condition along with a list of appliances and whether they are working. Consumer protection applies to the real estate agent, too. Texas licensees have an affirmative duty imposed by the Real Estate License Act to disclose known latent or hidden defects and can be held liable for false or misleading statements made about the property.

The DTPA protects consumers against false, misleading, or deceptive acts or practices of sellers or real estate agents.

In Texas, consumer rights are also protected by the **Texas Deceptive Trade Practices—Consumer Protection Act (DTPA),** Chapter 17, Subchapter E, Business and Commerce Code. This act declares, among other things, that "false, misleading or deceptive acts or practices" in the advertising, offering for sale, selling, or leasing of any real or personal property are unlawful. As set forth in the act, false, misleading, or deceptive acts or practices are included in a "Laundry List" of 23 items; some are stated below:

- Representing that something is new or original when it is not or that it is of a particular quality when it is not
- Advertising property with no intention of selling the property as advertised
- Making false statements of fact concerning the reasons for a price reduction
- Misrepresenting the authority of an agent to negotiate the final terms of a sales contract
- Representing that a warranty guarantees or confers rights or remedies not included
- Representing that work has been done on real or personal property when the work has not been done
- Failing to disclose information about goods or services that was known at the time of the transaction if such silence was intended to induce the customer into a transaction and the consumer would not have entered had the information been disclosed

In a DTPA suit, the consumer must prove that the deceptive act was the producing cause of damages. However, the DTPA does not require that the presence of fraud be proved; an innocent misrepresentation is actionable. For example, court cases have determined that using "as is" for property condition in a sales contract or a broker's claiming a statement was "mere opinion" does not relieve the broker of responsibility under the DTPA.

However, claims based on the rendering of professional services that involve providing advice, judgment, or opinion (such as an agent's preparing a competitive market analysis) are excluded from the DTPA—except for situations involving misrepresentation, unconscionable conduct, or breach of warranty. Additionally, with the exception of residential property, the DTPA does not apply to transactions that exceed $100,000 where there is a written contract and the consumer is represented by legal counsel.

By statute, a consumer may waive his or her rights to bring a suit under the DTPA. However, court opinions consistently uphold that "any waiver by a consumer of the provisions of the subchapter is contrary to public policy and is unenforceable and void." Therefore, all of the following strict requirements must be met for the waiver to be valid and enforceable:

- The waiver must be in writing and signed by the consumer.
- The consumer must not be in a significantly disparate bargaining position.
- The consumer must be represented by legal counsel (not referred by the defendant or an agent of the defendant) in seeking or acquiring the goods or services.
- The waiver must be conspicuous and in bold-face type of at least 10 points in size.

- The waiver must be in substantially the promulgated form under the heading "Waiver of Consumer Rights."

Either party to a lawsuit filed under the DTPA may file a motion to compel mediation of the dispute. Defenses to the DTPA include (1) a reasonable offer of settlement within specified time limits, (2) written notice to the consumer prior to consummation of the sale that the broker is relying on written information prepared by others, and (3) the impossibility of the broker's knowing that the information was false or inaccurate. The act also permits recovery of court costs and attorney fees if the lawsuit was ruled frivolous or harassing.

Recovery under the DTPA is limited to economic damages. However, if the defendant is found to have committed the act *knowingly,* then damages for mental anguish may also be awarded (and in some cases, up to three times the amount of economic damages). If the defendant is found to have committed the act *intentionally,* then the economic and mental anguish damages may be trebled. Note that an errors-and-omissions insurance policy purchased by a broker will not cover fraud or intentional violations of the DTPA. *St. Paul Insurance Company v. Bonded Realty, Inc.* 583 S.W.2d 619 (Tex. 1979) p. 141.

Under Section 15F of the License Act, parties to a contract and licensees are protected from liability for misrepresentation or concealment of material facts by each other or by a subagent unless the party or licensee knew of the falsity or concealment. Under the provisions of tort reform legislation passed in 1995, defendants who are only marginally at fault in a claim cannot be forced to pay for damages caused by other parties unless a defendant is found to be more than 50 percent responsible for damages, and each liable defendant will be liable to the consumer only for that defendant's percentage of responsibility. However, tort reform did not diminish the broker's liability for the acts of the broker's salespeople.

FRAUD IN REAL ESTATE AND STOCK TRANSACTIONS STATUTE

In addition to an agent's responsibilities under the Texas Real Estate License Act and the DTPA, the Fraud in Real Estate and Stock Transactions Statute, Article 27.01, Business and Commerce Code, states that any person who stands to gain financially from a transaction is assumed to have knowledge of all aspects of the transaction. Clearly this includes brokers and salespeople. Whereas common-law fraud is limited to the intent to deceive, among other elements, statutory fraud covers innocent misrepresentations as well as unfulfilled promises. The act provides for actual and punitive damages against not only the person making the misrepresentation or promise but against any person who benefits from the transaction, has actual knowledge of the falsity, and fails to reveal it. This means that one broker or seller who is aware of wrongful acts of another broker or seller can be liable for those acts if a benefit is received.

Extreme care should be taken in handling all phases of a real estate transaction. Carelessness in handling the documents connected with a real estate sale can result in expensive legal contests. A review of cases that involve lawsuits growing out of such transactions reveals that much litigation results from carelessness or ignorance of the law. In many such cases, costly court actions could have been avoided if the parties handling negotiations had exercised greater care and employed competent legal counsel.

Summary

Real estate brokerage is the business of bringing together people who wish to buy, sell, exchange, or lease real estate. An important part of real estate brokerage is the law of agency. A real estate broker is the agent, hired by the seller or by the buyer, to sell or find a particular parcel of real estate. The person who hires the broker is the principal. The principal and the agent have a fiduciary relationship under which the agent owes the principal the duties of care, obedience, accounting, loyalty, and disclosure. In the absence of a buyer representation agreement or a signed agreement for the broker to act as an intermediary, the broker's sales staff and cooperating brokers and their staffs are presumed to represent the seller.

The broker's compensation in a real estate sale generally takes the form of a commission, which is a percentage of the real estate's selling price. The broker is considered to have *earned* a commission when he or she procures a ready, willing, and able buyer for a seller. The commission is *payable* on closing or, under certain circumstances, on the seller's breach of contract.

A broker may hire salespeople to assist in this work. The salesperson works on the broker's behalf as either an employee or an independent contractor.

Many of the general operations of a real estate brokerage are regulated by the real estate license laws. In addition, state and federal antitrust laws prohibit brokers from conspiring to fix prices, boycott competitors, or allocate customers or markets.

In Texas, buyers of real estate are protected by the Texas Deceptive Trade Practices—Consumer Protection Act. This act prohibits real estate brokers and other providers of goods and services from deceiving or misleading consumers.

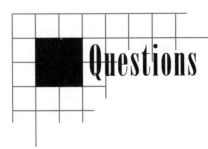

Questions

1. A real estate broker acting as the special agent of the seller
   a. is obligated to render faithful service to the seller.
   b. can disclose personal information to a buyer if it increases the likelihood of a sale.
   c. can agree to a change in price without the seller's approval.
   d. can accept a commission from the buyer without the seller's approval.

2. An agency relationship may be terminated by all of the following means **EXCEPT**
   a. the owner decides not to sell the house.
   b. the broker discovers that the market value of the property is such that he or she will not make an adequate commission.
   c. the owner dies.
   d. the broker secures a ready, willing, and able buyer for the seller's property.

3. A real estate broker will lose the right to a commission if he or she
   a. failed to advertise the property.
   b. was not licensed when a sale occurred.
   c. produced a ready, willing and able buyer.
   d. did not personally market and sell the listing.

4. A real estate broker who engages salespeople as independent contractors must
   a. withhold income tax and Social Security from all commissions earned by them.
   b. require them to attend sales meetings and to participate in office insurance plans if the broker requires other salespeople hired as employees to do so.
   c. refrain from controlling how the salesperson conducts his or her business activities.
   d. provide employee benefits.

5. The statement "a broker must be employed to recover a commission for his or her services" means that
   a. the broker must work in a real estate office.
   b. the seller must have signed an agreement to pay a commission to the broker for selling the property.
   c. the broker must have a salesperson employed in the office.
   d. the broker must have signed the listing agreement.

6. A real estate broker hired to sell a parcel of real estate must
   a. comply with the owner's instructions even if the broker believes they are unethical.
   b. be available at any time to show the property.
   c. comply with the law of agency.
   d. keep confidential a buyer's comment that he will pay up to $70,000 if the seller makes a counteroffer.

7. As an independent contractor for a real estate broker, a real estate salesperson has the authority to
   a. act as an agent for another person.
   b. assume only responsibilities assigned by the broker.
   c. act independently when he or she disagrees with the broker.
   d. make contracts and receive compensation directly from the principal.

8. *Reckless disregard for truth with the intent to obtain a financial advantage over another* is a definition of
   a. the Deceptive Trade Practices Act.
   b. fraud.
   c. procuring cause.
   d. puffing.

9. Alice is a real estate broker. Rich lists a home with Alice for $89,500. Later that same day, Robert comes into Alice's office and asks for general information about homes for sale in the $80,000 to $100,000 price range. Based on these facts, which of the following statements is true?
   a. Both Rich and Robert are Alice's customers.
   b. Rich is Alice's client; Robert is a customer.
   c. Alice owes fiduciary duties to both Rich and Robert.
   d. If Robert asks Alice to be a buyer's representative, Alice must decline because of the pre-existing agreement with Rich.

10. Mickie Michaels, a licensed broker, learns that his neighbor, Paul Cella, wishes to sell his house. Michaels knows the property well, and while Cella is out of town for a week, Michaels convinces Barney Schultz to buy the property. Michaels obtains Schultz's signature on a purchase offer, together with a check for an earnest money deposit. When Cella returns, Michaels presents Schultz's offer. In this situation
   a. Cella is not obligated to pay Michaels a commission.
   b. Schultz is obligated to pay Michaels a commission for locating the property.
   c. Cella must pay Michaels a commission.
   d. Michaels has become a subagent of Cella.

11. Which of the following statements best describes the role of an intermediary broker?
   a. The broker represents both the buyer and seller and may disclose confidential information from either unless instructed not to do so.
   b. The broker is paid by the seller and must not disclose any confidential information to the buyer.
   c. The broker is acting on behalf of both the buyer and seller and must not disclose any confidential information to either party without written permission.
   d. The broker is bound by the Texas Real Estate License Act to represent the buyer and must communicate with and carry out the buyer's instructions.

12. Which of the following would **NOT** be considered a violation of antitrust laws?
   a. Brokers representing the Temple, ABC, and All-American Property Management companies decide to de-escalate their current price war by charging more uniform rates.
   b. Salespeople Joe Black and Emma Marie Mitsubushi, working on behalf of two local firms, agree that Black should seek listings only from the east side of town and Mitsubushi should seek listings only from the west side of town.
   c. Brokers throughout the city set their commission rates unilaterally without consulting with competitors.
   d. A local association of apartment managers decides to charge a set rate for management services.

13. The legal relationship between broker and seller is generally a(n)
   a. special agency.
   b. general agency.
   c. ostensible agency.
   d. agency by ratification.

14. Broker Duncan Rivera lists Sam and Adele Kaufmann's house for $87,000. Adele has been transferred to another state, and the couple must sell their house within three months. To expedite the sale, Rivera tells a prospective buyer that the couple will accept at least $5,000 less for the house. In this situation
   a. Rivera has not violated his agency responsibilities to the Kaufmanns.
   b. Rivera should not have disclosed this information to the prospective buyer, because it is not in the sellers' best financial interests.
   c. Rivera has acted prudently as the sellers' agent.
   d. Rivera is only obligated to produce a ready, willing, and able buyer.

6 Fair Housing Laws and Ethical Practices

Key Terms

Americans with
  Disabilities Act
blockbusting
Canons of Professional
  Ethics and Conduct
Civil Rights Act of
  1866
Code of Ethics

Community
  Reinvestment Act
Equal Credit
  Opportunity Act
Fair Housing Act of
  1968
Home Mortgage
  Disclosure Act

redlining
steering
Texas Commission on
  Human Rights
Texas Fair Housing Act
U.S. Department of
  Housing and Urban
  Development

OVERVIEW

To ensure equal opportunity in housing, the federal and state governments have enacted fair housing laws that require licensees to follow ethical practices when dealing with the public. To achieve and maintain a favorable reputation in the community, a real estate licensee must demonstrate more than good business ability; his or her *ethics*, or business principles, must be above reproach as well. The Texas license laws require that licensees adhere to certain ethical practices, as do the codes of ethics subscribed to by members of professional real estate organizations. This chapter deals with fair housing laws and codes of ethical practices as they apply to the real estate business.

Section 7 of the Texas Real Estate License Act requires that all license applicants show evidence of satisfactory completion of three classroom hours of instruction on laws governing fair housing, community reinvestment, and equal credit opportunity. All three of these topics are discussed in this chapter.

EQUAL OPPORTUNITY IN HOUSING

Brokers and salespeople who offer residential property for sale anywhere in the United States must be aware of the federal, state, and local laws pertaining to human rights and nondiscrimination. These laws, under such titles as *open housing, fair housing,* and *equal opportunity housing,* generally prohibit undesirable and discriminatory activities. Their provisions affect every phase of the real estate sales process from listing to closing, and *all brokers and salespeople must comply with them.*

The goal of legislators who have enacted fair housing laws and regulations is to create an unbiased housing market—one in which every home seeker has the same opportunity to buy any home in the area he or she chooses, provided the home is within the home seeker's financial means. Potential licensees must be aware of undesirable and illegal housing practices so licensees can avoid them. Licensees must realize that failure to comply with fair housing practices is not only a criminal act but also grounds for license revocation or suspension.

Federal Fair Housing Laws

Efforts of the federal government to guarantee equal housing opportunities to all U.S. citizens began more than 100 years ago with passage of the **Civil Rights Act of 1866.** This law, an outgrowth of the Fourteenth Amendment, prohibits all racial discrimination. A summary of federal fair housing laws appears in Table 6.1.

Aside from a few isolated court decisions, little effort was directed to enforcing the principles of fair housing until 1962, when President John Kennedy issued *Executive Order No. 11063.* This order guaranteed nondiscrimination in all housing financed by FHA and VA loans. Because of the relatively small percentage of housing affected by Executive Order No. 11063, it had limited impact.

> "All citizens of the United States shall have the same right in every state and territory as is enjoyed by white citizens thereof to inherit, purchase, lease, sell, hold, and convey real and personal property."
> *Civil Rights Act of 1866*

The scope of the federal government's fair housing regulation was expanded by the *Civil Rights Act of 1964,* which prohibited discrimination in any housing program that receives whole or partial federal funding. However, because only a very small percentage of housing in the United States is government-funded, this law also had little impact on the housing industry.

Fair Housing Act of 1968. In 1968, two major events greatly advanced fair housing. The first was passage of the federal **Fair Housing Act of 1968,** which is contained in *Title VIII of the Civil Rights Act of 1968,* making it unlawful to discriminate on the basis of race, color, religion, or national origin when selling or leasing residential property only. Sex was added as a protected class by the *Housing and Community Development Act of 1974.* Although it is unlawful to discriminate in housing on the basis of sex, sexual orientation is not a protected classification under federal law. Some state or local laws may contain additional protected classes. Licensees must seek out this information and apply all fair housing laws. The federal Fair Housing Act covers dwellings and apartments, as well as vacant land acquired for the construction of residential buildings, and prohibits the following discriminatory acts:

- Refusing to sell, rent, or negotiate with any person or otherwise making a dwelling unavailable to any person
- Changing terms, conditions, or services for different individuals as a means of discrimination
- Practicing discrimination through any statement or advertisement that restricts the sale or rental of residential property

Table 6.1 *Summary of Federal Fair Housing Laws*

Law	Purpose
Civil Rights Act of 1866	Prohibits discrimination in housing based on race without exception
Executive Order No. 11063 (1962)	Prohibits discrimination in housing funded by FHA or VA loans
Civil Rights Act of 1964	Prohibits discrimination in federally funded housing programs
Title VIII of the Civil Rights Act of 1968 (Federal Fair Housing Act)	Prohibits discrimination in housing based on race, color, religion, or national origin, with certain exceptions
Housing and Community Development Act of 1974	Extends prohibitions to discrimination in housing based on sex
Fair Housing Amendments Act of 1988	Extends protection to cover persons with handicaps and families with children, with certain exceptions

- Representing to any person, as a means of discrimination, that a dwelling is not available for sale or rental
- Making a profit by inducing owners of housing to sell or rent because of the prospective entry into the neighborhood of persons of a particular race, color, religion, or national origin (also known as *blockbusting*)
- Altering the terms or conditions for a home loan to any person who wishes to purchase or repair a dwelling, or otherwise denying such a loan, as a means of discrimination
- Denying people membership or limiting their participation in any multiple-listing service, real estate brokers' organization, or other facility related to the sale or rental of a dwelling as a means of discrimination

The federal Fair Housing Act provides for certain exemptions. However, licensees should be aware that *no exemptions involve race and no exemptions apply when a real estate licensee is involved in a transaction.*

- The sale or rental of a single-family home is exempted when the home is owned by an individual who does not own more than three such homes at one time *and* when the following conditions exist: a broker, salesperson, or agent is not used and discriminatory advertising is not used. If the owner is not living in the dwelling at the time of the transaction or was not the most recent occupant, only one such sale by an individual is exempt from the law within any 24-month period.
- The rental of rooms or units is exempted in an owner-occupied, one-family to four-family dwelling.
- Dwelling units owned by religious organizations may be restricted to people of the same religion if membership in the organization is not restricted on the basis of race, color, or national origin.
- A private club may restrict the rental or occupancy of lodgings it owns to its members, as long as the lodgings are not operated commercially.

The federal Fair Housing Act does not require that housing be made available to any individual whose tenancy would constitute a direct threat to the health or safety of other individuals or that would result in substantial physical damage to the property of others.

Jones v. Mayer. The second significant fair housing development of 1968 was the U.S. Supreme Court decision in the case of *Jones v. Alfred H. Mayer Company,* 392 U.S. 409 (1968). In its ruling, the court affirmed that the Civil Rights Act of 1866 "prohibits all racial discrimination, private or public, in the sale and rental of property." Although the Fair Housing Act of 1968 permits some fair housing exemptions, the 1866 law prohibits all racial discrimination without exception. An aggrieved person may seek a remedy for racial discrimination under the 1866 law against *any* homeowner, regardless of whether the owner employed a real estate broker and/or advertised the property.

Amendments to Fair Housing Laws

The *1972 amendment to the federal Fair Housing Act of 1968* instituted the use of an equal housing opportunity poster. This poster (illustrated in Figure 6.1), which can be obtained from HUD, features the equal housing opportunity slogan, an equal housing statement pledging adherence to the Fair Housing Act and support of affirmative marketing and advertising programs, and the equal housing opportunity logo. When HUD investigates a broker for discriminatory practices, it considers failure to display the poster evidence of discrimination.

The *1988 amendment to the federal Fair Housing Act of 1968* added persons with a handicap or disability and persons having "familial status" to the list of unlawful discriminations.

Handicap has been defined as a physical or mental impairment or a history of such impairment that substantially limits one or more of a person's major life activities. Individuals who have AIDS are protected by the fair housing laws under the handicap classification. The federal fair housing law's protection of disabled persons does not include those who are current users of illegal or controlled substances. Nor are individuals who have been convicted of the illegal manufacture or distribution of a controlled substance protected under this law. However, the law does prohibit discrimination against those who are participating in addiction recovery programs. For instance, a landlord could lawfully discriminate against a cocaine addict, but not against a member of Alcoholics Anonymous. Both recovered and current mental patients are protected.

> The *Fair Housing Act* prohibits discrimination based on
>
> • race,
> • color,
> • religion,
> • sex,
> • handicap,
> • familial status,
> • national origin.

Tenants as well as buyers are protected from discrimination because of a handicap. Landlords must make reasonable accommodations to existing policies, practices, or services, such as permitting guide dogs in a normally no-pets building. Discrimination includes refusing to permit a person with a handicap to make reasonable modifications to the premises at his or her own expense. In the case of a rental, the landlord can require when the lease period ends, if it is reasonable to do so, that the person restore the interior of the premises to its previous condition if these modifications would make the property undesirable to the general population.

The law does not prohibit restricting occupancy exclusively to persons with a handicap in dwellings that are designed specifically for their accommodation. For new construction consisting of five or more units, the facility must

Figure 6.1   Equal Housing Opportunity Poster

U.S. Department of Housing and Urban Development

**EQUAL HOUSING
OPPORTUNITY**

**We Do Business in Accordance With the Federal Fair
Housing Law**
(The Fair Housing Amendments Act of 1988)

**It is Illegal to Discriminate Against Any Person
Because of Race, Color, Religion, Sex,
Handicap, Familial Status, or National Origin**

■ In the sale or rental of housing
   or residential lots

■ In advertising the sale or rental
   of housing

■ In the financing of housing

■ In the provision of real estate
   brokerage services

■ In the appraisal of housing

■ Blockbusting is also illegal

Anyone who feels he or she has been
discriminated against may file a complaint of
housing discrimination with the:
1-800-424-8590 (Toll Free)
1-800-424-8529 (TDD)

U.S. Department of Housing and
Urban Development
Assistant Secretary for Fair Housing and
Equal Opportunity
Washington, D.C. 20410

Previous editions are obsolete   form **HUD-928.1** (3-89)

be constructed so as to permit access and better usability by persons with a handicap.

Familial status has been defined as one or more individuals (under the age of 18) living with a parent or legal guardian or the designee of such parent or guardian. It also includes a person who is pregnant. Housing for older persons is exempt if it is occupied solely by persons age 62 and older or if 80 percent of its units are occupied by at least one person age 55 or older. Otherwise, single or multifamily housing must be made available for sale or rent to families with children, and landlords cannot restrict the number of occupants or advertise "adults only" with the intent or effect of eliminating families with children.

View the *Fair Housing Act* on the web at:
www.usdoj.gov/crt/housing

In Practice   For the civil rights laws to accomplish the goal of eliminating discrimination, licensees must apply them routinely. If a property owner requires that an agent discriminate in the sale of the property, the agent must refuse to accept the listing. If a buyer expresses a locational preference for housing based on race, the following response is recommended: "I cannot give you that kind of advice. I will show you several homes that meet your specifications. You will have to decide which one you want."

Blockbusting and Steering

Blockbusting and steering are illegal housing practices frequently discussed in connection with fair housing. Although not mentioned by name in the federal Fair Housing Act of 1968, both are prohibited by that law.

Blockbusting, sometimes referred to as *panic peddling,* means *inducing homeowners to sell by making representations regarding the entry or prospective entry of minority persons into the neighborhood.* The blockbuster frightens homeowners into selling and makes a profit by buying the homes cheaply and selling them at considerably higher prices to minority persons.

Steering is the *channeling* of home seekers to particular areas on the basis of race, religion, country of origin, or other protected class, either to maintain the homogeneity of an area or to change the character of an area in order to create a speculative situation. Steering often is difficult to detect, however, because the steering tactics can be so subtle that the home seeker is unaware that his or her choice has been limited. Steering also may be done unintentionally by agents who are not aware of their own biased assumptions. Nevertheless, an unintentional offense is still a violation of fair housing laws. A complainant does not have to prove guilty knowledge or specific intent—only the fact that discrimination occurred.

Less Favorable Treatment

One of the most common complaints of discrimination is the allegation that minority persons received less favorable treatment in the sale or rental of residential property. For example, a violation of the fair housing laws occurs when an agent ignores a minority buyer or seller; refers the buyer or seller to an agent of the same minority group; fails to use his or her best efforts; or fails to submit an offer because of race, religion, color, national origin, sex, handicap, or familial status. Licensees should document their services to *each* customer to establish the range of real estate offered and *keep detailed records* of all transactions and rentals in case a discrimination complaint is made.

Even an act that is done for everyone can be illegal if it is fair in form yet discriminatory in operation. An example of this is selling only to persons—regardless of race or national origin—who are in a specified group if that group has disproportionately fewer minority members (e.g., retired members of a trade union that until recently was all white).

Advertising

Printed or published advertisements of property for sale or rent cannot include language that indicates a preference, limitation, or discrimination with regard to any fair housing-protected classification. HUD's regulations cite examples that are considered discriminatory: "adult community, Catholic, no wheelchairs, integrated." References to a property's location also can imply discriminatory preference or limitation, such as its relation to landmarks that are associated with a nationality or religion, for example, "near temple." Pictorial representations using human models as residents or customers that depict one segment of the population while not including others in the protected classes are discriminatory. The media used for promoting property or real estate services cannot target one population to the exclusion of others.

However, advertising must be discriminatory *on its face* to be illegal. Statements that provide physical descriptions of the property (mother-in-law suite) or conduct required of residents (sober) are permissible. HUD has ruled as *acceptable* such advertising terms as "master bedroom, family room, play area, walking distance, beautiful view, no drugs, no smoking, credit check required."

Americans with Disabilities Act

Although the **Americans with Disabilities Act** (ADA) is not a housing or credit law, it still has a significant effect on the real estate industry. The ADA is important to licensees because it addresses the rights of individuals with disabilities in employment and public accommodations. Real estate brokers are often employers, and real estate brokerage offices are public spaces. The ADA requires that employers (including real estate licensees) make *reasonable accommodations* that enable an individual with a disability to perform essential job functions. Reasonable accommodations include making the work site accessible, restructuring a job, providing part-time or flexible work schedules, and modifying equipment that is used on the job. The provisions of the ADA apply to any employer with 15 or more employees.

> The *Americans with Disabilities Act* requires *reasonable accommodations* in employment and access to goods, services, and public buildings.

The ADA also provides for accessibility to goods and services for individuals with disabilities. While the federal civil rights laws have traditionally been viewed in the real estate industry as housing-related, the practices of licensees who deal with nonresidential property are significantly affected by the ADA. Building owners and managers must ensure that any obstacle restricting full and equal access to businesses and public services is eliminated. The ADA guidelines contain detailed specifications for designing parking spaces, curb ramps, elevators, drinking fountains, rest-room facilities, and directional signs to ensure maximum accessibility.

Enforcement of the Fair Housing Act

The fair housing laws allow any aggrieved party to file a complaint against discriminatory practices and to pursue enforcement through administrative proceedings, attorney general litigation, or private litigation. Complaints brought under the Civil Rights Act of 1866 must be taken directly to a federal court. Other fair housing complaints are enforced as follows:

Administrative proceedings. A complaint can be filed with the **Texas Commission on Human Rights** or with the **U.S. Department of Housing and Urban Development (HUD).** An aggrieved person who believes illegal discrimination has occurred may file a complaint within one year after the alleged act. If the complaint is filed with HUD, it will be referred to the Texas Commission on Human Rights because Texas has a HUD-approved "substantially equivalent" fair housing program that allows complaints to be heard at the state level rather than at the federal level. The Texas Commission on Human Rights has 100 days to investigate the complaint, to begin a process of conciliation (attempting to obtain an agreement ending the dispute), and to file a report of its findings. If no conciliation agreement is reached during the 100-day period, the Texas Commission on Human Rights must dismiss the complaint or file charges. If charges are filed, the aggrieved party has 20 days to exercise an election to take the matter to a state district court for a jury trial. If the aggrieved party does not choose to go to court, the case is assigned to an administrative law judge (ALJ). An

ALJ makes recommendations to the Texas Commission on Human Rights for resolution of the dispute. An ALJ has the authority to award actual damages to the aggrieved person and to impose monetary penalties. The penalties range from up to $10,000 for the first offense to $25,000 for the second violation within five years to $50,000 for further violations within seven years. An ALJ also has the authority to issue an injunction to order the offender to either take action (such as rent an apartment to the complaining party) or refrain from taking action (such as conducting business in a discriminatory manner).

Fair housing complaints are filed with the *Texas Commission on Human Rights.*

Litigation. *Through the attorney general:* If the aggrieved party elects to have a jury trial, the Texas Commission on Human Rights will notify the Texas Attorney General, who has 30 days to file a civil action in state district court on behalf of the complainant. *Through private litigation:* An aggrieved party may bring a private enforcement action in federal district court within two years of the discriminatory action. The private lawsuit can be filed even though an administrative complaint is filed with the Texas Commission on Human Rights. If a conciliation agreement is entered on the complaint or if a hearing commences before an ALJ, the private lawsuit must be terminated. The court can grant injunctions, unlimited actual and punitive damages, and other appropriate equitable remedies.

In addition to the **Texas Fair Housing Act,** some Texas cities currently enforce fair housing ordinances. The nearest HUD regional office can verify whether a city has a municipal ordinance that has been ruled substantially equivalent to the federal law.

Two other Texas statutes deal with fair housing or discrimination. One stipulates that, regardless of the provisions contained in a deed restriction, no state court can enforce a provision that is discriminatory. The second statute is part of the Real Estate License Act [Section 15(6)(AA)] and prohibits housing discrimination by a licensee. Violation of this statute subjects the licensee to potential civil action as well as license suspension or revocation.

Threats or Acts of Violence

The federal Fair Housing Act of 1968 contains criminal provisions that protect the rights of those who seek the benefits guaranteed under the open housing law. These provisions also protect owners, brokers, or salespeople who aid or encourage the enjoyment of open housing rights. Unlawful actions, threats, coercion, and intimidation are punishable by appropriate civil action. A victim should report the incident immediately to the local police and to the nearest office of the Federal Bureau of Investigation.

Implications for Brokers and Salespeople

The real estate industry is largely responsible for creating and maintaining an open housing market. Brokers and salespersons are a community's real estate experts. Along with the privilege of profiting from real estate transactions come the social and legal responsibilities to ensure that everyone's civil rights are protected. Licensees and the industry must be publicly conspicuous in their commitment to the principles of fair housing.

All parties deserve the same standard of service. Everyone has the right to expect equal treatment. A good test is to answer the question, "Are we doing this for everyone?" If an act is not performed consistently, or if an act affects some individuals differently from others, it could be construed as discriminatory. Standardized practices include careful record keeping for each customer: needs analysis, financial analysis, properties suggested, houses shown, documentation of all conversations. Besides helping to avoid fair housing violations, these practices are simply good business and may well translate into a larger client base.

HUD requires that its fair housing posters be displayed in any place of business where real estate is offered for sale or rent. Following HUD's advertising procedures and using the fair housing slogan and logo keep the public aware of the broker's commitment to equal opportunity.

From time to time, real estate offices may be visited by testers or *checkers*, undercover volunteers who investigate whether customers and clients are treated equally and are offered the same free choice within a given price range. The courts have held that such practice is permissible, as it is the only way to test compliance with the fair housing laws.

Fair housing *is* the law. The consequences for anyone who violates the law are serious. In addition to the financial penalties, a real estate broker's or salesperson's livelihood will be in danger if his or her license is suspended or revoked. Remember: that a fair housing offense was unintentional is no defense; only the fact that discrimination did occur has to be proven. Beyond being the law, fair housing is *good business*. It ensures the greatest number of properties available for sale and rent and the largest possible pool of potential purchasers and tenants.

FEDERAL FAIR LENDING LAWS

Equal Credit Opportunity Act

As enacted in 1974 and amended in 1976, the **Equal Credit Opportunity Act** (ECOA) was the first in a series of fair housing lending laws designed to make credit available to every financially qualified applicant. It prohibits lenders and others who grant or arrange credit to consumers from discriminating against credit applicants on the basis of race, color, religion, national origin, sex, marital status, age (provided the applicant is of legal age), or dependence on public assistance. Credit applicants must be judged *only* by criteria based on income, net worth, job stability, and credit rating. All rejected applicants must be notified, in writing and within 30 days, of the principal reasons for denial or termination of credit. The ECOA also provides that a borrower is entitled to a copy of the appraisal report if the borrower paid for the appraisal. The ECOA applies to a person or an institution that makes loans on a regular basis as a part of its usual business. It does not include a seller who agrees to carry back a note.

Home Mortgage Disclosure Act

The **Home Mortgage Disclosure Act** (HMDA), which became effective on December 31, 1975, requires that lenders with federally related loans disclose the number of loans applied for and loans made in different parts of their service areas. Prior to the disclosure law, some lenders limited the scope of their home loans to favored areas, a practice known as **redlining.** (Certain areas literally were excluded from eligibility for home loans as though "red lines" were drawn around them.) Congress felt that the practice of redlining was contributing to the decline of certain neighborhoods.

The Home Mortgage Disclosure Act affects any federally related home mortgage loan secured by a first lien on an owner-occupied one- to four-family dwelling. This act requires that all institutional mortgage lenders with assets in excess of $10 million and one or more offices in a given geographic area make annual reports by census tracts of all mortgage loans the institution makes or purchases. In addition, the regulation requires that each institution make its mortgage loan disclosure statement (prepared by the Federal Financial Examination Council) available to the general public. This law enables the government to detect lending or insuring patterns that might constitute redlining.

In 1992, the federal government began filing lawsuits against mortgage lenders who were violating the HMDA. Recent studies show these enforcement efforts have had a positive impact on the number of people in minority and lower-income areas who were able to obtain loans.

Community Reinvestment Act

In 1977, Congress passed yet another law dealing with lending practices—the **Community Reinvestment Act** (CRA). Prior to CRA enactment, lenders commonly made loans wherever they felt the risks were lowest and the returns were highest. However, the CRA requires that lenders serve their local communities first—to meet the deposit and credit needs of their low- and moderate-income housing communities, participate and invest in local community development and rehabilitation projects, and participate in loan programs for housing, small businesses, and small farms.

The Federal Reserve System's Regulation BB implements the CRA. Each affected lending institution is required to post in a public place in its facilities a Community Reinvestment Act Notice that discloses to potential customers the lending policies of the institution as well as informs customers of their rights under CRA. Additionally, the Community Reinvestment Act requires any federally supervised financial institution to prepare an annual statement containing

- a definition of the geographical boundaries of its community,
- an identification of the types of community reinvestment credit offered (such as residential housing loans, housing rehabilitation loans, small-business loans, commercial loans, and consumer loans), and
- comments from the public about the institution's performance in meeting its community's needs.

PROFESSIONAL ETHICS

Professional conduct involves more than just complying with the law. The Texas Real Estate License Act establishes those activities that are illegal and therefore prohibited. However, merely complying with the letter of the law may not be enough. *Ethics* refers to a system of *moral* principles, rules, and standards of conduct. The ethical system of a profession establishes conduct that goes beyond merely complying with the law. These moral principles address two sides of a profession:

1. They establish standards for integrity and competence in dealing with consumers of an industry's services.
2. They define a code of conduct for relations within the industry, among its professionals.

Figure 6.2　*Canons of Professional Ethics and Conduct—Texas Real Estate Commission*

Fidelity. A real estate broker or salesperson, while acting as an agent for another, is a fiduciary. Special obligations are imposed when such fiduciary relationships are created. They demand:

(1) that the primary duty of the real estate agent is to represent the interests of the agent's client, and the agent's position, in this respect, should be clear to all parties concerned in a real estate transaction; that, however, the agent, in performing duties to the client, shall treat other parties to a transaction fairly;

(2) that the real estate agent be faithful and observant to trust placed in the agent, and be scrupulous and meticulous in performing the agent's functions;

(3) that the real estate agent place no personal interest above that of the agent's client.

Integrity. A real estate broker or salesperson has a special obligation to exercise integrity in the discharge of the licensee's responsibilities, including employment of prudence and caution so as to avoid misrepresentation, in any wise, by acts of commission or omission.

Competency. It is the obligation of a real estate agent to be knowledgeable as a real estate brokerage practitioner. The agent should:

(1) be informed on market conditions affecting the real estate business and pledged to continuing education in the intricacies involved in marketing real estate for others;

(2) be informed on national, state and local issues and developments in the real estate industry.

(3) exercise judgment and skill in the performance of the work.

Consumer Information Form 1-1.

(a) The Texas Real Estate Commission adopts by reference Consumer Information Form 1-1 approved by the Texas Real Estate Commission in 1991. This document is published by and available from the Texas Real Estate Commission, P.O. Box 12188, Austin, Texas 78711-2188.

(b) Each real estate inspector or active real estate broker licensed by the Texas Real Estate Commission shall display Consumer Information Form 1-1 in a prominent location in each place of business the broker or inspector maintains.

Discriminatory Practices. No real estate licensee shall inquire about, respond to or facilitate inquiries about, or make a disclosure which indicates or is intended to indicate any preference, limitation or discrimination based on the following: race, color, religion, sex, national origin, ancestry, familial status, or handicap of an owner, previous or current occupant, potential purchaser, lessor, or potential lessee of real property. For the purpose of this section, handicap includes a person who had, may have had, has, or may have AIDS, HIV-related illnesses, or HIV infection as defined by the Centers for Disease Control of the United States Public Health Service.

Code of Ethics　**Canons of Professional Ethics and Conduct.** The importance of adhering to a set of ethical business standards cannot be overemphasized. The Texas Real Estate Commission has adopted a code of ethics as part of its rules to establish a basis for professional conduct of licensed real estate brokers and salespeople. Each applicant for a Texas broker's or salesperson's license must pledge that he or she will fully comply with the **Canons of Professional Ethics and Conduct** (see Figure 6.2).

In Practice   A Texas real estate broker was sued for breach of fiduciary duty based on the broker's failure to tell the owner that her listed property had been posted for foreclosure. The broker contended that his conduct was governed exclusively by the listing agreement. The court disagreed: Rules and regulations promulgated within an agency's authority have the force and effect of law [*Kinnard v. Homann*, 750 S.W. 2d 30 (1988)].

The NAR Code of Ethics is available on the NAR web site:

www.nar.realtor.com

NAR Code of Ethics. The National Association of REALTORS® publishes a **Code of Ethics,** along with interpretations of the Code known as *Standards of Practice*. Members of NAR and its affiliated state and local associations are expected to subscribe to this strict code of conduct. (Remember, not all licensees are members of NAR.) Similar to case law, interpretations of the Code establish precedents for local boards to follow in hearings that involve violations of the Code. Because the real estate business is only as good as its reputation, and reputations are built on sound business practices and fair dealings with clients, all licensees are obligated to conduct themselves in an ethical manner.

Summary

The federal regulations regarding equal opportunity in housing are contained principally in two laws. The Civil Rights Act of 1866 prohibits all racial discrimination, and the federal Fair Housing Act (Title VIII of the Civil Rights Act of 1968, as amended) prohibits discrimination on the basis of race, color, religion, sex, national origin, handicap, or familial status in the sale or rental of residential property. Discriminatory actions include refusing to deal with an individual or a specific group; changing any terms of a real estate or loan transaction; changing the services offered for any individual or group; making statements or advertisements that indicate discriminatory restrictions; and otherwise attempting to make a dwelling unavailable to any person or group because of race, color, religion, sex, national origin, handicap, or familial status.

Complaints under the federal Fair Housing Act may be reported to and investigated by the Department of Housing and Urban Development or the Texas Commission on Human Rights. Since Texas has passed the Texas Fair Housing Act, which is substantially equivalent to the federal law, complaints are heard by the Texas Commission on Human Rights or in state district courts. However, complaints under the Civil Rights Act of 1866 must be taken to a federal court.

The Home Mortgage Disclosure Act, the Equal Credit Opportunity Act, and the Community Reinvestment Act contribute to the fair availability of credit. All lenders are defined the same under each act.

A real estate business is only as good as its reputation. Real estate licensees can maintain good reputations by demonstrating good business ability and adhering to an ethical standard of business practices. Compliance with the Texas Real Estate Commission's Canons of Professional Ethics and Conduct is required of all Texas licensees. In addition, many licensees subscribe to a code of ethics as members of professional real estate organizations.

Questions

1. Which of the following acts is permitted under the federal Fair Housing Act?
   a. Advertising property for sale only to a special group
   b. Refusing to sell a home to a minority individual because of a poor credit history
   c. Telling an individual that an apartment has been rented when in fact it has not
   d. Showing a member of a minority group only those properties located in minority areas

2. Complaints relating to the Civil Rights Act of 1866
   a. must be taken directly to a federal court.
   b. are handled by HUD.
   c. are handled by state enforcement agencies.
   d. must be handled by local jurisdiction authority before appealing to federal court.

3. Under federal law, families with children may be refused rental or purchase in buildings where occupancy is reserved exclusively for those aged at least
   a. 55.   c. 62.
   b. 60.   d. 65.

4. Which of the following situations is considered to be discriminatory under the federal Fair Housing Act?
   a. The Penford Club of Metropole City will rent lodging only to graduates of Penford University who are members of this private club.
   b. A Catholic convent provides housing for Catholics only.
   c. The owner of a 20-unit apartment building refuses to rent apartments to women.
   d. An owner refuses to rent the other side of her duplex home to families with children.

5. "I hear *they're* moving in. There goes the neighborhood! Better put your house on the market before values drop!" This is an example of
   a. steering.
   b. redlining.
   c. blockbusting.
   d. channeling.

6. After a broker takes a listing to sell a residence, the owner specifies that he will not sell his home to any Asian family. The broker should do which of the following?
   a. Advertise the property exclusively in non-Asian-language newspapers.
   b. Explain to the owner that the instruction violates federal law and the broker cannot comply with it.
   c. Abide by the principal's instructions to fulfill the agency responsibility of *obedience.*
   d. Require that the owner sign a separate legal document stating the additional instruction as an amendment to the listing agreement.

7. Which of the following statements describes the Supreme Court's decision in the case of *Jones v. Alfred H. Mayer Company*?
   a. Racial discrimination is prohibited by any party in the sale or rental of real estate.
   b. Sales by individual residential homeowners are exempt from fair housing provisions, provided the owner does not use brokers.
   c. Laws against discrimination apply only to federally related transactions.
   d. Persons with disabilities are a protected class.

8. Why is the Civil Rights Act of 1866 unique?
   a. It protects the aged.
   b. It adds welfare recipients as a protected class.
   c. It contains "choose your neighbor" provisions.
   d. It provides no exceptions that would permit racial discrimination.

9. The act of channeling home seekers to a particular area either to maintain or to change the character of a neighborhood is
   a. blockbusting.
   b. redlining.
   c. steering.
   d. less favorable treatment.

10. A lender's refusal to lend money to potential homeowners attempting to purchase property located in predominantly African-American neighborhoods is known as
    a. blockbusting.
    b. redlining.
    c. steering.
    d. qualifying.

11. Under the Texas Fair Housing Act, violations of the fair housing laws are referred to and handled by
    a. federal courts.
    b. local boards of REALTORS®.
    c. the Texas Commission on Human Rights.
    d. HUD.

12. An exception that allows discrimination in the rental of rooms or units in an owner-occupied building with no more than four units is provided in
    a. the Civil Rights Act of 1964.
    b. the Civil Rights Act of 1866.
    c. *Jones v. Mayer.*
    d. the Fair Housing Act of 1968.

13. The Home Mortgage Disclosure Act requires that lenders disclose
    a. the geographic areas served by the lender.
    b. the amount of the loan-related closing costs.
    c. the annual percentage rate of each loan.
    d. the reason a loan was denied.

14. If a mortgage lender discriminates against a loan applicant on the basis of marital status, it violates what law?
    a. ADA
    b. Civil Rights Act of 1866
    c. ECOA
    d. Fair Housing Act

15. The Community Reinvestment Act (CRA) requires that lenders
    a. maintain a branch office in each geographic area where loans are made.
    b. reinvest at least 90 percent of their loan proceeds in properties located within the communities they serve.
    c. make loans within the communities from which they derive their deposits.
    d. make funds available for urban renewal projects.

16. The federal Fair Housing Act of 1988 added as protected groups
    a. families with children and persons with handicaps.
    b. senior citizens and persons with handicaps.
    c. single parents and those over age 65.
    d. persons unemployed and having a disability.

17. A real estate broker wants to achieve racial balance in residential housing. As an office policy, he requires that salespersons show prospective buyers from racial or ethnic minority groups only properties that are in areas of town where few members of their groups currently live. Which of the following statements is true regarding the broker's policy?
    a. While the policy may appear to constitute blockbusting, the practice is legal.
    b. Because the effect of the policy is discriminatory, it constitutes illegal steering regardless of the broker's intentions.
    c. The broker's policy constitutes redlining.
    d. While the broker's policy may appear to constitute steering, the practice is legal.

7 Texas Real Estate License Act

Key Terms

ARELLO
broker
core real estate course
mandatory continuing
  education (MCE)
nonresident licensee
real estate inspector
real estate recovery
  fund

residential rental
  locator
salesperson
salesperson annual
  education (SAE)
Texas Real Estate
  Commission (TREC)

Texas Real Estate
  Broker-Lawyer
  Committee
Texas Real Estate
  Research Center
  (Real Estate Center)

OVERVIEW

In Texas, broker and salesperson license applicants are required to pass an examination designed to test their knowledge of real estate principles and laws. Foremost among these laws is the *Texas Real Estate License Act*, which sets forth strict operating restrictions for licensees and penalties for noncompliance.

The license act is reproduced in its entirety in this chapter. The license law analysis form that precedes the end-of-chapter questions will help students learn the requirements of state law. The form can be used as a study device while reading through the state law or as a testing device after studying the license law.

REAL ESTATE LICENSE LAWS IN ALL STATES

All states, the District of Columbia, and Canadian provinces have enacted real estate license laws that regulate the activities of real estate brokers and salespeople. Details vary from state to state, but in many states the main provisions are similar and are based on the so-called pattern law recommended by the License Law Committee of the National Association of REALTORS®. In addition, **ARELLO**—the Association of Real Estate License Law

Officials—promotes uniform policies and standards in the fields of license law administration and enforcement.

Purposes of the License Law

Although a fee is charged for real estate licenses, the primary purpose of the license law is not to raise revenue. The purposes of the law are to (1) protect the public from dishonest or incompetent brokers or salespeople, (2) prescribe certain minimum standards and qualifications for licensing brokers and salespersons, (3) maintain high standards in the real estate profession, and (4) protect licensed brokers and salespersons from unfair or improper competition.

The Texas Real Estate Commission

Administration of the license act is vested in the **Texas Real Estate Commission (TREC),** which by statute is composed of nine members. Three are members of the public who may have no affiliation with real estate brokerage, and six are real estate broker-members. The commissioners are appointed by the governor with confirmation by the state senate.

The Sunset Act

Texas law provides for a periodic review of each state agency, commission, and board to evaluate its purpose, efficiency, and need. This review is performed by a statutory agency known as the *Sunset Commission,* which recommends retaining or abolishing the state entity under review. The Real Estate Commission has been reviewed three times under the *Sunset Act* and has received approval for retention each time; its next review is scheduled for 2007.

BASIC PROVISIONS OF THE TEXAS REAL ESTATE LICENSE ACT

Definitions of Broker and Salesperson

A licensed real estate *broker* is authorized to operate his or her own real estate brokerage business. A real estate **salesperson** with an active license is sponsored by and responsible to a licensed broker for the purposes of performing real estate brokerage transactions.

Licensing Procedure

All states require that an applicant for either the broker's or salesperson's license pass an examination to demonstrate knowledge of real estate principles and practices. In addition to the examination, Texas licensing requirements relate to age, citizenship, education, apprenticeship, and residency. Application forms, sources of acceptable real estate education, an exam study outline, practice exam questions, and information related to the activities of the Texas Real Estate Commission can be obtained from the TREC web site (http://www.trec.state.tx.us) or from TRECFax, a Fax-on-Demand retrieval system, by dialing 1-512-419-1623 from the handset on a fax machine. Licensees can receive TREC update notices automatically by subscribing through the TREC web site to an electronic list serve notification system. Information regarding license application procedures can also be obtained by calling the Texas Real Estate Commission at 1-800-250-8732 or by writing the Commission at P.O. Box 12188, Austin, TX 78711-2188.

Members of the real estate profession should be committed to promoting the profession and maintaining and improving the standards of the field. This is best done by carefully adhering to licensing and fair housing laws, pledging to comply with the Texas Real Estate Commission's Canons of Professional Ethics and Conduct, and taking advantage of every opportunity to expand professional knowledge and ability.

The licenses or registration certificates issued to qualified individuals and corporations are legal permits to operate a real estate brokerage business as described and permitted by state law. In Texas, a license is required to sell, purchase, rent, lease, auction, or exchange real estate for others and for compensation. To appraise, a person must be licensed by the Texas Real Estate Commission as a broker or salesperson *or* be certified or licensed by the Texas Appraiser Licensing and Certification Board; Chapter 14 discusses the requirements for licensure and certification of appraisers. Real estate licenses are issued for definite terms and must be renewed within specified time limits. Each license is a personal right and terminates on death of the licensee or dissolution of the corporation. While a license or registration certificate is in effect, the activities of each licensed person or entity are subject to control of the Texas Real Estate Commission as prescribed by the Texas Real Estate License Act. For this reason, every licensed person must be thoroughly familiar with the act.

Certain persons are exempt from the license law. Usually these are owners dealing with their own property; trustees, executors, receivers, and others operating under court orders; public officials; and attorneys at law.

Real Estate Brokers Do Not Give Legal Advice

Texas law prohibits nonmembers of the state bar from practicing law in the state. Although the legal rights and contractual obligations of the parties to a real estate transaction are the broker's fundamental concerns, it is not the broker's responsibility to offer legal advice. In fact, the license act authorizes the Texas Real Estate Commission to suspend or revoke a broker's or salesperson's license for the unlawful practice of law. To ensure valid sales contracts, licensees should advise sellers and buyers to secure legal counsel if they do not understand the provisions of the various contract forms that the act requires licensees to use.

THE TEXAS REAL ESTATE LICENSE ACT

The *Texas Real Estate License Act,* Article 6573a of Vernon's Texas Civil Statutes, was passed in 1949. This law was revised extensively in August 1967 and again in May 1975, with an increase in educational requirements, removal of surety bond provisions and the establishment of a **real estate recovery fund.** Further amendments were made in almost every biennial session of the Texas legislature, most recently in 2001.

Reproduction in full of the Texas Real Estate License Act on the following pages is intended to help applicants study the act. Headings have been added by the author, and some parts are emphasized in boldface type. This act must be interpreted as applied to each person or case by his or her legal counsel. It may be changed or amended by action of the state legislature and must be signed by the governor. To further understanding of the act, the *Rules of the Texas Real Estate Commission* interpret and define the act's provisions. The rules of the commission are subject to review by the legislature and may be amended by the commission. A copy of the Rules may be obtained from the TREC web site.

The Real Estate License Act, 2001 Revision (TRELA)

General Provisions   **Section 1.** (a) This Act shall be known and may be cited as "The Real Estate License Act."

(b) **It is unlawful** for a person to act in the capacity of, engage in the business of, or advertise or hold that person out as engaging in or conducting the business of a real estate broker or a real estate salesperson within this state without first obtaining a real estate license from the Texas Real Estate Commission. **It is unlawful** for a person licensed as a real estate salesperson to act or attempt to act as a real estate broker or salesperson unless that person is, at such time, associated with a licensed Texas real estate broker and acting for the licensed real estate broker.

(c) **Each real estate broker** licensed pursuant to this Act is responsible to the commission, members of the public, and the broker's clients for all acts and conduct performed under this Act by the broker or by a real estate salesperson associated with or acting for the broker.

(d) **No real estate salesperson** shall accept compensation for real estate sales and transactions from any person other than the broker under whom the salesperson is at the time licensed or under whom the salesperson was licensed when the salesperson earned the right to compensation.

(e) **No real estate salesperson** shall pay a commission to any person except through the broker under whom the salesperson is at the time licensed.

In Practice   Section 1 of the act establishes the requirement for a real estate license to be obtained by those who desire to practice brokerage as defined in Section 2. It also establishes the accountability of each broker to the Real Estate Commission, the public, and clients for acts performed by the broker or by a salesperson sponsored by the broker. This section prescribes the channels for payment of a commission to or by a salesperson. An amendment to the Rules in 1999 (535.1) provides that all real estate transactions conducted within the state will be regulated by the TRELA regardless of the location of the real estate. In addition, business conducted from another state by mail, telephone, the Internet, e-mail, or other medium is considered acting within Texas if all buyers, sellers, landlords, or tenants are legal residents of Texas and the real estate is located at least partially in Texas.

Definitions   **Section 2.** As used in this Act:

(1) **"Real estate"** means a leasehold, as well as any other interest or estate in land, whether corporeal, incorporeal, freehold, or nonfreehold, and whether the real estate is situated in this state or elsewhere. The term does not include an interest given as security for the performance of an obligation.

(2) **"Real estate broker"** means a person who, for another person and for a fee, commission, or other valuable consideration, or with the intention

or in the expectation or on the promise of receiving or collecting a fee, commission, or other valuable consideration from another person:

    (A) sells, exchanges, purchases, rents, or leases real estate;

    (B) offers to sell, exchange, purchase, rent, or lease real estate;

    (C) negotiates or attempts to negotiate the listing, sale, exchange, purchase, rental, or leasing of real estate;

    (D) lists or offers or attempts or agrees to list real estate for sales, rental, lease, exchange, or trade;

    (E) appraises or offers or attempts or agrees to appraise real estate;

    (F) auctions, or offers or attempts or agrees to auction, real estate;

    (G) buys or sells or offers to buy or sell, or otherwise deals in options on real estate;

    (H) aids, attempts, or offers to aid in locating or obtaining for purchase, rent, or lease any real estate;

    (I) procures or assists in the procuring of prospects for the purpose of effecting the sale, exchange, lease, or rental of real estate; or

    (J) procures or assists in the procuring of properties for the purpose of effecting the sale, exchange, lease, or rental of real estate.

(3) **"Broker"** also includes a person employed by or on behalf of the owner or owners of lots or other parcels of real estate, at a salary, fee, commission, or any other valuable consideration, to sell the real estate or any part thereof, in lots or parcels or other disposition thereof. It also includes a person who engages in the business of charging an advance fee or contracting for collection of a fee in connection with a contract whereby he undertakes primarily to promote the sale of real estate either through its listing in a publication issued primarily for such purpose, or for referral of information concerning the real estate to brokers, or both.

(4) **"Real estate salesperson"** means a person associated with a Texas-licensed real estate broker for the purposes of performing acts or transactions comprehended by the definition of "real estate broker" as defined in this Act.

(5) **"Person"** means an individual or any other entity including a government or governmental subdivision or agency, a limited liability company, a limited liability partnership, a partnership or a corporation, foreign or domestic.

(6) **"Commission"** means the Texas Real Estate Commission.

(7) If the sense requires it, words in the present tense include the future tense; in the masculine gender, include the feminine or neuter gender; in the singular number, include the plural number; in the plural number, include the singular number; the word "and" may be read "or"; and the word "or" may be read "and". This Act is substantive in character and is intended to be applied prospectively only.

In Practice   Section 2 contains the official definitions of terms used in the act. *Property, real property,* and *real estate* all have the same meaning when used in the license act. Of particular importance are the definitions of *broker* and *real estate salesperson* because they specifically describe those activities for which licensure is required. The act makes no distinction as to the type of activity that each is permitted to practice. The reason for the separate classification of licensure is to place the responsibility for the salesperson's actions on the broker.

Valuable consideration is defined to include money, gifts of merchandise having a retail value greater than $50, rent bonuses, and discounts (Rule 535.20).

Exemptions   **Section 3. Exemptions.** The provisions of this Act shall not apply to any of the following persons and transactions, and each and all of the following persons and transactions are hereby exempted from the provisions of this Act:

(1) an attorney at law licensed in this state or in any other state;

(2) an attorney in fact under a duly-executed power of attorney authorizing the consummation of a real estate transaction;

(3) a public official in the conduct of that person's official duties;

(4) a person calling the sale of real estate by auction under the authority of a license issued by this state provided the person does not perform any other act of a real estate broker or salesperson as defined by this Act;

(5) a person acting under a court order or under the authority of a will or a written trust instrument;

(6) a salesperson employed by an owner in the sale of structures and land on which said structures are situated, provided such structures are erected by the owner in the due course of the owner's business;

(7) an on-site manager of an apartment complex;

(8) transactions involving the sale, lease, or transfer of any mineral or mining interest in real property;

(9) an owner or the owner's employees in renting or leasing the owner's own real estate whether improved or unimproved;

(10) transactions involving the sale, lease, or transfer of cemetery lots;

(11) transactions involving the renting, leasing, or management of hotels or motels; or

(12) a partnership or limited liability partnership acting as a broker or real estate salesperson through a partner who is a licensed real estate broker.

In Practice   Section 3 of the act lists the exemptions from licensing requirements. Licensure is not required of one who buys and sells real property only for his or her own account. In addition, a license is not required for the performance of secretarial, clerical, or administrative tasks, as long as the person does not solicit business for the broker or hold himself or herself out as authorized to act as a real estate broker or salesperson. An unlicensed person may act as a host or hostess at a property being offered for sale by the broker, provided the unlicensed person does not engage in an activity for which a license is required. Under H.B. 1869 (2001), a manufactured home retailer is not required to hold a real estate license even if the home will be considered real property.

A Single Act Is a Violation   **Section 4.** A person who, directly or indirectly for another, with the intention or on the promise of receiving any valuable consideration, offers, attempts, or agrees to perform, or performs, a single act defined in Subdivisions 2 and 3, Section 2 of this Act, whether as a part of a transaction, or as an entire transaction, is deemed to be acting as a real estate broker or salesperson within the meaning of this Act. The commission of a single such act by a person required to be licensed or registered under this Act and not so licensed or registered shall constitute a violation of this Act.

Administration   **Section 5.** (a) **The administration** of the provisions of this Act is vested in a commission, to be known as the "Texas Real Estate Commission," consisting of nine members to be appointed by the governor with the advice and consent of two-thirds of the senate present. The commissioners hold office for staggered terms of six years with the terms of three members expiring January 31 of each odd-numbered year. Each member holds office until the member's successor is appointed and has qualified. Within 15 days after appointment, each member shall qualify by taking the constitutional oath of office and furnishing a bond payable to the Governor of Texas in the penal sum of $10,000, conditional on the faithful performance of the member's duties as prescribed by law. A vacancy for any cause shall be filled by the governor for the unexpired term. The governor shall designate as chairperson of the commission one member of the commission who is a licensed real estate broker. The chairperson serves in that capacity at the pleasure of the governor. At a regular meeting in February of each year, the commission shall elect from its own membership a vice-chairperson and secretary. A quorum of the commission consists of five members.

(b) (1) **All members, officers, employees, and agents of the commission** are subject to the code of ethics and standards of conduct imposed by Chapter 421, Acts of the 63rd Legislature, Regular Session, 1973 (Article 6252-9b, Vernon's Texas Civil Statutes). A state elected president, president-elect, vice-president, or secretary-treasurer, employee, or paid consultant of a Texas trade association in the real estate industry may not be a member of the commission or an employee of the commission who is exempt from the state's position classification plan or compensated at or above the amount prescribed by the General Appropriations Act for step 1, salary group 17, of the state position classification salary schedule. A person who is the spouse of an officer, manager, or paid consultant of a Texas trade association in the real estate industry may not be a commission member and may not be a commission employee who is exempt from the state's position classification plan or is compensated at or above the amount prescribed by the General Appropriations Act for step 1, salary group 17, of the state position classification salary schedule. For the purposes of this section, a Texas trade association is a nonprofit, cooperative, and voluntarily joined statewide association of business or professional competitors in this state designed to assist its members and its industry or profession in dealing with mutual business or professional problems and in promoting their common interest.

(2) A person may not serve as a member of the commission or act as the general counsel to the commission if the person is required to register as a lobbyist under Chapter 305, Government Code, because of the person's activities for compensation on behalf of a profession related to the operation of the commission.

(c) **Appointments** to the commission shall be made without regard to the race, color, handicap, sex, religion, age, or national origin of the appointees. Each member of the commission shall be a citizen of Texas and a qualified voter. Six members shall have been engaged in the real estate brokerage business as licensed real estate brokers as their major occupations for at least five years immediately preceding their appointments. Three members must be representatives of the general public. A person is not eligible for appointment as a public member of the commission if the person or the person's spouse:

(1) is registered, certified, or licensed by an occupational regulatory agency in the real estate industry;

(2) is employed by or participates in the management of a business entity or other organization regulated by the commission or receiving funds from the commission;

(3) owns or controls, directly or indirectly, more than a 10 percent interest in a business entity or other organization regulated by the commission or receiving funds from the commission; or

(4) uses or receives a substantial amount of tangible goods, services, or funds from the commission, other than compensation or reimbursement authorized by law for commission membership, attendance, or expenses.

(d) It is a ground for removal from the commission if a member:

(1) does not have at the time of appointment the qualifications required by Subsection (c) of this section for appointment to the commission;

(2) does not maintain during service on the commission the qualifications required by Subsection (c) of this section;

(3) violates a prohibition established by Subsection (b) of this section;

(4) cannot discharge the member's duties for a substantial part of the term for which the member is appointed because of illness or disability; or

(5) is absent from more than half of the regularly scheduled commission meetings that the member is eligible to attend during each calendar year, unless the absence is excused by majority vote of the commission.

(e) The validity of an action of the commission is not affected by the fact that it was taken when a ground for removal of a commission member existed.

(f) If the administrator has knowledge that a potential ground for removal exists, the administrator shall notify the chairperson of the commission of the ground. The chairperson shall then notify the governor that a potential ground for removal exists.

(g) Each member of the commission shall receive as compensation for each day actually spent on the member's official duties the sum of $75 and the actual and necessary expenses incurred in the performance of the member's official duties.

(h) **The commission shall have the authority** and power to make and enforce all rules and regulations necessary for the performance of its duties, to establish standards of conduct and ethics for its licensees in keeping with the purposes and intent of this Act or to insure compliance with the provisions of this Act. In addition to any other action, proceeding, or remedy authorized by law, the commission shall have the right to institute an action in its own name to enjoin any violation of any provision of this Act or any rule or regulation of the commission and in order for the commission to sustain such action it shall not be necessary to allege or prove, either that an adequate remedy at law does not exist, or that substantial or irreparable damage would result from the continued violation thereof. Either party to such action may appeal to the appellate court having jurisdiction of said cause. The commission shall not be required to give any appeal bond in any action or proceeding to enforce the provisions of this Act.

(i) **The commission is empowered** to select and name an administrator and to select and employ such other subordinate officers and employees as are necessary to administer this Act. The salaries of the administrator and the officers and employees shall be fixed by the commission not to exceed such amounts as are fixed by the applicable general appropriations bill. The commission may designate a subordinate officer as assistant administrator who shall be authorized to act for the administrator in the administrator's absence. The administrator or the administrator's designee shall develop a system of annual performance evaluations. All merit pay for commission employees must be based on the system established under this subsection. The administrator or the administrator's designee shall develop an intraagency career ladder program. The program shall require intraagency postings of all nonentry level positions concurrently with any public posting.

(j) **The commission shall adopt** a seal of a design which it shall prescribe. Copies of all records and papers in the office of the commission, duly certified and authenticated by the seal of the commission, shall be received in evidence in all courts with like effect as the original.

(k) **Except as provided** in Subsections (l) and (m) of this section, all money derived from fees, assessments, or charges under this Act, shall be paid by the commission into the State Treasury for safekeeping, and shall be placed by the State Treasurer in a separate fund to be available for the use of the commission in the administration of this Act on requisition by the commission. A necessary amount of the money so paid into the State Treasury is hereby specifically appropriated to the commission for the purpose of paying the salaries and expenses necessary and proper for the administration of this Act, including equipment and maintenance of supplies for the offices or quarters occupied by the commission, and necessary travel expenses for the commission or persons authorized to act for it when performing duties under this Act. The comptroller shall, on requisition of the commission, draw warrants from time to time on the State Treasurer for the amount specified in the requisition, not exceeding, however, the amount in the fund at the time of making a requisition. However, all money expended in the administration of this Act shall be specified and determined by itemized appropriation in the general departmental appropriation bill for the Texas Real Estate Commission, and not otherwise. The commission shall file annually with the governor and the presiding officer of each house of the legislature a complete and detailed written report accounting for all funds received and disbursed by the commission during the preceding fiscal year. The annual report must be in the form and reported in the time provided by the General Appropriations Act.

(l) **In the event that fees** collected under the Residential Service Company Act (Article 6573b, Vernon's Texas Civil Statutes), are insufficient to fund the legislative appropriation for that activity, funds from the real estate license fund are hereby authorized to be used for the administration of that Act. In no event, however, will the total expenditures for that activity exceed the legislative appropriation therefor.

(m) **The commission shall charge and collect** as a condition for issuance and for renewal of a real estate broker license the fee under Section 11(a)(14) of this Act. The commission shall charge and collect as a condition for issuance and for renewal of a registration under Section 9A of this Act the fee under Section 11(a)(14) of this Act. The commission shall charge and collect as a condition for issuance and for renewal of a real estate salesperson license the fee under Section 11(a)(15) of this Act. The commission shall transmit the fees under this subsection quarterly to Texas A&M University for deposit in a separate banking account. The money in the separate account shall be expended for the support and maintenance of the **Texas Real Estate Research Center** and for carrying out the purposes, objectives, and duties of the center. However, all money expended from the separate account shall be as determined by legislative appropriation.

(n) **The Texas Real Estate Commission is subject to Chapter 325, Government Code (Texas Sunset Act).** Unless continued in existence as provided by that chapter, the commission is abolished and this Act expires September 1, 2007.

(o) **The commission is subject to the open meetings law,** Chapter 271, Acts of the 60th Legislature, Regular Session, 1967, as amended (Article 6252-17, Vernon's Texas Civil Statutes), and the Administrative Procedure and Texas Register Act, as amended (Article 6252-13a, Vernon's Texas Civil Statutes).

(p) **The commission shall develop and implement policies** that provide the public with a reasonable opportunity to appear before the commission and to speak on any issue under the jurisdiction of the commission.

(q) **The commission by rule shall establish methods** by which consumers and service recipients are notified of the name, mailing address, and telephone number of the commission for the purpose of directing complaints to the commission. The commission may provide for that notification to be provided with the notification required by Section 8(q) of this Act or:

(1) on each registration form, application, or written contract for services of an individual or entity regulated under this Act;

(2) on a sign prominently displayed in the place of business of each individual or entity regulated under this Act; or

(3) in a bill for service provided by an individual or entity regulated under this Act.

(r) **The commission shall prepare information** of public interest describing the functions of the commission and the procedures by which complaints are filed with and resolved by the commission. The commission shall make the information available to the general public and appropriate state agencies.

(s) **The commission shall develop and implement policies** that clearly define the respective responsibilities of the governing body of the commission and the staff of the commission.

(t) **The commission may authorize specific employees** to conduct hearings and render final decisions in contested cases. The commission may employ a general counsel, attorneys, investigators, and support staff to administer and enforce this Act.

(u) **The administrator or the administrator's designee shall prepare** and maintain a written policy statement to assure implementation of a program of equal employment opportunity under which all personnel transactions are made without regard to race, color, handicap, sex, religion, age, or national origin. The policy statement must include:

(1) personnel policies, including policies relating to recruitment, evaluation, selection, appointment, training, and promotion of personnel;

(2) a comprehensive analysis of the commission work force that meets federal and state guidelines;

(3) procedures by which a determination can be made of significant underutilization in the commission work force of all persons for whom federal or state guidelines encourage a more equitable balance; and

(4) reasonable methods to appropriately address those areas of significant underutilization.

(v) **A policy statement prepared** under Subsection (u) must cover an annual period, be updated at least annually, and be filed with the governor's office.

(w) **The governor's office shall deliver** a biennial report to the legislature based on the information received under Subsection (v). The report may be made separately or as a part of other biennial reports made to the legislature.

(x) **The commission shall provide** to its members and employees, as often as necessary, information regarding their qualifications for office or employment under this Act and their responsibilities under applicable laws relating to standards of conduct for state officers or employees.

(y) **The commission shall prepare** and maintain a written plan that describes how a person who does not speak English or who has a physical, mental, or developmental disability can be provided reasonable access to the commission's programs.

(z) **The commission may not** adopt rules restricting competitive bidding or advertising by a person regulated by the commission except to prohibit false, misleading, or deceptive practices by the person. The commission may not include in its rules to prohibit false, misleading, or deceptive practices by a person regulated by the commission a rule that:

(1) restricts the use of any medium for advertising;

(2) restricts the person's personal appearance or use of the person's voice in an advertisement;

(3) relates to the size or duration of an advertisement by the person; or

(4) restricts the person's advertisement under a trade name.

In Practice

Section 5 provides for the composition of the Texas Real Estate Commission and administration of the act. It contains the provisions for the payment of license fees into the state treasury, except those fees earmarked to operate the **Texas Real Estate Research Center** (now the **Real Estate Center**) at Texas A&M University. This section of the act also provides the rule-making authority of the commission. These rules are quite extensive and have the net effect of law on licensees.

General Requirements for Licensure

Section 6. (a) **A person desiring to act as a real estate broker** in this state shall file an application for a license with the commission on a form prescribed by the commission. A person previously licensed as a broker may apply for inactive status. A person desiring to act as a real estate salesperson in this state must apply for a salesperson license on a form prescribed by the commission. If the person satisfies all requirements for a salesperson license, the commission may issue an inactive salesperson license to the person. The person may not act as a salesperson unless the person is sponsored by a licensed broker who has notified the commission and paid the fee for issuance of an active license to the salesperson as required by Section 13(b) of this Act.

(b) **To be eligible for a license, an individual** must be a citizen of the United States or a lawfully admitted alien, be at least 18 years of age, and be a legal resident of Texas at the time of the filing of an application, and must satisfy the commission as to the individual's honesty, trustworthiness, integrity, and competency. However, the competency of the individual, for the purpose of qualifying for the granting of a license, shall be judged solely on the basis of the examination referred to in Section 7 of this Act.

(c) **To be eligible for or to renew a license, a corporation** must designate one of its officers and a limited liability company must designate one of its managers to act for it. The designated person must be a licensed real estate broker as shown in the records of the commission. A corporation or limited liability company may not act as a real estate broker unless the designated person is a licensed real estate broker.

(d) **For an individual to be eligible for a registration or a renewal of a registration under Section 9A of this Act, the individual** must be a citizen of the United States or a lawfully admitted alien and be at least 18 years of age. For a corporation, limited liability company, partnership, limited liability partnership, or any other entity to be eligible for a registration or renewal of a registration under Section 9A of this Act, it must designate one of its officers, partners, or managers to act for it. The designated person must be an individual registered under Section 9A of this Act.

Section 6A. (a) **If, at any time** before a person applies for a license under this Act, the person requests the commission to determine whether the person's moral character complies with the commission's moral character requirements for licensing under this Act and the person pays a fee set by the commission for the moral character determination, the commission shall make its determination of the person's moral character.

(b) **Not later than the 30th day** after the day on which the commission makes its determination, the commission shall give the person notice of the determination.

(c) **If the person later applies** for a license under this Act, the commission may conduct a supplemental moral character check of the person. The supplemental check may cover only the time since the day on which the person requested the original moral character determination.

In Practice   Section 6 of the act establishes the eligibility requirements for applying for a broker's or salesperson's license. By Rule, an applicant must first obtain an evaluation of coursework from TREC and pay the fee set by law. Then under the provisions of H.B. 695 (2001), an applicant for a salesperson license will apply for an inactive license. To begin the practice of real estate after meeting all application and examination requirements, a new licensee will obtain a sponsoring broker and pay the fee ($20) for issuance of an active license. An applicant may submit a broker's sponsorship form at the time of initial application, with the payment of both the license fee and the fee for issuance of an active license.

Rule 541.1 lists criminal offenses that demonstrate inability to represent the interest of another with honesty, trustworthiness, and integrity; among those are "offenses involving fraud or misrepresentation" and "offenses involving moral turpitude."

Requirements for Licensing

Section 7. (a) **Competency as referred to in Section 6** of this Act shall be established by an examination prepared by or contracted for by the commission. The examination shall be given at such times and at such places within the state as the commission shall prescribe. The examination shall be of scope sufficient in the judgment of the commission to determine that a person is competent to act as a real estate broker or salesperson in a manner to protect the interest of the public. The examination for a salesperson license shall be less exacting and less stringent than the examination for a broker license. The commission shall furnish each applicant with study material and references on which the examination shall be based. When an applicant for a real estate license fails a qualifying examination, the applicant may apply for reexamination by filing a request therefor together with the proper fee. The examination requirement must be satisfied not later than six months after the date on which the application for a license is filed. Courses of study required for a license may include but are not limited to the following, which shall be considered **core real estate courses** for all purposes of this Act:

(1) **Principles of Real Estate** (or equivalent) shall include but not be limited to an overview of licensing as a real estate broker and salesperson, ethics of practice, titles to and conveyancing of real estate, legal descriptions, deeds, encumbrances and liens, distinctions between personal and real property, appraisal, finance and regulations, closing procedures, real estate mathematics, and at least three classroom hours of instruction on federal, state, and local laws relating to housing discrimination, housing credit discrimination, and community reinvestment.

(2) **Real Estate Appraisal** (or equivalent) shall include but not be limited to the central purposes and functions of an appraisal, social and economic determinant of value, appraisal case studies, cost, market data and income approaches to value estimates, final correlations, and reporting.

(3) **Real Estate Law** (or equivalent) shall include but not be limited to legal concepts of real estate, land description, real property rights and estates in land, contracts, conveyances, encumbrances, foreclosures, recording procedures, and evidence of titles.

(4) **Real Estate Finance** (or equivalent) shall include but not be limited to monetary systems, primary and secondary money markets, sources of mortgage loans, federal government programs, loan applications, processes and procedures, closing costs, alternative financial instruments, equal credit opportunity acts, community reinvestment act, and state housing agency.

(5) **Real Estate Marketing** (or equivalent) shall include but not be limited to real estate professionalism and ethics, characteristics of successful salespersons, time management, psychology of marketing, listing procedures, advertising, negotiating and closing, financing, and the Deceptive Trade Practices-Consumer Protection Act, as amended, Section 17.01 et seq., Business & Commerce Code.

(6) **Real Estate Mathematics** (or equivalent) shall include but not be limited to basic arithmetic skills and review of mathematical logic, percentages, interest, time-valued money, depreciation, amortization, proration, and estimation of closing statements.

(7) **Real Estate Brokerage** (or equivalent) shall include but not be limited to law of agency, planning and organization, operational policies and procedures, recruiting, selection and training of personnel, records and control, and real estate firm analysis and expansion criteria.

(8) **Property Management** (or equivalent) shall include but not be limited to role of property manager, landlord policies, operational guidelines, leases, lease negotiations, tenant relations, maintenance, reports, habitability laws, and the Fair Housing Act.

(9) **Real Estate Investments** (or equivalent) shall include but not be limited to real estate investment characteristics, techniques of investment analysis, time-valued money, discounted and nondiscounted investment criteria, leverage, tax shelters, depreciation, and applications to property tax.

(10) **Law of Agency** (or equivalent) shall include but not be limited to the principal-agent and master-servant relationships, the authority of an agent, the termination of an agent's authority, the fiduciary and other duties of an agent, employment law, deceptive trade practices, listing or buying representation procedures, and the disclosure of agency.

(11) **Law of Contracts** (or equivalent) shall include the elements of a contract, offer and acceptance, the statute of frauds, specific performance and remedies for breach, unauthorized practice of law, commission rules relating to use of adopted forms and owner disclosure requirements.

(b) **The commission by rule may:**

    (1) **prescribe the content of the core real estate courses** listed in Subsection (a) of this section; and

    (2) establish the title and content of additonal core real estate courses.

(c) **The commission shall waive** the examination of an applicant for a broker license who has, within one year previous to the filing of the application, been licensed in this state as a broker, and shall waive the examination of an applicant for a salesperson license who has, within one year previous to the filing of the application, been licensed in this state as either a broker or salesperson. The commission by rule may provide for the waiver of some or all of the requirements for a license under this Act for an applicant who was licensed under this Act within the six years preceding the date of filing the application.

(d) **Each applicant for a broker license** shall furnish the commission satisfactory evidence that the applicant has had not less than two years active experience in this state as a licensed real estate salesperson or broker during the 36-month period immediately preceding the filing of the application; and, in addition, shall furnish the commission satisfactory evidence of having completed successfully 60 semester hours, or equivalent classroom hours, of postsecondary education, of which a minimum of 18 semester hours or equivalent classroom hours must be completed in core real estate courses. The remaining 42 hours must be completed in core real estate courses or related courses accepted by the commission. These qualifications for a broker license may not be required of an applicant who, at the time of making the application, is duly licensed as a real estate broker by any other state in the United States if that state's requirements for licensure are comparable to those of Texas. As a prerequisite for applying for a broker license, those persons licensed as salespersons subject to the annual education requirements provided by Subsection (e) of this section shall, as part of the hours required by this subsection, furnish the commission satisfactory evidence of having completed all the requirements of Subsection (e) of this section.

(e) **Each applicant for a salesperson license** shall furnish the commission satisfactory evidence of having completed 12 semester hours, or equivalent classroom hours of postsecondary education, eight hours of which must be completed in core real estate courses, of which a minimum of four hours must be completed in Principles of Real Estate as described in Subsection (a)(1) of this section, a minimum of two hours must be completed in Law of Agency as described in Subsection (a)(10) of this section, and a minimum of two hours must be completed in Law of Contracts as described in Subsection (a)(11) of this section. The remaining four hours must be completed in core real estate courses or related courses. As a condition for the first renewal of a salesperson license, the applicant shall furnish the commission satisfactory evidence of having completed a minimum of 14 semester hours, or equivalent classroom hours, ten hours of which must be completed in core real estate courses. As a condition for the second renewal of a salesperson license, the applicant shall furnish the commission satisfactory evidence of having completed a minimum of 16 semester hours, or equivalent classroom hours, twelve hours of which must be completed in core real estate courses. As a condition for the third renewal of a salesperson license, the applicant shall furnish the commission satisfactory evidence of having completed a minimum of 18 semester hours, or equivalent classroom hours, fourteen hours of which must be completed in core real estate courses.

(f) **Insofar as is necessary for the administration of this Act,** the commission is authorized to inspect and accredit educational programs or courses of study in real estate and real estate inspection and to establish standards of accreditation for such programs conducted in the State of Texas, other than accredited colleges and universities. The commission shall determine the acceptability of real estate courses and real estate inspection courses offered to satisfy the requirements of this Act, and by rule may provide reasonable criteria for the approval of those courses. Schools, other than accredited colleges and universities, which are authorized to offer real estate educational courses pursuant to provisions of this section, shall be required to maintain a corporate surety bond, or other security acceptable to the commission, in the sum of $10,000, payable to the commission, for the benefit of a party who may suffer damages resulting from failure of a commission approved school or course to fulfill obligations attendant to the approval.

(g) **Notwithstanding any other provision of this Act,** each applicant for a broker license shall furnish the commission with satisfactory evidence:

(1) that the applicant has satisfied the requirements of Subsection (d) of this section;

(2) that the applicant is a licensed real estate broker in another state, has had not less than two years' active experience in the other state as a licensed real estate salesperson or broker during the 36-month period immediately preceding the filing of the application, and has satisfied the educational requirements for a broker license as provided by Subsection (d) of this section; or

(3) that the applicant has, within one year previous to the filing of the application, been licensed in this state as a broker.

(h) **Notwithstanding any other provision of this Act,** the commission shall waive the requirements of Subsection (e) of this section for an applicant for a salesperson license who has, within one year previous to the filing of the application, been licensed in this state as a broker or salesperson. However, with respect to an applicant for a salesperson license who was licensed as a salesperson within one year previous to the filing of the application but whose original license was issued under the provisions that the first, second, and third renewal of the license would be conditioned upon furnishing satisfactory evidence of successful completion of additional education, the commission shall require the applicant to furnish satisfactory evidence of successful completion of any additional education that would have been required if the license had been maintained without interruption during the previous year.

(i) **Not later than the 30th day** after the date on which a licensing examination is administered under this Act, the commission shall notify each examinee of the results of the examination. However, if an examination is graded or reviewed by a national testing service, the commission shall notify examinees of the results of the examination not later than the 14th day after the date on which the commission receives the results from the testing service. If the notice of examination results graded or reviewed by a national testing service will be delayed for longer than 90 days after the examination date, the commission shall notify the examinee of the reason for the delay before the 90th day. If requested in writing by a person who fails a licensing examination administered under this Act, the commission shall furnish the person with an analysis of the person's performance on the examination.

(j) **All license applicants** must complete at least three classroom hours of coursework on federal, state, and local laws governing housing discrimination, housing credit discrimination, and community reinvestment or at least three semester hours of coursework on constitutional law.

(k) **The commission may accept examinations** administered by a testing service as satisfying the examination requirements imposed under this Act. The commission may negotiate agreements with those testing services relating to examination development, test scheduling, examination site arrangements, and test administration, grading, reporting, and analysis. The commission may require a testing service to correspond directly with the license applicants regarding the administration of the examinations and may require that a testing service collect fees for administering the examinations directly from the applicants. The commission also may require a testing service to administer examinations at specific locations and specified frequencies. The commission shall retain the authority to establish the scope and type of all examinations. The commission shall adopt rules and standards as necessary to implement this section. In the absence of an agreement with a testing service, the commission shall administer any required qualifying examination in accordance with this Act.

Section 7A. (a) **To renew an active real estate broker license or an active real estate salesperson license** that is not subject to the annual education requirements of this Act, the licensee must provide the commission proof of attendance at at least 15 classroom hours of continuing education courses approved by the commission during the term of the current license. The commission by rule may prescribe the title, content, and duration of continuing education courses that a licensee must attend to renew a license and may provide for the substitution of relevant educational experience or correspondence courses approved by the commission instead of classroom attendance. In addition, supervised video instruction may be approved by the commission as a course counting as classroom hours of mandatory continuing education. At least six hours of instruction must be devoted to the rules of the commission, fair housing laws, landlord-tenant law and other Property Code issues, agency laws, antitrust laws, the Deceptive Trade Practices-Consumer Protection Act (Subchapter E, Chapter 17, Business & Commerce Code), disclosures to buyers, landlords, tenants, and sellers, current contract and addendum forms, the unauthorized practice of law, case studies involving violations of laws and regulations, current Federal Housing Administration and Department of Veterans Affairs regulations, tax laws, property tax consulting laws and legal issues, or other legal topics approved by the commission. The remaining hours may be devoted to other real estate-related topics approved by the commission. The commission may consider equivalent courses for continuing education credit. Property tax consulting laws and legal issues include but are not limited to the Tax Code, preparation of property tax reports, the unauthorized practice of law, agency laws, tax laws, laws concerning property taxes or assessments, deceptive trade practices, contract forms and addendum, and other legal topics approved by the commission. Real estate related courses approved by the State Bar of Texas for minimum continuing legal education participatory credit and core real estate courses under Section 7(a) of this Act shall automatically be approved as mandatory continuing education courses under this Act. The commission may not require examinations except for correspondence courses or courses offered by alternative delivery systems such as computers. Daily classroom course segments must be at least one hour long but not more than 10 hours long.

(b) **An applicant** for an active real estate broker license or an active real estate salesperson license who is not subject to the education requirements of Section 7 of this Act must provide the commission with proof of attendance of the number of classroom hours of continuing education that would have been required for a timely renewal as specified in Subsection (a) of this section during the two-year period preceding the filing of the application.

(c) **As a condition of returning to active status,** an inactive salesperson whose license is not subject to the annual education requirements of this Act must provide the commission with proof of attendance at at least 15 hours of continuing education as specified in Subsection (a) of this section during the two-year period preceding the filing of the application.

(d) **The commission may adopt rules and set and collect reasonable fees** to implement this section, including a fee not to exceed $400 for an application for approval of a provider of continuing education and a fee not to exceed $100 for an application for a course of study to be offered for continuing education. If the commission determines that an applicant satisfies the requirements of this section and any rules adopted by the commission under this section, the commission may authorize a provider to offer continuing education for a period of two years or authorize the offering of a course of study for a period of two years. (Effective August 31, 1991.)

(e) On or before September 25, 1991, the commission shall:

(1) identify each real estate broker that:

(A) has been licensed under this Act for at least 10 years as of September 1, 1991, and holds a license as a real estate broker on that date; and

(B) on June 1, 1991, has the principal place of real estate brokerage business, as designated on the real estate broker's license pursuant to Subsection (a) of Section 12 of this Act, located in a county with a population of 225,000 or less, according to the 1980 federal decennial census; and

(2) send a written notice to each real estate broker identified under Subdivision (1) of this subsection stating that the real estate broker may qualify to opt out of the mandatory continuing education requirements required by this Act in accordance with Subsection (f) of this section if the real estate broker has held a broker's license for ten years or more and holds a broker's license on September 1, 1991.

(f) **Notwithstanding any other provision of this Act,** a real estate broker identified and receiving a notice under Subsection (e) of this section who has held a broker's license for ten years or more and holds a broker's license on September 1, 1991, is not required to comply with the mandatory continuing education requirements of this section to renew the real estate broker's license if after October 1, 1991, and on or before October 30, 1991, the real estate broker:

(1) notifies the commission in writing that the real estate broker is opting out of those requirements; and

(2) pays a one-time fee to the commission in the amount determined by the commission to be adequate to recover the cost to process the application not to exceed $100.

(g) **The commission may adopt rules that establish procedures under which a license may be issued, renewed, or returned to active status** before the applicant completes the continuing education requirements of this section. The commission may prescribe an additional fee, not to exceed $200, for the issuance, renewal, or return to active status of a license before the applicant completes the continuing education requirements of this section and may require the applicant to complete the required continuing education not later than the 60th day after the date the license is issued, renewed, or returned to active status.

In Practice   Section 7 sets out the provisions for determining the competency of the applicant and the educational requirements for licensure. The applicant must satisfy the examination requirement within six months from the date the application is filed. According to the Rules of the Texas Real Estate Commission, the examinee must show a photo ID at the exam site and will be permitted to use a silent, nonprogrammable pocket-sized calculator without an alphabetic keyboard. The act describes eleven core courses and their content. The commission is permitted to establish additional core courses by rule rather than by statute; Promulgated Contract Forms and Residential Inspection for Real Estate Agents have both been established under this authority. Each applicant for a salesperson license is required to complete at least 60 classroom hours in Principles of Real Estate and 30 classroom hours each in Law of Agency and Law of Contracts. The requirements of Section

7(j) are built into every Principles of Real Estate course approved and accredited by TREC.

This section also provides for the completion of **salesperson annual education (SAE)** courses for all licensees and **mandatory continuing education (MCE)** courses for some brokers and all salespersons as prerequisites for license renewal. The MCE renewal hours do not become effective until a salesperson has completed the 90 classroom hours (six semester hours) of SAE courses required in the first three years after receiving a license. Persons affected by the MCE requirements must complete 15 classroom hours every two years prior to license renewal. At least six hours must be in topics required by the act, with the remaining nine hours devoted to real estate–related topics approved by the commission. Core real estate courses are also accepted for MCE credit. By Rule, if MCE hours have not been completed by the expiration date for license renewal, the licensee will be required to pay a $200 fee and complete MCE requirements within 60 days after the effective date of the new license. Table 7.1, shown at the end of this License Act section, summarizes pre-license and license-renewal requirements. Current rules provide a waiver of reexamination for persons licensed within two years prior to filing a new application. Rule 535.63 specifies the conditions under which the commission may waive education and experience requirements for persons licensed up to six years prior to filing an application.

By Rule, contents of salesperson and broker examinations are confidential. Removing or attempting to remove questions or answers from an examination site or providing or attempting to provide examination questions or answers to another person (whether an individual or a school) is grounds for disapproval of a pending application.

Real Estate Recovery Fund

Section 8. (a) **The commission shall establish a real estate recovery fund** which shall be set apart and maintained by the commission as provided in this section. The fund shall be used in the manner provided in this section for reimbursing aggrieved persons who suffer actual damages by reason of certain acts committed by a duly licensed real estate broker or salesperson, a duly registered person under Section 9A of this Act, or by an unlicensed employee or agent of a broker or salesperson, provided the registrant, broker, or salesperson was registered or licensed by the State of Texas at the time the act was committed and provided recovery is ordered by a court of competent jurisdiction against the registrant, broker, or salesperson. The use of the fund is limited to an act that constitutes a violation of Section 15(a)(3) or (6) of this Act if the judgment debtor was at the time of the violation a licensed real estate broker or salesperson. The use of the fund is limited to an act that constitutes a violation of Section 9A(c)(1) of this Act if the judgment debtor was at the time of the violation registered under Section 9A of this Act.

(b) **On application** for an original license pursuant to this Act, the applicant shall pay, in addition to the original license application fee, a fee of $10, which shall be deposited in the real estate recovery fund. On application for an original registration under Section 9A of this Act and for each renewal of such registration, the registrant shall pay, in addition to the registrant's original application fee or renewal fee, a fee of $50, which shall be deposited in the real estate recovery fund.

(c) **On determination by the commission at any time** that the balance remaining in the real estate recovery fund is less than $1 million, each real estate broker and each real estate salesperson, on the next renewal of the license, shall pay, in addition to the license renewal fee, a fee of $10, which shall be deposited in the real estate recovery fund, or a pro rata share of the amount necessary to bring the fund to $1.7 million, whichever is less. If on December 31 of any year the balance remaining in the real estate recovery fund is more than $3.5 million or more than the total amount of claims paid from the fund during the previous four fiscal years, whichever is greater, the amount of money in excess of the greater amount shall be transferred to the general revenue fund. To ensure the availability of a sufficient amount to pay anticipated claims on the fund, the commission by rule may provide for the collection of assessments at different times and under conditions other than those specified by this Act.

(d) **No action for a judgment** which subsequently results in an order for collection from the real estate recovery fund shall be started later than two years from the accrual of the cause of action. When an aggrieved person commences action for a judgment which may result in collection from the real estate recovery fund, the registrant, real estate broker, or real estate salesperson shall notify the commission in writing to this effect at the time of the commencement of the action.

(e) **When an aggrieved person recovers a valid judgment** in a court of competent jurisdiction against a registrant, real estate broker, or real estate salesperson, on the grounds described in Subsection (a) of this section that occurred on or after May 19, 1975, the aggrieved person may, after final judgment has been entered, execution returned nulla bona, and a judgment lien perfected, file a verified claim in the court in which the judgment was entered and, on 20 days' written notice to the commission, and to the judgment debtor, may apply to the court for an order directing payment out of the real estate recovery fund of the amount unpaid on the judgment, subject to the limitations stated in Subsection (n) of this section.

(f) **The court shall proceed** on the application forthwith. On the hearing on the application, the aggrieved person is required to show that:

(1) the judgment is based on facts allowing recovery under Subsection (a) of this section;

(2) the person is not a spouse of the debtor, or the personal representative of the spouse; and the person is not a registrant under Section 9A of this Act or a real estate broker or salesperson, as defined by this Act, who is seeking to recover a real estate commission or any compensation in the transaction or transactions for which the application for payment is made;

(3) based on the best available information, the judgment debtor lacks sufficient attachable assets in this state or any other state to satisfy the judgment; and

(4) the amount that may be realized from the sale of real or personal property or other assets liable to be sold or applied in satisfaction of the judgment and the balance remaining due on the judgment after application of the amount that may be realized.

(g) **A recovery on the judgment** against a single defendant made before payment from the recovery fund must be applied by the creditor first to actual damages.

(h) **The court shall make an order** directed to the commission requiring payment from the real estate recovery fund of whatever sum it finds to be payable on the claim, pursuant to and in accordance with the limitations contained in this section, if the court is satisfied, on the hearing, of the truth of all matters required to be shown by the aggrieved person by Subsection (f) of this section and that the aggrieved person has satisfied all of the requirements of Subsections (e) and (f) of this section. The commission may relitigate any issue material and relevant in the hearing on the application that was determined in the underlying action on which the judgment in favor of the applicant was based. If the court finds that the aggregate amount of claims against a registrant, real estate broker, or salesperson exceeds the limitations contained in this section, the court shall reduce proportionately the amount it finds payable on the claim.

(i) **A license or registration granted** under the provisions of this Act may be revoked by the commission on proof that the commission has made a payment from the real estate recovery fund of any amount toward satisfaction of a judgment against a registrant under Section 9A of this Act or a licensed real estate broker or salesperson. The commission may probate an order revoking a license. No registrant, broker, or salesperson is eligible to receive a new registration or license until the registrant, broker, or salesperson has repaid in full, plus interest at the current legal rate, the amount paid from the real estate recovery fund on the registrant's, broker's, or salesperson's account.

(j) **The sums received** by the real estate commission for deposit in the real estate recovery fund shall be held by the commission in trust for carrying out the purposes of the real estate recovery fund. These funds may be invested and reinvested in the same manner as funds of the Texas State Employees Retirement System, and the interest from these investments shall be deposited to the credit of the real estate recovery fund, provided, however, that no investments shall be made which will impair the necessary liquidity required to satisfy judgment payments awarded pursuant to this section.

(k) **When the real estate commission** receives notice of entry of a final judgment and a hearing is scheduled under Subsection (h) of this section, the commission may notify the Attorney General of Texas of its desire to enter an appearance, file a response, appear at the court hearing, defend the action, or take whatever other action it deems appropriate. In taking such action the real estate commission and the attorney general shall act only to protect the fund from spurious or unjust claims or to insure compliance with the requirements for recovery under this section.

(l) **When, on the order of the court,** the commission has paid from the real estate recovery fund any sum to the judgment creditor, the commission shall be subrogated to all of the rights of the judgment creditor to the extent of the amount paid. The judgment creditor shall assign all his right, title, and interest in the judgment up to the amount paid by the commission which amount shall have priority for repayment in the event of any subsequent recovery on the judgment. Any amount and interest recovered by the commission on the judgment shall be deposited to the fund.

(m) **The failure of an aggrieved person** to comply with the provisions of this section relating to the real estate recovery fund shall constitute a waiver of any rights under this section.

(n) **Notwithstanding any other provision,** payments from the real estate recovery fund are subject to the following conditions and limitations:

(1) payments may be made only pursuant to an order of a court of competent jurisdiction, as provided in Subsection (e) of this section, and in the manner prescribed by this section;

(2) payments for claims, including attorneys' fees, interest, and court costs, arising out of the same transaction shall be limited in the aggregate to $50,000 regardless of the number of claimants; and

(3) payments for claims based on judgments against any one licensed real estate broker, licensed real estate salesperson, or registrant under Section 9A of this Act may not exceed in the aggregate $100,000 until the fund has been reimbursed by the licensee or registrant for all amounts paid.

(o) **Nothing contained in this section shall limit the authority** of the commission to take disciplinary action against a registrant or licensee for a violation of this Act or the rules and regulations of the commission; nor shall the repayment in full of all obligations to the real estate recovery fund by a registrant or licensee nullify or modify the effect of any other disciplinary proceeding brought pursuant to this Act.

(p) **Any person receiving payment** out of the real estate recovery fund pursuant to Section 8 of this Act shall be entitled to receive reasonable attorney fees as determined by the court, subject to the limitations stated in Subsection (n) of this section.

(q) **A registrant, broker, or salesperson registered or licensed under this Act** shall notify consumers and service recipients of the availability of the real estate recovery fund established under this section for reimbursing certain aggrieved persons. The notice must include the name, mailing address, and telephone number of the commission and any other information required by commission rule. The notification may be provided with the notice required by Section 5(q) of this Act or:

(1) on a written contract for the services of a registrant, broker, or salesperson;

(2) on a brochure distributed by a registrant, broker, or salesperson;

(3) on a sign prominently displayed in the place of business of a registrant, salesperson, or broker; or

(4) in a bill or receipt for service provided by a registrant, broker, or salesperson.

In Practice   Section 8 provides for a **real estate recovery fund.** This fund is to be used to reimburse members of the public who have been financially injured or damaged by the actions of a real estate broker or salesperson. Persons desiring to benefit from this fund first must obtain a final money judgment against the offending licensee and then follow very specific requirements under the act in order to receive payment. On such payment, the commission may revoke the license of the offending licensee until the recovery fund has been reimbursed.

The minimum remaining balance requirement for the recovery fund is $1 million, with the collection of additional fees from licensees to bring the fund up to $1.7 million. Limits on payments from the recovery fund are $50,000 for claims arising from the same transaction and $100,000 for claims against any one real estate broker or salesperson.

License and Renewal

Section 9. (a) **When an applicant** has satisfactorily met all requirements and conditions of this Act, a license or certificate of registration shall be issued which may remain in force and effect so long as the holder of the certificate of registration or license remains in compliance with the obligations of this Act, which include payment of the renewal fee as provided in Section 11 of this Act. Each active salesperson license issued shall be delivered or mailed to the broker with whom the salesperson is associated and shall be kept under the broker's custody and control.

(b) **An applicant is not permitted to engage** in the real estate business either as a broker or salesperson until a license evidencing the applicant's authority to engage in the real estate business has been received. A person may not engage in the business of selling, buying, leasing, or transferring an easement or right-of-way for another for compensation until the person is licensed or registered under this Act.

(c) **The commission by rule may adopt** a system under which licenses and registrations expire on various dates during the year. Dates for payment of the renewal fee shall be adjusted accordingly. For the year in which the renewal date is changed, renewal fees payable shall be prorated on a monthly basis so each licensee or registrant shall pay only that portion of the fee which is allocable to the number of months during which the license or registration is valid. On renewal of the license or registration on the new renewal date, the total renewal fee is payable.

> Renewal notices are mailed three months before the expiration of the current license. Broker and 2-year salesperson licenses may be renewed with a credit card on the TREC Internet web site.

(d) **Any other provision of this Act notwithstanding,** the commission may issue licenses and registrations valid for a period not to exceed 24 months and may charge and collect renewal fees for such period; provided, however, that such renewal fees shall not, calculated on an annual basis, exceed the amounts established in Section 11 of this Act, and further provided that the educational conditions for renewal established in Subsection (e) of Section 7 of this Act shall not be waived by the commission.

> Licensees are required to provide a permanent mailing address to TREC and report any change in that address within 10 days after the change occurs. No fee is charged for a change of mailing address.

(e) **The commission shall require** in any application for a broker or salesperson license or a renewal of a broker or salesperson license the applicant to disclose whether the applicant has entered a plea of guilty or nolo contendere to, been found guilty of, or been convicted of a felony and the time for appeal has elapsed or the judgment or conviction has been affirmed on appeal, irrespective of an order granting probation following the conviction or suspending the imposition of sentence.

Right-of-Way Registration

Section 9A. (a) A person may not sell, buy, lease, or transfer an easement or right-of-way for another for compensation, or with the intention or in the expectation or on the promise of receiving or collecting compensation, for use in connection with telecommunication, utility, railroad, or pipeline service unless the person is:

(1) licensed as a real estate broker or real estate salesperson under this Act;

(2) exempt from this Act for the purpose of selling, buying, leasing, or transferring an easement or right-of-way; or

(3) registered with the commission under this section.

(b) The commission shall maintain a registry of persons who are registered under this section.

(c) The commission shall investigate a signed complaint received by the commission that relates to the acts of a person registered or required to be registered under this section. The commission may revoke or suspend the registration of a registrant under this section who:

(1) engaged in dishonest dealings, fraud, deceptive acts, misrepresentations, bad faith, unlawful discrimination, or untrustworthiness;

(2) failed within a reasonable time to make good a check to the commission after the commission has mailed a request for payment to the registrant's last known address as reflected in the commission records;

(3) failed to provide to a party in a transaction a written notice promulgated by the commission that is to be given before the party is obligated to sell, buy, lease, or transfer a right-of-way or easement and that contains the name of the registrant, the certificate number of the registrant, the name of the person the registrant represents, a statement advising the party that the party may seek representation from a lawyer or real estate broker in the transaction, and a statement generally advising the party that the right-of-way or easement may affect the value of the property; or

(4) disregarded or violated a provision of this Act or a rule of the commission relating to registrants under this section.

(d) The commission may adopt rules to administer and enforce this section.

In Practice

A *right-of-way agent,* a person who sells, buys, leases, or transfers an easement or right-of-way for another for compensation, is required to register with the Texas Real Estate Commission unless the person is licensed as a real estate broker or salesperson.

Failure and Refusal To License

Section 10. (a) **If the commission declines or fails to register or license an applicant,** it shall immediately give written notice of the refusal to the applicant. Before the applicant may appeal to a district court as provided in

Section 18 of this Act, the applicant must file within 10 days after the receipt of the notice an appeal from the ruling, requesting a time and place for a hearing before the commission. The commission shall set a time and place for the hearing within 30 days from the receipt of the appeal, giving 10 days' notice of the hearing to the applicant. The time of the hearing may be continued from time to time with the consent of the applicant. Following the hearing, the commission shall enter an order which is, in its opinion, appropriate in the matter concerned.

(b) **If an applicant fails to request a hearing as provided in this section,** the commission's ruling shall become final and not subject to review by the courts.

(c) **The commission may issue a probationary license.** The commission by rule shall adopt reasonable terms and conditions for a probationary license.

Fees **Section 11.** The commission shall charge and collect the following fees:

(1) a fee not to exceed $100 for the filing of an original application for a real estate broker license;

(2) a fee not to exceed $100 for annual renewal of a real estate broker license;

(3) a fee not to exceed $50 for the filing of an original application for a real estate salesperson license;

(4) a fee not to exceed $50 for annual renewal of a real estate salesperson license;

(5) a fee not to exceed $100 for an application for a license examination;

(6) a fee not to exceed $20 for filing a request for a license for each additional office or place of business;

(7) a fee not to exceed $20 for filing a request for a license or certificate of registration for a change of place of business, change of name, return to active status, or change of sponsoring broker;

(8) a fee not to exceed $20 for filing a request to replace a license or certificate of registration lost or destroyed;

(9) a fee not to exceed $400 for filing an application for approval of an education program under Section 7(f) of this Act;

(10) a fee not to exceed $200 a year for operation of an education program under Section 7(f) of this Act;

(11) a fee of $20 for transcript evaluation;

(12) a fee not to exceed $10 for preparing a license or registration history;

(13) a fee not to exceed $50 for the filing of an application for a moral character determination;

(14) an annual fee of $20 from each real estate broker and each registrant under Section 9A of this Act to be transmitted to Texas A&M University for the Texas Real Estate Research Center as provided by Section 5(m) of this Act;

(15) an annual fee of $17.50 from each real estate salesperson to be transmitted to Texas A&M University for the Texas Real Estate Research Center as provided by Section 5(m) of this Act;

(16) an annual fee of $80 from each registrant under Section 9A of this Act; and

(17) any fee authorized under Section 8 of this Act for the real estate recovery fund.

Section 11A. (a) **Each of the following fees** imposed by or under another section of this Act is increased by $200:

(1) fee for filing an original application for a real estate broker license; and

(2) fee for annual renewal of a real estate broker license.

(b) **Of each fee increase collected,** $50 shall be deposited to the credit of the foundation school fund and $150 shall be deposited to the credit of the general revenue fund. This subsection applies to the disposition of each fee increase regardless of any other provision of law providing for a different disposition of funds.

In Practice   Section 11 establishes the maximum fees to be charged for the various licensing functions of the commission. Actual fees assessed may be set by the commission at less than the maximum. The commission has the right to pass along credit card and on-line application processing fees to the applicant.

Broker Office Requirements

Section 12. (a) Each resident broker shall maintain a fixed office within this state. The address of the office shall be designated on the broker's license. Within 10 days after a move from a previously designated address, the broker shall submit an application for a new license, designating the new location of the broker's office, together with the required fee, whereupon the commission shall issue a license, reflecting the new location, provided the new location complies with the terms of this section.

(b) **If a broker maintains more than one place of business** within this state, the broker shall apply for, pay the required fee for, and obtain an additional license to be known as a branch office license for each additional office the broker maintains.

(c) **The license or licenses of the broker** shall at all times be prominently displayed in the licensee's place or places of business.

(d) **Each broker shall also prominently display** in the broker's place or in one of the broker's places of business the license of each real estate salesperson associated with the broker.

(e) **The certificate of registration** of a registrant under Section 9A of this Act shall at all times be prominently displayed in the registrant's place of business. Within 10 days after a move from a previously designated address, the registrant shall notify the commission of the move and obtain a new certificate of registration reflecting the new location.

Salesperson Change of Employment

Section 13. (a) When the association of a salesperson with the salesperson's sponsoring broker is terminated, the broker shall immediately return the salesperson license to the commission. The salesperson license then becomes inactive.

(b) **The salesperson license may be activated if,** before the license expires, a request, accompanied by the required fee, is filed with the commission by a licensed broker advising that the broker assumes sponsorship of the salesperson.

Section 13A. (a) **A real estate broker who holds a license issued under this Act** and who is not acting as a broker or sponsoring a salesperson may apply to the commission in writing to be placed on the inactive status list maintained by the commission. The broker must apply for inactive status before the expiration of the broker's license. The broker shall terminate the broker's association with any salesperson sponsored by the broker by giving written notice to the salesperson before the 30th day before the date the broker applies for inactive status. A person on inactive status under this section is required to pay the annual renewal fees.

(b) **A person on inactive status** under this section may not perform any activities regulated under this Act.

(c) **If the person has been on inactive status,** the commission shall remove the person from the list on application, payment of the required fee, and proof of attendance of at least 15 classroom hours of continuing education as specified in Subsection (a) of Section 7A of this Act during the two-year period preceding the filing of the application.

In Practice

Section 13 describes the procedures for obtaining an inactive license, along with the procedures for reactivation. The license of a salesperson immediately becomes inactive upon the death of the sponsoring broker or the expiration, suspension, revocation, or inactivation of the sponsoring broker's license. If the sponsoring broker is a corporation, limited liability company, or partnership, its dissolution or the loss of the license of the person designated as the broker also causes a salesperson's license to become inactive. Notification that license sponsorship has been terminated must be in writing—whether from a broker to a salesperson or from a salesperson to a broker.

Broker—Division of Fees and Nonresident Licensing

Section 14. (a) **It is unlawful for a licensed broker to employ** or compensate directly or indirectly a person for performing an act enumerated in the definition of real estate broker in Section 2 of this Act if the person is not a licensed broker or licensed salesperson in this state. However, a licensed broker may pay a commission to a licensed broker of another state if the foreign broker does not conduct in this state any of the negotiations for which the fee, compensation, or commission is paid.

(b) **A resident broker of another state** who furnishes the evidence required under Section 7(g) of this Act may apply for a license as a broker in this state. A resident of another state who is not licensed as a broker but who was formerly licensed as a salesperson or broker in this state may apply for a license in this state not later than the first anniversary of the date of the expiration of the previous license. An application by a nonresident is subject to the requirements under this Act for the type of license applied for. A **nonresident licensee** need not maintain a place of business in this state. The commission may in its discretion refuse to issue a license to an applicant who is not a resident of this state for the same reasons that it may refuse to license a resident of this state. The commission shall judge the competency of a nonresident applicant solely on the basis of the examination conducted under Section 7 of this Act.

(c) **Each nonresident applicant** shall file an irrevocable consent that legal actions may be commenced against him in the proper court of any county of this state in which a cause of action may arise, or in which the plaintiff may reside, by service of process or pleading authorized by the laws of this state, or by serving the administrator or assistant administrator of the commission. The consent shall stipulate that the service of process or pleading shall be valid and binding in all courts as if personal service had been made on the nonresident in this state. The consent shall be duly acknowledged, and if made by a corporation, shall be authenticated by its seal. A service of process or pleading served on the commission shall be by duplicate copies, one of which shall be filed in the office of the commission and the other forwarded by registered mail to the last known principal address which the commission has for the nonresident against whom the process or pleading is directed. No default in an action may be taken except on certification by the commission that a copy of the process or pleading was mailed to the defendant as provided in this section, and no default judgment may be taken in an action or proceeding until 20 days after the day of mailing of the process or pleading to the defendant.

Notwithstanding any other provision of this subsection, a nonresident of this state who resides in a city whose boundaries are contiguous at any point to the boundaries of a city of this state, and who has been an actual bona fide resident of that city for at least 60 days immediately preceding the filing of his application, is eligible to be licensed as a real estate broker or salesperson under this Act in the same manner as a resident of this state. If a person is licensed in this manner, the person shall at all times maintain a place of business either in the city in which the person resides or in the city in this state which is contiguous to the city in which the person resides, and the person may not maintain a place of business at another location in this state unless the person also complies with the requirements of Section 14(b) of this Act. The place of business must satisfy the requirements of Subsection (a) of Section 12 of this Act, but the place of business shall be deemed a definite place of business in this state within the meaning of Subsection (a) of Section 12.

In Practice Section 14 specifies the requirements for dividing a real estate commission. The broker may divide the fee with other brokers licensed in Texas, with salespersons under the broker's sponsorship, or with brokers licensed in another state or foreign country, provided the nonresident broker did not conduct any of the negotiations within Texas. This section also provides for the licensing of nonresident brokers. Texas does not accept a real estate license issued by any other state. Therefore, all persons desiring to practice real estate in Texas must satisfy all of the requirements of Section 7 of this act, whether such person is applying for nonresident licensure or is relocating his or her real estate brokerage practice in Texas after being licensed in another state.

Suspension and Revocation of Licenses

Section 15. (a) **The commission may, on its own motion, and shall, on the signed complaint in writing of any person,** provided the complaint, or the complaint together with evidence, documentary or otherwise, presented in connection with the complaint, provides reasonable cause, investigate the actions and records of a real estate broker or real estate salesperson. A service contract that a licensee under this Act enters into for services governed by this Act is not a good or service governed by Chapter 39, Business and Commerce Code. The commission may suspend or revoke a license issued under the provisions of this Act or take other disciplinary action authorized by this Act at any time when it has been determined that:

(1) **the licensee has entered a plea of guilty** or nolo contendere to, or been found guilty of, or been convicted of, a felony, in which fraud is an essential element, and the time for appeal has elapsed or the judgment or conviction has been affirmed on appeal, irrespective of an order granting probation following such conviction, suspending the imposition of sentence;

(2) **the licensee has procured,** or attempted to procure, a real estate license, for the licensee or a salesperson, by fraud, misrepresentation or deceit, or by making a material misstatement of fact in an application for a real estate license;

(3) **the licensee, when selling, buying, trading, or renting real property in the licensee's own name,** engaged in misrepresentation or dishonest or fraudulent action;

(4) **the licensee has failed within a reasonable time to make good a check** issued to the commission after the commission has mailed a request for payment by certified mail to the licensee's last known business address as reflected by the commission's records;

(5) **the licensee has disregarded or violated a provision of this Act;**

(6) **the licensee, while performing an act constituting an act of a broker or salesperson,** as defined by this Act, has been guilty of:

(A) **making a material misrepresentation, or failing to disclose to a potential purchaser any latent structural defect or any other defect known to the broker or salesperson.** Latent structural defects and other defects do not refer to trivial or insignificant defects but refer to those

> Licensees who hold more than a 10% interest in a property will be considered owners and must disclose their licensed status when dealing with their own property (Rule 535.144).

defects that would be a significant factor to a reasonable and prudent purchaser in making a decision to purchase;

(B) **making a false promise of a character likely to influence,** persuade, or induce any person to enter into a contract or agreement when the licensee could not or did not intend to keep such promise;

(C) **pursuing a continued and flagrant course of misrepresentation** or making of false promises through agents, salespersons, advertising, or otherwise;

(D) **failing to make clear, to all parties to a transaction, which party the licensee is acting for,** or receiving compensation from more than one party except with the full knowledge and consent of all parties;

(E) **failing within a reasonable time properly to account for or remit money** coming into the licensee's possession which belongs to others, or commingling money belonging to others with the licensee's own funds;

(F) **paying a commission or fees** to or dividing a commission or fees with anyone not licensed as a real estate broker or salesperson in this state or in any other state for compensation for services as a real estate agent;

(G) **failing to specify** a definite termination date that is not subject to prior notice in a contract, other than a contract to perform property management services, in which the licensee agrees to perform services for which a license is required under this Act;

(H) **accepting, receiving, or charging an undisclosed commission,** rebate, or direct profit on expenditures made for a principal;

(I) **soliciting, selling, or offering for sale real property under a scheme or program that constitutes a lottery or deceptive practice;**

(J) **acting in the dual capacity** of broker and undisclosed principal in a transaction;

(K) **guaranteeing, authorizing, or permitting a person to guarantee** that future profits will result from a resale of real property;

(L) **placing a sign on real property** offering it for sale, lease, or rent without the written consent of the owner or the owner's authorized agent;

(M) **inducing or attempting to induce a party to a contract** of sale or lease to break the contract for the purpose of substituting in lieu thereof a new contract;

(N) **negotiating or attempting to negotiate** the sale, exchange, lease, or rental of real property with an owner, lessor, buyer, or tenant, knowing that the owner, lessor, buyer, or tenant had a written outstanding contract, granting exclusive agency in connection with the transaction to another real estate broker;

(O) **offering real property for sale or for lease** without the knowledge and consent of the owner or the owner's authorized agent, or on terms other than those authorized by the owner or the owner's authorized agent;

(P) **publishing, or causing to be published,** an advertisement including, but not limited to, advertising by newspaper, radio, television, the Internet, or display which is misleading, or which is likely to deceive the public, or which in any manner tends to create a misleading impression, or

---

A real estate broker is responsible for all acts and conduct performed by a real estate salesperson associated with or acting for the broker. (Rule 535.141(c))

which fails to identify the person causing the advertisement to be published as a licensed real estate broker or agent;

(Q) **having knowingly withheld from or inserted in a statement of account or invoice,** a statement that made it inaccurate in a material particular;

(R) **publishing or circulating** an unjustified or unwarranted threat of legal proceedings, or other action;

(S) **establishing an association,** by employment or otherwise, with an unlicensed person who is expected or required to act as a real estate licensee, or aiding or abetting or conspiring with a person to circumvent the requirements of this Act;

(T) **failing or refusing on demand** to furnish copies of a document pertaining to a transaction dealing with real estate to a person whose signature is affixed to the document;

(U) **failing to advise a purchaser in writing** before the closing of a transaction that the purchaser should either have the abstract covering the real estate which is the subject of the contract examined by an attorney of the purchaser's own selection, or be furnished with or obtain a policy of title insurance;

(V) **conduct which constitutes dishonest dealings, bad faith, or untrustworthiness;**

(W) **acting negligently or incompetently** in performing an act for which a person is required to hold a real estate license;

(X) **disregarding or violating a provision of this Act;**

(Y) **failing within a reasonable time to deposit money** received as escrow agent in a real estate transaction, either in trust with a title company authorized to do business in this state, or in a custodial, trust, or escrow account maintained for that purpose in a banking institution authorized to do business in this state;

(Z) **disbursing money deposited** in a custodial, trust, or escrow account, as provided in Subsection (Y) before the transaction concerned has been consummated or finally otherwise terminated; or

(AA) **discriminating against an owner, potential purchaser,** lessor, or potential lessee on the basis of race, color, religion, sex, national origin, or ancestry, including directing prospective home buyers or lessees interested in equivalent properties to different areas according to the race, color, religion, sex, national origin, or ancestry of the potential owner or lessee;

(7) **the licensee has failed or refused on demand to produce a document,** book, or record in the licensee's possession concerning a real estate transaction conducted by the licensee for inspection by the commission or its authorized personnel or representative;

(8) **the licensee has failed within a reasonable time to provide information** requested by the commission as a result of a formal or informal complaint to the commission which would indicate a violation of this Act; or

(9) **the licensee has failed without just cause to surrender to the rightful owner,** on demand, a document or instrument coming into the licensee's possession.

(b) **The provisions of this section do not relieve a person from civil liability or from criminal prosecution under this Act or under the laws of this state.**

(c) **Notwithstanding Subsection (b) of this section,** a person is not subject to civil liability or criminal prosecution because the person did not inquire about, make a disclosure related to, or release information related to whether a previous or current occupant of real property had, may have had, has, or may have AIDS, HIV-related illnesses, or HIV infection as defined by the Centers for Disease Control of the U.S. Public Health Service.

(d) **The commission may not investigate** under this section a complaint submitted more than four years after the date of the incident involving a real estate broker or salesperson that is the subject of the complaint.

(e) **The commission may request** and, if necessary, compel by subpoena the attendance of witnesses for examination under oath and the production for inspection and copying of books, accounts, records, papers, correspondence, documents, and other evidence relevant to the investigation of alleged violations of this Act. If a person fails to comply with a subpoena issued under this subsection, the commission, acting through the attorney general, may file suit to enforce the subpoena in a district court in Travis County or in the county in which a hearing conducted by the commission may be held. The court, if it determines that good cause exists for the issuance of the subpoena, shall order compliance with the requirements of the subpoena. Failure to obey the order of the court may be punished by the court as contempt. (Added by S.B. No. 842, effective September 1, 1993.)

In Practice   Section 15 provides a list of possible actions by a licensee that can result in the revocation or suspension of a broker's or salesperson's license. Violation of other state laws could also result in license revocation; for example, on court order, TREC is authorized to revoke a license for nonpayment of awarded child support. Because landlord-tenant law permits extensions on leases, the requirement for a definite termination date in Section 15(a)(6)(G) does not apply to leases.

The term *advertisement* in Section 15(a)(6)(P) now includes, but is not limited to, all publications, radio or television broadcasts, all electronic media including e-mail and the Internet, business stationery, business cards, signs, and billboards. A listing may be solicited and accepted only in a broker's name, and any advertisements concerning listings must include broker identification. All signs must clearly identify that a real estate broker or agent published them; and, except for signs placed on property for sale or lease, the size of type or print for broker identification must be at least as large as the largest telephone number in the advertisement.

Section 15A. Repealed August 28, 1989.

Section 15B. (a) **Notwithstanding any other provision of the Act,** there shall be no undercover or covert investigations conducted by authority of this Act unless expressly authorized by the commission after due consideration of the circumstances and determination by the commission that such measures are necessary to carry out the purposes of this Act. No investigations of licensees or any other actions against licensees shall be initiated on the basis of anonymous complaints whether in writing or otherwise but shall be initiated only upon the commission's own motion or a signed written complaint from a person. Upon the adoption of such motion by the commission or upon receipt of such complaint, the licensee shall be notified promptly and in writing unless the commission itself, after due consideration, determines otherwise.

(b) **In addition to any other authority granted by this Act,** the commission may revoke or suspend a license, place on probation a person whose license has been suspended, or reprimand a licensee for a violation of this Act or a rule of the commission.

(c) **The commission may, upon majority vote,** rule that an order revoking, cancelling, or suspending a license be probated upon reasonable terms and conditions determined by the commission. (Added by S.B. No. 177, effective September 1, 1989.)

(d) **If a license suspension or revocation is probated,** the commission may require the licensee:

(1) to report regularly to the commission on matters that are the basis of the probation;

(2) to limit practice to the area prescribed by the commission; or

(3) to continue to renew professional education until the licensee attains a degree of skill satisfactory to the commission in those areas that are the basis of the probation.

(e) **The commission may authorize a commission employee** to file a signed written complaint against a licensee and to conduct an investigation if:

(1) a judgment against the licensee has been paid from a recovery fund established under this Act;

(2) the licensee is convicted of a criminal offense that may constitute grounds for the suspension or revocation of the licensee's license;

(3) the licensee fails to make good a check issued to the commission;

(4) the licensee fails to complete required continuing education within the period prescribed by commission rules adopted under Section 7A(g) of this Act; or

(5) the licensee fails to provide, within a reasonable time, information requested by the commission in connection with an application to renew a license.

In Practice   Section 15B prevents covert or undercover investigations except as expressly authorized by the commission and then only on due consideration of the circumstances. The commission is permitted to investigate only written and signed complaints or those initiated on its own motion. The commission is permitted to revoke or suspend a license or reprimand or place on probation a licensee who violates the act or the rules of the commission.

Agency Relationships   **Section 15C.** (Amended by S.B. No. 489, effective January 1, 1996.) (a) A licensee under this Act who represents a party in a proposed real estate transaction shall disclose that representation at the time of the licensee's first contact with:

(1) another party to the transaction; or

(2) another licensee who represents another party to the transaction.

(b) The disclosure required under Subsection (a) of this section may be made orally or in writing.

(c) A licensee who represents a party in a real estate transaction acts as that party's agent.

(d) Except as provided by Subsection (e) of this section, a licensee shall furnish to a party in a real estate transaction at the time of the first face-to-face meeting with the party the following written statement:

"Before working with a real estate broker, you should know that the duties of a broker depend on whom the broker represents. If you are a prospective seller or landlord (owner) or a prospective buyer or tenant (buyer), you should know that the broker who lists the property for sale or lease is the owner's agent. A broker who acts as a subagent represents the owner in cooperation with the listing broker. A broker who acts as a buyer's agent represents the buyer. A broker may act as an intermediary between the parties if the parties consent in writing. A broker can assist you in locating a property, preparing a contract or lease, or obtaining financing without representing you. A broker is obligated by law to treat you honestly.

"IF THE BROKER REPRESENTS THE OWNER: The broker becomes the owner's agent by entering into an agreement with the owner, usually through a written listing agreement, or by agreeing to act as a subagent by accepting an offer of subagency from the listing broker. A subagent may work in a different real estate office. A listing broker or subagent can assist the buyer but does not represent the buyer and must place the interests of the owner first. The buyer should not tell the owner's agent anything the buyer would not want the owner to know because an owner's agent must disclose to the owner any material information known to the agent.

"IF THE BROKER REPRESENTS THE BUYER: The broker becomes the buyer's agent by entering into an agreement to represent the buyer, usually through a written buyer representation agreement. A buyer's agent can assist the owner but does not represent the owner and must place the interests of the buyer first. The owner should not tell a buyer's agent anything the owner would not want the buyer to know because a buyer's agent must disclose to the buyer any material information known to the agent.

"IF THE BROKER ACTS AS AN INTERMEDIARY: A broker may act as an intermediary between the parties if the broker complies with The Texas Real Estate License Act. The broker must obtain the written consent of each party to the transaction to act as an intermediary. The written consent must state who will pay the broker and, in conspicuous bold or underlined print, set forth the broker's obligations as an intermediary. The broker is required to treat each party honestly and fairly and to comply with the Texas Real Estate License Act. A broker who acts as an intermediary in a transaction:

(1) shall treat all parties honestly;

(2) may not disclose that the owner will accept a price less than the asking price unless authorized in writing to do so by the owner;

(3) may not disclose that the buyer will pay a price greater than the price submitted in a written offer unless authorized in writing to do so by the buyer; and

(4) may not disclose any confidential information or any information that a party specifically instructs the broker in writing not to disclose unless authorized in writing to disclose the information or required to do so by the Texas Real Estate License Act or a court order or if the information materially relates to the condition of the property. With the parties' consent, a broker acting as an intermediary between the parties may appoint a person who is licensed under The Texas Real Estate License Act and associated with the broker to communicate with and carry out instructions of one party and another person who is licensed under that Act and associated with the broker to communicate with and carry out instructions of the other party.

"If you choose to have a broker represent you, you should enter into a written agreement with the broker that clearly establishes the broker's obligations and your obligations. The agreement should state how and by whom the broker will be paid. You have the right to choose the type of representation, if any, you wish to receive. Your payment of a fee to a broker does not necessarily establish that the broker represents you. If you have any questions regarding the duties and responsibilities of the broker, you should resolve those questions before proceeding."

(e) A licensee is not required to provide the written information under Subsection (d) of this section if:

(1) the proposed transaction is for a residential lease for not more than one year and no sale is being considered; or

(2) the licensee meets with a party who is represented by another licensee.

(f) In the written information required to be provided under Subsection (d) of this section, the licensee may substitute the word "buyer" with "tenant" and "seller" with "landlord" as appropriate.

(g) The written information required to be provided under Subsection (d) of this section may be printed in any format that uses at least 10-point type.

(h) A real estate broker may act as an intermediary between the parties if:

(1) the real estate broker obtains written consent from each party to the transaction for the real estate broker to act as an intermediary in the transaction; and

(2) the written consent of the parties under Subdivision (1) of this subsection states the source of any expected compensation to the real estate broker.

(i) A written listing agreement to represent a seller or landlord or a written agreement to represent a buyer or tenant which also authorizes a real estate broker to act as an intermediary in a transaction is sufficient to establish written consent of the party to the transaction if the written agreement sets forth, in conspicuous bold or underlined print, the real estate broker's obligations under Subsection (j) of this section.

(j) A real estate broker who acts as an intermediary between parties in a transaction:

(1) may not disclose to the buyer or tenant that the seller or landlord will accept a price less than the asking price unless otherwise instructed in a separate writing by the seller or landlord;

(2) may not disclose to the seller or landlord that the buyer or tenant will pay a price greater than the price submitted in a written offer to the seller or landlord unless otherwise instructed in a separate writing by the buyer or tenant;

(3) may not disclose any confidential information or any information a party specifically instructs the real estate broker in writing not to disclose unless otherwise instructed in a separate writing by the respective party or required to disclose such information by this Act or a court order or if the information materially relates to the condition of the property;

(4) shall treat all parties to the transaction honestly; and

(5) shall comply with this Act.

(k) If a real estate broker obtains the consent of the parties to act as an intermediary in a transaction in compliance with this section, the real estate broker may appoint, by providing written notice to the parties, one or more licensees associated with the broker to communicate with and carry out instructions of one party and one or more other licensees associated with the broker to communicate with and carry out instructions of the other party or parties. A real estate broker may appoint a licensee to communicate with and carry out instructions of a party under this subsection only if the written consent of the parties under Subsection (h) or (i) of this section authorizes the broker to make the appointment. The real estate broker and the appointed licensees shall comply with Subsection (j) of this section. However, during negotiations, an appointed licensee may provide opinions and advice to the party to whom the licensee is appointed.

(l) The duties of a licensee acting as an intermediary provided by this section supersede and are in lieu of a licensee's duties under common law or any other law.

(m) In this section:

(1) "Face-to-face meeting" means a meeting at which a substantive discussion occurs with respect to specific real property. The term does not include a meeting that occurs at a property being held open for prospective purchasers or tenants or a meeting that occurs after the parties to the transaction have signed a contract to sell, buy, rent, or lease the real property concerned.

(2) "Intermediary" means a broker who is employed to negotiate a transaction between the parties subject to the obligations in Subsection (j) of this section and for that purpose may be an agent of the parties to the transaction. The intermediary shall act fairly so as not to favor one party over the other. Appointment by the intermediary of associated licensees under Subsection (k) of this section to communicate with, carry out instructions of, and provide opinions and advice to the parties to whom the licensees are appointed is a fair and impartial act.

(3) "Licensee" means a real estate broker or real estate salesperson and includes a licensed associate of a licensee.

(4) "Party" means a prospective buyer, seller, landlord, or tenant or an authorized representative of a party, including a trustee, guardian, executor, administrator, receiver, or attorney-in-fact. The term does not include a licensee who represents a party.

(5) "Subagent" means a licensee who represents a principal through cooperation with and consent of a broker representing the principal and who is not sponsored by or associated with the principal's broker.

In Practice   Section 15C defines agency relationships and responsibilities as described in Chapter 5.

Section 15D. No licensed real estate broker, licensed real estate salesperson, or not for profit real estate board or association which provides information about real property sales prices or terms of sale for the purpose of facilitating the listing, selling, leasing, financing, or appraisal of real property shall be liable to any other person as a result of so providing such information unless the disclosure of same is otherwise specifically prohibited by statute.

Section 15E. Notwithstanding any other provision of this Act or any other law, a licensee shall have no duty to inquire about, make a disclosure related to, or release information related to whether a:

(1) previous or current occupant of real property had, may have had, has, or may have AIDS, HIV-related illnesses, or HIV infection as defined by the Centers for Disease Control of the U.S. Public Health Service; or

(2) death occurred on a property by natural causes, suicide, or accident unrelated to the condition of the property.

In Practice   Section 15E brings the Act into compliance with federal fair housing laws.

Section 15F. (Added by S.B. No. 489, effective January 1, 1996) (a) **A party is not liable for a misrepresentation or a concealment of a material fact** made by a licensee in a real estate transaction unless the party knew of the falsity of the misrepresentation or concealment and failed to disclose the party's knowledge of the falsity of the misrepresentation or concealment.

(b) A licensee is not liable for a misrepresentation or a concealment of a material fact made by a party in a real estate transaction unless the licensee knew of the falsity of the misrepresentation or concealment and failed to disclose the licensee's knowledge of the falsity of the misrepresentation or concealment.

(c) A party or a licensee is not liable for a misrepresentation or a concealment of a material fact made by a subagent in a real estate transaction unless the party or licensee knew of the falsity of the misrepresentation or concealment and failed to disclose the party's or licensee's knowledge of the falsity of the misrepresentation or concealment.

(d) The provisions of this section shall prevail over common law and any other law. This section does not diminish a real estate broker's responsibility for the acts or omissions of the broker's salespersons associated with or acting for the real estate broker, as provided by Section 1 of this Act.

(e) In this section, "licensee," "subagent," and "party" have the meaning assigned to those terms by Section 15C of this Act.

In Practice   Section 15F provides the parties and licensees protection from liability for the misrepresentation or concealment of material facts by each other or by a subagent unless the party or licensee knew of the falsity or concealment.

Licensee Not To Practice Law   **Section 16.** (a) **A license or registration granted under the provisions of this Act shall be suspended or revoked** by the commission on proof that the licensee or registrant, not being licensed and authorized to practice law in this state, for a consideration, reward, pecuniary benefit, present or anticipated, direct or indirect, or in connection with or as a part of the licensee's employment, agency, or fiduciary relationship as a licensee, drew a deed, note, deed of trust, will, or other written instrument that may transfer or anywise affect the title to or an interest in land, except as provided in the subsections below, or advised or counseled a person as to the validity or legal sufficiency of an instrument or as to the validity of title to real estate.

(b) **Notwithstanding the provisions of this Act or any other law, the completion of contract forms** which bind the sale, exchange, option, lease, or rental of any interest in real property by a registrant under Section 9A of this Act, a real estate broker, or a real estate salesperson incident to the performance of the acts of a broker as defined by this Act does not constitute the unauthorized or illegal practice of law in this state, provided the forms have been promulgated for use by the commission for the particular kind of transaction involved, or the forms have been prepared by an attorney at law licensed by this state and approved by said attorney for the particular kind of transaction involved, or the forms have been prepared by the property owner or prepared by an attorney and required by the property owner.

(c) **A Texas Real Estate Broker-Lawyer Committee** is hereby created which, in addition to other powers and duties delegated to it, shall draft and revise contract forms capable of standardization for use by real estate licensees and which will expedite real estate transactions and reduce controversies to a minimum while containing safeguards adequate to protect the interests of the principals to the transaction.

(d) **The Texas Real Estate Broker-Lawyer Committee** shall have 12 members including six members appointed by the commission and six members of the State Bar of Texas appointed by the President of the State Bar of Texas. The members of the committee shall hold office for staggered terms of six years with the terms of two commission appointees and two State Bar appointees expiring every two years. Each member shall hold office until the member's successor is appointed. A vacancy for any cause shall be filled for the expired term by the agency making the original appointment. Appointments to the committee shall be made without regard to race, creed, sex, religion, or national origin.

(e) **In the best interest of the public** the commission may adopt rules and regulations requiring real estate brokers and salespersons to use contract forms which have been prepared by the Texas Real Estate Broker-Lawyer Committee and promulgated by the commission; provided, however, that the commission shall not prohibit a real estate broker or salesperson from using a contract form or forms binding the sale, exchange, option, lease, or rental of any interest in real property which have been prepared by the property owner or prepared by an attorney and required by the property owner. For the purpose of this section, contract forms prepared by the Texas Real Estate Broker-Lawyer Committee appointed by the commission and the State Bar of Texas and promulgated by the commission prior to the effective date of this Act shall be deemed to have been prepared by the Texas Real Estate Broker-Lawyer Committee. The commission may suspend or revoke a license issued under the provisions of this article when it has determined that the licensee failed to use a contract form as required by the commission pursuant to this section.

In Practice   Section 16 defines the unauthorized practice of law by a real estate agent. Additionally, it provides for the creation of the **Texas Real Estate Broker-Lawyer Committee** and declares that the completion of promulgated (required) contract forms is not considered an unauthorized practice of law.

Hearings before Suspensions   **Section 17.** (a) **If the commission proposes to suspend or revoke** a person's license or registration, the person is entitled to a hearing before the commission or a hearings officer appointed by the commission. The commission shall prescribe procedures by which all decisions to suspend or revoke are made by or are appealable to the commission. The commission shall prescribe the time and place of the hearing. However, the hearing shall be held, if the licensee so desires, within the county where the licensee has the licensee's principal place of business, or if the licensee is a nonresident, the hearing may be called for and held in any county within this state. The hearing is governed by the procedures for a contested case under Chapter 2001, Government Code.

(b) **The commission may issue subpoenas** for the attendance of witnesses and the production of records or documents. Process issued by the commission may extend to all parts of the state and may be served by any person designated by the commission.

In Practice   Section 17 permits a licensee to have a public hearing before a license is suspended or revoked and specifies the procedures to be followed in this regard.

Appeal to Courts **Section 18. A person aggrieved by a ruling,** order, or decision of the commission has the right to appeal to a district court in the county where the hearing was held, and an appeal is governed by the procedures under the Administrative Procedure and Texas Register Act (Article 6252-13a, Vernon's Texas Civil Statutes).

Section 18A. (a) **Any listing contract form adopted by the commission** relating to the contractual obligations between a seller of real estate and a real estate broker or salesperson acting as an agent for the seller shall include a section that informs the parties to the contract that real estate commissions are negotiable.

(b) **When appropriate to the form,** it shall include a section explaining the availability of Texas coastal natural hazards information important to coastal residents.

Section 18B. (a) **If a person files a complaint with the commission** relating to a real estate broker or salesperson, the commission shall furnish to the person an explanation of the remedies that are available to the person under this Act and information about appropriate state or local agencies or officials with which the person may file a complaint. The commission shall furnish the same explanation and information to the person against whom the complaint is filed.

(b) The commission shall keep an information file about each complaint filed with the commission that the commission has authority to resolve.

(c) **If a written complaint is filed** with the commission that the commission has authority to resolve, the commission, at least quarterly and until final disposition of the complaint, shall notify the parties to the complaint of the status of the complaint unless the notice would jeopardize an undercover investigation authorized under Subsection (a) of Section 15B of this Act.

Section 18C. Repealed September 1, 1991.

In Practice   Section 18 provides that a licensee who is displeased by a ruling of the commission may appeal the decision to the district court. It also outlines the action taken by the commission when a written complaint is filed against a licensee.

Unlicensed Activity   **Section 19.** (a) **A person acting as a real estate broker or real estate salesperson** without first obtaining a license or a person required to register under Section 9A of this Act who sells, purchases, leases, or transfers a right-of-way or easement without first obtaining a certificate of registration under Section 9A of this Act commits an offense. An offense under this subsection is a Class A misdemeanor.

(b) **In case a person received money,** or the equivalent thereof, as a fee, commission, compensation, or profit by or in consequence of a violation of Subsection (a) of this section, the person shall, in addition, be liable to a penalty of not less than the amount of the sum of money so received and not more than three times the sum so received, as may be determined by the court, which penalty may be recovered in a court of competent jurisdiction by an aggrieved person.

(c) **When in the judgment of the Commission** a person has engaged, or is about to engage, in an act or practice which constitutes or will constitute a violation of a provision of this Act, the county attorney or district attorney in the county in which the violation has occurred or is about to occur, or in the county of the defendant's residence, or the attorney general may maintain an action in the name of the State of Texas in the district court of such county to abate and temporarily and permanently enjoin the acts and practices and to enforce compliance with this Act. The plaintiff in an action under this subsection is not required to give a bond, and court costs may not be adjudged against the plaintiff.

(d) **Notwithstanding any other provision of this section,** this Act, or any other law, if, in the judgment of the commission, a person has engaged or is about to engage in an act or practice that constitutes or will constitute a violation of this Act, the commission, acting through the attorney general, may maintain an action in the name of the state in district court in the county in which the violation has occurred or is about to occur, or in the county of the defendant's residence, to abate and temporarily or permanently enjoin those acts or practices and to enforce compliance with this Act. In an action under this subsection the commission is not required to give bond, and court costs may not be recovered against the commission. In addition to injunctive relief the commission may recover court costs, reasonable attorney's fees, and a civil penalty, payable to the state if a person received money or other consideration as a fee, commission, compensation, or profit by or in consequence of a violation of Subsection (a) of this section. The court shall set the civil penalty in an amount not less than the amount of the money so received, but not more than three times the amount so received.

Section 19A. (a) **If a person violates this Act** or a rule or order adopted by the commission under this Act, the commission may assess an administrative penalty against the person as provided by this section.

(b) **The penalty for each violation shall be set in an amount not to exceed $1,000.** Each day a violation continues or occurs may be considered a separate violation for purposes of penalty assessment if the commission finds that the person charged:

(1) engaged in an activity for which a real estate broker or real estate salesperson license is required without holding a license; and

(2) was not licensed by the commission as a real estate broker or real estate salesperson at any time in the four years preceding the date of the violation.

(c) **In determining the amount of the penalty,** the administrator named under Subsection (i) of Section 5 of this Act shall consider:

(1) the seriousness of the violation, including the nature, circumstances, extent, and gravity of the prohibited acts;

(2) the history of previous violations;

(3) the amount necessary to deter future violations;

(4) efforts to correct the violation; and

(5) any other matter that justice may require.

(d) **If, after investigation of a possible violation** and the facts surrounding that possible violation, the administrator determines that a violation has occurred, the administrator may issue a violation report stating the facts on which the conclusion that a violation occurred is based, recommending that an administrative penalty under this section be imposed on the person charged, and recommending the amount of that proposed penalty. The administrator shall base the recommended amount of the proposed penalty on the seriousness of the violation determined by the consideration of the factors set forth in Subsection (c) of this section. The commission may authorize the administrator to delegate to another commission employee the administrator's authority to act under this section.

(e) **Not later than the 14th day** after the date on which the report is issued, the administrator shall give written notice of the report to the person charged. The notice shall include a brief summary of the charges, a statement of the amount of the penalty recommended, and a statement of the right of the person charged to a hearing on the occurrence of the violation or the amount of the penalty, or both the occurrence of the violation and the amount of the penalty.

(f) **Not later than the 20th day** after the date on which notice is received, the person charged may accept the determination of the administrator made under Subsection (d) of this section, including the recommended penalty, or make a written request for a hearing on the determination.

(g) **If the person charged with the violation** accepts the determination of the administrator, the commission shall issue an order approving the determination and ordering the payment of the recommended penalty.

(h) **If the person charged requests a hearing or fails to timely respond to the notice,** the administrator shall set a hearing and give notice of the hearing. The hearing shall be held by a hearing examiner designated by the administrator. The hearing examiner shall make findings of fact and conclusions of law and promptly issue to the commission a proposal for decision as to the occurrence of the violation, including a recommendation as to the amount of the proposed penalty if a penalty is warranted. Based on the findings of fact, conclusions of law, and recommendations of the hearing examiner, the commission by order may find a violation has occurred and may assess a penalty or may find that no violation has occurred. All proceedings under this subsection are subject to Chapter 2001, Government Code. The commission may authorize the hearing examiner to conduct the hearing and enter a final decision.

(i) **The administrator shall give notice** of the commission's order to the person charged. The notice shall include:

(1) the findings of fact and conclusions of law separately stated;

(2) the amount of the penalty ordered, if any;

(3) a statement of the right of the person charged to judicial review of the commission's order, if any; and

(4) other information required by law.

(j) **Within the 30 day period** immediately following the date on which the order becomes final as provided by Subsection (c), Section 16, Administrative Procedure and Texas Register Act (Article 6252-13a, Vernon's Texas Civil Statutes), the person charged with the penalty shall:

(1) pay the penalty in full; or

(2) if the person files a petition for judicial review contesting either the amount of the penalty or the fact of the violation or contesting both the fact of the violation and the amount of the penalty:

(A) forward the amount to the administrator for placement in an escrow account; or

(B) in lieu of payment into escrow, post with the administrator a supersedeas bond in a form approved by the administrator for the amount of the penalty, the bond to be effective until all judicial review of the order or decision is final.

(k) **If a person charged is financially unable** either to forward the amount of the penalty for placement in an escrow account or post a supersedeas bond for the amount of the penalty, the person may satisfy the requirements of Subdivision (2) of Subsection (j) of this section by filing with the administrator an affidavit sworn by the person charged, stating that the person is financially unable either to forward the amount of the penalty or post a bond.

(l) **Failure to forward the money** to or to post the bond or file the affidavit with the administrator within the time provided by Subsection (j) of this section results in a waiver of all legal rights to judicial review. Also, if the person charged fails to pay the penalty in full as provided under Subdivision (1) of Subsection (j) of this section or forward the money, post the bond, or file the affidavit as provided by Subsection (j) or (k) of this section, the administrator may forward the matter to the attorney general for enforcement.

(m) **Judicial review of the order or decision of the commission** assessing the penalty shall be under the substantial evidence rule and shall be instituted by filing a petition with a district court in Travis County, as provided by Chapter 2001, Government Code.

(n) **If the penalty is reduced or not assessed by the court,** the administrator shall remit to the person charged the appropriate amount plus accrued interest if the penalty has been paid or shall execute a release of the bond if a supersedeas bond has been posted. The accrued interest on amounts remitted by the administrator under this subsection shall be paid at a rate equal to the rate charged on loans to depository institutions by the New York Federal Reserve Bank and shall be paid for the period beginning on the date the penalty is paid to the administrator under Subsection (j) of this section and ending on the date the penalty is remitted.

(o) **A penalty collected under this section for a violation** by a person licensed as a real estate broker or salesperson shall be deposited in the real estate recovery fund. A penalty collected under this section for a violation by a person licensed or registered as a real estate inspector shall be deposited in the real estate inspection recovery fund. A penalty collected under this section for a violation by a person who is not licensed under this Act shall be deposited in the real estate recovery fund or the real estate inspection recovery fund, as determined by the commission.

In Practice

Section 19 stipulates that a violation of the Act by *any* person (licensed or unlicensed) is a Class A misdemeanor. It is punishable by up to a $4,000 fine or imprisonment for a term not to exceed one year or both. Timely renewal of a real estate license is crucial to a licensee's avoiding charges under this Section. An aggrieved person may recover up to three times the amount of money paid to a broker if a salesperson's license had expired. Moreover, the state may recover a civil penalty of up to three times the amount of money paid to a broker.

Requirements for Compensation

Section 20. (a) **A person may not bring or maintain an action** for the collection of compensation for the performance in this state of an act set forth in Section 2 of this Act without alleging and proving that the person performing the brokerage services was a duly-licensed real estate broker or salesperson at the time the alleged services were commenced, or was a duly-licensed attorney at law in this state or in any other state.

(b) **An action may not be brought** in a court in this state for the recovery of a commission for the sale or purchase of real estate unless the promise or agreement on which the action is brought, or some memorandum thereof, is in writing and signed by the party to be charged or signed by a person lawfully authorized by the party to sign it.

(c) **When an offer to purchase real estate in this state is signed,** the real estate broker or salesperson shall advise the purchaser or purchasers, in writing, that the purchaser or purchasers should have the abstract covering the real estate which is the subject of the contract examined by an attorney of the purchaser's own selection, or that the purchaser or purchasers should be furnished with or obtain a policy of title insurance. Failure to advise the purchaser as provided in this subsection precludes the payment of or recovery of any commission agreed to be paid on the sale.

(d) **This section does not apply** to an agreement to share compensation between persons licensed under this Act. This section does not limit a cause of action between brokers for interference with business relationships.

> A licensee is required to obtain the consent of the licensee's principal before paying a portion of the licensee's fee to a party the licensee does not represent.

In Practice Section 20 addresses the requirements for recovery of a disputed commission as discussed in Chapter 5.

Section 21. Repealed September 1, 1991.

Section 22. Repealed July 1, 1991.

Real Estate Inspectors **Section 23. REAL ESTATE INSPECTORS.** (a) **DEFINITIONS.** In this section: (1) "Apprentice inspector" means a person who is in training under the direct supervision of a professional inspector or a real estate inspector to become qualified to perform real estate inspections.

(2) "Committee" means the Texas Real Estate Inspector Committee.

(3) "Core real estate inspection courses" means educational courses approved by the commission, including but not limited to structural, electrical, mechanical, plumbing, roofing, business, legal, standards of practice, report writing, appliances or ethics, all of which must relate to a real estate inspection.

(4) "Direct supervision" means the instruction and control by a professional inspector or real estate inspector licensed under this section who is:

(A) responsible for the actions of an individual performing a real estate inspection or preparing a report of a real estate inspection;

(B) available if and when needed to consult with or assist an individual performing a real estate inspection or preparing a report of a real estate inspection; and

(C) physically present at the time and place of the inspection.

(5) "Indirect supervision" means the instruction and control by a professional inspector licensed under this section who is:

(A) responsible for the actions of an individual performing or preparing a real estate inspection; and

(B) available if and when needed to consult with or assist an individual performing a real estate inspection or preparing a report of a real estate inspection, but who is not required to be physically present at the time and place of the inspection.

(6) "Inspector" means a person who is licensed as an apprentice inspector, real estate inspector, or professional inspector under this section.

(7) "License" means an apprentice license, a real estate inspector license or a professional inspector license issued under this section.

(8) "Licensee" means a person holding an apprentice inspector license, a real estate inspector license or a professional inspector license issued under this section.

(9) "Professional inspector" means a person who represents to the public that the person is trained and qualified to perform a real estate inspection and who accepts employment for the purpose of performing a real estate inspection for a buyer or seller of real property.

(10) "Real estate inspection" means a written or oral opinion as to the condition of the improvements to real property, including structural items, electrical items, mechanical systems, plumbing systems, or equipment.

(11) "Real estate inspector" means a person who represents to the public that the person is trained and qualified to perform real estate inspections under the indirect supervision of a professional inspector and who accepts employment for the purpose of performing a real estate inspection for a buyer or seller of real property.

(b) **TEXAS REAL ESTATE INSPECTOR COMMITTEE.** (1) The Texas Real Estate Inspector Committee is created. In addition to other powers and duties delegated to it by the commission, the committee shall recommend:

(A) rules for the licensing of inspectors in this state in accordance with this section;

(B) rules relating to the education and experience requirements for licensing as an inspector under this section;

(C) rules relating to the qualifying examination required for licensing as an inspector under this section;

(D) rules establishing a code of professional conduct and ethics for an inspector under this section;

(E) reasonable fees to implement this section, including an application fee for licensing, an examination fee, a renewal fee for a license, and any other fee required by law;

(F) rules relating to continuing education requirements for a licensed inspector;

(G) rules relating to the standards of practice for a real estate inspection;

(H) rules relating to granting or denying an application for the licensing of an inspector;

(I) the form and format for any applications and forms required under this section; and

(J) any other action by the commission as may provide a high degree of service and protection to the public when dealing with licensed inspectors.

(2) The committee is composed of nine members appointed by the commission. The members of the committee hold office for staggered terms of six years, with the terms of three members expiring February 1 of each odd-numbered year. Each member holds office until the member's successor is appointed. Appointments to the committee shall be made without regard to the sex, race, color, age, handicap, religion, or national origin of the appointees. In the event of a vacancy during a term, the commission shall appoint a replacement who meets the qualifications for appointment under this subdivision to fill the unexpired part of the term. A member of the committee must be a professional inspector actively engaged in the practice of real estate inspecting at the time of appointment and must have been primarily engaged in the practice of real estate inspecting for at least five years before the member's appointment. No more than three members of the committee may hold a real estate broker license. Each member of the committee is entitled to a per diem allowance and to reimbursement of travel expenses necessarily incurred in performing functions as a member of the committee, subject to any applicable limitation in the General Appropriations Act. The committee shall annually elect from its members a chairperson, a vice-chairperson, and secretary. A quorum of the committee consists of five members.

(3) The commission may remove a committee member if the member:

(A) does not have at the time of appointment the qualifications required by Subdivision (2) of this subsection;

(B) cannot discharge the member's duties for a substantial part of the term for which the member is appointed because of illness or disability; or

(C) is absent from more than half of the regularly scheduled committee meetings that the member is eligible to attend during each year, unless the absence is excused by the committee.

(4) The validity of an action of the committee is not affected by the fact that it was taken when a ground for removal of a committee member exists.

(5) If the administrator of the commission has knowledge that a potential ground for removal exists, the administrator shall notify the chairperson of the commission that a potential ground exists.

(6) The commission shall adopt procedural rules to be used by the committee in implementing its powers and duties.

(7) The committee is subject to the open meetings law, Chapter 271, Acts of the 60th Legislature, Regular Session, 1967 (Article 6252-17, Vernon's Texas Civil Statutes), the open records law, Chapter 424, Acts of the 63rd Legislature, Regular Session, 1973 (Article 6252-17a, Vernon's Texas

Civil Statutes), and the Administrative Procedure and Texas Register Act (Article 6252-13a, Vernon's Texas Civil Statutes).

(8) The committee shall meet semiannually and at the call of the commission. The committee may also meet at the call of a majority of its members.

(9) The committee shall act in an advisory capacity to develop and recommend to the commission rules under this section. The committee shall review commission rules relating to this section and recommend changes in the rules to the commission. The commission shall submit all proposed rules, all proposed rule changes and all requests for proposed rules or rule changes that relate to the regulation and licensing of inspectors under this section to the committee for development or recommendation. The commission may modify the rules developed by the committee if the commission finds such modifications are in the public interest. This section does not prohibit the commission from developing and adopting rules relating to the regulation and licensing of inspectors under this section if the committee fails to develop or recommend rules under this section within a reasonable period of time after the commission submits the proposed rules, rule changes or requests for proposed rules or rule changes to the committee. If the committee determines that a rule requested by the commission should not be developed or recommended for adoption by the commission, the committee shall submit a report on the matter to the commission. The chairperson of the commission and the chairperson of the committee shall then appoint three members each from their respective bodies to meet as an ad hoc committee to consider the report and recommend possible action by the commission. The chairperson of the commission or a member of the commission designated by the chairperson shall serve as the seventh member of the ad hoc committee. At least one member of the ad hoc committee must be a public member of the commission.

(c) **LICENSE REQUIRED.** (1) A person may not act as a professional inspector in this state for a buyer or seller of real property unless the person possesses a professional inspector license issued under this section.

(2) A person may not act or attempt to act as a real estate inspector in this state for a buyer or seller of real property unless the person possesses a real estate inspector license issued under this section and is under the indirect supervision of a professional inspector.

(3) A person may not act or attempt to act as an apprentice inspector in this state for a buyer or seller of real property unless the person is licensed under this section and is under the direct supervision of a real estate inspector or professional inspector.

(d) **ELIGIBILITY; APPLICATION.** (1) To be eligible for a license as an apprentice inspector, an applicant must be an individual, a citizen of the United States or a lawfully admitted alien, and a resident of this state at the time of the filing of the application. The applicant must be sponsored by a professional inspector licensed under this section. The applicant must be at least 18 years old. The applicant must satisfy the commission as to the applicant's honesty, trustworthiness, and integrity.

(2) To be eligible for a license as a real estate inspector, an applicant must have met the requirements and been licensed as an apprentice inspector for at least three months and have performed at least 25 real estate inspections under direct supervision before filing an application. The applicant must satisfy the commission as to the applicant's honesty, trustworthiness, integrity, and competency. An applicant for an original real estate inspector license must submit satisfactory evidence to the commission of successful completion of not less than 90 classroom hours of core real estate inspection courses. The commission by rule may specify the length and content of the core real estate inspection courses required by this subdivision. The commission shall determine the competency of an applicant on the basis of an examination required by Subsection (i) of this section. The applicant must be sponsored by a professional inspector licensed under this section. Notwithstanding this subdivision of this subsection, an applicant is eligible for and has satisfied all requirements for a license as a real estate inspector if the applicant was previously licensed as a real estate inspector during the preceding 24-month period immediately preceding the filing of the application, the applicant is sponsored by a professional inspector, and the applicant satisfies the commission as to the applicant's honesty, trustworthiness, and integrity.

(3) To be eligible for a license as a professional inspector, an applicant must have met the requirements and have been licensed as an apprentice inspector for at least three months and licensed as a real estate inspector for at least 12 months and have performed at least 175 real estate inspections under indirect supervision before filing an application. An applicant for an original professional inspector license must submit satisfactory evidence to the commission of successful completion of not less than 30 classroom hours of core real estate inspection courses and eight classroom hours related to the study of standards of practice, legal issues, or ethics related to the profession of real estate inspections. These classroom hours are in addition to those required for an apprentice inspector license or a real estate inspector license. The commission shall determine the competency of an applicant on the basis of an examination required by Subsection (i) of this section. Notwithstanding this subsection, an applicant is eligible for and has satisfied all requirements for a license as a professional inspector if the applicant was previously licensed as a professional inspector during the preceding 24-month period immediately preceding the filing of the application and the applicant satisfies the commission as to the applicant's honesty, trustworthiness, and integrity.

(4) The commission by rule shall provide for the substitution of relevant experience or additional education in lieu of the number of real estate inspections required by this section and in lieu of the requirement that the applicant be licensed as an apprentice inspector or a real estate inspector before issuance of a license as a real estate inspector or professional inspector. The rules adopted by the commission under this subdivision may not require an applicant to complete more than 60 additional classroom hours of core real estate inspection courses.

(5) An applicant must file an application for a license with the commission on forms prescribed by the commission.

(6) Before a licensed professional inspector may sponsor an apprentice inspector or a real estate inspector, the professional inspector must provide sufficient proof to the commission that the professional inspector has completed not less than 200 real estate inspections while licensed as a professional inspector under this Act.

(e) **ISSUANCE OF LICENSE.** The commission shall issue an apprentice license, a real estate inspector license, or a professional inspector license to an applicant who possesses the required qualifications, passes the appropriate examination if required, and pays the fee required by Subdivision (2) of Subsection (o) of this section.

(f) **EXPIRATION OF LICENSE; RENEWAL.** (1) A license issued under this section expires one year after the date it is issued.

(2) A person may renew an unexpired license by paying to the commission before the expiration date of the license the required renewal fee.

(3) If a person's license expires, the person may not renew the license. The person may obtain a new license by submitting to reexamination, if required, and complying with the requirements and procedures for obtaining an original license.

(4) At least 30 days before the expiration of a person's license the commission shall send written notice of the impending license expiration to the person at the person's last known address according to the records of the commission.

(g) **CHANGE OF ADDRESS.** A licensee under this section shall notify the commission and pay the required fee within 30 days after the date a change of place of business occurs.

(h) **FEES.** (1) The commission shall charge and collect reasonable and necessary fees to recover the cost of administering this section as follows:

(A) a fee not to exceed $75 for the filing of an original application for a license as an apprentice inspector;

(B) a fee not to exceed $125 for the filing of an original application for a license as a real estate inspector;

(C) a fee not to exceed $150 for the filing of an original application for a license as a professional inspector;

(D) a fee not to exceed $125 for the annual license renewal of an apprentice inspector;

(E) a fee not to exceed $175 for the annual license renewal of a real estate inspector;

(F) a fee not to exceed $200 for the annual license renewal of a professional inspector;

(G) a fee not to exceed $100 for taking a license examination;

(H) a fee not to exceed $20 for a request for a change of place of business or to replace a lost or destroyed license; and

(l) a fee not to exceed $20 for filing a request for issuance of a license because of a change of name, return to active status, or change in sponsoring professional inspector.

(2) All fees may be paid by cash, check, cashier's check, or money order.

(3) The fees shall be reviewed annually and reduced to the extent that the costs of administering this section are funded by the real estate inspector regulation account established under Subdivision (4) of Subsection (o) of this section.

(i) **EXAMINATION.** (1) The commission shall prescribe the licensing examinations, which shall be prepared by or contracted for by the commission. A licensing examination shall evaluate competency in the subject matter of all required core real estate inspection courses. The licensing examination shall be offered not less often than once every two months in Austin. If a license applicant fails the examination, the applicant may apply for reexamination by filing a request with the commission and paying the examination fee. Each license applicant must satisfy the examination requirement not later than six months after the date on which the license application is filed. A license applicant who fails to satisfy the examination requirement within six months after the date on which the license application is filed must submit a new license application with the commission and pay the examination fee to be eligible for examination. If a license applicant fails the examination three consecutive times in connection with the same application, the applicant may not apply for reexamination or submit a new license application with the commission for six months from the date he failed the last examination.

(2) Not later than the 30th day after the date on which a licensing examination is administered under this section, the commission shall notify each examinee of the results of the examination. However, if an examination is graded or reviewed by a national testing service, the commission shall notify examinees of the results of the examination not later than the 14th day after the date on which the commission receives the results from the testing service. If the notice of examination results graded or reviewed by a national testing service will be delayed for longer than 90 days after the examination date, the commission shall notify the examinee of the reason for the delay before the 90th day.

(3) If requested in writing by a person who fails a licensing examination administered under this section, the commission shall furnish the person with an analysis of the person's performance on the examination.

(j) **WAIVER FOR OUT-OF-STATE APPLICANTS.** The commission may waive any license requirement for an applicant with a valid license from another state having license requirements substantially equivalent to those of this state.

(k) **CONTINUING EDUCATION PROGRAMS.** The commission shall recognize, prepare, or administer continuing education programs for inspectors. Participation in the programs is mandatory. A real estate inspector must submit satisfactory evidence to the commission of successful completion of at least eight classroom hours of core real estate inspection courses annually before a license renewal is issued. A professional inspector must submit satisfactory evidence to the commission of successful completion of at least sixteen classroom hours of core real estate inspection courses annually before a license renewal is issued.

(l) **PROHIBITED ACTS.** A professional inspector, real estate inspector or an apprentice inspector licensed under this section may not:

(1) accept an assignment for real estate inspection if the employment or fee is contingent on the reporting of a specific, predetermined condition of the improvements to real property or is contingent on the reporting of specific findings other than those known by the inspector to be facts at the time of accepting the assignment;

(2) act in a manner or engage in a practice that is dishonest or fraudulent or that involves deceit or misrepresentation;

(3) perform a real estate inspection in a negligent or incompetent manner;

(4) act in the dual capacity of inspector and undisclosed principal in a transaction;

(5) act in the dual capacity of inspector and real estate broker or salesperson in a transaction;

(6) perform or agree to perform any repairs or maintenance in connection with a real estate inspection pursuant to the provisions of any earnest money contract, lease agreement, or exchange of real estate; or

(7) violate the rules adopted by the commission or any provisions of this section.

(m) **OFFENSES.** (1) A person commits an offense if the person knowingly or intentionally engages in the business of real estate inspecting without a license under this section or performs an inspection during a period in which the inspector's license is revoked or suspended.

(2) An offense under this subsection is a Class A misdemeanor.

(3) The commission may authorize the committee to conduct administrative hearings or recommend the entry of final orders, or both, in contested cases regarding a licensed inspector. The commission may authorize specific employees to conduct hearings and render final decisions in contested cases regarding a licensed inspector.

(4) The commission may investigate the actions of a licensed inspector and may, after notice and hearing in accordance with the provisions of Section 17 of this Act, reprimand, place on probation, suspend or revoke a license for a violation of this Act or a rule of the commission. If the commission revokes a license of a person, the person may not apply to the commission for one year after the revocation.

(n) **EXEMPTIONS.** This section does not apply to any electrician, plumber, carpenter, any person engaged in the business of structural pest control in compliance with the Texas Structural Pest Control Act (Article 135b-6, Vernon's Texas Civil Statutes), or any other person who repairs, maintains, or inspects improvements to real property and who does not represent to the public through personal solicitation or public advertising that the person is in the business of inspecting such improvements. The provisions of this section shall not be construed so as to prevent any person from performing any and all acts which the person is authorized to perform pursuant to a license or registration issued by this state or any governmental subdivision of this state.

(o) **REAL ESTATE INSPECTION RECOVERY FUND.** (1) The commission shall establish a real estate inspection recovery fund, which shall be set apart and maintained by the commission as provided by this subsection. The fund shall be used in the manner provided by this subsection for reimbursing aggrieved persons who suffer actual damages by reason of certain acts committed by a duly licensed inspector, provided the inspector was licensed by the State of Texas at the time the act was committed and provided recovery is ordered by a court of competent jurisdiction against the inspector. The use of the fund is limited to an act that is a violation of Subsection (l) of this section.

(2) When a person receives notice that he has successfully completed the licensing examination provided by Subsection (i) of this section, the person shall pay, in addition to any other fees required by this section, a fee not to exceed $200, which shall be deposited in the real estate inspection recovery fund prior to the commission's issuing the person an inspector license.

(3) If at any time the balance remaining in the real estate inspection recovery fund is less than $300,000, each inspector, on the next renewal of the person's license, shall pay, in addition to the license renewal fee, a fee of $75, or a pro rata share of the amount necessary to bring the fund to $450,000, whichever is less, which shall be deposited in the real estate inspection recovery fund. To ensure the availability of a sufficient amount to pay anticipated claims on the fund, the commission by rule may provide for the collection of assessments at different times and under conditions other than those specified by this Act.

(4) If on December 31 of any year the balance remaining in the real estate inspection recovery fund is greater than $600,000, the amount in excess of $600,000 shall be transferred to a separate account in the general revenue fund to be known as the real estate inspector regulation account. The money in the real estate inspector regulation account may be used only for the payment of costs incurred by the commission in the regulation of inspectors.

(5) No action for a judgment that results in an order for collection from the real estate inspection recovery fund shall be started later than two years from the accrual of the cause of action. When an aggrieved person commences action for a judgment that may result in collection from the real estate inspection recovery fund, the inspector shall notify the commission in writing to this effect at the time of the commencement of the action.

(6) When an aggrieved person recovers a valid judgment in a court of competent jurisdiction against an inspector on the grounds described in Subdivision (1) of this subsection, the aggrieved person may, after final judgment has been entered, execution returned nulla bona, and a judgment lien perfected, file a verified claim in the court in which the judgment was entered and, on 20 days' written notice to the commission and to the judgment debtor, may apply to the court where the judgment was rendered for

an order directing payment out of the real estate inspection recovery fund of the amount unpaid on the judgment, subject to the limitations stated in Subdivision (15) of this subsection.

(7) The court shall proceed on the application forthwith. On the hearing on the application, the aggrieved person is required to show:

(A) that the judgment is based on facts allowing recovery under Subdivision (1) of this subsection;

(B) that the person is not a spouse of the debtor, or the personal representative of the spouse and the person is not an inspector, as defined by this section;

(C) that based on the best information available, the judgment debtor lacks sufficient attachable assets in this state or any other state to satisfy the judgment; and

(D) the amount that may be realized from the sale of real or personal property or other assets liable to be sold or applied in satisfaction of the judgment and the balance remaining due on the judgment after application of the amount that may be realized.

(8) The court shall make an order directed to the commission requiring payment out of the real estate inspection recovery fund of whatever sum it finds to be payable on the claim, pursuant to and in accordance with the limitations contained in this subdivision, if the court is satisfied, on the hearing, of the truth of all matters required to be shown by the aggrieved person by Subdivision (7) of this subsection and that the aggrieved person has satisfied all of the requirements of Subdivisions (6) and (7) of this subsection. The commission may relitigate any issue material and relevant in the hearing on the application that was determined in the underlying action on which the judgment in favor of the applicant was based. If the court finds that the aggregate of claims against an inspector exceeds the limitations contained in this section, the court shall reduce proportionately the amount it finds payable on the claim.

(9) A recovery on the judgment against a single defendant made before payment from the real estate inspection recovery fund must be applied by the creditor first to actual damages.

(10) A license granted under the provisions of this section may be revoked by the commission on proof that the commission has made a payment from the real estate inspection recovery fund of any amount toward satisfaction of a judgment against a licensed real estate inspector. The commission may probate an order revoking a license. No inspector is eligible to receive a new license until the person has repaid in full, plus interest at the current legal rate, the amount paid from the real estate inspection recovery fund on the person's account.

(11) The sums received by the commission for deposit in the real estate inspection recovery fund shall be held by the commission in trust for carrying out the purpose of the real estate inspection recovery fund. These funds may be invested and reinvested in the same manner as funds of the Employees Retirement System of Texas, and the interest from these investments shall be deposited to the credit of the real estate inspection recovery fund. However, investments may not be made that will impair the necessary

liquidity required to satisfy judgment payments awarded pursuant to this subsection.

(12) When the commission receives notice of entry of a final judgment and a hearing is conducted under Subdivision (8) of this subsection, the commission may notify the Attorney General of Texas of the commission's desire to enter an appearance, file a response, appear at the court hearing, defend the action, or take whatever other action it deems appropriate. In taking such action the commission and the attorney general shall act only to protect the fund from spurious or unjust claims or to ensure compliance with the requirements for recovery under this subsection.

(13) When, on the order of the court, the commission has paid from the real estate inspection recovery fund any sum to the judgment creditor, the commission shall be subrogated to all of the rights of the judgment creditor to the extent of the amount paid. The judgment creditor shall assign all his right, title, and interest in the judgment up to the amount paid by the commission. The amount paid by the commission shall have priority for repayment in the event of any subsequent recovery on the judgment. Any amount in interest recovered by the commission on the judgment shall be deposited to the fund.

(14) The failure of an aggrieved person to comply with the provisions of this subsection relating to the real estate inspection recovery fund shall constitute a waiver of any rights under this subsection.

(15) Notwithstanding any other provision, payments from the real estate inspection recovery fund are subject to the following conditions and limitations:

(A) payments may be made only pursuant to an order of a court of competent jurisdiction, as provided by Subdivision (6) of this subsection, and in the manner prescribed by this subsection;

(B) payments for claims, including attorney fees, interest, and court costs, arising out of the same transaction shall be limited in the aggregate to $12,500 regardless of the number of claimants; and

(C) payments for claims based on judgments against a licensed inspector may not exceed in the aggregate $30,000 until the fund has been reimbursed by the licensee for all amounts paid.

(16) Nothing contained in this subsection shall limit the authority of the commission to take disciplinary action against a person licensed under this section for a violation of this section or the rules of the commission, nor shall the repayment in full of all obligations to the real estate inspection recovery fund by a person nullify or modify the effect of any other disciplinary proceeding brought pursuant to this section.

(17) A person receiving payment out of the real estate inspection recovery fund under Subdivision (15) of this subsection shall be entitled to receive reasonable attorney fees as determined by the court, subject to the limitations stated in that subdivision.

(18) An inspector licensed under this section shall notify consumers and service recipients of the availability of the real estate inspection recovery fund established under this section for reimbursing certain aggrieved per-

sons. The notice must include the name, mailing address, and telephone number of the commission and any other information required by commission rule. The notification may be provided:

(A) on a written contract for the services of an inspector;

(B) on a brochure distributed by an inspector;

(C) on a sign prominently displayed in the place of business of an inspector; or

(D) in a bill or receipt for service provided by an inspector.

(p) Inactive licenses. The commission by rule may adopt terms and conditions by which an inspector may apply for, renew, or place a license on inactive status and rules by which an inactive inspector may return to active status.

(q) The commission shall consider the recommendations of the Texas Real Estate Inspector Committee relating to the qualifications and licensure of inspectors to assure the public of a quality professional inspection system in real estate transactions in Texas.

(r) The commission by rule shall prescribe standard forms and adopt rules that require inspectors to use the forms to reduce discrepancies and create consistency in preparing reports of real estate inspections.

In Practice   Section 23 sets forth the educational and examination requirements for licensing real estate property inspectors. It provides for fees and the establishment of a real estate inspection recovery fund. All inspectors are required to use a standard report form.

Residential Rental Locators   **Section 24.**   RESIDENTIAL RENTAL LOCATORS. (a) In this section, **"residential rental locator"** means a person, other than the owner of the property or a person exempted by Section 3 of this Act, who offers, for consideration, to locate a unit in an apartment complex for lease to a prospective tenant.

(b) A person may not engage in business as a residential rental locator in this state unless the person holds a license issued under this Act to operate as a real estate broker or real estate salesperson and complies with the continuing education requirements under Section 7A of this Act.

(c) The commission by rule shall adopt regulations and establish standards relating to permissible forms of advertising by a person licensed under this section.

(d) Each residential rental locator shall post in a conspicuous place accessible to clients and prospective clients the locator's license, a statement that the locator is licensed by the commission, and the name, mailing address, and telephone number of the commission as provided by Section 5(q) of this Act.

(e) A violation of this section by a residential rental locator constitutes grounds under this Act for the suspension or revocation of the person's license and for the assessment of an administrative penalty under Section 19A of this Act.

(f) A person commits an offense if the person engages in business as a residential rental locator in this state without a license issued under this Act. An offense under this subsection is a Class A misdemeanor.

(g) Repealed September 1, 1997.

In Practice   A *residential rental locator* is defined by the License Act as one who offers, for consideration, to locate a unit in an apartment complex for lease to a prospective tenant. If the rental locator is not the owner of the property or an on-site property manager, he or she must be licensed as a real estate broker or salesperson.

Summary

The Texas Real Estate License Act was enacted by the Texas legislature to protect the public from dishonest brokers, salespersons, and registrants; prescribe certain licensing and registration standards; maintain high standards in the real estate profession; and protect licensed brokers from unfair or improper competition. The act stipulates who must be licensed or registered and who is exempt from licensing or registration; sets forth certain operating standards to which brokers, salespersons, and registrants must adhere; and creates certain licensing and registration procedures and requirements.

Prospective brokers, salespersons, and registrants will be operating and working under the Texas Real Estate License Act. Therefore, the law must be understood fully.

Table 7.1	Education Requirements for Salesperson and Broker Licenses		
Salesperson—Pre-License Requirements and Salesman Annual Education			
Requirements for an Active License	**First Annual Renewal**	**Second Annual Renewal**	**Third Annual Renewal**
12 semester hours (180 classroom hours) 4 semester hours (60 classroom hours) of Principles of Real Estate 2 semester hours (30 classroom hours) of Law of Agency 2 semester hours (30 classroom hours) of Law of Contracts 4 semester hours (60 classroom hours) of core* or related courses†	2 semester hours (30 classroom hours) Must have a total of 10 semester hours (150 classroom hours) in core real estate courses	2 semester hours (30 classroom hours) Must have a total of 12 semester hours (180 classroom hours) in core real estate courses	2 semester hours (30 classroom hours) Must have a total of 14 semester hours (210 classroom hours) in core real estate courses

Note: One semester hour equals 15 classroom hours.

Broker—Pre-License Requirements

60 semester hours (900 classroom hours)

18 semester hours (270 classroom hours) minimum of core real estate courses* (Equivalent to a two-year associate's degree plan in real estate)

Two-year apprenticeship required (two of last three years)

Mandatory Continuing Education (MCE)

All brokers and salespersons who have completed salesperson annual education (SAE) courses must complete 15 classroom hours of MCE during the license renewal period. At least six of these hours must be in legal topics required by the Commission with the remainder in topics approved by the Commission. (Some exemptions apply to brokers.)

---

* Core real estate courses—Principles, Agency, Appraisal, Law, Finance, Marketing, Mathematics, Brokerage, Property Management, Investments, Promulgated Contract Forms, Residential Inspection for Real Estate Agents, Law of Contracts.

† Related courses—An extensive list of approved related courses is available on the TREC web site: www.trec.state.tx.us (choose Education; R. E. Related Courses). Among the courses are Business Math, Government, Economics, and Marketing).

ANALYSIS FORM: TEXAS REAL ESTATE LICENSE ACT

Instructions: After studying the Texas Real Estate License Act, carefully complete the worksheet below. The information will be invaluable in preparation for the state license examination and in future real estate activities.

1. When was the Texas Real Estate License Act originally passed? _____

2. When was it last amended? _____

3. What are the requirements for licensure in Texas?

	For Broker's License	For Salesperson's License
a. Minimum age	_____	_____
b. Length of residence	_____	_____
c. Apprenticeship (years)	_____	_____
d. Education	_____	_____
e. Examination required?	_____	_____
f. Amount of payment into recovery fund	_____	_____

4. From the following list of real estate activities, check those that require a Texas real estate license or registration

_____ auction	_____ mortgage
_____ sell	_____ build
_____ exchange	_____ survey
_____ purchase	_____ repair
_____ rent	_____ subdivide
_____ owner who performs the above for himself or herself	_____ trade
	_____ garden
_____ owner's employee who performs the above for owners	_____ lease
	_____ buy
_____ assist in procuring prospects	_____ buy easements
_____ assist in finding listings	_____ inspect property condition
_____ appraise	
_____ collect rents	_____ locate renters

5. State the definition of a *broker* as given by state law. Know this definition and be able to list the activities that it includes.

_____

_____

6. State the definition of a *salesperson* as given by state law. Learn this definition.

_____

_____

7. What persons or transactions are *exempt* from licensure in Texas?

_____

_____

_____

8. What are the maximum fees in Texas?

	For Broker	For Salesperson
a. For original license application	_____	_____
b. For examination	_____	_____
c. For annual renewal	_____	_____
d. For each additional office	_____	_____
e. For change of place of business or sponsoring broker	_____	_____
f. For replacement of lost or destroyed license	_____	_____
g. For the Texas RE Research Center	_____	_____
h. For transcript evaluation	_____	_____

9. a. For what period is the license certificate issued? _____

b. When does it expire? _____

10. Examine Sections 15 and 16 of the act. Then list at least nine reasons why the Texas Real Estate Commission may discipline a broker or salesperson, refuse to issue a license or revoke or suspend a license.

a. _____

b. _____

c. _____

d. _____

e. _____

f. _____

g. _____

h. _____

i. _____

11. Acting as a broker or salesperson without first obtaining a license is a Class _____ misdemeanor, which is punishable by _____

_____

_____

12. The Texas Real Estate Commission consists of how many members?

_____

   What is their term of office?_____

_____

13. What are the requirements in regard to a broker's maintaining an
    office? _____

_____

_____

14. What provisions and/or requirements are made for the discharge or
    termination of employment of a real estate salesperson by a broker?

_____

_____

15. What constitutes the unauthorized practice of law by a licensee?

_____

_____

16. What is the Real Estate Recovery Fund? _____

_____

   What are the dollar limits on claims? _____

_____

   When is it used? _____

17. What are the educational requirements for becoming a real estate
    inspector? _____

_____

_____

   What constitutes a violation of the inspector's license law?

_____

_____

18. What is the composition of the Broker-Lawyer Committee? _____

_____

   What is its purpose? _____

_____

19. Section 7A outlines the requirements for continuing education for
    licensees. What are the requirements for Salesperson Annual
    Education (SAE) in the first three years of licensure? _____

_____

_____

   What are the requirements for Mandatory Continuing Education (MCE)?

_____

_____

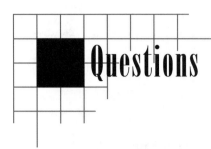

Questions

1. It is unlawful for a person to act in the capacity of or represent himself or herself as a real estate broker without first
    a. registering with the Texas Real Estate Commission.
    b. obtaining a license from the Texas Securities Commission.
    c. obtaining a license from the Texas Real Estate Commission.
    d. obtaining an office in an area zoned commercial.

2. It is unlawful for a person to act as a real estate salesperson unless
    a. such person is acting as the agent of the property owner.
    b. such person is associated with a licensed Texas real estate broker.
    c. the property owner or the prospective buyer gives such person a written statement acknowledging the unlicensed status of such person.
    d. such person is employed in a clerical capacity by a licensed real estate broker.

3. A real estate salesperson may
    a. accept compensation only from the broker under whom the salesperson is or was licensed.
    b. pay a "finder's fee" to anyone who provides a qualified lead.
    c. accept compensation from any licensed real estate broker.
    d. split his commission with any licensed attorney.

4. A real estate broker's license is **NOT** required of a person who
    a. agrees to negotiate a trade for another for a fee.
    b. offers to list real estate for sale.
    c. attempts to negotiate the rental of real estate for another in exchange for one month's rent.
    d. advertises and leases his/her own properties.

5. Persons required to hold a license under the license act include a(n)
    a. on-site manager of an apartment complex.
    b. real estate broker operating out of his or her home.
    c. person employed by a builder in the regular course of his or her business.
    d. lawyer, no matter what state he or she is licensed in.

6. The Texas Real Estate Commission is composed of
    a. nine members elected by the public in the general elections.
    b. six members appointed by the lieutenant governor.
    c. nine real estate brokers appointed by the governor.
    d. nine members, six of whom are brokers and three of whom are lay members, each appointed by the governor with senate approval.

7. The Real Estate Center at Texas A&M University is funded by
    a. $15.00 from brokers and $7.50 from salespersons, to be paid when a license is renewed.
    b. $20.00 from brokers and $17.50 from salespersons, each time a license is issued or renewed.
    c. $10.00 of each application fee for brokers and salespersons.
    d. a fee not to exceed $15.00 from each broker and salesperson annually.

8. An applicant for a Texas real estate salesperson's license must be
    a. at least 18 years old and be a legal Texas resident at the time of filing the application, or be a legally admitted alien.
    b. either 18 years old or have the disabilities of minority removed.
    c. either 18 years of age or be married.
    d. at least 21 years old and be a Texas resident for six months prior to filing the application.

9. Under the inspector licensing laws, the inspector
   a. may use any report form drawn up by the inspection firm or its attorney.
   b. must use a report form prescribed by TREC.
   c. may act as both inspector and real estate salesperson in a transaction.
   d. may act as both inspector and repairperson in a transaction.

10. Which of the following statements is true of payment that is made from the real estate recovery fund on account of a licensee's acts?
    a. The license is revoked automatically and a new one will not be issued until the fund has been reimbursed, with interest.
    b. The license will be revoked if the fund is not reimbursed within six months, with interest.
    c. The license may be revoked if payment is made from the recovery fund.
    d. The license is suspended immediately but will be reissued upon reimbursement of the fund, with interest.

11. Maximum license renewal fees are set by
    a. statute.
    b. the Texas Legislature in January of each year.
    c. the commission in January of each year.
    d. the commission each year based on budgetary needs.

12. A real estate salesperson's license must be
    a. displayed prominently in the broker's office.
    b. retained in a safe place by the licensee.
    c. carried by the licensee at all times.
    d. displayed both in the broker's office and in the licensee's residence.

13. A broker or salesperson who fails to give the statutory title notice to the buyer at or prior to closing
    a. will have the license suspended without reinstatement for two years.
    b. may have the license suspended or revoked and cannot collect a commission on the subject sale.
    c. is required to show cause as to why such disclosure was not made.
    d. must forfeit the entire commission on the subject transaction but in so doing is absolved of any other liability.

14. A licensee who draws an earnest money contract and does not use a form promulgated for that purpose
    a. shall have his or her license revoked or suspended.
    b. may have his or her license revoked or suspended.
    c. is acting in the best interest of the seller if no commission is charged.
    d. may do so provided proper disclosure is made to all parties.

15. A licensee must use the earnest money contract forms, addenda, and leases promulgated by the commission unless
    a. the forms do not fit the circumstances of the transaction.
    b. the agent is offering legal advice to the parties.
    c. an attorney prepares the forms and the property owner requires their use.
    d. the agent secures special permission from TREC.

16. To collect a commission through litigation, the seller's broker is **NOT** required to prove
    a. he or she was duly licensed at the time the services were commenced.
    b. the seller signed a written agreement to pay the fee.
    c. the required title notice was provided to the buyer.
    d. the buyer was aware of the commission amount.

17. The license act provides for
    a. a broker to act as an intermediary solely with the written consent of the buyer.
    b. a minimum of 15 classroom hours as a prerequisite to license renewal every two years after SAE requirements have been met.
    c. definite liability if a licensee fails to disclose that an owner has AIDS.
    d. a ten-year limit within which core courses taken at a college or approved proprietary school can be counted toward license requirements.

8 Interests in Real Estate

Key Terms

allodial system
defeasible fee estate
determinable fee
  estate
easement
easement appurtenant
easement by
  implication
easement by necessity
easement by
  prescription
easement in gross

eminent domain
encroachment
encumbrance
escheat
estate in land
fee simple
fee simple subject to a
  condition subsequent
feudal system
freehold estate
groundwater rights
homestead

license
life estate
littoral rights
police power
prior appropriation
remainder interest
restriction
reversionary interest
right-of-way
riparian rights
taxation

OVERVIEW

Ownership of a parcel of real estate is not necessarily absolute; it is dependent on the type of interest a person holds in the property. For example, one may own real property forever and be able to pass it on to heirs or this ownership may exist only as long as the owner lives. Real estate ownership may be restricted to exist only as long as the owner uses it for one specific purpose; likewise, it may be restricted to exist only as long as the owner *refrains from* using it for a specific purpose. In addition, the interest in real estate a person possesses may be reduced by the interests others possess in the property.

This chapter discusses the various interests in real estate and how they affect ownership and use. Government rights, encumbrances, water rights, and other interests of parties who do not own the property are also addressed.

HISTORICAL BACKGROUND

According to old English common law, the government or king held title to all lands under what was known as the **feudal system** of ownership. Through a series of social reforms in the seventeenth century, however, the feudal system evolved into the **allodial system** of ownership. Land held in the United States is under the allodial system. As firmly established by the Bill of Rights of the U.S. Constitution, property is owned by individual citizens.

GOVERNMENT POWERS

Individual ownership rights are subject to certain powers, or rights, held by federal, state, and local governments. Because they are intended to promote the general welfare of the community, these limitations on the ownership of real estate supersede the individual's rights. Such government rights include the following:

- **Taxation:** Taxation is a charge on real estate to raise funds to meet the public needs of a government (see Chapter 11).
- **Police power:** This is the power vested in a state to establish legislation to preserve order, protect the public health and safety, and promote the general welfare. There is no federal police power—it exists in this manner on a state level only. A state's police power is passed on to municipalities and counties through legislation called *enabling acts.* The use and enjoyment of property is subject to restrictions authorized by such legislation, including environmental protection laws and zoning and building ordinances that regulate the use, size, location, and construction of real estate (see Chapter 23).
- **Eminent domain:** The power of a government or public entity such as a utility or railroad company to take private property for a public use is *eminent domain.* The condemnor determines the location and the amount of land that is needed. However, the condemning entity cannot legally condemn more property than is reasonably required to serve the public use. Public agencies acquire real property *at market value* through direct negotiation and purchase from the owner. If the parties cannot agree on the amount of compensation, the condemnor may begin a *condemnation suit* through which the courts will determine the amount of compensation the landowner will receive.

    Some examples of acquisitions under eminent domain are street-widening projects, highways, public buildings, fire lanes, governmental rights-of-way, and easements. Decision-making power under the right of eminent domain generally is granted by state laws to quasi-public bodies, such as land clearance commissions and public housing or redevelopment authorities, as well as to publicly held companies such as railroads, public utilities, and mining companies.

    There are some limitations on government powers, too. Through the process of inverse condemnation, a landowner is entitled to compensation from the state when a state law or regulation reduces all or a portion of the value of a tract by 25 percent or more.
- **Escheat:** Although escheat actually is not a limitation on ownership, Texas law provides for ownership of real estate to revert, or escheat, to the state when an owner dies and leaves no heirs and no will disposing of his or her real estate. Additionally, if an owner has been absent for seven years and his or her whereabouts are unknown, property will escheat to the state if there are no heirs or will. Escheat occurs only when a property becomes ownerless. Escheated property is managed by the Texas General Land Office, and proceeds from its sale or lease are deposited into the Foundation School Fund.

> The four government powers can be remembered as **PETE**: *P*olice Power, *E*minent Domain, *T*axation and *E*scheat.

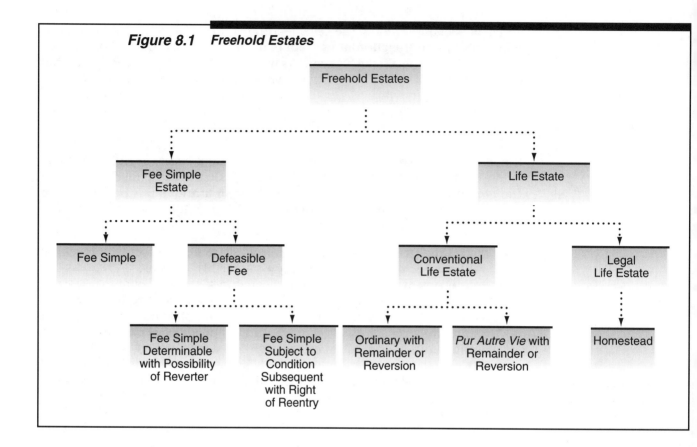

Figure 8.1   Freehold Estates

ESTATES IN LAND

The degree, quantity, nature, and extent of interest that a person has in real property is an **estate in land.** In the United States, estates in land are unique. Our present rights and interests in land are complete and free of state domination (except for the state's right to taxation, police power, and eminent domain, as previously mentioned).

Estates in land are divided into two major classifications: *freehold estates* and *leasehold estates* (those involving tenants). The freehold estates are illustrated in Figure 8.1. Leaseholds will be covered in Chapter 21.

Freehold estates are *estates of indeterminable length,* such as those existing for a lifetime or forever. These include (1) fee simple, (2) defeasible fee estates, (3) conventional life estates, and (4) legal life estates. Fee simple and defeasible fee estates continue for an indefinite period and are inheritable by the heirs of the owner. Life estates terminate upon the death of the person on whose life they are based.

Fee Simple Estate   An estate in **fee simple** is the *highest type of interest in real estate recognized by law.* A fee simple estate is one in which the holder is entitled to all rights incident to the property (complete ownership). There is no time limit on its existence—it is said to run forever. Because this estate is of unlimited duration, on the death of its owner it passes to his or her heirs or as provided in the owner's will. The fee simple estate is subject, however, to the governmental powers previously explained. The terms *fee, fee simple,* and *fee simple absolute* are basically the same. Such an estate can be freely *devised* (passed by a will) to a designated person known as the *devisee.*

Defeasible Fee Estate

A **defeasible fee estate,** also called a *fee simple defeasible* or a *qualified fee,* is an estate in which the holder has a fee simple title that may be divested on the occurrence or nonoccurrence of a specified event. There are two categories of defeasible fee estates: *fee simple determinable* and *fee simple subject to a condition subsequent.*

A **determinable fee estate,** sometimes referred to as a *fee on conditional limitation,* is a defeasible fee estate that may be inherited. However, this estate *will be determined* (come to an end) *immediately on the occurrence of a designated event,* the time of such occurrence being uncertain. In other words, the condition or event that will terminate the estate may be one that is certain to happen, but the time of its happening is uncertain. Such an estate also may be based on an uncertain condition or event.

When a parcel of real estate is conveyed and the deed specifically states that the land is granted so long as it is used for certain purposes (for example, as a schoolhouse or a church), the estate conveyed is a *determinable fee.* The words *so long as, until, while,* or *during* are the key to the creation of this estate. If the specified purpose ceases, title will revert (go back) to the original grantor or his or her heirs or to some specified third person (or such person's heirs). The person to whom such title will revert holds a future, or contingent, interest as long as the determinable fee is in effect. This future interest is called a *possibility of reverter,* and its holder is called a *remainderman.*

FOR EXAMPLE   A grant of land from an owner to her church "so long as the land is used only for religious purposes" is a determinable fee estate. If the church uses the land for a nonreligious purpose, title will revert automatically to the previous owner (or the heirs or successors).

A **fee simple subject to a condition subsequent,** the second type of defeasible fee estate, is similar to a determinable fee in that a grantor conveys a parcel of real estate subject to a condition of ownership, but it differs in the way the estate will terminate on violation of this condition. In a determinable fee, title to the subject property reverts back to the original owner (or his or her heirs) immediately and automatically when the condition of ownership is violated. In a fee simple subject to a condition subsequent, the estate does not automatically end on the occurrence or nonoccurrence of a stipulated condition. The grantor reserves for himself or herself only the right of reentry to the property. The estate does not actually terminate until the grantor goes to court to assert this right. The court orders a return of title to the previous owner, who can recover rent, profits, and damages for the period after the occurrence of the condition subsequent. The following terms are commonly used to establish a fee simple subject to a condition subsequent: *on the condition that, provided that,* or *if.*

FOR EXAMPLE   A grant of land "on the condition that" there be no sales of alcohol on the premises is a fee simple subject to a condition subsequent. If alcohol is sold on the property, the former owner has the right to reacquire full ownership. It will be necessary for the grantor (or the grantor's heirs or successors) to go to court to assert that right, however.

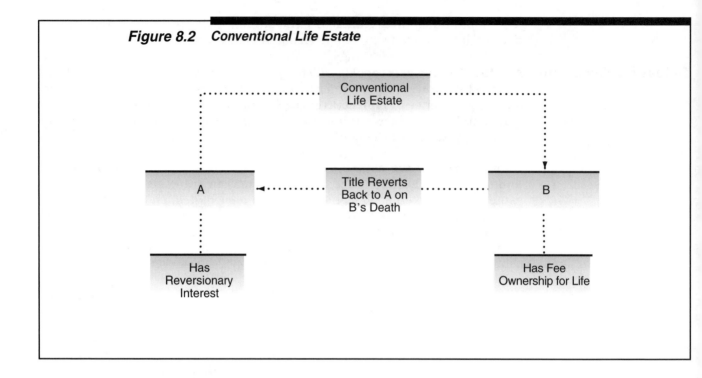

Figure 8.2   **Conventional Life Estate**

Conventional Life Estates

A conventional **life estate** is a freehold estate limited in duration to the life of the owner or the life of some other designated person or persons. Unlike other freehold estates, a life estate is not inheritable. It passes to future owners according to the provisions of the life estate.

A conventional life estate is established by a deed from an owner of a fee simple estate to an individual who is called the *life tenant*. The life tenant has full enjoyment of the ownership for the duration of his or her life. When the life tenant dies, the estate ends and its ownership passes to another designated individual or returns to the previous owner (see Figure 8.2).

FOR EXAMPLE *A, who has fee simple title, conveys a life estate to B for B's lifetime. B is the life tenant. On B's death, the life estate terminates. Subsequent ownership of the property would be determined by the provisions of the deed.*

A *pur autre vie* life estate is created when the grantor conveys property to the life tenant *for the life of another*, and the estate ends with the death of that third party. A pur autre vie life estate may be inherited by the life tenant's heirs, but only until the death of the person against whose life the estate is measured. A life estate pur autre vie is often created for a physically or mentally incapacitated person as an incentive for someone to care for him or her.

FOR EXAMPLE *A, who owns a fee simple estate, conveys a life estate in the property to B as the life tenant for the duration of the life of D, A's elderly relative. B is still the life tenant, but the measuring life is D's. On D's death, the life estate ends. If B should die while D is still alive, B's heirs may inherit the life estate. However, when D dies, the heirs' estate ends.*

Remainder and reversion. When creating a life estate, the original fee simple owner also must consider the future ownership of the property after the death of the life estate owner. The future interest may take one of two forms:

1. **Remainder interest:** When the deed or will that creates the life estate names a third party (or parties) to whom title will pass on the death of the life estate owner, then such third party is said to own the remainder interest or estate. The remainder interest is a nonpossessory estate—a *future* interest.
2. **Reversionary interest:** When the creator of a life estate (the original fee simple owner) does not convey the remainder interest to a third party (or parties), then on the death of the life estate owner full ownership reverts to the original fee simple owner—or if he or she is deceased, to the heirs or devisees set forth in the fee simple owner's will. This interest or estate is called a *reversion.*

Thus, on the death of the life estate owner or other designated person, the holder of the future interest, whether remainder or reversion, will be the owner of a fee simple estate and is commonly called the *remainderman.*

A life tenant is entitled to the rights of ownership. The life tenant can enjoy both possession and the ordinary use and profits arising from ownership, just as if the individual were a fee owner. A life tenant's rights are not absolute, however. He or she can enjoy the rights of the land but cannot encroach on those of the remainderman. For example, a life tenant cannot destroy a building or allow it to deteriorate, and a life tenant cannot remove oil, gas, or minerals without the remainderman's permission. In other words, the life tenant cannot perform any acts that would permanently injure the land or property. In legal terms, this injury is known as *waste.* If waste occurs, those who will eventually own the property can bring legal action against the life tenant for the damages or seek an injunction.

A life estate ownership may be sold, mortgaged, or leased; but the life interest will always terminate on the death of the person against whose life the estate is measured. Therefore, the value of a life estate is considerably less than that of a fee simple estate. If a life estate is mortgaged, a lender generally will require a credit life insurance policy that would pay the loan balance on the death of the person against whose life the estate is measured.

Legal Life Estates

Homestead. Created by the Texas Constitution, **homestead** is a legal life estate in *land that is owned and occupied as the family home.* The purpose of the Texas homestead law is to protect the family against eviction by general creditors and to protect spouses by requiring that both husband and wife join in executing any deed conveying homestead property or in any document creating a voluntary lien on the homestead property. A family can have only one homestead at any one time, and occupancy automatically creates the homestead—no filing is required.

The Texas homestead right is constitutional and therefore *cannot be waived* through any contractual agreement or change in state law. The homestead law includes the following requirements: (1) Every *head of a family* and every *single person* may hold a homestead. (2) The family or householder must occupy or intend to *occupy the premises as a home.* (3) The head of the family or householder must *own or lease the property.* The rights to occupy the homestead and protect it from forced sale continue for the life of the husband and wife and their survivor(s) and for minor children until they reach 18 years of age. If a homestead property is sold, the proceeds of the sale are exempt from creditors for a period of six months after the sale, allowing time for the purchase of another homestead property.

In Texas, a homestead may be either urban or rural but not both. A *rural homestead* is limited to 200 acres for a family and 100 acres for a single person, regardless of the value of the land or improvements on the land; the designated acreage must include the owner's home. An *urban homestead— that is, in a city, town, or village—*is limited to a lot (or contiguous lots) not to exceed ten acres. There is no limit on the value of the improvements on the lot or on any improvements subsequently built. The urban homestead may include both a home and a place of business for the head of the family or for the single householder, provided the total of both homestead claims does not exceed ten acres.

In Practice

Prior to the constitutional amendment passed in November 1999, the urban homestead was limited to one acre. For a complete copy of this bill and others passed during the last four legislative sessions, visit the Texas legislature's web site at www.capitol.state.tx.us.

The homestead may be selected from the separate property of either spouse or from the community property (see Chapter 9). If the homestead is selected from the separate property of a spouse and that spouse dies, the surviving spouse obtains a conditional life estate in that homestead. This can be troublesome if the decedent has children by a prior marriage and they desire to sell the separate property used as the homestead. Unless the surviving spouse leaves the homestead voluntarily or agrees to a settlement, the decedent's children will be unable to sell the property until the surviving spouse dies.

> **Homestead Limits**
> • Urban: 10 acres
> • Rural: 200 acres (family)

Homestead rights in property may be terminated by death, sale of the property, or abandonment. *Abandonment* has been defined as the discontinuance of use of the property coupled with an intention not to use it again as a home; the intention of the householder is a key factor. Sometimes a notice or declaration of abandonment is filed or recorded to confirm the release of homestead.

Homestead protection exemptions. In Texas, the homestead is exempt from forced sale by creditors for payment of most debts. However, there are a few lien rights that have been determined to be foreclosable against Texas homesteads.

> The Texas Residential Property Owners Protection Act of 2001 provides guidelines for the operation of homeowners' associations and protections for homeowners (S.B. 507).

- Taxes on the property.
- Purchase-money mortgages.
- Mechanics' and materialmen's claims for the cost of improvements on the homestead property.
- A homeowners' association assessment lien, if certain filing requirements have been met.
- An owelty lien, including a loan against the homestead to settle property claims in cases of divorce or death.
- Refinance of a lien against a homestead, including a federal tax lien.
- Home equity loans for any purpose, which will be discussed in Chapter 16.

- Reverse annuity mortgages, under which advances against a home's equity are provided to a borrower who is 62 years old or older.
- Conversion and refinance of a personal property lien secured by a manufactured home to a lien on real property, including the refinance of the purchase price of the home and the land and the cost of installing the home on the land (constitutional amendment, 2001).

A valid lien for labor or material on a homestead improvement (constructing new improvements or repairing or renovating existing improvements) must be based on a written contract, consented to by both spouses and acknowledged and signed before the work was performed or the materials delivered. Additional requirements provide that (a) the contract for the work and material must not be signed until five days after loan application; (b) the owner may rescind the contract up to three days after signing; and (c) the contract must be signed at the office of a third-party lender, an attorney, or a title company.

ENCUMBRANCES

A claim, charge, or liability that attaches to and is binding on real estate is an **encumbrance.** It is a right or an interest held by a party who is not the fee owner of the property. An encumbrance is anything that affects the title to or use of the property. An encumbrance may lessen the value or obstruct the use of the property, but it does not necessarily prevent a transfer of title.

Encumbrances may be divided into two general classifications: (1) liens (usually monetary), which affect the title, and (2) encumbrances, which affect the use of the property, such as restrictions, easements, licenses, and encroachments.

Liens
A claim against property that provides security for repayment of a debt or obligation of the property owner is a *lien.* If the obligation is not repaid, the lienholder, or creditor, has the right to have it paid from the proceeds of the sale of the debtor's property unless such property is exempt under the homestead laws. Real estate taxes, mortgages and trust deeds, judgments, and mechanics' liens (for people who have furnished labor or materials in the construction or repair of real estate) are possible liens against an owner's real estate. Liens will be discussed in detail in Chapter 11.

Restrictions
Private agreements placed in the public record that affect the use of land are *deed* **restrictions** *and covenants.* Deed restrictions typically would be imposed by a developer or subdivider to maintain specific standards in a subdivision. They would be listed in the original development plans for the subdivision filed in the public record and included in the seller's deed to the buyer. Restrictive covenants normally cover such things as lot size, building lines, type of architecture, and uses to which the property may be put.

Easements
A right acquired by one party to use the land of another party for a special purpose is an **easement.** Although this is the common definition of an easement, a party also may have an easement right in the air above a parcel of real estate.

Because an easement is a right to *use* land, it is classified as an interest in real estate, but it is not an estate in land. The holder of an easement has

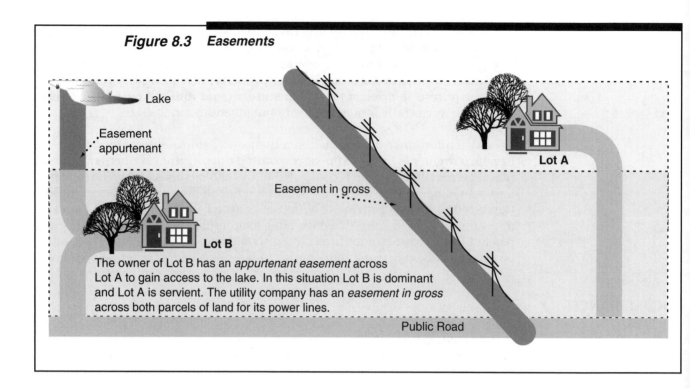

Figure 8.3   Easements

Lake

Easement
appurtenant

Easement in gross

Lot A

Lot B

The owner of Lot B has an *appurtenant easement* across
Lot A to gain access to the lake. In this situation Lot B is dominant
and Lot A is servient. The utility company has an *easement in gross*
across both parcels of land for its power lines.

Public Road

only a right; he or she does not have an estate or ownership interest in the
land over which the easement exists. An easement may be either appurtenant or in gross (see Figure 8.3).

Easement appurtenant. An easement that is *annexed to the ownership
and used for the benefit of another's parcel of land* is an **easement appurtenant.** For example, if *A* and *B* own adjacent properties in a resort community and only *A*'s property borders the lake, *A* may grant *B* a **right-of-way**
across *A*'s property to the beach. A right-of-way is the right acquired
through accepted usage or contract to *pass over* a designated portion of the
property of another.

For an easement appurtenant to exist, there must be two adjacent tracts of
land owned by different parties. The tract over which the access easement
runs is known as the *servient tenement;* the tract that is to benefit from the
easement is known as the *dominant tenement.*

An easement appurtenant is considered part of the dominant tenement; if
the dominant tenement is conveyed to another party, the easement passes
with the title. In legal terms it is said that the easement *runs with the land.*
However, ownership of the land over which an easement actually passes is
retained by the servient tenement. As a general rule, the dominant estate
owner has the duty to maintain the easement.

A *party wall easement,* another example of an easement appurtenant, is an
exterior wall of a building that straddles the boundary line between two
owners' lots, with half of the wall on each lot. Each lot owner owns the half
of the wall that is on his or her lot, each has an easement right in the other
half of the wall for support of his or her building, and each owner must pay
half of the expenses to build and maintain the wall. A written party-wall
agreement should be used to create these easement rights.

Easement in gross. *A mere personal interest* in or right to use the land of another is an **easement in gross.** Such an easement is not appurtenant to any ownership estate in land. Examples of easements in gross are the easement rights a railroad has in its right-of-way or the right-of-way for gas, electricity, and telephone lines. A person employed to acquire or sell easements or rights-of-way for others must be either licensed as a real estate broker or salesperson or registered with TREC. Commercial easements in gross may be assigned or conveyed and may be inherited. However, personal easements in gross usually are not assignable and terminate on the death of the easement owner.

Creating an easement. To create an easement there must be *two separate parties* because it is impossible for the owner of a parcel of property to have an easement over his or her own land. Easements commonly are created by written agreement between the parties establishing the easement right. Easements also may be created by *express grant* in a deed from the owner of the property over which the easement will run or by *express reservation* by the grantor in a deed of conveyance reserving an easement over the sold land. Three other ways that an easement can be created are *easement by necessity, easement by prescription,* and *easement by implication.*

Easement by necessity. When an owner sells part of the land that has no access to a street or public way except over the seller's remaining land, an **easement by necessity** arises because all owners have rights of ingress to and egress from their land—they cannot be landlocked. However, some parcels are already landlocked, and being landlocked does not by itself create a right to an easement by necessity. Two factors must be established through the courts: (1) Both parcels must at one time have been part of a single unit. (2) There must be an absolute necessity for the easement, and the necessity must have existed as of the severance of the two estates. Since 1995, county commissioners have been authorized under certain circumstances to condemn easements for landlocked property owners in rural areas.

Easement by prescription. When the claimant has made use of another's land for a certain period of time as defined by state law, an **easement by prescription** is acquired. This amounts to a limitation on the landowner's use of the property. In Texas, this *prescriptive period* is ten years. The claimant's use must have been continuous, exclusive, and without the owner's approval. Additionally, the use must be visible, open, and notorious, so that the owner readily could learn of it.

Through the concept of *tacking,* a party not in possession of real property for the entire required statutory period may successfully establish a claim of an easement by prescription. Successive periods of continuous and uninterrupted occupation by different parties may be tacked on, or combined, to reach the prescriptive period. To tack on one person's possession to that of another, the parties must be *successors in interest,* such as an ancestor and his or her heir, a landlord and tenant, or a seller and buyer.

FOR EXAMPLE For the past 12 years, *F* has driven his car across *J*'s front yard several times a day to reach his garage from a more comfortable angle. *F* has an easement by prescription.

For 15 years, *L* has driven across *J*'s front yard two or three times a year to reach her property when she's in a hurry. She does not have an easement by prescription because her use was not continuous.

For 6 years, *E* parked his car on *J*'s property, next to *J*'s garage. Five years ago, *E* sold his house to *N*, who continued to park his car next to *J*'s garage. Last year, *N* acquired an easement by prescription through tacking.

Easement by implication. An **easement by implication** arises when the parties' actions may imply that they intend to create an easement. For example, a person acquiring mineral rights on a property also acquires an implied easement to enter the property for the purpose of removing the minerals.

Terminating an easement. Easements may be terminated by any of the following four events:

1. Failure of purpose (when the purpose for which the easement was created no longer exists)
2. Merger (when the owner of either the dominant or the servient tenement becomes the owner of the other)
3. Release (when the dominant estate gives up the right to use the easement)
4. Abandonment (when the dominant estate stops using the easement)

License

A personal privilege to enter the land of another for a specific purpose is a **license.** A license is *not* an estate in land; it is a personal privilege or right of the party to whom it is given. A license differs from an easement in that *it can be terminated or canceled by the licensor* (the person who granted the license). If permission to use another's property is given orally or informally, it generally will be considered to be a license rather than a personal easement in gross. A license ceases on the death of either party and is revoked by the sale of the land by the licensor. Examples of license include permission to park in a neighbor's driveway and the privileges that are granted by the purchase of a ticket for the theater or a sports event.

If a property owner wishes to limit access to the land, he or she may do so by posting a "no trespassing" sign, enclosing the property with a fence, or marking trees or posts with "purple marks." Notice is not given by the "purple marks" unless signs outlining the meaning of the purple marks are placed at each vehicle entry point on the property (Section 30.03, Penal Code).

Encumbrances

- Liens
- Restrictions
- Easements
- Licenses
- Encroachments

Encroachments

When a building (or some portion of it) or a fence or a driveway *illegally extends beyond the land of its owner* and covers some land of an adjoining owner or a street or alley, an **encroachment** occurs. Encroachments usually are disclosed by a physical inspection of the property or by an improvement survey, which shows the location of all improvements located on a property and whether they extend over the lot lines. Note that encroachments usually are not disclosed by the title evidence normally provided in a real estate sale unless a survey is submitted while the examination is being made. If the building on a lot or the limbs of a tree encroach on neighboring land, the neighbor may be able to recover damages or secure removal of the portion that encroaches. Encroachments existing for more than ten years may give rise to easements by prescription.

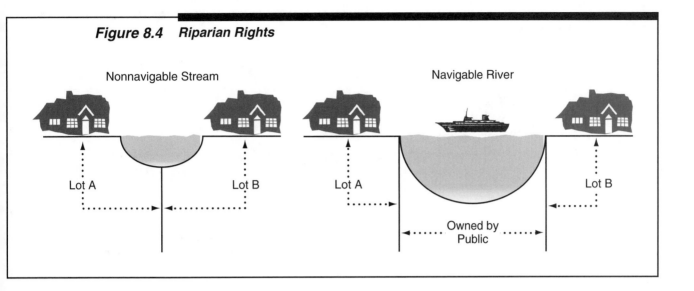

Figure 8.4   Riparian Rights

Nonnavigable Stream

Navigable River

Lot A   Lot B

Lot A   Lot B

Owned by
Public

In Practice   Because an undisclosed encroachment could render a title unmarketable, its existence should be noted in a listing agreement, and the sales contract governing the transaction should be made subject to the existence of the particular disclosed encroachment.

WATER RIGHTS

One of the interests that may attach to the ownership of real estate is the right to use adjacent bodies of water. Because the existence of a water supply directly affects the value of land, it is important that agents understand water rights. The ownership of water and the land adjacent to it is determined by either the doctrines of riparian and littoral rights or the doctrine of prior appropriation.

Riparian Rights Texas subscribes to the common-law doctrines of *riparian rights* and *littoral rights*. **Riparian rights** are granted to owners of land located along the course of a river or stream. The owner has the right to use the water for domestic purposes, provided he or she does not interrupt or alter the flow of the water or contaminate the water. Land patented from the state into private ownership before July 1, 1895, carries riparian rights. Land granted after that date does not and is subject to the Texas prior appropriation doctrine discussed later in this chapter. Since 1969, however, a riparian owner's right to use water has been limited by a state permit for the maximum actual water put to beneficial use without waste.

The law in Texas after 1895 provided that water in every river, stream, lake, canyon, ravine, and watershed is the property of the State of Texas unless a riparian owner can prove otherwise. Furthermore, the State of Texas classifies streams as being *navigable* or *nonnavigable*. An owner of land that borders a nonnavigable waterway may own the land under the water to the exact center of the waterway. Land adjoining navigable rivers usually is owned to the mean vegetation line, with the state holding title to the remaining land (see Figure 8.4). Navigable waters are considered public highways over which the public has an easement or right to travel.

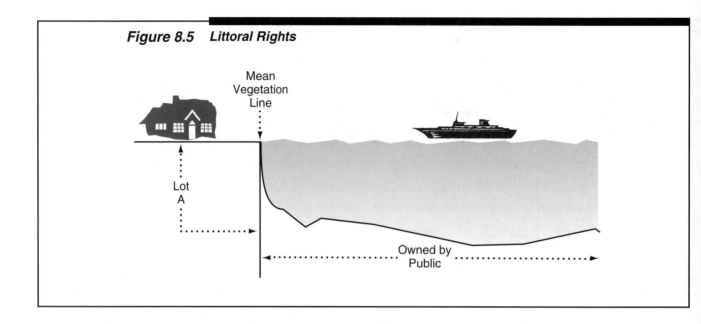

Figure 8.5 Littoral Rights

Mean
Vegetation
Line

Lot
A

Owned by
Public

The terms *navigable* and *nonnavigable* are very significant. In practice, it is sometimes surprising to find that a certain stream is classified as *navigable*. In dealing with property abutting or crossed by a stream, the stream's classification must be determined from an official source. Not only does this question affect boundary lines, it also affects mineral rights and royalties because the State of Texas owns these interests in navigable streams. However, in certain unusual situations, private ownership of the bed of a navigable river is recognized (see *Selkirk v. Standley,* 683 SW 2nd 793, 1985).

Littoral Rights

Closely related to riparian rights are the **littoral rights** of owners whose land borders on closed bodies of water, such as large, navigable lakes, and on oceans. Riparian and littoral rights are appurtenant (attached) to the land and cannot be retained when the property is sold. The right to use the water belongs to whoever owns the bordering land. Owners with littoral rights may enjoy unrestricted use of available water for domestic purposes but own the land adjacent to the water only up to the mean vegetation line (see Figure 8.5). All land below this point is owned by the government or other public authority, such as the Lower Colorado River Authority or various water districts.

*R*iparian refers to *r*ivers, streams and similar waterways. *L*ittoral refers to *l*akes, oceans, and similar bodies of water.

Where land adjoins streams or rivers, an owner is entitled to all *accretions*, increases in the land resulting from the deposit of soil by the natural action of the water. *Alluvion* is the term used for the land so created. Conversely, an owner may lose land through *erosion*, the gradual and imperceptible wearing away of the land caused by flowing water or other natural forces. This is contrasted to *avulsion*, the sudden removal of soil by an act of nature. A riparian owner generally does not lose title to land lost by avulsion—the boundary lines stay the same no matter how much soil is lost—whereas a riparian owner loses title to any land washed away by erosion or the changing of a river's course over a period of time.

Appropriation Rights

Under **prior appropriation,** *the right to use* any water, with the exception of limited domestic use, is controlled by the state rather than by the adjacent landowner. To secure water rights, a person must show a beneficial use for the water, such as crop irrigation, and file for and obtain a permit from the Texas Natural Resource Conservation Commission (TNRCC). The priority of the water right usually is determined by the oldest recorded permit date, subject to the adjudication of these rights by the state. After they are granted, water rights may be perfected through the legal processes prescribed by the state. When the water right is perfected, it generally becomes attached to the land of the person holding the permit. However, issuance of a water permit does not grant access to the water source. All access rights-of-way over the land of another (easements) must be obtained from the property owner.

Groundwater Rights   Groundwater is water under the earth's surface below the saturation point. Texas adheres to the *rule of capture* regarding **groundwater rights.** The rule of capture allows, with some exceptions, a landowner to pump as much groundwater as the landowner chooses—even if the use depletes the water supply and denies an adjoining property owner of a supply of water. However, a landowner may not maliciously take water for the sole purpose of injuring a neighbor nor may the landowner waste it. A landowner is liable for the subsidence (sinking) on another's land if it is caused by the negligent withdrawal of groundwater.

In Practice   Texas water ownership and rights may be very different in the future. Recent court decisions are setting new precedents for both surface-water and groundwater rights. A lawsuit in the Rio Grande Valley resulted in a system of water rights that are not tied to specific tracts of land. They are marketable in their own right and take on the character of real property that can be sold or leased. To take a proactive position toward the future of the water in Texas, Senate Bill 2 (2001) established a Texas Water Advisory Council. Some of the duties of the Council will be to promote surface-water and groundwater projects, to develop water conservation and drought management projects, and to implement approved regional and state water plans.

Open Beach Law   Texas's "open beach" law reserves to the public the perpetual right to use the public beaches. This right has been acquired by "prescription, dedication or presumption," as specified in Sections 61.016 and 61.017, Natural Resources Code. This easement is marked by the extreme seaward boundary of natural vegetation that spreads continuously inland. This means that even though fee simple title to a lot belongs to an individual, no structure is permitted to be built within the easement. In some circumstances, an entire lot can be located within the easement, in which case its owner must share its use with the public. Because of this severe limitation on use, the Natural Resources Code as cited requires that sellers provide to buyers a statutory notice relating to this easement. Failure to do so is, by statute, a violation of the Texas Deceptive Trade Practices Act.

Summary

An estate is the degree, quantity, nature, and extent of interest a person holds in land. The several types of estates are distinguished according to the degree of interest held. Freehold estates are estates of indeterminate length. Nonfreehold estates are those for which the length can be determined accurately. These are called *leasehold estates,* and they concern tenants.

Freehold estates are further divided into estates of inheritance and life estates. Estates of inheritance include fee simple and defeasible fee estates. There are two types of life estates: conventional life estates, which are created by acts of the parties, and legal life estates, which are created by law. Homestead gives rise to the legal life estate in Texas.

Encumbrances against real estate may be in the form of liens, deed restrictions, easements, licenses, and encroachments. A lien is a monetary encumbrance that affects the title. An easement is the right acquired by one person to use another's real estate. Easements are classified as interests in real estate but are not estates in land. Easements appurtenant involve two separately owned tracts. The tract benefited is the dominant tenement; the tract that is subject to the easement is the servient tenement. An easement in gross is a personal right, such as that granted to utility companies to maintain poles, wires, and pipelines.

Easements may be created by agreement, express grant, reservation in a deed, implication, necessity, or prescription. They can be terminated when the purpose of the easement no longer exists, by merger of both interests, by release, or by an intention to abandon the easement.

A license is permission to enter another's property for a specific purpose. A license usually is created orally, is of a temporary nature, and can be revoked.

An encroachment exists when an improvement on one property illegally extends beyond the land of its owner and covers some land of an adjoining owner.

Ownership of land encompasses not only the land itself but also the right to use the water on or adjacent to it. Texas subscribes to the common-law doctrine of riparian rights, which may permit the owner of land adjacent to a nonnavigable stream to hold ownership of the stream to its midpoint. Littoral rights are held by owners of land bordering large lakes and oceans and include rights to the water and ownership of the land up to the mean vegetation line. Water use may be decided by the doctrine of prior appropriation, under which water belongs to the state and is allocated to users who have obtained permits. Texas water law is really a combination of both doctrines. Groundwater ownership adheres to the rule of capture.

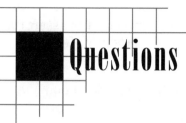

Questions

1. Passage of title of real property to the State of Texas in the absence of heirs is called
   a. police power.
   b. escheat.
   c. prior appropriation.
   d. eminent domain.

2. The right of a government body to take ownership of real estate for public use is called
   a. escheat.
   b. eminent domain.
   c. police power.
   d. caveat emptor.

3. Randy has constructed a fence that extends one foot over his lot line onto the property of a neighbor. The fence is an example of a(n)
   a. license.
   b. encroachment.
   c. easement by necessity.
   d. easement by prescription.

4. A Texas homeowner may be allowed certain protection from judgments of creditors as a result of the state
   a. homestead laws.
   b. police power rights.
   c. lien laws.
   d. equal credit laws.

5. A purchaser of real estate learned that his ownership rights will continue forever and that no other person claims to be the owner or has any ownership control over the property. This person owns a
   a. fee simple interest.
   b. life estate.
   c. determinable fee estate.
   d. defeasible fee estate.

6. Kenneth has permission from Ed to hike on Ed's land during the autumn months. Kenneth has a(n)
   a. easement by necessity.
   b. easement by prescription.
   c. license.
   d. restriction.

7. Which of the following is **NOT** true under the Texas homestead law?
   a. A single person may hold a homestead.
   b. The homestead may be either urban or rural.
   c. The homestead is exempt from forced sale by creditors, with a few exceptions.
   d. Homestead rights in property may be terminated by death of a spouse.

8. Janet Auden owned the fee simple title to a vacant lot adjacent to a hospital and was persuaded to make a gift of the lot to the hospital. She wanted to have some control over its use, so her attorney prepared her deed to convey ownership of the lot to the hospital "as long as it is used for hospital purposes." After completion of the gift, the hospital will own a
   a. fee simple estate.
   b. determinable fee estate.
   c. leasehold estate.
   d. reversionary interest.

9. If the owner of real estate in Texas does not take action to force removal of an encroachment before ten years have passed, then the encroachment may continue through a(n)
   a. easement by necessity.
   b. license.
   c. easement by prescription.
   d. right by prior appropriation.

10. Peter Desmond's driveway is regularly used by his neighbor to reach a garage located on the neighbor's property. Title to the neighbor's real estate includes an easement appurtenant that gives him the driveway right. Desmond's property is called the
    a. leasehold tenement.
    b. license tenement.
    c. dominant tenement.
    d. servient tenement.

11. A father conveys ownership of his residence to his son but reserves for himself a life estate in the residence. The interest the son owns during the father's lifetime is
    a. pur autre vie.
    b. a remainder.
    c. reversionary.
    d. a life tenancy.

12. Which one of the following **BEST** describes a conventional life estate?
    a. An estate conveyed to *A* for the life of *Z*, and on *Z*'s death to *B*
    b. An estate held by *A* and *B* in joint tenancy with right of survivorship
    c. A fee simple estate
    d. An estate in which there is no time limit on its existence

13. In Texas, for which claim may a residence **NOT** be subject to forced sale?
    a. The owner has not paid annual real estate taxes.
    b. Payments for a mortgage used to buy the residence are in arrears.
    c. The owner is three years behind on car payments.
    d. A mechanic has filed a claim for payment for improvements made to the residence.

14. Encumbrances on real estate
    a. may include liens, easements, and deed restrictions.
    b. make it impossible to sell the encumbered property.
    c. cannot affect the transfer of title.
    d. must all be removed before the title can be transferred.

15. If a grantor must go to court to assert the right of reentry to a property after a condition in the deed has been violated, the estate is a
    a. fee simple subject to a condition subsequent.
    b. determinable fee.
    c. fee simple.
    d. terminating estate.

16. Under riparian rights in Texas, Bert Burly, owner of land located along the course of a nonnavigable stream,
    a. may own the land under the water to the exact center of the waterway.
    b. has the right to use the water for any purpose, so long as he does not pollute it.
    c. may dam the stream for irrigation purposes.
    d. has no water rights because the stream is state property.

17. When a homeowner who is entitled by Texas law to a homestead exemption is sued by creditors, the creditors
    a. can have the court sell the home and apply the full proceeds of the sale to the debts.
    b. usually have no right to have the debtor's home sold.
    c. can force the debtor to sell the home to pay them.
    d. can have the sheriff serve an eviction notice.

18. An urban homestead is limited to a lot or lots not to exceed
    a. $10,000 in value.
    b. $100,000 in value.
    c. 1 acre.
    d. 10 acres.

9 How Ownership Is Held

Key Terms

beneficiary	general partnership	severalty
common elements	joint tenancy	syndicate
community property	limited liability	tenancy in common
community property	companies	time-sharing
right of survivorship	limited partnership	trust
condominium	partition	trustee
cooperative	partnership	trustor
co-ownership	right of survivorship	undivided interest
corporation	separate property	

OVERVIEW

Purchasers can consider many different forms of ownership before taking title to a parcel of real estate. The choice of ownership form will affect such matters as the owner's legal right to sell the real estate without the consent of others, the owner's right to choose who will own the property after his or her death, and the rights of creditors in the future. The choice in many cases also will have tax implications, both in terms of a possible gift tax resulting from a present transfer and in terms of future income and estate taxes.

This chapter discusses the many basic forms of real estate ownership available to individuals and business entities. The cooperative and condominium forms of ownership also are addressed.

FORMS OF OWNERSHIP

In Texas, a fee simple estate in land may be held by one owner or by two or more co-owners under one of three forms of ownership: (1) in **severalty,** which means that title is held by one owner; (2) in **co-ownership,** where title is held by two or more persons; or (3) in **trust,** where title is held by a third person for the benefit of another (or others), called the *beneficiary* (or *beneficiaries*).

The form by which property is owned is important to the real estate broker for two reasons: First, *the form of ownership existing when a property is sold determines who must sign the various documents involved* (listing contract, sales contract, and deed). Second, *the purchaser must determine in what form he or she wishes to take title.* For example, if one purchaser is taking title in his or her name alone, it is tenancy in severalty; two or more purchasers may take title as tenants in common or as joint tenants. Married purchasers' choices are governed by state laws. Texas law provides for married couples to own real estate under community property laws.

Forms of ownership are controlled by the laws of the state in which the land is located. When questions about these forms are raised by the parties to a transaction, the real estate broker should recommend that the parties seek legal advice.

OWNERSHIP IN SEVERALTY

When title to real estate is *vested in* (presently owned by) one entity, that person or organization is said to own the property *in severalty.* The root word is *sever,* which means "individually" or "severed from others." (In a similar use of the term, a judgment that reads "jointly and severally" literally means "collectively and individually.") This entity also is referred to as the *sole owner.* Businesses (partnerships, corporations, and limited liability companies) usually hold title to property in severalty with all real and personal property owned by the business. Texas has special laws that affect title held in severalty by either a husband or a wife. These laws are covered later in this chapter in the section entitled "Community Property Rights."

CO-OWNERSHIP

When title to one parcel of real estate is vested in two or more persons or organizations, those parties are said to be *co-owners,* or *concurrent owners,* of the property. Concurrent ownership means that the property is owned by two or more owners at the same time, each sharing in the rights of ownership, possession, and so forth. The forms of co-ownership most commonly recognized in Texas are (1) tenancy in common, (2) joint tenancy, and (3) community property. Each of these has unique legal characteristics and will be discussed separately.

Tenancy in Common   When a parcel of real estate is owned by two or more people as a **tenancy in common,** each of the owners holds an *undivided fractional interest* in the property. A tenancy in common has two important characteristics.

First, the ownership interest of a tenant in common is an **undivided interest;** there is a *unity of possession* among the co-owners. A tenant in common may hold, for example, a one-half or one-third interest in a property, but the physical property is not divided into a specific half or third. The deed creating a tenancy in common may or may not state the fractional interest held by each co-owner. If no fractions are stated and two people hold title to the property as co-owners, each has an undivided one-half interest. Likewise, if five people hold title, each owns an undivided one-fifth interest.

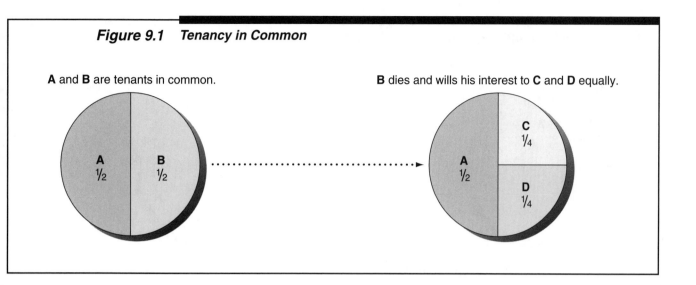

Figure 9.1   Tenancy in Common

A and B are tenants in common.

B dies and wills his interest to C and D equally.

The second important characteristic of a tenancy in common is that *each owner holds his or her undivided interest in severalty* and can sell, convey, mortgage, or transfer that interest *without the consent* of the other co-owners. On the death of a co-owner, his or her undivided interest passes to heirs or devisees (recipients by will) according to the will. If there is no will, this interest passes to the survivors according to the laws of "descent and distribution." The interest of a deceased tenant in common does not pass to another tenant in common unless the surviving co-owner is an heir, devisee, or purchaser (see Figure 9.1). In Texas, the spouse of a married tenant in common generally is required to sign a deed to a purchaser to release his or her rights. Both husband and wife *must* sign the deed to the homestead property, and both usually are required to sign the deed to community property unless one spouse is designated as the manager of such property.

When two or more people acquire title to a parcel of real estate and the deed of conveyance does not stipulate the character of the tenancy created, by operation of law the grantees usually acquire title as tenants in common. However, if the conveyance is made to a husband and wife with no further explanation, this assumption may not apply. In Texas, a conveyance made to a husband and wife creates a community property interest.

Joint Tenancy

Joint tenancy is the ownership of real estate by two or more people with the **right of survivorship** (see Figure 9.2). The right of survivorship is one of the distinguishing characteristics of joint tenancy. As each successive joint tenant dies, the surviving joint tenants acquire the interest of the deceased joint tenant. The last survivor takes title in severalty; on this person's death, the property goes to his or her heirs.

Forms of Co-Ownership

- Tenancy in common
- Joint tenancy
- Community property

Creating joint tenancies. In Texas, the law presumes that if two or more people hold an interest in property, the interest is held as tenants in common. Therefore, a joint tenancy relationship must be created by a written agreement of the joint owners. The written agreement must specifically state the intention to create a joint tenancy, and the grantees in a deed must be identified explicitly as joint tenants. For example, typical wording in a conveyance creating a joint tenancy is "to *A* and *B* as joint tenants and to the

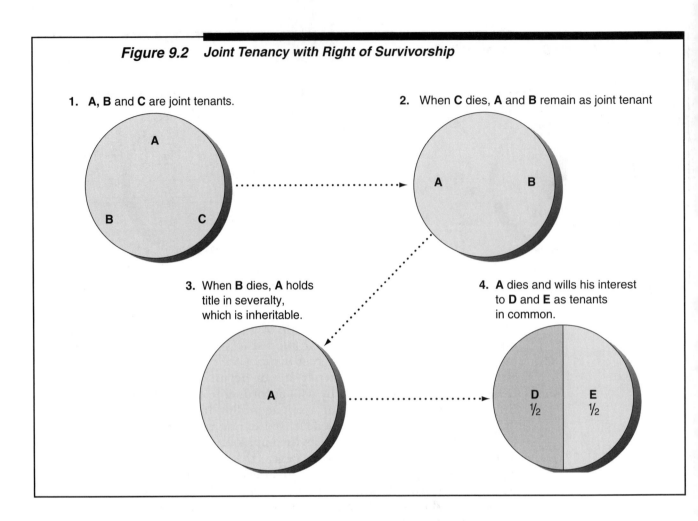

Figure 9.2   Joint Tenancy with Right of Survivorship

1. **A**, **B** and **C** are joint tenants.

2. When **C** dies, **A** and **B** remain as joint tenant

3. When **B** dies, **A** holds title in severalty, which is inheritable.

4. **A** dies and wills his interest to **D** and **E** as tenants in common.

survivor of them, his or her heirs and assigns." Particularly in community real estate, a property owner should consult an attorney before creating a joint tenancy with rights of survivorship in Texas.

A joint tenancy may be used by people who share a business and want the property to pass to the surviving business members to keep the company running. It also may be used when family members want property to pass to remaining immediate family members without its being diluted in various estates.

Common law dictates that four *unities* are required to create a joint tenancy: unity of *time*, unity of *title*, unity of *interest* and unity of *possession*. These four unities are present when title is acquired by *one deed, executed and delivered at one time and conveying equal interests to all the grantees who hold undivided possession of the property as joint tenants.* Because the 1987 legislative change that authorized written joint tenancy agreements did not mention the four unities, the four-unities requirement will have to be judicially determined in Texas, although the courts will probably uphold the common-law principle.

Terminating joint tenancies. A joint tenancy is destroyed when any one of the four essential unities of joint tenancy is terminated. Thus, although a joint tenant is free to convey his or her interest in the jointly held property,

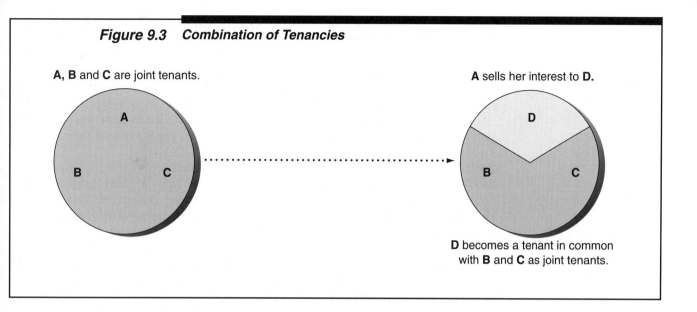

Figure 9.3   *Combination of Tenancies*

A, **B** and **C** are joint tenants.

A

B   C

A sells her interest to **D**.

D

B   C

D becomes a tenant in common
with **B** and **C** as joint tenants.

doing so will destroy the unity of interest and, in turn, the joint tenancy. For example, if *A, B,* and *C* hold title as joint tenants and *A* conveys her interest to *D*, then *D* will own an undivided one-third interest in severalty as a tenant in common with *B* and *C*, who will continue to own their undivided two-thirds interest as joint tenants (see Figure 9.3). Joint tenancies also may be terminated by operation of law, as in bankruptcy or foreclosure sale proceedings.

Termination of Co-Ownership by Partition Suit

Tenants in common or joint tenants who wish to terminate their co-ownership of real estate may file a suit in court to **partition** the land. The right of partition is a legal way to dissolve a co-ownership when the parties do not voluntarily agree to its termination. If the court determines that the land cannot actually be divided into parts *of equal value,* not size, it will order the real estate sold and divide the proceeds of the sale among the co-owners according to their fractional interests.

Community Property Rights

Texas community property laws are based on the concept that a husband and wife, rather than merging into one entity, are equal partners. Thus, any property acquired during a marriage (either formal or common law) is considered to be obtained by mutual effort. The concept of community property originated in Spanish law and has been adopted by only nine states (Arizona, California, Idaho, Louisiana, Nevada, New Mexico, Texas, Washington, and Wisconsin). The states' community property laws vary widely but they all recognize two kinds of property: separate property and community property.

Separate Property

Includes property acquired during marriage

- by gift,
- by inheritance,
- by purchase from separate funds,
- by personal injury settlement, or
- by written contract with a spouse.

Separate property is property owned solely by either spouse before the marriage or acquired by gift or inheritance after the marriage. Such separate property also includes any property purchased with separate funds after the marriage, proceeds from a personal injury settlement, or property separated during marriage by a written contract signed by both spouses (*contractual separate property*). In Texas, any income earned from separate property is community property, unless a signed agreement between the spouses provides that it be separate property. Property classified as sole and separate can be mortgaged or conveyed by the owning spouse without the signature of the nonowning spouse, unless such property is homestead property.

Even though property is separate property, an equitable interest exists for the nonowning spouse if there is (1) an enhancement in the value of the separate property from community property funds during the marriage or (2) community property funds are used to discharge all or part of the debt of the separate property. The equitable interest created is proportionate to the amount of payments made from community funds versus separate funds. Should a marriage terminate, the court is required to impose an equitable lien on community or separate property to secure the equitable interest.

If both spouses agree, all or part of their separate property can be converted to community property. In addition to statutorily prescribed language, the written agreement must identify the property being converted, specify that the property is being converted to community property, and be signed by both spouses.

Community property consists of all other property, real and personal, acquired by either spouse during the marriage. Any conveyance or encumbrance of community property requires the signatures of both spouses, unless one spouse is the manager of that particular piece of community property.

Although community property in Texas may be conveyed by a managing spouse alone, many attorneys and title companies require the signatures of both spouses "pro forma" ("for form") because of the possibility of commingling separate and community property funds. *Homestead rights can be conveyed only by the joint deed of husband and wife,* even if the homestead is the separate property of one spouse and title is held by that one spouse as sole owner.

On the death of one spouse who leaves no will, the survivor inherits all community property, *if* the surviving children and descendants are common to both spouses; otherwise, the surviving spouse retains his or her one-half interest in community property and the other half is distributed to the children of the deceased (see Chapter 17).

A **community property right of survivorship,** which provides for the existence of a community property estate with a right of survivorship, was established in 1987 through a Texas constitutional amendment. The community property right of survivorship differs from a joint tenancy in the parties' responsibilities for debts: in a joint tenancy, each party is liable for the *proportional* share of debts; in community property, both spouses may be jointly and severally liable for *all* community debts.

The agreement to create the community property right of survivorship must (1) be in writing, (2) be signed by both spouses, (3) describe the community property subject to the agreement, and (4) contain a phrase that demonstrates the intent, such as "with right of survivorship" or "will become the property of the survivor." A transfer at death is not a testamentary transfer; probate is eliminated, and all interest in the property goes automatically to the surviving spouse. Revocation of the right of survivorship requires a written agreement signed by both spouses or a written instrument signed by one spouse and delivered to the other spouse.

> In Texas, most property acquired by either spouse during marriage is *community property.* Additionally, income earned from separate property is generally community property.

In Practice   Because neither the community property right of survivorship agreement nor the revocation agreement must be filed in the county clerk's office, community property estates with rights of survivorship are not widely accepted by Texas title insurance companies and mortgage lenders and are, therefore, discouraged.

FOR EXAMPLE

- A deed conveys title to *A* and *B* (who are not a married couple). If the intention of the parties is not stated, ownership as tenants in common is created. If *A* dies, her one-half interest will pass to her heirs or according to her will.
- A deed conveying title one-third to *C* and two-thirds to *D* (who are not a married couple) creates a tenancy in common, with each owner having the fractional interest specified.
- A deed to *H* and *W* as husband and wife creates community property.
- A written joint tenancy agreement and a conveyance of real estate to two people (not husband and wife) by such wording as "to *Y* and *Z*, as joint tenants" may create a joint tenancy ownership. Upon the death of *Y*, title to the property passes to *Z* by right of survivorship.
- *M* and spouse hold title to an undivided one-half as community property, and *S* and spouse hold title to the other undivided one-half with a community property right of survivorship. The relationship among the owners of the two half interests is that of tenants in common. In this example, a combination of interests exists in one parcel of real estate.

TRUSTS

A *trust* is a device by which one person transfers ownership of property to someone else to hold or manage for the benefit of a third party. Perhaps a grandfather wishes to ensure the college education of his granddaughter, so he transfers his oil field into a trust. He instructs the grandchild's mother to use its income to pay for the grandchild's college tuition. In this case, the grandfather is the **trustor**—the person who creates the trust. The grand-daughter is the **beneficiary**—the person who benefits from the trust. The mother is the **trustee**—the party who holds legal title to the trust and is entrusted with carrying out the trustor's instructions regarding the purpose of the trust (see Figure 9.4). The trustee is a *fiduciary*, who acts in confidence or trust and has a special legal relationship with the beneficiary. The trustee's power and authority are limited by the terms of the trust agreement, will or deed in trust. The trustee can be either an individual or a corporation, such as a trust company.

Real estate can be owned under living trusts, testamentary trusts, and land trusts. In addition, real estate may be held by a number of people in a *real estate investment trust (REIT)*, discussed in Chapter 24.

Living and Testamentary Trusts   Property owners may provide for their own financial care and/or that of their families by establishing a trust. Such trusts may be created by agreement during a property owner's lifetime (living or *inter vivos*) or established by will after his or her death (testamentary).

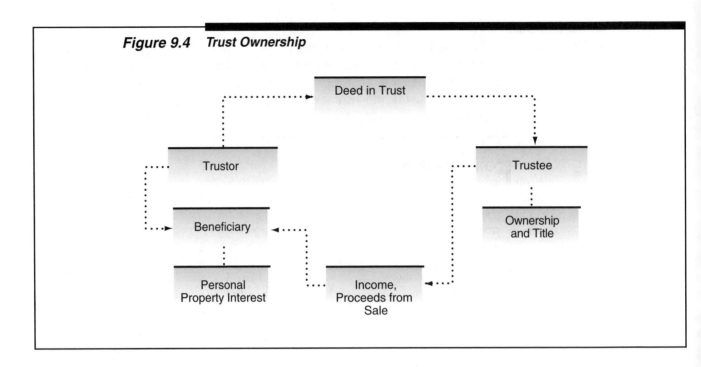

Figure 9.4   Trust Ownership

The person who creates the trust conveys real or personal property to a trustee (often a corporate trustee), with the understanding that the trustee will assume certain duties. These duties may include the care and investment of the trust assets to produce an income. After paying the trust's operating expenses and trustee's fees, the income is paid to or used for the benefit of the beneficiary. The trust may continue for the beneficiary's lifetime, or the assets may be distributed when the beneficiary reaches a certain age or when other conditions are met.

FOR EXAMPLE   Jack, a successful business executive, has a son (Carl) who is a well-known musician. Because Carl has little interest in financial matters, Jack irrevocably transferred certain securities and real estate to XYZ Trust Company to be administered by the company with the income going to Carl for life. On Carl's death, the property is to go into the music scholarship fund at a nearby university.

Land Trusts   Real estate is the only asset in a land trust, and the owner (trustor) is generally the beneficiary. One of the distinguishing characteristics of a land trust is that the *public records do not indicate the beneficiary's identity.* A land trust agreement is executed by the trustor and the trustee. Under this agreement the trustee has a *real property* interest, yet deals with the property only on the beneficiary's written direction. Although the beneficial interest in the trust real estate is considered to be *personal property,* the beneficiary retains management and control of the property and has the right of possession as well as the right to any income or proceeds from its sale.

A land trust generally continues for a definite term, such as 20 years. If the beneficiary does not extend the trust term when it expires, the trustee usually is obligated to sell the real estate and distribute the net proceeds to the beneficiary. Land trusts are normally used for speculative holding purposes and are popular among multiple owners who seek protection against the effects of divorce, judgments, or bankruptcy of the other owners.

OWNERSHIP OF REAL ESTATE BY BUSINESS ORGANIZATIONS

A business entity—for example, a corporation—is an organization that exists independently of the people who are members of the organization. Ownership by a business organization makes it possible for many people to hold an interest in the same parcel of real estate. Investors may be organized to finance a real estate project in various ways. Some methods provide for the real estate to be owned by the entity itself; others provide for direct ownership of the real estate by the investors. Business organizations may be categorized as partnerships, corporations, limited liability companies, or syndicates. The purchase or sale of real estate by any business organization involves complex legal questions, and legal counsel usually is required.

Partnerships   *An association of two or more people who operate a business as co-owners and share in the business's profits and losses* is a **partnership.** There are two kinds of partnerships, general and limited. In a **general partnership** all partners participate to some extent in the operation and management of the business and may be held personally liable for business losses and obligations. A **limited partnership** includes general partners as well as limited partners. The business is run by the general partner or partners. The limited partners do not participate, and each can be held liable for business losses *only* to the extent of his or her investment. However, documents must be filed with the office of the secretary of state of Texas to preserve the limited liability of the respective limited partners. The limited partnership is a popular method of organizing investors in a real estate project.

The agreement between partners may be oral or written, and title may be held in the names of the individual partners (as tenants in common or as joint tenants) or in the name of the partnership (as owners in severalty, according to the provisions of the *Uniform Partnership Act* and the *Uniform Limited Partnership Act).*

FOR EXAMPLE A partnership decides to sell some of its real property holdings. If the property is held by the partners as tenants in common, the signature of each partner will be required. If the property is held in the name of the partnership, only one signature will be required to convey the real estate.

General partnerships are dissolved and must be reorganized if one partner dies, withdraws, or goes bankrupt. In a limited partnership the agreement creating the partnership may provide for the continuation of the organization on the death or withdrawal of one of the partners.

The *Texas Uniform Partnership Act* also provides for the creation of *limited liability partnerships,* which must be registered with the secretary of state. A partner in a registered limited liability partnership is not individually liable for partnership debts and obligations arising from errors, omissions, negligence, incompetence, or malfeasance committed in the course of partnership business by another partner, unless the partner was directly involved or had knowledge of the misconduct at the time of the occurrence.

Corporations   A **corporation** is an artificial person, or legal entity, created under the authority of the laws of the state from which it receives its charter. Because a corporation is a legal entity, real estate ownership by a corporation is an *ownership in severalty.* A corporation is managed and operated by its *board* *of directors.* A corporation's charter sets forth the powers of the corporation, including its right to buy and sell real estate after passage of a resolution to that effect by its board of directors. Some charters permit a corporation to purchase real estate for any purpose; others limit such purchases to land that is needed to fulfill the entity's corporate purpose. A licensee should ask for a copy of the Corporate Resolution authorizing a sale before listing a property. However, a deed signed by an officer of the corporation is prima facie evidence that a resolution of the board of directors was adopted.

As a legal entity, a corporation exists in perpetuity until it is formally dissolved. The death of one of the officers or directors does not affect title to property that is owned by the corporation. Individuals participate, or invest, in a corporation by purchasing stock. Because stock is *personal property,* stockholders do not have a direct ownership interest in real estate owned by a corporation. Each stockholder's liability for the corporation's losses usually is limited to the amount of his or her investment. Officers and directors of corporations have limited liability when they rely on information, opinions, reports, and statements prepared by the corporation or other professional counsel and there is no evidence of fraud.

One of the main disadvantages of corporate ownership of income property is that the profits are subject to double taxation unless it is an S corporation. As a legal entity, a corporation must pay a franchise tax, file an income tax return, and pay tax on profits. In addition, the remaining profits distributed to stockholders as dividends are taxed again as part of the stockholders' individual incomes.

An *S Corporation,* once called a *subchapter S corporation,* allows a business to operate in corporate form but to be treated more like a partnership for tax purposes, avoiding the double taxation feature of corporate ownership. Profits and losses are passed through to each stockholder for reporting on an individual personal tax return. Although there is no limitation on the amount of corporate income for an S corporation, the number of shareholders is limited to 75. Its basic disadvantage is that aggregate losses that may be passed through to individual shareholders may equal only the amount of cash each shareholder paid for the stock plus any loans made to the company.

Limited Liability Companies

The 1991 Texas legislature enacted the *Texas Limited Liability Company Act* as a response to the concern over lawsuits filed against companies, juries' awards of significant sums of money, and attempts to pursue personal liability for officers and directors of corporations. A **limited liability company** (LLC) combines the most attractive features of limited partnerships and corporations. The members of an LLC enjoy the pass-through tax advantages of a partnership and the limited liability offered by a corporate form of ownership. Neither members nor managers are liable for company debts, obligations, or liabilities. In addition, an LLC offers flexible management structures without the complicated requirements of S corporations or the restrictions of limited partnerships. A membership interest is considered to be personal property, and a member has no interest in specific company property. A limited liability company must be registered with the Texas secretary of state.

Syndicates   Generally speaking, a **syndicate** is a *joining together of two or more people or firms to make and operate a real estate investment.* A syndicate is not in itself a legal entity; however, it may be organized into a number of ownership forms, including co-ownership (tenancy in common, joint tenancy), partnership, trust, or corporation. Real estate syndicates and other complex business arrangements will be discussed in Chapter 24.

COOPERATIVE AND CONDOMINIUM OWNERSHIP

During the first half of this century, the nation's population grew rapidly and concentrated in the large urban areas. This population concentration led to multiple-unit housing—highrise apartment buildings in the center city and lowrise apartment complexes in adjoining suburbs. Initially these buildings were occupied by tenants under the traditional rental system. But the urge to "own a part of the land," together with certain tax advantages that accrue to such ownership, gave rise at first to *cooperative* ownership and, more recently, to the *condominium* form of ownership of multiple-unit buildings.

Cooperative Ownership   Under the usual **cooperative** arrangement, title to land and building is held by the cooperative, which is a type of corporation. The building management sets a price for each apartment in the building. Each purchaser of an apartment in the building receives stock in the cooperative when he or she pays the agreed-on price for the apartment. The purchaser then becomes a stockholder of the cooperative and, *by virtue of that stock ownership, receives a proprietary lease* to his or her apartment for the life of the cooperative.

The cooperative building's real estate taxes are assessed against the cooperative as owner. The mortgage is signed by the cooperative, creating one lien on the entire parcel of real estate. Taxes, mortgage interest and principal, and operating and maintenance expenses on the property are shared by the tenants/shareholders in the form of monthly assessments similar to rent.

Thus, even though the cooperative tenants/owners do not actually own an interest in real estate (they own stock, which is *personal property*), for all practical purposes they control the property through their stock ownership and their voice in the management of the cooperative. For example, bylaws may provide that each prospective purchaser of an apartment lease must be approved by an administrative board.

FOR EXAMPLE   In a highly publicized incident, former President Richard Nixon's attempt to move into an exclusive Manhattan cooperative apartment building was blocked by the cooperative's board. In refusing to allow the controversial ex-President to purchase shares, the board cited the unwanted publicity and media attention other tenants would suffer.

One disadvantage of cooperative ownership is the possibility that if enough owners/occupants fail to make prompt payment of their monthly assessments, the cooperative might be forced to default. The entire property could be ordered sold by court order in a foreclosure suit. Such a sale usually would destroy the interests of all occupants/shareholders, even those who paid their assessments regularly. Another disadvantage is that some cooperatives provide that a tenant/owner can sell his or her interest back to the cooperative only at the original purchase price, so that the cooperative gains

Figure 9.5 *Condominium Ownership*

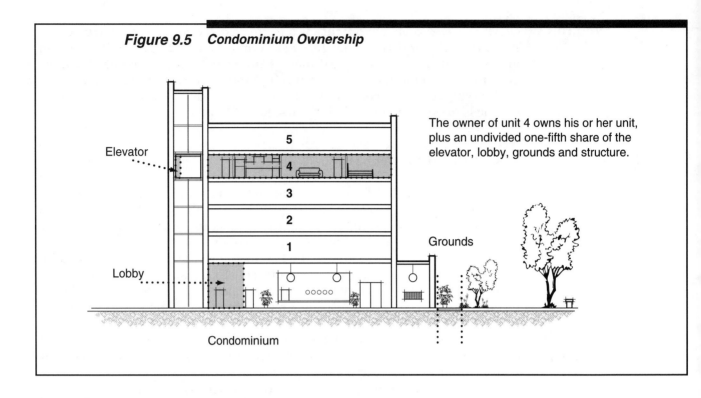

The owner of unit 4 owns his or her unit, plus an undivided one-fifth share of the elevator, lobby, grounds and structure.

Elevator

5
4
3
2
1

Lobby

Grounds

Condominium

Condominium Ownership

The **condominium** form of ownership of apartment buildings has gained increasing popularity in Texas in recent years, particularly in urban areas. A condominium in Texas may be created on lands owned in fee simple or held under a lease. Under the *Texas Uniform Condominium Act,* the owner of each apartment or unit holds a *fee simple title* to his or her unit (sometimes referred to as *owning from carpet to ceiling and paint to paint)* and also a specified share of the indivisible parts of the building and land, known as the **common elements** (see Figure 9.5). The individual unit owners in a condominium own these common elements together as *tenants in common.* The condominium legal documents usually limit this relationship among unit owners in that there is *no right to partition.*

any profits made on the resale. These limitations have diminished the appeal of this form of ownership and resulted in greater preference for the condominium form of ownership.

Ownership of a condominium generally breaks down into four subcategories. These are (1) full ownership of the airspace within the unit bounded by the surfaces of the floors, ceilings, and walls; (2) pro rata ownership of the limited common elements (bearing walls, porch, balcony, patio, stairs, and such that serve only the unit); (3) pro rata ownership of the general common elements (land, foundation, roof, pool, driveways, structure, clubhouse, and other items existing for common use); and (4) pro rata ownership in the homeowners' association.

The condominium form of ownership typically is used for residential buildings. It also is used for commercial property, office buildings, or multiuse buildings that contain offices and shops as well as residential units.

Creation of a condominium. To create a condominium (or *horizontal property regime,* as they are sometimes called), a condominium declaration and a condominium regime plat are recorded in the county in which the real estate is located. The condominium declaration sets out the rights and obligations of each unit owner.

The plat subdivides the land and building into apartment units, describes each apartment by unit number, and assigns a fractional share of the common elements to each unit. Texas law provides that the boundaries of the fee simple units are the interior surfaces of the perimeter walls, floors, and ceilings. In the event of settling, rising or lateral movement, or substantial reconstruction of the building, the law states that the existing physical boundaries shall be conclusively presumed to be the actual boundaries. The total of all units and their respective shares of common elements represents the entire parcel of real estate; the minimum number of units in a condominium is four.

Ownership. After the property is established as a condominium, each unit becomes a separate parcel of real estate that may be dealt with like any other parcel of real property. A condominium unit is *owned in fee simple and may be held by one or more people in any type of ownership or tenancy that is recognized by state law.*

Real estate taxes are assessed and collected on each unit as an individual property. Default in the payment of taxes or a mortgage loan by one unit owner may result in a foreclosure sale of that unit but does not affect the ownership of the other unit owners.

Operation and administration. The condominium property generally is administered by an association of unit owners according to the bylaws set forth in the declaration. The association may be governed by a board of directors or other official entity, it may manage the property on its own, or it may engage a professional property manager to perform this function.

Acting through its board of directors or other officers, the association must enforce any rules it adopts regarding the operation and use of the property. The association is responsible for the maintenance, repair, cleaning, and sanitation of the common elements and structural portions of the property. It also must maintain fire and extended-coverage insurance as well as liability insurance for these portions of the property. Expenses incurred in fulfilling these responsibilities are paid for by the unit owners in the form of monthly *assessments,* collected by the owners' association. (The owner of a condominium unit should obtain separate condominium insurance to provide for injuries or losses sustained within the unit.) Such fees are assessed each unit owner and are due monthly, quarterly, semiannually, or annually, depending on the provisions of the bylaws. If such assessments are not paid, the association usually has the option to seek a court-ordered judgment to have the property sold to cover the outstanding amount. Texas courts have held that this is an enforceable lien against the homestead, provided the condominium documents were filed properly prior to the creation of the homestead.

Termination of condominium ownership. If a condominium declaration provides for termination of condominium ownership, most or all of the unit owners must be party to a revocation agreement filed in the public record in the county where the property is located. All unit owners then would become tenants in common, each owning an undivided interest in the entire property that is equal to the percentage of ownership in the common elements he or she previously held.

Familiarity with the *Texas Uniform Condominium Act* is essential. Condominium ownership should not be confused with townhouse ownership, which typically includes fee simple ownership of the land beneath it. In a condominium interest, the land is held as part of the general common elements.

Time-shared ownership. **Time-sharing** is a variation of condominium ownership that permits multiple purchasers to buy undivided interests in real estate—usually a unit of a resort hotel or development—with a right to use the facility for a fixed or variable time period. Some time-sharing programs allow for a rotation system in which the tenant in common can occupy the unit at different times of the year in different years. Other programs sell only specific months or weeks of the year. For example, 12 individuals could own equal, undivided interests in one condominium unit, with each owner entitled to use the premises for a specified month out of each year. These interests can be either a title interest (fee simple) or merely a right to use (license). In the latter case, such right terminates after a specified time period.

According to *Real Estate Finance Today* (2000), vacation ownership resorts have increased from 500 to 5,000 worldwide in the past 20 years. During that same period, the number of families owning time-shares has jumped from 155,000 to more than 5 million.

Time-sharing enables a person to own a share in a vacation home in a desirable location for a fraction of the cost of full ownership and year-round maintenance. Maintenance and other common expenses are prorated among the unit owners.

Texas law requires the registration of time-share projects, and persons who sell time-share interests must hold a real estate broker's or salesperson's license. A contract to purchase a time-share interest may be canceled before the sixth day after the date a contract is signed; the purchaser cannot waive this right of cancellation. *A statutory notice to the purchaser of this right must be included with the purchase contract.* If the purchaser does not receive a copy of the contract when it is signed, the purchaser may cancel the contract before the sixth day after a copy of the contract is received. A developer or seller who violates the Timeshare Act is guilty of a Class A misdemeanor.

Summary

Sole ownership, or ownership in severalty, indicates that title is held by one person or entity. Title to real estate can be held concurrently by more than one person, called *co-ownership*, in several ways. In Texas, the most common forms of co-ownership are tenancy in common and community property.

Under tenancy in common, each party holds an undivided interest in severalty. An individual owner may sell his or her interest. On the death of an owner, that interest passes to the heirs or according to the will. There are no special requirements to create this interest. When two or more parties hold title to real estate, they will hold title as tenants in common unless there is an expressed intention otherwise. Joint tenancy involves two or more owners with the right of survivorship. The intention of the parties to establish a joint tenancy with right of survivorship must be stated clearly in an agreement between the parties. Historically, joint tenancy has required the four unities of time, title, interest, and possession.

Community property rights pertain only to land owned by husband and wife. Usually the property acquired by joint efforts during the marriage is community property, and one-half is owned by each spouse. Properties acquired by a spouse before the marriage and through bequests, inheritance, gifts, or agreements after the marriage are deemed separate property. Community property is a constitutional right in Texas. The constitution was amended in 1987 to permit a community property right of survivorship, which eliminates probate.

Real estate ownership also may be held in trust. In creating a trust, title to the property is conveyed by a trustor to a trustee under a living trust, a testamentary trust, or a land trust.

Various types of business organizations may own real estate. A corporation is a legal entity and holds title to real estate in severalty. Although a partnership is not, technically speaking, a legal entity (or legal "person") and is not subject to taxation, the Uniform Partnership Act and the Uniform Limited Partnership Act, adopted by Texas and most other states, enable a partnership to own property in the partnership's name. The partnership is a conduit, and tax consequences flow through to the partners. A new entity, the limited liability company, may permit businesses to avoid some unwarranted legal liabilities. A syndicate is an association of two or more people or firms to make an investment in real estate. A syndicate may be organized as a co-ownership, trust, corporation, or partnership.

Cooperative ownership of apartment buildings indicates title in one entity, the cooperative, which must pay taxes, mortgage interest and principal, and all operating expenses. Reimbursement comes from shareholders or beneficiaries through monthly assessments. Shareholders have proprietary, long-term leases to their apartments. Under condominium ownership, each owner holds fee simple title to his or her unit plus a share of the common elements. Each owner receives an individual tax bill and may mortgage the unit as desired. Expenses for operating the building are collected by an owners' association through monthly assessments. Time-sharing, a variation of condominium ownership, enables multiple purchasers to own a share in real estate or at least the right to use it for a certain part of each year.

Questions

1. Which of the following **BEST** describes ownership of a time-share?
   a. The purchaser will own a right to use facilities in a specified project for a specified length of time for a specified number of years.
   b. Two or more purchasers become members of a business organization and receive a proprietary lease to a condominium for the life of the corporation.
   c. Two or more people or firms join together to make and operate a real estate investment.
   d. An association of two or more people operate a business as co-owners and share in the business profits and losses.

2. A parcel of real estate was purchased by Howard Evers and Tinker Chance. The seller's deed received at the closing conveyed the property "to Howard Evers and Tinker Chance" without further explanation. Thus
   a. Evers and Chance are joint tenants.
   b. Evers and Chance are tenants in common.
   c. Evers and Chance hold community property rights.
   d. Evers and Chance hold equal shares in a land trust.

3. Martin, Barton, and Fargo are joint tenants owning a tract of land. Fargo conveys her interest to Vonder. After the conveyance, which relationship exists?
   a. Martin, Barton, and Vonder are joint tenants.
   b. Martin, Barton, and Vonder are all tenants in common.
   c. Martin, Barton, and Fargo are all tenants in common.
   d. Martin and Barton, are joint tenants; Vonder is a tenant in common.

4. The four unities of possession, interest, time, and title are associated with which of the following?
   a. Community property right of survivorship
   b. Ownership in severalty
   c. Tenancy in common
   d. Joint tenancy

5. A purchaser under the cooperative form of ownership receives
   a. a proprietary lease and the right to use the common elements.
   b. ownership of the airspace within the unit and a prorated portion of the common elements.
   c. the advantage of not having ownership interest destroyed by default of other occupants/shareholders.
   d. the statutory right to sell his or her interest back to the cooperative at the current market price.

6. Ownership of real property by one person without the ownership participation of others is called
   a. joint tenancy.
   b. severalty.
   c. solety.
   d. condominium.

7. The term *right of survivorship* is closely associated with a
   a. corporation.
   b. trust.
   c. joint tenancy.
   d. tenancy in common.

8. Because a corporation is a legal entity (an artificial person), real estate owned by it is owned in
   a. joint tenancy.
   b. partnership.
   c. severalty.
   d. survivorship tenancy.

9. Peterson and Kelley purchased a block of apartment buildings in Houston and, for business reasons, took ownership to the real estate under a land trust, as permitted in Texas. Under this ownership arrangement
   a. their identities will not appear in the public records.
   b. they will be unable to control the property or personally participate in the buildings' management.
   c. the land trust exists in perpetuity.
   d. legal title is held by the beneficiaries.

10. In a trust, the person in whom title is vested is called the
    a. trustee.
    b. trustor.
    c. beneficiary.
    d. vestee.

11. A property is owned by Fran, Gwen, and Hal as tenants in common. When Gwen dies, to whom will her interest pass?
    a. Fran and Hal equally
    b. Gwen's heirs
    c. Fran and Hal in joint tenancy
    d. The state, by the law of escheat

12. Alma lives in the elegant Howell Tower. If her possessory interest is evidenced by a proprietary lease, what does she own?
    a. Condominium unit
    b. Cooperative unit
    c. Time-share
    d. Leasehold

13. Gayle Dickins and Sam Swenson are engaged to be married. Any real estate that either owns at the time of marriage will remain that spouse's property in severalty, and property acquired after the wedding belongs to both of them equally. This form of ownership is
    a. joint tenancy.
    b. cooperative.
    c. community property.
    d. tenancy in common.

14. Harold Albertson owns a fee simple title to unit 12 and 4½ percent of the common elements. What does Albertson own?
    a. Cooperative
    b. Condominium
    c. Townhouse
    d. Land trust

15. A legal arrangement whereby title to property is held for the benefit of a beneficiary is a
    a. trust.
    b. limited partnership.
    c. general partnership.
    d. corporation.

16. *A*, *B*, and *C* were co-owners of a parcel of real estate. When *B* died, his interest passed, according to his will, to become part of his estate. Co-owner *B* was a(n)
    a. life tenant.
    b. joint tenant.
    c. tenant in common.
    d. owner in severalty.

17. Under community property, the co-owners
    a. are spouses.
    b. must own equal interests in all real and personal property.
    c. inherit the deceased spouse's one-half interest upon the death of one co-owner.
    d. are joint tenants with right of survivorship.

18. A condominium is created when
    a. the owner or developer files a declaration of condominium and a condominium regime plat in the public record.
    b. a condominium owners' association is established.
    c. all unit owners file documents in the public records asserting their decision.
    d. the construction of the improvements is completed.

19. Which of the following is true of a joint tenancy in Texas?
    a. Spouses may not own community property with right of survivorship.
    b. The conveyance must specifically state the intention to create a joint tenancy.
    c. Joint tenants need not hold an equal interest in the property.
    d. The death of one joint tenant destroys the joint tenancy relationship of other parties.

20. A married couple is selling its homestead, owned as community property. For the deed conveying the property to be valid, who must sign it?
    a. The husband
    b. The wife
    c. Both husband and wife
    d. Only the managing spouse

21. The term *separate property* is **MOST CLOSELY** associated with which of the following?
    a. Joint tenancy
    b. Tenancy in common
    c. Community property
    d. Partnership

22. An advantage for organizing a business as a limited liability company is its
    a. taxation as a corporation.
    b. ability to designate a proportional interest in the real property to each member.
    c. limits on the liability of members for company debts or other obligations.
    d. ability to operate without registering with the state.

10 Legal Descriptions

Key Terms

air lot
base line
bench mark
datum
legal description
metes and bounds
monument

point (place) of
  beginning
principal meridian
range
rectangular survey
  system

section
subdivision plat
township line
township square
township tier

OVERVIEW

People often refer to real estate by its street address, such as "1546 East Main Street." While that is usually enough for the average person to find a particular building, it is not precise enough to be used on documents affecting the ownership of land. Deeds, sales contracts, and other documents require that property be identified by a *legally sufficient* description.

This chapter explains how land is identified and measured and discusses the three forms of legal description used in the United States. Although one of these forms, the rectangular survey system, is not used in Texas, it is discussed because all states surrounding Texas use this method of legal description.

DESCRIBING LAND

One essential element of a valid real estate sales contract or of a deed is an accurate description of the land being conveyed. The real estate must be identifiable from the wording of the deed and with reference to only those documents named in the deed. The courts usually have held that a description of the real estate in question is sufficient from a legal standpoint if a competent surveyor can locate it.

Most state courts accept a street address as being sufficient to locate or identify a parcel of real estate, but not to serve as a legal description. However, the legal description in a deed or mortgage may be followed by the words *commonly known as* and the street address. A **legal description** is an *exact way of describing real estate in a contract, deed, mortgage, or other document that will be accepted by a court of law.*

The average parcel of land has been conveyed and transferred many times in the past. Its description in a deed, mortgage, or other instrument should be the same as that used in the previous instrument of conveyance. Discrepancies, errors, and legal problems can be avoided or minimized if this practice is followed in drawing up subsequent conveyances.

Methods of Describing Real Estate in Texas

Texas Land History   Land in Texas has been under the sovereignty of the king of Spain, the Republic of Mexico, the Republic of Texas and, since 1845, the State of Texas. The original grants from these sovereignties identified the land by metes-and-bounds descriptions, which give the distances and directions of the boundaries of the tract of land.

During the sovereignty of the Republic of Texas (1836-1845) and after the formation of the State of Texas, the term *section* was used to designate a unit of land in surveying and laying out the state's public lands.

Three basic methods are used to describe real estate in the United States: (1) *metes and bounds*, (2) *rectangular (government) survey,* and (3) *recorded subdivision plat* (lot and block). (Figure 10.3 shows which states use metes and bounds and which states use the rectangular survey method for describing property.) A fourth method, usable under limited conditions, is *by reference to a previously recorded document.* However, it is essential with this method that no partial sales or subsequent acquisitions have occurred since the date of the referenced document.

Metes and Bounds   The **metes-and-bounds** description is the oldest type of legal description. In it, the surveyor describes the perimeter of the subject property in terms of *distance, direction,* and *boundaries.* Such a description generally starts at a section corner or some other permanent reference marker established by the original surveyor of record. From this point, the surveyor sets out the distance and direction to reach the **point (place) of beginning** (POB) for a particular parcel. The legal description proceeds around the boundaries of the tract by reference to directions and linear measurements (measured in feet to the nearest one-hundredth of a foot). Surveyors describe direction with reference to north or south, except when the direction is *due* east or *due* west. The bearing of most boundary lines is northbound or southbound, with the variance from due north or due south measured in degrees, minutes, and seconds to the east or west. Due north and due south are 0°; due east and due west are 90° (see Figure 10.1).

In the metes-and-bounds legal description below, the east property boundary heads south at a 15° angle toward the east. After the direction of the boundary line is given, the surveyor states how far in that direction the boundary extends (distance). A metes-and-bounds description always ends at the POB so that the tract being described is fully enclosed (the survey "closes").

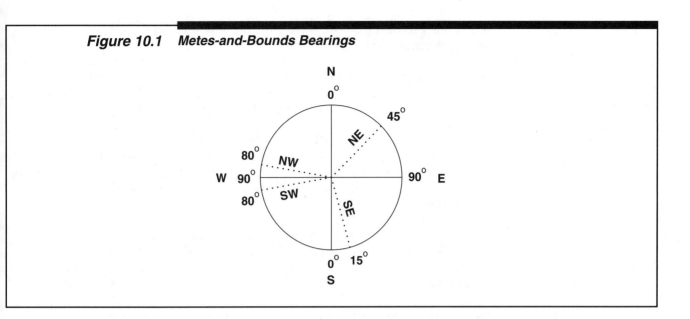

Figure 10.1   **Metes-and-Bounds Bearings**

Monuments are fixed objects used to establish real estate boundaries and placed at the corners or at points where directions change. Monuments are sometimes natural objects, such as trees, streams, or piles of stones; but they are generally man-made objects, such as iron pipes, posts, or stakes. In a metes-and-bounds description, the actual distance between monuments takes precedence over linear measurements set forth in the description if the two measurements differ; measurements often include the words *more or less*. Natural objects generally take precedence over man-made monuments, but court action may be required to resolve discrepancies in monument distances. An example of a metes-and-bounds description of a parcel of land (pictured in Figure 10.2) is

> A possible problem with natural monuments is that they are not necessarily permanent—trees may die, streams may change course, and stones may be moved.

> A tract of land located in Travis County, Texas, described as follows: Beginning at the intersection of the east line of Jones Road and the south line of Skull Drive; thence East along the south line of Skull Drive 200 feet to a 1/2″ rebar; thence South 15° East 216.5 feet, more or less, to the center of Red Skull Creek; thence Northwesterly along the center line of said creek to its intersection with the east line of Jones Road; thence North 105 feet, more or less, along the east line of Jones Road to the place of beginning.

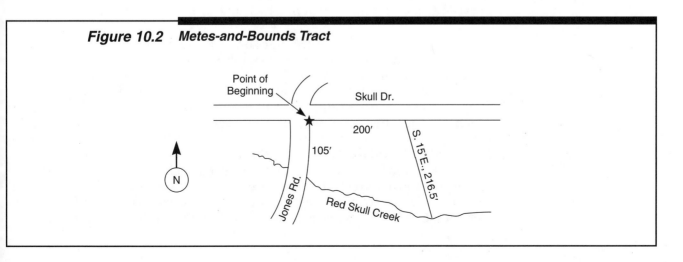

Figure 10.2   **Metes-and-Bounds Tract**

When used to describe property within a town or city, a metes-and-bounds description may begin as follows:

> Beginning at a point on the Southerly side of Kent Street, 100 feet Easterly from the corner formed by the intersection of the Southerly side of Kent Street and the Easterly side of Broadway; thence. . . .

In this description, the POB is given by reference to the corner intersection. *The description must close by returning to the POB.* The reference point of the street intersection is not included in the land described but is the point of beginning, sometimes called the *point of commencement* (POC), of this description.

Metes-and-bounds descriptions are highly complicated and should be handled with extreme care. When they include compass directions of the various lines and concave or convex curved lines, they can be difficult to understand. In such cases, the advice of a surveyor should be sought.

Rectangular (Government) Survey System Used in Other States

The **rectangular survey system,** sometimes called the *government survey method,* was established by Congress in 1785 to standardize the description of land acquired by the federal government. The system is based on sets of two intersecting lines: principal meridians and base lines. The **principal meridians** run north and south, and the **base lines** run east and west. Both are located by reference to degrees of longitude and latitude. Each principal meridian has a name or number and is crossed by a base line. These lines are pictured in Figure 10.3. Each principal meridian and its corresponding base line are used to survey a definite area of land, indicated on the map by boundary lines.

> The directions of township lines and range lines may be easily remembered by thinking of the words this way:
>
> **T**ownship lines
> **R**ange lines

Ranges. The land on either side of a principal meridian is divided into *six-mile-wide strips* by lines that run north and south, parallel to the meridian. These north-south strips of land are called **ranges** and are designated by consecutive numbers east or west of the principal meridian. For example, Range 3 East is a strip of land between 12 and 18 miles east of its principal meridian.

Township tiers. Lines running east and west parallel to the base line and six miles apart are referred to as **township lines** and form *strips* of land called township tiers. These **township tiers** are designated by consecutive numbers north or south of the base line. For instance, the strip of land between 6 and 12 miles north of a base line is Township 2 North.

Township squares. When the horizontal township lines and the vertical range lines intersect, they form **township squares,** which are the basic units of the rectangular survey system. Theoretically, townships are 6 miles square and contain 36 square miles (23,040 acres). Each township is given a legal description by using (1) the designation of the township strip in which the township is located, (2) the designation of the range strip, and (3) the name or number of the principal meridian for that area. For example, a township described as Township 3 North, Range 4 East of the Indian Meridian is in the third strip, or tier, north of the base line. The strip (or tier) designates the township number and direction. The township is also located in the fourth range strip (those running north and south) east of the Indian Meridian. Finally, reference is made to the Indian Meridian because the land

Figure 10.3   Public Land Survey Systems of the United States

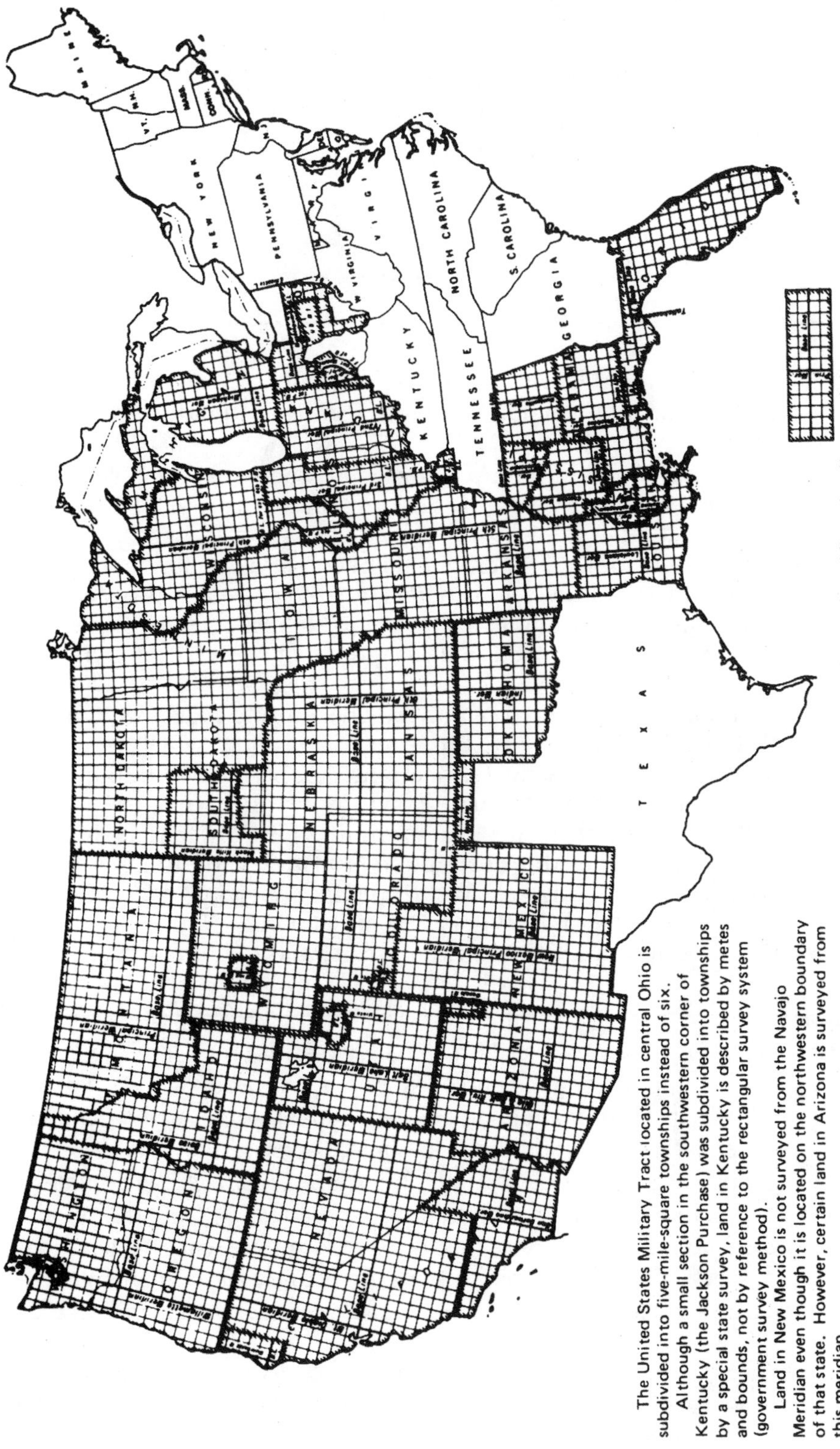

The United States Military Tract located in central Ohio is subdivided into five-mile-square townships instead of six.

Although a small section in the southwestern corner of Kentucky (the Jackson Purchase) was subdivided into townships by a special state survey, land in Kentucky is described by metes and bounds, not by reference to the rectangular survey system (government survey method).

Land in New Mexico is not surveyed from the Navajo Meridian even though it is located on the northwestern boundary of that state. However, certain land in Arizona is surveyed from this meridian.

Alaska uses the rectangular survey system. Its principal meridians are Copper River, Fairbanks, Seward, Umiat, and Kateel River.

Land in Hawaii is surveyed through the metes and bounds method.

Principal meridians, baselines, and the areas they describe are illustrated as shown above.

Areas in which metes and bounds descriptions are used are left blank.

Figure 10.4   *Sections in a Township*

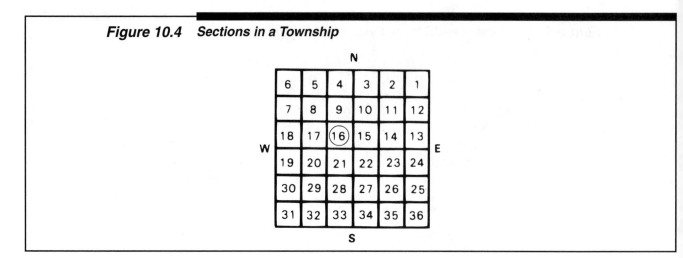

being described is within the boundary of land surveyed from that meridian. This description is abbreviated as *T3N, R4E Indian Meridian.*

Sections. Each township contains 36 **sections.** Each section is one square mile, or 640 acres. Sections are numbered 1 through 36, as shown in Figure 10.4. Section 1 is always in the northeast, or upper-right-hand, corner. By law each section number 16 has been set aside for school purposes and is referred to as a *school section.* The sale or rental proceeds from this land originally were available for township school use. As previously mentioned, the word *section* is used in descriptions of some Texas public land.

Sections (see Figure 10.5) may be divided into halves (320 acres) or quarters (160 acres). The southeast quarter of a section, which is a 160-acre tract, is abbreviated SE¼. Quarter-sections can be divided into quarters or halves, and such parts can be further divided by quarters. The SE¼ of SE¼ of SE¼ of Section 1 would be a 10-acre square in the lower-right-hand corner of Section 1. Sometimes this description is written without the word *of:* SE¼, SE¼, SE¼, Section 1. It is possible to combine portions of a section, such as: NE¼ of SW¼ and N½ of NW¼ of SE¼ of Section 1. Notice that because *and* is in this description, there are two parcels, and the total area is 60 acres.

In Practice   Texas uses the "section" measurement in rural legal descriptions; otherwise, the rectangular survey system is not used in Texas. In some counties (primarily those bordering adjacent states), some legal descriptions have the appearance of using the rectangular survey system. However, the township and range description (TWP 3N, R 3E, Section 22) is completed with "as described by metes and bounds as follows. . . ." In reality, because most sections in Texas are not exactly 1 mile square, each section does not equal exactly 640 acres. Most sections are actually larger than 640 acres.

MATH CONCEPTS   Calculate the number of acres and square feet in the following land description: N½, NW¼, NE¼ of Section 12, Block 9, SS&F Survey, Potter County, Texas.

1 section = 640 acres × ¼ × ¼ × ½ = 20 acres
20 acres × 43,560 square feet per acre = 871,200 square feet

Figure 10.5 *Divisions of a Section*

5,280 Feet

1,320 20 Chains	1,320 80 Rods	2,640 40 Chains 160 Rods			
2,640 W 1/2 of NW 1/4 (80 Acres)	E 1/2 of NW 1/4 (80 Acres)	NE 1/4 (160 Acres)			
1,320 NW 1/4 of SW 1/4 (40 Acres)	NE 1/4 of SW 1/4 (40 Acres)	N 1/2 of NW 1/4 of SE 1/4 (20 Acres) 20 Acres	W 1/2 of NE 1/4 of SE 1/4 20 Acres 1 Furlong	20 Acres	
1,320 SW 1/4 of SW 1/4 (40 Acres) 80 rods	40 Acres 440 Yards	(10 Acres) (10 Acres) 660 Feet 660 Feet	5 Acres 5 Acres	5 Acres Acs. SE 1/4 of SE 1/4 of SE 1/4 10 Acres	5 Acs.

Recorded Subdivision Plat

The third method of land description is by *lot and block number*, referring to a **subdivision plat** placed in the public records of the county where the land is located.

The first step in subdividing land is the preparation of a *subdivision plat* by a licensed surveyor, as illustrated in Figure 10.6. On this plat, the land is divided into blocks and lots, and streets or access roads for public use are indicated. The blocks and lots are assigned numbers or letters. Lot sizes and street details must be indicated completely and must comply with all local ordinances and requirements. When properly signed and approved, the sub-division plat may be recorded in the county in which the land is located; it thereby becomes part of the legal description. In Texas, it is a misdemeanor to describe a tract by lot and block if the subdivision plat has not been recorded in the county where the property is located.

> Texas properties are described
>
> • by metes and bounds *or*
> • by recorded subdivision plat

In describing a lot from a recorded subdivision plat, the lot and block number, name or number of the subdivision, and name of the county and state are used. For example: "Lots 2, 3, and 4 in Block 5 of L. Robinson's Subdivision, City of Austin, Travis County, Texas."

Some subdivided lands are further divided by a later resubdivision. For example, if Alan Roswell bought two full blocks of John Welch's subdivision and resubdivided this land into different-sized lots, then Roswell might convey as follows: "Lot 1 in Block A of Roswell's resubdivision of Blocks 2 and 3 of John Welch's Hometown Subdivision, City of Austin, Travis County, Texas." Cities and counties can specify the smallest tract that may be conveyed without having a subdivision plat prepared, approved, and recorded.

Preparation and Use of a Survey

Legal descriptions should not be changed, altered, or combined without adequate information from a competent authority such as a licensed surveyor or title attorney. To avoid ambiguity, legal descriptions *must* include the name of the county and state in which the land is located.

Figure 10.6   Subdivision Plat Map

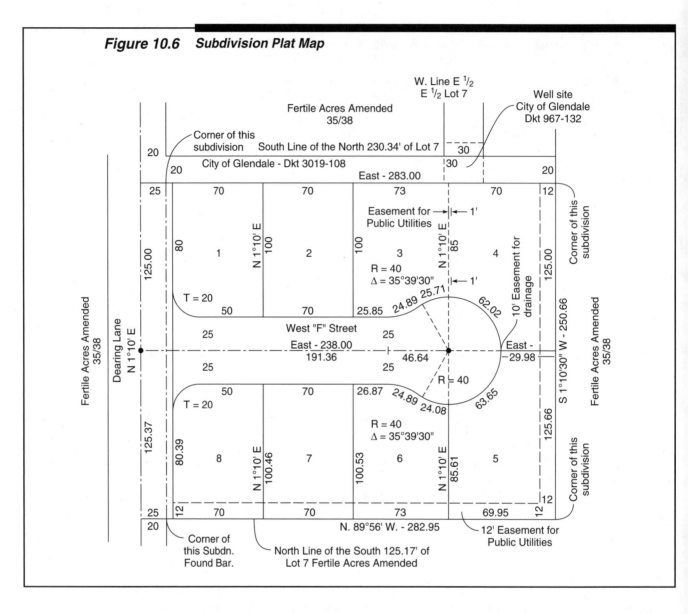

A licensed surveyor is trained and authorized to locate a given parcel of land and to determine its legal description. The surveyor does this by preparing a *survey,* which sets forth the legal description of the property, and a *survey sketch,* which shows the location and dimensions of the parcel. When a survey also shows the location, size, and shape of buildings located on the lot, it is referred to as an *improvement survey.* Surveys are required in many real estate transactions, for example:

- conveying a portion of a given tract of land,
- conveying real estate as security for a mortgage loan,
- showing the location of new construction,
- locating roads and highways, and
- determining the legal description of the land on which a particular building is located.

In Practice   Once they are recorded, legal descriptions affect title to real estate. Therefore, they should be prepared only by a licensed surveyor or a real estate attorney. Real estate licensees who attempt to draft legal descriptions create potential risk for themselves, their clients, and their customers. Further, when entered on a document of conveyance, legal descriptions should be copied with care. For example, a legal description that is worded incorrectly in a sales contract may obligate the seller to convey (or the buyer to purchase) more or less land than intended. Title problems can arise for the buyer when seeking to convey the property at a future date. Even if the contract can be corrected before the sale is closed, the licensee risks losing a commission. In addition, he or she may be held liable for damages suffered by an injured party because of an improperly worded legal description.

MEASURING ELEVATIONS

Just as surface rights must be identified, surveyed, and described, so must rights to the property above the earth's surface. Recall from Chapter 2 that *land* includes the space above the earth's surface. In the same way that land may be measured and divided into parcels, the air itself may be divided. The owner of a parcel of land may subdivide the air above his or her land into **air lots,** which are composed of airspace within specific boundaries located over a parcel of land. This type of description is found in titles to tall buildings located on air rights, generally over railroad tracks, and in legal descriptions for condominiums.

Datum. A point, line, or surface from which elevations are measured or indicated is a **datum.** For the purpose of the United States Geological Survey (USGS), *datum* is defined as the mean sea level at New York harbor. Surveyors would use a datum in determining the height of a structure or establishing the grade of a street.

Virtually all large cities have established a local official datum that is used in place of the USGS datum. For instance, the city of Austin has two local datum markers. One is in a brass plate at the Old Post Office Building at 7th and Lavaca streets. The other is in the relocated Post Office Building at 7th and Colorado streets. These datum points have been used for reference in Austin for all surveys since the early 1900s.

Bench Marks. To aid surveyors, **bench marks,** permanent reference markers such as an iron post or brass plate embedded in a sidewalk, have been established throughout the United States (see Figure 10.7). Cities with local datums also have designated local bench marks, which are given official status when assigned a permanent identifying number. Local bench marks simplify surveyors' work, for each bench mark has its own recognized official elevation, or datum, and measurements may be based on them rather than on the basic bench mark, which may be miles away. For example, the top of a fire hydrant, a local bench mark, has a datum reference of 3,681.58 feet, which serves as a vertical reference point for other surveys in the area.

Figure 10.7   *Bench Mark*

Legal description of a condominium interest. As discussed in Chapter 9, the Texas Uniform Condominium Act requires that a licensed surveyor prepare a condominium regime plat showing the elevations of floor and ceiling surfaces and the boundaries of a condominium apartment with reference to an official datum. A unit's floor, for instance, might be 60 feet above the datum, and its ceiling, 69 feet. Typically, a separate plat is prepared for each floor in the condominium building.

The following is an example of a legal description for a condominium unit that includes a fractional share of the common elements of the building and land:

> UNIT 15 as delineated on survey of the following described parcel of real estate (hereinafter referred to as Development Parcel): The north 99 feet of the west 1/2 of Block 4 (except that part, if any, taken and used for street), in Sutton's Division Number 5, a subdivision out of the City of Austin, Travis County, Texas, according to a plat thereof of record in Book 45, at page 125 of the Plat Records of Travis County, Texas, which survey is attached as Exhibit A to Declaration made by Travis Bank and Trust Company as Trustee under Trust No. 1250, said declaration being of record in Volume 4506 at page 1325 of the Deed Records of Travis County, Texas, together with an undivided 5% interest in said Development Parcel (excepting from said Development Parcel all the property and space comprising all the units thereof as defined and set forth in said Declaration and Survey).

Subsurface rights can be legally described in the same manner as air rights. However, they are measured *below* the datum rather than above it. Subsurface rights are used not only for coal mining, petroleum drilling, and utility line location but also for multistory buildings that have several floors below ground level.

UNDERSTANDING LAND UNITS AND MEASUREMENTS

It is important to know and understand land units and measurements because they are an integral part of legal descriptions. Some commonly used measurements are listed in Table 10.1.

Table 10.1	*Units of Land Measurement*
vara	33⅓ inches (by Texas statute)
rod	16.5 feet; 5.50 yards
chain	66 feet; 4 rods; 100 links
mile	5,280 feet; 1,760 yards; 320 rods
sq. mile	640 acres (5,280 × 5,280 = 27,878,400 ÷ 43,560)
acre	43,560 sq. feet; 160 sq. rods
section	640 acres
sq. foot	144 sq. inches
sq. yard	9 sq. feet
cu. yard	27 cu. feet

MATH CONCEPTS

Land Acquisition Costs. To calculate the cost of purchasing land, use the same unit in which the cost is given. Costs quoted per square foot must be multiplied by the proper number of square feet; costs quoted per acre must be multiplied by the proper number of acres; and so on.

To calculate the cost of a parcel of land of three acres at $1.10 per square foot, convert the acreage to square feet before multiplying:

43,560 square feet per acre × 3 acres = 130,680 square feet
130,680 square feet × $1.10 per square foot = $143,748

To calculate the cost of a parcel of land of 17,500 square feet at $60,000 per acre, convert the cost per acre into the cost per square foot before multiplying by the number of square feet in the parcel:

$60,000 per acre ÷ 43,560 square feet per acre = $1.38 (rounded) per square foot
17,500 square feet × $1.38 per square foot = $24,150

Summary

Documents affecting or conveying interests in real estate must contain an accurate legal description of the property involved. The three methods of describing land used in the United States are (1) metes and bounds, (2) rectangular (government) survey, and (3) recorded subdivision plat.

A legal description is a precise method of identifying a parcel of land. A property's description always should be the same as the one used in previous documents.

Texas is one of the 20 oldest states. These states (and parts of Ohio) use metes-and-bounds descriptions rather than the rectangular survey system. In a metes-and-bounds description, the actual location of monuments takes precedence over the written linear measurement in a document. When property is being described by metes and bounds, the description always must enclose a tract of land; that is, the boundary line must end where it started, at the point of beginning.

Sections are measurements used in some Texas land descriptions. A section consists of 640 acres, more or less, and can be divided into quarter-sections (160 acres), quarter of quarter-sections (40 acres), and so on.

Land in every state can be subdivided into lots and blocks by means of a recorded subdivision plat. An approved subdivision plat is filed for record in the county clerk's office of the county in which the land is located. The plat shows the division into blocks; gives the size, location, and designation of lots; and specifies the location and size of streets to be dedicated to public use. It is possible to resubdivide portions of a previously recorded subdivision. By referring to a subdivision plat, the legal description of a building site in a town or city can be given by lot, block, and subdivision.

The services of licensed surveyors are necessary in the conduct of the real estate business. A survey is the usual method of certifying the legal description of a certain parcel of land. A survey that also shows the location, size, and shape of the buildings located on the lot is referred to as an *improvement survey*. Improvement surveys customarily are required in the purchase of real estate when a mortgage or new construction is involved.

Air lots, condominium descriptions, and other measurements of vertical elevations may be computed from the United States Geological Survey datum, which is the mean sea level in New York harbor. Most large cities have established a local datum or elevation. Brass plates and other bench marks are placed at intervals within an area and reflect official elevations.

Questions

1. What is the legal description of the shaded area in the following diagram?
   a. S½ of the SE¼ of the NE¼
   b. S½ of the SE¼ of the SE¼ of the NE¼
   c. SE¼ of the SE¼ of the NE¼
   d. NE¼ of the SE¼

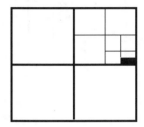

2. The N½ of the SW¼ of a section contains
   a. 40 acres.
   b. 20 acres.
   c. 160 acres.
   d. 80 acres.

3. A street address identifying a parcel of real estate
   a. is generally by itself an adequate legal description.
   b. is not an adequate legal description.
   c. is the same as a recorded plat description.
   d. is the basic monument used in a metes-and-bounds legal description.

4. A system of describing real estate that uses feet, degrees, and natural markers as monuments is
   a. the rectangular survey.
   b. metes and bounds.
   c. the government survey.
   d. the recorded subdivision plat.

5. A portion of airspace within specific boundaries located over a parcel of land is called an
   a. elevated parcel.
   b. vertical description.
   c. air lot.
   d. datum.

6. In a metes-and-bounds description
   a. linear measurements take precedence over the position of monuments.
   b. the measurements given in the recorded description take precedence over the actual distance between monuments.
   c. the actual distance between monuments takes precedence over linear measurements set forth in a description.
   d. man-made monuments take precedence over natural monuments.

7. A map of a subdivision that has been recorded in the office of the county clerk is called a
   a. rectangular survey plat.
   b. metes-and-bounds description.
   c. recorded subdivision plat.
   d. subdivision survey.

8. A survey showing the location, size, and shape of buildings located on a lot, in addition to the legal description, is called a(n)
   a. survey sketch.
   b. improvement survey.
   c. complete and accurate survey.
   d. surveyor's survey.

9. John purchased a one-acre parcel from Sarah for $2.15 per square foot. What was the selling price of the parcel?
   a. $344
   b. $774
   c. $1,376
   d. $93,654

10. If a farm described as "the NW¼ of the SE¼ of Section 10" sold for $1,500 an acre, what would the total sales price be?
    a. $15,000
    b. $30,000
    c. $45,000
    d. $60,000

11. The following metes-and-bounds description contains a major error. After reading the description, check the statement that accurately describes the error.

    A tract of land located in Travis County, Texas, described as follows: Beginning at the intersection of the east line of Jones Road and the south line of Skull Drive; thence East along the south line of Skull Drive 200 feet; thence South 15° East 216.5 feet, more or less, to the center of Red Skull Creek; thence Northwesterly along the center line of said creek to its intersection with the east line of Jones Road; thence North 105 feet, more or less, along the east line of Jones Road.

    a. The use of *more or less* makes the description inadequate.
    b. Red Skull Creek is not a proper monument.
    c. The description is incomplete because it does not enclose a parcel of land by returning to the point of beginning.
    d. The linear measurements between monuments are inaccurate.

12. An acre contains
    a. 160 square feet.
    b. 43,560 square feet.
    c. 640 square feet.
    d. 5,280 square feet.

13. How many acres does the following tract contain?

    Beginning at the NW corner of the SW¼, thence South along the west line to the SW corner of the section, then East along the south line of the section 2,640 feet, more or less, to the SE corner of the said SW¼, then in a straight line to the POB.

    a. 100 acres
    b. 160 acres
    c. 90 acres
    d. 80 acres

14. A *datum* is
    a. used in the description of an air lot.
    b. the basic unit of the rectangular survey system.
    c. the description of a subdivision recorded in the county clerk's office.
    d. a legal description by which property can be definitely located.

15. Which of these shaded areas depicts the NE¼ of the SE¼ of the SW¼?

    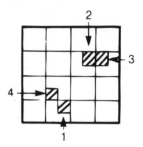

    a. Area 1
    b. Area 2
    c. Area 3
    d. Area 4

16. A *rod* is
    a. 16.5 feet.
    b. a measurement used for rectangular surveys.
    c. 9 square feet.
    d. a measurement used for reporting elevation.

Answer questions 17-19 by referring to the plat map for Mesquite Manor Subdivision, shown in Figure 10.8.

17. Which of the following lots has the most frontage on Adobe Lane?
    a. Lot 10, Block B
    b. Lot 11, Block B
    c. Lot 1, Block A
    d. Lot 2, Block A

18. "Beginning at the intersection of the east line of Goodrich Boulevard and the south line of Adobe Lane and running South along the east line of Goodrich Boulevard a distance of 230 feet; thence East parallel to the north line of Cactus Road a distance of 195 feet; thence Northeasterly on a course N 22° E a distance of 135 feet; and thence Northwesterly along the south line of Adobe Lane to the point of beginning." Which lots are described here?
    a. Lots 13, 14 and 15, Block A
    b. Lots 9, 10 and 11, Block B
    c. Lots 1, 2, 3 and 15, Block A
    d. Lots 7, 8 and 9, Block A

19. How many lots on the plat have easements?
    a. Two
    b. Three
    c. Four
    d. Five

20. A legal description for a parcel of real estate to be conveyed should be prepared by a(n)
    a. developer of the subdivision.
    b. county tax appraiser.
    c. attorney or licensed surveyor.
    d. attorney only.

21. A section of land contains
    a. 160 acres.
    b. 320 acres.
    c. 640 acres.
    d. 43,560 square feet.

22. What is the legal description of the shaded area in the following diagram?

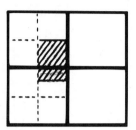

    a. SW¼ of the NE¼ and the N½ of the SE¼ of the SW¼
    b. N½ of the NE¼ of the SW¼ and the SE¼ of the NW¼
    c. SW¼ of the SE¼ of the NW¼ and the N½ of the NE¼ of the SW¼
    d. S½ of the SW¼ of the NE¼ and the NE¼ of the NW¼ of the SE¼

23. Terri purchased 4.5 acres of land for $78,400. An adjoining owner wants to purchase a strip of her land measuring 150 feet by 100 feet. What should this strip cost the adjoining owner if Terri sells it for the same price per square foot she originally paid for it?
    a. $3,000
    b. $6,000
    c. $7,800
    d. $9,400

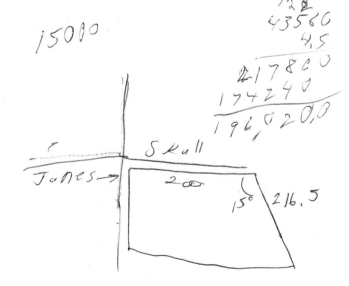

Figure 10.8 ***Plat of Mesquite Manor Subdivision***

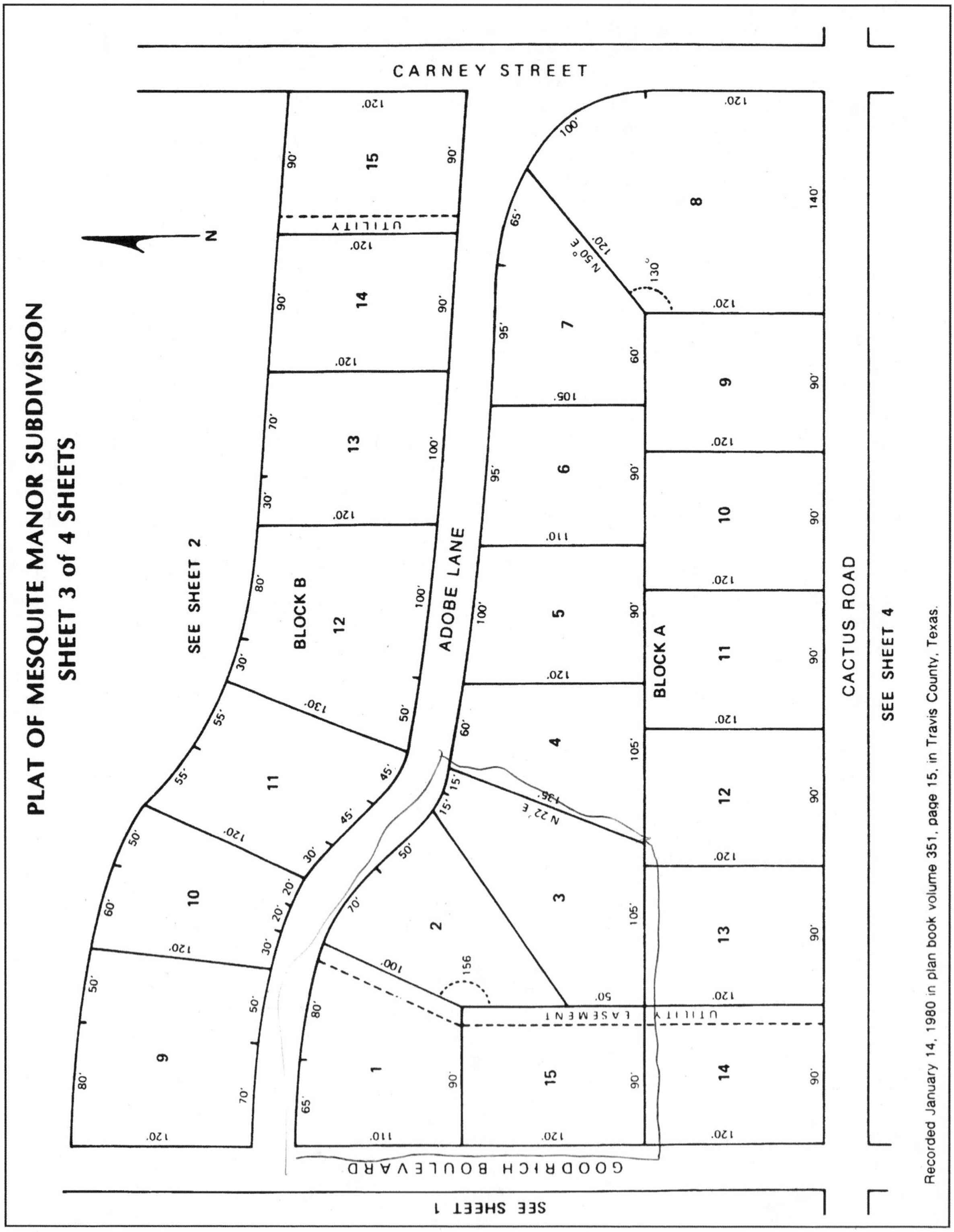

11 Real Estate Taxes and Other Liens

OVERVIEW

As discussed in previous chapters, ownership interest in real estate can be diminished by the interests of others. Specifically, taxing bodies, creditors, and courts can lessen an ownership interest by making a claim—called a *lien*—against property to secure payment of taxes, debts, and other obligations.

This chapter discusses the nature of liens, focusing on real estate tax liens, which affect every owner of real estate. In addition, the chapter describes liens other than taxes that involve real and personal property.

LIENS

A **lien** is a charge against property that provides security for a debt. It is an encumbrance that represents an interest in ownership; it does not constitute ownership in the property. The interest gives the lienholder the right to force the sale of or confiscate the property if the owner defaults on the debt, subject to the Texas homestead laws. Liens distinguish themselves from

Table 11.1 Real Estate Related Liens

	General	Specific	Voluntary	Involuntary
Ad Valorem Real Estate Tax Lien		✓		✓
Special Assessment (Improvement Tax) Lien		✓	✓ or	✓
Mortgage Lien		✓	✓	
Deed of Trust Lien		✓	✓	
Mechanic's Lien		✓		✓
Judgment Lien	✓			✓
Estate Tax Lien	✓			✓
Inheritance Tax Lien	✓			✓
Vendor's Lien		✓		✓
Vendee's Lien		✓		✓
Bail Bond Lien		✓	✓	
Income Tax Lien	✓			✓
Federal Judgment Lien	✓			✓

> All liens are encumbrances, but not all encumbrances are liens.

other encumbrances because, although they attach to the property, they do so because of a debt. Other encumbrances may be physical in nature, such as the easements and encroachments discussed in Chapter 8.

The lien created by a deed of trust is enforced through the power-of-sale provisions in that document, which permit the trustee to sell the subject property for the benefit of the beneficiary. This is a public sale, called a *nonjudicial foreclosure sale,* and is not conducted under the supervision of any court. Otherwise, liens are enforced by court order. A creditor must institute a legal action for the court to sell the real estate in question for full or partial satisfaction of the debt.

> The four ways of creating a lien may be remembered by the acronym **VISE:** *Voluntary, Involuntary, Statutory,* and *Equitable.*

A lien may be voluntary or involuntary. A **voluntary lien** is created by the lienee's action, such as taking out a mortgage loan. An **involuntary lien** is created by law and is either statutory or equitable. A **statutory lien** is created by statute; federal tax liens, ad valorem tax liens, judgment liens, and mechanics' and materialmen's liens are statutory liens. An **equitable lien** arises out of common law. A real estate tax lien, for example, is an involuntary, statutory lien; that is, it is created by statute without any action by the property owner. A vendor's lien or a vendee's lien is an involuntary, equitable lien on the debtor's property.

Liens may be further classified as to the property they affect (see Table 11.1). **General liens** usually affect all of a debtor's property, both real and personal, and include judgments, estate and inheritance taxes, debts of a deceased person, Internal Revenue Service taxes, and federal judgment liens. **Specific liens** usually are secured by a particular parcel of real estate and affect only that property. These include mechanics' liens, mortgages, taxes, special assessments, vendors' liens, vendees' liens, and surety bail bond liens.

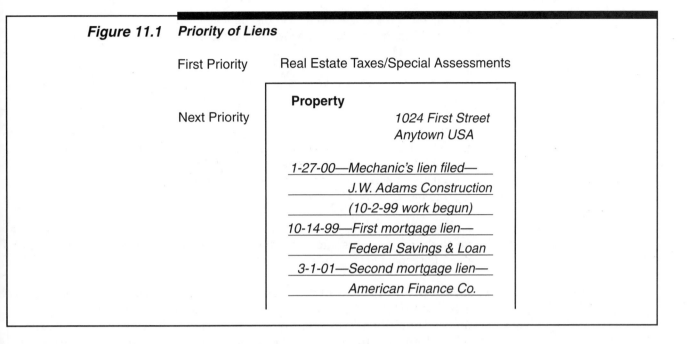

Figure 11.1 Priority of Liens

First Priority   Real Estate Taxes/Special Assessments

Next Priority

Property
1024 First Street
Anytown USA

1-27-00—Mechanic's lien filed—
J.W. Adams Construction
(10-2-99 work begun)
10-14-99—First mortgage lien—
Federal Savings & Loan
3-1-01—Second mortgage lien—
American Finance Co.

Effect of Liens on Title   Although the fee simple estate held by a typical real estate owner can be reduced in value by the lien and encumbrance rights of others, the owner still is free to convey title to a willing purchaser. This purchaser, however, will buy the property subject to any liens and encumbrances of the seller. This is because, after they are properly established, liens will *run with the land*; that is, they will bind successive owners if steps are not taken to clear them.

Remember, specific liens attach to property, not to the property owner. Thus, although a purchaser who buys real estate under a delinquent specific lien is not responsible for payment of the debt secured by the lien, he or she risks losing the property if the creditor takes court action to enforce payment of the lien.

Priority of liens. Real estate taxes and special assessments generally take **priority** over all other liens. This means that if the property goes through a court sale to satisfy unpaid debts or obligations, outstanding real estate taxes and special assessments are the *first* to be paid from the proceeds. The remainder is used to pay other outstanding liens in the order of their priority, which (with the exception of mechanics' liens, discussed later in this chapter) is established from the date of their recording in public records of the county where the property is located (see Figure 11.1). Finally, IRS tax liens do not have a specific priority; as general liens they attach to all property owned by the taxpayer, wherever it may be located.

FOR EXAMPLE Mottley Mansion is sold to satisfy a judgment resulting from a mechanic's lien ($25,000) for work begun on February 7, 2001, subject to a first mortgage lien ($295,000) recorded January 22, 1999, and to this year's outstanding real estate taxes ($10,000). If Mottley Mansion is sold at the foreclosure sale for $390,000, the proceeds of the sale will be distributed in the following order:

1. $10,000 to the taxing bodies for this year's outstanding real estate taxes
2. $295,000 to the mortgage lender for the entire amount of the mortgage loan outstanding as of the date of the sale

3. $25,000 to the creditor named in the judgment lien
4. $60,000 to the foreclosed landowner (the proceeds remaining after paying the first three items)

However, if Mottley Mansion sold for $310,000, the proceeds would be distributed as follows:

1. $10,000 to the taxing bodies for this year's outstanding real estate taxes
2. $295,000 to the mortgage lender for the entire amount of the mortgage loan outstanding as of the date of the sale
3. $5,000 to the creditor named in the judgment lien
4. $0 to the foreclosed landowner

Although the creditor is not repaid in full, this outcome is considered fair because the creditor's interest arose later than the others and the creditor *should have known* about the lien interests ahead of it and of the risk involved.

Subordination agreements are written agreements between lienholders to change the priority of mortgage, judgment, and other liens. For example, a landowner might agree to sell a parcel of land to a developer whose purpose is to build an apartment complex. To allow the developer to obtain a construction loan with a first-lien position, the landowner would have to agree to a subordination agreement and accept a second-lien position if full purchase price for the lot is not received. Priority and recording of liens will be discussed further in Chapter 18, "Title Records."

Tax Liens

As discussed in Chapter 8, ownership of real estate is subject to certain government powers. One of these powers is the right of state and local governments to impose **tax liens** for the support of their governmental functions. Because the location of real estate is permanently fixed, the government can levy taxes with high confidence that the taxes will be collected. The annual taxes levied on real estate usually have priority over other previously recorded liens and may be enforced by the court sale of real estate free of such other liens.

Real estate taxes can be divided into two types: (1) **ad valorem** (according to value) **tax** and (2) **special assessment,** or *improvement tax*. Both taxes are levied against specific parcels of property and automatically become liens on those properties.

Ad Valorem (General) Tax

The ad valorem tax is made up of duties levied on real estate by various governmental agencies and municipalities such as cities, towns, villages, and counties. Other taxing bodies are school districts or boards (including local elementary and high schools, junior and community colleges), drainage districts, hospital districts, water districts, and sanitary districts. Municipal authorities operating recreational preserves such as forest preserves and parks also are authorized by state legislatures to levy real estate taxes. Ad valorem taxes are levied for the *general support or operation* of the government agency authorized to impose the levy. These taxes are called *ad valorem* because the amount of the tax is *calculated on the appraised value of the property being taxed.* Ad valorem taxes are specific, involuntary statutory liens.

Exemptions from Ad Valorem Real Estate Taxes

The Texas Property Tax Code provides for several exemptions (reductions from appraised value) that result in lower taxes. Some general comments are made here, but for specific data consult county, city, and school local tax assessors because the state law permits great latitude in this matter.

Public or nonprofit property. Under Texas law, certain real estate is exempt from taxation. For example, property owned by cities, various municipal organizations (such as schools, parks, playgrounds), the state and federal governments, and religious corporations, hospitals, or educational institutions are tax-exempt, provided they are for charity and nonprofit. Usually, unless the property is used for tax-exempt purposes by the exempted group or organization, it is subject to tax.

Homestead. As discussed in Chapter 8, Texas law also grants a homestead value reduction commonly known as an *exemption*. If a homeowner files a proper *homestead exemption application* form with the appraisal district, the taxable value of his or her residence may be reduced $15,000 for school tax purposes. Other taxing districts also allow for optional homestead tax exemptions of varying amounts.

Senior citizens. School districts are required to grant a $10,000 "over-65 value exemption," commonly called the "age exemption"; other taxing authorities or districts may elect to grant exemptions or tax reductions to property owners over age 65. Once the over-65 exemption is in place, the property has a tax ceiling for calculation of school taxes. The school taxes cannot increase as long as the homeowner lives in the home and does not "improve" the home other than routine maintenance and repairs. Tax freezes are portable to a new residence at a dollar amount proportional to the old tax freeze value.

A person age 65 or older can make tax payments in four equal installments, without penalty or interest, on property owned and occupied as a homestead. If a homeowner age 65 or older owes delinquent taxes on the home he lives in, the homeowner may defer the payment of taxes until he no longer owns or lives in the home. At that time, all taxes and interest at the rate of 8 percent a year become due; no penalties accrue after the tax deferral affidavit is filed, provided that the taxes that were deferred are paid by the 91st day after the deferral expires. The surviving spouse of an individual receiving the over-65 exemption is entitled to that exemption for the same property if the surviving spouse is age 55 or older when the deceased spouse dies. A person qualifies for the over-65 exemption on the 65th birthday; effective January 1, 2000, a person who qualifies for the age exemption after January 1 of a tax year will receive that exemption for the entire year.

Disability status. School districts are required to grant a $10,000 exemption to persons having a physical or other recognized disability; it is optional for other taxing authorities. The taxpayer may be required to provide documentation of disability. A taxpayer cannot obtain both the senior citizen's exemption and the disability exemption at the same time. Additional tax exemptions accrue to a disabled Texas veteran or the surviving spouse or child of a disabled veteran. Persons with disability status and persons whose property was affected by a government-declared disaster may pay taxes in four installments.

Agricultural Valuations

Alternate methods of valuation are available for property that is used for agriculture. They are productivity valuations rather than market valuations. A property owner must apply for the special valuations and qualify by meeting the conditions in the paragraphs below.

Agricultural. Article 8, Section 1-d, of the Texas Constitution provides for a special valuation for land that qualifies for appraisal as agricultural property. For this special valuation, agriculture must be the primary source of income. Such property is appraised based on its agricultural value rather than its market value. If the property is sold or its use is changed, the land is subject to a maximum three-year rollback lien to recover the difference between taxes based on the special valuation and taxes at market value plus interest at the rate for delinquent taxes for each year. This method is seldom used in Texas compared with 1-d-1.

Open space. Article 8, Section 1-d-1, of the Texas constitution provides for special valuation through the "open space" provision. This is easier to qualify for than the agricultural special valuation, although except for timberland, both relate to the same type of property. For this special valuation, the primary source of income does not have to be farming. If the use of the subject property is changed, the land is subject to a maximum five-year tax rollback lien to recover the difference between taxes based on the special valuation and taxes at market value plus interest at 7 percent for each year. The owner who changes the use of the land is responsible for the rollback tax.

In Practice

The real estate licensee must determine from official sources the basis for the ad valorem taxes. For example, taxes assessed against the subject property may be substantially less than normal because of the benefit of a particular tax exemption. However, the new owner may not qualify for a continuation of the exemption. A licensee who fails to determine this status might incur considerable liability from a surprised—and disgruntled—buyer.

Tax Valuation

Real estate is valued, or appraised, for tax purposes by appraisal districts in each county. The land must be appraised separately from the building. Texas state law requires that real property be appraised at its true, or market, value. Texas law provides for property to be reappraised *at least* every three years. The increase in appraised value of residential property on which a homestead exemption has been filed is capped at a maximum of 10 percent a year. This is cumulative since the last reappraisal. Appraisal districts must maintain both the market value and capped value in their records.

The district appraiser sets the valuation of each parcel of property within the county at 100 percent of its market value. The various tax assessors (such as county, city, school, hospital district, water district, and so forth) then assess, or levy, taxes on property lying within their district based on two factors: (1) the taxable value within the district and (2) the budgeted expense requirements of that specific district. A "tax rate" then is determined, such as "55 cents per $100 of appraised value," and the property owner is assessed accordingly as further explained on the next page.

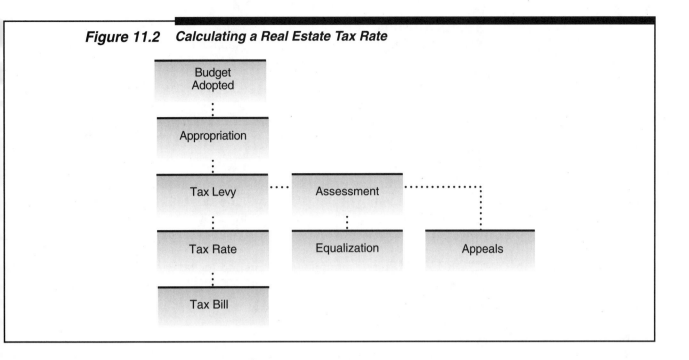

Figure 11.2 **Calculating a Real Estate Tax Rate**

Property owners who claim that errors were made in appraising their property may present their objections and supporting documentation to the district appraiser's office for review. If the property owner is not satisfied with the determination of the appraiser's office, the claim may be presented to a local **appraisal review board.** Protests or appeals ultimately may be taken to court. Such cases generally involve a proceeding whereby the court reviews the certified records of the tax officials.

Tax rate calculation. The process of arriving at a real estate tax rate begins with the *adoption of a budget* by each county, city, school board, or other taxing district (see Figure 11.2). Each budget covers the financial requirements of the taxing body for the coming fiscal year, which may be the January-to-December calendar year or some other 12-month period designated by statute. The budget must include an estimate of all expenditures for the year and indicate the amount of income expected from all fees, revenue sharing, and other sources. The net amount remaining to be raised from real estate taxes is determined from these figures.

The next step is *appropriation,* the action taken by each taxing body that authorizes the expenditure of funds and provides for the sources of such monies. Appropriation generally involves the adoption of an ordinance or the passage of a law setting forth the specifics of the proposed taxation.

The amount to be raised from the general real estate tax then is imposed on property owners through a *tax levy* (the formal action taken to impose the tax) by a vote of the taxing district's governing body.

The *tax rate* for each individual taxing body is computed separately. To arrive at a tax rate, the total monies needed for the coming fiscal year are divided by the total appraisal of all applicable real and personal property located within the jurisdiction of the taxing body.

FOR EXAMPLE A taxing district's budget indicates that $275,000 must be raised from tax revenues, and the appraisal roll (appraiser's record) of all taxable real and personal property within this district equals $15,000,000. The tax is computed thus:

$$\$275,000 \div \$15,000,000 = \$.01833$$

The tax rate is expressed in dollars per $100 of value. Therefore, the tax rate computed in the foregoing example would be expressed as $1.833 per $100 of assessed value.

Tax bills. A property owner's tax bill is computed by applying the tax rate to the taxable value of the property. One tax bill may incorporate all real estate taxes levied by the various taxing districts. In some areas, separate bills are prepared by each taxing district.

FOR EXAMPLE If a property is appraised for tax purposes at $90,000 with no exemptions and a tax rate of $1.833 per $100, the tax will be computed as follows:

$$(\$90,000 \div \$100) \times \$1.833 = \$1,649.70$$

In Texas, the general real estate tax becomes a lien on January 1 of the year of the tax. The delinquent date for annual taxes is February 1 of the year following the tax year (1999 taxes are delinquent as of February 1, 2000). Penalties and interest are added after the delinquent date. Discounts may be allowed by local option as follows for taxes paid in advance: 3 percent discount if paid by October 31, 2 percent if paid by November 30, and 1 percent if paid by December 31. By state law, the annual tax is payable on or after October 1, but provision may be made at the option of the taxing district or governing body that when half of the tax is paid by November 30, the balance may be paid without penalty on or before June 30 of the next year. Any balance not paid by June 30 is subject to a 12 percent penalty plus 1 percent interest per month. A tax collector may accept payment for taxes by credit card and include a fee for processing the payment, not to exceed 5 percent of the amount being paid.

In Practice   Effective August 30, 1999, H.B. 51 authorizes school boards to adopt policies permitting (1) the over-65 taxpayer to perform service for the district at minimum wage instead of paying school property taxes; (2) individuals to perform teaching services in high school or junior high school in lieu of taxes; (3) companies to have their employees perform teaching services in high school or junior high school in lieu of taxes. The procedures for performing services in lieu of paying taxes are outlined in the statute.

Enforcement of Tax Liens   To be enforceable, real estate taxes must be valid; that is, they must be (1) levied properly, (2) used for a legal purpose, and (3) applied equitably to all affected property. Tax liens generally are given priority over all other liens against a property. In Texas, real estate can be sold only after the foreclosure of the tax lien in a court of competent jurisdiction.

Tax sales usually are held pursuant to a published notice after a court has rendered a judgment for the tax, penalties, and interest and ordered the

A mortgage foreclosure does not clear tax liens on the property.

property to be sold. The sale is conducted by the sheriff or constable at a public sale. The purchaser must pay at least the amount of delinquent tax, penalty, interest, and costs (the aggregate judgment amount) or the appraised value of the property, whichever is less. Under a 1997 change in the law, all unpaid taxes, including the current year's taxes prorated to the date of sale, can be recovered from the proceeds of the sale with all penalty and interest accrued to the date of the sale.

Under Texas law, the successful bidder receives a deed from the sheriff or constable conducting the sale. The deed conveys all right, title, and interest of the defaulted taxpayer, including the defendant's right to the use and possession of the property. The deed, however, is subject to the property owner's right of redemption. Under what is known as an **equitable right of redemption,** the delinquent taxpayer can redeem the property at any time *prior* to the tax sale by paying the delinquent taxes plus interest and charges (court costs or attorney fees). In addition to the equitable right of redemption, Texas law provides for a period of redemption *after* the tax sale during which the defaulted owner may redeem the property by paying the amount paid at the tax sale, plus interest and other charges. This is known as the **statutory right of redemption.** Under this redemption right, if the property is the residence homestead of the defaulted taxpayer or if it is designated for agricultural use, the owner may redeem the property within two years after the sheriff's deed was recorded (for other properties, the redemption period is limited to six months).

The cost of the statutory right of redemption is an additional 25 percent of the purchase price if redeemed during the first year and 50 percent if redeemed during the second year. The 1997 legislature has limited this additional cost to redemptions from third-party purchasers. Taxing entities are no longer entitled to receive the additional 25 or 50 percent.

As mentioned above, only the right, title, and interest of the defaulted taxpayer are conveyed to the purchaser at a tax sale. Property that is not sold at a tax sale due to a lack of bidders is "struck off," or sold to a taxing unit that is a party to the judgment. This taxing unit takes title to the property (as trustee) for the use and benefit of itself and all other taxing units that established tax liens in the suit. One or more of the taxing units may use the property for its own benefit; if the trustee taxing unit does not resell the property within six months after the expiration of the redemption period, any taxing unit that is entitled to receive proceeds from the sale may force a public sale of the property. A 1997 amendment allows for a private sale of the property but only by the trustee taxing unit.

In Practice   In Texas, property that is a residence homestead or designated for agricultural use may be redeemed during the two-year period following a sale of land because of a tax lien. A property sold after foreclosure of a homeowners' association lien may be redeemed not later than 180 days after written notice of the sale is mailed to the owner (S.B. 507, 2001). There is no right of redemption if the foreclosure sale is made pursuant to a nonjudicial deed-of-trust enforcement of a mortgage loan or a judicial enforcement of a vendor's lien.

Special Assessment (Improvement Tax)

Special assessments are taxes levied on real estate that require that property owners pay for improvements that benefit the real estate they own. These taxes often are levied to pay for such improvements as streets, alleys, street lighting, curbs, and similar items and are enforced in the same manner as general real estate taxes. The following steps are taken to achieve the *specific improvements:*

1. Property owners may petition for an improvement; or a proper legislative authority, such as the city council or board of trustees, may initiate the proposal for an improvement.
2. Notices are given to the owners of the property affected, and hearings are held.
3. After the preliminary legal steps are taken, the legislative body authorized by statute to act in such cases adopts an *ordinance* that details the nature of the improvement, its cost, and a description of the area to be assessed.
4. The **assessment roll** spreads the assessment over the various parcels of real estate that will benefit, and hearings are held to *confirm the roll.* The amount of the assessment for each parcel usually is determined by one of the two following criteria: (1) estimated benefit each tract will receive by reason of the assessment or (2) front footage. Regardless of the basis used, the assessment usually varies from parcel to parcel because all will not benefit equally from the improvement.
5. The assessment becomes a lien on the land assessed.
6. Once the improvement is completed, a *warrant* is issued by the proper authority, often the clerk of the court that approved the roll. This warrant gives the local collector the authority to issue special assessment bills and begin collection.

> A homestead may not be subjected to a forced sale for nonpayment of a public improvement district assessment, according to a Texas Attorney General Opinion (June 2001).

In Texas, an assessment becomes a *lien* following the confirmation of the roll. As a rule, special assessments are due and payable in equal annual installments over a period of five to ten years. Interest is charged each property owner on the total amount of his or her assessment. The first installment generally becomes due during the year following confirmation. The bill will include yearly interest on the entire assessment. As subsequent installments are billed in following years, each bill will include a year's interest on the unpaid balance. Property owners have the right to prepay any or all installments and thus avoid the interest charges.

In Practice   Whereas real property taxes on a personal residence are deductible items for income tax purposes, special assessment taxes are not. The annual interest charged in connection with special real estate assessments is deductible, however.

Utility District Tax

If property being sold is located within a utility district, Section 50.301 of the Texas Water Code provides for the seller to furnish to the buyer a statutory notice relating to the bonded indebtedness and the tax rate of the district. A utility district is created by a developer of property not within the boundaries of a town or city. The district furnishes water and sewer services to property owners within its boundaries. These utilities are paid for by bonds, and the bonds are retired by the levying of taxes. Unpaid taxes can result in the creation of liens. If the seller fails to provide the required notice to the buyer, the statute provides remedies to an injured buyer, including rescission of the contract prior to closing or a set-aside for damages of up to $5,000 after closing. The licensee should obtain the specific form for each district from the county clerk or the district itself for *each* transaction. To reduce potential liability risk for a real estate licensee, an agent is permitted to use water district taxes as of January 1 of that year; information provided by the water district is deemed to be conclusive.

LIENS OTHER THAN TAXES

Aside from real estate tax and special assessment liens, other types of liens also may be charged against real property, either voluntarily or involuntarily. These include mortgage liens, mechanics' liens, judgments, estate and inheritance tax liens, vendors' liens, vendees' liens, surety bail bond liens, IRS tax liens, federal judgment liens, and Uniform Commercial Code (UCC) liens.

Mortgage (Deed of Trust or Purchase-Money) Liens

In general, a **mortgage** or **purchase-money lien** is a voluntary, specific lien on real estate given to a lender by a borrower as security for a mortgage loan. It becomes a lien on real property when the mortgage funds are disbursed. The lender then files or records the mortgage or deed of trust in the office of the county clerk where the property is located.

Mortgage lenders generally require a preferred lien, referred to as a *first mortgage lien;* this means that no other major liens against the property (aside from real estate taxes) take priority over the mortgage lien. Mortgages and mortgage liens will be discussed in detail in Chapter 15, "Real Estate Financing: Principles."

Mechanics' Liens

A **mechanic's lien** is a specific, involuntary lien that gives security to persons or companies that perform labor or furnish material to improve real property. A mechanic's lien is available to contractors, subcontractors, architects, engineers, surveyors, laborers, and other providers. The mechanic's lien right is based on the *enhancement of value theory*—because the labor performed and material furnished enhanced the value, the property should be security for payment. If the property owner does not pay voluntarily, the lien can be enforced with a foreclosure sale.

To be entitled to a mechanic's lien, the provider must have worked under contract (express or implied) with the owner or owner's authorized representative. If the property to be subject to the lien is a homestead, both spouses must sign the contract. A mechanic's lien is filed when the owner has not fully paid for the work or when the general contractor has been paid but has not paid the subcontractors or suppliers of materials. *A person claiming a mechanic's lien must file a notice of lien in the public record of the county where the property is located within a limited time after the work has been completed.*

Even though the claimant's notice of lien may be filed within a specified period after the work is completed, a mechanic's lien usually takes effect (establishes priority) from the time labor was performed or the material was supplied in whole or in part. As shown in Figure 11.1, a mechanic's lien may take priority over previously recorded liens such as mortgages. Enforcement of the mechanic's lien is by a foreclosure suit and a court order to have the sheriff sell the real estate to satisfy the claimant. There is no right of redemption after the court sale. *A purchaser of property that has been recently constructed, altered, or repaired should be cautious about possible unrecorded mechanics' liens against such property.*

If improvements have been ordered by a third party, such as a tenant, a property owner should execute a document called a *notice of nonresponsibility* to avoid possible mechanics' liens. By posting this notice in a conspicuous place on the property and recording a verified copy of it in the public record, the owner gives notice that he or she is not responsible for the work done.

Subcontractors' liens. A landowner usually hires a **general contractor** to perform a particular construction job and pays this person all fees and expenses. The general contractor in turn hires a number of **subcontractors** to actually furnish the materials and perform the labor. Both the general contractor and subcontractors are entitled to mechanics' liens if they are not paid in full. Payment in full to the general contractor will not necessarily free a landowner from the lien rights of unknown, unpaid suppliers and laborers. Thus an owner must protect himself or herself against known as well as unknown mechanics and materialmen. Because an owner does not actually hire these subcontractors (they are said not to be "in privity with the owner"), the owner would not be aware of them or the extent of the work or materials they provide. Subcontractors, therefore, generally are required to serve a landowner with personal notice of their individual lien claims.

Property owners are required to pay contractors for properly performed work or properly stored materials within 45 days (in some cases up to 61 days) after receiving a request for payment. The contractor has seven days from receipt of that payment to pay his or her subcontractor for services reflected in that payment.

Homeowner protection. Under sections 53.101 through 53.105 of the Texas Property Code, the property owner is required to hold a *10 percent retainage* of the total construction bill for 30 days following completion of work. Failure to do so may subject the owner to additional liability to subcontractors. As additional protection against liens by subcontractors who might not have been paid, an original contractor must give a *"final bills paid affidavit"* to a property owner on receipt of the final payment for completed construction. On a residential homestead construction project in excess of $5,000, a contractor must deposit trust funds received from the owner into an escrow account at a financial institution and account for deposits and disbursements. Because mechanic's lien statutes are very complex, always refer questions to an attorney.

Judgments   A **judgment** is a *decree issued by a court.* When the decree provides for the awarding of money and sets forth the amount of money owed by the debtor to the creditor, the judgment is referred to as a *money judgment.*

A judgment becomes a *general, involuntary, statutory lien on both real and personal property* owned by the debtor, although judgment liens do not normally attach to homestead property in Texas. A judgment takes its priority as a lien on the debtor's property from the date the judgment was abstracted and filed for record in the county clerk's office, creating an *abstract of judgment*. Usually a lien covers only property located within the county in which the abstract of judgment is issued. Therefore, notices of the lien must be filed in other counties where the debtor owns property when a creditor wishes to extend the lien coverage. For a creditor to pursue collection on the judgment, the court must issue a legal document called a *writ of execution* directing the sheriff to seize and sell as much of the debtor's nonexempt real or personal property as is necessary to pay the debt and the expenses of the sale. When the property is sold to satisfy the debt, the debtor should demand a legal document known as a *release of judgment*, which should be filed with the county clerk so that the record will be cleared of the judgment.

An abstract of judgment lien is valid for ten years; if the judgment lien holder has attempted to enforce the judgment through an execution, it may be extended for an additional ten-year period. If an abstract of judgment has not been extended within the ten-year period, it goes dormant and is no longer a valid lien. A 1995 change in the law (Section 31.006 of the Civil Practices and Remedies Code) provides a procedure for renewing a dormant judgment for an additional two-year period.

Judgments against community property that is a homestead cannot be executed by a court sale unless a mechanic's lien has been perfected on the property in accordance with law or unless another exemption from forced sale by creditors applies, as discussed in Chapter 8. If nonhomestead community property is owned in the sole name of the husband, the wife's community property interest can be made subject to a judgment lien against the wife, by adequate evidence that the property is community property. The reverse also is true.

Attachments. To prevent a debtor from conveying title to his or her unsecured real estate (realty that is not mortgaged or is similarly unencumbered) while a court suit is being decided, a creditor may seek a writ of **attachment** by which the court retains custody of the property until the suit is concluded. To obtain an attachment, a creditor first must post with the court a surety bond or deposit sufficient to cover any possible loss or damage the debtor may sustain during the period the court has custody of the property, in case the judgment is not awarded to the creditor.

Lis pendens. A judgment or other decree affecting real estate is rendered at the conclusion of a lawsuit. Generally there is a considerable time lag between the filing of a lawsuit and the rendering of a judgment. Therefore, when a suit is filed that affects title to a specific parcel of real estate (such as a foreclosure suit), a notice known as a *lis pendens* (Latin for "litigation pending") is recorded. A lis pendens is not a lien but rather a *notice of a possible future lien*. Recording of the lis pendens gives notice to all interested parties, such as prospective purchasers and lenders, and establishes a priority for the later lien, which is dated back to the date the lis pendens was filed for record.

Estate and Inheritance Tax Liens

Federal **estate taxes** and state **inheritance taxes** (as well as the debts of deceased persons) are *general, statutory, involuntary liens* that encumber a deceased person's real and personal property. These are normally paid or cleared in probate court proceedings. Probate and issues of inheritance will be discussed in Chapter 17, "Transfer of Title."

Vendors' Liens In Texas, the seller (vendor) has, by statute, a **vendor's lien** when he or she has not received in cash the full purchase price from the buyer (vendee) of the real estate. A vendor's lien is a claim on the real estate and is used only as security for the purchase-money debt. This is a *specific, equitable, involuntary lien* for the amount of unpaid balance due the seller or third-party lender. In the latter case, the seller assigns the vendor's lien to the lender. The lien is usually reserved in the deed; but even if it is not, Texas law imposes one.

In most sales, the grantor reserves a vendor's lien on the property as additional security for a note that is secured by a purchaser's deed of trust or mortgage. A seller in Texas can do this by including in the deed of conveyance a clause in the following general form:

> It is expressly agreed and stipulated that the vendor's lien is retained against the above-described property until the above-described note and interest thereon are fully paid, when this deed shall become absolute.

A seller enforces a vendor's lien by filing suit to have the real estate sold to pay the amount due. Recording the grantor's deed creates a vendor's lien, which then is valid against the grantee, spouse, heirs, and devisees and subsequent creditors and purchasers. This lien is created whether or not the vendor (seller) finances the sale. If the sale is not vendor-financed, the lien is assigned or transferred to the third-party lender.

Vendees' Liens A **vendee's lien** is a *buyer's claim* against a seller's property in cases where the seller failed to deliver title. This usually occurs when property is purchased under an installment contract or contract for deed and the seller fails to deliver title after all other terms of the contract have been satisfied. A vendee's lien is a *specific, equitable, involuntary lien* for any money paid plus the value of any improvements made to the property by the buyer. It arises because of the doctrine or theory of *equitable title* in favor of the buyer.

Surety Bail Bond Lien A real estate owner charged with a crime for which he or she must face trial may choose to put up real estate instead of cash as surety for bail. In Texas, the execution and recording of such a **surety bail bond lien** creates a legal requirement that the owner of surety provide assurance that he or she has a net worth at least twice the amount of the sum of the bail. This voluntary lien is enforceable by the sheriff or other court officer if the accused person does not appear in court as required. A surety bail bond lien cannot be levied against a homestead property.

IRS Tax Lien An **IRS** (Internal Revenue Service) **tax lien** results from a person's failure to pay any portion of federal IRS taxes owed, such as income and withholding taxes. A federal tax lien is a *general, statutory, involuntary lien* on all real and personal property owned by the delinquent taxpayer.

Federal Judgment Liens A **federal judgment lien** becomes a lien on all property of the judgment debtor upon the government's filing of a certified copy of the judgment or an abstract of judgment for such debts as unpaid student loans and deficiencies on government-insured or government-guaranteed loans. The judgment is filed in the county in which a debtor owns real property. The lien is effective for 20 years and applies to all judgments entered on or after May 21, 1981. The judgment lien may be extended once for an additional 20 years by filing a notice of renewal in the county clerk's records.

UNIFORM COMMERCIAL CODE

The **Uniform Commercial Code** (UCC) is a body of law that attempts to codify and make uniform throughout the country all laws relating to commercial transactions. The main relevance of the UCC to real property is in the area of personal property and fixtures. Section 9 of the Texas Business and Commerce Code is the Texas version of the UCC as it applies to pledging personal property or fixtures to secure a loan or credit purchase.

To create a security interest in personal property, including personal property that will become fixtures, Section 9 of the code requires the use of a **security agreement,** which must contain a complete description of the items against which the lien applies. A short notice of this agreement, called a **financing statement,** which includes the legal description of the real estate involved, must be filed in the county clerk's office where mortgages are recorded. The recording of the financing statement constitutes notice to subsequent purchasers and mortgagees of the security interest in personal property and fixtures on the real estate. Many mortgagees require the signing and recording of a financing statement when the mortgaged premises include personal property or readily removable fixtures (washers, dryers, and the like) as part of the security for the mortgage debt. If the financing statement has been recorded properly, on the borrower's default the creditor could repossess the personal property and remove it from the property.

Summary

Liens are claims, or charges, of creditors or tax officials against the real and personal property of a debtor. A lien is a type of encumbrance. Liens are either general, covering all real and personal property of a debtor/owner, or specific, covering only the specific parcel of real estate described in the mortgage, tax bill, building or repair contract, or other document.

The priority of liens generally is determined by the order in which they are placed in the public record of the county in which the debtor's property is located. Exceptions to this are IRS tax liens, real estate tax liens, and mechanics' liens.

Real estate taxes are levied annually by local taxing authorities. Tax liens generally have priority over other liens. Payments are required before stated dates, after which penalties accrue. An owner may lose title to property for nonpayment of taxes because such tax-delinquent property can be sold at a tax sale. Texas allows a maximum two-year period during which a defaulted owner can redeem his or her real estate after a tax sale on residential homestead or agricultural property.

Special assessment taxes are levied on real estate that benefits from improvements, such as new sidewalks, curbs, or paving, to cover the cost of these improvements. Assessments usually are payable annually over a five-year or ten-year period, together with interest due on the balance of the assessment each year.

Mortgage (deed of trust or purchase-money) liens are voluntary, specific liens given to lenders to secure payment for mortgage loans. Mechanics' liens protect general contractors, subcontractors, material suppliers, architects, engineers, and surveyors whose work enhances the value of real estate.

A judgment is a court decree obtained by a creditor, usually for a monetary award from a debtor. The abstract of judgment lien can be enforced by issuance of a writ of execution and sale by the sheriff to pay the judgment amount and costs.

Attachment is a means of preventing a defendant from conveying his or her real estate before completion of a suit in which a judgment is sought. Lis pendens is a recorded notice of a lawsuit that is awaiting trial in court and may result in a judgment that will affect title to a parcel of real estate.

Federal estate taxes and state inheritance taxes are general liens against a deceased owner's property. They usually are paid or cleared in probate court proceedings.

Vendors' liens and vendees' liens are claims against a specific parcel of real estate. A vendor's lien is a seller's claim against a purchaser who has not paid the entire purchase price in cash. A vendee's lien is a purchaser's claim against a seller who has not conveyed title under the terms of an installment contract.

Internal Revenue Service tax liens are general liens against the property of a person who is delinquent in payment of IRS taxes. Federal judgment liens are general liens resulting from attempts to collect debts owed to the federal government.

Under the Uniform Commercial Code, security interests in personal property must be recorded using a security agreement and a financing statement. The recording of a financing statement gives notice to purchasers and mortgagees of the security interests in personal property and fixtures on the specific parcel of real estate.

Questions

1. Which of the following **BEST** refers to the type of lien that affects all real and personal property of a debtor?
   a. Specific lien
   b. Involuntary lien
   c. General lien
   d. Statutory lien

2. General contractor Ralph Hammond was hired to build a room addition to Tom and Harriet Elkin's home. Hammond completed the work several weeks ago but still has not been paid. In this situation, Hammond is entitled to a mechanic's lien. Which of the following is correct concerning his lien?
   a. It is a general lien.
   b. It is a voluntary lien.
   c. Hammond must file a notice of his lien in the public records.
   d. Hammond cannot file a notice of lien because he failed to withhold the 10 percent retainage for 30 days.

3. In Texas after homestead real estate has been sold by the state or county to satisfy a delinquent real estate tax lien, the owner usually has a right to
   a. be paid for any improvement made during ownership.
   b. remain in possession indefinitely.
   c. redeem the property from sale within a two-year period.
   d. have the sale canceled.

4. Donny Prelate sold Ernest Tully a parcel of real estate. Title has passed, but to date Tully has not paid the purchase price in full as originally agreed. If Prelate does not receive payment, which of the following is he entitled to enforce?
   a. Vendee's lien
   b. Lis pendens
   c. Vendor's lien
   d. Judgment

5. *Priority of liens* refers to which of the following?
   a. The order in which a debtor assumes responsibility for payment of obligations
   b. The order in which liens will be paid if property is sold by court order to satisfy a debt
   c. The dates liens are filed for record
   d. The fact that specific liens have a greater priority than general liens

6. Which of the following is a lien on real estate to secure payment for specific municipal improvements to a parcel of real estate?
   a. Mechanic's lien
   b. Special assessment
   c. Ad valorem lien
   d. Utility lien

7. Which of the following entities do **NOT** levy general real estate taxes?
   a. Counties
   b. Texas legislature
   c. Cities
   d. Hospital districts

8. A specific parcel of real estate is appraised for tax purposes at $80,000 market value. The tax rate for the county in which the property is located is $1.50 per $100 of value. The tax bill will be
   a. $1,000.
   b. $1,100.
   c. $1,200.
   d. $1,400.

9. Which of the following taxes is (are) used to distribute the cost of public services among real estate owners?
   a. Personal property tax
   b. Sales tax
   c. Real property tax
   d. Special assessment

10. A mechanic's lien claim arises when, on the owner's order, a general contractor has performed work or provided material to improve a parcel of real estate but has not been paid. Such a contractor has a right to

    a. tear out the work.
    b. file a notice of nonresponsiblity.
    c. record a notice of the lien and file a court suit within the time required by state law.
    d. have the owner's personal property sold to satisfy the lien.

11. Which of the following is (are) considered a lien on real estate?

    a. Easements running with the land
    b. Unpaid mortgage loans
    c. An attachment
    d. An encroachment

12. A mortgage lien and a judgment lien have which of the following characteristics in common?

    a. Both are general liens.
    b. Both are involuntary liens.
    c. Both are voluntary liens.
    d. Both may involve a debtor-creditor relationship.

13. Which of the following is classified as a general lien?

    a. Vendor's lien
    b. Judgment lien
    c. Real estate tax lien
    d. Mechanic's lien

14. Which of the following liens usually is given higher priority?

    a. A mortgage dated last year
    b. The current real estate tax
    c. A mechanic's lien for work started before the mortgage was made
    d. A judgment rendered yesterday

15. The right of a defaulted taxpayer to recover his or her property before its sale for unpaid taxes is the

    a. statutory right of reinstatement.
    b. equitable right of appeal.
    c. statutory right of redemption.
    d. equitable right of redemption.

16. Which of the following statements most accurately describes special assessment liens?

    a. They are general liens.
    b. They are paid on a monthly basis.
    c. They take priority over mechanics' liens.
    d. They cannot be prepaid in full without penalty.

17. Which of the following is a voluntary, specific lien?

    a. Mechanic's lien
    b. Mortgage lien
    c. Vendor's lien
    d. Federal judgment lien

18. General contractor Kim Kelly is suing homeowner Bob Baker for nonpayment for services; suit will be filed in the next few weeks. Recently Kelly learned that Baker has listed his property with a local real estate broker for sale. In this instance which of the following **PROBABLY** will be used by Kelly and her attorneys to protect her interest?

    a. Notice of responsibility
    b. Lis pendens
    c. Vendee's lien
    d. Vendor's lien

19. To give notice of a security interest in personal property items, a lienholder must record which of the following?

    a. Security agreement
    b. Financing statement
    c. Vendor's lien
    d. Quitclaim deed

20. Which of the following is a specific, involuntary, statutory lien?

    a. Real estate tax lien
    b. Income tax lien
    c. Estate tax lien
    d. Judgment lien

21. All of the following would probably be exempt from real estate taxes **EXCEPT** a(n)

    a. public hospital.
    b. golf course operated by the city's park department.
    c. community church.
    d. apartment building.

12 Real Estate Contracts

OVERVIEW

"Get it in writing" is a phrase commonly used to warn one party to an agreement to protect his or her interests by entering into a written contract with the other party, outlining the rights and obligations of both. The real estate business makes use of many different types of contracts, including listing agreements, leases, and sales contracts. Brokers and salespeople must understand the content and uses of such agreements and must be able to explain them to buyers and sellers.

This chapter first deals with the legal principles governing contracts in general. Then it examines some of the special types of contracts used in the real estate business.

CONTRACTS

Brokers and salespeople use many types of contracts and agreements in the course of their business to carry out their responsibilities to sellers, buyers, and the general public. Among these are listing agreements, sales contracts, option agreements, installment contracts, leases, and escrow agreements.

Before studying these specific types of contracts, students first must understand *contract law,* the general body of law that governs the operation of such agreements. The following discussion provides an introduction to that portion of the law.

CONTRACT DEFINED

> A *contract* is a voluntary, legally enforceable promise between two competent parties to perform some legal act in exchange for consideration.

A **contract** is a voluntary agreement between legally competent parties to perform or refrain from performing some legal act, supported by legal consideration. In essence, a contract is an enforceable promise that must be performed and for which, if a breach of promise occurs, the law provides a remedy.

Depending on the situation and the nature or language of the agreement, a contract may be (1) express or implied; (2) unilateral or bilateral; (3) executory or executed; and (4) valid, unenforceable, voidable, or void. These terms are used to describe the type, status, and legal effect of a contract and are discussed in the sections that follow.

Express and Implied Contracts

Depending on how a contract is created, it may be express or implied. In an **express contract** the parties state the terms and show their intentions in words. An express contract may be oral or written. In an **implied contract** the agreement of the parties is demonstrated by their acts and conduct.

In Practice

In the typical agency relationships, a listing agreement is an express contract between the seller and the broker, and a buyer representation agreement is an express contract between the buyer and the broker. Both contracts name the broker as the fiduciary representative of the principal. However, the courts have held that under certain situations a broker also may have an implied contract to represent the opposing principal in the transaction. For example, a broker took a listing for a residence and showed it to several potential purchasers, one of whom requested that a physical inspection of the property be made. The broker complied but mistakenly hired an unqualified person to make the inspection. The interested party bought the property, discovered a serious physical defect, and sued the broker. The court ruled that, although the broker was the agent of the seller, in complying with the buyer's request, by implication he had accepted an agency agreement to represent the purchaser. By hiring an inspector who was not competent to do the job, the broker violated his duty to the purchaser under this implied agreement.

Bilateral and Unilateral Contracts

According to the nature of the agreement made, contracts also may be classified as either bilateral or unilateral. In a **bilateral contract,** both parties promise to do something; one promise is given in exchange for another. A real estate sales contract is a bilateral contract because the seller promises to sell a parcel of real estate and deliver title to the property to the buyer, who promises to pay a certain sum of money for the property. Today most real estate contracts are interpreted by the courts to be bilateral, that is, an exchange of promises.

Bi- means "two"—a *bilateral contract* must have two promises.

Uni- means "one"—a *unilateral contract* has only one promise.

Alternatively, a **unilateral contract** is a one-sided agreement whereby one party makes a promise in order to induce a second party to do something. The second party is not legally obligated to act; however, if the second party does comply, the first party is obligated to keep the promise. An offer of a reward is an example of a unilateral contract. For example, if a person runs a newspaper ad offering a reward for the return of a lost pet, that person is promising to pay if the act of returning the pet is fulfilled. A contract giving one party the option or right to purchase at specified terms also is an example of a unilateral contract because the seller cannot compel the buyer to perform; the unilateral *option agreement* is discussed later in this chapter.

Executed and Executory Contracts

A contract may be classified as either executed or executory, depending on whether the agreement is completely performed. A fully **executed contract** is one in which both parties have fulfilled their promises and thus have performed the contract. An **executory contract** exists when something remains to be done by one or both parties; that is, the agreement is *partially* performed.

Validity of Contracts

A contract can be described as valid, void, voidable, or unenforceable, depending on the circumstances. These contracts are summarized in Table 12.1.

A **valid contract** complies with all the essential elements and is binding and enforceable on both parties. (The essential elements of a contract are discussed later in this chapter.)

A **void contract** has no legal force or effect because it does not meet the essential elements of a contract. For example, one essential condition for a contract to be valid is that it be for a legal purpose. Thus, a "contract" to commit a crime is void; it is not a contract at all.

A **voidable contract** seems on the surface to be valid but may be rescinded, or disaffirmed, by the party who might be injured if the contract were to be enforced (in some cases this might be both parties). For example, a contract entered into with a minor or one in which fraud can be proven is usually voidable. A minor generally is permitted to disaffirm a real estate contract at any time while he or she is underage (a minor) or within a reasonable time after reaching legal age. A voidable contract will be considered by the courts to be a valid contract if the party who has the option to disaffirm the agreement does not do so within a prescribed period of time.

An **unenforceable contract** has all of the elements of a valid contract; however, neither party can sue the other to force performance. For example, an oral listing agreement is unenforceable. A broker who takes an oral listing risks being unable to sue a seller if the broker sells the seller's property but is not paid a commission as promised. Unenforceable contracts are said to be "valid as between the parties," because after the agreement is fully executed or performed and both parties are satisfied, neither would have reason to initiate a lawsuit to force performance.

Essential Elements for a Valid Contract

The five essential elements for a valid and enforceable contract in Texas are described below.

1. **Competent parties:** The buyer and the seller must be of legal age and free from a mental handicap that would make them incompetent. In Texas, people are considered to be of legal age if they are at least

Table 12.1   Legal Effects of Contracts

Type of Contract	Legal Effect	Example
Valid	Binding and enforceable on both parties	Agreement complying with essentials of a valid contract
Void	No legal effect	Contract for an illegal purpose
Voidable	Valid, but may be disaffirmed by one party	Contract with a minor
Unenforceable	Valid between the parties, but neither may force performance	Certain oral agreements

---

18 years old, or are married, or have had their minority status removed by a court. Contracts with the mentally infirm can be either void or voidable; they are void if the person has been adjudicated to be incompetent. To make a valid contract, a fiduciary, corporate officer, or agent must have legal authority given by a written document. *↳ trust & confidence*

2. **Offer and acceptance:** This requirement, also called *mutual assent,* means that a "meeting of the minds" must occur. *Offer* and *acceptance* are technical legal terms. Courts look to the objective intent of the parties to determine whether they meant to enter into a binding agreement. The agreement terms must be fairly definite and understood by both parties.

   Offer and acceptance requires that a contract must be entered into as the free and voluntary act of each party. Contracts signed by a person under duress (use of force), menace (threat of violence), or undue influence or as a result of misrepresentation or fraud are voidable (may be canceled) by the injured party or by a court. Extreme care should be taken when one or more of the parties to a contract is elderly, sick, in great distress, or under the influence of drugs or alcohol.

> Offer and acceptance are not present if *misrepresentation, fraud, undue influence,* or *duress* are involved.

3. **Consideration:** Courts will not enforce gratuitous (free) promises. This means that a promise will not be legally enforced against a person making the promise unless the person to whom the promise was made has given up something (consideration) in exchange. So, if Bob promises to pay Alice $75,000 for her house, the promise would not be enforceable because Alice has made no promise to do anything in return. However, if Alice promises to tender the deed to her house in exchange for the $75,000, her promise serves as consideration; and Bob's promise would be enforceable against him by Alice. Consideration is something of legal value (usually one party suffering a legal detriment), bargained for and given in exchange for a promise or an act. Any return promise to perform that has been bargained for and exchanged is legally sufficient to satisfy the consideration element. Consideration is a complex legal concept.

4. **Legality of object:** To be valid, a contract must not contemplate a purpose that is illegal or against public policy.

5. **Agreement in writing and signed:** The *Texas Statute of Frauds* requires that certain types of contracts be in writing to be enforceable. The statute provides the following requirements to prevent fraudulent proof of a fictitious oral contract: (a) the signature of the party to be charged is required; (b) a spouse's signature must be included when necessary to release marital rights, such as community property and homestead rights; (c) an agent may sign for a principal if the agent has proper written authority, such as a power of attorney; and (d) when sellers are co-owners, all co-owners must sign. A written agreement establishes the interest of the purchaser and his or her rights to enforce that interest by court action. Thus, it prevents the seller from selling the property to another person who might offer a higher price. The signed contract agreement also obligates the buyer to complete the transaction according to the terms agreed on in the contract.

acceptance by a seller conveys equitable title

right to acquire

The *Uniform Electronic Transactions Act* (S.B. 393, 2001) permits electronic records and electronic signatures in electronic transactions to be legally enforceable. If a law requires a record to be in writing and all parties to the transaction have previously agreed to conduct transactions by electronic means, an electronic record satisfies the law. If the law requires a signature, an electronic signature satisfies the law. An electronic signature is an electronic sound, symbol, or process attached to a record and executed or adopted by a person with the intent to sign the record. An electronic record is received when (1) it enters an information processing system that the recipient has designated and (2) it is in a form capable of being processed by that system.

Accurate description of the property. In addition to the five elements for all contracts as listed above, a real estate sales contract must contain an accurate legal description of the property being conveyed. The test that most courts use is whether the subject property can be identified with reasonable certainty. Since 1982, the grantee's address must be included in any document conveying real property in Texas.

Performance of Contract

Each party to a contract has certain rights and duties to fulfill. The question of when a contract must be performed is an important factor. Many contracts call for a specific time at which or by which the agreed-on acts must be completely performed. In addition, contracts may provide that "time is of the essence." This means that the contract must be performed within the time limit specified and that any party who has not performed on time is liable for breach of contract. Time *is* of the essence in an option agreement and in the Texas promulgated forms "Addendum for Sale of Other Property by Buyer" and "Addendum for 'Back-Up' Contract."

When a contract does not specify a date or time frame for performance, the acts it requires must be performed within a reasonable time. The interpretation of what constitutes a reasonable time will depend on the situation. Generally, if the act can be done immediately—such as a payment of money—it must be performed immediately, unless the parties agree otherwise. Only the option provision in the Texas sales contracts and a few addenda promulgated by the Texas Real Estate Commission specify that "time is of the essence"; therefore, most activities related to real estate contracts must be performed within a "reasonable time."

required & approved

Not taken out of context ←

If contract terms are vague and one party sues the other based on one of these terms, the courts will make the presumption that the document is a valid contract. The courts will make every effort to enforce it by determining the intent of the parties from within the "four corners" of the contract itself, with all provisions considered together in the original context.

Furthermore, the *parol evidence rule* prevents the admission into court of any prior or simultaneous oral or written agreements that contradict the terms of the written contract. If, for example, the buyer and seller orally agree that the seller will pay the appraisal fee but the final contract states that the buyer will pay, then the written contract prevails.

In Practice	The courts generally interpret the agreement against the party who prepared it. For example, a broker is responsible for preparing all listing agreements for his or her firm. If there were any doubt as to whether a listing agreement was an exclusive agency or an exclusive right to sell, the courts probably would construe it to be an exclusive agency, thus ruling against the broker who prepared the document.

Assignment and Novation

Often, after entering into a contract, one party may want to withdraw without actually terminating the agreement. This may be accomplished through either assignment or novation.

Assignment refers to a transfer of rights and/or duties under a contract. Generally *rights* may be assigned to a third party unless the agreement forbids such an assignment or unless the agreement contains a personal obligation. *Duties* also may be assigned, or delegated, but the original obligor remains secondarily liable for them (after the new obligor), unless he or she is specifically released from this responsibility. The purchase of a home on assumption or subject to an existing loan is an assignment. A contract that requires some personal quality or unique ability of one of the parties may not be assigned. Examples of such a contract are an owner-financed sale, which may not be assigned without express permission from the seller, and a listing agreement, which is a personal service contract. Most contracts include a clause that either permits or forbids assignment.

Assignment = substitution of parties

Novation = substitution of contracts

A contract also may be performed by **novation,** or the substitution of a new contract for an existing agreement with the intent of extinguishing the old contract. The new agreement may be between the same parties, or a new party may be substituted for either (the latter case is *novation of the parties*). The parties' intent must be to discharge the old obligation. The new agreement must be supported by consideration and must conform with all the essential elements of a valid contract. For example, a novation would occur if a buyer got behind on his or her payments and the lender modified the note terms to reflect a new payback arrangement. Whether or not a novation has occurred is determined by the courts.

Discharge of Contract

A contract may be *completely performed*, with all terms carried out, or it may be *breached* (broken) if one party defaults. In addition, a contract may be *discharged* by other methods. These include

- *partial performance of the terms along with a written acceptance* by the person for whom acts have not been done or to whom money has not been paid.
- *substantial performance,* in which one party has substantially performed the contract but does not complete all the details exactly as the contract requires. Such performance—for example, under construction contracts—may be sufficient to force payment, with certain adjustments for any damages suffered by the other party.
- *impossibility of performance,* in which an act required by the contract cannot be accomplished legally.
- *mutual agreement* of the parties to cancel.
- *operation of law,* as in the voiding of a contract by a minor, or as a result of fraud or the expiration of the statute of limitations or as a result of a contract's being altered without the written consent of all parties involved.

Default—breach of contract.   A **breach** of contract is a violation of any of the terms or conditions of a contract without legal excuse, as when a seller breaches a sales contract by not delivering title to the buyer under the conditions stated in the agreement. If either party breaches, or defaults, the defaulting party assumes certain burdens and the nondefaulting party has certain rights.

If the *seller defaults* on a real estate contract, the buyer has three alternatives. The buyer may

1. *rescind, or cancel, the contract* and recover his or her earnest money as liquidated damages; **or**
2. *file a court suit,* known as a suit for **specific performance,** to force the seller to perform the contract; **or**
3. *sue the seller for compensatory damage* (a personal judgment) **or** *the buyer may choose both options 2 and 3.*

In Practice   The damaged buyer who terminates the contract and recovers earnest money has no additional remedies. A suit for damages is seldom used when the seller defaults, however, because in most cases the buyer can collect only a minimal amount in damages.

If the *buyer defaults,* the seller, under statutory law, has four alternatives. He or she may

1. *declare the contract forfeited.* The right to forfeit usually is provided in the terms of the contract, and the seller usually is entitled to retain the earnest money and all payments received from the buyer; **or**
2. *rescind the contract;* that is, cancel or terminate the contract as if it had never been made. This requires that the seller return all payments the buyer has made; **or**
3. *sue for specific performance.* In some cases this may require the seller to tender, or offer, a valid deed to the buyer to show the seller's compliance with the contract terms; **or**
4. *sue for compensatory damages* **or** *the seller may choose both options 3 and 4.*

In Practice   A damaged seller who declares the contract forfeited or who rescinds the contract has no additional remedies.

Statute of limitations. The law of Texas allows a specific time limit during which parties to a contract may bring legal suit to enforce their rights. Any party who does not take steps to enforce his or her rights within this **statute of limitations** may lose those rights. Under Texas law, any action for the specific performance of a written contract for the conveyance of real property must be commenced within *four years* from the date of the breach; the limitation for oral contracts is two years. A suit brought for a DTPA violation must be begun within two years from the date a buyer could reasonably have discovered the deceptive act.

CONTRACTS USED IN THE REAL ESTATE BUSINESS

As mentioned earlier, the types of written agreements most commonly used by brokers and salespeople are listing agreements, buyer representation agreements, real estate sales contracts, option agreements, contracts for deed, leases, and escrow agreements.

Sales Contracts   The sales contract is the most important document in the transfer of real estate because it sets forth all details of the agreement between a buyer and a seller and establishes their legal rights and obligations. It is even more important than the deed because *the contract dictates the content of the deed.*

Offer and acceptance. One of the essential elements of a valid sales contract is a meeting of the minds whereby the buyer and seller agree on the terms of the sale. This is usually accomplished through the process of offer and acceptance.

A broker lists an owner's real estate for sale at the price and conditions set by the owner. A prospective buyer who wants to purchase the property at those terms, or at some other terms, is found. A contract is signed by the prospective buyer and presented by the broker to the seller. This is an *offer.* If the seller agrees to the offer *exactly as it was made* and signs the contract, the offer has been *accepted.* After appropriate *notification of acceptance* is given (explained below), the contract is *valid.* The licensee would then deliver a fully signed copy of the contract to the buyer, although it is not a requirement for validity of the contract.

An acceptance must not change or qualify the terms of an offer. If it does, the modification becomes a *counteroffer,* which voids the original offer.

Any attempt by the seller to change the terms proposed by the buyer creates a **counteroffer.** The buyer is relieved of his or her original offer because the seller has, in effect, rejected it. The buyer can accept the seller's counteroffer or reject it and, if desired, make another counteroffer. Any change in the last offer made results in a counteroffer, until one party finally agrees to the other party's last offer and both parties initial all changes and sign the final contract. Then acceptance must be communicated as detailed below.

An offer or counteroffer *may be withdrawn at any time before it has been accepted* (even if the person making the offer or counteroffer agreed to keep the offer open for a set period of time). In addition, an offer is not considered to be accepted until the person making the offer has been *notified of the other party's acceptance.* In a transaction involving subagency, notification of contract acceptance must be given directly to the buyer after seller acceptance because the buyer has no agent; but notification of acceptance, to the seller can be given to the seller's broker or the salesperson working for the seller. In a buyer brokerage transaction, notification of acceptance is complete when the other party's agent has been notified. The real estate broker or salesperson *must* transmit all offers, acceptances, or other responses as soon as possible to avoid questions that might arise regarding whether an acceptance, rejection, or counteroffer has effectively taken place. Notification of contract acceptance may be made orally, with written confirmation recommended to avoid future disputes. The *effective date* of the contract is the date on which the communication of acceptance was made. Notifications between the parties after contract acceptance (for such items as inspection and repair reports) must be in writing and may be mailed, hand delivered or transmitted by fax.

> A counteroffer is created by
> • offeree's rejection or
> • offeror's revocation.

In Practice   There are two items of special importance regarding offer and acceptance: (1) According to the TREC Enforcement Division, all contract offers that are delivered to the seller's agent must be presented to the seller—unless the seller has specifically instructed the listing broker not to bring offers below a certain price or the seller has a binding contract on the property and has instructed the agent *in writing* not to bring additional offers. (2) Although a real estate broker and an escrow agent may sign agreements on the contract form, they are not parties to the contract.

Equitable title. A buyer who signs a contract to purchase real estate does not receive fee title to the land; only a deed can convey fee title. However, after both buyer and seller have signed a sales contract, the buyer acquires an interest in the land known as **equitable title.** Acquisition of equitable title may give the buyer an insurable interest in the property. If the parties decide not to go through with the purchase and sale and if the contract has been recorded, the buyer will be required to give the seller a quitclaim deed to release the buyer's equitable interest in the land.

Destruction of premises. Once both parties sign the sales contract, who bears the loss of any damage to, or destruction of, the property by fire or other casualty prior to closing? The contract forms promulgated by the Texas Real Estate Commission place this risk of loss on the seller, who would probably be aided by insurance proceeds. If the seller does not repair the property, the purchaser may terminate the contract or accept the damaged property and an assignment of the insurance proceeds.

Earnest money deposits. It is customary for a purchaser to put down a cash deposit when making an offer to purchase real estate. This cash deposit, commonly referred to as an **earnest money deposit,** *gives evidence of the purchaser's intent to carry out the terms of the contract.* Earnest money is not required to have a valid contract, but a reasonable amount of earnest money helps to ensure a closing. Earnest money does not fulfill the requirement for consideration in a contract.

The amount of the deposit is a matter to be agreed on by the parties, although the selling broker may be asked to suggest an amount. Under the terms of many listing agreements, a real estate broker is required to obtain a reasonable amount as earnest money. Generally the deposit should be sufficient to discourage the buyer from defaulting, to compensate the seller for taking the property off the market, and to cover any expenses the seller and broker might incur if the buyer defaults.

Until an offer is accepted and notification is given to the other party, the earnest money check is not deposited. After the offer is accepted, the broker must deposit the earnest money by the close of the second working day after execution of the contract. The buyer may not get a refund of the money until the transaction has been completed, the buyer terminates the contract under the option provision, or the seller defaults on the contract. *Under no circumstances does the earnest money belong to the broker.*

Generally, earnest money is held by a title insurance company or similar institution. If it is held by the broker, it must be in a special *trust*, or *escrow, account.* This money cannot be *commingled,* or mixed, with a broker's personal funds. Likewise, a broker may not use such funds for his or her personal use, an illegal act known as *conversion.* A broker does not need a special escrow account for each earnest money deposit received; one such account into which all such funds are deposited is sufficient. A broker must maintain full, complete, and accurate records of all earnest money deposits, and a broker's license may be suspended or revoked for failure to account properly for such deposits.

Computation of time. In computing a period of time prescribed or allowed for negotiating a contract or for meeting a contract obligation, the time period generally begins on the day after the act, event, or default in controversy. It concludes on the last day of the computed period. Calendar days, not business days, are used. For example, if the last day to exercise a contract option is Saturday, December 25, the buyer would not have the right to exercise the option after that date.

Promulgated contract forms. The Texas Real Estate License Act provides for the establishment of the **Texas Real Estate Broker-Lawyer Committee.** The purpose of this special committee is the drafting and revising of standard contract forms to be used by real estate licensees because most real estate transactions are basically similar in nature. Once the forms have been drafted by the Broker-Lawyer Committee, the Texas Real Estate Commission has the option of approving or promulgating the forms for use by brokers and their salespeople. When a contract form or addendum has been *promulgated* by the commission, it *must* be used by a licensee for that particular contract situation. There are four exceptions to this requirement [Rule 537.11(b)]:

1. Transactions in which the licensee is functioning solely as a principal, not as an agent
2. Transactions in which an agency of the United States government requires that a different form be used

3. Transactions for which a contract form has been prepared by the property owner or prepared by an attorney and required by the property owner
4. Transactions for which no standard contract form has been promulgated by the Texas Real Estate Commission and for which the licensee uses a form prepared by an attorney at law licensed by this state and approved by the attorney for the particular kind of transactions involved or prepared by the Texas Real Estate Broker-Lawyer Committee and made available for trial use by licensees with the consent of the Texas Real Estate Commission

As public records, the promulgated contract forms are available to any person. However, TREC contract forms are intended for use only by licensed real estate brokers or salespersons who are trained in their correct use. Mistakes in the use of a form may result in financial loss or a contract that is unenforceable. A notice on TREC's web site advises nonlicensees who obtain the forms for use in a real estate transaction to contact a real estate licensee or an attorney for assistance.

Broker's authority. Specific guidelines have been drawn by statute regarding the authority of real estate licensees to prepare contracts for their clients and customers. A licensed real estate broker is not authorized to practice law—that is, to prepare legal documents such as deeds and mortgages. Sections 16(a) and (b) of the license act limit the broker's authority to prepare documents.

The rules of the commission, 22 TAC 537.11(d), clarify what is meant by Section 16 of the act:

A licensee may not undertake to draw or prepare documents fixing and defining the legal rights of the principals to a transaction. In negotiating real estate transactions, the licensee may fill in forms for such transactions, using exclusively forms which have been approved and promulgated by the Texas Real Estate Commission or such forms as are otherwise permitted by these rules. When filling in such a form, the licensee may only fill in the blanks provided and may not add to or strike matter from such form, except that licensees shall add factual statements and business details desired by the principals and shall strike only such matter as is desired by the principals and as is necessary to conform the instrument to the intent of the parties. A licensee may not add to a promulgated contract form factual statements or business details for which a contract addendum, lease or other form has been promulgated by the commission for mandatory use. Nothing herein shall be deemed to prevent the licensee from explaining to the principals the meaning of the factual statements and business details contained in the said instrument so long as the licensee does not offer or give legal advice.

In Practice   If a licensee fills in the blanks of a promulgated contract form, that does not constitute the unauthorized practice of law—provided the forms are used correctly. Notice that the rule cited above prohibits a licensee from paraphrasing provisions contained in a promulgated addendum or lease and inserting such into the base contract. This means that the licensee must use the appropriate promulgated addendum or lease form or one that is required by a party to the contract.

Table 12.2   *Forms Promulgated by the Texas Real Estate Commission*

Contract Forms (Abbreviated Titles)
- One to Four Family Residential Contract
- Unimproved Property
- New Home, Incomplete Construction
- New Home, Completed Construction
- Farm and Ranch
- Residential Condominium Contract

Special Conditions Addenda and Forms
- Sale of Other Property by Buyer Addendum
- Back-up Contract Addendum
- Release of Liability Addendum
- Seller Financing Addendum
- Environmental Assessment Addendum
- Abstract of Title Addendum
- Condominium Resale Certificate
- Coastal Area Property Addendum
- Property Located Seaward Addendum
- Agreement for Mediation Addendum
- Property Subject to Membership in an Owner's Association Addendum
- Subdivision Information, including Resale Certificate for Property Subject to Membership in an Owner's Association
- Notice of Termination of Contract
- Amendment to Contract
- Loan Assumption Addendum
- Third Party Financing Addendum

Temporary Residential Lease Forms
- Seller's Lease
- Buyer's Lease

Sample Real Estate Sales Contract

As shown in Table 12.2, the commission has promulgated 6 earnest money contract forms, 16 special conditions addenda and forms, and 2 temporary leases. Figure 12.1 is an example of the real estate contract most frequently used in Texas. Study the sample contract and the corresponding summary of each clause provided below. A HUD-1 closing statement for the transaction represented by this contract is located in Chapter 20 (Figure 20.1).

1. *Parties:* identifies the seller and buyer as well as establishes the intent to sell and to buy
2. *Property:* sets forth the legal description and thus identifies the property to be sold by this contract; lists fixtures that are a part of the property
3. *Sales Price:* establishes the cash down, loan amount, and sales price
4. *Financing:* stipulates the source of borrowed funds (details of the financing are specified in an addendum to the contract—Third Party Financing Condition Addendum, Loan Assumption Addendum, or Seller Financing Addendum)
5. *Earnest Money:* specifies the amount of earnest money and identifies the escrow agent

6. *Title Policy and Survey:* identifies which party is to pay for the title policy; notes the exceptions to title if a title policy is furnished; stipulates requirements for a title commitment; provides survey options; specifies procedures for a buyer to object to documents required in this paragraph; and includes required notices to buyer

7. *Property Condition:* specifies a buyer's right to have the property inspected; provides for the seller's disclosure of property condition and lead-based paint and hazards; specifies any limitations on the buyer's acceptance of property condition; establishes procedures for completion of repairs; and includes notices to the buyer

8. *Brokers' Fees:* notes that payments of brokers' fees are described in separate written agreements

9. *Closing:* establishes the target date for closing of the sale and identifies buyer and seller responsibilities at closing

10. *Possession:* specifies when the buyer may take possession of the property

11. *Special Provisions:* clarifies any business details of the sale not covered by the provisions of the printed earnest money contract form and not included in another TREC form; cannot include items that may constitute unauthorized practice of law

12. *Settlement and Other Expenses:* identifies which party is to pay a specific expense at closing

13. *Prorations:* specifies which items are to be prorated and fixes the timing of such proration *through* the day of closing; provides for an adjustment of the tax proration after closing, when necessary

14. *Casualty Loss:* specifies which party is to bear the risk of loss prior to closing and addresses the results of any such loss

15. *Default:* specifies the remedies available to each party in the event the other party breaches the contractual agreements

16. *Mediation:* encourages peaceable resolution of disputes through mediation

17. *Attorney's Fees:* specifies how the expenses of litigation are to be treated

18. *Escrow:* specifies the conditions under which the escrow agent agrees to be the holder of the earnest money and stipulates how such money is to be handled in the event the transaction does not close

19. *Representations:* lists statements made by the seller as to the status of the property and affords certain protections to the buyer should these statements prove false

20. *Federal Tax Requirements:* outlines the procedures to be followed by the buyer if the seller is a "foreign person," as defined by applicable law

21. *Notices:* states requirements for delivery of notices affecting the contract

22. *Agreement of Parties:* clarifies the understanding that no other agreements are to be relied on and identifies any TREC addenda or other forms to be a part of this contract

23. *Termination Option:* provides the buyer with an unrestricted right to terminate the contract, for a specified fee within a specified number of days after the effective date

24. *Consult an Attorney:* provides notice to both parties that real estate licensees cannot give legal advice and advises both parties to seek legal counsel for advice; includes Date of Final Acceptance (establishing the effective date of the contract) and the signature block

Figure 12.1   *Residential Sales Contract*

PROMULGATED BY THE TEXAS REAL ESTATE COMMISSION (TREC)

10-29-01

ONE TO FOUR FAMILY RESIDENTIAL CONTRACT (RESALE)

NOTICE: Not For Use For Condominium Transactions

1. **PARTIES:** John Iuro and wife, Joanne Iuro _____ (Seller) agrees to sell and convey to Blake Redemann and wife, Connie Redemann _____(Buyer) and Buyer agrees to buy from Seller the Property described below.

2. **PROPERTY:**
   A. LAND: Lot __15_____, Block _7____, Cedar Oaks _____ Addition, City of _Dallas_____ , _Dallas_____ County, Texas, known as _3040 North Racine 75340_____ _____(address/zip code), or as described on attached exhibit.
   B. IMPROVEMENTS: The house, garage and all other fixtures and improvements attached to the above-described real property, including without limitation, the following permanently installed and built-in items, if any: all equipment and appliances, valances, screens, shutters, awnings, wall-to-wall carpeting, mirrors, ceiling fans, attic fans, mail boxes, television antennas and satellite dish system and equipment, heating and air-conditioning units, security and fire detection equipment, wiring, plumbing and lighting fixtures, chandeliers, water softener system, kitchen equipment, garage door openers, cleaning equipment, shrubbery, landscaping, outdoor cooking equipment, and all other property owned by Seller and attached to the above described real property.
   C. ACCESSORIES: The following described related accessories, if any: window air conditioning units, stove, fireplace screens, curtains and rods, blinds, window shades, draperies and rods, controls for satellite dish system, controls for garage door openers, entry gate controls, mailbox keys, above ground pool, swimming pool equipment and maintenance accessories, and artificial fireplace logs.
   D. EXCLUSIONS: The following improvements and accessories will be retained by Seller and excluded: _____N/A_____ _____.

   The land, improvements and accessories are collectively referred to as the "Property".

3. **SALES PRICE:**
   A. Cash portion of Sales Price payable by Buyer at closing.................. $_____45,000.00_____
   B. Sum of all financing described below (excluding any VA funding fee or FHA or private mortgage insurance premium) .... $_____70,000.00_____
   C. Sales Price (Sum of A and B)... $_____115,000.00_____

4. **FINANCING:** The portion of Sales Price not payable in cash will be paid as follows: (Check applicable boxes below)
   ☒ A. THIRD PARTY FINANCING: One or more third party mortgage loans in the total amount of $_70,000.00_____. If the Property does not satisfy the lenders' underwriting requirements for the loan(s), this contract will terminate and the earnest money will be refunded to Buyer. (Check one box only)
       ☒(1) This contract is subject to Buyer being approved for the financing described in the attached Third Party Financing Condition Addendum.
       ☐(2) This contract is not subject to Buyer being approved for financing and does not involve FHA or VA financing.
   ☐ B. ASSUMPTION: The assumption of the unpaid principal balance of one or more promissory notes described in the attached TREC Loan Assumption Addendum.
   ☐ C. SELLER FINANCING: A promissory note from Buyer to Seller of $_____, bearing _____ % interest per annum, secured by vendor's and deed of trust liens, and containing the terms and conditions described in the attached TREC Seller Financing Addendum. If an owner policy of title insurance is furnished, Buyer shall furnish Seller with a mortgagee policy of title insurance.

5. **EARNEST MONEY:** Upon execution of this contract by both parties, Buyer shall deposit $_15,000.00__ as earnest money with _ABC Title Co._____, as escrow agent, at _1234 Settlement Street, Dallas, Tx 75340_____ (address). Buyer shall deposit additional earnest money of $__N/A_____ with escrow agent on or before _____, 20____. If Buyer fails to deposit the earnest money as required by this contract, Buyer will be in default.

Initialed for identification by Buyer_____ and Seller _____   **01A** TREC NO. 20-5

Figure 12.1   Residential Sales Contract (Continued)

Contract Concerning _____ 3040 North Racine 75340 _____ Page Two   10-29-01
                                                 (Address of Property)

6. TITLE POLICY AND SURVEY:
 A. TITLE POLICY: Seller shall furnish to Buyer at ☒Seller's ☐Buyer's expense an owner policy of
    title insurance (Title Policy) issued by ___ABC Title Company_____
    _____ (Title Company) in the amount of
    the Sales Price, dated at or after closing, insuring Buyer against loss under the provisions of
    the Title Policy, subject to the promulgated exclusions (including existing building and zoning
    ordinances) and the following exceptions:
    (1) Restrictive covenants common to the platted subdivision in which the Property is located.
    (2) The standard printed exception for standby fees, taxes and assessments.
    (3) Liens created as part of the financing described in Paragraph 4.
    (4) Utility easements created by the dedication deed or plat of the subdivision in which the
        Property is located.
    (5) Reservations or exceptions otherwise permitted by this contract or as may be approved by
        Buyer in writing.
    (6) The standard printed exception as to marital rights.
    (7) The standard printed exception as to waters, tidelands, beaches, streams, and related
        matters.
    (8) The standard printed exception as to discrepancies, conflicts, shortages in area or boundary
        lines, encroachments or protrusions, or overlapping improvements. Buyer, at Buyer's expense,
        may have the exception amended to read, "shortages in area".
 B. COMMITMENT: Within 20 days after the Title Company receives a copy of this contract, Seller
    shall furnish to Buyer a commitment for title insurance (Commitment) and, at Buyer's
    expense, legible copies of restrictive covenants and documents evidencing exceptions in the
    Commitment (Exception Documents) other than the standard printed exceptions.   Seller
    authorizes the Title Company to mail or hand deliver the Commitment and Exception
    Documents to Buyer at Buyer's address shown in Paragraph 21.   If the Commitment and
    Exception Documents are not delivered to Buyer within the specified time, the time for
    delivery will be automatically extended up to 15 days or the Closing Date, whichever is
    earlier.
 C. SURVEY: The survey must be made by a registered professional land surveyor acceptable to
    the Title Company and any lender. (Check one box only)
    ☐ (1) Within _____ days after the effective date of this contract, Seller, at Seller's expense,
           shall furnish a new survey to Buyer.
    ☒ (2) Within ___3___ days after the effective date of this contract, Buyer, at Buyer's expense,
           shall obtain a new survey.
    ☐ (3) Within _____ days after the effective date of this contract, Seller shall furnish Seller's
           existing survey of the Property to Buyer and the Title Company, along with Seller's
           affidavit acceptable to the Title Company for approval of the survey. If the survey is
           not approved by the Title Company or Buyer's lender, a new survey will be obtained at
           ☐ Seller's ☐ Buyer's expense no later than 3 days prior to the Closing Date.
 D. OBJECTIONS: Within _____ days after Buyer receives the Commitment, Exception Documents
    and the survey, Buyer may object in writing to defects, exceptions, or encumbrances to title:
    disclosed on the survey other than items 6A(1) through (7) above; disclosed in the
    Commitment other than items 6A(1) through (8) above; or which prohibit the following use or
    activity: ___N/A_____ .
    Buyer's failure to object within the time allowed will constitute a waiver of Buyer's right to
    object; except that the requirements in Schedule C of the Commitment are not waived. Seller
    shall cure the timely objections of Buyer or any third party lender within 15 days after Seller
    receives the objections and the Closing Date will be extended as necessary. If objections are
    not cured by the extended Closing Date, this contract will terminate and the earnest money
    will be refunded to Buyer unless Buyer waives the objections.
 E. TITLE NOTICES:
    (1) ABSTRACT OR TITLE POLICY: Broker advises Buyer to have an abstract of title covering
        the Property examined by an attorney of Buyer's selection, or Buyer should be furnished
        with or obtain a Title Policy. If a Title Policy is furnished, the Commitment should be
        promptly reviewed by an attorney of Buyer's choice due to the time limitations on Buyer's
        right to object.
    (2) MANDATORY OWNERS' ASSOCIATION MEMBERSHIP: The Property ☐ is ☒ is not subject
        to mandatory membership in an owners' association. If the Property is subject to
        mandatory membership in an owners' association, Seller notifies Buyer under §5.012,

Initialed for identification by Buyer_____ and Seller _____   **01A** TREC NO. 20-5

Figure 12.1   Residential Sales Contract (Continued)

Contract Concerning _____**3040 North Racine 75340**_____ Page Three   10-29-01
(Address of Property)

Texas Property Code, that, as a purchaser of property in the residential community in which the Property is located, you are obligated to be a member of the owners' association. Restrictive covenants governing the use and occupancy of the Property and a dedicatory instrument governing the establishment, maintenance, and operation of this residential community have been or will be recorded in the Real Property Records of the county in which the Property is located. Copies of the restrictive covenants and dedicatory instrument may be obtained from the county clerk. You are obligated to pay assessments to the owners' association. The amount of the assessments is subject to change. Your failure to pay the assessments could result in a lien on and the foreclosure of the Property.

  (3) STATUTORY TAX DISTRICTS: If the Property is situated in a utility or other statutorily created district providing water, sewer, drainage, or flood control facilities and services, Chapter 49, Texas Water Code requires Seller to deliver and Buyer to sign the statutory notice relating to the tax rate, bonded indebtedness, or standby fee of the district prior to final execution of this contract.

  (4) TIDE WATERS: If the Property abuts the tidally influenced waters of the state, §33.135, Texas Natural Resources Code, requires a notice regarding coastal area property to be included in the contract. An addendum containing the notice promulgated by TREC or required by the parties must be used.

  (5) ANNEXATION: If the Property is located outside the limits of a municipality, Seller notifies Buyer under §5.011, Texas Property Code, that the Property may now or later be included in the extraterritorial jurisdiction of a municipality and may now or later be subject to annexation by the municipality. Each municipality maintains a map that depicts its boundaries and extraterritorial jurisdiction. To determine if the Property is located within a municipality's extraterritorial jurisdiction or is likely to be located within a municipality's extraterritorial jurisdiction, contact all municipalities located in the general proximity of the Property for further information.

7. PROPERTY CONDITION:

  A. INSPECTIONS, ACCESS AND UTILITIES: Buyer may have the Property inspected by inspectors selected by Buyer and licensed by TREC or otherwise permitted by law to make inspections. Seller shall permit access to the Property at reasonable times for (1) inspections, (2) repairs, (3) treatments and (4) reinspections after repairs have been completed. Seller shall pay for turning on utilities for inspections and reinspections.

  B. SELLER'S DISCLOSURE NOTICE PURSUANT TO §5.008, TEXAS PROPERTY CODE (Notice): (Check one box only)

    ☒ (1) Buyer has received the Notice.

    ☐ (2) Buyer has not received the Notice. Within _____ days after the effective date of this contract, Seller shall deliver the Notice to Buyer. If Buyer does not receive the Notice, Buyer may terminate this contract at any time prior to the closing. If Seller delivers the Notice, Buyer may terminate this contract for any reason within 7 days after Buyer receives the Notice or prior to the closing, whichever first occurs.

    ☐ (3) The Texas Property Code does not require this Seller to furnish the Notice.

  C. SELLER'S DISCLOSURE OF LEAD-BASED PAINT AND LEAD-BASED PAINT HAZARDS is required by Federal law for a residential dwelling constructed prior to 1978.

  D. ACCEPTANCE OF PROPERTY CONDITION: Buyer accepts the Property in its present condition; provided Seller, at Seller's expense, shall complete the following specific repairs and treatments:_____
_____.

  E. LENDER REQUIRED REPAIRS AND TREATMENTS: Unless otherwise agreed in writing, neither party is obligated to pay for lender required repairs, which includes treatment for wood destroying insects. If the parties do not agree to pay for the lender required repairs or treatments, this contract will terminate and the earnest money will be refunded to Buyer. If the cost of lender required repairs and treatments exceeds 5% of the Sales Price, Buyer may terminate this contract.

  F. COMPLETION OF REPAIRS AND TREATMENTS. Unless otherwise agreed in writing, Seller shall complete all agreed repairs and treatments prior to the Closing Date. All required permits must be obtained, and repairs and treatments must be performed by persons who are licensed or otherwise authorized by law to provide such repairs or treatments. At Buyer's election, any transferable warranties received by Seller with respect to the repairs and treatments will be transferred to Buyer at Buyer's expense. If Seller fails to complete any agreed repairs and

Initialed for identification by Buyer_____ and Seller _____   **01A** TREC NO. 20-5

Figure 12.1   Residential Sales Contract (Continued)

Contract Concerning _____ **3040 North Racine   75340** _____ Page Four   10-29-01
(Address of Property)

treatments prior to the Closing Date, Buyer may do so and receive reimbursement from Seller at closing. The Closing Date will be extended up to 15 days, if necessary, to complete repairs and treatments.

G. ENVIRONMENTAL MATTERS. Buyer is advised that the presence of wetlands, toxic substances, including asbestos and wastes or other environmental hazards, or the presence of a threatened or endangered species or its habitat may affect Buyer's intended use of the Property. If Buyer is concerned about these matters, an addendum promulgated by TREC or required by the parties should be used.

H. RESIDENTIAL SERVICE CONTRACTS. Buyer may purchase a residential service contract from a residential service company licensed by TREC. If Buyer purchases a residential service contract, Seller shall reimburse Buyer at closing for the cost of the residential service contract in an amount not exceeding $__350.00__ . Buyer should review any residential service contract for the scope of coverage, exclusions and limitations. **The purchase of a residential service contract is optional. Similar coverage may be purchased from various companies authorized to do business in Texas.**

8. BROKERS' FEES: All obligations of the parties for payment of brokers' fees are contained in separate written agreements.

9. CLOSING:

A. The closing of the sale will be on or before ____**June 15**____, 20_XX_, or within 7 days after objections to matters disclosed in the Commitment or by the survey have been cured, whichever date is later (Closing Date). If either party fails to close the sale by the Closing Date, the non-defaulting party may exercise the remedies contained in Paragraph 15.

B. At closing:
(1) Seller shall execute and deliver a general warranty deed conveying title to the Property to Buyer and showing no additional exceptions to those permitted in Paragraph 6 and furnish tax statements or certificates showing no delinquent taxes on the Property.
(2) Buyer shall pay the Sales Price in good funds acceptable to the escrow agent.
(3) Seller and Buyer shall execute and deliver any notices, statements, certificates, affidavits, releases, loan documents and other documents required of them by this contract, the Commitment or law necessary for the closing of the sale and the issuance of the Title Policy.

C. Unless expressly prohibited by written agreement, Seller may continue to show the Property and receive, negotiate and accept back-up offers.

10. POSSESSION: Seller shall deliver to Buyer possession of the Property in its present or required condition, ordinary wear and tear excepted: ☒ upon closing and funding ☐ according to a temporary residential lease form promulgated by TREC or other written lease required by the parties. Any possession by Buyer prior to closing or by Seller after closing which is not authorized by a written lease will establish a tenancy at sufferance relationship between the parties. *Consult your insurance agent prior to change of ownership or possession because insurance coverage may be limited or terminated. The absence of a written lease or appropriate insurance coverage may expose the parties to economic loss.*

11. SPECIAL PROVISIONS: (Insert only factual statements and business details applicable to the sale. TREC rules prohibit licensees from adding factual statements or business details for which a contract addendum, lease or other form has been promulgated by TREC for mandatory use.)

Seller's contribution to buyer's expenses in paragraph 12A(3) shall apply to loan discount points.

12. SETTLEMENT AND OTHER EXPENSES:

A. The following expenses must be paid at or prior to closing:
(1) Expenses payable by Seller (Seller's Expenses): Releases of existing liens, including prepayment penalties and recording fees; release of Seller's loan liability; tax statements or certificates; preparation of deed; one-half of escrow fee; and other expenses payable by Seller under this contract.

Initialed for identification by Buyer_____ and Seller _____   **01A** TREC NO. 20-5

Figure 12.1 Residential Sales Contract (Continued)

Contract Concerning _____**3040 North Racine   75340**_____ Page Five   10-29-01
(Address of Property)

(2) Expenses payable by Buyer (Buyer's Expenses):
(a) Conventional/FHA Financing: Loan origination, discount, buy-down, and commitment fees (Loan Fees); appraisal fees; loan application fees; credit reports; preparation of loan documents; interest on the notes from date of disbursement to one month prior to dates of first monthly payments; recording fees; copies of easements and restrictions; mortgagee title policy with endorsements required by lender; loan-related inspection fees; photos, amortization schedules, one-half of escrow fee; all prepaid items, including required premiums for flood and hazard insurance, reserve deposits for insurance, ad valorem taxes and special governmental assessments; final compliance inspection; courier fee, repair inspections, underwriting fee and wire transfer, and other expenses payable by Buyer under this contract.
(b) VA Financing: Appraisal fees; all prepaid items, including required premiums for flood and hazard insurance, reserve deposits for other insurance, ad valorem taxes and special government assessments; mortgagee title policy; expenses incident to any loan, including credit reports, recording fees, loan origination fee and loan related inspection fees.
(3) Additional Expenses: Seller shall also pay an amount not to exceed $_**1,050.00**_ to be applied in the following order: Buyer's Expenses which Buyer is prohibited by FHA or VA from paying; Buyer's prepaid items; other Buyer's Expenses.

B. Buyer shall pay Private Mortgage Insurance Premium (PMI), VA Loan Funding Fee, or FHA Mortgage Insurance Premium (MIP) not to exceed $_**N/A**_ , which will be ❏ paid in cash at closing ❏ added to the amount of the loan or ❏ paid as follows: _____
_____ .

C. If any expense exceeds an amount expressly stated in this contract for such expense to be paid by a party, that party may terminate this contract unless the other party agrees to pay such excess. Buyer may not pay charges and fees expressly prohibited by FHA, VA, Texas Veterans Housing Assistance Program Loan or other governmental loan program regulations.

13. **PRORATIONS:** Taxes for the current year, interest, maintenance fees, assessments, dues and rents will be prorated through the Closing Date. If taxes for the current year vary from the amount prorated at closing, the parties shall adjust the prorations when tax statements for the current year are available. If taxes are not paid at or prior to closing, Buyer shall pay taxes for the current year.

14. **CASUALTY LOSS:** If any part of the Property is damaged or destroyed by fire or other casualty after the effective date of this contract, Seller shall restore the Property to its previous condition as soon as reasonably possible, but in any event by the Closing Date. If Seller fails to do so due to factors beyond Seller's control, Buyer may (a) terminate this contract and the earnest money will be refunded to Buyer (b) extend the time for performance up to 15 days and the Closing Date will be extended as necessary or (c) accept the Property in its damaged condition with an assignment of insurance proceeds and receive credit from Seller at closing in the amount of the deductible under the insurance policy. Seller's obligations under this paragraph are independent of any obligations of Seller under Paragraph 7.

15. **DEFAULT:** If Buyer fails to comply with this contract, Buyer will be in default, and Seller may (a) enforce specific performance, seek such other relief as may be provided by law, or both, or (b) terminate this contract and receive the earnest money as liquidated damages, thereby releasing both parties from this contract. If, due to factors beyond Seller's control, Seller fails within the time allowed to make any non-casualty repairs or deliver the Commitment, or survey, if required of Seller, Buyer may (a) extend the time for performance up to 15 days and the Closing Date will be extended as necessary or (b) terminate this contract as the sole remedy and receive the earnest money. If Seller fails to comply with this contract for any other reason, Seller will be in default and Buyer may (a) enforce specific performance, seek such other relief as may be provided by law, or both, or (b) terminate this contract and receive the earnest money, thereby releasing both parties from this contract.

16. **MEDIATION:** It is the policy of the State of Texas to encourage resolution of disputes through alternative dispute resolution procedures such as mediation. Any dispute between Seller and Buyer related to this contract which is not resolved through informal discussion ☒will ❏will not be submitted to a mutually acceptable mediation service or provider. The parties to the mediation shall bear the mediation costs equally. The covenants in this paragraph survive the closing. This

Initialed for identification by Buyer_____ and Seller _____   **01A** TREC NO. 20-5

Figure 12.1   Residential Sales Contract (Continued)

Contract Concerning _____ 3040 North Racine   75340 _____ Page Six   10-29-01
(Address of Property)

paragraph does not preclude a party from seeking equitable relief from a court of competent jurisdiction.

17. **ATTORNEY'S FEES:** The prevailing party in any legal proceeding related to this contract is entitled to recover reasonable attorney's fees and all costs of such proceeding incurred by the prevailing party.

18. **ESCROW:** The escrow agent is not (a) a party to this contract and does not have liability for the performance or nonperformance of any party to this contract, (b) liable for interest on the earnest money and (c) liable for the loss of any earnest money caused by the failure of any financial institution in which the earnest money has been deposited unless the financial institution is acting as escrow agent. At closing, the earnest money must be applied first to any cash down payment, then to Buyer's Expenses and any excess refunded to Buyer. If both parties make written demand for the earnest money, escrow agent may require payment of unpaid expenses incurred on behalf of the parties and a written release of liability of escrow agent from all parties. If one party makes written demand for the earnest money, escrow agent shall give notice of the demand by providing to the other party a copy of the demand. If escrow agent does not receive written objection to the demand from the other party within 30 days after notice to the other party, escrow agent may disburse the earnest money to the party making demand reduced by the amount of unpaid expenses incurred on behalf of the party receiving the earnest money and escrow agent may pay the same to the creditors. If escrow agent complies with the provisions of this paragraph, each party hereby releases escrow agent from all adverse claims related to the disbursal of the earnest money. Escrow agent's notice to the other party will be effective when deposited in the U. S. Mail, postage prepaid, certified mail, return receipt requested, addressed to the other party at such party's address shown below. Notice of objection to the demand will be deemed effective upon receipt by escrow agent.

19. **REPRESENTATIONS:** Seller represents that as of the Closing Date (a) there will be no liens, assessments, or security interests against the Property which will not be satisfied out of the sales proceeds unless securing payment of any loans assumed by Buyer and (b) assumed loans will not be in default. If any representation of Seller in this contract is untrue on the Closing Date, Buyer may terminate this contract and the earnest money will be refunded to Buyer. All representations contained in this contract will survive closing.

20. **FEDERAL TAX REQUIREMENTS:** If Seller is a "foreign person," as defined by applicable law, or if Seller fails to deliver an affidavit to Buyer that Seller is not a "foreign person," then Buyer shall withhold from the sales proceeds an amount sufficient to comply with applicable tax law and deliver the same to the Internal Revenue Service together with appropriate tax forms. Internal Revenue Service regulations require filing written reports if currency in excess of specified amounts is received in the transaction.

21. **NOTICES:** All notices from one party to the other must be in writing and are effective when mailed to, hand-delivered at, or transmitted by facsimile as follows:

To Buyer at:	To Seller at:
Blake Redemann and Connie Redemann	John Iuro and Joanne Iuro
7016 Hurst	3040 North Racine
Amarillo, TX 79109	Dallas, TX 75340
Telephone:(806) 372-4300	Telephone:(214) 497-1324
Facsimile:(806) 372-4301	Facsimile:(214) 497-2324

22. **AGREEMENT OF PARTIES:** This contract contains the entire agreement of the parties and cannot be changed except by their written agreement. Addenda which are a part of this contract are (check all applicable boxes):

☒ Third Party Financing Condition Addendum

❑ Seller Financing Addendum

❑ Loan Assumption Addendum

❑ Addendum for Property Subject to Mandatory Membership in an Owners' Association

Initialed for identification by Buyer_____ and Seller _____   **01A** TREC NO. 20-5

Figure 12.1   Residential Sales Contract (Continued)

Contract Concerning _____ 3040 North Racine 75340 _____ Page Seven 10-29-01
(Address of Property)

❑ Buyer's Temporary Residential Lease

❑ Seller's Temporary Residential Lease

❑ Addendum for Sale of Other Property by Buyer

❑ Addendum for "Back-Up" Contract

❑ Addendum for Seller's Disclosure of Information on Lead-based Paint and Lead-based Paint Hazards as Required by Federal Law

❑ Environmental Assessment, Threatened or Endangered Species and Wetlands Addendum

❑ Addendum for Coastal Area Property

❑ Addendum for Property Located Seaward of the Gulf Intracoastal Waterway

❑ Addendum for Release of Liability on Assumption of FHA, VA, or Conventional Loan/Restoration of Seller's Entitlement for VA Guaranteed Loan

❑ Other (list): _____

_____

23. **TERMINATION OPTION: This paragraph will be a part of this contract ONLY if both blanks are filled in and Buyer has paid the Option Fee.** Buyer has paid Seller $ 100.00 (Option Fee) for the unrestricted right to terminate this contract by giving notice of termination to Seller within 14 days after the effective date of this contract. If Buyer gives notice of termination within the time specified, the Option Fee will not be refunded, however, any earnest money will be refunded to Buyer. The Option Fee ❑will ☒will not be credited to the Sales Price at closing. For the purposes of this paragraph, time is of the essence; strict compliance with the time for performance stated herein is required.

24. **CONSULT AN ATTORNEY:** Real estate licensees cannot give legal advice. READ THIS CONTRACT CAREFULLY. If you do not understand the effect of this contract, consult an attorney BEFORE signing.

Buyer's
Attorney is:_____

_____

Telephone: (_____)_____

Facsimile: (_____)_____

Seller's
Attorney is:_____

_____

Telephone: (_____)_____

Facsimile: (_____)_____

EXECUTED the _____day of _____, 20_____ (EFFECTIVE DATE).
(BROKER: FILL IN THE DATE OF FINAL ACCEPTANCE.)

_____
Buyer

_____
Buyer

_____
Seller

_____
Seller

01A TREC NO. 20-5

Figure 12.1   **Residential Sales Contract (Continued)**

Contract Concerning _____ 3040 North Racine 75340 _____ Page Eight 10-29-01
(Address of Property)

SELLER'S RECEIPT

Receipt of $ __100.00__ (Option Fee) in the form of __personal check__ is acknowledged.

_____   _____
Seller   Date

BROKER INFORMATION AND RATIFICATION OF FEE

Listing Broker has agreed to pay Other Broker __N/A__ of the total sales price when Listing Broker's fee is received. Escrow Agent is authorized and directed to pay Other Broker from Listing Broker's fee at closing.

_____   Open Door Real Estate Company
Other Broker   Listing Broker

_____   332324   214-379-4300
License No.   Telephone   License No.   Telephone

represents ☐ Buyer only as Buyer's agent   represents   ☒ Seller and Buyer as an intermediary
            ☐ Seller as Listing Broker's subagent   ☐ Seller only as Seller's agent

_____   Renee Raymond   214-379-4300
Associate   Telephone   Listing Associate   Telephone

_____   1524 North Spring Drive 214-379-4309
Broker's Address   Listing Associate's Office Address Facsimile

_____   Nancy Nystrom   214-379-4300
Facsimile   Selling Associate   Telephone

                             1524 North Spring Drive 214-379-4309
                             Selling Associate's Office Address Facsimile

---

RECEIPT

Receipt of ☒ Contract and ☒ $ __15,000.00__ Earnest Money in the form of __personal check__
is acknowledged.
Escrow Agent: _____   Date: _____

By: _____

_____   Telephone (_____) _____
Address

_____   Facsimile: (_____) _____
City   State   Zip

01A TREC NO. 20-5

At the bottom of the contract negotiated between the buyer and the seller are the broker information and earnest money receipt paragraphs. The broker information section specifies the brokers involved in the transaction and the fee to be paid to the "other broker" by the listing broker. The Third Party Financing Condition Addendum in Figure 12.2 is one of the three addenda promulgated to expand the "financing" paragraph of the contract, providing conditions under which the buyer agrees to obtain financing.

Gulf Coast counties. Two promulgated addenda reflect the unique circumstances of property located in the Gulf Coast counties. The *Texas Open Beach Law* requires that the Gulf Coast beaches from the mean low tide to the vegetation line remain open to the public, as discussed in Chapter 8. The law requires that a contract for the sale of real property located seaward of the Gulf Intracoastal Waterway must include a prescribed statement regarding open beaches and the possibility that any structure that might become seaward of the vegetation line as a result of natural processes is subject to a lawsuit by the State of Texas for its removal. Prior to executing the contract, the buyer must also be advised to determine the rate of shoreline erosion in the vicinity of the property. The promulgated "Addendum for Property Located Seaward of the Gulf Intracoastal Waterway" contains the statutory notices.

If the property is sold without a contract, the seller must deliver the statutory notice to the buyer at or prior to closing of the sale. The buyer then must sign a receipt for the notice statement. If the seller fails to include the statement in the contract, the buyer has the option of terminating such contract without liability, and the earnest money is to be returned to the buyer. Furthermore, failure to provide the statement either in the contract or by a separate notice constitutes a violation of the Texas Deceptive Trade Practices Act.

Laws pertaining to wetland areas along the Gulf Coast require that sellers of property that adjoin or share a common boundary with tidally submerged lands must notify buyers of restrictions pertaining to the use and development of the property. The promulgated "Addendum for Coastal Area Property" contains the statutory notices.

Option Agreements

An **option** is a *contract by which an* optionor *(generally an owner) gives an* optionee *(a prospective purchaser or lessee) the right to buy or lease the owner's property at a fixed price within a stated period of time.*The optionee *must pay* an option fee for this option right. The optionee has no other obligation until he or she decides to either exercise the option right or allow the option right to expire. An option is enforceable by only one party—the optionee.

An option contract is not a sales contract. At the time the option is signed by the parties, the owner does not sell and the optionee does not buy. The parties merely agree that the optionee will have the *right* to buy and the owner will be *obligated* to sell *if* the optionee decides to exercise his or her right of option.

The option agreement requires that the optionor act only after the optionee gives notice that he or she elects to exercise the option and buy. If the option is not exercised within the time specified, the optionor's obligation and the

10-29-01

PROMULGATED BY THE TEXAS REAL ESTATE COMMISSION (TREC)

THIRD PARTY FINANCING CONDITION ADDENDUM

TO CONTRACT CONCERNING THE PROPERTY AT

3040 North Racine, Dallas, TX 75340
(Street Address and City)

Buyer shall apply promptly for all financing described below and make every reasonable effort to obtain financing approval. Financing approval will be deemed to have been obtained when the lender determines that Buyer has satisfied all of lender's financial requirements (those items relating to Buyer's assets, income and credit history). If financing (including any financed PMI premium) approval is not obtained within **30** days after the effective date, this contract will terminate and the earnest money will be refunded to Buyer. Each note must be secured by vendor's and deed of trust liens.

CHECK APPLICABLE BOXES:

☒ A. CONVENTIONAL FINANCING:
   ☒ (1) A first mortgage loan in the principal amount of $ **70,000.00** (excluding any financed PMI premium), due in full in **15** year(s), with interest not to exceed **10** % per annum for the first **15** year(s) of the loan with Loan Fees not to exceed **2½** % of the loan. The loan will be ☐ with ☒ without PMI.
   ☐ (2) A second mortgage loan in the principal amount of $_____ (excluding any financed PMI premium) due in full in _____ year(s), with interest not to exceed _____% per annum for the first _____ year(s) of the loan with Loan Fees not to exceed _____ % of the loan. The loan will be ☐ with ☐ without PMI.

☐ B. TEXAS VETERANS' HOUSING ASSISTANCE PROGRAM LOAN: A Texas Veteran's Housing Assistance Program Loan of $_____ for a period of at least _____years at the interest rate established by the Texas Veteran's Land Board at the time of closing.

☐ C. FHA INSURED FINANCING: A Section _____ FHA insured loan of not less than $_____ (excluding any financed MIP), amortizable monthly for not less than _____years, with interest not to exceed _____% per annum for the first _____year(s) of the loan with Loan Fees not to exceed _____ % of the loan. As required by HUD-FHA, if FHA valuation is unknown,"*It is expressly agreed that, notwithstanding any other provision of this contract, the purchaser (Buyer) shall not be obligated to complete the purchase of the Property described herein or to incur any penalty by forfeiture of earnest money deposits or otherwise unless the purchaser (Buyer) has been given in accordance with HUD/FHA or VA requirements a written statement issued by the Federal Housing Commissioner, Department of Veterans Affairs, or a Direct Endorsement Lender setting forth the appraised value of the Property of not less than $_____. The purchaser (Buyer) shall have the privilege and option of proceeding with consummation of the contract without regard to the amount of the appraised valuation. The appraised valuation is arrived at to determine the maximum mortgage the Department of Housing and Urban Development will insure. HUD does not warrant the value or the condition of the Property. The purchaser (Buyer) should satisfy himself/herself that the price and the condition of the Property are acceptable.*"

If the FHA appraised value of the Property (excluding closing costs and MIP) is less than the Sales Price, Seller may reduce the Sales Price to an amount equal to the FHA appraised value (excluding closing costs and MIP) and the sale will be closed at the lower Sales Price with proportionate adjustments to the down payment and loan amount.

Figure 12.2   Third Party Financing Condition Addendum (Continued)

Third Party Financing Condition Addendum Concerning   Page Two 10-29-01

3040 North Racine, Dallas, TX 75340
(Address of Property)

☐ D. VA GUARANTEED FINANCING: A VA guaranteed loan of not less than $_____ (excluding any financed Funding Fee), amortizable monthly for not less than_____years, with interest not to exceed_____% per annum for the first _____year(s) of the loan with Loan Fees not to exceed _____ % of the loan.

VA NOTICE TO BUYER: "*It is expressly agreed that, notwithstanding any other provisions of this contract, the Buyer shall not incur any penalty by forfeiture of earnest money or otherwise or be obligated to complete the purchase of the Property described herein, if the contract purchase price or cost exceeds the reasonable value of the Property established by the Department of Veterans Affairs. The Buyer shall, however, have the privilege and option of proceeding with the consummation of this contract without regard to the amount of the reasonable value established by the Department of Veterans Affairs.*"

If Buyer elects to complete the purchase at an amount in excess of the reasonable value established by VA, Buyer shall pay such excess amount in cash from a source which Buyer agrees to disclose to the VA and which Buyer represents will not be from borrowed funds except as approved by VA. If VA reasonable value of the Property is less than the Sales Price, Seller may reduce the Sales Price to an amount equal to the VA reasonable value and the sale will be closed at the lower Sales Price with proportionate adjustments to the down payment and the loan amount.

_____   _____
Buyer   Seller

_____   _____
Buyer   Seller

This form has been approved by the Texas Real Estate Commission for use with similarly approved or promulgated contract forms. Such approval relates to this form only. TREC forms are intended for use only by trained real estate licensees. No representation is made as to the legal validity or adequacy of any provision in any specific transactions. It is not suitable for complex transactions. Texas Real Estate Commission, P.O. Box 12188, Austin, TX 78711-2188, 1-800-250-8732 or (512) 459-6544 (http://www.trec.state.tx.us) TREC No. 40-0.

optionee's right will expire. The optionee cannot recover the consideration paid for the option right. However, the owner could elect (if desired) to apply the money paid for the option to the purchase price of the real estate if the optionee buys the property.

The Texas promulgated residential sales contract allows the buyer to create an option contract providing the unrestricted right to terminate the contract within the established period of the option. A buyer may terminate the contract during that period for any reason. *If* the option provision in the contract is selected, the buyer must pay an option fee which would not be refunded if he or she were to terminate the contract. Any earnest money would be refunded. Another common application of an option is a lease that includes an option for the tenant to purchase the property. Options on commercial real estate frequently are made dependent on the fulfillment of specific conditions, such as obtaining a zoning change or a building permit.

Contracts for Deed (Installment Contracts)

A real estate sale can be made under a **contract for deed,** *sometimes called a land contract,* an *installment contract,* or a *contract of sale.* Under a typical contract for deed, the seller (also known as the *vendor*) retains legal title. The buyer (called the *vendee*) takes possession and gets equitable title to the property, which establishes a homestead shield against the buyer's creditors. The buyer agrees to give the seller a down payment and pay regular monthly installments of principal and interest over a number of years. The buyer usually also pays real estate taxes, insurance premiums, repairs, and upkeep on the property. Although the buyer obtains possession under the contract, the seller is not obligated to execute and deliver a deed to the buyer until the terms of the contract have been satisfied. This frequently occurs when the buyer has accumulated enough down payment or enough time on his or her present job to obtain a new mortgage loan—or it may be when the note to the seller has been paid in full.

If the contract for deed conveys real property used as the purchaser's residence (excluding the sale of state land or a sale of land by the Veteran's Land Board), the seller must, before the contract is signed, satisfy many statutory requirements (S.B. 198, 2001). Among the requirements are

- providing copies of a current survey, a tax certificate, and an insurance policy, *and*
- disclosing property condition and information about utilities, road maintenance, encumbrances that affect title, and financing terms.

The purchaser has the right to cancel the contract *for any reason* on or before the fourteenth day after the effective date of the contract. Within 30 days of the execution of the contract for deed, the seller must record the contract and disclosure statements with the county clerk. The seller is further obligated to provide the purchaser with an annual accounting statement which reflects the amount paid, disbursements for taxes and insurance, and the balance remaining on the contract.

If the purchaser defaults under the terms of the contract, the seller must provide a specific statutory notice and give the purchaser 60 days to cure the default. If the purchaser fails to cure the default within the 60-day period and has paid 40 percent or more of the amount due or the equivalent of 48 monthly payments, the seller is granted the power to sell the property through a trustee designated by the seller. If the purchaser defaults before paying 40 percent of the amount due or the equivalent of 48 monthly payments, the seller may enforce the remedy of rescission or of forfeiture and acceleration of the debt.

Purchasers in a contract for deed sale should be aware of potential problems, such as the death of the seller prior to delivery of the deed or the filing of a judgment lien against the seller, which would attach to the subject land. Potential hazards to the seller include the purchaser's leasing the property to another party or possible damage to the property, resulting in a loss of property value if the buyer defaults. A contract for deed can be a useful sales and financing tool but it should never be used in an attempt to defeat a due-on-sale provision in a deed of trust or to hide a transaction from a lender. There is no promulgated contract for deed form in Texas; therefore, it is essential that both parties seek competent legal counsel.

Leases   A lease is a contract in which the owner agrees to give possession of all or part of certain real estate to another person for a specified time period in exchange for a rental fee. Leases are discussed in detail in Chapter 21.

Escrow Agreements (As Part of Closing or Settlement)   An *escrow* is a means by which the parties to a contract carry out the terms of their agreement. The parties appoint a disinterested third party to act as the *escrowee,* or *escrow agent.* This escrow agent must be someone who is not a party to the contract and will not benefit in any way from the contract.

Any real estate transaction can be closed through an escrow. The parties to the transaction enter into an **escrow agreement** (which may be part of the contract) that sets forth the duties of the escrow agent and the obligations and requirements of the parties to the transaction. An escrow agreement may be used in closing such real estate transactions as a sale, a mortgage loan, an exchange of property, a contract for deed, or a lease. In Texas, a title company typically acts as the escrow agent.

An escrow agreement requires that the seller deposit with the escrow agent the deed and other pertinent documents, such as leases, insurance policies, a survey, and a mortgage payoff letter (if the existing loan is to be paid in full and released of record). It also provides for the buyer to deposit the purchase price and an executed deed of trust and note if he or she is securing borrowed funds to purchase the property. The escrow agent is authorized to have the title examined, and if it is found to meet the conditions of the escrow agreement, the sale is concluded. Title then passes to the buyer, and the seller receives payment. The escrow procedure will be detailed more fully in Chapter 20.

The usual practice is to rely on the various provisions of the promulgated sales contract to establish the escrow agreement in a residential transaction. However, commercial transactions may include a separate set of instructions to the escrow agent that is signed by the contracting parties.

Summary

A contract may be defined as an agreement made by competent parties, with adequate consideration, to take or not take some proper, or legal, action. Contracts may be classified according to whether the parties' intentions are express or are implied by their actions. They also may be classified as bilateral, when both parties have obligated themselves to act, or unilateral, when one party is obligated to perform only if the other party acts. In addition, contracts may be classified according to their legal enforceability as valid, void, voidable, or unenforceable.

Many contracts specify a time for performance. In any case all contracts must be performed within a reasonable time. An executed contract is one that is fully performed. An executory contract is one that is partially performed.

The essentials of a valid contract are (1) legally competent parties, (2) offer and acceptance, (3) consideration, (4) legality of object, and (5) agreement in writing and signed by the parties. In Texas, a valid real estate contract also must include a description of the property.

In a number of circumstances, a contract may be canceled before it is fully performed. Furthermore, in certain types of contracts either party may transfer his or her rights and obligations under the agreement by assignment of the contract or by novation (substitution of a new contract).

If either party to a real estate sales contract defaults, several alternative actions are available. Contracts usually provide that the seller has the right to declare a sale canceled through forfeiture if the buyer defaults. In general, if either party has suffered a loss because of the other's default, he or she may sue for damages to cover the loss. If one party insists on completing the transaction, he or she may sue the defaulting party for specific performance of the terms of the contract; in this way, a court can order the other parties to comply with the agreement.

Contracts frequently used in the real estate business include listings, buyer representation agreements, sales contracts, options, contracts for deed, leases, and escrow agreements. A real estate sales contract binds a buyer and a seller to a definite transaction, as described in detail in the contract. The buyer is bound to purchase the property for the amount stated in the agreement. The seller is bound to deliver good and indefeasible title, free from liens and encumbrances (except those allowed by any "subject to" clause of the contract).

Under an option agreement the optionee purchases from the optionor, for a limited time period, the exclusive right to purchase or lease the optionor's property. For a potential purchaser or lessee, an option is a means of buying time to consider or complete arrangements for a transaction. A contract for deed is a sales/financing agreement under which a buyer purchases a seller's real estate on time; the buyer may take possession of and responsibility for the property but does *not* receive the deed until the terms of the contract are completed.

A real estate transaction may be completed through an escrow, a means by which the parties to a contract carry out the terms of their agreement. The parties appoint a third party to act as the escrowee, or escrow agent. In the sale of real estate, the seller's deed and the buyer's money are deposited with an escrow agent under an escrow agreement that sets forth the conditions to be met before the sale is consummated. The escrow agent records the deed and performs any other requirements of the escrow agreement, such as accumulating the buyer's funds and writing all of the checks.

1. C
2. C
3. A
4. D
5. D
6. B
7. C
8. B
9. B
10. A
11. B
12. D

13. B
14. D
15. B
16. C
17. A
18. B
19. A
20. D
21. B
22. D
23. B
24. A

Questions

1. A contract is said to be *bilateral* if
   a. one of the parties is a minor.
   b. only one party to the agreement is bound to act.
   c. all parties to the contract are bound to act.
   d. the contract has yet to be performed.

2. A contract for the sale of real estate that does not state the consideration to be paid for the property and is not signed by the parties is considered to be
   a. voidable.
   b. executory.
   c. void.
   d. enforceable.

3. Max makes an offer on Robert's house, Robert accepts and Max is notified of the acceptance. Both parties sign the sales contract. At this point, Max has what type of title to the property?
   a. Equitable
   b. Voidable
   c. Escrow
   d. Recorded

4. A seller gave an open listing to several brokers, specifically promising that if one of the brokers found a buyer for the seller's real estate, the seller would then pay a commission to that broker. This offer by the seller is what type of agreement?
   a. Executed
   b. Discharged
   c. Implied
   d. Unilateral

5. In the completion of a promulgated contract form, several words were crossed out and others inserted. To eliminate future controversy as to whether the changes were made before or after the contract was signed, the broker should
   a. write a letter to each party listing the changes.
   b. have each party write a letter to the other approving the changes.
   c. redraw the entire contract.
   d. have both parties initial or sign in the margin near each change.

6. If, after the sales contract is signed, the seller decides not to sell,
   a. the seller may cancel the contract and retain the buyer's earnest money deposit.
   b. the buyer may institute a suit for specific performance of the contract and/or for money damages.
   c. the buyer may both get his earnest money back and file for specific performance.
   d. the real estate agent forfeits a right to a commission.

7. Under the statute of frauds, contracts for the sale of real estate must be
   a. originated by a real estate broker.
   b. on preprinted forms.
   c. in writing to be enforceable.
   d. accompanied by earnest money deposits.

8. During the period after a real estate sales contract is signed but before title actually passes, the status of the contract is
   a. executed.
   b. executory.
   c. unilateral.
   d. implied.

9. Which of the following is **NOT** one of the elements essential to a valid contract?
   a. Offer and acceptance
   b. Earnest money
   c. Consideration
   d. Competent parties

10. Allen has a contract to buy property but would rather let his friend Mark buy it instead. If the contract allows, Mark can take over Allen's original obligation by the process known as
    a. assignment.
    b. subordination.
    c. novation.
    d. mutual consent.

11. John makes an offer to purchase certain property listed with broker Sam and leaves a deposit with the broker to show good faith. When the contract is accepted, Sam should
    a. immediately apply the deposit to the listing expenses.
    b. deposit the funds in an account as provided by state law within two working days.
    c. give the deposit to the seller when the offer is presented.
    d. put the deposit in his checking account.

12. Which of the following **BEST** describes the contract for deed or installment contract?
    a. A contract to buy land only
    b. A mortgage on land
    c. A means of conveying title immediately while the purchaser pays for the property in installments
    d. A method of selling real estate whereby the purchaser pays for the property in regular installments while the seller retains title to the property

13. When a real estate sales transaction is to be closed in escrow,
    a. the seller and escrow agent execute a separate escrow agreement.
    b. the buyer's purchase-money mortgage and note are deposited with the escrow agent.
    c. one of the parties to the contract is usually appointed as the escrow agent.
    d. the buyer sets forth the obligations of the escrow agent.

14. A contract may be discharged by all **EXCEPT** which of the following means?
    a. Impossibility of performance
    b. Agreement of the parties
    c. Default by one party
    d. Change in the marital status of one party

15. Broker Sam Manella has found a buyer for Joe Taylor's home. The buyer has entered into a real estate sales contract for the property for $1,000 less than the asking price and has deposited $5,000 earnest money with broker Manella. Taylor is out of town for the weekend, and Manella has been unable to inform him of the signed offer. At this point, the document is a(n)
    a. voidable contract.
    b. offer.
    c. executory agreement.
    d. implied contract.

16. A suit for specific performance of a real estate contract asks for
    a. money damages.
    b. a deficiency judgment.
    c. conveyance of the property.
    d. a new contract.

17. Caz Krys is selling his home to Burton Timmins. After the sales contract has been signed by both parties, but before the title has passed to the buyer, the home is destroyed in a fire. Who is likely to bear the loss?
    a. Caz Krys, the seller
    b. Burton Timmins, the buyer
    c. The buyer's mortgage lender
    d. The seller's mortgage lender

18. When a broker uses a client's earnest money deposit for his or her own personal use, the broker is guilty of
    a. commingling.
    b. conversion.
    c. cotenancy.
    d. conspiracy.

19. An option-to-purchase agreement
    a. is generally limited to a fixed price within a specified time period.
    b. requires option money that is refundable if the buyer does not buy.
    c. binds the buyer only.
    d. binds both buyer and seller.

20. The purchaser of real estate under a contract for deed
    a. generally pays no interest.
    b. is called a vendor.
    c. is not required to pay property taxes for the duration of the contract.
    d. is required to pay taxes and insurance on the property.

21. In Texas, who is authorized to draft deeds, mortgages, deeds of trust, and notes?
    a. A licensed real estate broker
    b. An attorney licensed to practice law
    c. The title company clerk
    d. The mortgage lender

22. Alice and Anne enter into a real estate sales contract. Under the contract's terms, Alice will pay Anne $500 a month for ten years. Anne will continue to hold legal title to the property. Alice will live in the property and pay all real estate taxes, insurance premiums, and regular upkeep costs. What kind of contract do Alice and Anne have?
    a. Option contract
    b. Contract for mortgage
    c. Unilateral contract
    d. Contract for deed

23. The Franklins offer in writing to purchase a house for $120,000, including its draperies, with the offer to expire on Saturday at noon. The Webers reply in writing on Thursday, accepting the $120,000 offer, but excluding the draperies. On Friday, while the Franklins consider this counteroffer, the Webers decide to accept the original offer, draperies included, and state that in writing. At this point, which of the following statements is true?
    a. The Franklins are legally bound to buy the house although they have the right to insist that the draperies be included.
    b. The Franklins are not bound to buy.
    c. The Franklins must buy the house and are not entitled to the draperies.
    d. The Franklins must buy the house, but may deduct the value of the draperies from the $120,000.

24. Between June 5 and September 23, Marcus suffered from a mental illness that caused delusions, hallucinations, and loss of memory. On July 1, Marcus signed a contract to purchase a property, with the closing set for October 31. On September 24, Marcus began psychiatric treatment; he was declared completely cured by October 15. Which of the following statements is true regarding Marcus's contract?
    a. The contract is voidable.
    b. The contract is void.
    c. The contract lacks offer and acceptance.
    d. The contract is fully valid and enforceable.

13 Listing Agreements

Key Terms

exclusive-agency listing
exclusive-right-to-sell
  listing

multiple-listing
  contract
net listing

open listing
Seller's Disclosure
  Notice

OVERVIEW

A retailer may employ the best salespeople in the business, maintain the most attractive shop in town, and spend thousands of dollars on public relations and advertising to further the company's image, only to go out of business because he or she does not have an adequate supply of goods on hand to sell. Such is the case in the real estate business. Without a well-stocked inventory of properly priced properties listed to sell, a broker or salesperson is no more than an office clerk without an income. The listing agreement that secures the broker's inventory can take many forms, each with its own rights and responsibilities for seller and agent.

This chapter examines these forms of listing agreements as well as some factors a broker or salesperson must consider when "taking a listing." The particular form of listing contract is chosen by the broker, who is a principal to the contract. The contract is subject to negotiation and alteration by either party. A multiple-listing service (MLS) provides listing contract forms, and these may vary from city to city. The student must become familiar with the specific forms supplied by the broker or the local MLS. Because the broker is a principal to the listing contract, the broker may draft it, but a legal review is certainly recommended to ensure adequate protection for the broker.

LISTING PROPERTY

Every real estate sale involves two parties: the seller and the buyer. The seller furnishes the real estate broker and salesperson with the necessary inventory, the *listing.* How complete and accurately priced this inventory is will determine the broker's ultimate success.

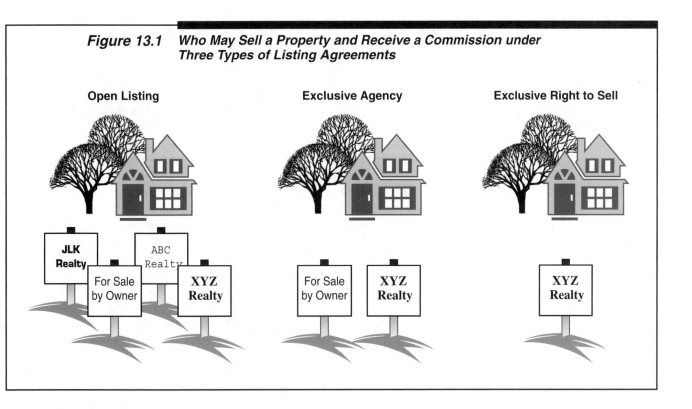

Figure 13.1   *Who May Sell a Property and Receive a Commission under Three Types of Listing Agreements*

The listing agreement is the contract of employment between a broker and a seller. It creates a *special agency* relationship between a broker (agent) and a seller (principal), whereby the agent is authorized to represent his or her principal's property for sale or lease, solicit offers, and submit the offers to the principal. Listing agreements in Texas must be in writing to be enforceable and must meet the requirements for a valid contract that were discussed in Chapter 12.

The provisions of the Texas Real Estate License Act state that only a broker can act as agent to list, sell, or rent another person's real estate. Throughout this chapter, unless otherwise stated, the terms *broker, agent,* and *firm* are intended to include both broker and salespersons. Whereas both have the authority to list, lease, and sell property and provide other services to a principal, these acts must be done in the name and under the supervision of the broker—*never in the name of the salesperson.*

Listing Agreements   The forms of listing agreements, or employment contracts, generally used are (1) exclusive-right-to-sell listing, (2) exclusive-agency listing, (3) open listing, and (4) net listing. Because a listing contract creates a personal obligation for the broker, it is not assignable (see Figure 13.1).

In Texas, if the broker is to be able to collect a commission, a listing must be *in writing* and must include the *seller's signed promise to pay the commission.* The broker also must prove that a valid license existed at the time the commission liability arose and that the statutory title notice was given as required. Unless these requirements are met, a broker cannot institute a lawsuit for recovery of commission (Section 20, Real Estate License Act).

<table>
<tr><td>

Exclusive-Right-To-Sell Listing

- One authorized agent
- Broker receives a commission regardless of who sells the property

</td><td>

Exclusive-right-to-sell listing.

In an **exclusive-right-to-sell listing,** one broker is appointed as sole agent of the seller and is given the exclusive right, or *authorization,* to offer the property in question. Under this form of contract, the seller must pay the broker a commission *regardless of who sells the property* if it is sold while the listing is in effect. In other words, if the seller gives a broker an exclusive-right-to-sell listing but finds a buyer without the broker's assistance, the seller still must pay the broker a commission. This is usually the most popular form of listing agreement among brokers. An example of this form of agreement is reproduced in Figure 13.2.

</td></tr>
</table>

<table>
<tr><td>

Exclusive-Agency Listing

- One authorized agent
- Broker receives a commission only if he or she is the procuring cause
- Seller retains the right to sell without obligation

</td><td>

Exclusive-agency listing.

In an **exclusive-agency listing,** *only one broker* is specifically authorized to act as the exclusive agent of the principal; the exclusive agent is entitled to a commission if any other broker sells the property. However, the *seller* under this form of agreement *retains the right to sell the property himself or herself* without a commission obligation to the broker. In other words, the seller is not obligated to pay a commission to the broker unless the broker has been the procuring cause of the sale. Most listing contracts taken by real estate agents are exclusive-right-to-sell agreements, and the Texas Association of REALTORS® has published an addendum that will convert the exclusive-right-to-sell to an exclusive-agency listing (see Figure 13.3).

</td></tr>
</table>

<table>
<tr><td>

Open Listing

- Multiple agents
- Only selling agent is entitled to a commission
- Seller retains the right to sell without obligation

</td><td>

Open listing.

In an **open listing,** the seller retains the right to employ any number of brokers to act as his or her agents. These brokers can act simultaneously, and the seller is obligated to pay a commission only to that broker who successfully produces a ready, willing, and able buyer. If the seller personally sells the property *without the aid of any of the brokers,* he or she is not obligated to pay any of them a commission. If a broker was in any way a procuring cause in the transaction, however, that broker may be entitled to a commission. A listing contract generally creates an open listing unless wording that specifically provides otherwise is included.

</td></tr>
</table>

<table>
<tr><td>

In a **net listing,** the broker is entitled to any amount exceeding the seller's stated net.

</td><td>

Net listing.

A **net listing** is a listing agreement in which the broker's commission is the difference between the sales proceeds and the net amount desired by the owner of the property. The agreement can take the form of an exclusive-right-to-sell, exclusive-agency, or open listing. TREC Rules state, "A broker may not take net listings unless the principal requires a net listing and the principal appears to be familiar with current market values of real property."

</td></tr>
</table>

FOR EXAMPLE   A seller explained her situation to her broker: "I want to sell my house, but I don't want to be bothered with percentages and bargaining and offers and counteroffers. I just need to walk out of this deal with $150,000 in my pocket. You sell the place for any price you want and keep anything over $150,000." The broker knows that comparable homes in the area are selling for more than $200,000. What should the broker do about this offer of a net listing?

Normally the broker is obligated to make diligent efforts to obtain the best price possible for the seller. The use of a net listing places an upper limit on the seller's expectancy and places the broker's interest above the seller's interest with reference to obtaining the best possible price. If a net listing is used, the listing agreement should assure the seller of not less than the desired price and limit the broker to a specified maximum commission. If possible, it is recommended that a broker suggest the property be listed for a full sales price that will include the broker's usual commission.

Figure 13.2 Exclusive-Right-To-Sell Agreement

TEXAS ASSOCIATION OF REALTORS®

RESIDENTIAL REAL ESTATE LISTING AGREEMENT
EXCLUSIVE RIGHT TO SELL

USE OF THIS FORM BY PERSONS WHO ARE NOT MEMBERS OF THE TEXAS ASSOCIATION OF REALTORS® IS NOT AUTHORIZED.
©Texas Association of REALTORS®, Inc. 2001

1. **PARTIES:** The parties to this agreement (this Listing) are:

   Seller: _____   Broker: _____

   Address: _____   Address: _____

   City, State, Zip: _____   City, State, Zip: _____

   Phone: _____   Phone: _____

   Fax: _____   Fax: _____

   E-mail: _____   E-mail: _____

   Seller appoints Broker as Seller's sole and exclusive agent and grants to Broker the exclusive right to sell the Property.

2. **PROPERTY:**

   A. "Property" means the following real property in Texas:

   Address: _____

   Legal Description: _____

   City: _____ County: _____ Zip:_____

   The Property ❑ is ❑ is not subject to a mandatory membership in an owners' association.

   If the Property is a condominium, attach the appropriate addendum.

   B. Except for items excluded in Paragraph 2C, Seller instructs Broker to market the Property together with all its fixtures, improvements, and the below specified accessories that include, without limitation, any of the following that are on the Property:

   (1) Improvements: all permanently installed equipment, appliances, valances, screens, shutters, awnings, wall-to-wall carpeting, mirrors, ceiling fans, attic fans, mail boxes, television antennas and satellite dish system and equipment, heating and air-conditioning units, security and fire detection equipment, wiring, plumbing and lighting fixtures, chandeliers, water softener system, built-in kitchen equipment, garage door openers, cleaning equipment, shrubbery, landscaping, outdoor cooking equipment, and all other property Seller owns that is permanently attached to the Property; and

   (2) Accessories: window air conditioning units, stove, fireplace screens, curtains and rods, blinds, window shades, draperies and rods, controls for satellite dish system, affixed and remote controls for garage door openers, entry gate controls, mailbox keys, above ground pool, swimming pool equipment and maintenance accessories, and artificial fireplace logs.

   C. Seller intends to retain the following: _____
   _____.

3. **LISTING PRICE:**

   A. Seller instructs Broker to market the Property at the following gross sales price: $_____ (Listing Price).

   B. Seller agrees to sell the Property for the Listing Price or any other price acceptable to Seller. Seller will pay all typical closing costs charged to sellers of residential real property in Texas (seller's typical closing costs are those set forth in the residential contracts promulgated by the Texas Real Estate Commission).

4. **TERM:**

   A. This Listing begins on _____ and ends at 11:59 p.m. on _____.

Figure 13.2   Exclusive-Right-To-Sell Agreement (Continued)

Residential Listing concerning _____

B. If Seller enters into a binding written contract to sell the Property before the date this Listing begins and the contract is binding on that date, this Listing will not commence and will be void.

5. BROKER'S FEE:

A. <u>Fee</u>: When earned and payable, Seller will pay Broker a fee of:

❑ (1) _____% of the sales price.

❑ (2) _____.

B. <u>Earned</u>: Broker's Fee is earned when any one of the following occurs during this Listing:
(1) Seller sells, exchanges, options, agrees to sell, agrees to exchange, or agrees to option the Property to anyone at any price on any terms;
(2) Broker individually or in cooperation with another broker procures a buyer ready, willing, and able to buy the Property at the Listing Price or at any other price acceptable to Seller; or
(3) Seller breaches this Listing.

C. <u>Payable</u>: Once earned, Broker's Fee is payable, either during this Listing or after it ends, at the earlier of:
(1) the closing and funding of any sale or exchange of the Property;
(2) Seller's refusal to sell the Property after Broker's Fee has been earned;
(3) Seller's breach of this Listing; or
(4) at such time as otherwise set forth in this Listing.

Broker's Fee is <u>not</u> payable if a sale of the Property does not close or fund as a result of: (i) Seller's failure, without fault of Seller, to deliver a title policy to a buyer; (ii) loss of ownership due to foreclosure or other legal proceeding; or (iii) Seller's failure to restore the Property, as a result of a casualty loss, to its previous condition by the closing date set forth in a contract for the sale of the Property.

D. <u>Other Fees</u>:

(1) If a buyer with whom Seller has entered into a contract for the sale of the Property during this Listing breaches the contract and Seller receives all or part of the earnest money, Seller will pay Broker the lesser of one-half of such amount or the amount of Broker's Fee stated in Paragraph 5A. Any amount paid under this Paragraph 5D(1) is in addition to any amount that Broker may be entitled to receive for subsequently selling the Property.

(2) If Seller collects the sales price and/or damages either by suit, compromise, settlement or otherwise from a buyer who breached a contract for the sale of the Property entered into during this Listing, Seller will pay Broker, after deducting attorneys' fees and other expenses of collection, an amount equal to the lesser of one-half of the amount collected after deductions or the amount of the Broker's Fee stated in Paragraph 5A. Any amount paid under this Paragraph 5D(2) is in addition to any amount that Broker may be entitled to receive for subsequently selling the Property.

(3) <u>Service Providers</u>: If Broker refers Seller or a prospective buyer to a service provider (for example, mover, cable company, telecommunications provider, utility, or contractor) Broker may receive a fee from the service provider for the referral. Any referral fee Broker receives under this Paragraph 5D(3) is in addition to any other compensation Broker may receive under this Listing.

(4) <u>Transaction Fees</u>: _____
_____

E. <u>Protection Period</u>:

(1) "Protection period" means that time starting the day after this Listing ends and continuing for _____ days.

(2) If Seller agrees to sell the Property during the protection period to any person whose attention has been called to the Property during this Listing, Seller will pay Broker, upon the closing of the sale, the amount that Broker would have been entitled to receive if this Listing were still in effect, if Broker, not later than 10 days after this Listing ends, sends Seller written notice specifying the names of the persons whose attention has been called to the Property during this Listing.

(3) "Person" means any person in any capacity whether an individual or entity. "Sell" means any transfer of any interest in the Property whether by agreement or option.

(4) This Paragraph 5E survives termination of this Listing. This Paragraph 5E will not apply if Seller agrees to sell the Property during the protection period and the Property is exclusively listed with another broker who is a member of the Texas Association of REALTORS® at the time the sale is negotiated and Seller is obligated to pay the other broker a fee for the sale.

Figure 13.2 Exclusive-Right-To-Sell Agreement (Continued)

Residential Listing concerning _____

F. <u>County</u>: All amounts payable to Broker are to be paid in cash in _____County, Texas.

G. <u>Escrow Authorization</u>: Seller authorizes, and Broker may so instruct, any escrow or closing agent authorized to close a transaction for the purchase or acquisition of the Property to collect and disburse to Broker all amounts payable to Broker under this Listing.

6. LISTING SERVICES:

❏ A. Broker will file this Listing with one or more Multiple Listing Services (MLS) by the earlier of the time required by MLS rules or 5 days after the date this Listing begins. Seller authorizes Broker to submit information about this Listing and the sale of the Property to the MLS.

> <u>Notice</u>: MLS rules require Broker to accurately and timely submit all information the MLS requires for participation, including sold data. Subscribers to the MLS may use the information for market evaluation or appraisal purposes. Subscribers are other brokers and other real estate professionals such as appraisers and may include the appraisal district. Any information filed with the MLS becomes the property of the MLS for all purposes. **Submission of information to MLS ensures that persons who use and benefit from MLS also contribute information.**

❏ B. Broker will not file this Listing with a Multiple Listing Service (MLS) or any other listing service.

7. ACCESS TO THE PROPERTY:

A. <u>Authorizing access</u>: Authorizing access to the Property means giving permission to another person to enter the Property, disclosing access codes to the Property to such person, and lending a key to the Property to such person either directly or through a keybox. To facilitate the showing and sale of the Property, Seller instructs Broker and Broker's associates to:
(1) access the Property at reasonable times; and
(2) authorize other brokers, inspectors, appraisers, and contractors to access the Property at reasonable times.

B. <u>Scheduling Companies</u>: Broker may engage the following companies to schedule appointments and to authorize others to access the Property:
_____.

C. **A keybox is a locked container placed on the Property holding a key to the Property. Keyboxes make it more convenient for cooperating brokers, home inspectors, appraisers, and contractors to show, inspect, or repair the Property. The keybox is locked and opened by a special combination, key, or a programmed access card so that whoever possesses the access device may access the Property, even in Seller's absence. The use of the keybox will probably increase the number of showings, but involves risks (for example, unauthorized entry, theft, property damage, or personal injury). Neither the Association of REALTORS® nor MLS requires the use of a keybox.**

(1) Broker ❏ is ❏ is not authorized to place a keybox on the Property.

(2) If a tenant occupies the Property at any time during this Listing, Seller will furnish Broker a written statement (for example, TAR No. 1411), signed by all tenants, authorizing the use of a keybox or Broker may remove the keybox from the Property.

D. <u>When authorizing access to the Property, using a keybox, or showing the Property, Broker, other brokers, their associates, any keybox provider, or any scheduling company are not responsible for personal injury or property loss to Seller or any other person. Seller will indemnify and hold such persons harmless from any personal injury or loss or damage that is not caused by such person's negligence. Seller assumes all risk of any loss, damage, and injury.</u>

8. COOPERATION WITH OTHER BROKERS: Broker will allow other brokers to show the Property to prospective buyers and if another broker procures an acceptable offer, Broker will offer to pay the other broker part of Broker's fee described in Paragraph 5A if the other broker:

❏ A. represents the buyer.

❏ B. _____.

> <u>Notice</u>: Seller may inquire about and discuss Broker's policy of cooperating with and compensating other brokers.

9. AGENCY RELATIONSHIPS: Broker will exclusively represent Seller in the sale of the Property. However, if a prospective buyer that Broker represents desires to purchase the Property, Seller consents to the following agency relationship with Broker. *(Check A or B only.)*

❏ A. <u>Intermediary Status</u>: Seller desires Broker to show the Property to interested prospective buyers that Broker represents. If a prospective buyer that Broker represents wishes to purchase the Property, Seller authorizes Broker to act as an intermediary as follows. *(Check (1) or (2) only.)*

Figure 13.2 **Exclusive-Right-To-Sell Agreement (Continued)**

Residential Listing concerning _____

- ☐ (1) <u>With the Possibility of Appointments</u>:
  - (a) If a prospective buyer that Broker represents is serviced by an associate other than the associate servicing Seller under this Listing, Broker will appoint the licensed associate then servicing Seller under this Listing to communicate with, carry out instructions of, and provide opinions and advice during negotiations to Seller. Broker will appoint the licensed associate then servicing the prospective buyer to the prospective buyer for the same purpose.
  - (b) If a prospective buyer that Broker represents is serviced by the same associate that is servicing Seller under this Listing, Broker will notify Seller that:
    - (i) Broker will assign another licensed associate to communicate with, carry out instructions of, and provide opinions and advice during negotiations to the prospective buyer and will appoint the licensed associate servicing the Seller under this Listing to Seller for the same purpose; or
    - (ii) Broker will make no appointments to either party and the associate servicing the parties will act solely as Broker's intermediary representative, who may facilitate the transaction but will not render opinions or advice during negotiations to either party.

- ☐ (2) <u>With No Appointments</u>: Broker will not appoint specific associates to either Seller or the prospective buyer. Any associate(s) servicing the parties will act solely as Broker's intermediary representative(s). The associate(s) may facilitate the transaction for the parties but will not render opinions or advice during negotiations to either party.

- ☐ B. <u>No Intermediary Status</u>:

  - ☐ (1) Seller does not wish Broker to show the Property to prospective buyers that Broker represents.

  - ☐ (2) Broker exclusively represents sellers and does not represent buyers.

Notice: **If Broker acts as an intermediary under Paragraph 9A, Broker and any of Broker's associates:**
  - ♦ **may not disclose to the prospective buyer that Seller will accept a price less than the asking price unless otherwise instructed in a separate writing by Seller;**
  - ♦ **may not disclose to Seller that the prospective buyer will pay a price greater than the price submitted in a written offer to Seller unless otherwise instructed in a separate writing by the prospective buyer;**
  - ♦ **may not disclose any confidential information or any information Seller or the prospective buyer specifically instructs Broker in writing not to disclose unless otherwise instructed in a separate writing by the respective party or required to disclose the information by the Real Estate License Act or a court order or if the information materially relates to the condition of the property;**
  - ♦ **shall treat all parties to the transaction honestly; and**
  - ♦ **shall comply with the Real Estate License Act.**

10. **CONFIDENTIAL INFORMATION:** During this Listing or after it ends, Broker may not knowingly disclose information obtained in confidence from Seller except as authorized by Seller or required by law. Broker may not disclose to Seller any confidential information regarding any other person Broker represents or previously represented except as required by law.

11. **BROKER'S AUTHORITY:**

  A. Broker will make reasonable efforts and act diligently to sell the Property.

  B. In addition to other authority granted by this Listing, Broker may:
    (1) advertise the Property by means and methods as Broker determines in any media, including the Internet;
    (2) place interior and exterior photographic images of the Property in any advertisements, including the Internet;
    (3) place a "For Sale" sign on the Property and remove all other signs offering the Property for sale or lease;
    (4) furnish comparative marketing and sales information about other properties to prospective buyers;
    (5) disseminate information about the Property to other brokers and to prospective buyers, including applicable disclosures or notices that Seller is required to make under law or a contract;
    (6) obtain information from any holder of a note secured by a lien on the Property;
    (7) accept and deposit earnest money in trust in accordance with a contract for the sale of the Property;
    (8) disclose the sales price and terms of sale to other brokers, appraisers, or other real estate professionals; and
    (9) place information about this Listing and a transaction for the Property on an electronic platform (an electronic platform is typically an Internet-based system where professionals related to the transaction, such as title companies and lenders, may receive, view, and input information).

  C. Broker is not authorized to execute any document in the name of or on behalf of Seller concerning the Property.

12. **SELLER'S REPRESENTATIONS:** Except as provided by Paragraph 15, Seller represents that:
  A. Seller has fee simple title to and peaceable possession of the Property and all its improvements and fixtures, unless rented, and the legal capacity to convey the Property;
  B. Seller is not bound by a listing agreement with another broker for the sale, exchange or lease of the Property that is or will be in effect during this Listing;
  C. any pool or spa and any required enclosures, fences, gates, and latches comply with all applicable laws and ordinances;

(TAR-1101) 7-6-01   Initialed for Identification by _____ Broker/Associate and _____, _____ Seller   Page 4 of 6

Figure 13.2   Exclusive-Right-To-Sell Agreement (Continued)

Residential Listing concerning _____

    D.   no person or entity has any right to purchase, lease, or acquire the Property by an option, right of refusal, or other agreement;
    E.   there are no delinquencies or defaults under any deed of trust, mortgage, or other encumbrance on the Property;
    F.   the Property is not subject to the jurisdiction of any court;
    G.   all information relating to the Property Seller provides to Broker is true and correct to the best of Seller's knowledge;
    H.   the name of any employer, relocation company, or other entity that provides benefits to Seller when selling the Property is:

       _____; and

    I.   Seller learned of Broker's firm by: _____.

13. SELLER'S ADDITIONAL PROMISES: Seller agrees to:
    A.   cooperate with Broker to facilitate the showing and marketing of the Property;
    B.   not rent or lease the Property during Listing without Broker's prior written approval;
    C.   not negotiate with any prospective buyer who may contact Seller directly, but refer all prospective buyers to Broker;
    D.   not enter into a listing agreement with another broker for the sale, exchange or lease of the Property to become effective during this Listing;
    E.   maintain any pool and all required enclosures in compliance with all applicable laws and ordinances;
    F.   provide Broker with copies of any leases or rental agreements pertaining to the Property and advise Broker of tenants moving in or out of the Property;
    G.   complete any disclosures or notices required by law or a contract to sell the Property; and
    H.   amend any applicable notices and disclosures if any material change occurs during this Listing.

14. LIMITATION OF LIABILITY

    A.   If the Property is or becomes vacant during this Listing, Seller must notify Seller's casualty insurance company and request a "Vacancy Clause" to cover the Property. Broker is not responsible for the security of the Property nor for inspecting the Property on any periodic basis.

    B.   Broker is not responsible or liable in any manner for personal injury to any person or for loss or damage to any person's real or personal property resulting from any act or omission not caused by Broker's negligence, including but not limited to:
       (1) other brokers, inspectors, appraisers, and contractors who are authorized to access the Property;
       (2) acts of third parties (for example, vandalism or theft);
       (3) freezing water pipes;
       (4) a dangerous condition on the Property; and
       (5) the Property's non-compliance with any law or ordinance.

    C.   Seller agrees to protect, defend, indemnify, and hold Broker harmless from any damages, costs, attorneys' fees, and expenses:
       (1) for which Broker is not responsible under this Listing;
       (2) that arise from Seller's failure to disclose any material or relevant information about the Property; and
       (3) that are caused by Seller giving incorrect information to Broker, other brokers, or prospective buyers.

15. SPECIAL PROVISIONS:

16. DEFAULT: If Seller breaches this Listing (including but not limited to leasing or selling the Property without Broker's prior consent) Seller is in default and will be liable to Broker for the amount of the Broker's fee specified in Paragraph 5A and any other fees Broker is entitled to receive under this Listing. If a sales price is not determinable in the event of an exchange or breach of this Listing, the Listing Price will be the sales price for purposes of computing Broker's Fee. If Broker breaches this Listing, Broker is in default and Seller may exercise any remedy at law.

17. MEDIATION: The parties agree to negotiate in good faith in an effort to resolve any dispute related to this Listing that may arise between the parties. If the dispute cannot be resolved by negotiation, the dispute will be submitted to mediation. The parties to the dispute will choose a mutually acceptable mediator and will share the cost of mediation equally.

18. ATTORNEYS' FEES: If Seller or Broker is a prevailing party in any legal proceeding brought as a result of a dispute under this Listing or any transaction related to or contemplated by this Listing, such party will be entitled to recover from the non-prevailing party all costs of such proceeding and reasonable attorneys' fees.

(TAR-1101) 7-6-01   Initialed for Identification by _____ Broker/Associate and _____, _____ Seller   Page 5 of 6

Figure 13.2   Exclusive-Right-To-Sell Agreement (Continued)

Residential Listing concerning _____

19. **ADDENDA AND OTHER DOCUMENTS:** Addenda that are part of this Listing and other documents that Seller may need to provide are:
   ☒ A.   Information About Brokerage Services;
   ☐ B.   Seller's Disclosure Notice (§5.008, Texas Property Code);
   ☐ C.   Seller's Disclosure of Information on Lead-Based Paint and Lead-Based Paint Hazard (if Property was built before 1978);
   ☐ D.   MUD Disclosure Notice (Chapter 49, Texas Water Code);
   ☐ E.   Request for Information from an Owner's Association;
   ☐ F.   Request for Mortgage Information;
   ☐ G.   Information about On-Site Sewer Facility;
   ☐ H.   Information about Special Flood Hazard Areas;
   ☐ I.   Condominium Addendum;
   ☐ J.   Keybox Authorization by Tenant; and
   ☐ K.   _____.

20. **AGREEMENT OF PARTIES:**
   A.   <u>Entire Agreement</u>: This Listing is the entire agreement of the parties and may not be changed except by written agreement.
   B.   <u>Assignability</u>: Neither party may assign this Listing without the written consent of the other party.
   C.   <u>Binding Effect</u>: Seller's obligation to pay Broker an earned fee is binding upon Seller and Seller's heirs, administrators, executors, successors, and permitted assignees.
   D.   <u>Joint and Several</u>: All Sellers executing this Listing are jointly and severally liable for the performance of all its terms.
   E.   <u>Governing Law</u>: Texas law governs the interpretation, validity, performance, and enforcement of this Listing.
   F.   <u>Severability</u>: If a court finds any clause in this Listing invalid or unenforceable, the remainder of this Listing will not be affected and all other provisions of this Listing will remain valid and enforceable.
   G.   <u>Notices</u>: Notices under this Listing will be sent to the parties as specified in Paragraph 1.

21. **ADDITIONAL NOTICES:**

   A.   **Broker's fees, or the sharing of fees between brokers are not fixed, controlled, recommended, suggested, or maintained by the Association of REALTORS®, MLS, or any listing service.**

   B.   **Fair housing laws require the Property to be shown and made available to all persons without regard to race, color, religion, national origin, sex, disability or familial status. Local ordinances may provide for additional protected classes (for example, creed, status as a student, marital status, sexual orientation, or age).**

   C.   **Seller may review the information Broker submits to an MLS or other listing service.**

   D.   **Broker advises Seller to safeguard and remove jewelry and other valuables from the Property.**

   E.   **Statutes or ordinances may regulate certain items on the Property (for example, swimming pools and septic systems). Non-compliance with the statutes or ordinances may delay a transaction and may result in fines, penalties, and liability to Seller.**

   F.   **Residential service contracts are available from licensed residential service companies. A residential service contract may provide for the repair or replacement of some appliances or electrical, plumbing, heating, or cooling systems. Exclusions and deductibles may apply. Some contracts may cover the Seller during the listing period.**

   G.   **Broker cannot give legal advice. READ THIS LISTING CAREFULLY. If you do not understand the effect of this Listing, consult an attorney BEFORE signing.**

_____ _____	_____ _____	
Broker's Printed Name License No.	Seller's Signature Date	
	Social Security or Tax ID No.: _____	

By: _____ _____   _____ _____
        Broker's or Associate's Signature   Date   Seller's Signature   Date
                                                                                  Social Security or Tax ID No: _____

Figure 13.3 *Addendum for Exclusive Agency*

TEXAS ASSOCIATION OF REALTORS'
ADDENDUM FOR EXCLUSIVE AGENCY

USE OF THIS FORM BY PERSONS WHO ARE NOT MEMBERS OF THE TEXAS ASSOCIATION OF REALTORS® IS NOT AUTHORIZED.
©Texas Association of REALTORS®, Inc. 2001

ADDENDUM TO LISTING AGREEMENT BETWEEN THE UNDERSIGNED PARTIES CONCERNING THE PROPERTY AT

_____

A. Definitions:

   (1) "Owner" means the seller or landlord of the above-referenced Property.

   (2) "Excluded Prospect" means a prospective buyer or tenant who:
   (a) has direct communication or negotiations with the Owner about the purchase or lease of the Property;
   (b) is procured through Owner's sole efforts; and
   (c) Owner identifies to be an Excluded Prospect as required by Paragraph D.

B. Exclusive Agency: Notwithstanding provisions in the above-referenced listing agreement (the Listing) to the contrary, Owner may sell or lease the Property to an Excluded Prospect if Owner does not use any other real estate broker to market or assist Owner to sell or lease the Property.

C. Broker's Fees: If Owner sells or leases the Property to an Excluded Prospect, Owner will not be obligated to pay the fees due to Broker under Paragraph 5A of the Listing, but Owner will pay Broker, at the time the Property is sold or leased, a fee equal to:

   (1) _____% of the sales price if the owner sells the Property;

   (2) _____% of the gross rent over the term of the lease if owner leases the Property; and

   (3) _____.

D. Naming of Excluded Prospects: For a person to qualify as an Excluded Prospect under this Addendum Owner must send Broker written notice identifying the Excluded Prospect by name, address, and telephone number. If Broker or any other broker shows the Property to a prospective buyer or tenant before Owner provides written notice to Broker that the prospective buyer or tenant is an Excluded Prospect, then the prospective buyer or tenant is not an Excluded Prospect.

E. Offers From Excluded Prospects: Owner will immediately notify Broker of:
   (1) Owner's receipt of an offer from an Excluded Prospect;
   (2) Owner's acceptance of an offer from an Excluded Prospect by providing Broker with a copy of the contract or lease; and
   (3) the closing or other termination of a binding contract for the sale or lease of the Property with an Excluded Prospect.

F. Effect on Listing upon Sale or Lease to Excluded Prospect: If Owner enters into a contract to sell or lease the Property to an Excluded Prospect, the Listing will terminate and Broker will have no further obligation to market the Property or to assist Owner in negotiating or closing the sale or lease.

G. Advertising: Owner ❑ may ❑ may not advertise the availability of the Property by signs, newspaper, Internet, or other media.

_____   _____
Broker's Name Printed   Owner's Signature   Date

By: _____   _____
Broker's or Associate's Signature   Date   Owner's Signature   Date

(TAR-1403) 7-6-01   Page 1 of 1

A *multiple-listing service (MLS)* is an arrangement in which brokers share their listings with other brokers in exchange for a share of the commission generated by a transaction.

Multiple listings. **Multiple-listing contracts** are used by those brokers who are members of a multiple-listing organization. Such an organization consists of a group of brokers within an area who agree to pool their listings.

The multiple-listing agreement is not actually a separate form of listing; it is, in effect, an *exclusive listing* (either an exclusive right to sell or an exclusive agency) with an additional authority and obligation given to the listing broker to *distribute the listing to other brokers who belong to the multiple-listing service (MLS)*. Usually, submission of a listing to this organization carries with it an offer of cooperation and compensation to any cooperating broker who produces a buyer. A cooperating broker who then submits an offer to the listing broker is deemed to have accepted the offer of cooperation according to the terms of that offer of cooperation. Cooperation can take the form of offers to subagents, buyer agents, or both, at the listing broker's discretion. All offers of cooperation must be accompanied by an offer of compensation; however, the listing broker may offer differing amounts to subagents and to buyer agents. A broker who has entered into a contract to represent a buyer must renounce the offer of subagency (as discussed in Chapter 5).

The contractual obligations among the member brokers of a multiple-listing organization vary widely. Most provide that on sale of the property *the commission is divided between the listing broker and the cooperating broker.* If a buyer's broker is to be paid by the seller, the listing contract must authorize the listing broker to divide the commission with the buyer's broker.

Most rules of MLSs say that the broker who secures the listing is not only authorized but *obligated* to turn the listing over to his or her MLS within a definite period of time so that it can be distributed to the other member brokers. The length of time varies as to how long the listing broker can offer the property exclusively without notifying the other member brokers.

A multiple listing offers advantages to broker, seller, and buyer alike. Brokers develop a sizable inventory of properties to be sold and are assured a portion of the commission if they list a property or participate in its sale. Sellers gain because their property is widely marketed through the MLS and because all members of the multiple-listing organization are eligible to sell their property. Buyers benefit because a larger selection of properties is available.

Termination of Listings

As discussed in Chapter 5, an agency relationship may be terminated for any number of reasons.

acts of the parties {

- Fulfillment of performance by the broker
- Expiration of the time period stated in the agreement
- Unilateral revocation by the owner or by the broker for just cause, such as abandonment by the broker or noncooperation of the seller for showings (although either party may be liable to the other for damages)
- Mutual consent

acts of law {

- Bankruptcy of the seller if title transferred to receiver
- Death or incapacity of either party
- Destruction of the property
- A change in property use by outside forces (such as a change in zoning)

Expiration of listing period. All listings must specify a definite period during which the broker is to be employed and must have a definite termination date, as provided by the License Act. The use of automatic extensions of time in exclusive listings is prohibited by Texas statute.

Obtaining Listings

senate bill 489 created intermediary and gave broker ability to appoint

On the first face-to-face meeting with the seller, the broker or salesperson must give the seller a written "Information About Brokerage Services" form that explains seller representation, subagency, buyer representation, and the intermediary position (see Chapter 5). The broker who lists the property for sale is the owner's agent unless the agent is already employed under a buyer representation agreement with a prospective purchaser. If a prospective purchaser has already been located for the property (as in the case of a "for sale by owner") and the broker is representing the buyer, a disclosure of buyer representation must be given to the seller at the time of the agent's first contact with the seller. The seller then would have the option to choose intermediary representation or to choose no representation at all.

All legal owners of the listed property or their authorized agents, as well as the listing salesperson and/or broker, should sign the listing agreement. The listing salesperson can sign the contract in the broker's name if so authorized by the broker. If the property being listed is homestead property, both spouses' names and signatures are required, even if the property is the separate property of one spouse.

tax appraisal records or deed will show all owners

Information needed for listing agreements. When a listing is taken, as much information as possible must be obtained on a parcel of real estate. This helps ensure that all possible contingencies can be anticipated and provided for, particularly when the listing will be shared with other brokers and salespeople in a multiple-listing arrangement. This information generally includes (where appropriate)

- names and addresses of owners (from the deed);
- legal description of the property (from the deed);
- size of the lot (frontage and depth, from the survey or plat records);
- zoning classification—especially important for vacant land (from city hall);
- number and sizes of rooms (from accurate measurements taken personally);
- construction and age of the building (from the tax office);
- information relative to the neighborhood—schools, churches, transportation, and so forth (fair housing laws must not be violated);
- current taxes and current tax exemptions (from each taxing authority);
- existing financing—including present balance, interest, payments, and loan assumability (from the note, deed of trust, and lender);
- utility payments (from owner's records);
- date of occupancy or possession;
- possibility of seller financing; and
- detailed list of personal and real property to be included or excluded.

Because verifiable written information supplied by others can be a broker's defense in a lawsuit involving the Texas Deceptive Trade Practices Act, the agent should verify pertinent information such as legal description, lot size, yearly taxes, and tax exemptions against data in the public records.

In Practice	Some brokers use a separate property profile or information sheet to record many of the foregoing property features. The broker should require that the owner review the property data and sign or initial the completed profile form. Remember, all marketing activities for the listed property must comply with federal, state, and local fair housing laws.

Property Disclosures and Notices

As an agent of the seller, a real estate broker is responsible for the disclosure of any material information regarding the property. To protect both the consumer and the real estate agent, the number of required disclosure notices to the customer is increasing. The applicable disclosure forms should be prepared when the property is listed.

- *Seller's Disclosure Notice:* The owner must disclose latent structural defects or any other known structural defects. Sellers of residential property of not more than one unit must deliver a **Seller's Disclosure Notice** to the buyer on or before the effective date of a contract for the sale of the property. Although the Notice is required in almost all residential transactions, there are a few exceptions, most notably the sale of a new property by a builder. Figure 13.4 shows the Texas Association of REALTORS® (TAR) Seller's Disclosure Notice. Licensees who are not TAR members would use a form approved by TREC and available on its web site.

  If a contract is entered into without the seller's providing the notice, the seller is given a limited time to provide the notice to the buyer. If the seller delivers the notice within the time frame, the buyer may still terminate the contract *for any reason* within seven days after receiving the notice. If the notice is not received within that time frame, the buyer may terminate the contract any time prior to closing [see Figure 12.1, ¶7B(2)]. The seller is required to complete the notice to the best of his or her knowledge; if information is unknown to the seller, that fact may be indicated on the notice. The seller and the seller's agent have no duty to disclose that a death by natural causes, suicide, or accident unrelated to the condition of the property occurred on the property. The seller and the real estate brokers in the transaction have no duty to disclose information about or the location of registered sex offenders.

  Under Section 62.045(e) of the Code of Criminal Procedure, sellers, builders, and landlords of single-family residential property, as well as the real estate agents in the transaction, are not responsible for obtaining or disclosing information about registered sex offenders. However, real estate agents, sellers, and landlords are not prohibited from providing such information. Sellers and real estate agents may direct prospects to a database at which prospects may search for such information. The Texas Department of Public Safety maintains a web site on which it maintains a registered sex offender database (www.txdps.state.tx.us; choose Online Services). TAR prints this web site address in a public information statement on the seller's disclosure notice that TAR publishes. Even though sellers' agents and buyers' agents are not *responsible* for disclosing information about registered sex offenders, they are not prohibited from doing so. They may, for business purposes or as a matter of policy, choose to provide such information. A listing agent providing such information to prospective buyers is advised to discuss this policy with the seller prior to taking a listing.

Figure 13.4 ***Seller's Disclosure Notice***

TEXAS ASSOCIATION OF REALTORS®

SELLER'S DISCLOSURE NOTICE

USE OF THIS FORM BY PERSONS WHO ARE NOT MEMBERS OF THE TEXAS ASSOCIATION OF REALTORS® IS NOT AUTHORIZED.
©**Texas Association of REALTORS®, Inc., 2001**

Section 5.008 of the Texas Property Code requires a seller of residential property of not more than one dwelling unit to deliver a Seller's Disclosure Notice to a purchaser on or before the effective date of a contract. **This form complies with and contains additional disclosures which exceed the minimum disclosures required by the Code.**

CONCERNING THE PROPERTY AT _____
(Street Address and City)

THIS NOTICE IS A DISCLOSURE OF SELLER'S KNOWLEDGE OF THE CONDITION OF THE PROPERTY AS OF THE DATE SIGNED BY SELLER AND IS NOT A SUBSTITUTE FOR ANY INSPECTIONS OR WARRANTIES THE BUYER MAY WISH TO OBTAIN. IT IS NOT A WARRANTY OF ANY KIND BY SELLER, SELLER'S AGENTS, OR ANY OTHER AGENT.

Seller ☐ is ☐ is not occupying the Property. If unoccupied (by Seller), how long since Seller has occupied the Property? _____

1.   The Property has the items below: *(Mark Yes (Y), No (N), or Unknown (U).)*

Y N U		Y N U		Y N U	
☐ ☐ ☐	Attic Fan(s)	☐ ☐ ☐	Gas Lines (Nat/LP)	☐ ☐ ☐	Public Sewer System
☐ ☐ ☐	Cable TV Wiring	☐ ☐ ☐	Intercom System	☐ ☐ ☐	Rain Gutters
☐ ☐ ☐	Ceiling Fan(s)	☐ ☐ ☐	Microwave	☐ ☐ ☐	Range
☐ ☐ ☐	Dishwasher	☐ ☐ ☐	Outdoor Grill	☐ ☐ ☐	Sauna
☐ ☐ ☐	Disposal	☐ ☐ ☐	Oven	☐ ☐ ☐	Spa or Hot Tub
☐ ☐ ☐	Evaporative Cooler	☐ ☐ ☐	Patio/Decking	☐ ☐ ☐	Trash Compactor
☐ ☐ ☐	Exhaust Fan(s)	☐ ☐ ☐	Plumbing System	☐ ☐ ☐	TV Antenna
☐ ☐ ☐	Fences	☐ ☐ ☐	Pool	☐ ☐ ☐	Wall/Window A/C Units
☐ ☐ ☐	Fire Detection Equipment	☐ ☐ ☐	Pool Equipment	☐ ☐ ☐	Washer/Dryer Hookups
☐ ☐ ☐	French Drain	☐ ☐ ☐	Pool Maintenance Accessories	☐ ☐ ☐	Window Screens
☐ ☐ ☐	Gas Fixtures	☐ ☐ ☐	Pool Heater		

Y N U			
☐ ☐ ☐	Central A/C	If yes:	☐ Electric ☐ Gas Number of Units _____
☐ ☐ ☐	Central Heat	If yes:	☐ Electric ☐ Gas ☐ Solar Number of Units _____
☐ ☐ ☐	Carport	If yes:	☐ Attached ☐ Not Attached
☐ ☐ ☐	Fireplace & Chimney	If yes:	☐ Woodburning ____ (No.) ☐ Mock _____ (No.) ☐ Direct Vent _____ (No.)
☐ ☐ ☐	Garage	If yes:	☐ Attached ☐ Not Attached
☐ ☐ ☐	Garage Door Openers	If yes:	Number of Units _____ Number of Controls_____
☐ ☐ ☐	Satellite Dish and Controls	If yes:	☐ Owned ☐ Leased from_____
☐ ☐ ☐	Security System	If yes:	☐ Owned ☐ Leased from_____
☐ ☐ ☐	Water Heater	If yes:	☐ Gas ☐ Electric ☐ Solar ☐ Other_____
☐ ☐ ☐	Water Softener	If yes:	☐ Owned ☐ Leased from_____
☐ ☐ ☐	Underground Lawn Sprinkler	If yes:	☐ Automatic ☐ Manual Areas covered_____
☐ ☐ ☐	Septic or other on-site sewer facility	If yes:	Attached is ☐ ☐ Information About On-Site Sewer Facility (TAR No.1407)

Water supply provided by: ☐ City   ☐ Well   ☐ MUD   ☐ Co-Op ☐ Other   ☐ Unknown
Was the dwelling built before 1978? ☐ Yes   ☐ No   ☐ Unknown
Roof Type:_____ Age:_____ (approx.)
Is there an overlay roof covering (shingles or roof covering placed over existing shingles or roof covering)? ☐ Yes   ☐ No   ☐ Unknown

Are you (Seller) aware of any of the items in Section 1 that are not in working condition, that have known defects, or that are in need of repair? ☐ Yes *(If you are aware.)*   ☐ No *(If you are not aware.)* If yes, describe. *(Attach additional sheets if necessary.)*
_____
_____
_____

This notice does not establish which items will or will not be conveyed in a sale. The terms of the contract will determine which items will and will not be conveyed.

(TAR 1406) 7-6-01   Initialed for Identification by Buyer _____, _____ and Seller _____, _____   Page 1 of 3

Figure 13.4   Seller's Disclosure Notice (Continued)

Seller's Disclosure Notice concerning_____

2.   Are you (Seller) aware of any known defects/malfunctions in any of the following? *(Mark Yes (Y) if you are aware, mark No (N) if you are not aware.)*

Y	N		Y	N		Y	N	
☐	☐	Basement	☐	☐	Exterior Walls	☐	☐	Plumbing/Sewers/ Septics
☐	☐	Ceilings	☐	☐	Floors	☐	☐	Roof
☐	☐	Doors	☐	☐	Foundation/Slab(s)	☐	☐	Sidewalks
☐	☐	Driveways	☐	☐	Interior Walls	☐	☐	Walls/Fences
☐	☐	Electrical Systems	☐	☐	Lighting Fixtures	☐	☐	Windows
☐	☐	Other Structural Components (describe):_____						

If the answer to any of the items in Section 2 is yes, explain. *(Attach additional sheets if necessary.)*_____
_____
_____
_____

3.   Are you (Seller) aware of any of the following conditions? *(Mark Yes (Y) if you are aware, mark No (N) if you are not aware.)*

Y	N	
☐	☐	Aluminum Wiring
☐	☐	Asbestos Components
☐	☐	Diseased Trees: ☐ Oak Wilt ☐ _____
☐	☐	Endangered Species/Habitat on Property
☐	☐	Fault Lines
☐	☐	Hazardous or Toxic Waste
☐	☐	Improper Drainage
☐	☐	Intermittent or Weather Springs
☐	☐	Landfill
☐	☐	Lead-Based Paint or Lead-Based Paint Hazards
☐	☐	Located in 100-year Floodplain
☐	☐	Previous Fires
☐	☐	Present Flood Insurance Coverage (If yes, attach Information About Special Flood Hazard Areas – TAR No. 1414)
☐	☐	Radon Gas
☐	☐	Settling
☐	☐	Soil Movement
☐	☐	Subsurface Structures or Pits
☐	☐	Underground Storage Tanks
☐	☐	Unrecorded Easements

Y	N	
☐	☐	Unplatted Easements
☐	☐	Urea-formaldehyde Insulation
☐	☐	Water Penetration
☐	☐	Wetlands on Property
☐	☐	Wood Rot
		Previous Flooding
☐	☐	Into the Improvements
☐	☐	Onto the Property
		Structural Repairs:
☐	☐	Previous Foundation Repairs
☐	☐	Previous Roof Repairs
☐	☐	Other Structural Repairs
		Termites or Other Wood-Destroying Insects:
☐	☐	Active Infestation
☐	☐	Previous Treatment
☐	☐	Previous Damage Repaired
☐	☐	Damage Needing Repair

If the answer to any of the conditions in Section 3 is yes, explain. *(Attach additional sheets if necessary.)*_____
_____
_____
_____

4.   Are you (Seller) aware of any item, equipment, or system in or on the Property that is in need of repair, which has not been previously disclosed in this notice? ☐ Yes *(If you are aware.)* ☐ No *(If you are not aware.)* If yes, explain. *(Attach additional sheets if necessary.)*_____
_____
_____
_____

5.   Are you (Seller) aware of any of the following? *(Mark Yes (Y) if you are aware, mark No (N) if you are not aware.)*

Y   N
☐   ☐   Room additions, structural modifications, or other alterations or repairs made without necessary permits or not in compliance with building codes in effect at that time.

☐   ☐   Homeowners' association or maintenance fees or assessments. If yes, complete:
Amount of fee or assessment: $_____ ☐ Mandatory   ☐ Voluntary
Due: ☐ monthly   ☐ quarterly   ☐ annually
Any unpaid fees or assessments for the Property: ☐ Yes   ☐ No   If yes, amount: $_____
Manager's Name:_____   Phone:_____

Figure 13.4 Seller's Disclosure Notice (Continued)

Seller's Disclosure Notice concerning_____

Y	N	
☐	☐	Any "common area" (facilities such as pools, tennis courts, walkways, or other) co-owned in undivided interest with others. If yes, complete: Any optional user fees for common facilities charged: ☐ Yes ☐ No If yes, describe:_____ _____
☐	☐	Any notices of violations of deed restrictions or governmental ordinances affecting the condition or use of the Property.
☐	☐	Any lawsuits or other legal proceedings directly or indirectly affecting the Property. If yes, describe: Condemnation proceedings:_____ Pending or threatened change in zoning or deed restrictions:_____ Other:_____
☐	☐	Death on the Property other than death caused by: natural causes, suicide, or accident unrelated to the Property's condition.
☐	☐	Any condition on the Property which materially affects the physical health or safety of an individual.
☐	☐	Any repairs or treatment, other than routine maintenance, made to the Property to eliminate environmental hazards such as asbestos, radon, lead-based paint, urea-formaldehyde, or mold?

If the answer to any of the items in Section 5 is yes, explain. *(Attach additional sheets if necessary.)*_____
_____
_____
_____

6.   List and attach any written inspection reports that you (Seller) have received in the last 4 years that were completed by persons who regularly provide inspections and who are either licensed as inspectors or otherwise permitted by law to perform inspections.

Date of Inspection	Type of Inspection	Name of Inspector/Company	Number of Pages
_____	_____	_____	_____
_____	_____	_____	_____
_____	_____	_____	_____

A buyer should not rely on the above-cited reports as a reflection of the current condition of the Property. A buyer should obtain inspections from inspectors of the buyer's own choice.

7.   Check any tax exemption(s) which you (Seller) currently claim for the Property: ☐ Homestead   ☐ Senior Citizen
                                                                                       ☐ Disabled   ☐ Disabled Veteran
                                                                                       ☐ Agricultural ☐ Unknown
                                                                                       ☐ Other_____

8.   Have you (Seller) ever collected any insurance payments pursuant to a claim made for damage to the Property and not used the proceeds to make the repairs for which the claim was submitted? ☐ Yes ☐ No If yes, explain_____
_____

9.   *NOTICES TO BUYER:*

   A.   *The Texas Department of Public Safety maintains a database that consumers may search, at no cost, to determine if registered sex offenders are located in certain zip code areas. To search the database, visit www.txdps.state.tx.us. For information concerning past criminal activity in certain areas or neighborhoods, contact the local police department.*

   B.   *The Listing Broker and any other broker advise you that this Seller's Disclosure Notice was completed by Seller as of the date signed. The brokers have relied on this notice as true and correct and have no reason to believe it to be false or inaccurate. YOU ARE ENCOURAGED TO HAVE AN INSPECTOR OF YOUR CHOICE INSPECT THE PROPERTY.*

_____   _____
Signature of Seller   Date   Signature of Seller   Date

The undersigned Buyer acknowledges receipt of the foregoing notice.

_____   _____
Signature of Buyer   Date   Signature of Buyer   Date

(TAR 1406) 7-6-01   Page 3 of 3

In Practice

An agent should not participate in filling out the required Seller's Disclosure Notice. It should be completed by the seller and signed by the seller. If the agent were to assist in preparing the form and were to mismark an item or provide false information, the agent could be liable for the misrepresentation.

- *Lead-Based Paint:* Exposure to lead from lead-based paint poses a risk to young children and to pregnant women, and all sellers and landlords of properties that were built prior to 1978 (with a few specific exceptions) must disclose to buyers or tenants any knowledge of lead-based paint or hazards in the property. A TREC-approved addendum permits a seller or landlord to indicate if he or she (1) has knowledge of the presence of lead-based paint, (2) has provided the buyer or tenant with copies of records or reports pertaining to lead-based paint, (3) has permitted the buyer up to 10 days to have the property inspected for lead-based paint or hazards, and (4) has provided the buyer or tenant with a copy of the EPA-approved pamphlet entitled *Protect Your Family from Lead in Your Home.* Real estate agents share responsibility for ensuring compliance and must retain for three years proof that the appropriate disclosures were made. The federal rules do not require testing, removal, or abatement of lead-based paint—just disclosure. If an inspection is desired, it must be conducted by a person certified by the Texas Department of Health as a lead inspector.

    Lead-based paint disclosures are not required on properties leased for less than 100 days, houses *exclusively* for the elderly or handicapped (unless there are children living there), zero bedroom units, or houses sold because of foreclosure. If properties have been inspected and found free of lead-based paint, disclosure does not have to be made. For more information on lead-based-paint hazards, visit the web site at www.hud.gov/offices/lead.

- *Notice of Additional Tax Liability:* Sellers of *vacant land* must include in the sales contract a statutorily prescribed disclosure notice regarding possible liability of the purchaser for additional taxes. The buyer is alerted that a change in ownership or a change in the use of the land may not permit the continued use of special appraisal methods that might previously have valued the land at less than its market value. The TREC Farm and Ranch Contract and the Unimproved Property Contract provide for this new disclosure. This disclosure requirement does not apply if the sales contract separately allocates responsibility between the seller and the purchaser for any future rollback tax liability. If it is required, however, and if a seller does not make the required disclosure, the seller will be responsible for the additional taxes and interest.

- *Conditions under Surface:* A seller of *unimproved land to be used for residential purposes* must disclose the location of any transportation pipelines for natural gas and related products under the property's surface. If the notice is not received on or before the effective date of the contract, the buyer may terminate the contract for any reason up to seven days after the effective date of the contract. This notice is not required if the seller is obligated to deliver a title commitment to the purchaser and if the purchaser has the right to terminate the contract if all objections to title are not cured.

- *Notice of Obligations Related to Membership in Property Owners' Association:* A seller of residential real property that is subject to membership

> If the promulgated sales contract is used in a transaction, many of these (and other) disclosures are made or referenced (see ¶6 and 7, Figure 12.1).

in a property owners' association is required to give a prospective purchaser a written notice stating that (1) the purchaser would be obligated to be a member of the association; (2) copies of restrictive covenants governing the use and occupancy of the property are filed in the county clerk's office; and (3) the purchaser would be obligated to pay assessments to the association, and failure to pay the assessments could result in a lien on and the foreclosure of the property (H.B. 2224, 1999). The notice (either as a part of the contract or on a separate document) must be delivered to the purchaser before the effective date of the contract. If it is not, the purchaser may terminate the contract for any reason within the earlier of seven days after the date the purchaser receives the notice or the date of closing. A property owner's association must provide, on request, a copy of the restrictions, the bylaws and rules of the association, and a "resale certificate" (S.B. 434, 1999).

- *Seller's Disclosure Regarding Potential Annexation:* Sellers of property outside the city limits must provide a written notice to a prospective purchaser that the property "may now or later be included in the extraterritorial jurisdiction of a municipality and may now or later be subject to annexation by the municipality" (S.B. 167, 1999). The statutory notice (on either the contract or a separate piece of paper) must be given before the effective date of the contract. If not, the buyer may terminate the contract for any reason within seven days after receiving the notice or on the day of closing, whichever is earlier. If a buyer wants more information regarding this possibility, he or she should contact all municipalities located in the general proximity of the property.

- *Addendum for Unimproved Property Located in a Certificated Service Area of a Utility Service Provider:* A seller of unimproved property located in a certificated service area of a utility service provider must give written notice to the purchaser prior to his or her signing a contract that the extension of water or sewer services might require additional expense to the purchaser and that there might be a delay in the utility's ability to provide the services. If the seller fails to give the notice, the purchaser may terminate the contract and, in some cases, sue the seller for damages and reasonable attorney's fees.

Sample Listing Agreement

The sample listing agreement shown in Figure 13.2 is a typical exclusive-right-to-sell agreement. There is no TREC-promulgated listing form; however, the topics listed below are included in most listing agreements.

- *Broker or Firm:* The name of the broker entering into the listing contract must be stated clearly and must be the same as that on the broker's license, whether an individual or a corporate license.
- *Owners:* The complete legal names of all parties having an ownership interest in the property must be specified. Note the form of co-ownership.
- *Property Description:* The legal description of the property and a statement of fixtures to be included or excluded from the sale must be given.
- *Type of Agency:* This form specifies that the agency to be created is an exclusive right to sell the subject property.
- *Listing Price:* The listing price is the gross selling price to be quoted to the public. It is set by the seller, using competitive market data supplied by the agent. The owner should clearly understand that certain sales expenses must be paid at closing. (The competitive market analysis [CMA] will be discussed in Chapter 14.)

1. A
2. C
3. A
4. C
5. C
6. B
7. B
8. A
9. C
10. A
11. B
12. B
13. B
14. C
15. B

- *Representations:* The owner certifies that no known title defects, adverse claims, or other known defects exist and that the owner has legal capacity to convey the property.
- *Evidence of Title:* The owner agrees to *furnish* a general warranty deed and either a title policy or an abstract of title to the property.
- *Brokerage Fee:* The amount of the brokerage fee is negotiated between the owner and broker.
- *Extension:* The extension clause provides a broker's protection period establishing the right to a fee, under certain circumstances, if the owner sells the property to one of the broker's prospects.
- *Broker's Authority:* The owner agrees to permit the broker to submit the property to the MLS if the broker is a member and to offer cooperation and compensation to other members of the MLS. Other authorizations may include advertising the property, using a lockbox, placing a yard sign, or disclosing the final sales price to MLS and taxing authorities.
- *Liabilities:* The owner agrees to hold the broker harmless for any loss to the property or any lapse of insurance coverage.
- *Discussion of Agency Relationships:* The broker discloses his or her representation of the seller and the agency relationships from which a potential buyer might choose.
- *Term:* This section specifies the beginning and ending dates of the listing contract.
- *Agreement:* The owner acknowledges that the broker will offer the property for sale according to the fair housing laws, that the listing contract has been read and understood, that a copy of the contract has been received, and that the contract is legally binding and cannot be assigned without written approval of the other party.

Summary

To acquire an inventory of properties to sell, brokers and salespersons must obtain listings. In Texas, listing agreements must be in writing for the broker to collect a commission. The various kinds of listing agreements include open listings, exclusive-agency listings, exclusive-right-to-sell listings, and net listings.

In an open listing, the broker's commission depends on his or her finding a buyer before the property is sold by the seller or another broker. Under an exclusive-agency listing the broker is given the exclusive right to represent the seller, but by selling the property without the broker's help, the seller can avoid paying the broker a commission. With an exclusive-right-to-sell listing, the seller appoints one broker to represent him or her and must pay that broker a commission regardless of whether it is the broker or the seller who finds a buyer, as long as the buyer is found within the listing period.

A multiple listing is a subtype of exclusive listing with the additional authority and obligation on the part of the listing broker to distribute the listing to other brokers in his or her multiple-listing organization. This constitutes a unilateral offer of cooperation and compensation.

A net listing is based on the net price the seller will receive if the property is sold. The broker under a net listing may retain as commission any amount over and above the seller's net. However, it is recommended that a broker suggest the property be listed for a full sales price that would include the broker's commission. A listing agreement may be terminated for the same reasons as any other agency relationship.

Questions

1. Which of the following statements is true of a listing contract?
   a. It is an employment contract for the personal and professional services of the broker.
   b. It obligates the seller to convey the property if the broker procures a ready, willing and able buyer.
   c. It obligates the broker to work diligently for both the seller and the buyer.
   d. It is a TREC-promulgated form.

2. Which statement describes a similarity between an exclusive-agency listing and an exclusive-right-to-sell listing?
   a. Under both types of listings, the seller retains the right to sell his or her real estate without the broker's help and without paying the broker a commission.
   b. Both are open listings.
   c. Both give the responsibility of representing the seller to one broker only.
   d. Under both, the seller authorizes only one particular salesperson to show his or her property.

3. Which statement describes a similarity between an open listing and an exclusive-agency listing?
   a. Under both, the seller avoids paying the broker a commission if the seller sells the property to someone the broker did not procure.
   b. Both listings grant a commission to any licensed broker who finds a buyer for the seller's property.
   c. Both are net listings.
   d. Under both the broker earns a commission regardless of who sells the property, as long as it is sold within the listing period.

4. A multiple listing
   a. involves more than one parcel of real estate.
   b. is the same as an open listing.
   c. allows the broker to distribute the listing information to other brokers for cooperation and compensation.
   d. allows the broker to offer the property for sale at the highest price possible and retain as the commission any amount over and above the amount requested by the seller.

5. All of the following would terminate an agency relationship **EXCEPT**
   a. expiration of the time period stated in the listing.
   b. death or incapacity of the broker.
   c. nonpayment of the commission by the seller.
   d. destruction of the improvements on the property.

6. A listing contract that requires that all other brokers honor the listing broker's contract but reserves the seller's right to sell directly to a buyer with no commission liability is a(n)
   a. open listing.
   b. exclusive-agency listing.
   c. exclusive-right-to-sell listing.
   d. net listing.

7. A listing agreement that runs for a set period and automatically renews itself for another listing period after the initial period ends is
   a. commonly used in conjunction with a multiple listing.
   b. illegal in Texas.
   c. known as an *open listing.*
   d. a unilateral offer of subagency.

8. The listing price for a property should be determined by the
   a. seller.
   b. salesperson.
   c. broker's competitive market analysis (CMA).
   d. appraised value.

9. All of the following provisions are usually included in listing agreements in Texas, **EXCEPT**
   a. the rate of commission.
   b. the date the agreement commences and the date it terminates.
   c. the minimum earnest money required by the seller.
   d. a disclosure of latent defects.

10. Johnson has his property under an exclusive-agency listing with broker Smith. If Johnson sells his property himself during the term of the listing without using Smith's services, he will owe Smith
    a. no commission.
    b. the full commission.
    c. a partial commission.
    d. only reimbursement for the broker's costs.

11. A seller lists his residence with a broker and stipulates that he wants to receive $85,000 from the sale but that the broker can sell the residence for as much as possible and keep the difference as a commission. The broker agrees, thus creating a(n)
    a. open listing.
    b. net listing.
    c. exclusive-right-to-sell listing.
    d. exclusive-agency listing.

12. Which statement best describes the Seller's Disclosure Notice?
    a. Sellers of residential property (single-family or multifamily housing) must provide the disclosure to a buyer.
    b. A buyer must receive a copy of the disclosure on or before the effective date of the contract, or the buyer may terminate the contract for any reason within seven days after receiving the notice.
    c. The seller has a duty to disclose death by natural causes or suicide that occurred on the property.
    d. Only visible structural defects need to be disclosed.

13. A listing taken by a real estate salesperson is an agreement between the seller and the
    a. salesperson.
    b. broker.
    c. salesperson and broker equally.
    d. local multiple-listing service.

14. A seller hired Nathan, a broker, under the terms of an open listing. While that listing was still in effect, the seller—without informing Nathan—hired Fred under an exclusive-right-to-sell listing for the same property. If Nathan produces a buyer for the property and the seller accepts that offer, then the seller must pay a
    a. full commission only to Nathan.
    b. full commission only to Fred.
    c. full commission to both Nathan and Fred.
    d. half commission to both Nathan and Fred.

15. Gayle listed his residence with a real estate broker. The broker brought an offer at full price from ready, willing, and able buyers, in accordance with the terms of the listing agreement. However, Gayle changed his mind and rejected the buyer's offer. In this situation, Gayle
    a. must sell the property.
    b. owes a commission to the broker.
    c. is liable to the buyers for specific performance.
    d. is liable to the buyers for compensatory damages.

14 Real Estate Appraisal

- estimate of a value on a specific date

Key Terms

appraisal	functional	reconciliation
capitalization rate	obsolescence	replacement cost
competitive market	gross income multiplier	reproduction cost
analysis	gross rent multiplier	sales comparison
cost approach	highest and best use	approach
depreciation	income approach	substitution
economic life	physical deterioration	value
external obsolescence	plottage value	

OVERVIEW

As stated earlier in the text, real estate is the business of value. Members of the general public informally estimate this value when they buy, sell or invest in real estate. A formal estimate of value is conducted by a practicing appraiser and serves as a basis for the pricing, financing, insuring, or leasing of real property.

This chapter examines value—what determines it, adds to it, and detracts from it. It also discusses in detail the various methods used by appraisal professionals to estimate the value of residential as well as commercial and industrial real estate.

In studying this chapter, the student must be careful not to confuse the job and practices of an appraiser with those of a real estate licensee who, as listing agent, makes an *estimate* of value for marketing purposes. Such an estimate is, of necessity and practicality, a very limited and narrow survey of the factors that constitute an objective value of the property.

In 1991, the Texas legislature enacted laws affecting the licensure and certification of appraisers. The requirements for becoming an appraiser also are discussed in this chapter.

APPRAISING

An **appraisal** is "the act or process of developing an opinion of value; an opinion of value." Based on his or her education, training, experience, and integrity, the appraiser attempts to project sellers' and buyers' past activities into a current estimate of real estate value. Because of the uniqueness of each property, comparisons of like properties often entail adjustments in arriving at a conclusion. Financial consideration by the layman for similar properties sometimes reflects sentiment, compassion, sympathy, bias, politics, specific needs, lack of understanding, and other factors not considered by the appraiser. A professional appraiser must remain impartial and objective in the process of estimating property value.

An appraisal cannot be guaranteed or proven. However, the opinion or estimate of value can be substantiated and justified. The final opinion or estimate of value is the result of a professional analysis of a considerable quantity of physical and economic facts. An appraisal must not be considered absolute but should be used as a basis of negotiation between parties involved in the property, whatever their interests. Formal appraisal reports are relied on in important decisions made by mortgage lenders, investors, public utilities, government agencies, businesses, and individuals. Home mortgage lenders, for instance, need to know a property's market value so that the loan-to-value ratio (the percentage of value to be loaned) will accurately reflect the property's value as collateral.

Not all estimates of real estate value are made by appraisal professionals; often the real estate agent must help a seller arrive at a market value for his or her property without the aid of a formal appraisal report. Thus it is necessary for everyone engaged in the real estate business to command at least a fundamental knowledge of real estate valuation.

Appraisal Regulations

Since 1939, a license has been required to appraise real property for a fee in Texas (unless otherwise exempted by law). In 1989, the *Financial Institutions Reform, Recovery, and Enforcement Act* (FIRREA) further required that any appraisal used in connection with a federally related transaction of $250,000 and above must be performed by a licensed or certified appraiser. *Federally related transactions* are real estate financial transactions that are above the transaction value *de minimus* ($250,000) in which a federal financial institution, regulatory agency, or secondary market participant engages. In 1991, the *Texas Appraiser Licensing and Certification Act* was passed to conform to the federal FIRREA guidelines. Either a TREC broker or salesperson license (for non-federally related transactions); a license, certification, or authorization by the Texas Appraiser Licensing and Certification Board (TALCB); or an exception under the law is required for all real property appraisals for a fee.

Texas law provides for five classifications of state appraiser certifications or licenses: Certified General Real Estate Appraiser, Certified Residential Real Estate Appraiser, State Licensed Real Estate Appraiser, Provisional Licensed Real Estate Appraiser, and Appraiser Trainee. The appraiser education, experience, and examination requirements, along with the scope of practice for which each classification is permitted, are shown in Table 14.1. The provisional license allows an applicant for appraiser trainee classification to take the state-licensed appraiser exam if he or she has met all

Texas Appraiser Licensing and Certification Board
SUMMARY OF REQUIREMENTS (as of 4/1/2001)
Complete requirements may be found in the Rules of the Texas Appraiser Licensing and Certification Board, particularly §§153.9–153.16 and §153.21.

Table 14.1   Texas Appraiser Licensing and Certification Board Summary of Requirements

Classification	Education	Experience	Examination	Comments	Authorized Tasks
CERTIFIED GENERAL Real Estate Appraiser	180 classroom hours of acceptable real estate appraisal related courses, including at least 90 hours of "fundamental" real estate appraisal courses with 30 hours of "non-residential" appraisal, and 15 hours of the Uniform Standards of Professional Appraisal Practice (USPAP) completed within two years of application. All Appraiser Qualifications Board (AQB) required subjects must have been covered.	3,000 hours of acceptable real estate appraisal experience over a minimum of 30 months (2½ years). A minimum of 1,500 hours must be in non-residential real estate appraising. Experience may be acquired anytime during the appraiser's career when that person had legal authority to perform real estate appraisals. Must conform to the Uniform Standards of Professional Appraisal Practice (USPAP).	Appraiser Qualifications Board (AQB) approved general certification examination. Exam is administered by Assessment Systems, Inc. (ASI), a national testing service. Current exam fee: $100 (to be paid to ASI).	Must submit completed "Application for Appraiser Certification or Licensing" (TALCB Form 1.5), together with total application and federal registry fees of $250. Just passing the exam does not certify an applicant. A person is not certified until ALL requirements have been met and the TALCB has issued the certification.	May appraise all types of real property without regard to transaction value or complexity in both federally related transactions (FRT) and non-FRT). **Must comply with the Uniform Standards of Professional Appraisal Practice (USPAP).**
CERTIFIED RESIDENTIAL Real Estate Appraiser	120 classroom hours of acceptable real estate appraisal related courses, including at least 40 hours of "fundamental" real estate appraisal courses, and 15 hours of Uniform Standards of Professional Appraisal Practice (USPAP) completed within two years of application. All AQB required subjects must have been covered.	2,500 hours of acceptable real estate appraisal experience over a minimum of 24 months (2 years). Experience may be acquired anytime during the appraiser's career when that person had legal authority to perform real estate appraisals. Must conform to USPAP.	AQB approved residential certification examination. Exam is administered by ASI. Current exam fee: $100 (to be paid to ASI).	Must submit completed "Application for Appraiser Certification or Licensing" (TALCB Form 1.5), together with total application and federal registry fees of $200. Just passing the exam does not certify an applicant. A person is not certified until ALL requirements have been met and the TALCB has issued the certification.	May appraise 1–4 unit residential real property without regard to transaction value or complexity in both federally related transactions (FRT) and non-federally related transactions (Non-FRT). May associate with a General Certified appraiser, who must sign the report, to appraise non-residential properties. **Must comply with USPAP.**
State LICENSED Real Estate Appraiser	90 classroom hours of acceptable real estate appraisal related courses, including at least 40 hours of "fundamental" real estate appraisal courses, and 15 hours of Uniform Standards of Professional Appraisal Practice (USPAP) completed within two years of application. All AQB required subjects must have been covered.	2,000 hours of acceptable real estate appraisal experience, which may be acquired anytime during the appraiser's career when that person had legal authority to perform real estate appraisals. Must conform to USPAP.	AQB approved state licensed exam. Exam is administered by ASI. Current exam fee: $100 (to be paid to ASI).	Must submit completed "Application for Appraiser Certification or Licensing" (TALCB Form 1.5), together with total application and federal registry fees of $175. Just passing the exam does not license an applicant. A person is not licensed until ALL requirements have been met and the TALCB has issued the license.	May appraise 1–4 unit real property with a transaction value less than $1M (non-complex) or $250K (complex) in both federally related transactions (FRT) and non-federally related transactions (Non-FRT). May associate with a General Certified appraiser, who must sign the report, to appraise non-residential properties. **Must comply with USPAP.**
PROVISIONAL LICENSED Real Estate Appraiser	90 classroom hours of acceptable real estate appraisal related courses, including at least 40 hours of "fundamental" real estate appraisal courses, and 15 hours of Uniform Standards of Professional Appraisal Practice (USPAP) completed within two years of application. All AQB required subjects must have been covered.	None. A Provisional Licensed person has 60 months after receiving the Provisional License in which to acquire 2,000 hours of acceptable real estate appraisal experience or the provisional license will be revoked. All appraisals must conform to USPAP.	AQB approved state licensed exam. Exam is administered by ASI. Current exam fee: $100 (to be paid to ASI).	Must complete ALL educational requirements AND fail to secure sponsorship as an Appraiser Trainee by two certified appraisers. **Then** must submit completed "Application for Provisional License" (TALCB Form 11.0) with total application and federal registry fees of $175, and two (2) completed "Affidavit Declining Sponsorship" forms (TALCB Form 12.0).	May appraise 1–4 unit real property with a transaction value less than $1M (non-complex) or $250K (complex) in both federally related transactions (FRT) and non-federally related transactions (Non-FRT). May associate with a General Certified appraiser, who must sign the report, to appraise non-residential properties. **Must comply with USPAP.**
Approved Appraiser TRAINEE	None	None	None	Must be sponsored by one or more current Texas certified (only) appraiser(s) who is responsible for the Trainee's actions. Must submit "Application for Approval as An Appraiser Trainee" (TALCB Form 4.4) together with total fees of $75.	Must appraise real property only under the active, personal and diligent direction and supervision of their sponsoring certified appraiser who shall sign the appraisal report. **Must comply with USPAP.**

Table 14.2 *Appraiser Requirements for Federally Related Transactions*		
Transaction Amount	**Residential**	**Nonresidential**
Less than $250,000 (non-federally related transaction)	TALCB-certified or -licensed appraiser, or TREC-licensed broker or salesperson	TALCB-certified or -licensed appraiser, or TREC-licensed broker or salesperson
Between $250,000 and $1,000,000	TALCB state-licensed, certified residential or certified general appraiser	TALCB-certified general appraiser*
Above $1,000,000	TALCB-certified residential or -certified general appraiser	TALCB-certified general appraiser*

* A certified residential or state licensed appraiser may associate with a certified general appraiser, who must sign the appraisal report, to appraise these types of properties.

requirements for licensing except the 2,000 hours of experience and if he or she has failed to secure sponsorship from at least two certified appraisers to obtain the experience. Table 14.2 reflects the license or certification required to appraise various types of properties in Texas. An appraisal in a non-federally related transaction may be conducted by a TREC-licensed broker or salesperson regardless of property type or dollar amount, although individual lenders or government agencies may still require state-certified or state-licensed appraisers in these transactions.

Except for the Appraiser Trainee, all applicants must meet certain education requirements, including at least 40 classroom hours of *"fundamental" real estate appraisal courses* in addition to 15 classroom hours of the Uniform Standards of Professional Appraisal Practice (USPAP). "Fundamental" appraisal courses are basic real estate appraisal courses, including principles of real estate appraisal, real estate appraisal practice, real estate appraisal procedures, highest and best use, report writing, rural appraisal, appraisal review, residential appraisal/valuation, agricultural property appraisal, sales comparison approach, cost approach, income capitalization, discounted cash flow analysis, real estate appraisal case studies, commercial appraisal, nonresidential real estate appraisal, and other courses specifically determined by the TALCB. Only two TREC "core" real estate courses are accepted to fulfill the education requirements above the required "fundamental" real estate appraisal hours: real estate principles and real estate appraisal (if not separately approved by the TALCB as a fundamental appraisal course). For additional information on licensure, visit the TALCB web site: www.talcb.state.tx.us.

After licensure, licensed and certified appraisers must complete 28 classroom hours of Appraiser Continuing Education (ACE) before each two-year license renewal. Each renewal must include at least seven classroom hours of USPAP. Although USPAP rules and regulations must be followed for *all* appraisals, USPAP standards do not apply to the activities of a real estate broker in the normal course of seeking listings or determining a competitive market value for a specific property.

THE APPRAISAL PROCESS

The key to an accurate appraisal lies in the methodical collection of accurate and verified data. The appraisal process is an orderly set of procedures used to collect and analyze data to arrive at an ultimate value conclusion. Figure 14.1 outlines the steps an appraiser takes in carrying out an appraisal assignment. The numbers in the following list correspond to the numbers on the diagram.

1. *State the problem:* The kind of value to be estimated must be specified and the valuation approach(es) most valid and reliable for the kind of property under appraisal must be selected. This includes the purpose of the appraisal.
2. *List the data needed and the sources:* Based on the approach(es) the appraiser uses, the types of data needed and the sources to be consulted are listed.
3. *Gather, record, and verify the necessary data:*
   a. *General data:* Detailed information concerning the economic, political, and social conditions of the region and/or city; comments on the effects of these data on the subject property must be obtained.
   b. *Specific data:* Detailed information about the subject property and improvements including comparative data relating to costs, sales, income, and expenses of similar properties.
   c. *Data for each approach:* Depending on the approach(es) used, comparative information relating to sales, income, and expenses and construction costs of comparable properties must be collected. All data should be verified, usually by checking the same information against two different sources. In the case of sales data, one source should be a person directly involved in the transaction.
4. *Determine the highest and best use:* The appraiser determines the most probable use that is legal, physically possible, and financially feasible.
5. *Estimate value by each of the three approaches:* The appraiser uses data collected in Step 3 to compute estimates of value by the cost approach, the sales comparison approach, and the income approach.
6. *Reconcile the estimated values for the final value estimate:* The appraiser analyzes the findings obtained from all three approaches to value, determining the most appropriate approach, for a particular property and determining the final estimate of value.
7. *Report the final value estimate:* After the three approaches have been reconciled and an opinion of value reached, the appraiser prepares a formal written report for the client. The statement may be a completed form, a letter, a short summary, or a lengthy written *narrative*, and it should contain the following information:
   a. The estimate of value and the date to which it applies
   b. The purpose for which the appraisal was made
   c. A description of the neighborhood and the subject property
   d. Factual data covering costs, sales, and income and expenses of similar, recently sold properties
   e. An analysis and interpretation of the data collected
   f. A presentation of one or more of the three approaches to value in enough detail to support the appraiser's final value conclusion

H.B. 1268 (2001) prohibits a lender from making the payment for an appraisal contingent on a specified value—thereby interfering with the appraiser's obligation to provide an independent and impartial opinion of value.

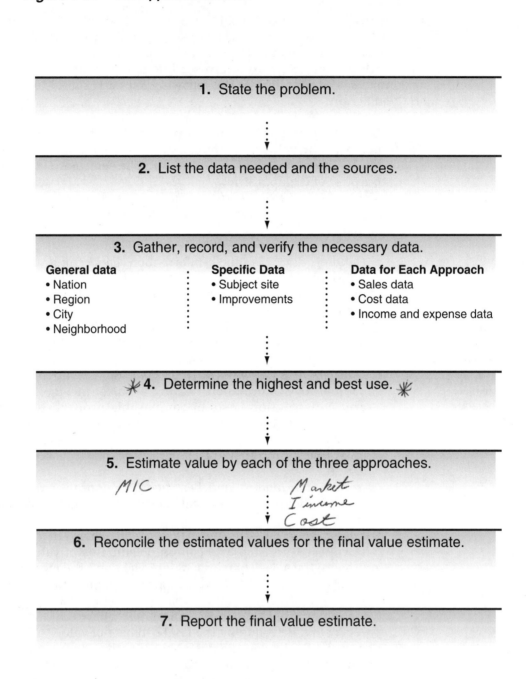

Figure 14.1   *The Appraisal Process*

1. State the problem.

2. List the data needed and the sources.

3. Gather, record, and verify the necessary data.

General data	**Specific Data**	**Data for Each Approach**
• Nation	• Subject site	• Sales data
• Region	• Improvements	• Cost data
• City		• Income and expense data
• Neighborhood		

4. Determine the highest and best use.

5. Estimate value by each of the three approaches.

MIC

Market
Income
Cost

6. Reconcile the estimated values for the final value estimate.

7. Report the final value estimate.

    g. Any qualifying conditions

    h. Supportive material such as charts, maps, photographs, floor plans, leases, and contracts

    i. The certification and signature of the appraiser

Figure 14.2 is the *Uniform Residential Appraisal Report* form required by many government agencies. In response to the effect of environmental risks on the value of real estate, USPAP requires that licensed and certified appraisers recognize and report environmental conditions as a part of the appraisal report.

VALUE

The four characteristics of value may be remembered by the acronym **DUST**: *D*emand, *U*tility, *S*carcity, and *T*ransferability.

To have **value** in the real estate market—that is, to have monetary worth based on desirability—a property must have the following four characteristics:

1. *Effective **D**emand:* the need or desire for possession or ownership backed up by the financial means to satisfy that need (Note: When the word *demand* is used in economics, *effective demand* is usually assumed.)
2. ***U**tility:* the capacity to satisfy human needs and desires
3. ***S**carcity:* a finite supply
4. ***T**ransferability:* the relative ease with which ownership rights are transferred from one person to another

Market Value

Although a given parcel of real estate may have many different kinds of value at the same time (as illustrated in Figure 14.3), generally the goal of an appraiser is to estimate *market value.* The market value of a parcel of real estate is the most probable price a property should bring in a competitive and open market under all conditions requisite to a fair sale, with the buyer and seller each acting prudently and knowledgeably and assuming the price is not affected by undue stimulus. Included in this definition are the following key points:

- Market value is the *most probable estimated price a property will bring—not the average price, highest price, or lowest price.*
- Both buyer and seller are motivated.
- Buyer and seller are *well informed* or *well advised,* with both acting in what they consider their own best interests.
- A reasonable time is allowed for exposure in the *open market.*
- Payment is made in terms of *cash* or its equivalent.
- The price represents the normal consideration for the property sold, unaffected by special financing or sales concessions.

Market value versus market price.

Market value is an estimated price based on an analysis of comparable sales and other pertinent market data. *Market price,* on the other hand, is what a property *actually* sells for—its selling price. Theoretically, the ideal market price is the same as the market value; however, sometimes a property may be sold below or above market value, for example, when a seller is forced to sell quickly, when a sale is arranged between relatives, or when buyers are less than fully informed. Thus the market price can be taken as accurate evidence of current market

Figure 14.2   **Uniform Residential Appraisal Report**

UNIFORM RESIDENTIAL APPRAISAL REPORT File No.

Property Description

SUBJECT

Property Address		City		State	Zip Code

Legal Description — County

Assessor's Parcel No. — Tax Year — R.E. Taxes $ — Special Assessments $

Borrower — Current Owner — Occupant: ☐ Owner ☐ Tenant ☐ Vacant

Property rights appraised ☐ Fee Simple ☐ Leasehold — Project Type ☐ PUD ☐ Condominium (HUD/VA only) — HOA$ /Mo.

Neighborhood or Project Name — Map Reference — Census Tract

Sale Price $ — Date of Sale — Description and $ amount of loan charges/concessions to be paid by seller

Lender/Client — Address

Appraiser — Address

NEIGHBORHOOD

Location	☐ Urban	☐ Suburban	☐ Rural	Predominant occupancy	Single family housing		Present land use %	Land use change

Location ☐ Urban ☐ Suburban ☐ Rural

Built up ☐ Over 75% ☐ 25-75% ☐ Under 25%

Growth rate ☐ Rapid ☐ Stable ☐ Slow

Property values ☐ Increasing ☐ Stable ☐ Declining

Demand/supply ☐ Shortage ☐ In balance ☐ Over supply

Marketing time ☐ Under 3 mos. ☐ 3-6 mos. ☐ Over 6 mos.

Predominant occupancy ☐ Owner ☐ Tenant ☐ Vacant (0-5%) ☐ Vacant (over 5%)

Single family housing PRICE $(000) AGE (yrs) — Low — High — Predominant

Present land use % — One family — 2-4 family — Multi-family — Commercial

Land use change ☐ Not likely ☐ Likely ☐ In process — To:

Note: Race and the racial composition of the neighborhood are not appraisal factors.

Neighborhood boundaries and characteristics:

Factors that affect the marketability of the properties in the neighborhood (proximity to employment and amenities, employment stability, appeal to market, etc.):

Market conditions in the subject neighborhood (including support for the above conclusions related to the trend of property values, demand/supply, and marketing time - - such as data on competitive properties for sale in the neighborhood, description of the prevalence of sales and financing concessions, etc.):

PUD

Project Information for PUDs (If applicable) - - Is the developer/builder in control of the Home Owners' Association (HOA)? ☐ Yes ☐ No

Approximate total number of units in the subject project _____ Approximate total number of units for sale in the subject project _____

Describe common elements and recreational facilities:

SUBJECT SITE

Dimensions _____ — Topography _____

Site area _____ — Corner Lot ☐ Yes ☐ No — Size _____

Specific zoning classification and description _____ — Shape _____

Zoning compliance ☐ Legal ☐ Legal nonconforming (Grandfathered use) ☐ Illegal ☐ No zoning — Drainage _____

Highest & best use as improved: ☐ Present use ☐ Other use (explain) — View _____

Utilities	Public	Other	Off-site Improvements	Type	Public	Private	
Electricity			Street				Landscaping
Gas			Curb/gutter				Driveway Surface
Water			Sidewalk				Apparent easements
Sanitary sewer			Street lights				FEMA Special Flood Hazard Area ☐ Yes ☐ No
Storm sewer			Alley				FEMA Zone — Map Date

FEMA Map No.

Comments (apparent adverse easements, encroachments, special assessments, slide areas, illegal or legal nonconforming zoning use, etc.):

DESCRIPTION OF IMPROVEMENTS

GENERAL DESCRIPTION	EXTERIOR DESCRIPTION	FOUNDATION	BASEMENT	INSULATION
No. of Units	Foundation	Slab	Area Sq. Ft.	Roof
No. of Stories	Exterior Walls	Crawl Space	% Finished	Ceiling
Type (Det./Att.)	Roof Surface	Basement	Ceiling	Walls
Design (Style)	Gutters & Dwnspts.	Sump Pump	Walls	Floor
Existing/Proposed	Window Type	Dampness	Floor	None
Age (Yrs.)	Storm/Screens	Settlement	Outside Entry	Unknown
Effective Age (Yrs.)	Manufactured House	Infestation		

ROOMS	Foyer	Living	Dining	Kitchen	Den	Family Rm.	Rec. Rm.	Bedrooms	# Baths	Laundry	Other	Area Sq. Ft.
Basement												
Level 1												
Level 2												

Finished area **above** grade contains: _____ Rooms; _____ Bedroom(s); _____ Bath(s); _____ Square Feet of Gross Living Area

INTERIOR	Materials/Condition	HEATING	KITCHEN EQUIP.	ATTIC	AMENITIES	CAR STORAGE:
Floors		Type	Refrigerator	None	Fireplace(s) #	None
Walls		Fuel	Range/Oven	Stairs	Patio	Garage # of cars
Trim/Finish		Condition	Disposal	Drop Stair	Deck	Attached
Bath Floor		COOLING	Dishwasher	Scuttle	Porch	Detached
Bath Wainscot		Central	Fan/Hood	Floor	Fence	Built-In
Doors		Other	Microwave	Heated	Pool	Carport
		Condition	Washer/Dryer	Finished		Driveway

COMMENTS

Additional features (special energy efficient items, etc.):

Condition of the improvements, depreciation (physical, functional, and external), repairs needed, quality of construction, remodeling/additions, etc.:

Adverse environmental conditions (such as, but not limited to, hazardous wastes, toxic substances, etc.) present in the improvements, on the site, or in the immediate vicinity of the subject property.:

Figure 14.2 Uniform Residential Appraisal Report (Continued)

UNIFORM RESIDENTIAL APPRAISAL REPORT File No. _____

Valuation Section

COST APPROACH

ESTIMATED SITE VALUE . . . . = $ _____

ESTIMATED REPRODUCTION COST-NEW-OF IMPROVEMENTS:

Dwelling _____ Sq. Ft @ $ _____ = $ _____

_____ Sq. Ft @ $ _____ = _____

= _____

Garage/Carport _____ Sq. Ft @ $ _____ = $ _____

Total Estimated Cost New . . . . = $ _____

Less   Physical   Functional   External

Depreciation _____ _____ _____ = $ _____

Depreciated Value of Improvements . . . . = $ _____

"As-is" Value of Site Improvements . . . . = $ _____

INDICATED VALUE BY COST APPROACH . . . . = $ _____

Comments on Cost Approach (such as, source of cost estimate, site value, square foot calculation and for HUD, VA and FmHA, the estimated remaining economic life of the property): _____

SALES COMPARISON ANALYSIS

ITEM	SUBJECT	COMPARABLE NO. 1		COMPARABLE NO. 2		COMPARABLE NO. 3	
Address							
Proximity to Subject							
Sales Price	$		$		$		$
Price/Gross Liv. Area	$ ☑	$	☑	$	☑	$	☑
Data and/or Verification Source							
VALUE ADJUSTMENTS	DESCRIPTION	DESCRIPTION	+ (-) $ Adjustment	DESCRIPTION	+ (-) $ Adjustment	DESCRIPTION	+ (-) $ Adjustment
Sales or Financing Concessions							
Date of Sale/Time							
Location							
Leasehold/Fee Simple							
Site							
View							
Design and Appeal							
Quality of Construction							
Age							
Condition							
Above Grade	Total Bdrms Baths	Total Bdrms Baths		Total Bdrms Baths		Total Bdrms Baths	
Room Count							
Gross Living Area	Sq. Ft.	Sq. Ft.		Sq. Ft.		Sq. Ft.	
Basement & Finished Rooms Below Grade							
Functional Utility							
Heating/Cooling							
Energy Efficient Items							
Garage/Carport							
Porch, Patio, Deck, Fireplace(s), etc.							
Fence, Pool, etc.							
Net Adj. (total)		☐ + ☐ - $		☐ + ☐ - $		☐ + ☐ - $	
Adjusted Sales Price of Comparable			$		$		$

Comments on Sales Comparison (including the subject property's compatibility to the neighborhood, etc.): _____

ITEM	SUBJECT	COMPARABLE NO. 1	COMPARABLE NO. 2	COMPARABLE NO. 3
Date, Price and Data Source, for prior sales within year of appraisal				

Analysis of any current agreement of sale, option, or listing of the subject property and analysis of any prior sales of subject and comparables within one year of the date of appraisal: _____

INDICATED VALUE BY SALES COMPARISON APPROACH . . . . $ _____

INDICATED VALUE BY INCOME APPROACH (If Applicable) Estimated Market Rent $ _____ /Mo. x Gross Rent Multiplier _____ = $ _____

This appraisal is made ☐ "as is" ☐ subject to the repairs, alterations, inspections or conditions listed below ☐ subject to completion per plans and specifications.

Conditions of Appraisal: _____

Final Reconciliation: _____

RECONCILIATION

The purpose of this appraisal is to estimate the market value of the real property that is the subject of this report, based on the above conditions and the certification, contingent and limiting conditions, and market value definition that are stated in the attached Freddie Mac Form 439/Fannie Mae Form 1004B (Revised _____).

I (WE) ESTIMATE THE MARKET VALUE, AS DEFINED, OF THE REAL PROPERTY THAT IS THE SUBJECT OF THIS REPORT, AS OF _____ (WHICH IS THE DATE OF INSPECTION AND THE EFFECTIVE DATE OF THIS REPORT) TO BE $ _____

APPRAISER:

Signature _____

Name _____

Date Report Signed _____

State Certification # _____ State _____

Or State License # _____ State _____

SUPERVISORY APPRAISER (ONLY IF REQUIRED):

Signature _____   ☐ Did   ☐ Did Not

Name _____   Inspect Property

Date Report Signed _____

State Certification # _____ State _____

Or State License # _____ State _____

Freddie Mac Form 70 6-93   10 CH.   PAGE 2 OF 2   Fannie Mae Form 1004 6-93

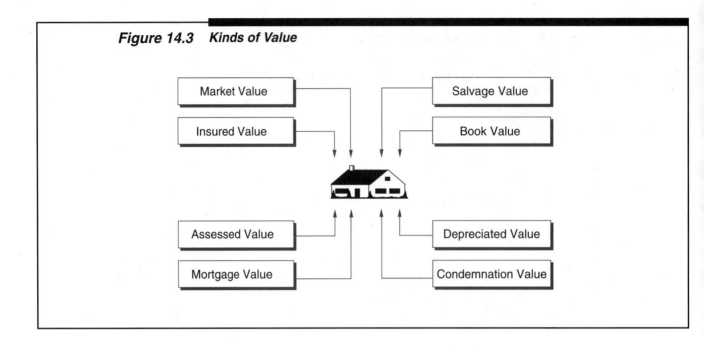

Figure 14.3　Kinds of Value

Market Value	Salvage Value
Insured Value	Book Value
Assessed Value	Depreciated Value
Mortgage Value	Condemnation Value

value *only* after considering the relationship of the buyer and the seller, the terms and conditions of the market, any financing or sales concessions made by the seller, and the effect of the passage of time since the sale was made.

Market value versus cost. It also is important to distinguish between market value and *cost.* One of the most common errors made in valuing property is the assumption that cost represents market value. Cost and market value *may* be equal and often are when the improvements on a property are new and represent the highest and best use of the land.

More often, however, cost does not equal market value. For example, two homes are identical in every respect except one is located on a street with heavy traffic and the other is on a quiet residential street. The value of the former may be less than that of the latter, although the cost of each may be exactly the same. Another example would be a situation in which the demand for homes greatly exceeds the available supply to such an extent that buyers actually pay more than it would cost to construct such homes because they want to secure housing without long delay. In this instance, market value easily could exceed cost.

> *Market value* is a reasonable *opinion* of a property's value. *Market price* is the *actual selling price* of a property. *Cost* is the original capital outlay for land, labor, materials and profit.

Basic Principles of Value

A number of economic principles affect the value of real estate. The most important of these principles are defined in the following subsections.

Highest and best use. The most probable use to which a property is suited that will result in its "highest value" is its **highest and best use.** The most probable use must be legal, physically possible, and financially feasible. The highest and best use of a site can change with social, political, and economic forces. For example, a parking lot in a busy downtown area may not maximize the land¾s profitability to the same extent as an office building.

Substitution. The principle of **substitution** states that the maximum value of a property tends to be set by the cost of purchasing an equally desirable and valuable substitute property. For example, if two similar houses are for sale in an area, the one with the lower asking price normally would be purchased first.

Supply and demand. This principle states that the value of a property will increase if the supply decreases and the demand either increases or remains constant—and vice versa. For example, the last lot to be sold in a residential area where the demand for homes is high probably would be worth more than the first lot sold in that area.

Conformity. Maximum value is realized if the use of land conforms to existing neighborhood standards. In single-family residential neighborhoods, for example, buildings should be similar in design, construction, size, and age. For example, the biggest house on the block tends to lose value to its neighbors; it is said to be *overbuilt* for the neighborhood. The reverse is sometimes true for the smallest house on the block.

Externalities. The principle of *externalities* states that influences outside a property may have a positive or negative effect on its value. For example, the federal government's participation in interest rate levels, mortgage loan guarantees, slum clearance, and rehabilitation has a powerful impact on stimulating or retarding supply and demand. At the neighborhood level, property values can be enhanced even by decorative features such as fresh paint, flowers, and plush lawns.

Anticipation. This principle holds that value can increase or decrease in anticipation of some future benefit or detriment affecting the property. For example, the value of a house may be affected by rumors that an adjacent property may be converted to commercial use in the near future.

Increasing and diminishing returns. Improvements to land and structures eventually will reach a point at which they no longer have a positive net effect on property values. As long as money spent on improvements produces an increase in income or value, the *law of increasing returns* is applicable. At the point where additional improvements produce no proportionate increase in income or value, the *law of diminishing returns* applies.

Plottage value. The increased utility and value resulting from the combining or consolidating of adjacent lots into one larger lot is the principle of **plottage value**. For example, two adjacent lots are each valued at $35,000; each one will accommodate a duplex. If the two lots are combined into one lot that will accommodate an eight-unit apartment complex, the land might be worth $90,000. The process of merging the two lots under one owner is known as *assemblage.*

Contribution. The value of any component of a property is measured by the amount it contributes to the value of the whole or the amount its absence detracts from that value. For example, the cost of installing an air-conditioning system and remodeling an older office building may be greater than is justified by the rental increase that may result from the improvement to the property.

Competition. This principle states that excess profits tend to attract competition. For example, the success of a retail store may attract investors to open similar stores in the area. This tends to mean less profit for all stores concerned unless the purchasing power in the area increases substantially.

Change. No physical or economic condition remains constant. Real estate is subject to natural phenomena such as tornadoes, fires, and the routine wear and tear of the elements. The real estate business is also subject to the demands of its market, just as any other business. An appraiser should be knowledgeable about the past and, perhaps, the predictable future effects of natural phenomena and the behavior of the marketplace.

THE THREE APPROACHES TO VALUE

To arrive at an accurate estimate of value three basic approaches, or techniques, are traditionally used by appraisers: the sales comparison approach, the cost approach, and the income approach. Each method serves as a check against the others and narrows the range within which the final estimate of value will fall. Each method is generally considered most reliable for specific types of property.

The Sales Comparison Approach

> The *sales comparison approach* compares the subject property with recently sold comparable properties and is based on the *principle of substitution.*

In the **sales comparison approach,** sometimes called the *market data approach,* an estimate of value is obtained by comparing the subject property (the property under appraisal) with recently sold comparable properties (properties similar to the subject). This approach is used most often by brokers and salespeople helping a seller set a price for residential real estate in an active market. Because no two parcels of real estate are exactly alike, each comparable property must be compared with the subject property, and the sales prices must be adjusted for any dissimilar features. The principal factors for which adjustments must be made fall into four basic categories:

1. *Date of sale:* An adjustment must be made if economic changes occur between the date of sale of the comparable property and the date of the appraisal.
2. *Location:* An adjustment may be necessary to compensate for locational differences. For example, similar properties might differ in price from neighborhood to neighborhood or even in more desirable locations within the same neighborhood.
3. *Physical features:* Physical features that may cause adjustments include age of building; size of lot; landscaping; construction; number of rooms; square feet of living space; interior and exterior condition; the presence or absence of a garage, fireplace, or air conditioner; and so forth.
4. *Terms and conditions of sale:* This consideration becomes important if a sale is not financed by a standard mortgage procedure.

After a careful analysis of the differences between comparable properties and the subject property, the appraiser assigns a dollar value to each difference. On the basis of their knowledge and experience, appraisers estimate dollar adjustments that reflect actual values extracted from the marketplace. The value of a feature present in the subject property but not in the comparable property is *added to* the sales price of the comparable. This presumes that, all other features being equal, a property having a feature (such

---

Table 14.3 Sales Comparison Approach to Value

	Subject Property: 155 Potter Dr.	Comparables A	B	C	D	E
Sales price		$118,000	$112,000	$121,000	$116,500	$110,000
Financing concessions	none	none	none	none	none	none
Date of sale		current	current	current	current	current
Location	good	same	inferior +6,500	same	same	same
Age	6 years	same	same	same	same	same
Size of lot	60′ × 135′	same	same	larger −5,000	same	larger −5,000
Landscaping	good	same	same	same	same	same
Construction	brick	same	same	same	same	same
Style	ranch	same	same	same	same	same
No. of rooms	6	same	same	same	same	same
No. of bedrooms	3	same	same	same	same	same
No. of baths	1½	same	same	same	same	same
Sq. ft. of living space	1,500	same	same	same	same	same
Other space (basement)	full basement	same	same	same	same	same
Condition—exterior	average	superior −1,500	inferior +1,000	superior −1,500	same	inferior +2,000
Condition—interior	good	same	same	superior −500	same	same
Garage	2-car attached	same	same	same	same	none +5,000
Other improvements	none	none	none	none	none	none
Net Adjustments		−1,500	+7,500	−7,000	-0-	+2,000
Adjusted Value		$116,500	$119,500	$114,000	$116,500	$112,000

Note: Because the value range of the properties in the comparison chart (excluding comparable B) is close, and comparable D required no adjustment, an appraiser would conclude that the indicated market value of the subject is $116,500.

---

as a fireplace or wet bar) not present in the comparable property tends to have a higher market value solely because of this feature. The feature need not be a physical amenity; it may be a locational or an aesthetic feature. Likewise, the value of a feature present in the comparable but not in the subject property is *subtracted from* the sales price of the comparable. The adjusted sales prices of the comparables represent the probable value range of the subject property. From this range a single market value estimate can be reached.

The sales comparison approach is essential in almost every appraisal of real estate. It is considered the most reliable of the three approaches in appraising residential property, where the amenities (intangible benefits) may be difficult to measure otherwise. An example of the sales comparison approach is shown in Table 14.3.

The Cost Approach

The **cost approach** to value is based on the property's reproduction cost. Because most people will not pay more for a property than it would cost to acquire a similar site and erect a similar structure on it, the current reproduction cost of the building plus the value of the land tends to set the upper limit of a property's value. The cost approach is sometimes called *appraisal by summation.*

Table 14.4   *Cost Approach to Value*

Land Valuation: Size 60′ × 135′ @ $450 per front foot		$ 27,000
Building Valuation: Replacement Cost 1,500 sq. ft. @ $65 per sq. ft. (Includes the combined cost of basic structure, floor coverings, heating and cooling equipment, fixtures, appliances, etc.	$97,500	
Plus site improvements: driveway, walks, landscaping, etc.	4,000	
Total Estimated Cost New of Improvements	$101,500	
Less Depreciation:		
Physical depreciation curable (items of deferred maintenance) roof	$4,000	
incurable (structural deterioration)	5,200	
Functional obsolescence	2,000	
External obsolescence	-0-	
Total Depreciation	−11,200	
Depreciated Value of Improvements		$ 90,300
Indicated Value by Cost Approach		$117,300

The cost approach consists of five steps as illustrated in Table 14.4:

The *cost approach* calculates the property value based on the improvement's reproduction cost or replacement cost.

1. Estimate the value of the land as if it were vacant and available to be put to its highest and best use.
2. Estimate the current cost of constructing the building(s) and site improvements.
3. Estimate the amount of accrued depreciation resulting from physical deterioration, functional obsolescence, and/or external obsolescence.
4. Deduct accrued depreciation from the estimated construction cost of a new building(s) and site improvements.
5. Add the estimated land value to the depreciated cost of the building(s) and site improvements to arrive at the total property value.

Land value (step 1) is most commonly estimated by using the sales comparison approach. That is, the location and improvements of the subject site are compared with those of similar nearby sites and adjustments are made for significant differences.

There are two ways to look at the construction of a building for appraisal purposes (step 2): reproduction cost and replacement cost. **Reproduction cost** is the dollar amount required to construct an *exact duplicate* of the subject building at current prices. **Replacement cost** of the subject property would be the construction cost at current prices of a property that is not necessarily an exact duplicate but serves the same purpose or function as the original. As an example, this approach permits the installation of less expensive hardwood kitchen cabinets instead of more expensive but outdated enameled steel cabinets. Replacement cost is used more frequently in appraising older structures because it eliminates obsolete features and takes advantage of current construction materials and techniques.

Determining reproduction or replacement cost.

An appraiser using the cost approach computes the reproduction or replacement cost of a building using one of the following three methods:

1. *Square-foot method:* The cost per square foot of a recently built comparable structure is multiplied by the number of square feet in the subject building. This is the most common method of cost estimation on a residential appraisal (see Table 14.4). Square-footage measurements are taken from the *exterior* surface of outside walls (brick to brick) for *finished areas* of the dwelling. Finished areas (living areas) include enclosed areas that are suitable for year-round use with walls, floors, and ceilings that are similar to the rest of the house. For some properties, the cost per *cubic foot* of a recently built comparable structure is multiplied by the number of cubic feet in the subject structure.

2. *Unit-in-place method:* The replacement cost of a structure is estimated based on the cost per unit of measure of individual building components, including the cost of material, labor, overhead, and profit. For example, insulation might be computed at $0.13 per square foot, drywall at $2.25 per square yard, and so on. The total in-place cost per unit is multiplied by the number of such units in each building component.

3. *Quantity-survey method:* An estimate is made of the quantities of raw materials needed to replace the subject structure (lumber, plaster, brick, and so on) as well as of the current price of such materials and their installation costs. For example, reproduction might be stated as 10,000 concrete slabs at $3.50 per slab, 1,500 doorknobs at $7.00 each, and so forth. These factors are added to the indirect costs (such as building permit, survey, payroll taxes, builder's profit) to arrive at the total replacement cost of the structure.

Depreciation.

In a real estate appraisal, **depreciation** refers to any condition that adversely diminishes the value of an *improvement* to real property. Land is not depreciated. For appraisal purposes (as opposed to depreciation for tax purposes, which will be discussed in Chapter 24), depreciation can be classified into three types:

Curable depreciation is depreciation that can be corrected at an economically feasible cost.

1. **Physical deterioration** is a loss in value due to wear and tear from use, age, weather, lack of maintenance, or even vandalism. Economically, physical deterioration can be either curable or incurable. *Curable:* A new roof would be a warranted expense on a 40-year-old brick building otherwise in good condition. *Incurable:* Replacing weather-worn siding near the end of a building's economic life may not warrant the financial investment. **Economic life** refers to the period over which a building can be profitably utilized.

2. **Functional obsolescence** is caused by a relative loss of building utility. This loss may be due to a deficiency such as a faulty building design, outmoded equipment, or a poorly arranged floor plan. The loss also could be due to an overimprovement (*superadequacy*) such as an in-ground swimming pool in the backyard of a $30,000 house.

Functional obsolescence can be curable or incurable. *Curable:* Outmoded plumbing fixtures are usually easily and fairly inexpensively replaced. *Incurable:* An office building that cannot accommodate a central air-conditioning system has an incurable deficiency.

3. **External obsolescence** is caused by factors not on the subject property (such as environmental, social, or economic forces) and is usually *incurable*. Proximity to a nuisance—a polluting factory or a deteriorating neighborhood, for instance—would be an unchangeable factor that could not be cured by the owner of the subject property. This type of depreciation is sometimes referred to as *locational obsolescence* or *economic obsolescence*.

In determining a property's depreciation most appraisers use the *breakdown method,* in which depreciation is broken down into all three classes, with separate estimates for curable and incurable factors in each class. Depreciation, however, is difficult to measure, and the older the building, the more difficult it is to estimate. Much of functional obsolescence and all of external obsolescence can be evaluated only by analyzing the actions of buyers in the marketplace.

In Practice	The cost approach is most helpful in the appraisal of special-purpose buildings such as schools, churches, and other public buildings. Such properties are difficult to appraise using other methods because local sales of comparables are seldom available and the properties usually do not generate income.

The Income Approach

The **income approach** to value is based on the premise that there is a relationship between the income a property can earn and the property's value. It assumes that the income derived from a property will, to a large extent, influence the value of that property. Residential one- to four-family properties are usually valued by the gross rent multiplier method, to be discussed later.

> The *income approach* estimates property value based on its rental income.

The *income capitalization approach* is used for valuation of income properties such as apartments, offices, and retail and commercial establishments. This approach makes use of both *direct capitalization* and *yield capitalization* methods. The direct capitalization method is the most commonly employed method for most income-producing properties. Table 14.5 illustrates the steps that an appraiser must go through to estimate value by the direct capitalization method:

1. Estimate annual potential *gross income.*
2. Based on market experience, deduct an appropriate allowance for vacancy and rent loss to arrive at the *effective gross income.*
3. Based on appropriate operating standards, deduct the annual *operating expenses* of the real estate from the effective gross income to arrive at the annual *net operating income.* Management costs are always included as operating expenses even if the current owner manages the property himself or herself. Mortgage loan payments (including principal and interest), however, are *not* considered operating expenses. For the property to be a viable investment, the net operating income

Table 14.5	*Income Capitalization Approach to Value*	
Gross Annual Income Estimate (potential rent income plus other income)		$60,000
Less vacancy and loss of rent (estimated) @ 5% *-/0%*		- 3,000
Effective Gross Income		$57,000
Expenses:		
Real estate taxes	$9,000	
Insurance	1,000	
Janitor	5,200	
Utilities (electricity, water, gas)	3,600	
Repairs	1,200	
Decorating	1,400	
Replacement of equipment	800	
Maintenance	1,200	
Legal and accounting	600	
Management *(15-25%)*	3,000	
Total Expenses		$27,000
Annual Net Operating Income *(NOI)*		$30,000
Capitalization rate = 10%		
Capitalization of annual net operating income	$30,000 0.10	
Indicated Value by Income Approach = $300,000		

Note: if the annual debt service exceeds $30,000, the property has "negative cash flow," which reduces its value accordingly.

should be sufficient to satisfy the debt service (make the loan payments) and leave some "positive cash flow" income for the owner.

4. Estimate the price a typical investor would pay for the income produced by this particular type and class of property. This is done by estimating the rate of return (or yield) that an investor will demand for the investment of his or her capital in this type of building. This rate of return is called the **capitalization rate** (or "cap" rate) and is determined by comparing the relationship of net income with the sales prices of similar properties that have sold in the current market. For example, a comparable property producing an annual net operating income of $15,000 is sold for $125,000. The capitalization rate is 12 percent ($15,000 ÷ $125,000). If other comparable properties sold at prices that yielded substantially the same rate, 12 percent is the rate the appraiser should apply to the subject property.

5. Finally, the capitalization rate is applied to the property's annual net operating income, resulting in the appraiser's estimate of the property's value.

With the appropriate capitalization rate and the projected annual net operating income, the appraiser can obtain an indication of value by the income approach in the following manner:

Net Operating Income ÷ Capitalization Rate = Value

Example: $20,000 income ÷ 12% cap rate = $166,700 value

> To calculate value by the *income approach*, remember the name **IRV**: *I*ncome = *R*ate × *V*alue.

This formula and its variations are important in dealing with income property. Variations are as follows:

$$\text{Income} = \text{Rate} \times \text{Value} \qquad \frac{\text{Income}}{\text{Rate}} = \text{Value} \qquad \frac{\text{Income}}{\text{Value}} = \text{Rate}$$

Another, and more accurate, method for estimating value by the income capitalization approach can be accomplished by using a yield capitalization method, such as *discounted cash flow analysis.* The application of yield capitalization is beyond the scope of this text.

In Practice   The most difficult step in the income approach to value is determining the appropriate capitalization rate for the property. This rate must be selected to reflect accurately the recapture of the original investment over the building's economic life, give the owner an acceptable rate of return on his or her investment, and provide for the repayment of borrowed capital. Note that an income property that carries with it a great deal of risk as an investment generally requires a higher rate of return than a property that is considered to be a safer investment.

Gross rent or income multipliers. Some properties, such as single-family homes, are not purchased primarily for the income they can produce. As a substitute for a more elaborate income capitalization analysis, the **gross rent multiplier** (GRM) method often is used in appraising such properties. The GRM relates the sales price of a property to its rental income; gross *monthly* income is used for residential property. The gross rent multiplier formula is as follows:

$$\frac{\text{Sales Price}}{\text{Gross Monthly Rental Income}} = \text{Gross Rent Multiplier}$$

For example, if a home recently sold for $82,000 and its gross monthly rental income was $750, the GRM for the property is computed in the following manner:

$$\frac{\$82,000}{\$750} = 109.3 \text{ GRM}$$

> **Multipliers**
>
> *GRM* uses gross *monthly* income; it applies primarily to residential properties.
>
> *GIM* uses gross *annual* income; it applies primarily to industrial and commercial properties.

To establish an accurate GRM, an appraiser must have recent sales and rental data from properties that are similar to the subject property. The resulting GRM then can be applied to the estimated fair market rental of the subject property to arrive at its market value (see Table 14.6). The formula is

$$\text{Gross Monthly Income} \times \text{GRM} = \text{Estimated Market Value}$$

However, gross *annual* income is used in appraising industrial and commercial properties. The ratio used to convert annual income into market value is called a **gross income multiplier** (GIM). The formula to determine a GIM follows:

$$\frac{\text{Sales Price}}{\text{Annual Gross Income}} = \text{Gross Income Multiplier}$$

Table 14.6	Gross Rent Multiplier			
	Comparable No.	**Sales Price**	**Monthly Rent**	**GRM**
	1	$93,600	$650	144
	2	78,500	450	174
	3	95,500	675	141
	4	82,000	565	145
	Subject	?	625	?

Note: Based on an analysis of these comparisons, a GRM of 145 seems reasonable for homes in this area. In the opinion of an appraiser, then, the estimated value of the subject property would be $625 × 145, or $90,625.

Much skill is required to use multipliers accurately because no fixed multiplier is available for all areas or all types of properties. Therefore, many appraisers view the technique simply as a quick, informal way to check the validity of a property value obtained by the other appraisal methods. In fact, GRMs and GIMs have been used less in recent years because this technique not only fails to take into consideration the tax situations of different possible investors but also fails to recognize alternative methods of financing.

Reconciliation   If the three approaches to value are applied to the same property, they normally will produce three separate indications of value. **Reconciliation** is the art of analyzing and effectively weighing the findings from the three approaches. Although each approach may serve as an independent guide to value, whenever possible all three approaches should be used as a check on the final estimate of value. The process of reconciliation is more complicated than simply taking the average of the three value estimates. An average implies that the data and logic applied in each of the approaches are equally valid and reliable and should therefore be given equal weight. In fact, certain approaches are more valid and reliable with certain kinds and ages of properties and certain time periods in the real estate cycle than with others.

For example, in appraising a residence the income approach is rarely used, and the cost approach is of limited value unless the home is relatively new; therefore, the sales comparison approach usually is given greatest weight in valuing single-family residences. In the appraisal of income or investment property, the income approach normally would be given the greatest weight. In the appraisal of churches, libraries, museums, schools, and other special-use properties where there are few sales and little or no income, the cost approach usually would be assigned the greatest weight. From this analysis, or reconciliation, a single estimate of market value is produced.

In Practice   In an effort to reduce costs and speed up loan processing, both Fannie Mae and Freddie Mac (secondary mortgage market entities) are permitting expedited appraisals. Requirements vary, but in some cases they require only that the appraiser first "drive by" the property to determine that a building exists on the property and there are no obvious major problems. Then the appraiser would estimate property value using only the sales comparison approach with appropriate adjustments on three comparable sales. The interior of the building would not be examined unless the appraiser saw a problem during the drive-by appraisal. For appraisals in the future, consideration is being given to using tax appraisal values (available electronically from the local appraisal district), supported by a satellite picture to ensure that a building exists on the property.

PRICING A PROPERTY

> A *competitive market analysis* is an analysis of market activity among comparable properties; it is *not* the same as a formal appraisal.

Generally, an appraisal is not conducted on a property until after a contract is received from a buyer. Therefore, initial pricing of the real estate to enable the seller's receiving the highest price in the least amount of time is of primary importance to a listing agent. It is the responsibility of the broker or salesperson to advise, counsel, and assist in the pricing process, but ultimately it is the *seller* who must determine a listing price for his or her property. Because the average seller does not have the background to make an informed decision about a fair market value, the real estate agent prepares a competitive market analysis that can provide guidance to the seller in this process.

Competitive market analysis. The **competitive market analysis (CMA)**, also known as a *comparative market analysis*, is a variation of the sales comparison approach that is prepared by real estate agents to assist sellers and buyers with the determination of listing prices and offering prices. If possible, a CMA should include homes that have sold within the past six months in the same neighborhood as the one being evaluated. Properties should be comparable to the subject property: similar in age, condition, size, amenities, number of rooms and existing mortgage type. As shown in Figure 14.4, the CMA also includes an analysis of homes currently on the market and homes for which the listings expired prior to sale. The CMA range of values for similar sold properties will show a seller what the home probably will sell for and will help an agent decide whether to accept a listing. The licensee *must* provide the following written statement to the person for whom a market analysis is prepared:

> THIS IS AN OPINION OF VALUE OR COMPARATIVE MARKET ANALYSIS AND SHOULD NOT BE CONSIDERED AN APPRAISAL. In making any decision that relies upon my work, you should know that I have not followed the guidelines for development of an appraisal or analysis contained in the Uniform Standards of Professional Appraisal Practice of the Appraisal Foundation.

If adequate comparable properties are not available, or if the seller feels his or her property is unique in some way, a full-scale real estate appraisal may be warranted. A broker should reject any listing in which the seller insists on a substantially exaggerated listing price after receiving the CMA or the appraisal estimate of value.

Seller's net return. A major concern of every seller is how much money he or she will realize from the sale. Assume that an estimate of value, determined from a CMA, is $155,000. After paying the broker's commission (estimated at 7 percent in this hypothetical situation) and the other applicable closing costs (estimated at $4,485 for the conventional loan in this illustration), the seller will net $139,665:

$155,000   estimate of value
−10,850   commission (at 7%)
− 4,485   other closing costs
$139,665   net to seller

More detailed information for calculating closing costs will be provided in Chapter 20, "Closing the Real Estate Transaction."

Summary

To appraise real estate means to develop an opinion of value. Although there are many types of value, the most common objective of an appraisal is to estimate market value—the most probable sales price of a property.

Although appraisals are concerned with values, costs, and prices, it is vital to understand the distinctions among the terms. Value is an estimate of future benefits, cost represents a measure of past expenditures, and price reflects the actual amount of money paid for a property.

The value of real estate is influenced by basic economic principles: highest and best use, substitution, supply and demand, conformity, externalities, anticipation, increasing and diminishing returns, plottage, contribution, competition, and change.

A professional appraiser analyzes a property through three approaches to value. In the sales comparison approach, the value of the subject property is compared with the values of others like it that have sold recently. Because no two properties are exactly alike, adjustments must be made to account for differences. With the cost approach, an appraiser calculates the cost of building a similar structure on a similar site. Then he or she subtracts depreciation (losses in value), which reflects the differences between new properties of this type and the present condition of the subject property. The three types of depreciation typically utilized in the appraisal process are physical deterioration, functional obsolescence, and external obsolescence. The income approach is an analysis based on the relationship between the rate of return that an investor requires and the net operating income that a property produces.

A special informal version of the income approach, called the *gross rent multiplier* (GRM), often is used to estimate the value of single-family residential properties that are not usually rented but could be. The GRM is computed by dividing the sales price of a property by its gross monthly rent.

Normally the application of the three approaches will result in three different estimates of value. In the process of reconciliation, the validity and reliability of each approach are weighed objectively to arrive at the single best and most supportable conclusion of value.

A real estate licensee prepares a competitive market analysis, an abbreviated variation of the sales comparison approach, to assist sellers in pricing property or to assist buyers in determining how much to offer for a property.

Figure 14.4 Competitive Market Analysis

COMPETITIVE MARKET ANALYSIS

PREPARED FOR: ____________ AREA: ____________ DATE: ____________

ADDRESS: ____________

PHONE: (H) ____________ (O) ____________ PREPARED BY: ____________

PROPERTY ADDRESS	BEDROOMS	BATHS	GARAGE	DINING	FAMILY	FIREPLACE	BASEMENT	POOL	CONSTRUCTION	AGE	SPECIAL FEATURES/ REMARKS	LISTED PRICE	SELLING PRICE	DAYS ON MARKET	DATE CLOSED	SQ. FT.	PRICE PER SQ. FT.
SUBJECT PROPERTY																	
SOLD PROPERTIES																	
PENDING PROPERTIES													X				
													X				
													X				
FOR SALE PROPERTIES																	
EXPIRED PROPERTIES																	

AVERAGE PRICE PER SQ. FT. SOLD $ ____________

AREA MARKET CONDITIONS: ____________

COMPETITIVE MARKET RANGE

HIGH $ ____________ LOW $ ____________

COMMENTS: ____________

1.
2. B
3. B
4. A
5. D
6. A
7. B
8. B
9. A
10. C
11. B
12. C
13. A
14. B
15. C
16. D
17. A
18. D
19. B
20. A
21. C
22. B

Questions

1. A competitive market analysis
   a. cannot help the seller set a price for his or her real estate.
   b. is a comparison of recently sold properties that are similar to a seller's parcel of real estate.
   c. is the same as an appraisal.
   d. should not be retained in the property's listing file because of its confidentiality.

2. The elements of value include which of the following?
   a. Anticipation
   b. Scarcity
   c. Competition
   d. Balance

3. 457 and 459 Tarpepper Street are adjacent vacant lots, each worth approximately $50,000. If the owner sells them as a combined parcel, however, they will be worth $120,000. What principle does this illustrate?
   a. Substitution
   b. Plottage
   c. Externalities
   d. Contribution

4. The amount of money a property brings in the marketplace is its
   a. market price.
   b. market value.
   c. intrinsic value.
   d. book value.

5. For appraisal purposes, accrued depreciation is caused by all of the following **EXCEPT**
   a. functional obsolescence.
   b. physical deterioration.
   c. external obsolescence.
   d. accelerated depreciation.

6. Howard constructs an eight-bedroom brick house with a tennis court, a greenhouse, and an indoor pool in a neighborhood of modest two-bedroom and three-bedroom frame houses on narrow lots. The value of Howard's house is likely to be affected by what principle?
   a. Conformity
   b. Assemblage
   c. Externalities
   d. Contribution

7. *Reconciliation* refers to which of the following?
   a. Separating the value of the land from the total value of the property to compute depreciation
   b. Analyzing the results obtained by the three approaches to value to determine a final estimate of value
   c. The process by which an appraiser determines the highest and best use for a parcel of land
   d. Averaging the results of the three approaches to determine a final estimate of value

8. One method an appraiser uses to determine a building's replacement cost involves an estimate of the raw materials needed to build the structure, plus labor and indirect costs. This is called the
   a. square-foot method.
   b. quantity-survey method.
   c. cubic-foot method.
   d. unit-in-place method.

9. If a property's annual net income is $37,500 and it is valued at $300,000, what is its capitalization rate?
   a. 12.5 percent
   b. 10.5 percent
   c. 15 percent
   d. 18 percent

10. Certain data must be determined by an appraiser before value can be computed by the income approach. Which one of the following is **NOT** required for this process?
    a. Annual net operating income
    b. Capitalization rate
    c. Accrued depreciation
    d. Annual gross income

11. The ceiling, or top limit, of value of an improved parcel of real estate usually is the
    a. sales price paid for a similar property.
    b. cost of buying a lot and erecting a similar building on it.
    c. capitalized value of present net rents.
    d. depreciated value of the building plus the cost of land.

12. An appraiser is asked to determine the value of an existing strip shopping center. Which approach to value will be given the most weight?
    a. Cost approach
    b. Sales comparison approach
    c. Income approach
    d. Reproduction approach

13. The market value of a parcel of real estate is
    a. an estimate of the most probable price it should bring.
    b. the amount of money paid for the property.
    c. its value without improvements.
    d. its cost.

14. Capitalization is the process by which annual net operating income is used to
    a. determine cost.
    b. estimate value.
    c. establish depreciation.
    d. determine potential tax value.

15. From the reproduction or replacement cost of the building, an appraiser deducts depreciation, which represents
    a. the remaining useful economic life of the building.
    b. remodeling costs to increase rentals.
    c. loss of value due to any cause.
    d. costs to modernize the building.

16. The effective gross annual income from a property is $112,000. Total expenses for this year are $53,700. What capitalization rate was used to obtain a valuation of $542,325?
    a. 9.75%   c. 10.50%
    b. 10.25%   d. 10.75%

17. In the sales comparison approach to value, the probable sales price of a building may be estimated by
    a. considering sales of similar properties.
    b. deducting accrued depreciation.
    c. determining construction cost.
    d. computing replacement cost of the structure.

18. Which of the following factors is **NOT** important in comparing properties under the sales comparison approach to value?
    a. Difference in dates of sale
    b. Difference in financing terms
    c. Difference in appearance and condition
    d. Difference in original cost

19. In the income approach to value
    a. the reproduction or replacement cost of the building must be computed.
    b. the capitalization rate, or rate of return, must be estimated.
    c. depreciation must be determined.
    d. sales of similar properties must be considered.

20. In the cost approach to value it is necessary to
    a. determine a dollar value for depreciation.
    b. estimate future expenses and operating costs.
    c. check sales prices of recently sold houses in the area.
    d. reconcile differing value estimates.

21. Which of the following formulas is used to determine the capitalization rate of an office building?
    a. Income = Rate × Value
    b. Income ÷ Rate = Value
    c. Income ÷ Value = Rate
    d. Rate = Value × Income

22. The appraised value of a residence with four bedrooms and one bathroom would probably be reduced because of
    a. external obsolescence.
    b. functional obsolescence.
    c. curable physical deterioration.
    d. incurable physical deterioration.

15 Real Estate Financing: Principles

Key Terms

acceleration clause	interest	redemption
alienation clause	lien theory	release deed
deed in lieu of	mortgage	release of lien
foreclosure	mortgagee	satisfaction of
deed of trust	mortgagor	mortgage
defeasance clause	negotiable instrument	title theory
deficiency judgment	power-of-sale clause	trust deed
foreclosure	prepayment penalty	usury
hypothecation	promissory note	

OVERVIEW

Rarely is a parcel of real estate purchased on a cash basis; almost every real estate transaction involves some type of financing. Thus an understanding of real estate financing is of prime importance to the real estate licensee. Usually the buyer in a real estate transaction borrows the major portion of the purchase price by securing a loan and pledging the real property involved as security (collateral) for the loan. This generally is known as a *mortgage loan.*

This chapter explores the principles of mortgage financing through the documents required to establish a valid lien—the promissory note and the deed of trust—and the foreclosure procedures followed if a borrower defaults under the terms of the deed of trust. The sources for mortgage money and some specifics regarding the most common types of loans are discussed in Chapter 16.

MORTGAGE THEORY

The concept of mortgage lending originated in England under Anglo-Saxon law. Originally, a borrower who needed to finance the purchase of land (the **mortgagor**) was forced to convey title to the property to the lender (the **mortgagee**) to ensure payment of the debt. If the obligation was not paid, the mortgagor automatically forfeited the land to the creditor, who was already the legal owner of the property.

Through the years English courts began to acknowledge that a mortgage was only a *security device* and the mortgagor was the true owner of the mortgaged real estate. Under this concept, real estate was merely given as *security* for the payment of a debt, which was represented by a *note*.

United States Mortgage Law

After gaining independence from England, the original 13 colonies adopted the English laws as their basic body of law. From their inception, American courts of equity considered a mortgage a voluntary lien on real estate, given to secure the payment of a debt or the performance of an obligation.

> **Remember:**
>
> The *"or"* gives to the *"ee."*
>
> The *mortgagor* (borrower) gives the mortgage document to the lender.
>
> The *mortgagee* (lender) receives the property as security.

Those states, including Texas, that interpret a mortgage purely as a lien on real property are called **lien theory** states. In such states, if a mortgagor defaults, the lender is required to foreclose the lien, offer the property for sale, and apply the funds received from the sale to reduce or extinguish the obligation. The owner, not the lender, has a right to rental income while property is posted for foreclosure. Although many lien theory states allow a statutory redemption period, *Texas law contains no provision for redemption of property sold under a deed of trust.*

Other states recognize a lender as the owner of mortgaged land. This ownership is subject to defeat on full payment of the debt or performance of the obligation. These states are called **title theory** states. Under title theory, a lender has the right to possession of and rents from the mortgaged property on default by the borrower.

SECURITY AND DEBT

Generally any interest in real estate that may be sold may be pledged as security for a debt. The basic principle of property law—that a person cannot convey greater rights in property than he or she actually has—applies equally to the right to mortgage. The owner of a fee simple estate can mortgage the fee, and the owner of a leasehold or subleasehold can mortgage that leasehold interest. For example, a large retail corporation renting space in a shopping center may mortgage its leasehold interest to finance some remodeling work.

As discussed in Chapter 9, the owner of a cooperative interest holds a personal property interest, not an interest in real estate. Although a cooperative owner has a leasehold interest, the nature of that leasehold is not generally acceptable to lenders as collateral. The owner of a condominium unit, however, can mortgage his or her fee interest in the condominium unit.

Mortgage Loan Instruments

There are two parts to a mortgage loan—the debt itself and the security for the debt. Therefore, when a property is to be mortgaged, the owner must execute, or sign, two separate instruments:

1. The **promissory note** is the promise, or agreement, to repay the debt in definite installments with interest. The mortgagor executes one or more promissory notes to total the amount of the debt. The note *creates* the debt.
2. The **mortgage** is the document that creates the lien, or conveys the property to the mortgagee as *security* for the debt. The **deed of trust** is the mortgage document generally used in Texas to secure payment of the debt. As backup security, a vendor's lien, a special type of

mortgage discussed in Chapter 11, is reserved in the warranty deed conveying title to the buyer. The vendor's lien is held by the seller until paid in full for the property. If third-party financing is obtained, this lien is usually assigned to the lender.

Hypothecation is the term used to describe the pledging of property as security for payment of a loan without giving up possession of the property. A pledge of security—the deed of trust—is not legally effective unless there is a debt to secure. *Both the note and the deed of trust must be executed to create an enforceable mortgage loan.*

PROVISIONS OF THE NOTE

The promissory note (or notes) executed by a borrower (known as the *maker* or *payor*) generally states the amount of the debt, the time and method of payment, and the rate of interest. If the note is used with a mortgage, it names the mortgagee as the payee; if it is used with a deed of trust, the note may be made payable to the bearer. It also may refer to, or repeat, several of the clauses that appear in the mortgage document or deed of trust. The note, like the mortgage or deed of trust, should be signed by all parties who have an interest in the property. Where homestead or community property is involved, both spouses have an interest in the property and must sign the note and deed of trust. An exception is community property where one spouse is designated as the manager of that particular piece of community property. Figure 15.1 is an example of a note commonly used with a deed of trust.

A note is a **negotiable instrument** like a check or bank draft. The individual who holds the note is referred to as the *payee*. He or she may transfer the right to receive payment to a third party in one of two ways: by signing the instrument over to the third party or, in some cases, by merely delivering the instrument to that person. The transferee, or new holder of the note, is known as a *holder in due course*.

Interest A charge for the use of money is called **interest.** A lender charges a borrower a certain percentage of the principal as interest for each year the debt is outstanding. The amount of interest due on any one installment payment date is calculated by computing the total yearly interest, based on the unpaid balance, and dividing that figure by the number of payments made each year. For example, if the current outstanding loan balance is $50,000 with interest at the rate of 12 percent per annum and constant monthly payments of $617.40, the interest and principal due on the next payment would be computed as follows:

$$\begin{array}{ll} \$50,\!000 \\ \underline{\times\quad .12} \\ \$\ 6,\!000 \text{ annual interest} \end{array} \qquad \begin{array}{l} \underline{\$500.00 \text{ month's interest}} \\ 12)\$6,\!000.00 \end{array}$$

$$\begin{array}{l} \$617.40 \\ \underline{-500.00} \\ \$117.40 \text{ month's principal reduction} \end{array}$$

Figure 15.1   Lien Note

NOTE

May 29th, 20XX

2222 MAIN STREET, ANYWHERE, TEXAS   70000
(Property Address)

1. BORROWER'S PROMISE TO PAY

In return for a loan that I have received, I promise to pay U.S. $ $84,000.00   (this amount is called "Principal"), plus interest, to the order of the Lender. The Lender is **FIRST STATE BANK, HAPPY.** I will make all payments under this Note in the form of cash, check or money order.

I understand that the Lender may transfer this Note. The Lender or anyone who takes this Note by transfer and who is entitled to receive payments under this Note is called the "Note Holder."

2. INTEREST

Interest will be charged on unpaid principal until the full amount of Principal has been paid. I will pay interest at a yearly rate of 7.875%

The interest rate required by this Section 2 is the rate I will pay both before and after any default described in Section 6(B) of this Note.

3. PAYMENTS

(A) Time and Place of Payments

I will pay principal and interest by making payments every month.

I will make my monthly payments on the   First   day of each month beginning on   JULY 1st , 20XX   . I will make these payments every month until I have paid all of the principal and interest and any other charges described below that I may owe under this Note. Each monthly payment will be applied as of its scheduled due date and will be applied to interest before Principal. If, on   JUNE 1st   , 20XX I still owe amounts under this Note, I will pay those amounts in full on that date, which is called the "Maturity Date."

I will make my monthly payments at   P.O. Box 7865, Amarillo, Texas 79114-7865 or at a different place if required by the Note Holder.

(B) Amount of Monthly Payments

My monthly payment will be in the amount of U.S. $ 796.70

4. BORROWER'S RIGHT TO PREPAY

I have the right to make payments of Principal at any time before they are due. A payment of Principal only is known as a "Prepayment." When I make a Prepayment, I will tell the Note Holder in writing that I am doing so. I may not designate a payment as a Prepayment if I have not made all the monthly payments due under the Note.

I may make a full Prepayment or partial Prepayments without paying a Prepayment charge. The Note Holder will use my Prepayments to reduce the amount of Principal that I owe under this Note. However, the Note Holder may apply my Prepayment to the accrued and unpaid interest on the Prepayment amount, before applying my Prepayment to reduce the Principal amount of the Note. If I make a partial Prepayment, there will be no changes in the due date or in the amount of my monthly payment unless the Note Holder agrees in writing to those changes.

5. LOAN CHARGES

If a law, which applies to this loan and which sets maximum loan charges, is finally interpreted so that the interest or other loan charges collected or to be collected in connection with this loan exceed the permitted limits, then: (a) any such loan charge shall be reduced by the amount necessary to reduce the charge to the permitted limit; and (b) any sums already collected from me which exceeded permitted limits will be refunded to me. The Note Holder may choose to make this refund by reducing the Principal I owe under this Note or by making a direct payment to me. If a refund reduces Principal, the reduction will be treated as a partial Prepayment.

6. BORROWER'S FAILURE TO PAY AS REQUIRED

(A) Late Charge for Overdue Payments

If the Note Holder has not received the full amount of any monthly payment by the end of **15** calendar days after the date it is due, I will pay a late charge to the Note Holder. The amount of the charge will be **5.000%** of my overdue payment of principal and interest. I will pay this late charge promptly but only once on each late payment.

Borrower's Initials _____ _____ _____

Figure 15.1   Lien Note (Continued)

(B) Default

If I do not pay the full amount of each monthly payment on the date it is due, I will be in default.

(C) Notice of Default

If I am in default, the Note Holder may send me a written notice telling me that if I do not pay the overdue amount by a certain date, the Note Holder may require me to pay immediately the full amount of Principal which has not been paid and all the interest that I owe on that amount. That date must be at least 30 days after the date on which the notice is mailed to me or delivered by other means.

(D) No Waiver By Note Holder

Even if, at a time when I am in default, the Note Holder does not require me to pay immediately in full as described above, the Note Holder will still have the right to do so if I am in default at a later time.

(E) Payment of Note Holder's Costs and Expenses

If the Note Holder has required me to pay immediately in full as described above, the Note Holder will have the right to be paid back by me for all of its costs and expenses in enforcing this Note to the extent not prohibited by applicable law. Those expenses include, for example, reasonable attorneys' fees.

7. GIVING OF NOTICES

Unless applicable law requires a different method, any notice that must be given to me under this Note will be given by delivering it or by mailing it by first class mail to me at the Property Address above or at a different address if I give the Note Holder a notice of my different address.

Any notice that must be given to the Note Holder under this Note will be given by delivering it or by mailing it by first class mail to the Note Holder at the address stated in Section 3(A) above or at a different address if I am given a notice of that different address.

8. OBLIGATIONS OF PERSONS UNDER THIS NOTE

If more than one person signs this Note, each person is fully and personally obligated to keep all of the promises made in this Note, including the promise to pay the full amount owed. Any person who is a guarantor, surety or endorser of this Note is also obligated to do these things. Any person who takes over these obligations, including the obligations of a guarantor, surety or endorser of this Note, is also obligated to keep all of the promises made in this Note. The Note Holder may enforce its rights under this Note against each person individually or against all of us together. This means that any one of us may be required to pay all of the amounts owed under this Note.

9. WAIVERS

I and any other person who has obligations under this Note waive the rights of Presentment and Notice of Dishonor. "Presentment" means the right to require the Note Holder to demand payment of amounts due. "Notice of Dishonor" means the right to require the Note Holder to give notice to other persons that amounts due have not been paid.

10. UNIFORM SECURED NOTE

This Note is a uniform instrument with limited variations in some jurisdictions. In addition to the protections given to the Note Holder under this Note, a Mortgage, Deed of Trust or Security Deed (the "Security Instrument"), dated the same date as this Note, protects the Note Holder from possible losses which might result if I do not keep the promises which I make in this Note. That Security Instrument describes how and under what conditions I may be required to make immediate payment in full of all amounts I owe under this Note. Some of those conditions are described as follows:

If all or any part of the Property or any interest in the Property is sold or transferred (or if Borrower is not a natural person and a beneficial interest in Borrower is sold or transferred) without Lender's prior written consent, Lender may require immediate payment in full of all sums secured by this Security Instrument. However, this option shall not be exercised by Lender if such exercise is prohibited by Applicable Law.

If Lender exercises this option, Lender shall give Borrower notice of acceleration. The notice shall provide a period of not less than 30 days from the date the notice is given in accordance with Section 15 within which Borrower must pay all sums secured by this Security Instrument. If Borrower fails to pay these sums prior to the expiration of this period, Lender may invoke any remedies permitted by this Security Instrument without further notice or demand on Borrower.

Borrower's Initials _____ _____ _____ _____

Figure 15.1   Lien Note (Continued)

WITNESS THE HAND(S) AND SEAL(S) OF THE UNDERSIGNED.

_____ (Seal)
                                    Borrower

_____ (Seal)
                                    Borrower

_____ (Seal)
                                    Borrower

_____ (Seal)
                                    Borrower

[Sign Original Only]

SAMPLE

Interest may be due either at the end of each payment period (known as payment *in arrears*) or at the beginning of each payment period (payment *in advance*). Whether interest is charged in arrears or in advance is specified in the note. In practice, the distinction becomes important if the property is sold before the debt is repaid in full, as will become evident in Chapter 20, "Closing the Real Estate Transaction." Most residential notes specify that interest is paid as it accrues (or in arrears).

In Practice   As discussed in Chapter 4, interest payments made under a mortgage loan on the taxpayer's residence are deductible for federal income tax purposes. This deduction in effect reduces the borrower's total cost of housing for the year. Under most types of amortized loans, the borrower pays mostly interest in the early years of the loan, and thus the borrower's tax liability will be reduced even more for these years than in the later years of the loan.

Usury. The maximum rate of interest that may be charged on mortgage loans is set by state law. Charging interest in excess of this rate is called **usury,** and lenders are penalized for making usurious loans. Usury laws were enacted to protect borrowers from unscrupulous lenders that charge unreasonably high interest rates.

Under Texas state law, the maximum rate of interest is determined by the buyer's use of the property. The parties to a written contract that is primarily for personal, family, household, or agricultural use may agree to any rate of interest that does not exceed 18 percent per year. This ceiling may be raised if a floating index calculated by the Federal Reserve Board and published by the consumer credit commissioner in the *Texas Register* exceeds 18 percent per year. In that event, the new usury ceiling is 24 percent per year, but the rate will "float" between 18 and 24 percent based on the published index.

The same ceiling provisions apply to contracts for business, commercial, investment, or similar-purpose loans for up to $250,000. If more than $250,000 is extended in credit, however, the maximum interest rate may rise, via the floating index, to 28 percent per year.

A lender that makes usurious loans in Texas is subject to substantial penalties, which may include a forfeiture of all principal and interest, as well as reasonable attorney fees and other costs.

Money available for borrowing is a commodity subject to the economic laws of supply and demand, and lenders are in business to make money by lending money and charging interest. When plenty of money is available, interest rates become fairly low. When money is scarce, interest rates go up. Because both lenders and consumers want to earn a fair return on their money, they invest their funds where they will yield the highest rate of interest. Banks, wanting the deposits of consumers, will raise interest rates paid to depositors to compete with higher yielding alternative investments. They then will raise interest rates charged to borrowers for home and consumer loans. The usury laws protect the consumer against unreasonably high interest rates, but they also free lenders to make loans at economically viable interest rates.

In Practice   Texas usury rates were established during a time of high interest rates. Because current rates are much lower than the usury limits, the usury law has little significance in today's lending market.

Prepayment   When a loan is paid in installments over a long term, the total interest paid by the borrower can be a larger amount of money than the loan principal. If such a loan is paid off ahead of its full term, the lender will collect less interest from the borrower. For this reason, some mortgage notes require that the borrower pay a **prepayment penalty** against the unearned portion of the interest for any payments made ahead of schedule. The premium charged may run from 1 percent of the balance due at the time of prepayment to all interest due for the first ten years of the loan. Some lenders allow the borrower to pay off 20 percent of the original loan in any one year without paying a premium; but if the loan is paid off in full, the borrower may be charged a percentage of the principal paid in excess of that allowance.

Texas law prohibits a prepayment penalty on any note having an interest rate of 10 percent or more. Prepayment penalties are also prohibited on all Federal Housing Administration (FHA) and Department of Veterans Affairs (VA) loans and on mortgages sold to Fannie Mae or Freddie Mac after September 1979 or pooled by Ginnie Mae.

PROVISIONS OF THE MORTGAGE DOCUMENT (OR DEED OF TRUST)

The *borrower* is the *trustor.*

The neutral *third party* is the *trustee.*

The *lender* is the *beneficiary.*

Deeds of trust. In Texas, lenders prefer to use a three-party security instrument known as a *deed of trust,* or **trust deed,** rather than a *regular two-party mortgage* document. The three parties involved in the deed of trust mortgage transaction are the borrower (the *mortgagor, trustor,* or *grantor*), the lender (the *mortgagee* or *beneficiary*), and a neutral third party (the *trustee*). A deed of trust conditionally conveys the real estate as security for the loan to the trustee, who acquires a *mortgage lien* on the real estate. The title remains in trust until the loan is paid off. The trustee is limited to carrying out the duties as directed by the beneficiary, or lender. The wording of the conveyance in the deed of trust sets forth actions that the trustee may take if the borrower defaults under any of the terms. Usually the lender chooses the trustee (who is generally an employee of the lender) and reserves the right to substitute trustees in the event of death or dismissal. Because Texas is a lien theory state, the borrower (rather than the lender) is considered the owner of the property.

See Figures 15.2 and 15.3 for a comparison of mortgages and deeds of trust. In Texas and other states where deeds of trust generally are preferred, foreclosure procedures for defaulted deeds of trust are usually simpler and speedier than those for regular mortgages.

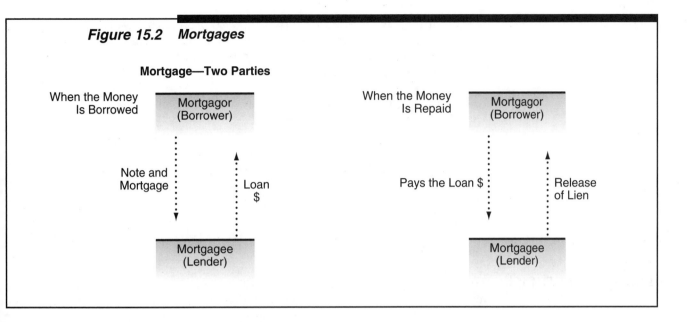

Figure 15.2   Mortgages

Mortgage—Two Parties

When the Money Is Borrowed
Mortgagor (Borrower)
Note and Mortgage
Loan $
Mortgagee (Lender)

When the Money Is Repaid
Mortgagor (Borrower)
Pays the Loan $
Release of Lien
Mortgagee (Lender)

The deed of trust refers to the terms of the note and clearly establishes that the conveyance of land is security for the debt. It identifies the lender and the trustee as well as the borrower. It includes an accurate legal description of the property and sets forth the obligations of the borrower and the rights of the lender. All parties who have an interest in the real estate should sign it. Figure 15.4 is a sample deed of trust. Deeds of trust provisions can vary significantly; an attorney should be consulted for specific interpretations.

Duties of the Mortgagor or Trustor

The borrower is required to fulfill many obligations. Usually these include

- payment of the debt in accordance with the terms of the note;
- payment of all real estate taxes on the property given as security;

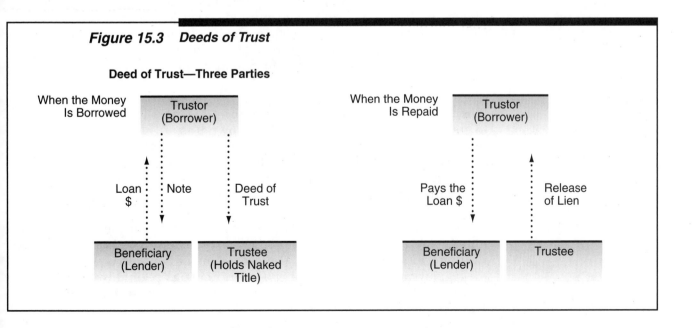

Figure 15.3   Deeds of Trust

Deed of Trust—Three Parties

When the Money Is Borrowed
Trustor (Borrower)
Loan $
Note
Deed of Trust
Beneficiary (Lender)
Trustee (Holds Naked Title)

When the Money Is Repaid
Trustor (Borrower)
Pays the Loan $
Release of Lien
Beneficiary (Lender)
Trustee

- maintenance of adequate insurance to protect the lender if the property is destroyed or damaged by fire, windstorm, or other hazard;
- maintenance of the property in good repair at all times;
- receipt of lender authorization before making any major alterations on the property; and
- not introducing hazardous material (as defined by the EPA) to the property.

Failure to meet any of these obligations can result in a borrower's default on the note. When this happens, the trust deed may provide for a grace period (30 days on the Fannie Mae/Freddie Mac deed of trust) during which the borrower can meet the obligation and cure the default. Otherwise, the lender has the right to foreclose on the deed of trust and collect on the note. The most frequent cause of default is the borrower's failure to meet monthly installments.

Provisions for Default

The provisions of deeds of trust include an **acceleration clause** to assist the lender in foreclosure. If a borrower defaults, the lender has the right to accelerate the maturity of the debt—to declare the unpaid balance of the debt due and payable *immediately*—even though the terms of the mortgage or deed of trust allow the borrower to amortize the debt in regular payments over a period of years. Without the acceleration clause, the lender would have to sue the borrower every time a payment was in default.

Other clauses in the deed of trust enable the lender to take care of the property in the event of the borrower's negligence or default. If the borrower does not pay taxes or insurance premiums or make necessary repairs on the property, the lender may step in and do so to protect his or her security (the real estate). Any money advanced by the lender to cure such defaults is either added to the unpaid debt or declared immediately due and payable from the borrower.

Assignment of the Mortgage

As mentioned earlier, a note is a negotiable instrument; it may be sold to a third party, or holder in due course. When a note is sold to a third party, the mortgagee endorses the note to the third party and executes an *assignment of deed of trust.* This assignment must be recorded. On payment in full, or satisfaction of the debt, the assignee who holds the note and deed of trust is required to sign the release, or satisfaction, of lien as discussed in the following section. In the event of a foreclosure, the assignee (not the original mortgagee) is required to file the suit.

When a lender sells a loan to an investor, the lender is under no obligation to notify the borrower *unless* the servicing rights are also sold. When servicing rights are sold, the federal Real Estate Settlement Procedures Act (RESPA) requires that both parties inform the mortgagor in writing and furnish a toll-free or collect-call phone number for questions related to the transfer of servicing.

Release of the Deed of Trust Lien

When all mortgage loan payments have been made and the note is paid in full, the mortgagor wants the public record to show that the debt has been paid and the lien released. By the provisions of the **defeasance clause** in the regular mortgage document, when the note has been fully paid the mortgagee is required to execute a **release of lien,** or **satisfaction of mortgage.** This document reconveys to the mortgagor (borrower) all interest in the real

Figure 15.4   Deed of Trust

——————————————— [Space Above This Line For Recording Data] ———————————————

DEED OF TRUST

GRANTOR   THIS DEED OF TRUST ("Security Instrument") is made on   May 29,   . The grantor is
John Doe and Jane Doe, husband and wife

TRUSTEE   ("Borrower"). The trustee is   Samuel Smith
, whose address is
P.O. Box 7865, Amarillo, TX. 79114-7865

BENEFICIARY   ("Trustee"). The beneficiary is   First State Bank, Happy, Texas
,
which is organized and existing under the laws of   Texas   , and whose
address is   P.O. Box 7865, Amarillo, TX. 79114-7865
("Lender"). Borrower owes Lender the principal sum of

NOTE AMOUNT   Eighty-Four Thousand and no/100 – – – –   Dollars (U.S. $ $84,000.00   ).
This debt is evidenced by Borrower's note dated the same date as this Security Instrument ("Note"), which provides for
monthly payments, with the full debt, if not paid earlier, due and payable on   June 1, 2012   .
This Security Instrument secures to Lender: (a) the repayment of the debt evidenced by the Note, with interest, and all renewals,
extensions and modifications of the Note; (b) the payment of all other sums, with interest, advanced under paragraph 7 to
protect the security of this Security Instrument; and (c) the performance of Borrower's covenants and agreements under this
Security Instrument and the Note. For this purpose, Borrower irrevocably grants and conveys to Trustee, in trust, with power of
sale, the following described property located in   Randall   County, Texas:

LEGAL DESCRIPTION   Lot 10, Block 5 of Sometimes Addition, an addition to the City of Anywhere, Randall County,
Texas, according to the map or plat thereof recorded in Volume 9999, Page 1111, deed records
of Randall County, Texas.

Item #: 005 7777 9999
which has the address of   2222 Main Street, Anywhere   [Street, City],
Texas   70000
[Zip Code]   ("Property Address");

TEXAS-Single Family-Fannie Mae/Freddie Mac UNIFORM INSTRUMENT   Page 1 of 6
Form 3044 9/90
Amended 5/91

VMP® -6R(TX) (9105)   VMP MORTGAGE FORMS - (313)293-8100 - (800)521-7291   Initials: _____

Figure 15.4   Deed of Trust (Continued)

TOGETHER WITH all the improvements now or hereafter erected on the property, and all easements, appurtenances, and fixtures now or hereafter a part of the property. All replacements and additions shall also be covered by this Security Instrument. All of the foregoing is referred to in this Security Instrument as the "Property."

BORROWER COVENANTS that Borrower is lawfully seised of the estate hereby conveyed and has the right to grant and convey the Property and that the Property is unencumbered, except for encumbrances of record. Borrower warrants and will defend generally the title to the Property against all claims and demands, subject to any encumbrances of record.

THIS SECURITY INSTRUMENT combines uniform covenants for national use and non-uniform covenants with limited variations by jurisdiction to constitute a uniform security instrument covering real property.

UNIFORM COVENANTS. Borrower and Lender covenant and agree as follows:

1. Payment of Principal and Interest; Prepayment and Late Charges. Borrower shall promptly pay when due the principal of and interest on the debt evidenced by the Note and any prepayment and late charges due under the Note.

TAX AND INSURANCE RESERVES

2. Funds for Taxes and Insurance. Subject to applicable law or to a written waiver by Lender, Borrower shall pay to Lender on the day monthly payments are due under the Note, until the Note is paid in full, a sum ("Funds") for: (a) yearly taxes and assessments which may attain priority over this Security Instrument as a lien on the Property; (b) yearly leasehold payments or ground rents on the Property, if any; (c) yearly hazard or property insurance premiums; (d) yearly flood insurance premiums, if any; (e) yearly mortgage insurance premiums, if any; and (f) any sums payable by Borrower to Lender, in accordance with the provisions of paragraph 8, in lieu of the payment of mortgage insurance premiums. These items are called "Escrow Items." Lender may, at any time, collect and hold Funds in an amount not to exceed the maximum amount a lender for a federally related mortgage loan may require for Borrower's escrow account under the federal Real Estate Settlement Procedures Act of 1974 as amended from time to time, 12 U.S.C. Section 2601 *et seq.* ("RESPA"), unless another law that applies to the Funds sets a lesser amount. If so, Lender may, at any time, collect and hold Funds in an amount not to exceed the lesser amount. Lender may estimate the amount of Funds due on the basis of current data and reasonable estimates of expenditures of future Escrow Items or otherwise in accordance with applicable law.

The Funds shall be held in an institution whose deposits are insured by a federal agency, instrumentality, or entity (including Lender, if Lender is such an institution) or in any Federal Home Loan Bank. Lender shall apply the Funds to pay the Escrow Items. Lender may not charge Borrower for holding and applying the Funds, annually analyzing the escrow account, or verifying the Escrow Items, unless Lender pays Borrower interest on the Funds and applicable law permits Lender to make such a charge. However, Lender may require Borrower to pay a one-time charge for an independent real estate tax reporting service used by Lender in connection with this loan, unless applicable law provides otherwise. Unless an agreement is made or applicable law requires interest to be paid, Lender shall not be required to pay Borrower any interest or earnings on the Funds. Borrower and Lender may agree in writing, however, that interest shall be paid on the Funds. Lender shall give to Borrower, without charge, an annual accounting of the Funds showing credits and debits to the Funds and the purpose for which each debit to the Funds was made. The Funds are pledged as additional security for all sums secured by this Security Instrument.

If the Funds held by Lender exceed the amounts permitted to be held by applicable law, Lender shall account to Borrower for the excess Funds in accordance with the requirements of applicable law. If the amount of the Funds held by Lender at any time is not sufficient to pay the Escrow Items when due, Lender may so notify Borrower in writing, and, in such case Borrower shall pay to Lender the amount necessary to make up the deficiency. Borrower shall make up the deficiency in no more than twelve monthly payments, at Lender's sole discretion.

Upon payment in full of all sums secured by this Security Instrument, Lender shall promptly refund to Borrower any Funds held by Lender. If, under paragraph 21, Lender shall acquire or sell the Property, Lender, prior to the acquisition or sale of the Property, shall apply any Funds held by Lender at the time of acquisition or sale as a credit against the sums secured by this Security Instrument.

3. Application of Payments. Unless applicable law provides otherwise, all payments received by Lender under paragraphs 1 and 2 shall be applied: first, to any prepayment charges due under the Note; second, to amounts payable under paragraph 2; third, to interest due; fourth, to principal due; and last, to any late charges due under the Note.

4. Charges; Liens. Borrower shall pay all taxes, assessments, charges, fines and impositions attributable to the Property which may attain priority over this Security Instrument, and leasehold payments or ground rents, if any. Borrower shall pay these obligations in the manner provided in paragraph 2, or if not paid in that manner, Borrower shall pay them on time directly to the person owed payment. Borrower shall promptly furnish to Lender all notices of amounts to be paid under this paragraph. If Borrower makes these payments directly, Borrower shall promptly furnish to Lender receipts evidencing the payments.

Borrower shall promptly discharge any lien which has priority over this Security Instrument unless Borrower: (a) agrees in writing to the payment of the obligation secured by the lien in a manner acceptable to Lender; (b) contests in good faith the lien by, or defends against enforcement of the lien in, legal proceedings which in the Lender's opinion operate to prevent the enforcement of the lien; or (c) secures from the holder of the lien an agreement satisfactory to Lender subordinating the lien to this Security Instrument. If Lender determines that any part of the Property is subject to a lien which may attain priority over this Security Instrument, Lender may give Borrower a notice identifying the lien. Borrower shall satisfy the lien or take one or more of the actions set forth above within 10 days of the giving of notice.

Form 3044   9/90

VMP -6R(TX) (9106)   Page 2 of 6   Initials:_____

Figure 15.4   Deed of Trust (Continued)

5. Hazard or Property Insurance. Borrower shall keep the improvements now existing or hereafter erected on the Property insured against loss by fire, hazards included within the term "extended coverage" and any other hazards, including floods or flooding, for which Lender requires insurance. This insurance shall be maintained in the amounts and for the periods that Lender requires. The insurance carrier providing the insurance shall be chosen by Borrower subject to Lender's approval which shall not be unreasonably withheld. If Borrower fails to maintain coverage described above, Lender may, at Lender's option, obtain coverage to protect Lender's rights in the Property in accordance with paragraph 7.

All insurance policies and renewals shall be acceptable to Lender and shall include a standard mortgage clause. Lender shall have the right to hold the policies and renewals. If Lender requires, Borrower shall promptly give to Lender all receipts of paid premiums and renewal notices. In the event of loss, Borrower shall give prompt notice to the insurance carrier and Lender. Lender may make proof of loss if not made promptly by Borrower.

Unless Lender and Borrower otherwise agree in writing, insurance proceeds shall be applied to restoration or repair of the Property damaged, if the restoration or repair is economically feasible and Lender's security is not lessened. If the restoration or repair is not economically feasible or Lender's security would be lessened, the insurance proceeds shall be applied to the sums secured by this Security Instrument, whether or not then due, with any excess paid to Borrower. If Borrower abandons the Property, or does not answer within 30 days a notice from Lender that the insurance carrier has offered to settle a claim, then Lender may collect the insurance proceeds. Lender may use the proceeds to repair or restore the Property or to pay sums secured by this Security Instrument, whether or not then due. The 30-day period will begin when the notice is given.

Unless Lender and Borrower otherwise agree in writing, any application of proceeds to principal shall not extend or postpone the due date of the monthly payments referred to in paragraphs 1 and 2 or change the amount of the payments. If under paragraph 21 the Property is acquired by Lender, Borrower's right to any insurance policies and proceeds resulting from damage to the Property prior to the acquisition shall pass to Lender to the extent of the sums secured by this Security Instrument immediately prior to the acquisition.

6. Occupancy, Preservation, Maintenance and Protection of the Property; Borrower's Loan Application; Leaseholds. Borrower shall occupy, establish, and use the Property as Borrower's principal residence within sixty days after the execution of this Security Instrument and shall continue to occupy the Property as Borrower's principal residence for at least one year after the date of occupancy, unless Lender otherwise agrees in writing, which consent shall not be unreasonably withheld, or unless extenuating circumstances exist which are beyond Borrower's control. Borrower shall not destroy, damage or impair the Property, allow the Property to deteriorate, or commit waste on the Property. Borrower shall be in default if any forfeiture action or proceeding, whether civil or criminal, is begun that in Lender's good faith judgment could result in forfeiture of the Property or otherwise materially impair the lien created by this Security Instrument or Lender's security interest. Borrower may cure such a default and reinstate, as provided in paragraph 18, by causing the action or proceeding to be dismissed with a ruling that, in Lender's good faith determination, precludes forfeiture of the Borrower's interest in the Property or other material impairment of the lien created by this Security Instrument or Lender's security interest. Borrower shall also be in default if Borrower, during the loan application process, gave materially false or inaccurate information or statements to Lender (or failed to provide Lender with any material information) in connection with the loan evidenced by the Note, including, but not limited to, representations concerning Borrower's occupancy of the Property as a principal residence. If this Security Instrument is on a leasehold, Borrower shall comply with all the provisions of the lease. If Borrower acquires fee title to the Property, the leasehold and the fee title shall not merge unless Lender agrees to the merger in writing.

7. Protection of Lender's Rights in the Property. If Borrower fails to perform the covenants and agreements contained in this Security Instrument, or there is a legal proceeding that may significantly affect Lender's rights in the Property (such as a proceeding in bankruptcy, probate, for condemnation or forfeiture or to enforce laws or regulations), then Lender may do and pay for whatever is necessary to protect the value of the Property and Lender's rights in the Property. Lender's actions may include paying any sums secured by a lien which has priority over this Security Instrument, appearing in court, paying reasonable attorneys' fees and entering on the Property to make repairs. Although Lender may take action under this paragraph 7, Lender does not have to do so.

Any amounts disbursed by Lender under this paragraph 7 shall become additional debt of Borrower secured by this Security Instrument. Unless Borrower and Lender agree to other terms of payment, these amounts shall bear interest from the date of disbursement at the Note rate and shall be payable, with interest, upon notice from Lender to Borrower requesting payment.

8. Mortgage Insurance. If Lender required mortgage insurance as a condition of making the loan secured by this Security Instrument, Borrower shall pay the premiums required to maintain the mortgage insurance in effect. If, for any reason, the mortgage insurance coverage required by Lender lapses or ceases to be in effect, Borrower shall pay the premiums required to obtain coverage substantially equivalent to the mortgage insurance previously in effect, at a cost substantially equivalent to the cost to Borrower of the mortgage insurance previously in effect, from an alternate mortgage insurer approved by Lender. If substantially equivalent mortgage insurance coverage is not available, Borrower shall pay to Lender each month a sum equal to one-twelfth of the yearly mortgage insurance premium being paid by Borrower when the insurance coverage lapsed or ceased to be in effect. Lender will accept, use and retain these payments as a loss reserve in lieu of mortgage insurance. Loss reserve

Form 3044   9/90

Initials:_____

Figure 15.4   Deed of Trust (Continued)

payments may no longer be required, at the option of Lender, if mortgage insurance coverage (in the amount and for the period that Lender requires) provided by an insurer approved by Lender again becomes available and is obtained. Borrower shall pay the premiums required to maintain mortgage insurance in effect, or to provide a loss reserve, until the requirement for mortgage insurance ends in accordance with any written agreement between Borrower and Lender or applicable law.

    9. Inspection. Lender or its agent may make reasonable entries upon and inspections of the Property. Lender shall give Borrower notice at the time of or prior to an inspection specifying reasonable cause for the inspection.

    10. Condemnation. The proceeds of any award or claim for damages, direct or consequential, in connection with any condemnation or other taking of any part of the Property, or for conveyance in lieu of condemnation, are hereby assigned and shall be paid to Lender.

    In the event of a total taking of the Property, the proceeds shall be applied to the sums secured by this Security Instrument, whether or not then due, with any excess paid to Borrower. In the event of a partial taking of the Property in which the fair market value of the Property immediately before the taking is equal to or greater than the amount of the sums secured by this Security Instrument immediately before the taking, unless Borrower and Lender otherwise agree in writing, the sums secured by this Security Instrument shall be reduced by the amount of the proceeds multiplied by the following fraction: (a) the total amount of the sums secured immediately before the taking, divided by (b) the fair market value of the Property immediately before the taking. Any balance shall be paid to Borrower. In the event of a partial taking of the Property in which the fair market value of the Property immediately before the taking is less than the amount of the sums secured immediately before the taking, unless Borrower and Lender otherwise agree in writing or unless applicable law otherwise provides, the proceeds shall be applied to the sums secured by this Security Instrument whether or not the sums are then due.

    If the Property is abandoned by Borrower, or if, after notice by Lender to Borrower that the condemnor offers to make an award or settle a claim for damages, Borrower fails to respond to Lender within 30 days after the date the notice is given, Lender is authorized to collect and apply the proceeds, at its option, either to restoration or repair of the Property or to the sums secured by this Security Instrument, whether or not then due.

    Unless Lender and Borrower otherwise agree in writing, any application of proceeds to principal shall not extend or postpone the due date of the monthly payments referred to in paragraphs 1 and 2 or change the amount of such payments.

    11. Borrower Not Released; Forbearance By Lender Not a Waiver. Extension of the time for payment or modification of amortization of the sums secured by this Security Instrument granted by Lender to any successor in interest of Borrower shall not operate to release the liability of the original Borrower or Borrower's successors in interest. Lender shall not be required to commence proceedings against any successor in interest or refuse to extend time for payment or otherwise modify amortization of the sums secured by this Security Instrument by reason of any demand made by the original Borrower or Borrower's successors in interest. Any forbearance by Lender in exercising any right or remedy shall not be a waiver of or preclude the exercise of any right or remedy.

    12. Successors and Assigns Bound; Joint and Several Liability; Co-signers. The covenants and agreements of this Security Instrument shall bind and benefit the successors and assigns of Lender and Borrower, subject to the provisions of paragraph 17. Borrower's covenants and agreements shall be joint and several. Any Borrower who co-signs this Security Instrument but does not execute the Note: (a) is co-signing this Security Instrument only to mortgage, grant and convey that Borrower's interest in the Property under the terms of this Security Instrument; (b) is not personally obligated to pay the sums secured by this Security Instrument; and (c) agrees that Lender and any other Borrower may agree to extend, modify, forbear or make any accommodations with regard to the terms of this Security Instrument or the Note without that Borrower's consent.

    13. Loan Charges. If the loan secured by this Security Instrument is subject to a law which sets maximum loan charges, and that law is finally interpreted so that the interest or other loan charges collected or to be collected in connection with the loan exceed the permitted limits, then: (a) any such loan charge shall be reduced by the amount necessary to reduce the charge to the permitted limit; and (b) any sums already collected from Borrower which exceeded permitted limits will be refunded to Borrower. Lender may choose to make this refund by reducing the principal owed under the Note or by making a direct payment to Borrower. If a refund reduces principal, the reduction will be treated as a partial prepayment without any prepayment charge under the Note.

    14. Notices. Any notice to Borrower provided for in this Security Instrument shall be given by delivering it or by mailing it by first class mail unless applicable law requires use of another method. The notice shall be directed to the Property Address or any other address Borrower designates by notice to Lender. Any notice to Lender shall be given by first class mail to Lender's address stated herein or any other address Lender designates by notice to Borrower. Any notice provided for in this Security Instrument shall be deemed to have been given to Borrower or Lender when given as provided in this paragraph.

    15. Governing Law; Severability. This Security Instrument shall be governed by federal law and the law of the jurisdiction in which the Property is located. In the event that any provision or clause of this Security Instrument or the Note conflicts with applicable law, such conflict shall not affect other provisions of this Security Instrument or the Note which can be given effect without the conflicting provision. To this end the provisions of this Security Instrument and the Note are declared to be severable.

    16. Borrower's Copy. Borrower shall be given one conformed copy of the Note and of this Security Instrument.

Form 3044   9/90

VMP -6R(TX) (9105)   Page 4 of 6   Initials:_____

Figure 15.4 Deed of Trust (Continued)

ALIENATION (DUE-ON-SALE) CLAUSE

17. Transfer of the Property or a Beneficial Interest in Borrower. If all or any part of the Property or any interest in it is sold or transferred (or if a beneficial interest in Borrower is sold or transferred and Borrower is not a natural person) without Lender's prior written consent, Lender may, at its option, require immediate payment in full of all sums secured by this Security Instrument. However, this option shall not be exercised by Lender if exercise is prohibited by federal law as of the date of this Security Instrument.

If Lender exercises this option, Lender shall give Borrower notice of acceleration. The notice shall provide a period of not less than 30 days from the date the notice is delivered or mailed within which Borrower must pay all sums secured by this Security Instrument. If Borrower fails to pay these sums prior to the expiration of this period, Lender may invoke any remedies permitted by this Security Instrument without further notice or demand on Borrower.

18. Borrower's Right to Reinstate. If Borrower meets certain conditions, Borrower shall have the right to have enforcement of this Security Instrument discontinued at any time prior to the earlier of: (a) 5 days (or such other period as applicable law may specify for reinstatement) before sale of the Property pursuant to any power of sale contained in this Security Instrument; or (b) entry of a judgment enforcing this Security Instrument. Those conditions are that Borrower: (a) pays Lender all sums which then would be due under this Security Instrument and the Note as if no acceleration had occurred; (b) cures any default of any other covenants or agreements; (c) pays all expenses incurred in enforcing this Security Instrument, including, but not limited to, reasonable attorneys' fees; and (d) takes such action as Lender may reasonably require to assure that the lien of this Security Instrument, Lender's rights in the Property and Borrower's obligation to pay the sums secured by this Security Instrument shall continue unchanged. Upon reinstatement by Borrower, this Security Instrument and the obligations secured hereby shall remain fully effective as if no acceleration had occurred. However, this right to reinstate shall not apply in the case of acceleration under paragraph 17.

19. Sale of Note; Change of Loan Servicer. The Note or a partial interest in the Note (together with this Security Instrument) may be sold one or more times without prior notice to Borrower. A sale may result in a change in the entity (known as the "Loan Servicer") that collects monthly payments due under the Note and this Security Instrument. There also may be one or more changes of the Loan Servicer unrelated to a sale of the Note. If there is a change of the Loan Servicer, Borrower will be given written notice of the change in accordance with paragraph 14 above and applicable law. The notice will state the name and address of the new Loan Servicer and the address to which payments should be made. The notice will also contain any other information required by applicable law.

20. Hazardous Substances. Borrower shall not cause or permit the presence, use, disposal, storage, or release of any Hazardous Substances on or in the Property. Borrower shall not do, nor allow anyone else to do, anything affecting the Property that is in violation of any Environmental Law. The preceding two sentences shall not apply to the presence, use, or storage on the Property of small quantities of Hazardous Substances that are generally recognized to be appropriate to normal residential uses and to maintenance of the Property.

Borrower shall promptly give Lender written notice of any investigation, claim, demand, lawsuit or other action by any governmental or regulatory agency or private party involving the Property and any Hazardous Substance or Environmental Law of which Borrower has actual knowledge. If Borrower learns, or is notified by any governmental or regulatory authority, that any removal or other remediation of any Hazardous Substance affecting the Property is necessary, Borrower shall promptly take all necessary remedial actions in accordance with Environmental Law.

As used in this paragraph 20, "Hazardous Substances" are those substances defined as toxic or hazardous substances by Environmental Law and the following substances: gasoline, kerosene, other flammable or toxic petroleum products, toxic pesticides and herbicides, volatile solvents, materials containing asbestos or formaldehyde, and radioactive materials. As used in this paragraph 20, "Environmental Law" means federal laws and laws of the jurisdiction where the Property is located that relate to health, safety or environmental protection.

NON-UNIFORM COVENANTS. Borrower and Lender further covenant and agree as follows:

ACCELERATION CLAUSE

21. Acceleration; Remedies. Lender shall give notice to Borrower prior to acceleration following Borrower's breach of any covenant or agreement in this Security Instrument (but not prior to acceleration under paragraph 17 unless applicable law provides otherwise). The notice shall specify: (a) the default; (b) the action required to cure the default; (c) a date, not less than 30 days from the date the notice is given to Borrower, by which the default must be cured; and (d) that failure to cure the default on or before the date specified in the notice will result in acceleration of the sums secured by this Security Instrument and sale of the Property. The notice shall further inform Borrower of the right to reinstate after acceleration and the right to bring a court action to assert the non-existence of a default or any other defense of Borrower to acceleration and sale. If the default is not cured on or before the date specified in the notice, Lender, at its option, may require immediate payment in full of all sums secured by this Security Instrument without further demand and may invoke the power of sale and any other remedies permitted by applicable law. Lender shall be entitled to collect all expenses incurred in pursuing the remedies provided in this paragraph 21, including, but not limited to, reasonable attorneys' fees and costs of title evidence.

POWER-OF-SALE CLAUSE

If Lender invokes the power of sale, Lender or Trustee shall give notice of the time, place and terms of sale by posting and recording the notice at least 21 days prior to sale as provided by applicable law. Lender shall mail a copy of the notice of sale to Borrower in the manner prescribed by applicable law. Sale shall be made at public vendue between the hours of 10 a.m. and 4 p.m. on the first Tuesday of the month. Borrower authorizes Trustee to sell the Property to the highest bidder for cash in one or more parcels and in any order Trustee determines. Lender or its designee may purchase the Property at any sale.

Trustee shall deliver to the purchaser Trustee's deed conveying indefeasible title to the Property with covenants of general warranty. Borrower covenants and agrees to defend generally the purchaser's title to the Property against all claims and demands. The recitals in the Trustee's deed shall be prima facie evidence of the truth of the statements made therein. Trustee shall apply the proceeds of the sale in the following order: (a) to all expenses of the sale, including, but not limited to, reasonable Trustee's and attorneys' fees; (b) to all sums secured by this Security Instrument; and (c) any excess to the person or persons legally entitled to it.

If the Property is sold pursuant to this paragraph 21, Borrower or any person holding possession of the Property through Borrower shall immediately surrender possession of the Property to the purchaser at that sale. If possession is not surrendered, Borrower or such person shall be a tenant at sufferance and may be removed by writ of possession.

Form 3044 9/90

VMP -6R(TX) (9105) ®   Page 5 of 6   Initials: _____

Figure 15.4   Deed of Trust (Continued)

RELEASE

22. Release. Upon payment of all sums secured by this Security Instrument, Lender shall release this Security Instrument without charge to Borrower. Borrower shall pay any recordation costs.

23. Substitute Trustee. Lender, at its option and with or without cause, may from time to time remove Trustee and appoint, by power of attorney or otherwise, a successor trustee to any Trustee appointed hereunder. Without conveyance of the Property, the successor trustee shall succeed to all the title, power and duties conferred upon Trustee herein and by applicable law.

24. Subrogation. Any of the proceeds of the Note used to take up outstanding liens against all or any part of the Property have been advanced by Lender at Borrower's request and upon Borrower's representation that such amounts are due and are secured by valid liens against the Property. Lender shall be subrogated to any and all rights, superior titles, liens and equities owned or claimed by any owner or holder of any outstanding liens and debts, regardless of whether said liens or debts are acquired by Lender by assignment or are released by the holder thereof upon payment.

25. Partial Invalidity. In the event any portion of the sums intended to be secured by this Security Instrument cannot be lawfully secured hereby, payments in reduction of such sums shall be applied first to those portions not secured hereby.

26. Waiver of Notice of Intention to Accelerate. Borrower waives the right to notice of intention to require immediate payment in full of all sums secured by this Security Instrument except as provided in paragraph 21.

27. Riders to this Security Instrument. If one or more riders are executed by Borrower and recorded together with this Security Instrument, the covenants and agreements of each such rider shall be incorporated into and shall amend and supplement the covenants and agreements of this Security Instrument as if the rider(s) were a part of this Security Instrument.
[Check applicable box(es)]

☐ Adjustable Rate Rider   ☐ Condominium Rider   ☐ 1-4 Family Rider
☐ Graduated Payment Rider ☐ Planned Unit Development Rider ☐ Biweekly Payment Rider
☐ Balloon Rider   ☐ Rate Improvement Rider   ☐ Second Home Rider
☐ V.A. Rider   ☐ Other(s) [specify]

28. Purchase Money; Vendor's Lien; Renewal and Extension. [Complete as appropriate]

BY SIGNING BELOW, Borrower accepts and agrees to the terms and covenants contained in this Security Instrument and in any rider(s) executed by Borrower and recorded with it.
Witnesses:

_____(Seal)
JOHN DOE   -Borrower

_____(Seal)
JANE DOE   -Borrower

_____(Seal)   _____(Seal)
                 -Borrower   -Borrower

STATE OF TEXAS,   Randall   County ss:

BEFORE ME, the undersigned, a Notary Public in and for said County and State, on this day personally appeared

John Doe and Jane Doe
                                                                    , known to me
to be the person(s) whose name(s)   are   subscribed to the foregoing instrument, and acknowledged to me
that   they   executed the same for the purposes and consideration therein expressed.
GIVEN UNDER MY HAND AND SEAL OF OFFICE, this   29th   day of   May, 1997.

_____
Notary Public

estate that was conveyed to the mortgagee (lender) by the original recorded mortgage lien document. Remember that this interest is a lien interest and not a title interest. By having this release entered in the public record, the owner shows that the mortgage lien has been removed from the property. If a mortgage or deed of trust has been assigned by a recorded assignment, the release must be executed by the assignee mortgagee.

When a real estate loan secured by a deed of trust has been repaid, the beneficiary (lender) requests in writing that the trustee convey the property back to the grantor (borrower). The trustee then executes a release of lien and delivers a **release deed,** sometimes called a *deed of reconveyance*, to the trustor conveying the same rights and powers that the trustee was given under the trust deed. The release deed should be acknowledged and recorded in the county clerk's records in the county where the property is located.

Tax and Insurance Reserves

Many lenders require that borrowers provide a reserve fund, called an *escrow account*, to make future payments for real estate taxes, property insurance premiums, and, when applicable, homeowner's dues and mortgage insurance premiums. RESPA limits the amount of tax and insurance reserves that a lender may require. When the mortgage or deed of trust loan is made, the borrower starts the escrow account by depositing funds to cover the amount of year-to-date unpaid real estate taxes, including the month of closing and two months' tax reserve. If a new insurance policy has been purchased, the insurance premium reserve will be started with the deposit of two months of the annual insurance premium liability. An aggregate adjustment will then be made to the initial escrow amount collected to ensure that at least once each year the escrow account does not exceed two times the monthly escrow payment. Thereafter, the monthly loan payments required of the borrower will include *principal* and *interest* and one month's *tax* and *insurance* reserves (PITI).

Assignment of Rents

When a mortgage or trust deed is executed, the borrower may make an assignment of rents to the lender, to become effective on the borrower's default. The rent assignment may be included in the mortgage or deed of trust, or it may be made as a separate document. In either case, the rent assignment should be drafted in language that clearly indicates that the parties intend to assign the rents, not merely pledge them as security for the loan.

Buying "Subject to" or Assuming a Seller's Loan Secured by a Mortgage or Deed of Trust

A person who purchases real estate that has an outstanding loan on it secured by a mortgage or deed of trust may take the property subject to the mortgage or may assume it and agree to pay the debt. This technical distinction becomes important if the buyer defaults and the mortgage or deed of trust is foreclosed.

When the property is sold *subject to* the mortgage or deed of trust, the courts hold that the purchaser is not personally obligated to pay the debt in full. The purchaser has bought the real estate knowing that he or she must make the loan payments and that on default, the lender will foreclose and the property will be sold to pay the debt. If the sale does not pay off the entire debt, the purchaser is not liable for the difference. However, the original seller might still have some liability for that difference.

In contrast, when the grantee not only purchases the property but *assumes and agrees to pay* the seller's debt, the grantee becomes personally obligated for the payment of the *entire debt*. If the deed of trust or mortgage is foreclosed and the sale does not bring enough money to pay the debt in full, a deficiency judgment against the assumer may be obtained for the unpaid balance of the note. Unless the lender agrees to the assumption and a release of liability is given to the original borrower, the original borrower also will be liable for the unpaid balance. When a mortgage loan is assumed, most lending institutions charge a transfer fee to the purchaser to cover the costs of changing their records.

FOR EXAMPLE   Jane is being transferred out of town. When she bought her house, interest rates were very low; but rates have risen dramatically since that time. Buyers may be attracted by the prospect of *assuming* her mortgage to retain a more favorable interest rate, thereby saving money.

Alienation clause. Frequently, when a real estate loan is made, the lender wishes to prevent some future purchaser of the property from being able to assume that loan, particularly at its old rate of interest. For this reason most lenders include an **alienation clause** (also known as a *resale clause* or *due-on-sale clause*) in the note and deed of trust. An alienation clause provides that, on the sale of the property by the original borrower to a buyer who wants to assume the loan, the lender has the choice of either declaring the entire loan balance immediately due and payable or permitting the buyer to assume the loan at current market interest rates. This operates much like the acceleration clause that allows the lender to demand payment of the note in full if the provisions of the note or deed of trust are breached.

Deed of Trust To Secure Assumption

As shown earlier, a deed of trust is an instrument used to tie the payment of a note to a piece of property in such a manner that a default on the note or the deed of trust permits the holder thereof to foreclose and regain legal title to the encumbered property. In a broader sense, however, the deed of trust is a collateralizing instrument; it ties the performance of an *obligation* to a certain piece of property.

Another type of deed of trust is the *deed of trust to secure assumption*, a document developed to protect the seller who allows someone to assume his or her loan. If the buyer subsequently defaults in payment of the note assumed, the seller has the obligation to pay the delinquent sums to the lender. The buyer must then reimburse the seller within five days; otherwise, the seller may foreclose under the power-of-sale clause in the deed of trust to secure assumption.

From the buyer's perspective, however, the deed of trust to secure assumption may create problems in obtaining a subsequent second lien on the property. For example, a prospective lender on a second lien note *may* require the subordination of the deed of trust to secure assumption as a condition of making the second lien loan. Some lenders perceive the deed of trust to secure assumption as a lien on the property; others, merely the granting of the right of foreclosure to another party. Therefore, sellers and buyers should consult a competent attorney if an assumption of loan is involved.

Recording Mortgages and Deeds of Trust

Although the deed of trust is normally recorded, it does not have to be recorded to be valid. However, recording the deed of trust in the county clerk's office where the real estate is located gives constructive notice to the world of the borrower's obligations and establishes the lien's priority. Promissory notes are not recorded.

First and Second Mortgages or Deeds of Trust

Mortgages and other liens normally have priority in the order in which they have been recorded. A mortgage or deed of trust on land that has no prior mortgage lien on it is a *first mortgage* or *first deed of trust.* If the owner of this land later executes another loan on the same property, for additional funds, the new loan becomes a *second mortgage (deed of trust),* or *junior lien,* when recorded. The second lien is subject to the first lien; the first has prior claim to the value of the land pledged as security. Because second loans represent a greater risk to the lender, they usually are issued at higher interest rates.

The priority of mortgage or deed of trust liens may be changed by the execution of a *subordination agreement,* in which the first lender subordinates his or her lien to that of the second lender, as discussed in Chapter 11. To be valid, such an agreement must be signed by both lenders.

FORECLOSURE

If a borrower defaults in making payments or fulfilling any of the obligations set forth in the deed of trust, the lender can enforce his or her rights through a foreclosure. A **foreclosure** is a legal procedure whereby the property that is pledged as security in the mortgage document or deed of trust is sold to satisfy the debt. Such a foreclosure under a deed of trust is called a *power of sale,* which means that the foreclosure is done out of court. The foreclosure procedure brings the rights of all parties to a conclusion and passes title in the subject property to either the person holding the deed of trust or a third party who purchases the realty at a *foreclosure sale.* Property thus sold is *free of the mortgage and all junior liens.*

Methods of Foreclosure

The two general types of foreclosure proceedings recognized in Texas are judicial and nonjudicial foreclosure.

Judicial foreclosure *(for a home equity lien or a vendor's lien).* A judicial foreclosure proceeding provides that the property pledged as security may be sold by court order after the mortgagee gives sufficient public notice. On a borrower's default the lender may *accelerate* the due date of all remaining monthly payments. The lender's attorney must then file suit and obtain a judgment ordering foreclosure of the lien. A public sale is advertised and held, and the real estate is sold to the highest bidder. The Texas Supreme Court has promulgated rules of civil procedure for expedited foreclosure proceedings for home equity loans.

Nonjudicial foreclosure *(for a deed of trust lien).* Texas allows nonjudicial foreclosure procedures through the **power-of-sale clause** contained in the deed of trust. This provision allows the trustee to satisfy the debt without going through court proceedings. In Texas, foreclosure sales occur on the first Tuesday of each month between the hours of 10 A.M. and 4 P.M. Written notice of the proposed sale must be given at least 21 days preceding the date of the sale by (1) posting it at the door of the courthouse in the county in which the sale is to be conducted, (2) filing it in the office of the county clerk, and (3) sending it by certified mail to each debtor obligated to pay the debt. The notice must state at which courthouse entrance the sale will take place and the earliest time that the sale will occur; the sale may not be started more than three hours after the stated time. If the real property is the debtor's residence, both the Fannie Mae/Freddie Mac note and deed of trust allow the defaulting property owner 30 days to cure the default before notice of sale is given. (State law requires at least 20 days' notice.) Foreclosure under a power-of-sale clause greatly simplifies and expedites foreclosure and eliminates costly court fees. The successful bidder at the sale receives a trustee's deed to the real estate. The deed executed by the trustee *conveys whatever title the borrower had.* The title passes as is, but free of the former defaulted debt. There are no warranties, but it is possible to procure a title insurance policy.

Deed in Lieu of Foreclosure

With a **deed in lieu of foreclosure,** a defaulting borrower negotiates with a lender to transfer voluntarily the property's title to the lender—thus avoiding costly foreclosure proceedings and a possible deficiency judgment. This is sometimes called a *friendly foreclosure* because it is by agreement rather than by civil action. The major disadvantage of this default settlement is that the mortgagee takes the real estate subject to all junior liens, whereas a power-of-sale foreclosure eliminates all such liens. (Foreclosure of a vendor's lien does not extinguish junior liens, however, unless those lienholders were named in the foreclosure suit.) By accepting a deed in lieu of foreclosure, the lender usually loses any rights pertaining to FHA or private mortgage insurance or VA guarantees.

Redemption

Texas recognizes the *equitable right of* **redemption** prior to a mortgage foreclosure sale. If, after default but *before the foreclosure sale,* the borrower or any other person who has an interest in the real estate (such as another creditor) pays the lender the amount in default, plus costs, the debt usually will be reinstated. However, in some cases the person who redeems may be required to repay the accelerated loan in full. If a person other than the mortgagor or trustor redeems the real estate, the borrower becomes responsible to that person for the amount of the redemption.

Although a defaulted borrower may redeem the property at any time before the sale, Texas law contains *no* provisions for *statutory redemption* of property after a sale to satisfy a home equity lien or a power-of-sale clause in a deed of trust. Following a foreclosure and a court sale, the deed will be executed and delivered to the purchaser by the officer conducting the sale.

However, as discussed in Chapter 11, if the foreclosure sale is held to satisfy a tax lien on a residence, Texas does have a two-year statutory redemption period on homestead property (six months on nonhomestead property). Or if foreclosure occurs on a homeowners' association lien, there is a 180 day statutory period for redemption.

Deficiency Judgment

Under Texas law, if the foreclosure sale of real estate securing a deed of trust does not produce enough money to pay the loan balance in full, all expenses of sale, and accrued unpaid interest, the lender may be entitled to a *personal judgment* against the borrower for the unpaid balance. Such a judgment is called a **deficiency judgment.** It may also be obtained against any endorsers or guarantors of the note and any owners of the mortgaged property who may have assumed the debt by written agreement. If the foreclosure sales price exceeds the amount needed for principal, interest, and expenses, any surplus funds are paid to the borrower.

Summary

Mortgage and deed of trust loans provide the principal sources of financing for real estate operations. Mortgage loans involve a borrower, called the *mortgagor,* and a lender, the *mortgagee.* Deed of trust loans involve a third party, called the *trustee,* in addition to the borrower (in this case the *trustor*) and the lender (the *beneficiary*).

States that recognize the lender as the owner of mortgaged property are known as *title theory states.* Others recognize the borrower as the owner of mortgaged property and are known as *lien theory states.* Texas is a lien theory state.

A borrower of funds for the purchase of a home is required to execute a note, agreeing to repay the debt, and a mortgage or deed of trust, placing a lien on the real estate to secure his or her note. This transaction is normally recorded in the public records to give notice to the world of the lender's interest.

The note also sets the rate of interest at which the loan is made and that the mortgagor or trustor must pay as a charge for borrowing the money. Charging more than the maximum interest rate allowed by state statute is called *usury* and is illegal. The mortgage document or deed of trust secures the debt and sets forth the obligations of the borrower and the rights of the lender. Payment in full of the note by its terms entitles the borrower to a release, or satisfaction, of lien, which is recorded to clear the lien from the public records. Default by the borrower may result in acceleration of payments, a foreclosure sale, and loss of title.

Questions

1. A promissory note
   a. is a negotiable instrument.
   b. may not be sold by the lender to a third party.
   c. is recorded in the county clerk's records.
   d. is security for the loan.

2. The person who obtains a real estate loan by signing a note and a mortgage (deed of trust) is called the
   a. trustee.
   b. beneficiary.
   c. mortgagee.
   d. mortgagor.

3. The Stevensons sold their farmland to the Crawfords but retained the rights to and ownership of all coal and other minerals in the land. The Crawfords obtained a mortgage loan from their bank and executed a mortgage to the bank as security. Which of the following statements is true regarding this transaction?
   a. The Crawfords' mortgage covers the land and the minerals.
   b. The Crawfords' mortgage covers the land but not the minerals.
   c. The Crawfords' mortgage covers only the minerals.
   d. If the Crawfords default, the bank automatically acquires the mineral rights.

4. The lender under a deed of trust is known as the
   a. trustor.
   b. trustee.
   c. beneficiary.
   d. vendee.

5. A borrower obtains a $76,000 mortgage loan at 11½ percent interest. If the monthly payments of $785 are credited first on interest and then on principal, what will the balance of the principal be after the borrower makes the first payment?
   a. $75,215.00
   b. $75,943.33
   c. $75,543.66
   d. $75,305.28

6. A mortgage or deed of trust document requires that the mortgagor perform certain duties. Which of the following is **NOT** one of these?
   a. Maintain the property in good condition at all times
   b. Obtain the mortgagee's permission before renting a room to a boarder
   c. Maintain adequate insurance on the property
   d. Obtain the lender's permission before making major alterations to the property

7. Which of the following is **NOT** a necessary element of a deed of trust mortgage?
   a. Consideration
   b. Signature of trustee
   c. Legal capacity of parties
   d. Written document

8. A state law provides that lenders cannot charge more than 18 percent interest on a loan. This law is called
   a. a Truth-in-Lending law.
   b. a usury law.
   c. the statute of frauds.
   d. RESPA.

9. Prior to the foreclosure sale, a defaulting borrower seeks to pay off the debt plus any accrued interest and costs under the right of
   a. equitable redemption.
   b. statutory redemption.
   c. hypothecation.
   d. defeasance.

10. The clause in a note that gives the lender the right to have all future installments become due on default is the
    a. escalation clause.
    b. defeasance clause.
    c. alienation clause.
    d. acceleration clause.

11. What document is given to the trustor when the deed of trust debt is completely repaid?
   a. Satisfaction of mortgage
   b. Defeasance certificate
   c. Deed of trust
   d. Release deed

12. Which of the following allows a mortgagee to proceed to a foreclosure sale without having to go to court first?
   a. Waiver of redemption right
   b. Power of sale
   c. Alienation clause
   d. Acceleration clause

13. Pledging property for a loan without giving up possession is best described as
   a. hypothecation.   c. novation.
   b. alienation.   d. defeasance.

14. The provisions of a nonjudicial foreclosure include all the following **EXCEPT**
   a. written notice must be posted at the courthouse at least 21 days before the sale.
   b. homestead property owners must be given 45 days to cure the default before notice of sale is given.
   c. notice of the proposed sale must be sent to each debtor at least 21 days before the sale.
   d. notice of the sale must state at which courthouse entrance the sale will take place.

15. In a foreclosure through a power of sale clause, who actually conducts the foreclosure?
   a. Mortgagee   c. Trustee
   b. Mortgagor   d. Trustor

16. The borrower under a deed of trust is known as the
   a. trustor.   c. beneficiary.
   b. trustee.   d. vendee.

16 Real Estate Financing: Practice

Key Terms

adjustable-rate
  mortgage
balloon payment
biweekly payment plan
blanket mortgage
buydown mortgage
computerized loan
  origination
construction loan
contract for deed
conventional loan
discount points
equity loan
Fannie Mae
Farm Service Agency
Federal Reserve
  System (the "Fed")

FHA loan
flexible-payment loan
Freddie Mac
fully amortized loan
Ginnie Mae
loan origination fee
mortgage-backed
  securities
open-end mortgage
package mortgage
primary mortgage
  market
private mortgage
  insurance
purchase-money
  mortgage

Regulation Z
reverse-annuity
  mortgage
sale-and-leaseback
secondary mortgage
  market
shared-appreciation
  mortgage
straight (term) loan
Texas Department of
  Housing and
  Community Affairs
VA loan
warehousing agency
wraparound loan

OVERVIEW

Without mortgage loans, the American dream of owning one's home would be possible for very few people. Through programs of the Department of Housing and Urban Development (HUD), the Department of Veterans Affairs (VA), and agencies such as Ginnie Mae, the federal government has assisted the American citizen by providing affordable housing money.

This chapter explores the alternative types of financing and payment plans. The chapter also examines the various primary and secondary sources for mortgage money and looks at the role of the federal government in real estate financing.

SOURCES OF REAL ESTATE FINANCING—THE PRIMARY MORTGAGE MARKET

The funds used to finance the purchase of real estate come from a variety of sources in the **primary mortgage market**—lenders who supply funds to borrowers as an investment. Mortgage loans generally are made by institutional lenders such as savings associations, commercial banks, mutual savings banks, insurance companies, mortgage banking companies, mortgage brokers, and credit unions.

There are government sources of real estate financing as well. Many local government bodies issue interest-bearing certificates, called *bond issues,* to finance real estate projects and community improvements. In Texas, the Department of Housing and Community Affairs and regional or local housing authorities have the authority to make mortgages and temporary loans to assist people with low or moderate incomes.

Savings Associations

Savings associations (also called savings and loan associations or S&Ls) are active participants in the home loan mortgage market, specializing in long-term residential loans. All savings associations must be chartered, either by the federal government or by the state in which they are located. The principal function of a savings association has been to promote thrift and home ownership. Generally real estate mortgages and real estate-related assets are the main source of investment for savings associations. Since July 1, 1991, these institutions have been required to maintain 70 percent of their loan portfolios in housing-related loans, such as residential mortgage loans, residential construction loans, home equity loans, and mortgage-backed securities. Traditionally they are the most flexible of all the lending institutions in regard to their mortgage lending procedures. In addition, savings associations participate in FHA-insured and VA-guaranteed loans.

Commercial Banks

Commercial banks are an important source of real estate financing. Historically, bank loan departments have handled such short-term loans as construction, home improvement, and manufactured housing loans. However, commercial banks are also originating an increasing number of home mortgages and play a significant role in issuing VA and FHA loans. Like the savings associations, banks must be chartered by the state or federal government. The *Federal Deposit Insurance Corporation (FDIC)* protects depositors in both savings associations and commercial banks.

Mutual Savings Banks

Mutual savings banks operate like savings associations. They issue no stock and are mutually owned by their investors, the depositors themselves. Although mutual savings banks do offer limited checking account privileges, they are primarily savings institutions and are highly active in the mortgage market, investing in loans secured by income property as well as residential real estate. In addition, because mutual savings banks usually seek low-risk loan investments, they often prefer to originate FHA-insured or VA-guaranteed loans.

Insurance Companies

Insurance companies amass large sums of money from the premiums paid by their policyholders. Although a certain portion of this money is held in reserve to satisfy claims and cover operating expenses, much of it is invested in profit-earning enterprises such as long-term real estate loans.

Most insurance companies invest their money in large, long-term loans that finance commercial and industrial properties. They also invest in residential mortgage and deed of trust loans by purchasing large blocks of government-backed (FHA-insured and VA-guaranteed) loans from Fannie Mae and other agencies that warehouse such loans for resale in the *secondary mortgage market* (discussed later in this chapter).

In addition, many insurance companies seek to ensure further the safety of their investments by insisting on equity positions (known as *equity kickers*) in many projects they finance. They may require a partnership arrangement with a project developer or subdivider as a condition for making a loan.

Mortgage Banking Companies

Mortgage banking companies use money borrowed from other institutions and/or funds of their own to make real estate loans. They make loans in the name of the mortgage banker with the intention of selling them to investors either on a loan-by-loan basis or pooled together as a security. Many mortgage bankers will sell only the loans and retain the servicing, which generates revenue for long periods of time. Other mortgage bankers will retain servicing until a certain volume is reached to optimize its value for a sale to another loan servicer. A mortgage banking company is generally organized as a stock company or as a wholly owned subsidiary of a bank or savings association, subject to the regulations of the bank or savings association.

Mortgage Brokers

Mortgage brokers are not lenders but are often instrumental in obtaining financing. Mortgage brokers are individuals who act as intermediaries to bring borrowers and lenders together. They locate potential borrowers, process preliminary loan applications, and submit the applications to lenders for final approval. The loans are generally closed in the name of the lender, not the mortgage broker. Frequently they work with or for mortgage banking companies in these activities. They do not service loans once they are made. Many mortgage brokers are also real estate brokers who offer these financing services in addition to their regular brokerage activities; however, full disclosure must be made to all parties to the transaction. Mortgage brokers and loan officers working under a mortgage broker must meet specified educational and/or experience requirements and obtain a license from the state; no examination is required (S.B. 1074, 1999).

Credit Unions

Credit unions are cooperative organizations in which members place money in savings accounts, usually at higher interest rates than other savings institutions offer. In the past, most credit unions made only short-term consumer and home improvement loans, but in recent years they have branched out into originating longer-term first and second mortgage and deed of trust loans. They generally sell their long-term loans in the secondary market.

APPLICATION FOR CREDIT

All mortgage lenders require that prospective borrowers file an application for credit that provides the lender with the basic information needed to evaluate the acceptability of the proposed loan. All residential lenders are required to use the Uniform Residential Loan Application for *all* loans (FHA, VA, FSA, and conventional) secured by one-family to four-family properties (see Figure 16.1). The application includes information regarding the pur-

Form 1003

pose of the loan, the amount, the rate of interest, and the proposed terms of repayment. This is considered a preliminary offer of a loan agreement; final terms may require lengthy negotiations.

The lender must qualify the buyer, the title, and the property. Within the application, a prospective borrower must submit personal information to the lender, including employment, earnings, assets, and financial obligations. Details of the real estate that will be the security for the loan must be provided, including legal description, improvements, title, survey, and taxes. For loans on income property or those made to corporations, additional information is required, such as financial and operating statements, schedules of leases and tenants, and balance sheets.

The lender carefully investigates the application information, studying credit reports and an appraisal of the property before deciding whether to grant the loan. Some lenders issue a written *loan commitment*, which creates a contract to make a loan and sets forth the details. Under some circumstances, lenders charge a fee for this commitment. There are standardized forms for use by mortgage brokers for representing that an applicant is pre-approved or has prequalified for a loan (H.B. 1493, 2001).

In Practice   Although lenders compute loan qualifying ratios for prospective home-buyers, "credit scoring" has become a major factor in lending decision making. Fair, Isaac and Company (FICO) created a system for reducing the loan application creditworthiness elements into one number, a FICO score. FICO scores have proven to be a reliable indicator of the risk of mortgage default. Fannie Mae and Freddie Mac have set 620 as the minimum FICO score for their automated secondary market purchases. A score below 620 would require manual underwriting review. The "calculator" section on many real estate web sites, such as homepath.com, can help a buyer or agent determine how much house a purchaser can buy and what the maximum qualifying payment would be.

Computerized Loan Origination and Automated Underwriting

A **computerized loan origination (CLO)** system is an electronic network for handling loan applications through remote computer terminals linked to several lenders' computers. With a CLO system, a real estate broker or salesperson can call up a menu of mortgage lenders, interest rates, and loan terms, then help a buyer select a lender and apply for a loan right from the brokerage office.

The licensee may assist the applicant in answering the on-screen questions and in understanding the services offered. The broker in whose office the terminal is located may earn fees of up to one half point of the loan amount. The *borrower*, not the mortgage broker or lender, *must pay the fee*. The fee amount may be financed, however. While multiple lenders may be represented on an office's CLO computer, consumers must be informed that other lenders are available. A CLO system enhances an applicant's ability to

Figure 16.1   *Uniform Residential Loan Application*

Uniform Residential Loan Application

This application is designed to be completed by the applicant(s) with the Lender's assistance. Applicants should complete this form as "Borrower" or "Co-Borrower," as applicable. Co-Borrower information must also be provided (and the appropriate box checked) when [X] the income or assets of a person other than the "Borrower" (including the Borrower's spouse) will be used as a basis for loan qualification or [X] the income or assets of the Borrower's spouse will not be used as a basis for loan qualification, but his or her liabilities must be considered because the Borrower resides in a community property state, the security property is located in a community property state, or the Borrower is relying on other property located in a community property state as a basis for repayment of the loan.

I. TYPE OF MORTGAGE AND TERMS OF LOAN

Mortgage Applied for:	[ ] VA [X] Conventional [ ] Other: [ ] FHA [ ] FmHA	Agency Case Number	Lender Case Number DEMOCONV

Amount $ 80,000.00	Interest Rate 7.375 %	No. of Months 360	Amortization Type:	[X] Fixed Rate [ ] GPM	[ ] Other (explain): [ ] ARM (type):

II. PROPERTY INFORMATION AND PURPOSE OF LOAN

Subject Property Address (street, city, state, ZIP) 1456 HOUSE TEXAS	No. of Units 1

Legal Description of Subject Property (attach description if necessary)	Year Built 1994

Purpose of Loan [X] Purchase [ ] Construction [ ] Other (explain): [ ] Refinance [ ] Construction-Permanent	Property will be: [X] Primary Residence [ ] Secondary Residence [ ] Investment

Complete this line if construction or construction-permanent loan.

Year Lot Acquired	Original Cost $	Amount Existing Liens $	(a) Present Value of Lot $	(b) Cost of Improvements $	Total (a + b) $

Complete this line if this is a refinance loan.

Year Acquired	Original Cost $	Amount Existing Liens $	Purpose of Refinance	Describe Improvements [ ] made [ ] to be made Cost: $

Title will be held in what Name(s) JOHN DOE AND JANE DOE	Manner in which Title will be held TENANTS IN COMMON	Estate will be held in: [X] Fee Simple [ ] Leasehold (show expiration date)

Source of Down Payment, Settlement Charges and/or Subordinate Financing (explain) CASH ASSETS

III. BORROWER INFORMATION

	Borrower	Co-Borrower
Name (include Jr. or Sr. if applicable)	JOHN DOE	JANE DOE
Social Security Number	123-45-6789	101-12-1314
Home Phone (incl. area code)	806-355-0000	806-355-0000
Age	35	34
Yrs. School	16	16
Marital status	[X] Married [ ] Separated [ ] Unmarried	[X] Married [ ] Separated [ ] Unmarried
Dependents (not listed by Co-Borrower)	no. 2 ages 8, 6	no. 2 ages
Present Address (street, city, state, ZIP)	[X] Own [ ] Rent 5.00 No. Yrs. 1234 ANY STREET AMARILLO, TEXAS 79109	[X] Own [ ] Rent 5.00 No. Yrs. 1234 ANY STREET AMARILLO, TEXAS 79109

If residing at present address for less than two years, complete the following:

Former Address (street, city, state, ZIP)	[ ] Own [ ] Rent No. Yrs.	Former Address (street, city, state, ZIP)	[ ] Own [ ] Rent No. Yrs.

Former Address (street, city, state, ZIP)	[ ] Own [ ] Rent No. Yrs.	Former Address (street, city, state, ZIP)	[ ] Own [ ] Rent No. Yrs.

IV. EMPLOYMENT INFORMATION

	Borrower	Co-Borrower
Name & Address of Employer	MASON AND HANGER [ ] Self Employed P. O. BOX 30020 AMARILLO, TEXAS 79177	AMARILLO I S D [ ] Self Employed 7200 I 40 WEST AMARILLO, TEXAS 79106
Yrs. on this job	7.00	5.00
Yrs. employed in this line of work/profession	7.00	5.00
Position/Title/Type of Business	SECURITY COURIER GOVERNME	TEACHER EDUCATION
Business Phone (incl. area code)	806-477-0000	806-353-0000

If employed in current position for less than two years or if currently employed in more than one position, complete the following:

	Borrower	Co-Borrower
Name & Address of Employer	[ ] Self Employed	[ ] Self Employed
Dates (from - to)		
Monthly Income	$	$
Position/Title/Type of Business		
Business Phone (incl. area code)		

	Borrower	Co-Borrower
Name & Address of Employer	[ ] Self Employed	[ ] Self Employed
Dates (from - to)		
Monthly Income	$	$
Position/Title/Type of Business		
Business Phone (incl. area code)		

Borrower's Signature: X	Date	Co-Borrower's Signature: X	Date

(VMP)-21 (9210).09   VMP MORTGAGE FORMS - (800)521-7291   Freddie Mac Form 65 10/92   Fannie Mae Form 1003 10/92

Page 1 of 4

Figure 16.1 Uniform Residential Loan Application (Continued)

V. MONTHLY INCOME AND COMBINED HOUSING EXPENSE INFORMATION

Gross Monthly Income	Borrower	Co-Borrower	Total	Combined Monthly Housing Expense	Present	Proposed
Base Empl. Income*	$ 3800.00	$ 2200.00	$ 6000.00	Rent	$	
Overtime				First Mortgage (P&I)	1666.00	$ 552.54
Bonuses				Other Financing (P&I)		
Commissions				Hazard Insurance		75.00
Dividends/Interest				Real Estate Taxes		166.67
Net Rental Income				Mortgage Insurance		
Other (before completing, see the notice in "describe other income," below)				Homeowner Assn. Dues		
				Other:		
Total	$ 3800.00	$ 2200.00	$ 6000.00	Total	$ 1666.00	$ 794.21

* Self Employed Borrower(s) may be required to provide additional documentation such as tax returns and financial statements.

Describe Other Income	Notice: Alimony, child support, or separate maintenance income need not be revealed if the Borrower (B)	Monthly Amount
B/C	or Co-Borrower (C) does not choose to have it considered for repaying this loan.	$

VI. ASSETS AND LIABILITIES

This Statement and any applicable supporting schedules may be completed jointly by both married and unmarried Co-Borrowers if their assets and liabilities are sufficiently joined so that the Statement can be meaningfully and fairly presented on a combined basis; otherwise separate Statements and Schedules are required. If the Co-Borrower section was completed about a spouse, this Statement and supporting schedules must be completed about that spouse also.

Completed [XX] Jointly [ ] Not Jointly

ASSETS Description	Cash or Market Value	Liabilities and Pledged Assets. List the creditor's name, address and account number for all outstanding debts, including automobile loans, revolving charge accounts, real estate loans, alimony, child support, stock pledges, etc. Use continuation sheet, if necessary. Indicate by (*) those liabilities which will be satisfied upon sale of real estate owned or upon refinancing of the subject property.	Monthly Pmt. & Mos. Left to Pay	Unpaid Balance
Cash deposit toward purchase held by: STEWART TITLE CO.	$	LIABILITIES	$ Pmt./Mos.	$
List checking and savings accounts below		Name and address of Company MBNA AMERICA PO BOX 15019 WILMINGTON, DE		
Name and address of Bank, S&L, or Credit Union FIRST STATE BANK HAPPY, TEXAS P. O. BOX 7865 AMARILLO, TEXAS 79114-7865				
222222222	$ 5000.00	Acct. no.	80 / 63	5000.00
Acct. no. 111111111	$ 1000.00	Name and address of Company CAR LOAN COMPANY	$ Pmt./Mos.	$
Name and address of Bank, S&L, or Credit Union AETNA				
401K		Acct. no.	526 / 19	10000.00
Acct. no. 5555555555	$ 20000.00	Name and address of Company BOAT LOAN	$ Pmt./Mos.	$
Name and address of Bank, S&L, or Credit Union				
		Acct. no. BOAT LOAN	219 / 46	10000.00
		Name and address of Company	$ Pmt./Mos.	$
Acct. no.	$			
Name and address of Bank, S&L, or Credit Union				
		Acct. no.		
		Name and address of Company	$ Pmt./Mos.	$
Acct. no.	$			
Stocks & Bonds (Company name/number & description) MASSACHUSETTS MUTUAL	$ 10000.00			
		Acct. no.		
		Name and address of Company	$ Pmt./Mos.	$
Life insurance net cash value Face amount: $	$			
Subtotal Liquid Assets	$ 36000.00			
Real estate owned (enter market value from schedule of real estate owned)	$	Acct. no.		
Vested interest in retirement fund	$	Name and address of Company	$ Pmt./Mos.	$
Net worth of business(es) owned (attach financial statement)	$			
Automobiles owned (make and year) CAR 1 CAR 11	$ 20000.00 35000.00	Acct. no.		
Other Assets (itemize) PERSONAL PROPERTY	$ 50000.00	Alimony/Child Support/Separate Maintenance Payments Owed to:	$	
		Job Related Expense (child care, union dues, etc.)	$	
		Total Monthly Payments	$ 825	
Total Assets a.	$ 141000.00	Net Worth (a minus b) ▶ $ 116000.00	Total Liabilities b.	$ 25000.00

Borrower's Signature: Date	Co-Borrower's Signature: Date
X	X

Page 2 of 4

VMP-21 (9210).09

Fannie Mae Form 1003 10/92
Freddie Mac Form 65 10/92

Figure 16.1   **Uniform Residential Loan Application (Continued)**

VI. ASSETS AND LIABILITIES (cont.)

Schedule of Real Estate Owned (If additional properties are owned, use continuation sheet.)

Property Address (enter S if sold, PS if pending sale or R if rental being held for income)	Type of Property	Present Market Value	Amount of Mortgages & Liens	Gross Rental Income	Mortgage Payments	Insurance, Maintenance, Taxes & Misc.	Net Rental Income
		$	$	$	$	$	$
Totals		$	$	$	$	$	$

List any additional names under which credit has previously been received and indicate appropriate creditor name(s) and account number(s):

Alternate Name	Creditor Name	Account Number

VII. DETAILS OF TRANSACTION

a.	Purchase price	$ 100000.00
b.	Alterations, improvements, repairs	
c.	Land (if acquired separately)	
d.	Refinance (incl. debts to be paid off)	
e.	Estimated prepaid items	1875.04
f.	Estimated closing costs	1672.00
g.	PMI, MIP, Funding Fee	
h.	Discount (if Borrower will pay)	
i.	Total costs (add items a through h)	103547.04
j.	Subordinate financing	
k.	Borrower's closing costs paid by Seller	
l.	Other Credits (explain)	
m.	Loan amount (exclude PMI, MIP, Funding Fee financed)	80000.00
n.	PMI, MIP, Funding Fee financed	
o.	Loan amount (add m & n)	80000.00
p.	Cash from/ to Borrower (subtract j, k, l & o from i)	23547.04

VIII. DECLARATIONS

If you answer "Yes" to any questions a through i, please use continuation sheet for explanation.

		Borrower Yes	Borrower No	Co-Borrower Yes	Co-Borrower No
a.	Are there any outstanding judgments against you?		XX		XX
b.	Have you been declared bankrupt within the past 7 years?		XX		XX
c.	Have you had property foreclosed upon or given title or deed in lieu thereof in the last 7 years?		XX		XX
d.	Are you a party to a lawsuit?		XX		XX
e.	Have you directly or indirectly been obligated on any loan which resulted in foreclosure, transfer of title in lieu of foreclosure, or judgment? (This would include such loans as home mortgage loans, SBA loans, home improvement loans, educational loans, manufactured (mobile) home loans, any mortgage, financial obligation, bond, or loan guarantee. If "Yes," provide details, including date, name and address of Lender, FHA or VA case number, if any, and reasons for the action.)		XX		XX
f.	Are you presently delinquent or in default on any Federal debt or any other loan, mortgage, financial obligation, bond, or loan guarantee? If "Yes," give details as described in the preceding question.		XX		XX
g.	Are you obligated to pay alimony, child support, or separate maintenance?		XX		XX
h.	Is any part of the down payment borrowed?		XX		XX
i.	Are you a co-maker or endorser on a note?		XX		XX
j.	Are you a U.S. citizen?	XX		XX	
k.	Are you a permanent resident alien?		XX		XX
l.	Do you intend to occupy the property as your primary residence? If "Yes," complete question m below.	XX		XX	
m.	Have you had an ownership interest in a property in the last three years?		XX		XX
	(1) What type of property did you own -- principal residence (PR), second home (SH), or investment property (IP)?	PR		PR	
	(2) How did you hold title to the home -- solely by yourself (S), jointly with your spouse (SP), or jointly with another person (O)?	SP		SP	

IX. ACKNOWLEDGMENT AND AGREEMENT

The undersigned specifically acknowledge(s) and agree(s) that: (1) the loan requested by this application will be secured by a first mortgage or deed of trust on the property described herein; (2) the property will not be used for any illegal or prohibited purpose or use; (3) all statements made in this application are made for the purpose of obtaining the loan indicated herein; (4) occupation of the property will be as indicated above; (5) verification or reverification of any information contained in the application may be made at any time by the Lender, its agents, successors and assigns, either directly or through a credit reporting agency, from any source named in this application, and the original copy of this application will be retained by the Lender, even if the loan is not approved; (6) the Lender, its agents, successors and assigns will rely on the information contained in the application and I/we have a continuing obligation to amend and/or supplement the information provided in this application if any of the material facts which I/we have represented herein should change prior to closing; (7) in the event my/our payments on the loan indicated in this application become delinquent, the Lender, its agents, successors and assigns, may, in addition to all their other rights and remedies, report my/our name(s) and account information to a credit reporting agency; (8) ownership of the loan may be transferred to successor or assign of the Lender without notice to me and/or the administration of the loan account may be transferred to an agent, successor or assign of the Lender with prior notice to me; (9) the Lender, its agents, successors and assigns make no representations or warranties, express or implied, to the Borrower(s) regarding the property, the condition of the property, or the value of the property.

Certification: I/We certify that the information provided in this application is true and correct as of the date set forth opposite my/our signature(s) on this application and acknowledge my/our understanding that any intentional or negligent misrepresentation(s) of the information contained in this application may result in civil liability and/or criminal penalties including, but not limited to, fine or imprisonment or both under the provisions of Title 18, United States Code, Section 1001, et seq. and liability for monetary damages to the Lender, its agents, successors and assigns, insurers and any other person who may suffer any loss due to reliance upon any misrepresentation which I/we have made on this application.

Borrower's Signature	Date	Co-Borrower's Signature	Date
X		X	

X. INFORMATION FOR GOVERNMENT MONITORING PURPOSES

The following information is requested by the Federal Government for certain types of loans related to a dwelling, in order to monitor the Lender's compliance with equal credit opportunity, fair housing and home mortgage disclosure laws. You are not required to furnish this information, but are encouraged to do so. The law provides that a Lender may neither discriminate on the basis of this information, nor on whether you choose to furnish it. However, if you choose not to furnish it, under Federal regulations this Lender is required to note race and sex on the basis of visual observation or surname. If you do not wish to furnish the above information, please check the box below. (Lender must review the above material to assure that the disclosures satisfy all requirements to which the Lender is subject under applicable state law for the particular type of loan applied for.)

BORROWER

Race/National Origin: [ ] I do not wish to furnish this information
[ ] American Indian or Alaskan Native   [ ] Asian or Pacific Islander   [XX] White, not of Hispanic origin
[ ] Black, not of Hispanic origin   [ ] Hispanic
[ ] Other (specify) _____

Sex: [ ] Female   [XX] Male

CO-BORROWER

Race/National Origin: [ ] I do not wish to furnish this information
[ ] American Indian or Alaskan Native   [ ] Asian or Pacific Islander   [XX] White, not of Hispanic origin
[ ] Black, not of Hispanic origin   [ ] Hispanic
[ ] Other (specify) _____

Sex: [XX] Female   [ ] Male

To be Completed by Interviewer
This application was taken by:
[XX] face-to-face interview
[ ] by mail
[ ] by telephone

Interviewer's Name (print or type)

Interviewer's Signature   Date

Interviewer's Phone Number (incl. area code)
806-352-2265

Name and Address of Interviewer's Employer
First State Bank Happy, Texas
3131 Bell Street, Suite 202
Amarillo, Texas 79106

comparison shop for a loan. One-stop shopping real estate services and federal regulations pertaining to CLOs are discussed in Chapter 20.

On the lender's side, new automated underwriting procedures can shorten loan approvals from weeks to minutes. Automated underwriting also tends to lower the cost of loan application and approval by reducing a lender's time spent on the approval process by as much as 60 percent. Freddie Mac uses a system called *Loan Prospector.* Fannie Mae has a system called *Desktop Underwriter* that reduces approval time to minutes, based on the borrower's credit report, a paycheck stub, and a drive-by appraisal of the property. Complex or difficult mortgages can be processed in less than 72 hours. Through automated underwriting, one of a borrower's biggest headaches in buying a home—waiting for loan approval—is eliminated. In addition, a prospective buyer can strengthen his or her purchase offer by including proof of loan approval.

In Practice   On-line mortgage lenders are putting even more loan choices into buyers' hands. According to a study published in the *Origination News in 2001,* 12 percent of all mortgage originations will take place over the Internet by 2005. Because buyers rely on agents for advice on finding a mortgage, it benefits a licensee to stay informed about the latest Internet resources available from various on-line lenders.

PAYMENT PLANS

Although most mortgage and deed of trust loans are *fully amortized loans,* other payment plans may be more appropriate under certain circumstances—such as the straight payment, the flexible payment, and the balloon payment. These payment plans are illustrated in Figure 16.2.

Fully Amortized Payment   In a **fully amortized loan** payment plan, the mortgagor pays a *constant amount,* usually monthly. The mortgagee credits each payment first to the interest owed and then applies the balance to reduce the principal amount over a term of years. Although the amount of each principal and interest payment is the same, the portion applied toward repayment of the principal grows; and the interest due declines as the unpaid balance of the loan is reduced. At the end of the term (usually 15, 20, or 30 years), the full amount of the principal and all interest due is reduced to zero. Such loans also are called *direct reduction loans.*

MATH CONCEPTS

Amortizing a Loan.
The monthly principal and interest (P&I) payment on a $100,000 loan at 9 percent amortized over 30 years is $805 (see Table 16.1: $100,000 ÷ $1,000 x $8.05.) To determine the principal balance remaining after the first payment, (1) calculate the interest portion of the payment, (2) deduct that amount from the P&I payment, and (3) subtract the resulting principal reduction from the principal balance.

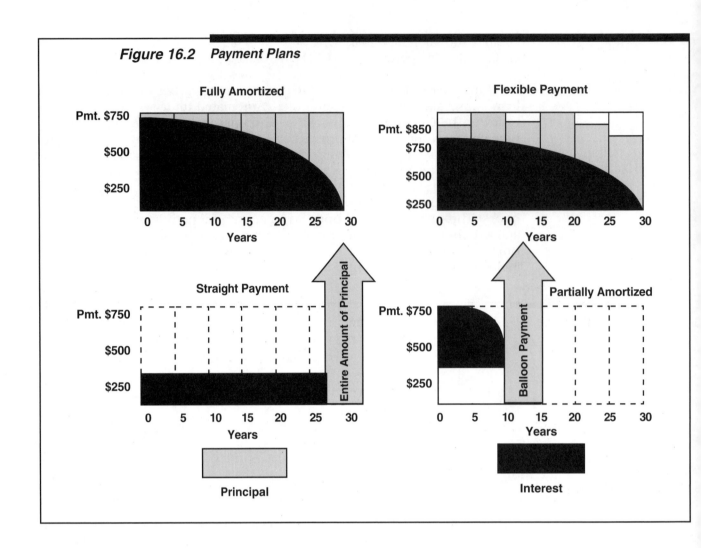

Figure 16.2   **Payment Plans**

To compute one month's interest, use the formula $I = P \times R \times T$, where

I = Interest
P = Principal
R = Rate
T = Time

$$\$100,000 \times .09 \times \tfrac{1}{12} = \$750.00 \text{ interest}$$

To compute the principal portion of the payment:

$$\$805.00 - \$750.00 = \$55.00 \text{ applied to the principal}$$

The principal balance used to calculate the next month's payment is $99,945.00.

$$\$100,000 - \$55.00 = \$99,945.00$$

Most amortized mortgage and deed of trust loans are paid in monthly installments. If the borrower wishes to pay off the loan more quickly and reduce the total interest costs, he may

- pay additional amounts that are applied directly to the principal (with the consent of the lender) *or*
- negotiate a **biweekly payment plan** that calls for 26 half-month payments a year (reducing the principal balance approximately twice each month and resulting in one full month's additional payment each year).

Straight Payment A mortgagor may choose a *straight payment* plan that calls for periodic payments of interest, with the principal to be *paid in full at the end of the loan term.* This is known as a **straight, or term, loan.** Most lenders will require an interest-rate adjustment provision on a long-term loan. Term loans are generally used for home improvement loans, second mortgages, and investor loans rather than for residential first mortgage loans.

Flexible Payment The mortgagor may elect to take advantage of a **flexible-payment loan,** generally used to enable younger buyers and buyers in times of high interest rates to purchase real estate. Under this plan, a mortgagor makes lower monthly payments for the first few years of the loan (typically the first five years) and larger payments for the remainder of the term, when the mortgagor's income is expected to increase.

Balloon Payment When a mortgage or deed of trust loan requires periodic payments that will not fully amortize the amount of the loan by the time the final payment is due, the final payment is larger than the others. This is called a **balloon payment,** and this type of loan is a *partially amortized loan.* For example, the payments on a loan made for $80,000 at 11½ percent interest may be computed on a 30-year amortization schedule but paid over a 20-year term, with a final balloon payment due at the end of the 20th year. In this case, each monthly payment would be $792.24 (the amount taken from a 30-year amortization schedule), with a final balloon payment of $56,340 (the amount of principal still owing after 20 years). It is presumed that if the payments are made promptly, the lender will extend the balloon payment for another limited term. The lender, however, is not legally obligated to grant this extension and can require payment in full when the note is due. A balloon payment is frequently used in seller-financing transactions.

CONVENTIONAL, FHA, AND VA LOANS

Most first mortgage or deed of trust loans advanced for residential purposes are 15-year to 30-year fully amortized loans classified as conventional, FHA, or VA loans. These are discussed in detail in the following subsections.

Conventional Loans A **conventional loan** is one that is not underwritten by a federal agency. Lenders rely primarily on their own appraisal of the security and their own credit reports and information concerning the credit reliability of the prospective borrower. Conventional loans may be "conforming" or "nonconforming." Most conventional loans are *conforming* loans, meeting Fannie Mae and Freddie Mac guidelines so they can easily be sold in the secondary market. *Nonconforming* loans can be made by any lender to be held in its own portfolio or sold to a private mortgage packager. Borrower qualifications for most conventional loans are somewhat more stringent than for FHA or VA loans.

A Credit

> *High* down payment =
> *Low* LTV and *Low* lender
> risk

A buyer's maximum house payment (PITI) for a conventional loan is generally 25 to 28 percent of gross monthly income; total debts cannot exceed 33 to 36 percent, which includes the house payment, all installment and revolving account payments, and child support. Because loan underwriting guidelines can vary, check with a local lender for its particular requirements. A conventional loan calculator is available at www.mortgagequotes.lycos.com/calc.html.

Table 16.1 **Mortgage Factor Chart**

Term Rate	10 Years	15 Years	20 Years	25 Years	30 Years
4	10.13	7.40	6.06	5.28	4.78
4⅛	10.19	7.46	6.13	5.35	4.85
4¼	10.25	7.53	6.20	5.42	4.92
4⅜	10.31	7.59	6.26	5.49	5.00
4½	10.37	7.65	6.33	5.56	5.07
4⅝	10.43	7.72	6.40	5.63	5.15
4¾	10.49	7.78	6.47	5.71	5.22
4⅞	10.55	7.85	6.54	5.78	5.30
5	10.61	7.91	6.60	5.85	5.37
5⅛	10.67	7.98	6.67	5.92	5.45
5¼	10.73	8.04	6.74	6.00	5.53
5⅜	10.80	8.11	6.81	6.07	5.60
5½	10.86	8.18	6.88	6.15	5.68
5⅝	10.92	8.24	6.95	6.22	5.76
5¾	10.98	8.31	7.03	6.30	5.84
5⅞	11.04	8.38	7.10	6.37	5.92
6	11.10	8.44	7.16	6.44	6.00
6⅛	11.16	8.51	7.24	6.52	6.08
6¼	11.23	8.57	7.31	6.60	6.16
6⅜	11.29	8.64	7.38	6.67	6.24
6½	11.35	8.71	7.46	6.75	6.32
6⅝	11.42	8.78	7.53	6.83	6.40
6¾	11.48	8.85	7.60	6.91	6.49
6⅞	11.55	8.92	7.68	6.99	6.57
7	11.61	8.98	7.75	7.06	6.65
7⅛	11.68	9.06	7.83	7.15	6.74
7¼	11.74	9.12	7.90	7.22	6.82
7⅜	11.81	9.20	7.98	7.31	6.91
7½	11.87	9.27	8.05	7.38	6.99
7⅝	11.94	9.34	8.13	7.47	7.08
7¾	12.00	9.41	8.20	7.55	7.16
7⅞	12.07	9.48	8.29	7.64	7.25
8	12.14	9.56	8.37	7.72	7.34
8⅛	12.20	9.63	8.45	7.81	7.43
8¼	12.27	9.71	8.53	7.89	7.52
8⅜	12.34	9.78	8.60	7.97	7.61
8½	12.40	9.85	8.68	8.06	7.69
8⅝	12.47	9.93	8.76	8.14	7.78
8¾	12.54	10.00	8.84	8.23	7.87
8⅞	12.61	10.07	8.92	8.31	7.96
9	12.67	10.15	9.00	8.40	8.05
9⅛	12.74	10.22	9.08	8.48	8.14
9¼	12.81	10.30	9.16	8.57	8.23
9⅜	12.88	10.37	9.24	8.66	8.32
9½	12.94	10.45	9.33	8.74	8.41
9⅝	13.01	10.52	9.41	8.83	8.50
9¾	13.08	10.60	9.49	8.92	8.60
9⅞	13.15	10.67	9.57	9.00	8.69
10	13.22	10.75	9.66	9.09	8.78
10⅛	13.29	10.83	9.74	9.18	8.87
10¼	13.36	10.90	9.82	9.27	8.97
10⅜	13.43	10.98	9.90	9.36	9.06
10½	13.50	11.06	9.99	9.45	9.15
10⅝	13.57	11.14	10.07	9.54	9.25
10¾	13.64	11.21	10.16	9.63	9.34

How To Use This Chart

To use this chart, start by finding the appropriate interest rate. Then follow that row over to the column for the appropriate loan term. This number is the *interest rate factor* required each month to amortize a $1,000 loan. To calculate the principal and interest (PI) payment, multiply the interest rate factor by the number of 1,000s in the total loan.

For example, if the interest rate is 10 percent for a term of 30 years, the interest rate factor is 8.78. If the total loan is $100,000, the loan contains 100 1,000s. Therefore

100 × 8.78 = $878 PI only

To estimate a mortgage loan amount using the amortization chart, divide the PI payment by the appropriate interest rate factor. Using the same facts as in the first example:

$878 ÷ 8.78 = $100 1,000's, or $100,000

Historically, the *loan-to-value ratio (LTV)* on a conventional loan has been 80 percent of the value of the property or less—lower than on FHA-insured or VA-guaranteed loans. The VA guarantees loans up to 100 percent of value; FHA insures loans up to 97 percent. The LTV, the ratio of debt to value of the property, is calculated by dividing the amount of the loan by the value of the property.

MATH CONCEPTS

Determining LTV.
If a property has an appraised value of $100,000, secured by an $80,000 loan, the LTV is 80 percent; $80,000 ÷ $100,000 = 80%.

Private Mortgage Insurance

According to Fannie Mae records, 3%-down loans are foreclosed four times more often than 10%-down loans.

One way a borrower can obtain a loan with a lower down payment is under a **private mortgage insurance** (PMI) program. The borrower purchases insurance from a private mortgage insurance company as additional security to insure the lender against borrower default. LTVs of up to 95 percent of the appraised property value are possible with mortgage insurance. And new offerings through GE Capital and Fannie Mae's Community Home Buyer's Programs include 97 percent loans.

PMI insures a certain percentage of a loan, usually 25 to 30 percent, which limits the lender's exposure to only 70 to 75 percent in the event of a default. On all loans sold to Fannie Mae and Freddie Mac and on all other conventional loans if closed after July 29, 1999, borrowers must be sent an annual notice that they may cancel the PMI when the loan balance is 80 percent or less of the *original value* of the property. (Texas law requires notification when the loan-to-*current value* reaches 80 percent.) Depending on the size of the mortgage and the risk, automatic cancellation is required when the loan reaches 77 to 78 percent of the original property value.

Discount Points

From a borrower's point of view, a deed of trust loan is a means of financing an expenditure; from a lender's point of view, it is an investment. To continually replenish their supplies of funds, lending institutions will often sell the loans to investors instead of holding them for the full term. However, the interest rate that a lender charges for a loan might be less than the *yield* (true rate of return) an investor demands. To make up the difference, the lender charges the borrower **discount points.**

A **point** is *not* 1 percent of the purchase price; a point is 1 percent of the *loan amount*.

FOR EXAMPLE An investor is offered two loans—one made at an interest rate of 10 percent and the other at 10½ percent. If both loans were offered to an investor at the same price, the investor would choose the 10½ percent loan.

Discount points, then, represent the percentage by which the face amount of a mortgage loan is discounted, or reduced, when it is sold to an investor to make its interest rate yield competitive in the current money market. Without this discount, an investor would not be interested in the lower-rate loan. As a general rule of thumb, each point of discount raises the effective yield by ⅛ of 1 percent; the actual amount depends on the term and type of loan obtained.

For the borrower, one discount point equals 1 percent of the loan amount and is charged as prepaid interest at closing. Buyers and sellers negotiate to determine the portion of the points to be paid by each party.

Calculating Discount Points.
A house sells for $100,000, and the borrower seeks an 80 percent LTV loan. Each point charged on the $80,000 loan would be $800 ($80,000 x .01). If the lender charges 3 discount points, the total discount points due to the lender at closing would be $2,400 ($80,000 x .03). The lender's yield would be increased by ⅜% (⅛% × 3 points).

Loan Origination Fee

A **loan origination fee** is a charge made by the lender for the expense involved in taking the loan application and processing and closing the loan. The loan origination fee is usually 1 percent of the loan amount, but the amount can vary with the complexity of the transaction and the supply and demand forces for mortgage money. A loan origination fee is not prepaid interest and is, therefore, collected in addition to any discount points charged on the loan.

FHA-Insured Loans

The Federal Housing Administration (FHA), which operates under the Department of Housing and Urban Development (HUD), neither builds homes nor lends money itself. The common term **FHA loan** refers to a loan that is *insured* by the agency.

The most popular FHA program is Title II, Section 203(b), which provides fixed-interest rate loans for 10 to 30 years on one- to four-family residences. Interest rates are competitive with other types of loans, even though they are high-LTV loans. Four of the technical requirements that must be met before the FHA will insure a loan are summarized below.

1. In addition to paying interest, the borrower is charged *a one-time mortgage insurance premium* for the FHA insurance and *a monthly mortgage insurance premium*. The rate for the one-time, up-front mortgage insurance premium (UFMIP) is 1.5 percent of the loan amount. The UFMIP premium may be paid at closing by the borrower or by someone else, or it may be added to the loan amount. A monthly mortgage insurance premium rate of ½ percent of the base loan amount is collected on a monthly basis (annual premium divided by 12) for all FHA loans except 15-year loans with an LTV ratio less than 90 percent, for which the rate is .25 percent. When homeowners build a 22 percent equity in their homes (based on the original value of the property), the annual premium will be eliminated. Depending on the interest rate and down payment, a borrower can generally eliminate the annual premium by the eleventh year of the loan. FHA will continue to insure the mortgage after the premium has been dropped.
2. FHA regulations set *standards* for type and construction of buildings, quality of neighborhoods, and credit requirements for borrowers.
3. For loans on properties built before 1978, the FHA requires that buyers sign a lead-based-paint notice on or before the date of the sales contract.
4. The mortgaged real estate must be appraised by an *approved FHA appraiser*. The downpayment calculation excludes closing costs and is based on a fixed percentage of the lesser of the property's purchase price or appraised value, which is called *acquisition cost*. Only two LTV calculations apply when figuring an FHA loan amount in Texas:

98.75% for homes $50,000 or less
97.75% for homes over $50,000

A borrower is required to pay at least 3 percent of the acquisition cost in cash at closing toward the downpayment and closing costs (excluding loan discount points, prepaid expenses, or other loan-related expenses). The 3 percent can be a gift from a family member, a grant, bond proceeds, or a combination of these funding sources. FHA single-family loans must include a consumer disclosure (within three days after loan application) that compares the costs of an FHA loan with that of a conventional loan.

Maximum loan calculation notes:

- The maximum FHA loan amount is established by regions.
- For homes less than one year old that were not built to FHA standards and do not carry a ten-year warranty plan, the loan ratio is 90 percent of the appraised value or selling price, whichever is less.
- If the contract purchase price of a property exceeds the FHA-appraised value, the buyer may pay the difference in cash as part of the down payment.

The *203(b) veteran's preference* permits a qualified veteran to make a smaller down payment than would normally be required. Other types of FHA-insured loans include one-year adjustable-rate mortgages, home improvement and rehabilitation loans, loans for the purchase of condominiums, and reverse-annuity mortgages.

FHA loan qualifying. To qualify for an FHA-insured loan, the buyer must have a house payment (PITI) of no more than 29 percent of gross monthly income. The buyer's total debts cannot exceed 41 percent of gross monthly income; included in this amount must be the house payment, installment accounts (ten or more payments remaining), all revolving accounts, and child support payments. FHA qualifying procedures are more lenient than for conventional or VA loans. Automated underwriting systems will usually approve ratios up to 33 percent and 53 percent if credit scores are in the 600s and the buyer has 1½ months of residual cash available after closing. For more information, visit the HUD web site at www.hud.gov/qualify.cfm.

Discount points. The lender of an FHA-insured loan can charge discount points in addition to the 1 percent *loan origination fee.* The payment of points is a matter of negotiation between the seller and the buyer. However, if the seller pays more than 6 percent of the costs normally paid by the buyer (such as discount points, the loan origination fee, the mortgage insurance premium, buydown fees, or other normal buyer-paid closing costs), the lender is to treat such payments as sales concessions, and the price of the property for purposes of the loan will have to be reduced.

Prepayment privileges. When a deed of trust loan is insured by the FHA and the real estate given as security is a single-family dwelling or an apartment building with no more than four units where the owner occupies one of the units, the borrower retains the privilege of prepaying the debt without penalty. The borrower must give the lender a written notice of intention to exercise this privilege at least 30 days before the anticipated prepayment, or the lender has the option of charging up to 30 days' interest. A borrower who pays off an FHA loan may petition to get a partial refund on the "up-front" mortgage insurance paid at closing.

Assumption rules. The assumption rules for FHA-insured loans vary, depending on the date that the loan was originated.

- FHA-insured loans originated prior to December 1986 generally have no restrictions on their assumption; the seller remains liable until the loan is paid off unless released by the lender or FHA.
- For FHA-insured loans originated between December 1, 1986, and December 15, 1989, a creditworthiness review of the person proposing to assume is required. If the original loan was for the purchase of a principal residence, this review is required if the assumption occurs during the first 12 months of the loan's origination or assumption. If the original loan was for the purchase of an investment property, the review is required if the assumption occurs during the first 24 months of the loan's origination or assumption. The seller remains liable for five years unless released by the lender or FHA.
- For FHA-insured loans originated December 15, 1989, and thereafter, there are no assumptions without complete buyer qualification, and there are no longer any investor loans. All FHA loans made under the 203(b) program will be for owner-occupied properties only. The seller is released of all liability.

VA-Guaranteed (GI) Loans

The Department of Veterans Affairs (VA) is authorized to guarantee loans to purchase or construct homes for eligible veterans and their spouses (including unremarried spouses of veterans whose deaths were service-related). The VA also guarantees loans to purchase manufactured homes and land on which to place them. A veteran who meets any of the time-in-service criteria shown in Table 16.2 is eligible for a VA loan. VA-guaranteed loans assist veterans in financing the purchase of homes with little or no down payments. Residential property must be owner-occupied.

Table 16.2	VA Requirements for Eligibility		
Period of Service		**Dates**	**Minimum Service**
WW II		9/16/40–7/25/47	90 days
Peacetime		7/26/47–6/26/50	181 days
Korean War		6/27/50–1/31/55	90 days
Post-Korean Era		2/1/55–8/4/64	181 days
Vietnam War		8/5/64–5/7/75	90 days
Post-Vietnam Era		5/8/75–9/7/80	181 days
Enlisted Personnel		after 9/7/80	24 months
Commissioned Officers		after 10/16/81	24 months
Persian Gulf War		after 8/2/90	24 months
If on active duty			90 days
Reserves and National Guard		after 10/28/92	6 years
If veteran is still on active duty			181 days

Table 16.3   *VA Loans: Guaranty Sliding Scale*

Loan Amount	Guaranty
$45,000 and less	50% of loan
$45,001–$56,250	$22,500
$56,251–$90,000	40% of loan
$90,001–$144,000	$36,000
$144,001 and up	25% of loan up to $50,750

Like the term *FHA loan, VA loan* is something of a misnomer. The VA normally does not lend money; it guarantees loans made by lending institutions approved by the agency. Therefore, the term **VA loan** refers to a loan that is not made by the agency, but *guaranteed by it.*

There is no VA limit on the amount of the loan a veteran can obtain; that is determined by the lender. The VA simply limits the amount of the loan it will guarantee. Because Ginnie Mae requires at least a 25 percent guaranty from the VA for a loan to be included in a Ginnie Mae security, most lenders will follow that guideline in making a VA-guaranteed loan to enable them to participate in the secondary market. Table 16.3 shows the VA Guaranty Sliding Scale; the amount of the guaranty increases with the amount of the loan and combines fixed dollar amounts and percentages of loan amounts. On a $95,000 VA loan, $36,000 is the amount of the guaranty—the amount the lender would receive from the VA in case of a default and foreclosure if the sale did not bring enough to cover the outstanding balance. For example, if the $95,000 loan were in default, the property could sell at foreclosure for as little as $59,000 ($95,000 – $36,000), and the lender would recoup the full value of the loan (disregarding the costs of foreclosure).

To determine what portion of a mortgage loan the VA will guarantee, the veteran must apply for a *certificate of eligibility.* This certificate does not mean that the veteran will automatically receive a mortgage. It merely sets forth the maximum guaranty to which the veteran is entitled. For individuals with full eligibility, no down payment is required for a loan up to the maximum guaranty limit.

The VA also issues a *certificate of reasonable value* (CRV) for the property being purchased, stating its current market value based on a VA-approved appraisal. The CRV places a ceiling on the amount of a VA loan allowed for the property. If the purchase price is greater than the amount cited in the CRV, the veteran must pay the difference in cash.

The VA purchaser pays a *loan origination fee* (up to 1 percent) to the lender, as well as a *funding fee* to the Department of Veterans Affairs. Funding fees to a veteran with active service getting a first-time VA loan vary from 2 percent with less than a 5 percent down payment to 1.25 percent with a 10 percent or more down payment—on subsequent VA loans, 3 percent for no down payment to 1.25 percent with a 10 percent or more down payment. Different funding fees apply to National Guard and Reserves (2.75 percent to 2 percent on first use; 3 percent to 2 percent on subsequent use) and persons refinancing loans (.50 percent). The funding fee can be added to the loan amount—except on VA refinance loans. Reasonable *discount points* may be charged on a VA-guaranteed loan. Either the veteran or the seller may pay the points, but they may not be financed in the loan.

Table 16.4 is a comparison of conventional, FHA, and VA loan programs.

VA loan qualifying. According to the VA, two methods must be employed to determine a veteran's ability to qualify for a loan—*debt-to-income ratio* and *residual income*. The combined total of monthly debts shall not exceed 41 percent of the veteran-borrower's gross monthly income; debts include the house payment, all installment accounts, all revolving accounts, minimum payments on paid-out revolving accounts, child support, and child care. *Residual income* is defined as the amount of monthly income remaining after all the debts listed above, income tax, Social Security tax, and maintenance and utilities are deducted. A regional chart showing residual incomes based on family size and loan amounts can be obtained from a local lender. For more information on VA loans, visit the web site at www.homeloans.va.gov

Prepayment privileges. As with an FHA loan, the borrower on a VA-guaranteed loan can prepay the debt at any time without penalty. The borrower must give the lender a written notice of intention to exercise this privilege at least 30 days before the anticipated prepayment, or the lender has the option of charging up to 30 days' interest.

Assumption rules. VA-guaranteed loans can be assumed by purchasers who do not qualify as veterans, and the balance of the veteran's entitlement will still be available for a new VA-guaranteed loan. However, if the seller-veteran wishes to have the full guaranty entitlement reinstated, an assumption must be by another qualified veteran who agrees to substitute his or her eligibility, or the old loan must be paid off. The assumption rules for VA-guaranteed loans vary, depending on the date that the loan was originated. For example:

- For loans made prior to March 1, 1988, the veteran-seller could sell on assumption without prior approval from the VA and remain liable for loan repayment or require the purchaser to be approved by the VA and obtain a release from further liability on the loan.
- For loans made after March 1, 1988, the assumption borrower must have prior approval from the VA or the loan holder. The original veteran is given a release of liability. However, this procedure does not restore the veteran's entitlement to be used on another loan.

Farm Service Agency

The **Farm Service Agency (FSA),** formerly the Farmer's Home Administration (FmHA), is a federal agency of the Department of Agriculture. The FSA offers direct and guaranteed farm ownership and operating loan programs to farmers who are temporarily unable to obtain private, commercial credit. Often, these are beginning farmers who cannot qualify for conventional loans because they have insufficient net worth. Under the guaranteed-loan program, the agency guarantees loans made by conventional agricultural lenders for up to 95 percent of principal. The lender may sell the loan to a third party; however, the lender is always responsible for servicing the loan.

Table 16.4 *Comparison of Loan Programs*

Conventional	Federal Housing Administration	Department of Veterans Affairs
1. Financing is available to veterans and nonveterans.	1. Financing is available to veterans and nonveterans.	1. Financing available only to veterans and certain unremarried widows and widowers.
2. Financing for 1-family to 4-family dwellings; owner-occupied or investor loans.	2. Financing programs are for owner-occupied (1-family to 4-family), residential dwellings.	2. Financing is limited to owner-occupied residential (1-family to 4-family) dwellings; must sign occupancy certificate.
3. Generally requires a larger down payment than FHA or VA.	3. Requires a larger down payment than VA.	3. Normally does not require down payment.
4. Most lenders require appraisal by a licensed or certified appraiser, even though not required if less than $250,000.	4. Like VA, there are prescribed valuation procedures for the approved appraisers to follow.	4. Methods of valuation differ—VA issues a certificate of reasonable value (CRV).
5. Maximum loan based on appraisal valuation; buyer may pay in cash the amount exceeding appraised value.	5. FHA valuation sets the maximum loan FHA will insure but does not limit the sales price.	5. With regard to home loans, the law requires that the VA loan not exceed the appraised value of the home.
6. No prepayment penalty if interest is 10% or more, sold to Fannie Mae or Freddie Mac after 9/79 or pooled by Ginnie Mae.	6. No prepayment penalty.	6. No prepayment penalty.
7. On foreclosure, the lender receives the amount of insurance coverage and sells the property.	7. On default, foreclosure, and claim, the FHA lender usually gets U.S. debentures.	7. Following default, foreclosure and claim, the lender usually receives cash (if VA elects to take the house).
8. Insures loans over 80% LTV with private mortgage insurance (PMI). PMI may be paid by buyer in cash or added to note.	8. Insures the loan by way of mutual mortgage insurance; premiums paid by buyer or seller. If by buyer, may be paid in cash or added to note.	8. Guarantees loans according to a sliding scale.
9. Second-lien financing is permitted concurrently with first lien as long as minimum down payment requirements are met.	9. No secondary financing is permitted until after closing.	9. Secondary financing is permitted in exceptional cases.
10. Buyer may pay loan origination fee and discount points.	10. Buyer pays a 1% loan origination fee.	10. Buyer may pay discount points but cannot finance them in the loan; he or she may pay up to 1% in loan origination fees.
11. Loans are generally nonassumable; a lender may permit assumption with a qualified assumptor.	11. Loans made prior to 12/1/86 are fully assumable; seller remains liable until the loan is paid off. Loans made between 12/1/86 and 12/15/89 are fully assumable after 12 months on owner-occupied loans; seller remains liable for 5 years. Loans made since 12/15/89 require prior approval of assumptor; seller is released from liability.	11. VA loan can be assumed without VA approval for loans made prior to 3/1/88; otherwise, approval is required.
	12. An up-front mortgage insurance premium of 1.5% may be paid by the borrower or someone else or added to the loan. Initially, a ½% monthly premium is also charged.	12. For loans originated after 3/1/88, release of liability is automatic if VA approves the assumption.
		13. A funding fee from 1.25% to 3% must be paid to VA in addition to other fees. It may be paid by the seller or buyer. If paid by the buyer, it may be paid in cash or added to the note. The note cannot exceed $203,000.

In Practice	Regulations and requirements regarding conventional, FHA, VA, and FSA loans change frequently. Check with local lenders for current information regarding these loan programs.

TEXAS LOAN PROGRAMS

Department of Housing and Community Affairs

Several programs are available through the **Texas Department of Housing and Community Affairs (TDHCA)** to finance the acquisition, construction, or rehabilitation of housing that meets the needs of low- and moderate-income persons and families. By generating funds through bond issues, the Housing Finance Division helps lower-income working families buy homes through two programs:

1. The *Texas First-Time Homebuyer Program* channels below-market interest rate mortgage money through participating Texas lending institutions to very-low- to moderate-income families who are purchasing their first home or who have not owned a home in the past three years.
2. The *Down Payment Assistance Program* helps very-low- and low-income families purchase a home by providing an interest-free loan ranging from $5,000 to $10,000—depending on the county in which the property is located and the individual borrower qualifications. This loan is for downpayment and eligible closing costs, and it creates a second lien on the property. The borrower repays the loan when the home is either sold or refinanced or when the first lien is paid off. Funding for this program is limited and may not be available at all times.

For more information about these programs and others available through the TDHCA, write to the Texas Department of Housing and Community Affairs, 811 Barton Springs Road, Austin, TX 78704; call 1-800-792-1119; or visit the web site at www.tdhca.state.tx.us.

Texas Veteran's Land Board

The Texas Veteran's Land Board (a division of the General Land Office of Texas) administers a program to assist Texas veterans in purchasing a principal residence and/or land and in financing home improvements. To qualify as a *Texas veteran*, a loan applicant must have entered the service from Texas or must have lived in Texas for at least two years preceding the filing of the loan application or must be the unmarried surviving spouse of a qualified veteran who died in the line of duty or is missing in action.

Veteran's Housing Assistance Program. The *Veteran's Housing Assistance Program (VHAP)* provides funds to purchase a principal residence, the veteran's homestead. The home can be either an existing home or a new home. Although the Veteran's Land Board has set no limit on the amount of acreage bought with the home, lenders may have a maximum number of acres they will finance. Currently, the maximum VHAP loan is $150,000. If additional loan funds are needed, the Texas veteran can couple a loan made under the VHAP with a new conventional, FHA, or VA loan. Such a loan package encompasses two notes of equal dignity, which means that neither is a first lien or a second lien. Both notes are secured by a single deed of trust. One note is payable to the VHAP, and the companion note is payable to the participating lender. However, the borrower makes only one monthly payment to the participating lender, which services the loan for VHAP.

VHAP loans are funded from the proceeds of bond sales, and the interest rates on VHAP loans are based on the yield of the bonds. Interest rates on VHAP loans are traditionally below other mortgage interest rates. However, different bond series may bear different rates of interest, and in a declining market, the interest on a VHAP loan could be considerably higher than the rate on a companion loan. Although no loan discount fees are charged, a loan participation fee must be paid by the seller. The borrower pays a 1 percent loan origination fee and a nominal application fee. The amount of down payment and the underwriting standards are governed by the type of participating loan. For example, the VA requires no down payment, and a conventional lender might require a 10 percent down payment.

When the market interest rates on home loans are above the rate charged by VHAP and the buyer is qualified to use this program, it should be investigated.

Veteran's Land Program. Another program administered by the Texas Veteran's Land Board provides a maximum of $40,000 to qualified Texas veterans for the purchase of land. The veteran selects a tract of land of at least five acres and files the required application and contract of sale with the land board. After an appraisal and loan processing, the land board pays the seller cash for the tract of land and simultaneously sells it to the veteran buyer on a contract for deed. The guidelines for this program are subject to change, but currently the veteran buyer must make a 5 percent cash down payment plus pay nominal closing costs, as set by the Land Board.

A veteran who has already used the Texas Veteran's Land Program for a land purchase may also apply for a Veteran's Housing Assistance Program loan.

Home Improvement Loan Program. In addition to the two loans discussed above, a veteran is permitted to borrow up to $25,000 for 20 years on a home improvement loan. Land Board guidelines are subject to change, and these programs are subject to the availability of funds. In Texas, call 1-800-252-VETS (1-800-252-8387) or visit the web site at www.glo.state.tx.us for up-to-date information.

OTHER FINANCING TECHNIQUES

Because borrowers often have different needs, a variety of other financing techniques have been created. Still other techniques apply to various types of collateral. Some of these special-purpose financing techniques will be discussed in this section. To avoid unexpected results, both the licensee and borrower must understand the long-term effect of a loan being considered.

Adjustable-Rate Mortgages (ARMs)

Adjustable-rate mortgages (ARMs) are originated at one rate of interest, with the rate fluctuating up or down during the loan term based on a certain economic indicator. Because the interest may change, so may the mortgagor's loan payments. The amount of interest-rate adjustment is governed by the movement of an index, such as Treasury notes or bills, that is beyond the control of the lender. Details of how, when, and how much the interest rate will change are included in the note. A *convertible feature* on most ARMs allows a borrower to convert to a fixed-rate loan during specified periods of the loan.

FOR EXAMPLE An adjustable-rate loan starts at 8 percent a year (which would be lower than a fixed-rate loan available at that time). The note states that the lender may adjust that rate no more often than once a year (the *adjustment period*) and by no more than 2 percent each year (the *periodic rate cap*). The *aggregate rate cap* provides for no more than a 5 percent increase/decrease over the 30-year term of the loan. Thus, the 8 percent loan could go no higher than 13 percent, no matter what happened to the lender's cost of money. And unless the loan terms stipulated a specific floor for the interest rate, it could go as low as 3 percent.

In times of rising interest rates, ARMs allow the lender to keep a loan profitable over the length of its term; in times of falling interest rates, the mortgagor can take advantage of lower mortgage rates without refinancing the loan. Lenders favor loans that do not have fixed interest rates—because with fixed-rate loans, they are making long-term loans based on short-term deposits. Even if a traditional fixed-rate loan is available, some borrowers choose the flexible-rate loan because the initial rate is generally lower and the borrower may believe there is a greater chance for long-term rates to decrease rather than increase.

Buydown Mortgages

With a **buydown mortgage,** the interest rate starts well below the market rate. The lender charges a buydown fee, which pays a portion of the mortgage loan interest in advance for the purpose of temporarily reducing the interest rate. The buydown fee is like a loan discount fee in that it increases the lender's yield on a loan. Typical buydown arrangements provide for a reduced interest rate over the first one to two years of the loan term and generally do not involve deferred interest or negative amortization.

FOR EXAMPLE A homebuilder wishes to stimulate sales by offering a lower-than-market rate. Or a first-time homebuyer may have difficulty qualifying for a loan at the prevailing rates, and relatives or the sellers want to help the buyer qualify. If the loan market interest rate is 10 percent, a "2-1" buydown would result in first-year loan payments at 8 percent interest (10 percent minus 2 percent); the second year, at 9 percent; the third and subsequent years, at 10 percent.

Purchase-Money Mortgages (Deeds of Trust)

A **purchase-money mortgage** is a note and deed of trust *created at the time of purchase*. The term is used in two ways: First, it may refer to *any* security instrument originating at the time of sale. More often, it refers to the instrument given by the purchaser to a seller who "takes back" a note for part or all of the purchase price. It may be a first or a junior lien, depending on whether prior mortgage liens exist. In the event of a foreclosure, a purchase-money deed of trust is valid against the homestead.

FOR EXAMPLE A buyer wants to purchase a property for $200,000. He has $40,000 for a down payment and agrees to assume the existing mortgage of $80,000. The owner agrees to take back a purchase-money second mortgage in the amount of $80,000. At closing, the buyer will execute a note and deed of trust in favor of the owner.

Equity Loans

Equity loans were first made available to Texas citizens on January 1, 1998, following a constitutional amendment to Texas homestead laws. In an equity loan, the lender agrees to make a loan based on the amount of equity in a borrower's home. It allows the homeowner to use the funds that result from rising home prices and the first-loan paydown. Equity loans are popular as a source of funds for home improvement, college expenses, new business start-ups, and additional real estate investment.

Texas equity loans have many protective restrictions for home owners, only a few of which are given here

- The maximum loan-to-value ratio is 80 percent, closing costs cannot exceed 3 percent, and no negative amortization can occur.
- A decrease in market value cannot trigger loan acceleration, and prepayment penalties are prohibited.
- In the event of default on the equity loan, the lender must pursue a judicial foreclosure; and the loan is nonrecourse (there is no personal liability beyond the homestead property).
- Only one equity loan can be in place at a time, and only one equity loan can be made in a given year.
- An equity loan cannot be closed sooner than 12 days after loan application, and the owner has a 3-day right of rescission after the credit has been extended.
- If the lender fails to comply with any of the detailed technical requirements for making an equity loan, the lender will forfeit all principal and interest on that loan.

Reverse-Annuity Mortgages

Reverse-annuity mortgages (RAMs) were made available to citizens of Texas on January 1, 1998, following the November 1997 constitutional amendment to the Texas homestead laws. As revised by constitutional amendments in 1999, RAMs enable homeowners who are 62 years old or older to borrow against the equity in their homes and receive periodic payments needed to help meet living costs. The loan balance of the reverse mortgage increases as funds are advanced from the lender and as interest and other charges accrue. No repayment will be due on the funds advanced until

- the property is sold;
- the borrowers move from the home for longer than 12 months without prior approval from the lender;
- all borrowers have died; *or*
- the borrower defaults on any of the terms of the deed of trust, commits fraud in connection with the loan, or fails to maintain the priority of the lender's lien.

The lender cannot require repayment from any asset other than the home, and the obligation to repay the loan is limited to the market value of the home without recourse for personal liability against the owner.

Shared-Appreciation Mortgages (SAMs, Deeds of Trust)

With a **shared-appreciation mortgage** (SAM), the lender originates a deed of trust loan at a favorable interest rate (several points below the current rate) in return for a guaranteed share of the gain (if any) the borrower realizes when the property is sold. SAMs are primarily made to developers of large real estate projects.

Package Mortgages (Deeds of Trust)

A **package mortgage** includes not only the real estate but also all personal property and appliances installed on the premises. In recent years, this kind of loan has been used extensively to finance furnished condominium units. Package loans usually include furniture; drapes; carpets; and the kitchen range, refrigerator, washer, dryer, and other appliances as part of the sales price of the home. A deed of trust may serve as a security agreement on the personal property and fixtures to be placed in or attached to the real property. Otherwise, the Texas Business and Commerce Code (described in Chapter 11) governs the pledging of personal property, with a UCC financing statement to secure the loan.

Blanket Mortgages (Deeds of Trust)

A **blanket mortgage** or deed of trust pledges *more than one parcel or lot.* It is usually used to finance subdivision developments; however, it can finance the purchase of improved properties or consolidate loans as well. A blanket loan usually includes a *partial release clause* that permits the borrower to obtain the release of any one lot or parcel from the lien by paying a specified amount of the loan. The lender issues a partial release for each parcel as it is released from the mortgage lien. The release form includes a provision that the lien will continue to cover all unreleased lots.

Wraparound Loan

A **wraparound loan** enables a borrower to obtain additional financing from a second lender *without paying off the first loan.* The second lender gives the borrower a new, increased loan at a higher interest rate and assumes payment of the existing loan. The total amount of the new loan includes the existing loan as well as the additional funds needed by the borrower. The borrower makes payments to the new lender on the larger loan, and the new lender makes payments on the original loan out of the borrower's payments. The buyer should require a protective clause in the loan documents granting him or her the right to make payments directly to the original lender in the event of a potential default on the original loan by the second lender.

FOR EXAMPLE A buyer purchases a property for $100,000 with $15,000 down. The seller, acting as a lender, gives the buyer a wraparound note for $85,000 at 13 percent, and the buyer makes payments of $920.83 to the seller. The seller's original $50,000 mortgage at 10 percent has payments of $438.79. The seller continues to make those payments to the original lender and realizes a net monthly income of $482.04 ($920.83 – $438.79).

A wraparound loan is possible only if the original loan documents permit it. A due-on-sale clause (alienation clause) in the original deed of trust may prevent a sale with a wraparound loan.

Open-End Mortgages (Deeds of Trust)

An **open-end mortgage** or deed of trust loan secures a *note* executed by the borrower to the lender, as well as any future *advances* of funds made by the lender to the borrower. The interest rate on the initial amount borrowed is fixed, but interest on future advances may be at the market rate then in effect. Often a less costly alternative to a home improvement loan, this financing technique allows the borrower to "open" the mortgage or deed of trust to increase the debt to its original amount, or the amount stated in the note, after the debt has been reduced by payments over a period of time. The mortgage usually states the maximum amount that can be secured, the terms and conditions under which the loan can be opened, and the provisions for repayment.

Construction Loans

A **construction loan** is made to *finance the construction of improvements* on real estate (homes, apartments, office buildings, and so forth). Under a construction loan, the lender commits the full amount of the loan but disburses the funds throughout the construction period. These payments are known as *draws*. Draws are made to the general contractor or the owner for that part of the construction work that has been completed since the previous payment. Prior to each payment, the lender inspects the work. The general contractor must provide the lender with adequate waivers releasing all mechanics' lien rights for the work covered by the payments.

This kind of loan generally bears a higher-than-market interest rate because of the risks assumed by the lender. These risks include the inadequate release of mechanics' liens, possible delays in completing the building, or the financial failure of the contractor or subcontractors. Construction loans are generally *short-term* or *interim financing*. The borrower is expected to arrange for a permanent loan (also known as a *takeout loan*) that will repay or "take out" the construction financing lender when the work is completed.

Sale and Leaseback

Sale-and-leaseback arrangements are used to finance large commercial or industrial properties. The land and building, usually used by the seller for business purposes, are sold to an investor, such as an insurance company. The real estate is then leased back by the buyer (the investor) to the seller, who continues to conduct business on the property as a tenant. The buyer becomes the lessor, and the original owner becomes the lessee. This enables a business firm that has money invested in a plant to free that money so it can be used as working capital.

Contract for Deed (Installment Contract)

As discussed in Chapter 12, a **contract for deed** can be effectively used when mortgage financing is unavailable or too expensive or when the purchaser has insufficient down payment. The Texas Veteran's Land Board sells land through its Veteran's Land Program with a contract for deed. Title to property purchased on a contract for deed normally does not transfer to the purchaser until the full price has been paid.

In Practice

When complex financing situations exist, a real estate broker should advise parties to consult with legal and tax experts.

GOVERNMENT INFLUENCE IN MORTGAGE LENDING

Aside from FHA-insured and VA-guaranteed loan programs, the federal government influences mortgage lending through the Federal Reserve System as well as through various federal agencies, such as the Farm Service Agency. It also deals in the secondary mortgage market through Ginnie Mae.

Federal Reserve System

The **Federal Reserve System (the "Fed"),** the nation's central bank, operates to maintain sound credit conditions, help counteract inflationary and deflationary trends, and create a favorable economic climate. The Federal Reserve System divides the country into 12 federal reserve districts, each served by a federal reserve bank. All nationally chartered banks must join the Federal Reserve and purchase stock in its district reserve banks.

The Fed regulates the flow of money and interest rates in the marketplace indirectly by controlling *reserve requirements* and *discount rates* for member banks and by its *open market operations.*

Reserve. The Federal Reserve requires that each member bank keep a certain amount of its assets on hand as reserve funds, unavailable for loans or any other use. This requirement not only protects customer deposits but also provides a means of manipulating the flow of cash in the money market.

In setting its reserve requirements, the Federal Reserve in effect establishes the amount of money that member banks can use to make loans. When the reserve requirement is increased and the amount of money available for lending decreases, interest rates (the amount lenders charge for the use of their money) rise. By causing interest rates to rise, the government can slow down an overactive economy, limiting the number of loans that would have been directed toward major purchases of goods and services. The opposite is also true: By decreasing the reserve requirements, the Fed can encourage more lending, causing the amount of money circulated in the marketplace to rise and interest rates to drop.

Discount rates. Federal Reserve member banks are permitted to borrow money from the district reserve banks to maintain their liquidity but not to expand their lending operations. The interest rate charged by the district banks for the use of this money is called the *discount rate.* This rate is the basis on which banks determine the percentage rate of interest they will charge their loan customers. The *prime rate*, the short-term interest rate charged to a bank's largest, most creditworthy customers, is strongly influenced by the Fed's discount rate. In turn, the prime rate is often the basis for determining a bank's interest rates on other loans, including mortgages. In theory, when the Federal Reserve discount rate is high, bank interest rates are high, fewer loans will be made, and less money will circulate in the marketplace. Conversely, a lower discount rate results in lower interest rates, more bank loans, and more money in circulation.

Open market operations. The Fed's open market operations encompass the movement of cash into or out of the commercial banks through the buying or selling of government bonds. When the Fed buys bonds, the banks receive an influx of cash that can be used to make more loans and thus lift the economy.

The Secondary Market

In addition to the *primary mortgage market*, where loans are originated, there is a **secondary mortgage market.** Here, loans are bought and sold only after they have been closed and funded by a primary mortgage market lender. Lenders routinely sell loans to avoid interest rate risks and to realize profits on the sales. This secondary market activity helps lenders raise capital to continue making mortgage loans. Secondary market activity is especially desirable when money is in short supply; it stimulates both the housing construction market and the primary mortgage market by expanding the types of loans available.

When a loan is sold, the original lender may continue to collect the payments from the borrower. The lender then passes the payments along to the investor who purchased the loan and charges the investor a fee for servicing the loan.

Warehousing agencies purchase a number of mortgage loans and assemble them into packages called *pools*. Securities that represent shares in these pooled mortgages are then sold to investors. Loans are eligible for sale to the secondary market only when the collateral, borrower, and documentation meet certain requirements to provide a degree of safety for the investors. The major secondary market entities are discussed in the following paragraphs.

Fannie Mae. Chartered as the Federal National Mortgage Association (FNMA), **Fannie Mae** is a privately owned corporation that issues its own common stock and provides a secondary market for mortgage loans—conventional, FHA, and VA loans. Fannie Mae will buy individual loans or *pools* of mortgages from a lender in exchange for *mortgage-backed securities*, which the lender may keep or sell. Fannie Mae guarantees payment of all interest and principal to the holder of the securities. Fannie Mae's mission is to increase the availability and affordability of homes for low-, moderate-, and middle-income Americans. For more information, visit the web site at www.fanniemae.com.

 WWWeb.Link
www.fanniemae.com

Ginnie Mae. Chartered as the Government National Mortgage Association (GNMA), **Ginnie Mae** is a wholly-owned corporation within the Department of Housing and Urban Development (HUD). Ginnie Mae guarantees investment securities issued by private institutions (such as banks and mortgage companies) and backed by pools of FHA, VA, and FSA mortgage loans. The *Ginnie Mae pass-through certificate* is a security interest in a pool of mortgages that provides for a monthly "pass-through" of principal and interest payments directly to the certificate holder. The certificates are guaranteed by Ginnie Mae and backed by the full faith and credit of the United States.

Under its Targeted Lending Initiative, Ginnie Mae provides financial incentives to lenders to help raise homeownership levels in selected urban areas. To increase lender activity and expand the availability of mortgage capital, Ginnie Mae reduces its guaranty fee on loans made in traditionally underserved areas in one of 72 designated communities around the nation. For more information about Ginnie Mae, visit the web site at www.ginniemae.gov.

 WWWeb.Link
www.ginniemae.gov

Freddie Mac. Chartered as the Federal Home Loan Mortgage Corporation (FHLMC), **Freddie Mac** is a private corporation that provides a secondary market for conventional loans primarily. Freddie Mac has the authority to purchase mortgages, pool them, and sell bonds in the open market with the mortgages as security. Note, however, that FHLMC does not guarantee payment of Freddie Mac mortgages.

Most lenders use the standardized forms and follow the guidelines issued by Freddie Mac because use of FHLMC forms is mandatory for lenders who wish to sell mortgages in the agency's secondary mortgage market. The standardized documents include loan applications, credit reports, and appraisal forms. The Freddie Mac web address is www.freddiemac.com.

Private mortgage packagers. *Private mortgage packagers* also purchase and pool mortgages from loan originators selling to the secondary market. Some specialize in areas not serviced by Fannie Mae, Freddie Mac, or Ginnie Mae, such as jumbo loans with balances that exceed limits set by the other secondary markets.

In Practice Because real estate mortgage loans are now traded on the stock exchanges as **mortgage-backed securities,** interest rates and loan discount rates are extremely sensitive to the pressures of the money markets. Now loan discounts can change significantly during the course of a business day, whereas they once remained relatively stable for weeks or even months at a time.

FINANCING LEGISLATION

The federal government regulates the lending practices of mortgage lenders through several pieces of legislation, among them the Truth-in-Lending Act, the Equal Credit Opportunity Act, the Community Reinvestment Act, and the Real Estate Settlement Procedures Act. The Federal Reserve is responsible for supervision of the first three laws; HUD administers the Real Estate Settlement Procedures Act.

Regulation Z (Truth-in-Lending) **Regulation Z** of the *Truth-in-Lending Act* requires that credit institutions inform borrowers of the true cost of obtaining credit. Its purpose is to permit borrowers to compare the costs of various lenders and avoid the uninformed use of credit. Regulation Z applies when credit is extended to individuals for personal, family, or household uses and the amount of credit is $25,000 or less. Regardless of the amount, however, *Regulation Z always applies when a credit transaction is secured by a residence.* The regulation does not apply to business or commercial loans or to agricultural loans over $25,000.

Regulation Z mandates that the customer be fully informed of all finance charges and the true annual interest rate before a transaction is consummated. The finance charges disclosed must include the costs that are incurred in a transaction *solely* because there is a loan involved—such as loan origination fees, finders' fees, service charges, loan insurance or guaranty fees, and points, as well as interest. In the case of a mortgage loan made to finance the purchase of a dwelling, the lender must compute and disclose the annual percentage rate (APR) but does not have to indicate the total interest payable during the term of the loan (although most standard Regulation Z disclosure forms do include the "total finance charge"). The lender does not have to include as part of the finance charge actual costs such as title fees, legal fees, appraisal fees, credit reports, survey fees, and closing expenses.

Three-day right of rescission. In most consumer credit transactions covered by Regulation Z, the borrower has three days in which to rescind the transaction by merely notifying the lender. However, this right of rescission does not apply to residential first mortgage loans that finance the acquisition or initial construction of a dwelling or to loans carried by a seller who does not make more than five loans a year involving a dwelling as security. Junior liens against real estate are subject to the right of rescission.

Advertising. Regulation Z provides strict regulation of real estate advertisements that include mortgage financing terms. General phrases like "liberal terms available" may be used; however, if details are given, they must comply with this act. The APR—which includes all charges rather than the interest rate alone—must be stated.

Specific credit terms, such as the down payment, monthly payment, dollar amount of the finance charge, or term of the loan, may not be advertised unless the following information is set forth as well: cash price; required down payment; number, amount, and due dates of all payments; and annual percentage rate. The total of all payments to be made over the term of the mortgage also must be specified unless the advertised credit refers to a first mortgage or trust deed to finance acquisition of a dwelling.

Penalties. Regulation Z imposes penalties for noncompliance. A fine of up to $10,000 may be imposed for engaging in an unfair or deceptive practice. The penalty for violation of an administrative order enforcing Regulation Z is $10,000 for each day the violation continues. In addition, a creditor may be liable to a consumer for twice the amount of the finance charge, for a minimum of $100 and a maximum of $1,000, plus court costs, attorney fees, and any actual damages. Willful violation is a misdemeanor punishable by a fine of up to $5,000 or one year's imprisonment, or both.

Federal Equal Credit Opportunity Act

The federal *Equal Credit Opportunity Act* (ECOA), discussed in Chapter 6, prohibits lenders and others who grant or arrange credit to consumers from discriminating against credit applicants on the basis of race, color, religion, national origin, sex, marital status, age (provided the applicant is of legal age), or dependency on public assistance. In addition, lenders and other creditors must inform all rejected credit applicants, in writing, of the principal reasons why credit was denied or terminated.

Real Estate Settlement Procedures Act

The federal *Real Estate Settlement Procedures Act* (RESPA) was created to ensure that the buyer and seller in a residential real estate transaction involving a new first mortgage loan have knowledge of all settlement costs. This important federal law will be discussed in detail in Chapter 20.

Community Reinvestment Act

As discussed in Chapter 6, the *Community Reinvestment Act* ensures that financial institutions meet their communities' needs for low- and moderate-income housing.

Texas Security Laws

The *Texas Security Laws* include provisions to control and regulate the offering and sale of securities. In some instances, a real estate syndication might actually be selling securities instead of interests in real estate. To protect the public, who may be solicited to participate but may not be sophisticated investors, real estate securities must be registered with state officials and/or with the federal Securities & Exchange Commission when they meet the defined conditions of a public offering. The number of prospects solicited, the total number of investors or participants, the financial background and sophistication of the investors, and the value or price per unit of investment are pertinent facts. Salespersons of such real estate securities may be required to obtain special licenses.

Summary

Home mortgage loans are originated in the primary market—most commonly by savings associations, commercial banks, mortgage banks, or mortgage brokers. Loans through these institutions may be set up as fully amortized loans, straight loans, flexible-payment loans, or partially amortized balloon loans.

There are many types of mortgages and deed of trust loans, including conventional loans and those insured by the FHA or guaranteed by the VA. FHA and VA loans must meet certain requirements for the borrower to obtain the benefits of the government backing, which induces the lender to lend its funds. The interest rates for these loans may be lower than those charged for conventional loans. Lenders may also charge discount points. Borrowers in Texas may take advantage of special home-loan programs available through regional and local housing authorities, the Department of Housing and Community Affairs, and the Texas Veteran's Land Board.

Other types of real estate financing include adjustable-rate mortgages (ARMs), purchase-money mortgages or deeds of trust, home equity loans, reverse-annuity mortgages, shared-appreciation mortgages (SAMs), blanket mortgages, package mortgages, open-end mortgages, wraparound mortgages, construction loans, sale-and-leaseback agreements, and contracts for deed.

The federal government affects interest rates and the availability of money to finance real estate through the Federal Reserve Board's discount rate, reserve requirements, and open market operations. It also participates in the secondary mortgage market, composed of the investors who ultimately purchase and hold the loans as investments. These investors include insurance companies, investment funds, and pension plans. Fannie Mae, Ginnie Mae, and Freddie Mac take an active role in creating a secondary market by regularly purchasing mortgage and trust deed loans from originators and retaining, or warehousing, them until investment purchasers are available or by guaranteeing investment securities backed by pools of loans.

Regulation Z, implementing the federal Truth-in-Lending Act, requires that lenders inform prospective borrowers of all finance charges involved in such a loan if they use their homes as security for credit. Severe penalties are provided for noncompliance. The federal Equal Credit Opportunity Act prohibits creditors from discriminating against credit applicants on the basis of race, color, religion, national origin, sex, marital status, age, or dependency on public assistance. The Real Estate Settlement Procedures Act requires that lenders inform both buyers and sellers in advance of all fees and charges required for the settlement or closing of a residential real estate transaction. Other important financing legislation includes the Community Reinvestment Act and the Texas Security Laws.

Questions

1. The McBains are purchasing a lakefront summer home in a new resort development. The house is completely equipped, and the McBains have obtained a deed of trust loan that covers the purchase price of the residence, including the furnishings and appliances. This kind of financing is called a(n)
   a. wraparound deed of trust.
   b. package deed of trust.
   c. blanket deed of trust.
   d. unconventional loan.

2. With a fully amortized mortgage or deed of trust loan
   a. the total payment is the same each month, but the allocation to interest is different each month.
   b. the interest portion of each payment remains the same throughout the entire term of the loan.
   c. periodic payments are made, but the final payment is larger.
   d. the total payment varies each month but a fixed amount is credited toward the principal.

3. What does Freddie Mac do?
   a. Guarantees mortgages by the full faith and credit of the federal government
   b. Buys and pools blocks of conventional mortgages, selling bonds with such mortgages as security
   c. Acts in tandem with Ginnie Mae to provide special assistance in times of tight money
   d. Buys and sells VA and FHA mortgages

4. Fran purchased her home more than 30 years ago. Today, she receives monthly checks from the bank that supplement her income. Fran has most likely obtained a(n)
   a. shared-appreciation mortgage.
   b. adjustable-rate mortgage.
   c. reverse-annuity mortgage.
   d. package loan.

5. A developer has obtained a large loan to finance the construction of a planned unit development. Which statement is **NOT** true?
   a. This is a short-term loan, and the developer has arranged for long-term financing to repay it when the construction is completed.
   b. The borrowed money is disbursed in installments, ensuring that all subcontractors and laborers have been paid properly before disbursing each installment of the loan.
   c. The lender inspects the construction that has been completed to date.
   d. The construction loan is called a *take-out loan.*

6. The Carters purchased a residence for $95,000. They made a down payment of $15,000 and agreed to assume the seller's existing mortgage, which had a current balance of $23,000. The Carters financed the remaining $57,000 of the purchase price by executing a mortgage and note to the seller. This type of loan, by which the seller becomes the mortgagee, is called a
   a. wraparound mortgage.
   b. package mortgage.
   c. balloon note.
   d. purchase-money mortgage.

7. When the Federal Reserve Board raises its discount rate, which of the following should happen?
   a. Interest rates will rise.
   b. Interest rates will fall.
   c. The amount of money circulated in the marketplace will increase.
   d. Lenders will be willing to make more mortgage loans.

8. Discount points on a mortgage are computed as a percentage of the
   a. selling price.
   b. amount borrowed.
   c. closing costs.
   d. down payment.

9. Which of the following **BEST** defines the secondary mortgage market?
   a. Lenders who deal exclusively in second mortgages
   b. A market where loans are bought and sold after they have been originated
   c. The major lender of residential mortgages and trust deeds
   d. The major lender of FHA and VA loans

10. Terrence purchased a new residence for $175,000. He made a down payment of $15,000 and obtained a $160,000 mortgage loan. The builder of the house paid the lender 3 percent of the loan balance for the first year and 2 percent for the second year. This represented a total savings for Terrence of $8,000. What type of mortgage does this represent?
    a. Wraparound
    b. Package
    c. Blanket
    d. Buydown

11. Funds for FHA-insured loans are usually provided by
    a. the Federal Housing Administration (FHA).
    b. the Federal Deposit Insurance Corporation (FDIC).
    c. approved lending institutions.
    d. Fannie Mae.

12. The federal Equal Credit Opportunity Act prohibits lenders from discriminating against potential borrowers on the basis of all of the following **EXCEPT**
    a. sex.
    b. national origin.
    c. source of income.
    d. amount of income.

13. A charge of three discount points on a $120,000 loan equals
    a. $450.
    b. $3,600.
    c. $4,500.
    d. $36,000.

14. Under the provisions of Regulation Z (the Truth-in-Lending Act), the annual percentage rate (APR) of a finance charge includes all of the following components **EXCEPT**
    a. discount points paid by borrower.
    b. broker's commission.
    c. loan origination fee.
    d. interest rate.

15. Which of the following is **NOT** a secondary market?
    a. Fannie Mae
    b. Ginnie Mae
    c. FHA
    d. FHLMC

16. A developer received a loan that covers five parcels of real estate and provides for the release of the mortgage lien on each parcel when certain payments are made on the loan. This type of loan arrangement is called a
    a. purchase-money loan.
    b. blanket loan.
    c. package loan.
    d. wraparound loan.

17. A borrower obtains a $100,000 mortgage loan for 30 years at 7½ percent interest. If the monthly payments of $902.77 are credited first to interest and then to principal, what will be the balance of the principal after the borrower makes the first payment?
    a. $99,772.00
    b. $99,722.23
    c. $99,097.32
    d. $100,000.00

18. Using Table 16.1, what is the monthly interest rate factor required to amortize a loan at 8⅛ percent over a term of 25 years?
    a. 7.72
    b. 7.81
    c. 7.89
    d. 8.06

19. Using Table 16.1, calculate the principal and interest payment necessary to amortize a loan of $135,000 at 7¾ percent interest over 15 years.
    a. $1,111.85
    b. $1,270.35
    c. $1,279.80
    d. $1,639.16

20. Hellon borrowed $85,000, to be repaid in monthly installments of $823.76 at 11½ percent annual interest. How much of her first month's payment was applied to reducing the principal amount of the loan?
    a. $8.15
    b. $9.18
    c. $91.80
    d. $814.58

21. If a lender agrees to make a loan based on an 80 percent LTV, what is the amount of the loan if the property appraises for $114,500 and the sales price is $116,900?
    a. $83,200
    b. $91,300
    c. $91,600
    d. $92,900

Transfer of Title

Key Terms

acknowledgment	grantee	quitclaim deed
adverse possession	granting clause	special warranty deed
bargain and sale deed	grantor	testate
bequest	habendum clause	testator
codicil	heir	title
deed	holographic will	trustee's deed
deed in trust	intestate	voluntary alienation
delivery and	involuntary alienation	warranty clause
acceptance	last will and testament	warranty deed
formal will	probate	

OVERVIEW

A parcel of real estate may be transferred from one owner to another in a number of different ways. It may be given *voluntarily,* such as by sale or gift, or it may be taken *involuntarily,* by operation of law. It also may be transferred by the living or by will or descent after an owner dies. In every instance, however, a transfer of title to a parcel of real estate is a complex legal procedure involving a number of laws and documents.

This chapter discusses the four methods of title transfer. Also discussed are the various legal documents of conveyance with which the real estate broker or salesperson must be familiar.

TITLE

Title to real estate means the right to or ownership of the land; in addition, it represents the *evidence* of ownership. So the term *title* has two functions: it represents the "bundle of rights" the owner possesses in the real estate, and it denotes the facts that, if proven, would enable a person to recover or retain ownership or possession of a parcel of real estate.

The laws of each state govern real estate transactions for land located within its boundaries. Each state has the authority to pass legislative acts that affect the methods of transferring title or other interests in real estate. Title to real estate may be transferred in Texas by (1) voluntary alienation, (2) involuntary alienation, (3) will, and (4) descent.

VOLUNTARY ALIENATION

> To remember which party gives title and which one receives: The "*or*" gives to the "*ee*" —the *grantor* gives title to the *grantee*.
>
> A *deed* is the instrument that conveys property from the grantor to the grantee.

Voluntary alienation (transfer) of title may be made by either gift or sale. To transfer title by voluntary alienation during his or her lifetime, an owner must use some form of deed of conveyance.

A **deed** is a *written instrument by which an owner of real estate intentionally conveys to a purchaser his or her right, title, or interest in a parcel of real estate.* All deeds must be in writing in accordance with the requirements of the statute of frauds. The owner (who sells or gives the land) is referred to as the **grantor,** and the purchaser (who acquires the title) is called the **grantee.** A deed is executed (or signed) by the grantor.

Requirements for a Valid Conveyance

The minimum general requirements for an instrument to qualify as a deed in Texas are that it must (1) name the grantor and grantee, (2) state that consideration was given, (3) contain a description of the property sufficient to identify it, (4) contain words of conveyance, (5) be in writing and signed by the grantor or properly authorized agent, and (6) be delivered to the grantee or his or her agent and accepted.

Figure 17.1 is an example of a "cash warranty deed" used in Texas. Some of the paragraphs in that deed are *required* for a valid deed; others, though not required, are generally expressed in a deed for clarification purposes, when applicable.

Grantor. A grantor must be of sound mind and of lawful age. According to Texas law, a person reaches majority at the age of 18. A person under 18 who is married is considered to be of legal age to buy and sell real estate even though such person may be divorced prior to age 18. Service in the armed forces also removes the minority status. To release homestead rights in Texas, the grantor's spouse is required to join in and sign any deed of conveyance.

A deed executed by an *infant* (one who has not reached majority) is considered to be *voidable,* not void. The rule is that an infant (or minor) can disaffirm, or repudiate, his or her conveyance of real estate after reaching majority, at which time he or she has a reasonable period in which to disaffirm. What constitutes a reasonable time varies with the particular case.

A grantor generally is held to have sufficient mental capacity to execute a deed if he or she is capable of understanding the act. A deed executed by a person considered to be mentally incompetent is only *voidable*—it is not void. However, in some states, including Texas, a deed executed by a person who is *judged* legally incompetent is considered to be void. In Texas, legally incompetent people can neither contract nor convey; the court must appoint a guardian.

Figure 17.1 *Warranty Deed Conveying a Life Estate*

CASH WARRANTY DEED

Date: MAY 29, 1996

GRANTOR

Grantor: JAMES R. ELDER

Grantor's Mailing Address:

> 4205 PETUNIA
> SUNNYSIDE, GRANT COUNTY, TEXAS 79055

GRANTEE

Grantee: JOHN Q. YOUNGER, WITH FULL POSSESSION, USE, AND BENEFIT FOR HIS LIFE

Grantee's Mailing Address:

> 8205 MARIGOLD
> SUNNYSIDE, GRANT COUNTY, TEXAS 79055

CONSIDERATION

Consideration: TEN DOLLARS AND OTHER VALUABLE CONSIDERATION

LEGAL DESCRIPTION

Property (including any improvements):

> LOT 3, BLOCK 12, BLACK ACRE UNIT NO. 15, AN ADDITION TO THE CITY OF SUNNYSIDE, GRANT COUNTY, TEXAS, ACCORDING TO THE RECORDED MAP OR PLAT THEREOF.

Prior Liens:

> NONE

RESERVATION AND EXCEPTIONS

Reservations From and Exceptions To Conveyance and Warranty:

> EASEMENTS, RIGHTS OF WAY, AND PRESCRIPTIVE RIGHTS OF RECORD; ALL PRESENTLY RECORDED RESTRICTIONS, RESERVATIONS, COVENANTS, CONDITIONS, OIL AND GAS LEASES, MINERAL SEVERANCES, AND OTHER INSTRUMENTS, OTHER THAN LIENS AND CONVEYANCES, THAT AFFECT THE PROPERTY; RIGHTS OF ADJOINING OWNERS IN ANY WALLS AND FENCES SITUATED ON A COMMON BOUNDARY; ANY DISCREPANCIES, CONFLICTS, OR SHORTAGES IN AREA OR BOUNDARY LINES; AND ANY ENCROACHMENTS OR OVERLAPPING OF IMPROVEMENTS.

GRANTING CLAUSE

HABENDUM AND WARRANTY CLAUSE

Grantor, for the consideration and subject to the prior liens and the reservations from and exceptions to conveyance and warranty, grants, sells, and conveys to Grantee the property, together with all and singular the rights and appurtenances thereto in any wise belonging, to have and to hold it to Grantee for his life. Grantor binds Grantor and Grantor's heirs, executors, administrators, and successors to warrant and forever defend all and singular the property to Grantee for his life against every person whomsoever lawfully claiming or to claim the same or any part thereof, except as to the prior liens and the reservations from and exceptions to conveyance and warranty.

When the context requires, singular nouns and pronouns include the plural.

SIGNATURE OF GRANTOR

_____

JAMES R. ELDER

STATE OF TEXAS

COUNTY OF _____

This instrument was acknowledged before me on May 29, 1996 by JAMES R. ELDER.

ACKNOWLEDGMENT (REQUIRED FOR FILING)

_____

NOTARY PUBLIC, STATE OF TEXAS

Warranty Deed
Page 1

A grantor's name must be spelled correctly and consistently throughout the deed. If for any reason a grantor's name has been changed from that by which title originally was acquired, he or she must show both names. It is customary for such a grantor to be described as, for example, "John Smith, now known as John White." In these circumstances, a grantor should first state the name under which the title was acquired and then indicate his or her current name.

Grantee. To be valid, a deed must name a grantee and do so in such a way that he or she is readily identifiable. A deed naming as the grantee a wholly fictitious person—a company that does not exist legally or a society or club that is not properly incorporated—is considered void.

Consideration. To be valid, all deeds must contain a clause acknowledging the grantor's receipt of consideration. When a deed conveys real estate as a gift to a relative, "love and affection" may be sufficient consideration. However, in deeds conveying property as a gift, it is customary in Texas to recite a *nominal* consideration, such as "$10.00 and other good and valuable consideration." The full dollar amount of consideration is seldom set forth in the deed, except when the instrument is executed by a corporation or trustee or pursuant to court order.

Description of real estate. For a deed to be valid, it must contain an accurate legal description of the real estate conveyed.

Reservations and exceptions ("subject to" clauses). A grantor may *reserve* some right in the land for his or her own use (minerals, royalties, easements, for example). A grantor also may place certain restrictions on a grantee's use of the property. For example, a developer may restrict the number of houses that can be built on a one-acre lot in a subdivision. Such restrictions may be stated in the deed or contained in a previously recorded document (such as the subdivider's master deed or plat with restrictive covenants) that is expressly cited in the deed. Many of these deed restrictions have time limits, often including renewal clauses.

In addition to any reservations, a deed should specifically note any encumbrances or limitations that affect the title being conveyed. Such *exceptions* to clear title may include mortgage liens, taxes, restrictions, minerals or mineral leases, and easements that run with the land. For example, a deed may grant title to a grantee "subject to general real estate taxes for the year 2002 and subsequent years."

Granting clause (words of conveyance). A deed of conveyance transfers a present interest in real estate. Therefore, it must contain words that state the grantor's intention to convey the property at this time; an expression of intent to convey at some future time is inadequate. Such words of grant, or conveyance, are contained in the **granting clause.** Depending on the type of deed and the obligations agreed to by the grantor, the wording is generally "convey and warrant," "grant," "grant, bargain, and sell," or "remise, release, and quitclaim."

If more than one grantee is involved, the granting clause should cover the creation of their specific rights in the property. The clause might state, for example, that the grantees will take title as joint tenants or tenants in common. The wording is especially important in creating a joint tenancy.

The granting clause also should indicate what interest in the property is being conveyed by the grantor. Deeds that convey the entire fee simple interest of the grantor usually contain such wording as "to Jacqueline Smith and to her heirs and assigns forever." If the grantor is conveying less than his or her complete interest, such as a life estate to property, the wording must indicate this limitation on the grantee's interest. For example, a deed creating a life estate would convey property "to Jacqueline Smith for the duration of her natural life." See Figure 17.1 for an example of granting and habendum clauses conveying a life estate.

Habendum and warranty clauses. When it is necessary to define or limit the ownership interest of the grantee, a **habendum clause** follows the granting clause. The habendum clause begins with the words "to have and to hold." Its provisions must agree with those set down in the granting clause. When a discrepancy between the two clauses exists, the provisions in the granting clause usually are followed. The **warranty clause** states the nature of the grantor's warranties—for example, "forever" in a general warranty deed; "by or through me" in a special warranty deed; "without warranty" in a bargain and sale deed.

Signature of grantor. To be valid, a deed must be signed by *all grantors* named in the deed. When a grantor's spouse has been named as a grantor, the spouse also must sign the deed to release homestead rights. In Texas, witnesses to the grantor's signature are not necessary and no seal is required, but the signatures must be acknowledged (notarized) to permit recording.

Texas law permits a grantor's signature to be signed by an attorney-in-fact acting under a power of attorney that has been recorded in the county where the property is located. An *attorney-in-fact* is any person who has been given power of attorney (specific written authority) to sign legal instruments for a grantor. Because the power of attorney terminates on the death of the person granting such authority, adequate evidence must be submitted that the grantor was alive at the time the attorney-in-fact signed the deed and that the grantor was legally competent when the power was granted.

Texas law permits a grantor who is unable to write to sign his or her name by *mark*. With this type of signature, two persons other than the notary public taking the acknowledgment usually must witness the grantor's execution of the deed and sign as witnesses.

Transfer of title requires both *delivery and acceptance* of the deed.

Delivery and acceptance. A title is not considered transferred until the deed is actually **delivered** to **and accepted** by the grantee. The grantor may deliver the deed to the grantee personally or through a third party. *Title is said to "pass" only when a deed is delivered.* The effective date of the transfer of title from the grantor and to the grantee is the date of delivery of the deed itself. When a deed is delivered in escrow, the date of delivery is usually the date that the deed was deposited with the escrow agent.

Furthermore, delivery and acceptance are generally presumed if a deed has been recorded by the county clerk. However, delivery is a very technical aspect of the validity of a deed and usually is strictly construed by the courts. Brokers should consult legal counsel with questions regarding delivery.

Acknowledgment. An **acknowledgment** is a formal declaration that the person who signs a written document does so *voluntarily* and that his or her signature is genuine. The declaration is made before a *notary public* or authorized public officer, such as a clerk of the district court or judge or clerk of the county court. An acknowledgment usually states that the person signing the deed or other document is known to the officer or has produced sufficient identification to prevent a forgery.

Acknowledgment is not essential to the *validity* of a deed in Texas, although it is customary to acknowledge the execution of a deed. However, from a purely practical point of view, a deed that is not acknowledged is not a satisfactory instrument because it cannot be recorded. Although an unrecorded deed is valid between the grantor and the grantee, it often is not a valid conveyance against subsequent innocent purchasers who do record a deed. To help ensure good title, a grantee always should require acknowledgment of the grantor's signature on a deed. In Texas, an instrument is admissible as evidence in court even if the acknowledgment is invalid.

Execution of Corporate Deeds

Under the law, a corporation is considered a legal entity. The laws affecting corporations' rights to convey real estate vary from state to state. Two basic rules must be followed in Texas:

1. A corporation can convey real estate only by authority granted in its *bylaws* or on a proper resolution passed by its *board of directors*. If all or a substantial portion of a corporation's real estate is being conveyed, a resolution authorizing the sale usually must be secured from the *stockholders*.
2. Deeds to real estate can be *signed only by an authorized officer.* The authority of the officer must be granted by a resolution properly passed by the board of directors, but the signing of a deed by a corporate officer is prima facie evidence of a resolution's existence.

Rules pertaining to religious corporations and not-for-profit corporations vary widely. Because the legal requirements must be followed explicitly, it is advisable to consult an attorney for all corporate conveyances.

Types of Deeds

There are several forms of deeds. The seven most commonly used in Texas are

1. warranty deed (or general warranty deed),
2. special warranty deed,
3. bargain and sale deed (deed without warranty),
4. quitclaim deed,
5. deed in trust,
6. trustee's deed, and
7. deed executed pursuant to a court order.

Other instruments affect title to property but do not convey title. These include *mortgages* and *trust deeds (deeds of trust).* These documents are not intended to convey title but are financing instruments that establish real estate as security for the payment of a debt.

General warranty deeds. For a purchaser of real estate a **warranty deed** (shown in Figures 17.1 and 17.2) provides the *greatest protection* of any

Figure 17.2   *Warranty Deed with Vendor's Lien*

WARRANTY DEED WITH VENDOR'S LIEN

Date: MAY 29, 1996

Grantor: JAMES R. ELDER

Grantor's Mailing Address:

     4205 PETUNIA
     SUNNYSIDE, GRANT COUNTY, TEXAS 79055

Grantee: JOHN Q. YOUNGER

Grantee's Mailing Address:

     8205 MARIGOLD
     SUNNYSIDE, GRANT COUNTY, TEXAS 79055

Consideration: TEN DOLLARS AND A NOTE OF EVEN DATE THAT IS IN THE PRINCIPAL AMOUNT OF $80,000.00, IS EXECUTED BY GRANTEE, AND PAYABLE TO THE ORDER OF SUNNYSIDE NATIONAL BANK. THE NOTE IS SECURED BY A VENDOR'S LIEN RETAINED IN FAVOR OF SUNNYSIDE NATIONAL BANK IN THIS DEED AND BY A DEED OF TRUST OF EVEN DATE FROM GRANTEE TO AL L. SMILES, TRUSTEE.

Property (including any improvements):

     LOT 3, BLOCK 12, BLACK ACRE UNIT NO. 15, AN ADDITION TO THE CITY OF SUNNYSIDE, GRANT COUNTY, TEXAS, ACCORDING TO THE RECORDED MAP OR PLAT THEREOF.

Prior Liens:

     NONE

Reservations From and Exceptions to Conveyance and Warranty:

     EASEMENTS, RIGHTS OF WAY, AND PRESCRIPTIVE RIGHTS OF RECORD; ALL PRESENTLY RECORDED RESTRICTIONS, RESERVATIONS, COVENANTS, CONDITIONS, OIL AND GAS LEASES, MINERAL SEVERANCES, AND OTHER INSTRUMENTS, OTHER THAN LIENS AND CONVEYANCES, THAT AFFECT THE PROPERTY; RIGHTS OF ADJOINING OWNERS IN ANY WALLS AND FENCES SITUATED ON A COMMON BOUNDARY; ANY DISCREPANCIES, CONFLICTS, OR SHORTAGES IN AREA OR BOUNDARY LINES; AND ANY ENCROACHMENTS OR OVERLAPPING OF IMPROVEMENTS.

Grantor, for the consideration and subject to the prior liens and the reservations from and exceptions to conveyance and warranty, grants, sells, and conveys to Grantee the property, together with all and singular the rights and appurtenances thereto in any wise belonging, to have and to hold it to Grantee, Grantee's heirs, executors, administrators, successors, or assigns forever. Grantor binds Grantor and Grantor's heirs, executors, administrators, and successors to warrant and forever defend all and singular the property to Grantee and Grantee's heirs, executors, administrators, successors, and assigns against every person whomsoever lawfully claiming or to claim the same or any part thereof, except as to the prior liens and the reservations from and exceptions to conveyance and warranty.

Grantor transfers the vendor's lien against and superior title to the property to SUNNYSIDE NATIONAL BANK. The vendor's lien against and superior title to the property are retained until each note described is fully paid according to its terms, at which time this deed shall become absolute.

When the context requires, singular nouns and pronouns include the plural.

                            ————————————————————————
                                      JAMES R. ELDER

STATE OF TEXAS

COUNTY OF _____

     This instrument was acknowledged before me on May 29, 1996 by JAMES R. ELDER.

                     ————————————————————————
                     NOTARY PUBLIC, STATE OF TEXAS

Warranty Deed With Vendor's Lien
Page 1

deed. It is referred to as a *warranty deed* or *general warranty deed* because the grantor is legally bound by certain covenants or warranties. In some states, but not in Texas, the grantor's warranties are expressly written into the deed itself. In Texas, the warranties usually are implied by the use of certain words specified in the state statutes. Some of the specific words include "convey and warrant," "warrant generally," and "grant, bargain, and sell." The five basic implied warranties are as follows:

1. *Covenant of seisin:* The grantor warrants that he or she is the owner of the property and has the right to convey title to it. The grantee may recover damages up to the full purchase price if this covenant is broken.
2. *Covenant against encumbrances:* The grantor warrants that the property is free from any liens or encumbrances except those specifically stated in the deed. Encumbrances include such items as mortgages, mechanics' liens, and easements. If this covenant is breached, the grantee may sue for expenses to remove the encumbrance.
3. *Covenant of quiet enjoyment:* The grantor guarantees that the grantee's title is good against third parties who might bring court actions to establish superior title to the property. If the grantee's title is found to be inferior, the grantor is liable for damages.
4. *Covenant of further assurance:* The grantor promises to obtain and deliver any instrument needed to make the title good. For example, if the grantor's spouse has failed to sign away homestead rights, the grantor must deliver a *quitclaim deed* executed by the spouse to clear the title.
5. *Covenant of warranty forever:* The grantor guarantees that if, at any time in the future, the title fails, he or she will compensate the grantee for the loss sustained.

In Texas, the grantor in a deed is not obliged to insert a covenant of warranty of title. However, unless otherwise negated by express language in the deed, the word *grant* or *convey* creates implied warranties to the grantee and to his or her heirs and assigns for the first two covenants listed above. The last three covenants are derived from language in the deed such as "warrant and forever defend the grantee against every person lawfully claiming" an interest in the land. Covenants in a general warranty deed are not limited to matters that occurred during the time the grantor owned the property; they extend back to the origin of the title. If possible, a seller should provide no greater warranties than he or she received.

Special warranty deeds. A conveyance that carries only one covenant is a ***special warranty deed.*** The grantor warrants *only* that the property was not encumbered during the time he or she held title except as noted in the deed and that he or she has done nothing during ownership to cloud or damage the title. Special warranty deeds generally contain the words "remise, release, alienate, and convey" in the granting clause. Any additional warranties to be included must be stated specifically in the deed. The full consideration for the property also is stated in the deed.

A special warranty deed is usually used by fiduciaries such as trustees, executors, and corporations, and sometimes by grantors who have acquired title at tax sales. It is based on the theory that a fiduciary or corporation has no knowledge to warrant against acts of its predecessors in title and does

General Warranty Deed

Two basic warranties in Texas:

1. Covenant of seisin
2. Covenant against encumbrances

Special Warranty Deed

Covenant against defects occurring during the grantor's ownership not want the exposure to liability. Fiduciaries may hold title for a limited time without having a personal interest in the proceeds.

Bargain and sale deed. The **bargain and sale deed,** sometimes called a *deed without warranty,* uses the words "grant and release" or "grant, bargain, and sell" in the granting clause. A bargain and sale deed contains no warranties against encumbrances; however, it does *imply* that the grantor holds title and possession of the property. Because the warranty is not specifically stated, the grantee has little legal recourse if defects later appear in the title. Figure 17.3 illustrates the bargain and sale deed, the deed without warranty.

> **Bargain and Sale Deed**
>
> - Contains no express warranties
> - Implies that grantor holds title and possession

Quitclaim deeds. A **quitclaim deed** provides the grantee with the least protection of any deed. It carries no covenants or warranties and conveys only such interest that the grantor may have when the deed is delivered. If the grantor has no interest, the grantee will acquire nothing, nor will the grantee acquire any right of warranty claim against the grantor. On the other hand, a quitclaim deed can convey title as effectively as a warranty deed if the grantor has good title when he or she delivers the deed. However, it provides none of the guarantees that a warranty deed does. Through a quitclaim deed, the grantor only "remises, releases, and quitclaims" his or her interest in the property, if any. A title insurance policy cannot be written on a property if it is being conveyed through a quitclaim deed.

> **Quitclaim Deed**
>
> No express or implied covenants or warranties; no words of conveyance

A quitclaim deed frequently is used to cure a title defect, called a *cloud on the title.* For example, it might convey an easement, it might reconvey equitable title back to a seller, or it might divide property in a divorce proceeding. If the name of the grantee is misspelled on a warranty deed placed in the public record, a quitclaim deed with the correct spelling might be executed to the grantee to perfect the title. A quitclaim deed is also used when a grantor allegedly has *inherited* property but is not certain that the decedent's title was valid. A warranty deed in such an instance could carry with it obligations of warranty, whereas a quitclaim deed would convey only the grantor's interest.

Deeds in trust. A **deed in trust** is the means by which a *trustor* conveys real estate to a *trustee* for the benefit of a *beneficiary.* The real estate is held by the trustee to fulfill the purpose of the trust, with ownership powers (to sell, mortgage, subdivide, etc.) granted to the trustee.

Trustee's deed. A deed of conveyance executed by a trustee is a **trustee's deed.** It usually is used when a trustee named in a will, trust agreement, or deed of trust sells or conveys property out of the trust. The trustee's deed sets forth the fact that the trustee executes the instrument in accordance with the powers and authority granted to him or her by the trust instrument or the deed of trust.

Deeds executed pursuant to court order. This classification covers such deed forms as executors' deeds, masters' deeds, administrators' deeds, sheriffs' deeds, and many others. These statutory deed forms are used to convey title to property that is transferred by court order or perhaps by will if provided in the will. The forms of such deeds must conform to the laws of Texas.

Figure 17.3   Bargain and Sale Deed (Deed Without Warranty)

DEED WITHOUT WARRANTY

Date: MAY 29, 1996

Grantor: JAMES R. ELDER

Grantor's Mailing Address:

4205 PETUNIA
SUNNYSIDE, GRANT COUNTY, TEXAS 79055

Grantee: JOHN Q. YOUNGER

Grantee's Mailing Address:

8205 MARIGOLD
SUNNYSIDE, GRANT COUNTY, TEXAS 79055

Consideration: TEN DOLLARS AND OTHER VALUABLE CONSIDERATION

Property (including any improvements):

LOT 3, BLOCK 12, BLACK ACRE UNIT NO. 15, AN ADDITION TO THE CITY OF SUNNYSIDE, GRANT COUNTY, TEXAS, ACCORDING TO THE RECORDED MAP OR PLAT THEREOF.

Prior Liens:

NONE

Reservations From and Exceptions To Conveyance:

EASEMENTS, RIGHTS OF WAY, AND PRESCRIPTIVE RIGHTS OF RECORD; ALL PRESENTLY RECORDED RESTRICTIONS, RESERVATIONS, COVENANTS, CONDITIONS, OIL AND GAS LEASES, MINERAL SEVERANCES, AND OTHER INSTRUMENTS, OTHER THAN LIENS AND CONVEYANCES, THAT AFFECT THE PROPERTY; RIGHTS OF ADJOINING OWNERS IN ANY WALLS AND FENCES SITUATED ON A COMMON BOUNDARY; ANY DISCREPANCIES, CONFLICTS, OR SHORTAGES IN AREA OR BOUNDARY LINES; AND ANY ENCROACHMENTS OR OVERLAPPING OF IMPROVEMENTS.

Grantor, for the consideration and subject to the prior liens and the reservations from and exceptions to conveyance, conveys to Grantee the property without express or implied warranty, and all warranties that might arise by common law and the warranties in Section 5.023 of the Texas Property Code (or its successor) are excluded.

When the context requires, singular nouns and pronouns include the plural.

_____
JAMES R. ELDER

STATE OF TEXAS

COUNTY OF _____

This instrument was acknowledged before me on May 29, 1996 by JAMES R. ELDER.

_____
NOTARY PUBLIC, STATE OF TEXAS

Deed Without Warranty
Page 1

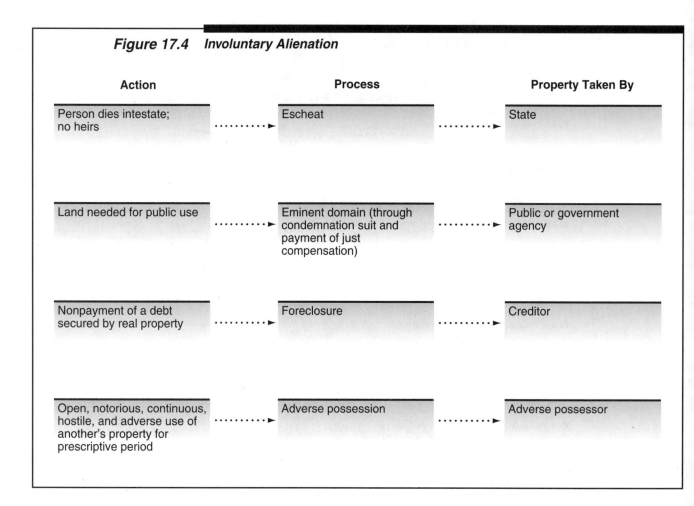

Figure 17.4   Involuntary Alienation

Action	Process	Property Taken By
Person dies intestate; no heirs	Escheat	State
Land needed for public use	Eminent domain (through condemnation suit and payment of just compensation)	Public or government agency
Nonpayment of a debt secured by real property	Foreclosure	Creditor
Open, notorious, continuous, hostile, and adverse use of another's property for prescriptive period	Adverse possession	Adverse possessor

One characteristic of such instruments is that the *full consideration* usually is stated in the deed. Because the court has authorized the sale of the property for a given amount of consideration, this amount should be stated *exactly* in the document. By Texas statute, the party executing this kind of deed may be entitled to a sales fee or commission based on a percentage of the full consideration.

INVOLUNTARY ALIENATION

In addition to voluntary alienation by gift or sale as just discussed, title to property can be transferred by **involuntary alienation,** that is, without the owner's consent (see Figure 17.4). Such transfers usually are carried out by operation of law and include several concepts studied earlier in this text: *escheat, eminent domain, tax or mortgage foreclosure, and erosion.*

Adverse possession is another means of involuntary transfer. An owner who does not use his or her land or does not inspect it for a number of years may lose title to another person who has some claim to the land, takes possession, and uses the land. The possession of the claimant must be open, notorious, hostile, and uninterrupted for a period of 3, 5, 10, or 25 years as set by Texas state law and summarized in Figure 17.5. The intent of the adverse possession laws is not to legally "steal" someone's property but rather to clear up boundary and title disputes.

Figure 17.5 Adverse Possession

3-Year Statute	5-Year Statute	10-Year Statute	25-Year Statute
Requirements: • Have title or color of title • Possess a general or special warranty deed	**Requirements:** • Cultivate, use, or enjoy the property • Pay taxes • Register a deed (may be a quitclaim or bargain and sale deed)	**Requirements:** • Cultivate, use, or enjoy the property	**Requirements:** • Have a deed that is recorded in the county • Act in good faith
	Does not require: • Color of title or chain of title • Indefeasible title	**Does not require:** • A deed or other form of conveyance	**Does not require:** • A valid deed; the grantor may not have had legal capacity to sign the deed
Example: *A* sells to *B* who does not record a deed and lives out of town; the property is vacant. *A* sells to *C* who does not record a deed, believes he has good title, and moves into the house. More than 3 years later, *B* moves to town and wants his house. *C* can legally claim title under the 3-year adverse possession statute. The adverse possessor must have a deed that appears to be legal title but may not be filed.		**Example:** *Farmer M* knows *Farmer T* is farming a portion of his land; he says nothing because it benefits him. Eleven years later and after having a "disagreement" with *Farmer T, Farmer M* files a suit for trespassing. The court awards the property to the "occupant" of the land for the last ten years, *Farmer T.*	

Adverse Possession

The acquiring of title to real property owned by someone else by open, notorious, hostile, and continuous possession for a statutory period of time.

The *3-year statute* requires that the adverse possessor have title or color of title. *Title* is defined as a regular chain of transfers beginning with the original land grant from the government. *Color of title* means a consecutive chain of transfers (that may not be regular) down to the adverse possessor. An irregular chain is one in which an instrument was not recorded or some other defect occurred that was not the result of dishonesty or unfairness. The adverse possessor must be capable of producing a chain of documents that prove in all fairness that title should be in him or her.

The *5-year statute* requires that the claimant pay the taxes on the property; cultivate, use, or enjoy the property; and claim the property under a recorded deed. The major difference between the 3-year and 5-year statutes is the requirement of a chain of title from the sovereignty. Under the 5-year statute, the adverse possessor is not required to produce a chain of title. The claimant must produce a recorded deed and proof of payment of taxes to support the other elements of adverse possession.

The *10-year statute* is the general adverse possession provision. It requires adverse possession for a 10-year period by one who uses, cultivates, or enjoys the property. A deed or chain of title in support of the claim is not necessary. The adverse claimant is limited to the acquisition of 160 acres unless there is some type of written memorandum of title that increases the number of acres.

Finally, the *25-year statute* requires that the adverse possessor have adverse possession of the property for 25 years, be in good faith, and have a recorded deed that purports to convey title to the claimant. Generally, adverse possession cannot be claimed against public property, minors, the insane, or the imprisoned; however, the 25-year statute runs against title holders who may be minors, insane, or suffering from some other disability. The 25-year statute allows the running of the time period even though the record owner from whom the adverse possessor received the property may have been under a legal disability at the time. Although this provision is used infrequently, the 25-year time period is the absolute bar against claims of others.

> Once title is *perfected* through adverse possession, the statutes confer "full title, precluding all claims." Basically, the adverse possessor acquires fee simple title.

Through the principle of *tacking,* successive periods of adverse possession can be combined by successive adverse possessors, thus enabling a person who is not in possession for the entire required time period to establish a valid claim.

Through adverse possession, the law recognizes that the use of land is an important function of its ownership. If a property owner discovers a use that might later be claimed as adverse possession, the property owner should give permission to use the land and file the permission document with the county clerk. Permission stops adverse possession. A claimant who cannot prove title through adverse possession may acquire an easement by prescription (see Chapter 8). When a transaction involves the possibility of title by adverse possession, the parties should seek competent legal counsel.

TRANSFER OF A DECEDENT'S PROPERTY

When a person dies **intestate** (without having left a valid will), the decedent's real estate and personal property pass to his or her heirs according to the *statute of descent and distribution.* In effect, the state makes a will for such decedents. In contrast, a person who dies **testate** has prepared a will indicating how property will be disposed of after his or her death.

Legally, a decedent's title to his or her real estate immediately passes either to the heirs by descent or to the persons named in the will. However, if there is a dispute among the devisees, the will must be probated. All claims against the estate must be satisfied.

Probate Proceedings

Probate is a legal process by which a court determines the validity of a will and establishes the assets of a decedent and who will inherit those assets. Probate proceedings must take place in the county where the real estate in question is located. If the will is upheld, the property is distributed according to the will's provisions. If a person has died intestate, the court determines who inherits by reviewing a *proof of heirship.* This statement, usually prepared by an attorney, gives personal information regarding the decedent's spouse, children, and relatives. This affidavit must be signed by a nonrelative who has known the family for a long time. From this document the court decides which parties will receive what portion of the estate.

To initiate probate proceedings, the custodian of the will, an heir, or another interested party must petition the court. The court then holds a hearing to determine the validity of the will and/or the order of descent, should no valid will exist. If for any reason a will is declared invalid by the court, any property owned by the decedent passes by the laws of descent. After the heirs are established, the court appoints an *administrator* (an *administratrix* if a woman) to oversee the administration and distribution of the estate (if no *executor/executrix* was named in a will).

The court gives the administrator (if there is no will) or executor (if there is a will) the authority to appraise the assets of the estate and satisfy all debts that are owed by the decedent. He or she also is responsible for paying federal estate taxes and, in Texas, state inheritance taxes. After all these liens against the property have been satisfied, the executor or administrator distributes the remaining assets of the estate according to the provisions of the will or the state law of descent.

In Practice   A broker entering into a listing agreement with the executor or administrator of an estate in probate should be aware that the amount of commission will be fixed by the court and that such commission is payable only from the proceeds of the sale. The broker will not be able to collect a commission unless the court approves the sale. In addition, the broker should be aware of who owns the property and has the authority to sign the listing agreement. If the previous owner died intestate, it may not be immediately obvious which heirs own the property.

Transfer of Title by Will

A **last will and testament** is an instrument made by an owner to voluntarily convey title to the owner's property after his or her death. A will takes effect only after the death of the decedent; until that time, any property covered by the will can be conveyed by the owner and thus be removed from the owner's estate. In Texas, a surviving spouse automatically owns one-half of the couple's community property acquired during the marriage. A will is not necessary to protect the surviving spouse's one-half interest in the community property.

Testator: a person who makes a will

Devise: gift of real property by will

Bequest or *legacy:* gift of personal property by will

A person who has died and left a will is said to have *died testate.* A party who makes a will is known as a **testator;** the gift of real property by will is known as a *devise,* and a person who receives property by will is known as a *devisee.* In addition, a gift of personal property is known as a *legacy* or **bequest;** the person receiving the personal property is known as a *legatee.*

A will differs from a deed in that a deed conveys a present interest in real estate during the lifetime of the grantor, whereas a will conveys no interest in the property until after the death of the testator. To be valid, a deed *must* be delivered during the grantor's lifetime. The parties named in a will have no rights or interests as long as the testator is still alive; they acquire interest or title only after the owner's death.

Legal requirements for making a will. The legal capacity to make a will is given by Texas law to every person who is of sound mind and is 18 years of age or who is lawfully married or a member of maritime services, the U.S. armed forces, or auxiliaries thereto.

The testator must be of *sound mind* at the time he or she executes the will. There are no rigid tests to determine the capacity to make a will. Usually the courts hold that the testator must have sufficient mental capacity to understand the nature and extent of his or her property, the identity of the natural heirs, and the fact that execution of the will means that the property passes to those named in the will at his or her death. The courts also hold that the drawing of a will must be a voluntary act, free of any undue influence by other people. A will made by someone who had previously been declared mentally incompetent by the courts would be void.

Because a will must be valid to convey title to real estate effectively, it must be executed and prepared in accordance with the laws of the state where the real estate is located. In Texas a **formal,** or witnessed, **will** must be in writing and signed by the testator in the presence of two or more credible witnesses above the age of 14 who will subscribe their names as witnesses. The witnesses should be persons not named as devisees or legatees in the will. The testator may modify his or her executed will by means of a **codicil,** which must be in the same form as the will it amends. A will may be revoked at any time prior to the death of the testator. Texas law also recognizes a **holographic will**—one that is wholly in the handwriting of the maker. The document must indicate that the decedent intended the writing to be the last will and testament. Witnesses to the execution of the will are not required.

If for any reason a will is declared invalid by the probate court, the real estate of the decedent will pass by the intestate laws of descent.

Transfer of Title by Descent (Intestate Succession)

By law, the title to real estate and personal property of an intestate decedent passes to his or her heirs. Under the descent statutes, the primary **heirs** of the deceased are his or her spouse and close blood relatives such as children, parents, brothers, sisters, aunts, uncles, and, in some cases, first and second cousins. The closeness of the relationship to the decedent determines the specific rights of the heirs. As previously discussed, the relative's right to inherit must be established by proof of heirship during the probate process.

Texas law makes provisions for adopted children. When they have been legally adopted, they usually are considered heirs of the adopting parents but will not be considered heirs of ancestors of the adopting parents. Illegitimate children inherit from the mother but not from the father, unless he has admitted parentage in writing or parentage has been established legally. Of course, if he legally adopts the child, that child will inherit as an adopted child.

Requirements for a Valid Formal Will

- Legal age
- Sound mind
- Proper wording
- No undue influence
- Signed
- Witnessed

Note: Property of an intestate decedent will be distributed according to the laws of the state in which the *property* is located.

Community property. Effective September 1, 1993, community property passes on the death of one spouse without a will in one of two ways: (1) to the surviving spouse, if all surviving children and descendants of the deceased spouse are also children or descendants of the surviving spouse, or (2) one-half to the surviving spouse and one-half to the children or descendants of the deceased spouse if there are any children or descendants of the decedent that are not the children or descendants of the surviving spouse. Community property passes charged with any debts that are against it.

Separate property. The *Texas Law of Descent and Distribution* provides that real estate (other than community property) located in Texas and owned as separate property by a deceased owner who died intestate is distributed as digested briefly in the following list. *Descendants* means living descendants (blood or adopted), however remote, of the deceased. Distribution is always *per stirpes;* that is, children receive a proportionate share of their deceased parent's share.

1. If the deceased leaves a spouse and children or descendants of deceased children, the spouse takes one-third of the real estate for life and the balance is shared equally by the children.
2. If there is no surviving spouse and if the deceased leaves one or more children, the children take the real estate equally among them. If there are descendants of a deceased child, such descendants would take the share that their deceased parent would have received.
3. When the deceased does not leave children or their descendants but does leave a spouse and parents, brothers, sisters, or descendants of deceased brothers or sisters, the spouse takes one-half of the real estate and the other half passes in *one* of the following ways: (a) to both parents equally, (b) half to the surviving parent and the other half to the brothers and sisters and their descendants, (c) all to the surviving parents if there are no living descendants, or (d) all to the decedent's brothers and sisters or their descendants.
4. If the deceased leaves a spouse but no children or descendants of children and no parents or descendants of parents, the spouse takes all of the estate.
5. If the decedent leaves no spouse or descendants (as in the case of an unmarried person), the decedent's entire ownership of real estate passes as indicated in item 3.
6. If none of the foregoing exist, one-half of the real estate passes to the paternal kin and the other half to the maternal kindred. The statute contains detailed instructions for finding heirs by tracing back through maternal and paternal grandparents.
7. If the deceased leaves no surviving spouse and no kindred or heirs, the real estate escheats to the state.

Summary

Title to real estate is the right to, and evidence of ownership of, the land. It may be transferred in four ways: (1) voluntary alienation, (2) involuntary alienation, (3) will, and (4) descent.

The voluntary transfer of an owner's title is made by a deed, executed (signed) by the owner as grantor to the purchaser as grantee. The form and execution of a deed must comply with the statutory requirements of the state of Texas.

The requirements for a valid deed in Texas are a grantor with legal capacity to contract, a readily identifiable grantee, a recital of consideration, a legal description of the property, a granting clause, the signature of the grantor, and delivery and acceptance. To permit recording, the deed should be acknowledged before a notary public or other officer to provide evidence that the signature is genuine and the signing was voluntary. For purposes of clarification, deeds often include paragraphs to describe exceptions and reservations on the title ("subject to" clauses), limitations on conveyance of a fee simple estate, and habendum and warranty clauses.

The obligation of a grantor is determined by the form of the deed, that is, whether it is a general warranty deed, special warranty deed, or quitclaim deed. The words of conveyance in the granting clause are important in determining the form of deed.

A general warranty deed provides the greatest protection of any deed by binding the grantor to certain covenants or warranties. A special warranty deed warrants only that the title to the real estate has not been encumbered by the grantor except as stated in the deed. A quitclaim deed carries with it no warranties whatsoever and conveys only the interest, *if any,* the grantor possesses in the property.

An owner's title may be transferred without his or her permission by a court action, such as a foreclosure or judgment sale, a tax sale, condemnation under the right of eminent domain, adverse possession, or escheat. Land also may be transferred by the natural forces of water and wind through accretion or erosion.

The real estate of an owner who makes a valid will (who dies testate) passes to the devisees on the death of the testator. The title of an owner who dies without a will (intestate) passes according to the provisions of the law of descent and distribution of the state in which the real estate is located.

Questions

1. Title to real estate may be transferred during a person's lifetime by which of the following means?
   a. Escheat
   b. Descent
   c. Involuntary alienation
   d. Devise

2. Every deed must be signed by the
   a. grantor.
   b. grantee.
   c. grantor and grantee.
   d. devisee.

3. Harry Hughes, age 15, recently inherited many parcels of real estate from his late father and has decided to sell one of them. If Hughes signed a deed conveying his interest in the property to a purchaser without the signature of his legal guardian, such a conveyance would be
   a. valid.   c. invalid.
   b. void.   d. voidable.

4. To voluntarily transfer his or her right, title, or interest in real estate, an owner may use all the various deeds of conveyance **EXCEPT** a
   a. sheriff's deed.
   b. warranty deed.
   c. quitclaim deed.
   d. deed in trust.

5. Title to an owner's real estate can be transferred at the death of the owner by which one of the following documents?
   a. Special warranty deed
   b. Trustee's deed
   c. Last will and testament
   d. Quitclaim deed

6. Ken signed a deed transferring ownership of a property to Larry. To provide evidence that Ken's signature was genuine, Ken executed a declaration before a notary. This declaration is known as an
   a. affidavit.   c. affirmation.
   b. acknowledgment.   d. estoppel.

7. Matilda Fairbanks inherited acreage in a distant Texas county, never went to see the acreage, and did not use the ground. Harold Sampson moved his mobile home onto the land, had a water well drilled, and lived there for 26 years. Sampson might become the owner of the land if he has complied with Texas law regarding
   a. adverse possession.
   b. avulsion.
   c. voluntary alienation.
   d. descent and distribution.

8. A grantee receives the greatest protection with what type of deed?
   a. Quitclaim   c. Bargain and sale
   b. General warranty   d. Special warranty

9. Alvin Rosewell executes a deed to Sylvia Sanchez as grantee, has it acknowledged, and receives payment from the buyer. Rosewell holds the deed, however, and arranges to meet Sanchez the next morning at the courthouse to deliver the deed to her. In this situation at this time
   a. Sanchez owns the property because she has paid for it.
   b. title to the property will not officially pass until Sanchez has been given the deed the next morning.
   c. title to the property will not pass until Sanchez has received the deed and recorded it the next morning.
   d. Sanchez will own the property when she has signed the deed the next morning.

10. Claude Johnson, a bachelor, died owning real estate that he devised by will to his niece, Annette. In essence, at what point does title pass to his niece?
    a. Immediately upon Johnson's death
    b. After Annette has paid all inheritance taxes
    c. After the executor executes a new deed to the property
    d. When Annette executes a new deed to the property

11. A person who pays for and receives a quitclaim deed
    a. will receive whatever title the grantor possessed in the property.
    b. can force the grantor to make the title good by a suit in court.
    c. receives the greatest protection of any deed.
    d. receives fee simple title.

12. Hap conveys property to Kasey by deed. The deed contains the following: (1) Kasey's name spelled out in full; (2) a statement that Hap has received $10 and Kasey's love and affection; (3) a statement that the property is conveyed to Kasey "to have and to hold." Which of the following correctly identifies, in order, these three elements of the deed?
    a. Grantee; consideration; granting clause
    b. Grantee; consideration; habendum clause
    c. Grantor; habendum clause; legal description
    d. Grantee; acknowledgment; habendum clause

13. An owner of Texas real estate, who was adjudged legally incompetent, later made a will during his stay at a nursing home. He died and was survived by a wife and three children. His real estate will pass
    a. to his wife.
    b. to the heirs mentioned in his will.
    c. by the laws of descent and distribution as if no will had been made at all.
    d. to the state.

14. A warranty deed usually implicitly obligates the grantor to the following warranties **EXCEPT**
    a. seisin.
    b. escheat.
    c. against encumbrances.
    d. further assurance.

15. Entrepreneur Harley Wilcox is purchasing a large apartment building in a choice urban location. For financial and professional reasons Wilcox wants to hold the property as beneficiary under a land trust. Which of the following instruments would be used to create this trust?
    a. Trust deed
    b. Deed of trust to secure assumption
    c. Trustee's deed
    d. Deed in trust

16. Which of the following is **NOT** a way in which title to real estate may be transferred by involuntary alienation?
    a. Eminent domain   c. Erosion
    b. Escheat   d. Seisin

17. A person who died leaving a valid will is called a(n)
    a. devisee.   c. legatee.
    b. testator.   d. intestator.

18. The statute or act that creates the need for a deed to be in writing is the
    a. law of descent and distribution.
    b. statute of frauds.
    c. statute of limitations.
    d. Texas Real Estate License Act.

19. An instrument authorizing one person to act for another is called a(n)
    a. power of attorney.
    b. release deed.
    c. quitclaim deed.
    d. acknowledgment.

18 | Title Records

Key Terms

abstract of title	evidence of title	recording
actual notice	good and indefeasible	subrogation
attorney's opinion of	title	suit to quiet title
title	league	title insurance
chain of title	marketable title	title search
constructive notice	priority	

OVERVIEW

For the protection of real estate owners, taxing bodies, creditors, and the general public, public records are maintained in every county in Texas. Such records help to establish official ownership, give notice of encumbrances, and establish priority of liens. The placing of documents in the public record is known as **recording.**

This chapter discusses the necessity for recording and the various types of title evidence that may be determined by an examination of the public records.

PUBLIC RECORDS AND RECORDING

In Texas, public records are maintained by designated officials, as required by state law. These include records maintained by the general land office, county clerks, surveyors, district clerks, county assessor-collectors, county treasurers, city clerks, and clerks of various courts of record. Records involving taxes, special assessments, ordinances, zoning, and building also fall into this category.

The principle expressed by the original statute of frauds has been enacted into all state laws, so no transfer of real estate is enforceable unless it is in writing. Written instruments are required for all transfers of title or interest, whether by deed, mortgage, or lease (unless the lease is for one year or less).

In addition to the statute of frauds, which requires that instruments affecting interests in real estate be in writing, the legislature also has passed laws that require owners or parties interested in real estate to record, or file, in the public records all documents affecting their interests in real estate in order to give *legal, public, and constructive notice* to the world of their interests. These statutory enactments are commonly referred to as *recording acts.*

Under the provisions of the *Uniform Electronic Transactions Act* (2001), a county clerk *may* accept instruments by electronic filing and record the instruments electronically. An agent should check with the local county clerk to determine that county's processes for electronic notarization and recording of electronic documents. Although permitted by law, electronic filing is not likely to be available throughout the state for several years.

Necessity for Recording

Before purchasing a fee simple estate to a parcel of real estate, a prospective buyer wants to be sure that the seller can convey good title to the property. The present owner undoubtedly purchased his or her interest from a previous owner, so the same question of *kind and condition* of title has been inquired into many times in the past. As long as taxes are paid and liens do not become delinquent, it is expected that a fee simple title will remain marketable.

Texas law provides that a *deed or mortgage is not effective as far as later purchasers* are concerned until such documents have been *recorded*. Thus the public records should reveal the condition of the title, and a purchaser should be able to rely on a search of such public records.

Recording Acts

To give constructive notice under the Texas recording acts, all instruments affecting any estate, right, title, or interest in land *must be recorded in the office of the county clerk in the county where the land is located.* The purpose of this requirement is to give to everyone interested in the title to a property notice of the various interests of all other parties. From a practical point of view, the recording acts give legal *priority* to those interests that are recorded first (first in time is first in priority).

> To give *notice* to third parties, written documents that affect land *must* be recorded in the county where the land is located.

To be *eligible for recording,* an instrument must be drawn and executed in conformity with the provisions of the recording statutes of the state in which the real estate is located. Texas requires that the instrument be signed and acknowledged before a notary public or other officer with the authority to take acknowledgments. Since 1837, all deeds to Texas land must be in English. Deeds made prior to that date may be in Spanish if an English translation is attached. The address to which the recorded document is to be returned must be indicated clearly on that document under penalty of law.

Notice

Anyone who has an interest in a parcel of real estate can take certain steps, called *giving notice,* to ensure that knowledge of the interest is accessible to the public. Through the legal maxim of *caveat emptor,* the courts charge a prospective real estate buyer or mortgagee (lender) with the responsibility of inspecting the property and searching the public records to ascertain the interests of other parties. The two basic types of notice are *constructive notice* and *actual notice.*

Constructive notice is a concept based on the legal presumption that information may be obtained by an individual through diligent inquiry. Properly

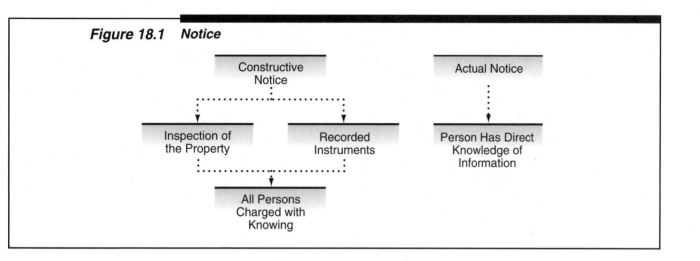

Figure 18.1   Notice

recording documents in the public record serves as constructive notice to the world of an individual's rights or interest. So does the physical possession of a property. Because the information or evidence is readily available to the world, a prospective purchaser or lender is responsible for discovering the interest.

In contrast, **actual notice** means that not only is the information available but someone has been given the information and actually knows it (see Figure 18.1). After an individual has searched the public records and inspected the property, he or she has actual notice. Actual notice is also known as *direct knowledge.* If it can be proved that an individual has actual knowledge of information concerning a parcel of real estate, he or she cannot use a lack of constructive notice (such as an unrecorded deed or an owner who is not in possession) to justify a claim.

Priority refers to the order of rights in time. Many complicated situations can arise that affect the priority of rights in a parcel of real estate—who recorded first; which party was in possession first; who had actual or constructive notice. For instance, a purchaser may receive a deed and take possession of the property but not record the deed. By taking possession a purchaser gives notice that he or she has an interest in the land. Such a purchaser's rights would be considered superior to the rights of a subsequent purchaser who acquired a deed from the original owner at a later date and recorded the deed but did not inspect the property to determine who was in possession. How the courts rule in any situation depends on the specific facts of the case. These are strictly legal questions that should be referred to lawyers.

FOR EXAMPLE

• In May, Bob purchased a property from Allen and received a deed. Bob never recorded the deed, but began farming operations on the property in June. In November, Allen (who was forgetful) again sold the property, this time to Carol. Carol accepted the deed and promptly recorded it. However, because Carol never inspected the property to see whether someone was in possession, Bob has the superior right to the property even though he never recorded the deed. By taking possession, a purchaser gives constructive notice of his or her interest in the land. Carol has recourse against Allen for this second sale of the property.

• Bill Wilson mortgaged his land to Jane Fry, and she failed to record the mortgage. Wilson later mortgaged the same land to Edgar Morse, who *knew* of the existence of the earlier mortgage. In this case, Morse is charged with actual knowledge of the existing mortgage, so his mortgage is a second mortgage, with Fry's mortgage having a prior claim on the property.

Unrecorded Documents

Certain types of liens are not recorded in the public records. Real estate taxes and special assessments are direct liens on specific parcels of real estate and need not be recorded in the county clerk's office. Other liens, such as inheritance taxes and franchise taxes, are placed by statutory authority against all real estate owned either by a decedent at the time of death or by a corporation at the time the franchise tax became a lien; these liens also are not recorded.

Notice of these liens must be gained from sources other than the county clerk's office. Evidence of the payment of real estate taxes and special assessments can be gathered from paid tax receipts and letters from municipalities. Creative measures are often required to get information about "off the record" liens.

Chain of Title

Chain of title is the record of a property's ownership. A search of the grantor-grantee indexes reveals a complete line of fee title owners from the original grant (from the sovereignty of the soil) to the most current property owner—linking each owner to the next so that a chain is formed.

> *Chain* of title: linking one owner to the next without a *gap* in the chain

If ownership cannot be traced through an unbroken chain, it is said that there is a *gap* in the chain. In these cases, the cloud on the title makes it necessary to establish ownership by a court action called a **suit to quiet title.** For instance, a suit might be required when a grantor acquired title under one name and conveyed it under another. Or there may be a forged deed in the chain, after which no subsequent grantee would have acquired legal title.

Title Search and Abstract of Title

A **title search** is an examination of all public records in the county to determine whether any defects exist in the chain of title. The records of the conveyances of ownership are examined beginning with the present owner. Then the title is traced backward to its origin. A search for title insurance purposes may be traced backward just to the ownership interest that could document a claim through the 25-year statute of adverse possession.

> *Abstract of title*: a condensed history of documents found in the public records

Other public records are examined to identify wills, judicial proceedings, and other encumbrances that may affect title. These include a variety of taxes, special assessments, and other recorded liens.

An **abstract of title** is a condensed history of all the instruments found in the title search that affect a particular parcel of land. A person who prepares this report is called an *abstracter*. The abstracter searches all the public records, then summarizes the various events and proceedings that affected the title throughout its history. The report begins with the original grant, then provides a chronological list of recorded instruments. All recorded liens and encumbrances are included, along with their current status.

Origin of Texas Land Titles

While Texas land was under control of the Spanish crown, royal grants of land were made to nobles, generals, explorers, adventurers, and colonists.

The originals of these grants, which were signed and authenticated, were called the *protocol* and were made a part of the official record. An authenticated extract of the grant, called a *testimonio,* was given to the owner as evidence of his or her title. While the Republic of Mexico was the sovereign government, colonists called *empresarios* were given grants of land. The best known of these was Stephen F. Austin. The *protocols* or the *testimonios* have become a part of the archives of the Texas General Land Office and are the basis or source of titles of land described therein.

Land was granted to an individual settler by the Mexican government in a large tract called a **league.** A league consisted of a square, each side being 5,000 varas (a *vara* by Texas statute is 33⅓ inches), or 13,888.89 feet. The area is 4,428.4 acres, or 6.919 square miles. A married colonist was entitled to a league, and a single man was given one-third league, or 1,476 acres. These were known in the records by the name of the colonist; for example, *Walter Scott's League.* Grants or patents from the Republic or the State of Texas are referred to as *surveys* and are known by the original owner's name; for example, the *Amos Waters Survey.* To identify each survey or league, the General Land Office of Texas has assigned a state abstract number to every grant of land from the Spanish crown, the Mexican government, the Republic of Texas, or the State of Texas. A separate set of numbers is used for each county. A smaller unit of measurement was the *labór* (a Spanish term pronounced la-*bór*), which was 177½ acres.

During the sovereignty of the Republic of Texas and continuing after the formation of the state, settlers were offered tracts of land of 640 acres or fractions thereof. These were surveyed and laid out as square sections.

EVIDENCE OF TITLE

Although the grantor in a general warranty deed warrants that he or she is the owner of the property and that all encumbrances have been disclosed, a deed is not considered satisfactory evidence of title. It contains no proof of the kind or condition of the grantor's title at the time of conveyance. The grantee needs some assurance that he or she is actually acquiring ownership and that the title is good and indefeasible. Therefore, an abstract of title and attorney's opinion of title or a title insurance policy would be used to provide **evidence of title.**

Abstract of Title and Attorney's Opinion of Title

If an **attorney's opinion of title** is used to provide *evidence of title,* an *abstracter* is hired to prepare an *abstract of title.* The abstracter concludes with a certificate indicating which records were searched and which records were not searched in preparation of the report. In summarizing a deed in the chain of title, the abstracter might note the recorder's book and page number, the date of the deed, the recording date, the names of the grantor and grantee, a brief description of the property, the type of deed, and any conditions or restrictions contained in the deed.

Proof of Good Title:

- Abstract of title and attorney's opinion
- Title insurance

Abstracters must exercise due care because they can be liable for negligence for any failure to include or accurately record all pertinent data. An *abstracter does not pass judgment on or guarantee the condition of the title.* Therefore, once the abstract is brought up to date, it is submitted to the buyer's attorney, who must examine the entire abstract. Following this detailed examination, the attorney must evaluate all the facts and prepare a written report for the purchaser on the condition of the ownership. This report, the *attorney's opinion of title*, should be prepared by an attorney thoroughly familiar with real estate law.

The attorney's opinion of title does not protect against defects that cannot be discovered from the public records, and mistakes can be made in creating the abstract or the attorney's opinion. Therefore, most lenders require title insurance as satisfactory evidence of title.

Title Insurance

A **title insurance** policy is a contract by which the policyholder is protected from losses arising from defects in the title. Unlike other insurance policies that insure against future losses, title insurance protects the insured from an event that occurred before the policy was issued. A title insurance company determines whether the title is insurable based on a review of the public records. If the title is insurable and a policy is written, a title insurance company agrees, subject to the terms of its policy, to indemnify (that is, to compensate or reimburse) the insured (the owner, mortgagee, or other interest holder) against any losses sustained as a result of defects in the title other than those exceptions listed in the policy. Under the contract, the title insurance company will defend the title at its own expense as well as pay any claims against the property if the title proves to be defective. Title insurance guarantees indemnification (reimbursement) for losses; it does not guarantee continued ownership. When a title company makes a payment to settle a claim covered by a policy, the company acquires by the right of **subrogation** all the remedies and rights of the insured party against anyone responsible for the settled claim.

Types of policies. Title companies issue various forms of title insurance policies, the most common of which are the *owner's* title insurance policy (with separate forms for residential and commercial use), the *mortgagee's* title insurance policy, the *leasehold* title insurance policy, and the *certificate of sale* title insurance policy. As the names indicate, each of these policies is issued to insure specific interests. For example, a residential owner's title policy assures the new homeowner that the title is as stated subject only to certain specified exceptions. Title insurance provides for reimbursement up to the purchase price on the owner's policy. Upon sale of the subject property, an owner's policy is automatically converted to a warrantor's policy, which will continue *in perpetuity* at no cost.

A mortgagee's title insurance policy assures a lender that it has a valid first lien (or perhaps a second lien) against the property. Reimbursement on the mortgagee's policy is limited to the outstanding loan balance; the lender's coverage decreases as the loan balance decreases. The mortgagee's policy transfers with each sale of the loan note. A leasehold title insurance policy assures a lessee that he or she has a valid lease. A certificate of sale policy is issued to a purchaser in a court sale and ensures the purchaser's interest in property sold under a court order.

The title commitment. In most cases, as soon as a property goes under contract, the real estate agent will deliver a copy of the sales contract to a title company to begin the title search. On completion of the examination, the title company issues a commitment to issue a title policy. According to the provisions of the promulgated Texas sales contracts, the seller has 20

The most common title insurance policies are the

- *owner's title policy,* insuring the owner has good title, *and*
- *mortgagee's title policy,* insuring the lender has a valid lien.

days from the date the title company receives the contract to accomplish the following:

- Deliver to the buyer a "commitment for title insurance" *and*
- Deliver, at buyer's expense, copies of restrictive covenants and documents evidencing exceptions in the commitment other than the standard printed exceptions.

If the commitment is not delivered within 20 days, the time for its delivery is automatically extended up to 15 days. The commitment for title insurance discloses to the prospective buyer the condition of the title and the exceptions to title that would not be covered by the policy. It includes (1) the name of the insured party; (2) the legal description of the real estate; (3) the estate or interest covered; (4) a schedule of all exceptions, consisting of encumbrances and defects found in the public records; and (5) conditions and stipulations under which the policy is issued.

Coverage. A *standard coverage* policy usually insures against defects that may be found in the public records plus such items as forged documents, improperly delivered deeds, lack of good and indefeasible title, and liens for labor and material that were contracted for by the seller and that have inception before the policy date. Lack of access to and from the property is also a covered risk. However, the buyer, seller, or agent must prove there is access through a survey or other means; otherwise, the title company will generally delete the insuring provision covering access to and from the land. A title company *may* accept an existing survey when providing area and boundary coverage, regardless of the age of the survey or the party for whom it was prepared (S.B. 1707, 2001). Exactly which defects the title company will insure against depends on the type of policy it issues and the endorsements requested by the mortgagee (see Table 18.1).

An *owner's policy usually will exclude coverage* against unrecorded documents, unrecorded defects of which the policyholder has knowledge, rights of eminent domain, claims arising by reason of bankruptcy or insolvency, and questions of survey.

Endorsements may be requested by the lender to cover additional risks that may be discovered only through inspection of the property, inquiries of persons in actual possession of the land, or examination of an accurate survey. The company does not agree to insure against any defects in or liens against the title that are found by the title examination and listed in the policy.

Premiums for title insurance policies are set by the State Board of Insurance and are paid only once, at closing.

The Title: Marketable or Good and Indefeasible

In most states, title to real property is generally considered satisfactory when it is marketable. A **marketable title** is one that is so free from significant defects that the purchaser can be assured against having to defend the title and would willingly accept it. It is title that is reasonably free from doubt that would affect the market value of the real estate. Although marketable title is not statutorily defined in Texas, generally a marketable title must (1) be free from any significant liens and encumbrances, (2) disclose no serious defects and not be dependent on doubtful questions of law or fact to prove its validity, (3) not expose a purchaser to the hazard of litigation or threaten

Table 18.1	Title Insurance Policy	
Standard Coverage	**Endorsements**	**Not Covered**
1. Defects found in public records	1. Property inspection	1. Defects and liens listed in policy
2. Forged documents	2. Rights of parties in possession	2. Unrecorded defects
3. Incompetent grantors	3. Examination of survey	3. Rights of eminent domain
4. Incorrect marital statements	4. Unrecorded liens not known of by policyholder	4. Questions of survey
5. Improperly delivered deeds	5. EPA lien endorsement	5. Claims arising by reason of bankruptcy or insolvency
6. Lack of access to and from land	6. Homestead or community property or survivorship rights	
7. Lack of good and indefeasible title	7. Guaranty against rollback taxes	

the quiet enjoyment of the property, and (4) convince a reasonably well-informed and prudent person acting on business principles and willful knowledge of the facts and their legal significance that he or she in turn could sell or mortgage the property at a fair market value.

> Texas title insurance policies insure *good and indefeasible title.*

Title insurance companies in Texas insure **good and indefeasible title,** rather than marketable title. A good and indefeasible title is a title that cannot be defeated by a superior claim, set aside, or made void. It is more than just a marketable title. As noted in Table 18.1, it guarantees against defects in the public records, forged documents, incompetent grantors, and more. *Marketable title* is free from any claim—but *good and indefeasible title* insures that, if there is a claim, the claim can be defeated.

Summary

1. B
2. B
3. C
4. A
5. D
6. B
7. C
8. B
9. D
10. A

11. B
12. A
13. D
14. A
15. A
16. C
17. A
18. A

The purpose of the recording acts is to give legal, public, and constructive notice to the world of parties' interests in real estate. The recording provisions have been adopted to create system and order in the transfer of real estate. Without them it would be virtually impossible to transfer real estate from one party to another. The interests and rights of the various parties in a particular parcel of land must be recorded so that such rights will be legally effective against third parties who do not have knowledge, or notice, of the rights.

Possession of real estate generally is interpreted as constructive notice of the rights of the person in possession. Actual notice is knowledge acquired directly and personally by an individual.

A deed of conveyance is evidence that a grantor has conveyed his or her interest in land, but it is not evidence of the kind or condition of the title. The purpose of a deed is to transfer a grantor's interest in real estate to a grantee. It does not *prove* that the grantor has any interest at all, even if he or she conveys the interest by means of a warranty deed that carries with it the implied covenants of warranty.

Two forms of title evidence are used in Texas. These are (1) abstract of title and attorney's opinion and (2) owner's title insurance policy.

If a seller provides an abstract of title and attorney's opinion of title as evidence of title, an abstracter first searches the documents that affect title to the subject property and then prepares an abstract with an abstracter's certificate, indicating which records were examined. The attorney for the buyer examines the abstract and issues an opinion of title.

A title insurance policy is a contract by which the policyholder is protected from losses arising from defects in the title. If the title is insurable and a policy is written, a title insurance company agrees to reimburse the insured against any losses sustained as a result of defects in the title other than those exceptions listed in the policy.

Marketable title is generally one that is so free from significant defects that the purchaser can be assured against having to defend the title. Texas title insurance policies insure good and indefeasible title. Should there be a claim against the title, the claim can be defeated.

Questions

1. Jim Anderson bought Ward Cleaver's home, and Cleaver delivered his deed to Anderson. Because it was a warranty deed, Anderson can assume which of the following?
   a. There are no outstanding mortgages or liens on the property.
   b. Cleaver warrants that he had title.
   c. Cleaver had good and marketable title.
   d. Cleaver's warranty through the deed itself is adequate protection.

2. An owner's title insurance policy with standard coverage generally covers all **EXCEPT** which of the following?
   a. Forged documents
   b. Rights of parties in possession
   c. Incompetent grantors
   d. Improperly delivered deeds

3. A mortgagee's title policy protects which parties against loss?
   a. Buyers
   b. Sellers
   c. Lenders
   d. Buyers and lenders

4. Phil Simpson bought Larry Fine's house, received a deed, and moved into the residence but neglected to record the document. One week later, Fine died and his heirs in another city, unaware that the property had been sold, conveyed title to Melvin Howard, who recorded the deed. Who owns the property?
   a. Phil Simpson
   b. Melvin Howard
   c. Larry Fine's heirs
   d. Both Simpson and Howard

5. Which **ONE** characteristic distinguishes *good and indefeasible title* from *marketable title*?
   a. It is free from significant liens and encumbrances.
   b. It discloses no serious defects regarding validity.
   c. It convinces a reasonably well-informed and prudent person that he or she could sell the property.
   d. It cannot be defeated by a superior claim.

6. Albert and Danielle Latour purchased a ranch house near El Paso. To provide evidence of their ownership, the Latours obtained a title insurance policy. The Latours' policy
   a. guarantees that they own the property.
   b. will reimburse, up to the amount of the policy, losses that the Latours sustain as a result of incompetent grantors.
   c. will terminate when they sell the property in the future.
   d. does not guarantee good and indefeasible title.

7. A purchaser went to the county clerk's office to check the records. She found that the seller was the grantee in the last recorded deed and that no mortgage was on record against the property. Thus, the purchaser may assume which of the following?
   a. All taxes are paid, and no judgments are outstanding.
   b. The seller has good title.
   c. The seller did not mortgage the property.
   d. The seller inherited the property free and clear.

8. When the title examination is completed, the title insurance company notifies the parties in writing of the condition of the title. This notification is referred to as
   a. a chain of title.
   b. commitment for title insurance.
   c. an abstract.
   d. an escrow statement.

9. An abstract is usually examined by the
   a. broker.
   b. abstract company.
   c. purchaser.
   d. attorney for the purchaser.

10. The person who prepares an abstract of title for a parcel of real estate
    a. writes a brief history of the title after inspecting the county records for documents affecting the title.
    b. ensures the condition of the title.
    c. issues a title insurance policy.
    d. gives an opinion of the status of the title.

11. A purchaser of real estate is charged with knowledge of all recorded documents, so he or she must have current title evidence to indicate the rights and interests revealed by public records. The purchaser also is charged with the responsibility to
    a. make improvements on the property.
    b. learn the rights of the parties in possession.
    c. inspect the property after closing.
    d. purchase additional insurance to protect the title.

12. Which statement **BEST** explains why instruments affecting real estate are recorded?
    a. Recording gives constructive notice to the world of the rights and interests in a particular parcel of real estate.
    b. Failing to record will void the transfer.
    c. The instruments must be recorded to comply with the terms of the statute of frauds.
    d. Recording proves the execution of the instrument.

13. When a claim is settled by a title insurance company, the company acquires all rights and claims of the insured against any other person who is responsible for the loss. This is called
    a. escrow.   c. subordination.
    b. abstract of title.   d. subrogation.

14. The documents referred to as *title evidence* include
    a. title insurance policies.
    b. general warranty deeds.
    c. quitclaim deeds.
    d. security agreements.

15. Written instruments affecting real estate should be recorded in
    a. the county clerk's office where the real estate is located.
    b. the state auditor's office.
    c. the city tax office.
    d. both state and county tax offices.

16. *Chain of title* refers to which of the following?
    a. A summary or history of all instruments and legal proceedings affecting a specific parcel of land
    b. An instrument or document that protects the insured parties (subject to specific exceptions) against defects in the examination of the record and hidden risks, such as forgeries, undisclosed heirs, errors in the public records
    c. The succession of conveyances from some starting point whereby the present owner derives his or her title
    d. Documentary proof that title is free of encumbrances

17. The date and time a document was recorded establish which of the following?
    a. Priority
    b. Chain of title
    c. Subrogation
    d. Good and indefeasible title

18. Kelly sells a portion of her property to Lew. Lew promptly records the deed in the appropriate county office. If Kelly tries to sell the same portion of her property to Melvin, which of the following statements is true?

   a. Melvin has been given constructive notice of the prior sale because Lew promptly recorded the deed.

   b. Melvin has been given actual notice of the prior sale because Lew promptly recorded the deed.

   c. Because Melvin's purchase of the portion of Kelly's property is the more recent, it will have priority over Lew's interest, regardless of when Lew recorded the deed.

   d. Because Kelly is selling the property a second time, the courts will request a quitclaim deed from Lew.

Real Estate Mathematics

Key Terms

amortization	linear	percent
area	loan discount	profit
interest	loss	volume

OVERVIEW

The *Real Estate License Act* requires that a Real Estate Principles course include instruction in real estate mathematics. The study of real estate mathematics goes beyond that requirement, however, for mathematics plays an important role in the real estate business. Math is involved in nearly every aspect of a typical transaction, from the moment a listing agreement is filled out until the final monies are paid at the closing.

This review is designed to familiarize students with some basic mathematical formulas that are important in day-to-day transactions and that are included on state licensing examinations. Some of this material is covered in detail elsewhere in the text, in which cases reference is made to the appropriate chapter. If additional help is required in working these problems, the text *Mastering Real Estate Mathematics*, Sixth Edition, by Ventolo, Tamper, and Allaway can be ordered from Real Estate Education Company®.

CALCULATORS

Calculators are permitted when taking the state licensing examination. The calculator must be silent, hand-held, battery operated, and nonprinting. A calculator that will add (+), subtract (–), multiply (×), and divide (÷) is sufficient for licensing examinations. Because calculators are available in many sizes, shapes, and colors, choose a calculator that is comfortable for you and allow yourself time to learn to use it correctly before you take the licensing examination. At some point in your profession, you might want to purchase a business or financial calculator with at least the following keys: N (number of interest compounding periods/number of payments), I (interest rate per period), PV (present value of money/loan), PMT (amount of payment), and FV (future value of money). Regardless of the calculator you select, follow the user's manual and set the decimal to float or to a minimum of five decimals. This will enable you to arrive at an answer with enough decimals to match multiple choice answers on exams.

FRACTIONS

$\underline{7}$ Numerator
8 Denominator

The denominator shows the number of equal parts in the whole or total. The numerator shows the number of those parts with which you are working. In the example above, the whole or total has been divided into eight equal parts and you have seven of those equal parts.

Proper fractions. The fraction ⅞ is an example of a proper fraction. A proper fraction is one in which the numerator is smaller than the denominator—it is less than a whole, or one.

Improper fractions. $\underline{11}$ Numerator
8 Denominator

An improper fraction is one in which the numerator is larger than the denominator—it is more than one.

Mixed numbers. A mixed number is a whole number plus a fraction; for example, 11½ is a mixed number.

Converting fractions to decimals. Fractions will sometimes be used in real estate math problems. These problems are most easily solved when the fractions are converted to decimals. *FORMULA: To convert a fraction to a decimal, the numerator is divided by the denominator.* Using the previous three fractions, you can calculate the decimal equivalent:

$$⅞ = 7 \div 8 = 0.875$$
$$11/8 = 11 \div 8 = 1.375$$
$$11½ = 1 \div 2 = 0.5 + 11 = 11.5$$

Once fractions have been converted to decimals, other calculations can easily be completed using the calculator.

PERCENTAGES

Many real estate computations are based on the calculation of percentages. A **percent** expresses a portion of a whole; *percent* means "per hundred." The whole or total always represents 100 percent.

$$5\% = 5 \text{ parts of } 100$$
$$75\% = 75 \text{ parts of } 100$$
$$120\% = 100 \text{ parts of } 100 \text{ plus } 20 \text{ parts of another } 100$$

To solve a problem involving percentages, the percentage must be converted to either a decimal or a fraction. To *convert a percentage to a decimal,* move the decimal two places to the left and drop the percent sign—or divide the number by 100:

$$5\% = 0.05$$
$$75\% = 0.75$$
$$120\% = 1.20$$

To *convert a decimal to a percentage* if an answer requires that a number be expressed as a percentage, move the decimal in the number two places to the right and add the percent sign—or multiply the number by 100:

$$0.0875 = 8.75\% \text{ or } 8\tfrac{3}{4}\% \qquad 0.05 = 5\% \qquad 0.2 = 20\% \qquad 1.82 = 182\%$$

Percentage formulas. Percentage problems contain three elements: *rate* (percentage), *total,* and *part.* There are three formulas for solving all percentage problems:

$$\textbf{Total} \times \textbf{Rate} = \textbf{Part}$$

$$\textbf{Part} \div \textbf{Rate} = \textbf{Total}$$

$$\textbf{Part} \div \textbf{Total} = \textbf{Rate}$$

A simple way of remembering these formulas is

- **MULTIPLY** when **PART** is the **UNKNOWN.**
- **DIVIDE** when **PART** is the **KNOWN.**
- When you divide, always enter **PART** into the calculator **first.**

Another tool to use in place of the three formulas is the T Bar.

$$\frac{\textbf{PART}}{\textbf{TOTAL} \mid \textbf{RATE}}$$

The procedure for using the T Bar is as follows:

1. Enter the two known items in the correct places.
2. If the line between the two items is vertical, multiply to solve for the missing item.
3. If the line between the two items is horizontal, divide to solve for the missing item. When you divide, the top (numerator/*Part*) always goes into the calculator first, divided by the bottom (denominator/*Total* or *Rate*).

The following examples show how the formulas and the T Bar can be used to solve percentage problems:

Example: There are 200 homes in your prospecting area. If 5 percent of them sold last year, how many homes sold last year?

$$200 \text{ (Total)} \times 5\% \text{ (Rate)} = \text{Part}$$
$$200 \times 0.05 = \textbf{10 homes (answer)}$$

or

$$\frac{\text{PART} = ?}{200 \text{ (Total)} \quad 5\% = 0.05 \text{ (Rate)}}$$

$200 \times 0.05 = \textbf{10 homes (answer)}$

Example: A broker received $10,200 for the sale of a house. If the commission rate was 6 percent, what was the total sales price?

$10,200 \text{ (Part)} \div 6\% \text{ (Rate)} = \text{Sales Price (Total)}$
$10,200 \div 0.06 = \textbf{\$170,000 sales price (answer)}$

or

$$\frac{\$10,200}{\text{Total} = ? \quad | \quad 6\% = 0.06}$$

$10,200 \div 0.06 = \textbf{\$170,000 sales price (answer)}$

Example: If a broker received a $7,700 commission on a $110,000 sale, what was the commission rate?

$7,700 \text{ (Part)} \div \$110,000 \text{ (Total)} = \text{Rate}$
$7,700 \div \$110,000 = 0.07 = \textbf{7\% commission rate}$

or

$$\frac{\$7,700}{\$110,000 \quad | \quad \text{Rate} = ?}$$

$7,700 \div \$110,000 = 0.07 = \textbf{7\% commission rate}$

Solving Word Problems

Solving word problems requires careful attention to the following steps:

- ***Read*** the problem carefully and completely. Never touch the calculator until you have read the entire problem.
- ***Analyze*** the problem to determine what is being asked, which facts are given that *will* be needed to solve for the answer, and which facts are given that *will not* be needed to solve for the answer. Eliminate any information and/or numbers given that are not needed to solve the problem. Take the remaining information and/or numbers and determine which will be needed first, second, etc., depending on the number of steps it will take to solve the problem.
- ***Choose*** the proper formula(s) and steps needed to solve the problem.
- ***Insert*** the known elements and calculate the answer.
- ***Check*** your answer to be sure you keyed in the numbers and functions properly on the calculator. Be sure you finished the problem. For example, when the problem asks for the salesperson's share of the commission, do not stop at the broker's share of the commission and mark that answer just because it is one of the choices.

Percentage Problems

Commission. The full commission is a percentage of the sales price unless otherwise stated in the problem. Remember that commission rates charged to clients, commission splits between brokers, and commission splits between the broker and a salesperson are always negotiable.

Example: A seller listed his home for $200,000 and agreed to pay a full commission rate of 5 percent. The home sold 4 weeks later for 90 percent of the list price. The listing broker agreed to give the selling broker 50 percent of the commission. The listing broker paid the listing salesperson 50 percent of her share of the commission, and the selling broker paid the selling salesperson 60 percent of his share of the commission. How much commission did the selling salesperson receive?

Step 1: Calculate the sales price using the formula for *Part:* ***Total*** × ***Rate = Part***

$200,000 listing price (Total) × 90% (Rate) = Sales Price (Part)
$200,000 × 0.9 = $180,000 sales price

or

$$\frac{\text{Part} = ?}{\text{\$200,000 (Total)} \mid 90\% = 0.9 \text{ (Rate)}}$$

$200,000 × 0.9 = $180,000 sales price

Step 2: Calculate the full commission using the formula for *Part.*

$180,000 (Total Sales Price) × 5% (Commission Rate) = Full Commission (Part)
$180,000 × 0.05 = $9,000 full commission

or

$$\frac{\text{Part} = ?}{\text{\$180,000 (Total)} \mid 5\% = 0.05 \text{ (Rate)}}$$

$180,000 × .05 = $9,000 full commission

Step 3: Calculate the selling broker's share using the formula for *Part.*

$9,000 Full Commission (Total) × 50% (Rate) = Selling Broker's Share (Part)
$9,000 × 0.5 = $4,500 selling broker's commission

or

$$\frac{\text{Part} = ?}{\text{\$9,000 (Total)} \mid 50\% = 0.50 \text{ (Rate)}}$$

$9,000 × 0.5 = $4,500 selling broker's commission

Step 4: Calculate the selling salesperson's commission using the formula for *Part.*

$4,500 Selling Broker's Share (Total) × 60% (Rate) = Selling Salesperson (Part)
$4,500 × 0.6 = **$2,700 selling salesperson's commission (answer)**

or

$$\frac{\text{Part} = ?}{\text{\$4,500 (Total)} \mid 60\% = 0.6 \text{ (Part)}}$$

$4,500 × 0.6 = **$2,700 selling salesperson's commission (answer)**

Seller's net. The amount of money left after the real estate commission is deducted from the sales price is called the seller's *net after commission.*

Example: After deducting $5,850 in closing costs and a 5 percent broker's commission, the sellers received their original cost of $175,000 plus a $4,400 profit. What was the sales price of the property?

Step 1: Calculate the seller's *net after commission.*

$175,000 Original Cost + $4,400 Profit + $5,850 Closing Costs = $185,250 net after commission

Step 2: Calculate the *rate after commission.*

100% (Total Rate) - 5% (Commission Rate) = 95% Rate after Commission

Step 3: Calculate the total sales price using the formula for *Total*: ***Part ÷ Rate = Total.***

$185,250 Net after Commission (Part) ÷ 95% Rate after Commission = Sales Price (Total)

$185,250 ÷ 0.95 = **$195,000 Sales Price (answer)**

or

$185,250 Net after Commission (Part)	
Total = ?	95% = 0.95 Rate after Commission

$185,250 ÷ 0.95 = **$195,000 Sales Price (answer)**

To check the answer, take 5 percent of the sales price, or,

$195,000 × 0.05 = $9,750

which, if subtracted from the sales price of $195,000, leaves the seller's desired net after commission of $185,250.

PROFIT

A **profit** is made when an item is sold for more than the purchase price. If an item is sold for less than the purchase price, there is a **loss** on the sale. Use the percentage formulas to calculate profit or loss.

Example: A home was listed for $125,000. It sold for $123,200, which resulted in a 10 percent profit over the original cost. What was the original cost?

Step 1: Calculate the *rate* that the sales price represents.

100% Original Cost + 10% Profit = 110% Sales Price

Step 2: Calculate the original cost using the formula for *Total*: **Part ÷ Rate = Total.**

$123,200 Sales Price (Part) ÷ 110% (Rate) = Original Cost (Total)
$123,200 ÷ 1.10 = $112,000 **original cost (answer)**

or

$$\frac{\$123,200 \text{ Sales Price (Part)}}{\text{Original Cost (Total)} = ? \;\bigg|\; 110\% = 1.10 \text{ (Rate)}}$$

$123,200 ÷ 1.10 = **$112,000 Original Cost (answer)**

Note that in the case of a profit, the "part" is larger than the "total."

INTEREST

Interest is the cost of using money. The amount of interest paid is determined by the agreed-on annual interest rate, the amount of money borrowed (loan amount) or amount of money still owed (loan balance), and the period of time the money is held. The formulas for percentage calculations also are used for *interest* computations. For more information about interest calculations, see Chapter 16.

Note: Using a calculator with a "%" key, a percentage problem can be computed without moving the decimals "two to the left" or "two to the right." On most calculators, simply enter the first number and depress the appropriate function key; then enter the second number and depress "%." The answer that appears on the calculator is decimally correct. Check the user's manual for instructions on the use of the "%" key on your calculator.

Example: What is the annual interest on a $10,000 loan on which the interest rate is 12 percent?

$10,000 (Total) × 12% (Rate) = Interest (Part)
$10,000 × 0.12 = **$1,200 interest (answer)**

or

$$\frac{\text{Part} = ?}{\$10,000 \text{ (Total)} \;\bigg|\; 12\% = 0.12 \text{ (Rate)}}$$

$10,000 × 0.12 = **$1,200 interest (answer)**

In the preceding problem, the interest was calculated for one year. When interest is not calculated for a full year, the formula must have a "time" factor. Therefore, the following formula is generally used for interest computations:

Principal (total) × Rate × Time (in months) = Interest (Part)

Example: How much interest would be charged if the loan could be paid off in seven months?

$10,000 × 0.12 × 7/12 = Interest
$10,000 × 0.12 × .583333 = **$700 interest (answer)**

or

$$\frac{\text{Part} = ?}{\$10{,}000\text{ (Total)} \quad | \quad 12\% = 0.12\text{ (Annual Rate)} \quad | \quad 7/12\text{ (Time)}}$$

$$\$10{,}000 \times 0.12 \times 7/12 = \textbf{\$700 interest (answer)}$$

As explained earlier in this chapter, the percentage calculations illustrated above are used to solve most real estate mathematics problems. You can see that both the formula method and the T Bar method yield the same results. Therefore, use the method that makes more sense to you. For the sake of simplicity, the remaining problems in this chapter will be solved using the formula method only. If you prefer the T Bar, just draw the graphic beside each problem.

AMORTIZATION

The process of paying off a loan in equal installments of principal and interest is known as **amortization.** The interest is calculated each month on the remaining loan balance, and "time" is 1 month or 1/12. The payment is first applied to the accrued interest with the remaining balance applied to reduce the principal (See Chapter 16).

Example: What is the balance after two payments on a loan in the original amount of $150,000 with monthly payments of $1,449.00 at 10 percent over a 20-year period?

First month:

$150,000 loan (Total) × 10% (Rate) × 1/12 (Time) =
$1,250 interest first month (Part)

$1,449.00	total payment
−1,250.00	interest first month
$199.00	principal reduction first month

Second month:

$150,000.00	original loan
−199.00	first month's reduction
$149,801.00	second month's beginning balance

$149,801.00 loan balance (Total) × 10% (Rate) × 1/12 (Time) =
$1,248.34 interest second month (Part)

$1,449.00	total payment
−1,248.34	interest second month
$200.66	principal reduction second month

$149,801.00	second month's beginning balance
−200.66	second month's reduction
$149,600.34	**balance after second month's payment, beginning of third month (answer)**

LOAN DISCOUNT

The **loan discount** is a method of increasing the lender's yield on a loan without increasing the interest rate. One point equals 1 percent of the loan amount (see Chapter 16). Use the formula for *Part* to compute a loan discount amount.

Example: The lender will charge a 1-point origination fee and 2½ loan discount points. What will be the total due for points on an $98,000 loan?

$98,000 (Total) × 3½% (1% + 2½% Rate) = Total Points (Part)
$98,000 × 0.035 = **$3,430 total due for points (answer)**

PROPERTY TAXES AND INSURANCE PREMIUMS

Property taxes and insurance premiums usually are expressed as rates per unit of value. For example, taxes might be computed in a certain county at the rate of $2.50 per $100 of appraised value. An insurance premium on a $65,000 home might be computed at $8.646 per $1,000 of insurable value. Use the formula for *Part* to compute taxes or insurance premiums.

Example: A house has been appraised at $90,000 and is taxed at an annual rate of $2.50 per $100 appraised valuation. What is the yearly tax?

$90,000 appraised value (Total) × [$2.50 ÷ $100] (Rate) =
Total Annual Tax (Part)
$90,000 × .0250 = **$2,250 total annual tax (answer)**

See Chapter 11 for a further discussion of tax computations.

MEASUREMENTS

Linear. Linear measurement is measurement of a line. When the terms per foot, per linear foot, per running foot, or per front foot are used, determine the total length of the object. To measure front footage of a lot, use the street footage. To measure linear feet for a fence, measure the sides to be fenced. If two dimensions are given for a tract of land, the first dimension is the frontage if they are not labeled.

Example: A rectangular lot is 50 feet × 150 feet. The cost to fence this lot is priced per linear/running foot. How many linear/running feet will be used to calculate the price of the fence, assuming the entire lot is to be enclosed in the fence?

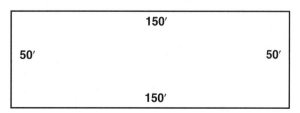

50 feet + 150 feet + 50 feet + 150 feet = **400 linear/running feet (answer)**

Example: A parcel of land that fronts on I-45 in Houston is for sale at $5,000 per front foot. What would it cost to purchase this parcel of land if the dimensions are 150′ by 100′?

150 front feet × $5,000 per front foot = **$750,000 cost to purchase (answer)**

Area and volume. Area is the two-dimensional surface of an object. Area is quoted in square units (feet, yards, acres). A real estate agent would use this formula to compute the area of a parcel of land or figure the square footage of living area in a house. To *compute the area of a square or rectangular parcel*, use the formula:

$$area = length \times width$$

Example: How many square feet are in a room 15′6″ × 30′9″?

Step 1: Convert "inches" to a decimal figure by dividing by 12 inches per foot.

6″ ÷ 12 = 0.5′ 9″ ÷ 12 = 0.75′

Step 2: Calculate the area.

15.5′ × 30.75′ = **476.625 square feet (answer)**

Remember: Area is always expressed in square units.

Example: If carpet costs $63 per square yard to install, what would it cost to carpet the room in the previous example?

476.625 square feet ÷ 9 square feet/square yard = 52.958333 square yards
52.958333 square yards × $63 per square yard = **$3,336.37 carpet cost (answer)**

To compute the amount of surface in a triangular-shaped area, use the formula:

$$area\ of\ a\ triangle = \text{½ (base} \times \text{height)}$$
or
$$area\ of\ a\ triangle = (base \times height) \div 2$$

The *base* of a triangle is the bottom, the side on which the triangle rests. The *height* is an imaginary straight line extending from the point of the uppermost angle straight down to the base.

Example: How many square feet are contained in a triangular parcel of land that is 400 feet on the base and 200 feet high?

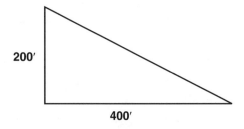

(400′ × 200′) ÷ 2 = **40,000 square feet (answer)**

Example: How many acres are in a 3-sided tract of land that is 300′ on the base and 400′ high?

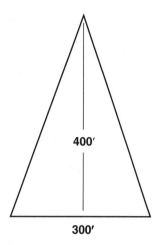

(300′ × 400′) ÷ 2 = 60,000 square feet ÷ 43,560 sq. ft./acre =
1.377 acres (answer)

To compute the area of an irregular room, a house, or parcel of land, divide the shape into regular rectangles, squares, or triangles. Next, compute the area of each regular figure and add the areas together to obtain the total area.

Volume is the space inside a three-dimensional object. It is used, for example, in measuring the interior airspace of a room to determine the required capacity for a heating unit or to calculate the amount of concrete needed on a construction project. *Remember: Volume is always expressed in cubic units.*

The formula for *computing volume* is

volume = length × width × height

Example: A building is 500 feet long, 400 feet wide, and 25 feet high. How many cubic feet of space are in this building?

500′ × 400′ × 25′ = **5,000,000 cubic feet (answer)**

Example: How many cubic yards of concrete would it take to build a sidewalk measuring 120′ long, 2′ 6″ wide and 3 inches thick?

Step 1: Convert inches to feet.

6″ = 6/12′ = 0.5′   3″ = 3/12′ = 0.25′

Step 2: Calculate cubic feet and convert to cubic yards.

120′ × 2.5′ × 0.25′ = 75 cubic feet

75 cubic feet ÷ 27 cubic feet/cubic yard = **2.78 cubic yards (answer)**

To compute the volume of a triangular prism, such as the airspace under a gable roof or in an A-frame cabin, use the formula:

$$volume = 1/2\ (length \times width \times height)$$

Example: A building is 40 feet by 25 feet with a 10-foot-high ceiling. The building has a gable roof that is 8 feet high at the tallest point. How many cubic feet are in this structure, including the roof?

Step 1: Divide the structure into two parts: the rectangular dwelling unit and the triangular prism roof unit.

Dwelling unit: 40′ (length) by 25′ (width) by 10′ (height)
Roof unit: 40′ (length) by 25′ (width) by 8′ (height)

Step 2: Calculate the area of each portion and combine the totals.

40′ × 25′ × 10′ = 10,000 cubic feet

½ (40′ × 25′ × 8′) = 4,000 cubic feet

10,000 cubic feet + 4,000 cubic feet = **14,000 total cubic feet (answer)**

PRORATING

Most closings involve the division of financial responsibility between the buyer and seller for such items as loan interest, taxes, rents, fuel, and utility bills. These allowances are called *prorations.* Prorations are necessary to ensure that expenses are divided fairly between the seller and the buyer. For example, the seller may owe current taxes that have not been billed; the buyer would want this settled at the closing. If the buyer assumes the seller's existing loan, the seller usually owes the buyer for interest from the first of the month *through* the date of closing.

Accrued expense items are items to be prorated that are owed by the seller but eventually will be paid by the buyer (such as interest on an assumed loan or accrued taxes). Therefore, the seller pays the buyer for these expenses at closing.

Prepaid expense items are items to be prorated that have been prepaid by the seller but not fully used up (such as a prepaid insurance policy). The buyer owes the seller for these expenses. *Prepaid income items,* such as rental income, would be prorated and the income for the unused days transferred to the buyer from the seller at closing.

Some general guidelines in computing prorations are listed below:

- The seller owns the property on the day of closing; the seller is charged expenses for that day and gets income for that day. This is called prorating *through* the day of closing, which is a requirement of the Texas promulgated sales contracts.
- Prorations are based on either a statutory year or a calendar year. A *statutory* or *banker's year* is based on a 360-day year, using 30 days in

each month. A *calendar year* is based on a 365-day year, using the actual number of days in each month.

- The buyer pays the seller for prepaid expense items; the seller pays the buyer for accrued expense items. The party receiving the money "gets the credit"; the party paying the money is "debited" (see Figure 19.1).

Proration steps. When an item is to be prorated, these steps should be followed:

Step 1: The charge must first be broken down into yearly, monthly, and daily amounts, depending on the type of charge. Using a *statutory year*, a total annual charge would be divided by 360 to arrive at a daily charge; a monthly charge, by 30. Using a *calendar year*, a total annual charge would be divided by 365 to arrive at a daily charge; a monthly charge, by the actual number of days in the month of closing.

Step 2: The prorated time period is calculated using the actual number of months and days.

Step 3: The monthly and daily amounts are then multiplied by the number of years, months, and days in the prorated time period to determine the accrued or unearned amount to be credited or debited at closing.

Mortgage interest proration. *Example:* A buyer purchases a home for $175,000 and plans to assume the seller's existing loan for $146,750 with monthly payments of $1,449 at 10 percent. The closing date is set for August 18. Because interest on a mortgage loan is collected in arrears, the August 1 payment covered July's interest. Therefore, the seller has not yet made a payment to cover August's interest, and the seller will owe a portion of the interest to the buyer for the next house payment.

Step 1: The initial step is to calculate the *dollars per day* for the interest on the mortgage. Carry all computations to three decimal places until a final figure is reached, then round off to the nearest penny.

$146,750 (Total) × 10% (Rate) × 1/12 = $1,222.916 interest for the month of closing

Using a 30-day month and 360-day *statutory year* (required for computations of prepaid interest on sales to Fannie Mae and Freddie Mac if this were a new loan), divide the monthly charge by 30 to get the daily premium:

$1,222.916 ÷ 30 days = $40.763 daily charge

Step 2: Next, calculate the time period for which the seller owes the buyer:

18 days in August *through the day of closing*

Step 3: Finally, multiply the daily interest amount by the number of days to be charged to the seller:

$40.763 daily charge × 18 days = **$733.73 prorated interest**, **using a** *statutory year* **(answer);** a *debit* to the seller and a *credit* to the buyer

Figure 19.1   The Debit/Credit Flow

Using a *calendar year* (which would be normally be used on an assumption's accrued interest computation), the proration would be

Step 1: Calculate the charge per day (31 days in August):

$$\$1,222.916 \div 31 \text{ days} = \$39.449 \text{ daily charge}$$

Step 2: Calculate the time period: August 1 through August 18 = 18 days

Step 3: Multiply the daily charge by the number of days:

$$\$39.449 \times 18 \text{ days} = \$710.08 \text{ \textbf{prorated interest,}}$$
$$\textbf{using a } \textit{calendar year} \textbf{ (answer)}$$

Tax proration. Real estate taxes are assessed from January 1 through December 31. Because taxes are usually paid in arrears, the seller will owe the buyer for accrued taxes from January 1 *through* the day of closing. If the current tax bill has not been issued, the proration is generally computed on the previous year's bill.

Example: A sale is to be closed on September 17, and current real estate taxes of $1,200 are to be prorated accordingly.

Step 1: First determine the prorated cost of the real estate tax per month and day; assume a *statutory year.*

$$\$1,200 \text{ annual taxes} \div 12 \text{ months} = \$100 \text{ taxes per month}$$
$$\$100 \text{ monthly taxes} \div 30 \text{ days} = \$3.333 \text{ taxes per day}$$

Step 2: The accrued period is 8 months and 17 days (January through August = 8 months; September 1 through September 17 = 17 days).

1. C
2. B
3. C
4. B
5. D
6. C
7. D
8. D
9. A
10. A
11. C
12. B
13. B
14. B
15. B
16. B
17. B
18. A
19. C
20. C
21. D

Step 3: Next, multiply the monthly and daily charges by the accrued period and add the totals to determine the prorated real estate tax:

$100	$ 3.333	$800.000
× 8 months	× 17 days	+ 56.661
$800	$56.661	$856.661

$856.66 prorated taxes, using the *statutory year* (answer)

This amount represents the seller's accrued *earned* tax; it will be *a credit to the buyer and a debit to the seller* on the closing statement (shown in Figure 20.1).

Another procedure for calculating the proration for the *statutory year* is this: January 1 to September 17 runs 257 days (January's 30 days, February's 30 days, and so on). A tax bill of $1,200 ÷ 360 days = $3.333 per day. $3.333 × 257 days = $856.58. Note the slight difference in results ($856.66 and $856.58) from rounding.

The following method would be used to compute this proration according to the *calendar-year method:* the accrued period from January 1 to September 17 runs 260 days (January's 31 days, February's 28 days, and so on). A tax bill of $1,200 ÷ 365 days = $3.288 per day. $3.288 × 260 days = $854.880, or $854.88.

For more information about prorations, see Chapter 20.

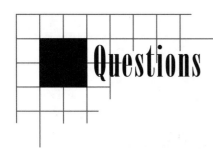

Questions

1. If the bank gave John a 90 percent loan on a house valued at $88,500, how much additional cash must he produce as a down payment if he already had paid $4,500 in earnest money?
   a. $3,500
   b. $4,000
   c. $4,350
   d. $8,850

2. What did the owners originally pay for their home if they sold it for $98,672, which gave them a 12 percent profit over their original cost?
   a. $86,830
   b. $88,100
   c. $89,700
   d. $110,510

3. Four women pooled their savings and purchased a 6-unit apartment building for $350,000. If one person invested $80,000 and two contributed $87,500 each, what percentage of ownership was left for the fourth investor?
   a. 20%
   b. 25%
   c. 27%
   d. 30%

4. Jacob wants to determine the principal amount still owed on his mortgage loan. He knows that the interest portion of his last monthly payment was $391.42. If he is paying interest at the rate of 11½ percent, what was the outstanding balance of the loan before that last payment was made?
   a. $43,713.00
   b. $40,843.83
   c. $36,427.50
   d. $34,284.70

5. The home at 1358 DeKalb Street is valued at $95,000. The local tax rate is $1.71 per $100. What is the amount of the monthly taxes?
   a. $1,111.50
   b. $926.30
   c. $111.15
   d. $135.38

6. What is the total cost of a driveway 15′ wide, 40′ long, and 4″ thick if the concrete costs $60.00 per cubic yard and the labor costs $1.25 per square foot?
   a. $527.25
   b. $693.75
   c. $1,194.00
   d. $1,581.75

7. An owner agrees to list his property on the condition that he will receive at least $47,300 after paying a 5 percent broker's commission and paying $1,150 in closing costs. At what price must it sell?
   a. $48,450
   b. $50,815
   c. $50,875
   d. $51,000

8. The Loving Gift Shop pays rent of $600 per month plus 2.5 percent of gross annual sales in excess of $50,000. What was the average monthly rent last year if gross annual sales were $75,000?
   a. $1,125.00
   b. $756.25
   c. $600.00
   d. $652.08

9. Two brokers split the 6 percent commission equally on a $73,000 home. The selling salesperson, Joe, was paid 70 percent of his broker's share. The listing salesperson, Janice, was paid 30 percent of her broker's share. How much did Janice receive?
   a. $657
   b. $4,380
   c. $1,533
   d. $1,314

10. How much interest will the seller owe the buyer for a closing date of August 10 if the outstanding loan balance is $43,580? The interest rate on this assumable loan is 10½ percent and the last payment was paid on August 1. Prorations are to be done *through* the day of closing, using a *statutory year.*
    a. $127.11
    b. $254.22
    c. $508.43
    d. $381.33

11. The buyer has agreed to pay $175,000 for a property. If she makes a 10 percent down payment, how much will she owe at closing for points if there are 2.5 loan discount points and a 1-point origination fee?
    a. $1,575.00
    b. $3,937.50
    c. $5,512.50
    d. $6,125.00

12. Calculate eight months' interest on a $5,000 interest-only loan at 9½ percent.
    a. $475.00
    c. $237.50
    b. $316.67
    d. $39.58

13. The Burns family has sold its home and closing is set for May 23. If last year's tax bill totaled $1,282 and was paid, how much will the tax proration be? Prorate *through* the day of closing using a *calendar year.*
    a. $498.70
    c. $609.98
    b. $502.22
    d. $613.42

14. What is the monthly net operating income on an investment of $115,000 if the rate of return is 12½ percent?
    a. $1,150.00
    c. $7,666.67
    b. $1,197.92
    d. $14,375.00

15. What is the interest rate on a $10,000 loan with semiannual interest of $450?
    a. 7%
    c. 11%
    b. 9%
    d. 13.5%

16. An office building produces $68,580 annual net operating income. What price would you pay for this property to show a minimum return of 12 percent on your investment?
    a. $489,857
    c. $685,800
    b. $571,500
    d. $768,096

17. If a broker received a 6.5 percent commission that was $5,200, what was the sales price of the house?
    a. $80,400
    c. $77,200
    b. $80,000
    d. $86,600

18. Bill earns an annual income of $60,000; Betty earns $2,400 per month. How much can Bill and Betty pay monthly for their mortgage payment if the lender uses a 28 percent qualifying ratio?
    a. $2,072
    c. $2,352
    b. $1,400
    d. $672

19. What percentage of profit would you make if you paid $10,500 for a lot, built a home on the lot at a cost of $93,000, and then sold the house and lot for $134,550?
    a. 13%
    c. 30%
    b. 23%
    d. 45%

20. A fence is being built to enclose a lot 125′ by 350′. If there will be one 10′ gate, how many running feet of fence will it take to enclose the lot?
    a. 465
    c. 940
    b. 600
    d. 960

21. A 100-acre farm is divided into lots for homes. The streets require ⅛ of the whole farm. If there are 140 lots, how many square feet are in each lot?
    a. 43,560
    c. 31,114
    b. 35,004
    d. 27,225

20 Closing the Real Estate Transaction

Key Terms

accrued item	doctrine of relation	prorate
closing	back	Real Estate Settlement
closing agent	escrow	Procedures Act
closing statement	escrow agent	(RESPA)
credit	HUD-1	Uniform Settlement
debit	prepaid item	Statement

OVERVIEW

After securing and servicing a listing, advertising the property, finding and qualifying potential buyers, and negotiating for and obtaining a signed sales contract on the seller's property, a real estate licensee is one step away from receiving a commission. That last step is the real estate closing, a procedure that includes both title and financial considerations.

This chapter discusses both aspects of real estate closing, focusing on the licensee's role in this concluding phase of a real estate transaction. Special emphasis is placed on the computations required to settle all necessary expenses between buyer and seller and between seller and broker; a detailed example of a real estate closing illustrates these computations.

CLOSING THE TRANSACTION—PRECLOSING PROCEDURES

Closing, or settlement, is the consummation of the real estate transaction. It is the time when the title to the real estate is transferred in exchange for payment of the purchase price. In many transactions, it is also the closing of the buyer's loan—the signing of the loan documents and the disbursal of mortgage funds by the lender.

A sales contract is the blueprint for the completion of a real estate transaction. A contract should be complete and should provide for all possibilities to avoid misunderstandings that could delay or even prevent closing of the sale. Before closing, the parties should assure themselves that the various conditions and stipulations of their sales contract have been met and that the closing statement correctly reflects all agreements regarding monies involved.

Buyer's Issues The buyer will want to ensure that the seller can deliver good title and that the property will be in the promised condition. This involves inspecting

- the title evidence;
- the seller's deed;
- any documents demonstrating the removal of undesired liens and encumbrances;
- the survey;
- the results of any required inspections, such as termite or structural inspections, or required repairs; and
- any leases if tenants reside on the premises.

Title evidence. The buyer and the buyer's lender will want assurance that the seller's title complies with the requirements of the sales contract. The seller is usually required to produce a current *abstract of title* from an abstracter or a *title commitment* from a title insurance company. When an abstract of title is used, the buyer's attorney examines it and issues an opinion of title. This opinion, like the title commitment, sets forth the status of the seller's title. It discloses all liens, encumbrances, easements, conditions, or restrictions that appear on the record and to which the seller's title is subject. The Texas Real Estate License Act *requires* that a broker advise a purchaser in writing, at or prior to closing, to have the abstract examined by an attorney or to obtain a title insurance policy. This "advice" is printed on the Texas promulgated sales contract forms.

There are usually three searches of the public records to check the status of the seller's title. The first (to prepare the title commitment or abstract) shows the status of the seller's title on the date of the sales contract. The second search is made on the day of closing and covers the date when the deed is delivered to the purchaser. A third search is conducted prior to recording the papers to be sure that nothing affecting the property has been recorded since the last search was made. If title insurance is purchased, the cost of all title searches is included in the cost of the mortgagee's (lender's) policy and the mortgagor's (owner's) policy.

Releasing existing liens. When the purchaser pays cash or obtains a new loan to purchase the property, the seller's existing loan is paid in full and released of record. The exact amount required to pay the existing loan is provided in a current *payoff statement* from the lender, effective as of the date of closing. This payoff statement notes the unpaid amount of principal, interest due through the date of loan payoff, the fee for issuing the release of lien, credits (if any) for tax and insurance reserves, and the amount of any prepayment penalties. The same procedure would be followed for any other liens that must be released before the buyer takes title.

In a transaction in which the buyer assumes the seller's existing mortgage loan, the buyer will want to know the exact balance of the loan as of the closing date. It is recommended that the buyer obtain an *estoppel certificate* and waiver of acceleration from the lender, stating the exact balance due, the last interest payment made, and the fact that the lender permits the assumption.

Survey. An improvement survey gives information about the exact location and dimensions of the land and any improvements on it. In addition, the survey should set out in full any existing easements and encroachments. Whether or not the sales contract calls for a survey, lenders usually require one.

Checking the premises. The buyer should inspect the property to determine the interests of any parties in possession or other interests that cannot be determined from inspecting the public record.

If a final walk-through has been requested in the purchase contract, it usually occurs on the day of closing or shortly before. At that time, the buyer checks to see that all fixtures and personal property included in the transaction are still present, that no damage has been done to the property, and that any required repairs have been properly completed.

Seller's Issues Because the seller's main interest is in receiving payment for the property, he or she will want to be sure that the buyer has obtained the necessary financing and has sufficient funds to complete the sale. The seller will also want to be certain that he or she has complied with all the buyer's inspection and repair requirements so the transaction can be completed.

CONDUCTING THE CLOSING

> *Closing* is the point at which ownership of a property is transferred in exchange for the selling price.

Generally speaking, the closing of a real estate transaction involves a gathering of interested parties at which the promises made in the *real estate sales contract* are kept, or *executed;* that is, the seller's deed is delivered in exchange for the purchase price. In many sales transactions, two closings actually take place at this time: (1) the closing of the sale and (2) the closing of the buyer's loan—the signing of the loan documents and disbursement of mortgage funds by the lender. A closing that involves all interested parties is often called a *round table close.*

Where Closings Are Held and Who Attends Closings may be held at a number of locations, including the title company, the lending institution, or the office of one of the parties' attorneys or the broker. In Texas, the closing usually takes place at a title company. Those attending may include any (not necessarily all) of the following interested parties:

- Buyer
- Seller
- Real estate agent (broker and/or salesperson)
- Attorney(s) for the seller and/or buyer
- Representatives and/or attorneys for the lending institution(s) involved
- Representative of the title insurance company

Closing agent. One person usually calculates the official settlement, or division of charges and expenses between the parties and conducts the proceedings at a closing. In some areas real estate brokers preside, but more commonly the buyer's or seller's attorney or a representative of a title company serves as the **closing agent.** Some title companies and law firms employ paralegal assistants who conduct closings for their firms.

Preparation for closing involves ordering and reviewing an array of documents, such as the title insurance policy, the survey, the property insurance policy, and other items. The closing agent prepares the closing statements and arranges the time and place of closing with all parties.

In Practice   In Texas, title companies are not permitted to prepare legal documents. This is the practice of law and must be done by an attorney, who often is retained by the title company for such purpose.

The exchange. When all parties are satisfied that everything is in order, the exchange is made and the closing agent collects all funds. After the closing, the agent writes all disbursement checks arising from the closing, prepares the final disbursement sheet to prove that money paid in equals money paid out, and transmits the appropriate documents to the county clerk for recording.

Closing in Escrow

> In an *escrow closing*, a third party coordinates the closing activities on behalf of the buyer and seller.

An **escrow** is a method of closing in which a disinterested third party is authorized to act as escrow agent and is given the responsibility to coordinate the closing activities. The **escrow agent** also may be called the *escrow holder.* The escrow agent may be an attorney, a title company, a trust company, an escrow company, or the escrow department of a lending institution. Although a real estate brokerage can offer escrow services, a broker cannot be a disinterested party in a transaction from which he or she expects to collect a commission. Because the escrow agent is placed in a position of great trust, Texas has laws regulating escrow agents and limiting who may serve in this capacity. An escrow agent must be licensed by the state insurance board and must obtain and maintain a surety bond.

The Escrow Procedure

When a transaction will be closed in escrow, the buyer and seller choose an escrow agent. If a TREC-promulgated sales contract form has been used, the escrow agreement is a part of that contract. The agreement sets forth the details of the transaction and the instructions to the escrow agent. After the contract is signed, the broker turns over the earnest money to the escrow agent, who deposits it in a special trust, or escrow, account. The License Act and TREC rules require that the broker deposit the earnest money by the end of the second business day after the contract has been signed by all parties.

Buyer and seller deposit all pertinent documents with the escrow agent before the specified date of closing. The *seller* usually deposits

- the deed conveying the property to the buyer,
- title evidence (abstract or title insurance policy),
- the payoff letter (a letter from the mortgagee of the existing mortgage, setting forth the amount needed to pay the loan in full or the exact amount the buyer will assume),
- affidavits of title, and
- other instruments or documents necessary to clear the title or complete the transaction.

Among the seller's affidavits is an *affidavit as to debts and liens,* a sworn statement in which the seller assures the title company (and the buyer) that there are no unpaid bills for repairs or improvements and there are no undisclosed defects in the title. Required by the title insurance company before it will issue an owner's policy to the buyer, this affidavit establishes the right for the title company to sue the seller if his or her statements in the affidavit prove incorrect.

Prior to closing in escrow, the *buyer* deposits

- the balance of the cash needed to complete the purchase, usually in the form of a certified check;
- loan documents (if the buyer is securing a new loan);
- a hazard insurance policy, including flood insurance (where required);
- a survey, if requested in the contract or required by the lender; and
- other documents needed to complete the transaction.

$1,500 limit to accept personal check

The escrow agent has the authority to examine the title evidence. When clear title is shown in the name of the buyer and all other conditions of the escrow agreement have been met, the agent generally is authorized to disburse the purchase price to the seller, minus all seller's expenses. The agent then records the deed and deed of trust (if a new loan has been obtained by the purchaser).

If the escrow agent's examination of the title discloses liens, a portion of the purchase price can be withheld from the seller to pay the liens and clear the title.

If the seller cannot clear his or her title, or if for any reason the sale cannot be consummated, the escrow agreement generally provides that the parties be returned to their former status, as if no sale had occurred. The escrow agent returns the deed to the seller and refunds the purchase money to the buyer after obtaining a release of liability from the seller, buyer, and broker.

There are several advantages of closing a sale in escrow: (1) the buyer's money will not be paid to the seller until the seller's title is acceptable, (2) the seller is assured of getting the purchase price because the buyer's check must clear before title passes, and (3) neither party need be present when title is passed.

Under the "Good Funds Rule" of the Texas State Board of Insurance, the title company must require that the buyer provide a bank cashier's check or certified personal check at closing if the amount due at closing is $1,500 or more.

Doctrine of relation back. If a seller deposits his or her deed with an escrow agent under the terms of a valid escrow agreement and thereafter the conditions of the escrow are satisfied, the *deed passes title to the purchaser as of the date it was delivered to the escrow agent.* This is called the **doctrine of relation back**—the title relates back to the date on which the deed was deposited in escrow. If the conditions of the escrow agreement have not been met, however, the deed is not considered delivered and title does not pass to the purchaser.

> When a seller delivers title into escrow, but dies before closing of escrow, the conveyance still will be accomplished.

In Practice   Fees charged by the escrow agent typically are split between buyer and seller. However, a purchaser under new VA financing is not allowed to pay any escrow fees, so all such costs are the sole responsibility of the seller.

Broker's Role at Closing

After the contract is signed and the earnest money is delivered to the title company, the loan company, title company, and attorneys take over. However, the broker's service generally continues all the way through closing. The broker makes sure all details are taken care of so the closing can proceed smoothly. This means ensuring that arrangements are made for obtaining title evidence, surveys, appraisals, inspections, repairs, and other items listed in the contract. At the closing itself, the broker's role can vary from simply collecting the commission to conducting the proceedings. In addition, if neither the person who conducts the closing nor the lender provides IRS Form 1099-S to the seller, the broker is required to do so if the transaction is reportable under IRS rules. In most cases, capital gains on a principal residence are not reportable because they do not exceed the $250,000-single or $500,000-married exclusion discussed in Chapter 4. Closings on other types of property generally would be reportable.

In Practice   Licensees should avoid recommending a specific person or company for any inspection or testing services. If a buyer suffers any injury as a result of a provider's negligence, the licensee also may be liable. The better practice is to give clients the sources for names of several professionals who offer high-quality services.

Lender's Interest in Closing

Whether a buyer obtains new financing or assumes the seller's existing loan, the lender wants to protect its security interest in the property by ensuring that tax and insurance payments are maintained. Lenders want their mortgage lien to have priority over other liens. They also want to ensure that insurance is kept up to date in case property is damaged or destroyed. For this reason, the lender usually requires a title insurance policy and a fire and hazard insurance policy (along with a receipt for the premium). In addition, a lender may require other information: a survey, a termite or other inspection report, or a certificate of occupancy (for a newly constructed building). A lender may also request that a reserve account be established for tax and insurance payments.

RESPA

The federal **Real Estate Settlement Procedures Act (RESPA)** was enacted to protect consumers from abusive lending practices. RESPA also aids consumers during the mortgage loan settlement process. It ensures that consumers are provided with accurate and timely information about the actual costs of closing a transaction. It also eliminates kickbacks and other referral fees that tend to inflate the costs of settlement unnecessarily and it prohibits lenders from requiring excessive escrow account deposits. RESPA is administered by HUD, and additional information about RESPA can be obtained on the web site at www.hud.gov/fha/sfh/res/respa_hm.html.

RESPA requirements apply when a purchase is financed by a federally related mortgage loan. *Federally related loans* include loans made by banks, savings associations, or other lenders whose deposits are insured by federal agencies. It also includes loans insured by the FHA and guaranteed by the VA; loans administered by HUD; and loans intended to be sold by the lenders to Fannie Mae, Ginnie Mae, or Freddie Mac.

RESPA regulations apply to first-lien residential mortgage loans made to finance the purchase of one-family to four-family homes, cooperatives, and condominiums for either owner occupancy or investment. RESPA also governs subordinate loans (including loans for home equity and home improvement), refinancings, and reverse mortgages.

RESPA applies to all federally related residential mortgage loans *except* (1) a loan on property of 25 acres or more; (2) a loan for business, commercial, or agricultural purposes; (3) a temporary construction loan; (4) a loan on vacant land; (5) assumption without lender approval; (6) a conversion of a federally related mortgage loan to different terms, if a new note is not required; and (7) transfer of a loan in the secondary market.

Disclosure requirements. Lenders and closing agents have certain disclosure obligations at the time of loan application and loan closing:

- *Special Information Booklet:* Lenders must give a copy of a HUD Special Information Booklet to every person from whom they receive or for whom they prepare a loan application (except for refinancings). The HUD booklet must be given at the time the application is received or within three days afterward. This booklet provides the borrower with general information about closing costs and explains the various RESPA provisions, including a line-by-line discussion of the Uniform Settlement Statement.
- *Good-faith estimate of settlement costs:* At the time of the loan application or within three business days thereafter, the lender must provide the borrower with a good-faith estimate of the settlement costs the borrower is likely to incur. This estimate may be a specific figure or a range of costs based on comparable past transactions in the area. In addition, if the lender requires use of a particular attorney or title company to conduct the closing, the lender must state whether it has any business relationship with that firm and must estimate the charges for this service.
- *Uniform Settlement Statement (HUD Form 1):* RESPA provides that loan closing information must be detailed on a special HUD form, the **Uniform Settlement Statement,** or **HUD-1.** A copy of this form is illustrated in Figure 20.1 at the end of the chapter. The completed statement must itemize all charges to be collected at closing, whether required by the lender or a third party. Items required by the lender that are paid for prior to the closing must be marked "paid outside of closing" (POC). Items paid by the buyer or seller outside closing, not required by the lender, are not included on the HUD-1. The HUD-1 statement must be made available for inspection by the borrower one day prior to closing if requested. No fee can be charged for preparation

of the HUD-1 or related statements required by RESPA or the Truth-in-Lending Act.

- *Escrow account disclosure:* Lenders and loan servicers must provide disclosure statements to borrowers at closing concerning (a) the possibility of a future transfer of loan servicing (collection of and accounting for loan payments and escrow accounts) to another company and (b) the rights of the borrower if that occurs.

Prohibitions and restrictions. RESPA affords consumer protection through its restrictions placed on brokers, lenders, and title companies.

- *Prohibition against kickbacks:* RESPA explicitly prohibits the payment of kickbacks, or unearned fees, in any real estate settlement service. It prohibits referral fees *when no services are actually rendered.* For example, an insurance agency would be prohibited from paying a kickback to a lender for the lender's referring one of its customers to the agency. This prohibition does *not* include fee splitting among cooperating brokers or members of multiple-listing services, brokerage referral arrangements, the division of a commission between a broker and his or her salespeople, or referrals made by an employee to generate business for the company itself.
- *Selection of the title company:* RESPA makes it illegal for the seller to require that a buyer use a specific title company if the property is purchased with the assistance of a federally related mortgage loan.
- *Limitation on escrow (or reserve) account:* RESPA rules allow a lender or a company servicing a mortgage to collect each month for deposit into an escrow account a sum equal to one month's annual property taxes, insurance premiums, and other recurring items such as homeowners' dues and mortgage insurance premiums. Under the *aggregate analysis accounting method,* the company can also maintain a cushion equal to two months' worth of those payments as long as at least once each year the escrow account total does not exceed two times the monthly escrow payment. No cushion can be held for monthly FHA mortgage insurance premiums.
- *Computerized loan origination:* A broker may charge a fee for using a computerized loan origination (CLO) system to help a buyer select and originate a mortgage as long as the fee is disclosed on the good-faith estimate of closing costs and is reasonably related to the value of services provided. (See Chapter 16 for more information on CLOs.)
- *Controlled Business Arrangements (CBA):* A service that is increasing in popularity is one-stop shopping for consumers of real estate services. A real estate firm, title insurance company, mortgage broker, home inspection company, or even moving company may agree to offer a package of services to consumers. CBAs are permitted *as long as a consumer is clearly informed of the relationship among the service providers and that other providers are available.* Fees may not be exchanged among the affiliated companies simply for referring business to one another.

RESPA's Consumer Protections

- Settlement cost booklet
- Good-faith estimate of closing costs
- Uniform Settlement Statement
- Prohibition of kickbacks and unearned fees
- Escrow account limitations
- CLO regulation
- CBA disclosure

In Practice   Revisions have been proposed to several RESPA rules. Consult a lender, a title company, or the RESPA Web site for recent changes.

Table 20.1 *Credits and Debits at Closing*

Items Credited to Buyer (debited to seller)	Items Credited to Seller (debited to buyer)
1. Buyer's earnest money†	1. Sales price
2. Unpaid principal balance of outstanding mortgage being assumed by buyer*	2. Prorated premium for unearned (prepaid) portion of fire insurance
3. Earned interest on existing assumed mortgage not yet payable (accrued)	3. Insurance and tax reserve (if any) when outstanding mortgage is being assumed by buyer (prepaid)
4. Earned portion of general real estate tax not yet due (accrued)	4. Prepaid water charge and similar expense
5. Unearned portion of current rent collected in advance	5. Unearned portion of general real estate tax, if paid in advance
6. Earned janitor's salary (and sometimes vacation allowance)	
7. Tenants' security deposits*	
8. Principal amount of new loan†	
9. Seller-financed purchase-money loan	

*These items are not prorated.
†Note: Buyer's items 1 and 8 are not debited to seller.

PREPARATION OF CLOSING STATEMENTS

In addition to the purchase price, a typical real estate sales transaction involves numerous expenses for both parties. Some expenses are buyer's charges, others are seller's charges, and still others are split between the parties. On items prepaid by the seller for which reimbursement is due or expenses accrued by the seller and later billed to the buyer, charges must be **prorated** (divided) between the buyer and the seller. After accounting for the purchase price, loan amounts, expenses, and prorated items on the HUD-1 Uniform Settlement Statement, the buyer will know how much money to take to the closing and the seller will know how much money he or she will get at the closing.

How the Closing Statement Works

The completion of a **closing statement** involves an accounting of the parties' debits and credits. A **debit** is a charge, an amount that the party being debited owes and must pay at the closing. A **credit** is an amount a person gets at closing for an expense that he or she has already paid and for which he or she must be reimbursed. See Table 20.1 for a listing of credits and debits at closing.

Normal Closing Charges (Debits)

Common expenses incurred in a real estate transaction include the following items:

Broker's commission. The responsibility for paying the broker's commission will have been determined by previous agreement. If the broker is the agent for the seller, the seller is normally responsible for paying the commission. If an agency agreement exists between a broker and the buyer or if two agents are involved (one for the seller and one for the buyer), the commis-

> A *debit* is an amount to be paid by the buyer or seller; a *credit* is an amount to be received by the buyer or seller.

sion still may be paid by the seller or it may be apportioned as an expense between both parties.

Attorney fees. In most cases, attorney fees are charged to the seller for the preparation of the deed and a release of lien (if the seller's note is being paid off at closing or the buyer is assuming liability for the note). The buyer pays attorney fees for the preparation of the note and deed of trust.

Recording expenses. The charges for recording all of the documents must be paid to the county clerk. Each party pays those charges specified in the sales contract. If not specified in the contract, the *seller* usually pays for recording charges (filing fees) necessary to clear all defects and furnish clear title. Items usually charged to the *seller* include recording of release of liens, quitclaim deeds, affidavits, and satisfaction of mechanic's lien claims. The *purchaser* usually pays for recording charges that arise from the actual transfer of the title—the deed and the deed of trust or mortgage. In Texas, the charges are set by each county. The normal charge for the first page is $3 to $9; for each succeeding page, $2 to $3.

Title expenses. Under the provisions of the Texas promulgated sales contract form, the seller is required to furnish evidence of good title. If a property is closed on an abstract, the seller usually pays for the expenses of having the abstract prepared or brought up to date; the buyer pays for his or her attorney to inspect the abstract and issue an opinion of title. If the property closes on a title policy, the seller generally pays for the owner's title policy; if a new loan is involved, the buyer pays for the mortgagee's title policy. However, the promulgated contract form actually allows either party to pay for the owner's title policy. The premiums for title policies are set by the Texas State Board of Insurance.

Loan fees. When the purchaser is securing a new loan to finance the purchase, the lender usually will charge a loan origination fee of 1 percent of the loan. The fee usually is paid by the purchaser at the time the transaction is closed. If the buyer assumes the seller's existing loan, an assumption fee will be charged to the buyer.

The lender may also charge discount points, the payment of which is negotiated between the buyer and the seller on the sales contract. In addition, the terms of some mortgage loans require that the seller pay a prepayment charge or penalty for paying off the mortgage loan in advance of its due date.

Tax reserves and insurance reserves (escrows). The mortgage lender usually requires that the borrower establish and maintain an *escrow account* so the lender will have sufficient funds to pay general real estate taxes and to renew insurance policies when these items become due. To set up the reserve, the borrower is required to make a lump-sum payment to the lender when the loan is closed. The amount first paid into this reserve account is limited by RESPA to the amount of year-to-date unpaid real estate taxes (including the month of closing) and two months' reserves for taxes, insurance, and other expenses to be paid by the lender or servicer. Because the lender or servicer must ensure that at least once each year the escrow account does not exceed two times the monthly escrow payment, an aggregate adjustment then must be made to the total to be deposited into the escrow account at the time of closing. The escrow deposit and the interest from the date of closing to the end of the month preceding the buyer's first regular payment are called the *prepaids.*

Appraisal fees. When the buyer obtains a loan, it is customary for the buyer to pay for a lender-required appraisal. However, in most cases, either the buyer or the seller *may* pay the appraisal fees, as negotiated in the sales contract. In the case of a VA appraisal, the seller must pay for the appraisal unless it is ordered in the name of the veteran-buyer. A residential loan appraisal may cost from $325 to $400.

Settlement or closing fees. When a transaction is closed through a title company, a closing fee is charged for the services of the closing agent or escrow agent. A title company will furnish a real estate agent with an estimate of its customary charges for these services.

Survey fees. If the purchaser obtains new mortgage financing, he or she often pays the survey fees, because the survey is a lender requirement.

Prorations

Prorations of expenses between buyer and seller are necessary to ensure that expenses are divided fairly. Expenses that are most frequently prorated include interest on an assumed loan, taxes, rents, and utility bills.

Accrued items are expenses that are owed by the seller, but later will be paid by the buyer. Accrued expenses include taxes, interest on an assumed mortgage, and water bills. The seller is debited (charged) for these items at closing and the buyer gets the credit.

Prepaid items are expenses to be prorated, such as fuel oil in a tank, that have been prepaid by the seller but not fully used up. Therefore, the buyer is debited at closing and the seller gets the credit.

FOR EXAMPLE A sale is to be closed on June 25. Taxes are paid in arrears and will not be billed until late September. Therefore, the seller needs to pay the buyer for taxes from January 1 through June 25 because the buyer will pay the full year's taxes when they come due. If the buyer assumes the seller's existing mortgage, the seller will also owe the buyer the accrued interest for June 1 through June 25. The buyer will make the July payment, which includes interest for the month of June because interest is paid in arrears. Both the taxes and mortgage interest would be debits to the seller and credits to the buyer.

General rules for prorating. The provisions of the sales contract establish which items will be prorated and the agreements involved in that process. The Texas promulgated contract forms state in paragraph 13, "Taxes for the current year, interest, maintenance fees, assessments, dues and rents will be prorated through the Closing Date."

The general rules that guide the computation of prorations include the following:

- The seller owns the property on the day of closing, and prorations or apportionments are made *through the day of closing* if the promulgated contract forms are used. This means that the seller pays expenses and receives income for the day of closing.

- Prorations may be based on a statutory year (*360 days in a year and 30 days in a month*) or a calendar year (*365 days in a year and actual days in each month*), depending on local custom. Most tax and interest prorations in Texas are based on the calendar year.
- Accrued *general real estate taxes* that are not yet due are prorated at the closing. When the amount of the current real estate tax cannot be determined definitely, the proration usually is based on the last obtainable tax bill. The Texas promulgated sales contract provides that "If taxes vary from the amount prorated at closing, the parties shall adjust the prorations when tax statements for the current year are available." *Special assessments* for such municipal improvements as sewers, water mains, or streets are usually charged in full to the seller and are not prorated at closing.
- *Rents* usually are prorated on the basis of the *actual* number of days in the month of closing. The seller receives the rents for the day of closing and pays all expenses for that day. If any rents for the current month are uncollected when the sale is closed, the buyer may collect the rents if possible and remit a pro rata share to the seller.
- Payments made by tenants in advance to cover the *last month's rent* or the *security deposit* are *not* prorated. Some leases may require the tenant's consent to transfer the deposit.
- Unpaid *wages of building employees* are prorated if the sale is closed between wage payment dates.

The arithmetic of prorating. Accurate prorating involves four considerations:

1. The nature of the item being prorated
2. Whether it is an accrued item that requires the determination of an earned amount
3. Whether it is a prepaid item that requires the determination of an unearned amount—a refund to the seller
4. Whether the proration is for a *360-day statutory year* or a *365-day calendar year*

The steps for calculating the prorated amount are

- *Step 1*: Divide the yearly charge by 12 to determine a monthly charge for the item. For a daily charge, divide the yearly charge by 360 for a *statutory-year* proration or by 365 for a *calendar-year* proration.
- *Step 2*: Determine the actual number of months and/or days in the proration period.
- *Step 3:* Multiply the number of months and/or days in the prorated time period by the monthly and/or daily charges to determine the amount that will be used in the settlement statement.

In some cases when a sale is closed on the 15th of the month, the one-half month's charge is computed by simply dividing the monthly charge by two.

The final proration figure will vary slightly, depending on which computation method is used. The final figure also will vary according to the number of decimal places to which the division is carried. *All computations in this text carry the division to three decimal places.* The third decimal place is rounded off to the nearest cent only after the final proration figure is determined.

For examples of proration calculations, see the section on prorating in Chapter 19.

In Practice   On state brokers' and salespersons' examinations, prorations usually are based on a 30-day month (360-day year) unless specified otherwise in the problem. Note that local customs regarding prorations may differ. Prepaid interest calculations for new loans to be sold to Fannie Mae and Freddie Mac must be computed using a 360-day year. Ginnie Mae requires a 365-day year computation. Many title insurance companies provide proration charts that detail tax factors for each day in the year. To determine a tax proration using one of these charts, multiply the factor given for the closing date by the annual real estate tax.

RESPA UNIFORM SETTLEMENT STATEMENT

The Uniform Settlement Statement, HUD-1, is required by RESPA for almost all transactions. The sample transaction presented on the following pages illustrates the calculations involved in a real estate closing and the resulting HUD-1 form (Figure 20.1). The sales contract for this transaction is shown in Chapter 12 (Figure 12.1).

To complete the buyer's side of the closing statement, first the buyer's expenses are listed on page 2 of the HUD-1 form. Then the buyer's expenses are transferred to page 1 and added to the sales price for a "gross amount due from borrower." The borrower's credits are totaled next: earnest money, which has already been paid by the buyer; the balance of a loan to be assumed or the amount of a new loan; and the prorated amounts for items unpaid by the seller (taxes or mortgage interest). The credits are subtracted from the debits, and the difference between the two is the amount of money the buyer needs to take to closing.

A similar procedure is followed to determine how much money the seller actually will receive. The seller's debits and credits are each totaled. The seller's debits include the balance of any mortgage loan or other lien to be paid off at closing. The credits include the purchase price plus the buyer's share of any prorated items that the seller has prepaid. Finally, the total of the seller's charges is subtracted from the total credits to arrive at the amount the seller will receive at closing.

Case Study

John and Joanne Iuro listed their home at 3040 North Racine Avenue with the Open Door Real Estate Company. The listing price was $118,500 and possession could be given within four weeks after all parties had signed the contract. Under the terms of the listing agreement, the sellers agreed to pay the broker a commission of 7 percent of the sales price.

On May 16, the Open Door Real Estate Company submitted a contract offer to the Iuros from Blake and Connie Redemann, husband and wife. The Redemanns offered $115,000 and agreed to obtain a new mortgage loan. The Iuros signed the contract on May 18. Closing was set for June 15 at the office of the ABC Title Company. The title company holds earnest money in the amount of $15,000. (*Use a 360-day year for prorations.*)

Seller's Settlement

The unpaid balance of the Iuros' mortgage after the seller makes the June 1 payment will be $57,700. Payments are $680 per month with interest at 11 percent per annum on the unpaid balance.

The seller submitted evidence of title in the form of title insurance. The cost of the title policy was $1,086. Recording charges of $22 were paid for the recording of the release of seller's lien. In addition, the seller must pay $75 for the closing fee to the title company, $115 attorney fee for document preparation, $27 for tax certificates, $20 for a courier fee, and 1½ discount points on the buyer's new loan. All of these amounts will be paid from the closing proceeds.

Buyer's Settlement

The buyers' new loan is from Thrift Federal Savings in the amount of $70,000 at 10 percent interest. In connection with this loan, they will be charged $325 to have the property appraised by Swift Appraisal and $75 for a credit report from the Acme Credit Bureau—both of these amounts were paid at the time of loan application and will appear as "POC" on the HUD-1. The buyers' attorney will charge $150 to prepare the note and deed of trust. The buyer is to pay a 1 percent loan origination fee. The survey fee of $375 is to be paid by the buyer. Finally, the Redemanns will have to pay $43 for recording the deed of trust and the deed, $175 for a mortgagee's title insurance policy to cover the lender's interest in the property, $75 for the escrow closing fee to the title company, and $20 for courier fees.

In addition, the following prorations and/or deposits into the escrow account will be made:

- Interest in advance for the last 16 days of June, $311.10, because the first payment will not be due until August 1 and that payment will cover interest for the month of July only
- Tax reserves for 9 months, consisting of the seller's payment to the buyer for the prorated share of taxes from January 1 through June 15 plus the buyer's expense for the period from June 16 through July 31 (because the first payment is not until August 1, and it will cover August taxes) plus the escrow account deposit of $287.50 for two months of the anticipated annual real estate taxes ($1,725)
- Insurance reserves for two months of the annual insurance premium of $550

Computing the Prorations and Charges

The figures below illustrate some of the various steps in computing the prorations and other amounts to be included in the settlement.

1. *Closing date:* June 15

2. *Commission:* 7% × $115,000 (sales price) = $8,050

Figure 20.1   Settlement Statement

A. **Settlement Statement**

U.S. Department of Housing and Urban Development

OMB Approval No. 2502-0265

B. Type of Loan

1. ☐ FHA 2. ☐ FmHA 3. ☒ Conv. Unins. 4. ☐ VA 5. ☐ Conv. Ins.	6. File Number: **GF# 123456**	7. Loan Number: **000-0000**	8. Mortgage Insurance Case Number:

C. Note: This form is furnished to give you a statement of actual settlement costs. Amounts paid to and by the settlement agent are shown. Items marked "(p.o.c.)" were paid outside the closing; they are shown here for informational purposes and are not included in the totals.

D. Name & Address of Borrower: **Blake Redemann and wife,** **Connie Redemann** **7016 Hurst** **Amarillo, TX 79109**	E. Name & Address of Seller: **John Iuro and wife,** **Joanne Iuro** **3040 N. Racine** **Dallas, TX 75340** **Tax ID# 000-00-0000**	F. Name & Address of Lender: **Thrift Federal Savings** **567 Lender's Place** **Dallas, TX 75240**

G. Property Location: **3040 North Racine** **Dallas, TX 75340**	H. Settlement Agent: **ABC Title Co.** Place of Settlement: **1234 Settlement Street** **Dallas, TX 75240**	Tax I.D. No: **000-00-0000** I. Settlement Date: **06/15/XX**

J. Summary of Borrower's Transaction		K. Summary of Seller's Transaction	
100. Gross Amount Due From Borrower		**400. Gross Amount Due To Seller**	
101. Contract sales price	$115,000.00	401. Contract sales price	$115,000.00
102. Personal property		402. Personal property	
103. Settlement charges to borrower (line 1400)	$3,555.36	403.	
104.		404.	
105.		405.	
Adjustments for items paid by seller in advance		Adjustments for items paid by seller in advance	
106. City/town taxes to		406. City/town taxes to	
107. County taxes to		407. County taxes to	
108. Assessments to		408. Assessments to	
109.		409.	
110.		410.	
111.		411.	
112.		412.	
120. Gross Amount Due From Borrower	$118,555.36	**420. Gross Amount Due To Seller**	$115,000.00
200. Amounts Paid By Or In Behalf Of Borrower		**500. Reductions In Amount Due To Seller**	
201. Deposit or earnest money	$15,000.00	501. Excess deposit (see instructions)	
202. Principal amount of new loan(s)	$70,000.00	502. Settlement charges to seller (line 1400)	$10,445.00
203. Existing loan(s) taken subject to		503. Existing loan(s) taken subject to	
204.		504. Payoff of first mortgage loan	$57,964.47
205.		505. Payoff of second mortgage loan	
206.		506.	
207.		507.	
208.		508.	
209.		509.	
Adjustments for items unpaid by seller		Adjustments for items unpaid by seller	
210. City/town taxes **01-01-XX** to **06-15-XX**	$284.16	510. City/town taxes **01-01-XX** to **06-15-XX**	$284.16
211. County taxes **01-01-XX** to **06-15-XX**	$174.20	511. County taxes **01-01-XX** to **06-15-XX**	$174.20
212. Assessments to		512. Assessments to	
213. **School Taxes**	$332.31	513. **School Taxes**	$332.31
214.		514.	
215.		515.	
216.		516.	
217.		517.	
218.		518.	
219.		519.	
220. Total Paid By/For Borrower	$85,790.67	**520. Total Reduction Amount Due Seller**	$69,200.14
300. Cash At Settlement From/To Borrower		**600. Cash At Settlement To/From Seller**	
301. Gross Amount due from borrower (line 120)	$118,555.36	601. Gross amount due to seller (line 420)	$115,000.00
302. Less amounts paid by/for borrower (line 220)	($85,790.67)	602. Less reductions in amt. due seller (line 520)	($69,200.14)
	$32,764.69		$45,799.86
303. Cash ☒ From ☐ To Borrower		603. Cash ☒ To ☐ From Seller	

Previous editions are obsolete

HUD-1

Figure 20.1   Settlement Statement (Continued)

L. Settlement Charges

	Paid From Borrowers Funds at Settlement	Paid From Seller's Funds at Settlement
700. Total Sales/Broker's Commission based on price $ 115,000.00 @ 7 % = $8,050.00		
Division of Commission (line 700) as follows:		
701. $ **$8,050.00** to **Open Door Real Estate Company**		
702. $ to		
703. Commission paid at Settlement		$8,050.00
704.		
800. Items Payable In Connection With Loan		
801. Loan Origination Fee 1 %	$700.00	
802. Loan Discount 1.5 %		$1,050.00
803. Appraisal Fee $325 to **Swift Appraisal**	POC	
804. Credit Report $50 to **Acme Credit Bureau**	POC	
805. Lender's Inspection Fee		
806. Mortgage Insurance Application Fee to		
807. Assumption Fee		
808.		
809.		
810.		
811.		
900. Items Required By Lender To Be Paid In Advance		
901. Interest from **6-15-XX** to **7-01-XX** @$ **19.444** /day **(16 days)**	$311.10	
902. Mortgage Insurance Premium for 0 months to		
903. Hazard Insurance Premium for 1 years to **Basic Insurance**	$550.00	
904. years to		
905.		
1000. Reserves Deposited With Lender		
1001. Hazard insurance 2 months@$ **$45.83** per month	$91.66	
1002. Mortgage insurance months@$ per month		
1003. City property taxes 9 months@$ **$51.67** per month	$465.03	
1004. County property taxes 9 months@$ **$31.66** per month	$248.94	
1005. Annual assessments months@$ per month		
1006. School Property Taxes 9 months@$ **$60.42** per month	$543.78	
1007. months@$ per month		
1008. Aggregate Adjustment months@$ per month	– $229.15	
1100. Title Charges		
1101. Settlement or closing fee to		
1102. Abstract or title search to		
1103. Title examination to		
1104. Title insurance binder to		
1105. Document preparation to		
1106. Notary fees to		
1107. Attorney's fees to		$115.00
(includes above items numbers:)		
1108. Title insurance to **ABC Title Co.**	$175.00	$1,086.00
(includes above items numbers:)		
1109. Lender's coverage $ **$70,000.00/$175.00**		
1110. Owner's coverage $ **$115,000.00/$1,086.00**		
1111. Escrow Fee ABC Title Co.	$75.00	$75.00
1112. Attorneys Fees (Note and Deed of Trust)	$150.00	
1113. Federal Express - Courier	$20.00	$20.00
1200. Government Recording and Transfer Charges		
1201. Recording fees: Deed $ **$20.00** ; Mortgage $ **$23.00** ; Releases $ **$22.00**	$43.00	$22.00
1202. City/county tax/stamps: Deed $; Mortgage $		
1203. State tax/stamps: Deed $; Mortgage $		
1204. Tax Certificates to **Dallas County**		$27.00
1205.		

Figure 20.1   Settlement Statement (Continued)

1300. Additional Settlement Charges		
1301. Survey to Excel Surveying	$375.00	
1302. Pest inspection to		
1303.		
1304.		
1305.		
1400. Total Settlement Charges (enter on lines 103, Section J and 502, Section K)	**$3,555.36**	**$10,445.00**

Seller's and Purchaser's signature hereon acknowledges his/their approval of tax prorations, and signifies their understanding that prorations were based on figures for preceding year, or estimates for current year, and in event of any change for current year, all necessary adjustments must be made between Seller and Purchaser direct; likewise any DEFICIT in delinquent taxes will be reimbursed to Title Company by the Seller.

I have carefully reviewed the HUD-1 Settlement Statement and to the best of my knowledge and belief, it is a true and accurate statement of all receipts and disbursements made on my account or by me in this transaction. I further certify that I have received a completed copy of pages 1, 2 and 3 of this HUD-1 Settlement Statement.

_____   _____
Blade Redemann   John Iuro

_____   _____
Connie Redemann   Joanne Iuro

SETTLEMENT AGENT CERTIFICATION
The HUD-1 Settlement Statement which I have prepared is a true and accurate account of this transaction. I have caused the funds to be disbursed in accordance with this statement.

_____   _____
     Settlement Agent   Date
Warning: It is a crime to knowingly make false statements to the United States on this or any other similar form. Penalties upon conviction can include a fine and imprisonment. For details see: Title 18 U.S. Code Section 1001 and Section 1010.

Seller's Taxpayer Identification Number Solicitation and Certification
You are required by law to provide the Settlement Agent named above with your correct taxpayer identification number. If you do not provide the Settlement Agent with your correct taxpayer identification number, you may be subject to civil or criminal penalties imposed by law. **Under Penalties of perjury, I certify that the number shown on this statement is my correct taxpayer identification number.**

_____   _____
     Seller's Signature   Date

Previous editions are obsolete   HUD-1

3. *Mortgage interest:*
   11% × $57,700 (principal due after 6/1 payment) = $6,347 interest per year

   $6,347 ÷ 360 days = $17.631 interest per day
   15 days of accrued interest to be paid by the seller
   15 × $17.631 = $264.465, or $264.47 *interest owed by the seller*

4. *Real estate taxes* (estimated based on last year's tax bill of $1,725):
   $1,725.00 ÷ 12 months = $143.75 per month
   $143.75 ÷ 30 days = $4.792 per day

   The earned period is from January 1 to and including June 15 and equals 5 months, 15 days:

   $143.75 × 5 months = $718.750
   $4.792 × 15 days = $ 71.880
   $790.630 or *$790.63 seller owes buyer*

   The buyer's share of prepaid taxes for June 16 through July 31 equals 15 days (including June 16) plus 1 month:

   $4.792 × 15 days = $ 71.880
   $143.75 × 1 month = 143.750
   $215.630 *buyer's prepaid taxes*

The Uniform Settlement Statement is divided into 12 sections. In Section J, the summary of the borrower's transaction, the buyer's/borrower's debits are listed in lines 100 through 116 and totaled on line 120 (gross amount due from borrower). The total of the borrower's settlement costs itemized in Section L of the statement is entered on line 103 as one of the buyer's charges. The buyer's credits are listed on lines 201 through 219 and totaled on line 220 (total paid by/for borrower). Then the buyer's credits are subtracted from the charges to arrive at the cash due from the borrower to close (line 303).

In Section K, the summary of the seller's transaction, the seller's credits are entered on lines 400 through 416 and totaled on line 420 (gross amount due to seller). The seller's debits are entered on lines 501 through 519 and totaled on line 520 (total reduction amount due seller). The total of the seller's settlement charges from Section L is on line 502. Then the debits are subtracted from the credits to arrive at the cash due to the seller in order to close (line 603)—unless the total is a negative number, and then it would be cash *from* the seller to close.

Section L is a summary of all the settlement charges for the transaction; the buyer's expenses are listed in one column and the seller's expenses are listed in the other. If an attorney's fee is listed as a lump sum in line 1107, the settlement should list by line number the services that were included in that total fee.

Line 1009 requires an aggregate adjustment that is calculated by the lender to ensure that at least once each year the escrow account does not exceed two times the monthly escrow payment; the amount will always be $0 or a negative number. The aggregate adjustment is deducted from the "Reserves Deposited with Lender" charged to the borrower. For this case study, the aggregate adjustment is computed as follows:

1. Calculate an initial trial balance: Project deposits and disbursements based on starting an escrow account at zero balance. Add ¹⁄₁₂ of the taxes and insurance into the escrow account each month; deduct taxes in December and an insurance premium in the month of closing.
2. Identify the lowest monthly balance from Year 1 (–$777.10), convert it to positive dollars ($777.10), and add to the allowable monthly cushion (two months' taxes and two months' insurance) ($379.16). The result is the maximum allowable starting balance for the escrow account ($1,156.26).
3. Deduct the total of the "Reserves Deposited with Lender" section shown on the HUD-1 ($1,385.41) from the maximum allowable starting balance in Step 2 ($1,156.26). The result is the aggregate adjustment: –$229.15.

Summary

Closing a sale involves both title procedures and financial matters. The broker, as the agent of the seller, must be present at the closing to see that the sale actually is concluded and to account for the earnest money deposit if deposited in the broker's account.

The federal Real Estate Settlement Procedures Act (RESPA) requires disclosure of all settlement costs when a real estate purchase is financed by a federally related mortgage loan. RESPA requires lenders to use a Uniform Settlement Statement to detail the financial particulars of a transaction.

The buyer's attorney may examine the title evidence to ensure that the seller's title is acceptable. The gap in time between the date of the abstract or title commitment and the closing date is covered by the seller's affidavit as to debts and liens.

The sale may be closed in escrow so that the buyer can be assured of receiving good title as described in the sales contract and the seller can be assured that all funds due him or her are held in cash by the escrow agent.

The actual amount to be paid by the buyer at the closing is computed by preparation of a closing, or settlement, statement. This lists the sales price, earnest money deposit, expenses, and prorations between buyer and seller. The HUD-1 closing statement shows the net amount due to the seller and from the buyer at closing. The form is signed by both parties to evidence their approval.

1. C
2. A
3. D
4. C
5. B
6. C
7. A
8. C
9. B
10. B
11. C
12. B
13. D
14. A
15. B
16. C
17. D
18. A
19. C
20. A
21. B

Questions

1. Which statement is true of real estate closings in Texas?
   a. The buyer usually receives the rents for the day of closing.
   b. The buyer must reimburse the seller for any title evidence provided by the seller.
   c. The seller usually pays the expenses for the day of closing.
   d. The seller must pay all the closing expenses.

2. Security deposits on rental property being sold should be listed on a closing statement as a credit to the
   a. buyer.
   b. seller.
   c. lender.
   d. broker.

3. The purpose of RESPA (Real Estate Settlement Procedures Act) is to
   a. make sure buyers do not borrow more than they can pay.
   b. make real estate brokers more responsive to buyers' needs.
   c. help buyers know how much money is required.
   d. see that buyers and sellers know all settlement costs.

4. Some amounts included in a closing statement are not prorated but are listed at the full amount. Which of the following is always prorated?
   a. Special assessments
   b. The unpaid principal balance of the seller's mortgage assumed by the buyer
   c. Interest on the seller's mortgage assumed by the buyer that has accrued since the last interest was paid
   d. Rent security deposit

5. All encumbrances and liens shown on the report of title, other than those waived or agreed to by the purchaser and listed in the contract, must be removed so that the title can be delivered free and clear. The removal of such encumbrances is the duty of the
   a. buyer.
   b. seller.
   c. title company.
   d. lender.

6. Legal title passes from the seller to the buyer
   a. on the date of execution of the deed.
   b. when the closing statement has been signed.
   c. when the deed is delivered and accepted.
   d. when the contract is signed.

7. Which one of the following items would **NOT** be prorated between buyer and seller at the closing on an apartment complex?
   a. Recording charges
   b. General taxes
   c. Mortgage interest
   d. Rental income

Questions 8 through 13 pertain to certain items as they normally would appear on a closing statement.

8. The sales price of the property is a
   a. credit only to the seller.
   b. debit only to the buyer.
   c. credit to the seller and a debit to the buyer.
   d. credit to the buyer and a debit to the seller.

9. The earnest money left on deposit with the broker or title company is a
   a. credit to the seller.
   b. credit to the buyer.
   c. debit to the seller.
   d. debit to the buyer.

10. The principal amount of the purchaser's new mortgage loan is a
    a. credit to the seller.
    b. credit to the buyer.
    c. debit to the seller.
    d. debit to the buyer.

11. Unpaid real estate taxes are a
    a. credit only to the buyer.
    b. debit only to the seller.
    c. credit to the buyer and debit to the seller.
    d. credit to the seller and debit to the buyer.

12. The broker's commission is usually shown as a
    a. debit to the buyer.
    b. debit to the seller.
    c. credit to the seller.
    d. credit to the buyer.

13. The interest proration on an existing assumed mortgage is a
    a. credit only to the seller.
    b. debit only to the buyer.
    c. credit to the seller and debit to the buyer.
    d. credit to the buyer and debit to the seller.

14. The *doctrine of relation back* is most closely associated with which of the following?
    a. Escrow   c. Title evidence
    b. Prorations   d. Subrogation

15. The RESPA Uniform Settlement Statement must be used to illustrate all settlement charges for
    a. transactions financed by VA and FHA loans only.
    b. residential transactions financed by federally related mortgage loans.
    c. all transactions in which mortgage financing is involved.
    d. all transactions involving commercial property.

16. Which of the following would a lender generally **NOT** require to be produced at or prior to the closing?
    a. Title insurance policy
    b. Appraisal
    c. Homestead declaration
    d. Survey

17. When a transaction is to be closed in escrow, the seller generally deposits all **EXCEPT** which of the following items with the escrow agent before the closing date?
    a. Deed to the property
    b. Title evidence
    c. Payoff letter
    d. New hazard insurance policy

18. The annual real estate taxes amount to $1,800, payable in arrears. If closing is set for June 15, which of the following is true, using a *statutory year*?
    a. Credit buyer $825; debit seller $825.
    b. Credit seller $825; debit buyer $825.
    c. Credit buyer $975; debit seller $975.
    d. Credit seller $975; debit buyer $975.

19. The seller collected rent of $400, payable in advance, from a tenant on November 1. At closing on November 15 the
    a. seller owes the buyer $400.
    b. buyer owes the seller $400.
    c. seller owes the buyer $200.
    d. buyer owes the seller $200.

20. A buyer of a $100,000 home has paid $12,000 as earnest money and has a loan commitment for 70 percent of the purchase price. Disregarding closing costs, how much more cash does the buyer need to bring to the closing?
    a. $18,000
    b. $30,000
    c. $58,000
    d. $61,600

21. Which of the following statements is true of a computerized loan origination (CLO) system?
    a. The mortgage broker or lender may pay any fee charged by the real estate broker in whose office the CLO terminal is located.
    b. The borrower must pay the fee charged by the real estate broker in whose office the CLO terminal is located.
    c. The real estate broker in whose office the CLO terminal is located may charge a fee of up to two points for the use of the system.
    d. The fee charged by the real estate broker for using the CLO terminal may not be financed as part of the loan.

21 Leases

Key Terms

actual eviction
constructive eviction
estate for years
estate from period to
  period
forcible entry and
  detainer
gross lease

ground lease
holdover tenancy
lease
leasehold estate
month-to-month
  tenancy
net lease
percentage lease

periodic estate
reversionary right
security deposit
sublease
suit for possession
tenancy at sufferance
tenancy at will

OVERVIEW

When an owner of real property does not wish to use the property personally or wants to derive income from its ownership, he or she can allow it to be used by another person in exchange for consideration. The person who makes periodic payments for the use of the property *leases* it from the owner. Generally, any type of real property may be leased; the apartment dweller as well as the commercial or industrial tenant may find it advantageous to lease real estate for a given period of time rather than purchase it.

This chapter examines the various leasehold estates a landlord (lessor) and a tenant (lessee) may enter into and the types and specific provisions of lease agreements commonly used in the real estate business. In discussing leases the terms *owner, landlord,* and *lessor* are equivalent. Similarly, *renter, tenant,* and *lessee* describe the same person.

Real estate licensees are prohibited by the license act from preparing any document that transfers any interest in real estate. This includes leases. Therefore a real estate licensee must use whatever lease form may be promulgated by the Texas Real Estate Commission. If none has been promulgated that fits a specific need, then guidelines provided by Section 16 of the license act and Rule 537.11 of the commission should be followed.

LEASING REAL ESTATE

A **lease** is a contract between an owner of real estate (known as the *lessor*) and a tenant (the *lessee*) that transfers the right to exclusive possession and use of the owner's property to the tenant for a specified period of time. This agreement generally sets forth the length of time the contract is to run, the amount to be paid by the lessee for the right to use the property, and other rights and obligations of the parties.

Almost one-third of renters say they prefer to rent, even though they could afford to buy a home, according to Fannie Mae.

In effect, the lease agreement is a combination of a conveyance (of an interest in the real estate) and a contract (to pay rent and assume other obligations). The landlord (lessor) grants the tenant (lessee) the right to occupy the premises and use them for purposes stated in the lease. In return, the landlord retains the right to receive payment for the use of the premises as well as a **reversionary right** to retake possession after the lease term has expired. The lessor's interest in leased property is called a *leased fee estate plus reversionary right.*

Several laws that have been previously discussed apply to leases on real property as well as to sales.

- The fair housing laws affect landlords and tenants just as they do sellers and buyers. All persons must have access to housing of their choice without differentiation in the terms and conditions because of their race, color, religion, national origin, sex, handicap, or familial status. Withholding an apartment that is available for rent, segregating certain persons in separate sections of an apartment complex or parts of a building, and requiring different amounts of rent or security deposits from persons in the protected classes all constitute violations of the law. The fair housing laws require that the same tenant criteria be applied to families with children that are applied to adults. A landlord cannot charge a higher rent or security deposit because one of the tenants is a child. Tenants with disabilities must be permitted to make reasonable modifications to a property at their own expense. However, if the modifications would interfere with a future tenant's use, the landlord may require that the premises be restored to their original condition at the end of the lease term. (For additional fair housing protections, see Chapter 6.)
- The *Americans with Disabilities Act* (ADA) applies to commercial, nonresidential property in which public goods or services are provided. The ADA requires that such properties either be free of architectural barriers or provide reasonable accommodations for people with disabilities. (For more information about the ADA, see Chapters 6 and 22.)
- The *Texas Statute of Frauds* requires that a *lease for a term of more than one year be written* to be enforceable. It must be signed by the parties to be charged with its performance—both the lessor and the lessee. A lease for one year or less usually is enforceable if it is entered into orally. However, it is prudent to have *all* leases in writing to avoid relying on the memory of two parties whose recall of the lease essentials may differ.
- An "Information About Brokerage Services" form must be given to prospective tenants at the first face-to-face meeting regarding a residential lease for more than one year or when the purchase of the property is contemplated (see Chapter 5).

- A lead-based paint disclosure and a pamphlet, "Protecting Your Family," must be given to tenants in properties built prior to 1978 (with a few specific exceptions) (see Chapter 13).

Leasehold Estates

When a landowner leases his or her real estate to a tenant, the tenant's right to occupy the land for the duration of the lease is called a **leasehold estate**. A leasehold estate is an estate in land that generally is considered personal property. However, when the contract is a lease for life or for 99 years, under which the tenant assumes many of the landowner's obligations, the tenant gets some of the benefits and privileges of a property owner. In addition, the Internal Revenue Service permits certain tax advantages for leases longer than 30 years.

In the discussion of interests and estates in Chapter 8, freehold estates were differentiated from leasehold estates. Just as there are several types of freehold (ownership) estates, there are also various leasehold estates. The four most important are (1) estate for years, (2) periodic estate (or estate from period to period), (3) tenancy at will, and (4) tenancy at sufferance.

Estate for Years

A leasehold that continues for a *definite period of time,* whether for years, months, weeks, or even days, is an **estate for years.** An estate for years always has a specific starting and ending time and does not automatically renew at the end of the lease period. When the definite term specified in a written or an oral lease expires, the lessee is required to vacate the premises and surrender possession to the lessor. No notice is required to terminate the lease at the end of the lease period because a specific expiration date already is provided. A lease for years may be terminated prior to the expiration date by the mutual consent of both parties, but otherwise neither party may terminate without showing that the lease agreement has been breached. Typically, an estate for years gives the lessee the right to occupy and use the leased property—subject, of course, to the terms and covenants contained in the lease agreement itself, which is generally a written document. This right of occupancy is exclusive, which bars even the owner from possession or occupancy.

> *Estate for years* = Any definite period (e.g., lease on office space)

Periodic Estate

Periodic estates, sometimes called **estates from period to period** or from month to month, are created when the landlord and tenant enter into an agreement that continues for an *indefinite length of time without a specific expiration date.* Rent, however, is payable at definite intervals. These tenancies generally are created by agreement or operation of law to run for a certain amount of time; for instance, month to month, week to week, or year to year. The agreement is automatically renewed for similar succeeding periods until one of the parties gives notice to terminate. In effect the payment and acceptance of rent extend the lease for another period. A **month-to-month tenancy,** for example, is created when a tenant takes possession with no definite termination date and pays rent on a monthly basis.

If the lease agreement on an estate for years provides for the conversion to a periodic tenancy, no negotiations are necessary. The tenant simply exercises his or her option to begin leasing on a month-to-month basis. If the lease does not provide for a conversion and the tenant remains in possession after the lease term expires, a **holdover tenancy,** or *tenancy at sufferance*, is created. The landlord may either evict the tenant or accept the tenant's rent, which is considered proof of acceptance of the periodic estate.

Periodic estate = Indefinite term; automatically renewing (e.g., month-to-month lease on a single-family dwelling)

The courts customarily hold that a tenant who holds over can do so for a term equal to the term of the original lease, provided the period is for one year or less. The courts usually have ruled that a holdover tenancy cannot exist for longer than one year. Thus, if the original lease were for six months and the tenancy were held over, the courts usually would consider the holdover to be for a like period, that is, six months. However, if the original lease were for five years, the holdover tenancy could not exceed one year.

To *terminate* a periodic estate, either the landlord or the tenant must give *proper notice.* Normally to terminate an estate from week to week, one week's notice is required; to terminate an estate from month to month or longer, one month's notice is required unless there is an agreement to the contrary.

Tenancy at Will

A **tenancy at will** is a leasehold estate that exists for as long as both the lessor and lessee desire it to last. Therefore, it is a tenancy of indefinite duration. It continues until it is terminated by either party's giving proper notice or by the death of either the landlord or the tenant. A tenancy at will may be created by express agreement or by operation of law; during its existence, the tenant has all the rights and obligations of a lessor-lessee relationship, including the duty to pay rent at regular intervals.

Tenancy at will = Indefinite term; with landlord's oral or written consent (e.g., possession of property as long as tenant and landlord both desire it)

FOR EXAMPLE At the end of a lease period, a landlord informs a tenant that in a few months the city is going to demolish the apartment building to make way for an expressway. The landlord gives the tenant the option to move or to continue to occupy the premises until demolition begins. If the tenant agrees to stay, a tenancy at will is created.

In a tenancy at will the tenant remains in possession rightfully; the landlord or tenant "wills" that possession can continue.

Tenancy at Sufferance

A **tenancy at sufferance** arises when a tenant who lawfully possessed real property continues in possession of the premises without the landlord's consent after the rights expire. In this situation the landlord does not want the tenant in possession but "suffers" or permits the tenant to remain. Two examples of estates at sufferance are (1) when a tenant for years *fails to surrender* possession at the expiration of the lease and (2) when a borrower continues in possession after a foreclosure sale. Eviction procedures will be discussed later in this chapter.

Tenancy at sufferance = Tenant's previously lawful possession continued without landlord's consent (e.g., a holdover tenant who does not surrender the property at the lease's termination)

In Practice

The requirement in Section 15 of the Texas Real Estate License Act that all contracts must have a definite termination date that is not subject to prior notice does not apply to lease agreements. Landlord and tenant law permits tenancies without definite termination dates—periodic estates, tenancies at will, and tenancies at sufferance.

COMMON LEASE PROVISIONS

In determining the validity of a lease, the courts apply the rules governing contracts. If the intention to convey temporary possession of a certain parcel of real estate from one person to another is expressed, the courts generally hold that a lease has been created. Texas and most other states require no special wording to establish the landlord-tenant relationship. The lease may be written, oral, or implied, depending on the circumstances. The lease shown as Figure 21.1 has been approved for use by members of the Texas Association of REALTORS® for leasing residential real estate. Another popular residential lease used in Texas is the TAA lease form used by members of the Texas Apartment Association.

Because the requirements for a valid lease are essentially the same as those for any other contract, the essentials of a valid lease are as follows:

- *Offer and acceptance:* The parties must reach a mutual agreement on all the terms of the contract.
- *Consideration:* Rent is the normal consideration granted for the right to occupy the leased premises; however, the payment of rent is not essential as long as consideration was granted in creation of the lease itself. Some courts have construed rent as being any consideration that supports the lease, thus not limiting its definition to the payment of monthly rent (as will be illustrated later in discussions of gross, net, and percentage leases).
- *Capacity to contract:* The parties must have the legal capacity to contract.
- *Legal objectives:* The objectives of the lease must be legal.
- *Legal description:* The leased premises must be clearly described. The legal description of the real estate should be used if the lease covers land, such as a ground lease or a single-family residence. If the lease is for a multifamily residential property, the street address and apartment designation are acceptable.

As discussed earlier in this chapter, the Texas Statute of Frauds requires that leases for longer than one year be in writing because a lease is considered to be a conveyance of an interest in real estate. The tenant's signature usually is *not essential if the tenant has taken possession.* Of course, both parties must sign the lease if it is to be enforceable against each party. The courts consider a lease to be a contract and not subject to subsequent changes in the rent or other terms unless these changes are in writing and signed in the same manner as the original lease.

After a valid lease has been signed, the lessor, as the owner of the real estate, is usually bound by the *implied covenant of quiet possession.* Under this covenant, the lessor guarantees that the lessee may take possession of the leased premises and that he or she will not be evicted from these premises by any person who successfully claims to have a title superior to that of the lessor.

Use of Premises   A lessor may restrict a lessee's use of the premises through provisions included in the lease. This is most important in leases for stores or commercial space. For example, a lease may provide that the leased premises are to be used *only* for the purpose of a real estate office *and for no other.* In the absence of such limitations, a lessee may use the premises for any *lawful* purpose.

Figure 21.1 *Residential Lease Agreement*

TEXAS ASSOCIATION OF REALTORS®
RESIDENTIAL LEASE AGREEMENT
USE OF THIS FORM BY PERSONS WHO ARE NOT MEMBERS OF THE TEXAS ASSOCIATION OF REALTORS® IS NOT AUTHORIZED.
©**Texas Association of REALTORS®, Inc. 1997**

NOTICE:
Landlord's broker, _____, ❑ will ❑ will not act as the property manager.
Future inquires about this Lease, rental payments, and security deposits should be directed to ❑ Landlord's broker ❑ Landlord.
Landlord's broker ❑ does ❑ does not have authority to bind Landlord to this Lease under another agreement or power of attorney.

---

1. **PARTIES:** The parties to this agreement (Lease) are the owner of the Property_____
_____(Landlord) and _____
_____ (Tenant).

2. **PROPERTY:** Landlord leases to Tenant that certain real property known as_____
_____(address)_____(city) Texas_____ (zip code)
or as described on attached exhibit together with all its improvements including the following non-real estate items_____
_____, (the Property)
also described as (legal description recommended if lease is for one year or more):_____
_____ .

3. **TERM:** This Lease commences on _____ (Commencement Date) and ends on
_____(Termination Date).

4. **AUTOMATIC RENEWAL AND NOTICE OF TERMINATION:** This lease will automatically renew on a month-to-month basis
unless either party provides the other party written notice of termination at least thirty (30) days before the Termination Date or the
end of any renewal period.   VERBAL NOTICE IS NOT SUFFICIENT UNDER ANY CIRCUMSTANCES.   If this Lease is
automatically renewed on a month-to-month basis, either party may terminate the renewal of this Lease by providing   written
notice to the other party and the renewal will terminate:

  ❑ A. on the last day of the month in which the notice is given if notice is given on the first day of the month. If the notice is given
        on a day other than the first day of the month, the renewal will terminate on the last day of the month following the month in
        which the notice is given.

  ❑ B. on the date designated in the notice but not sooner than thirty (30) days after the notice is given and, if necessary, rent will
        be prorated on a daily basis.

If neither of the above choices is checked, box A will be deemed checked. Time is of the essence for providing notice of
termination (strict compliance with dates by which notice must be provided is required).

5. **RENT:**

  A. <u>Monthly Rent</u>: Tenant will pay monthly rent in the amount of _____ for each full month during
     this Lease. The first full month's rent is due and payable no later than _____.
     Thereafter, Tenant will pay the monthly rent on or before the first day of each month during this Lease. Weekends and
     holidays do not delay or excuse Tenant's obligation to timely pay rent.

  B. <u>Prorated Rent</u>: Tenant will pay as prorated rent from the Commencement Date to the first day of the following month the sum
     of _____ on or before _____.

  C. <u>Place of Payment</u>: Tenant will pay all rent to _____ (name of
     payee) at _____
     (address) in _____ (city) _____ (state) _____ (zip) or at
     such other place as Landlord may designate from time to time in writing.

  D. <u>Method of Payment</u>: Tenant must pay all rent timely and without demand, deduction, or offset, except as permitted by this
     Lease. Time is of the essence for the payment of rent (strict compliance with rental due dates is required). Tenant must pay
     all rent by check, money order, cashier's check, or other means acceptable to Landlord. If multiple Tenants occupy the

(TAR-2001) 10-01-97   Initialed for Identification by Tenants: _____, _____, _____, _____ and Landlord _____, _____   Page 1 of 8

Figure 21.1 **Residential Lease Agreement (Continued)**

Residential Lease concerning_____

Property, Landlord may require Tenants to pay monthly rents by one check or draft. By providing written notice to Tenant, Landlord may require Tenant to pay the amounts due under this Lease by certified funds.

   E. Common Areas: Landlord is not obligated to pay any non-mandatory or user fees for Tenant's use of any common areas or facilities (such as pool or tennis courts).

   F. Rent Increases: There will be no rent increases through the Termination Date. If this Lease is renewed automatically on a month-to-month basis, Landlord may increase the rent during the renewal period by providing written notice to Tenant that becomes effective the month following the 30th day after the notice is provided.

6. **LATE CHARGES:** If Tenant fails to timely pay any month's rent, Tenant will pay Landlord an initial late charge of _____ plus additional late charges of _____ per day thereafter until rent is paid in full. If Landlord receives the monthly rent by the _____ day of the month, Landlord will waive the late charges for that month. Any waiver of late charges under this paragraph will not affect or diminish any other right or remedy Landlord may exercise for Tenant's failure to timely pay rent (including reporting late payments to consumer reporting agencies).

7. **RETURNED CHECKS:** Tenant will pay _____ (*not to exceed $25*) for each check Tenant tenders to Landlord which is returned by the institution on which it is drawn for any reason, plus initial and additional late charges until Landlord has received payment.

8. **APPLICATION OF FUNDS:** Landlord will apply all funds received from Tenant first to any non-rent obligations of Tenant including late charges, returned check charges, charge-backs for repairs, brokerage fees, and periodic utilities, then to rent regardless of any notations on a check.

9. **PETS:** THERE WILL BE NO PETS, unless authorized by a separate written pet agreement. Tenant must not permit any pet, including mammals, reptiles, birds, fish, rodents, or insects on the Property, even temporarily, unless otherwise agreed by a separate written pet agreement. If Tenant violates the pet restrictions of this Lease, Tenant will pay Landlord a fee of _____ per day per pet for each day Tenant violates the pet restrictions as additional rent for any unauthorized pet. Landlord may remove or cause to be removed any unauthorized pet and deliver it to appropriate local authorities by providing at least 24-hour written notice to Tenant of Landlord's intention to remove the unauthorized pet. Landlord will not be liable for any harm, injury, death, or sickness to any unauthorized pet. Tenant is responsible and liable for any damage or required cleaning to the Property caused by any unauthorized pet and for all costs Landlord may incur in removing or causing any unauthorized pet to be removed.

10. **DELAY OF OCCUPANCY:** If Tenant is unable to occupy the Property on the Commencement Date because of construction on the Property or a prior tenant's holding over of the Property, Landlord will not be liable to Tenant for such delay and this Lease will remain enforceable. Landlord will abate rent on a daily basis during any delay. If Tenant is unable to occupy the Property after the third (3rd) day after the Commencement Date because of construction on the Property or a prior tenant's holding over of the Property, Tenant may terminate this Lease by giving written notice to Landlord before the Property becomes available to be occupied by Tenant, and Landlord will refund to Tenant the security deposit and any rent paid. These conditions do not apply to any delay in occupancy caused by cleaning or repairs.

11. **SECURITY DEPOSIT:**

   A. Security Deposit: Upon execution of this Lease, Tenant will pay a security deposit to Landlord in the amount of _____. "Security deposit" has the meaning assigned to that term in §92.102 of the Texas Property Code. No interest will be paid to Tenant on the security deposit. Landlord may place the security deposit in an interest bearing account and any interest earned will be paid to Landlord or Landlord's representative. **Notice: §92.108 of the Texas Property Code provides that Tenant may not withhold payment of any portion of the last month's rent on grounds that the security deposit is security for unpaid rent. Bad faith violations of §92.108 may subject Tenant to liability up to three times the rent wrongfully withheld and the Landlord's reasonable attorney's fees.**

   B. Refund: Subchapter C of Chapter 92 of the Texas Property Code governs the obligations of the parties regarding the security deposit. Tenant must give Landlord at least thirty (30) days written notice of surrender before Landlord is obligated to refund or account for the security deposit. **Notice: The Texas Property Code does not obligate Landlord to return or account for the security deposit until 30 days after Tenant surrenders the Property (vacating and returning all keys and access devices) and gives Landlord a written statement of Tenant's forwarding address.**

   C. Deductions:

      (1) Landlord may deduct reasonable charges from the security deposit for:

         (a) unpaid or accelerated rent;

(TAR-2001) 10-01-97   Initialed for Identification by Tenants: _____, _____, _____, _____ and Landlord _____, _____   Page 2 of 8

Figure 21.1 Residential Lease Agreement (Continued)

Residential Lease concerning_____

    (b) late charges;
    (c) unpaid utilities;
    (d) costs of cleaning, deodorizing, and repairing the Property and its contents for which Tenant is responsible;
    (e) pet violation charges;
    (f) replacing unreturned keys, garage door openers or other security devices;
    (g) the removal of unauthorized locks or fixtures installed by Tenant;
    (h) insufficient light bulbs;
    (i) packing, removing, and storing abandoned property;
    (j) removing abandoned or illegally parked vehicles;
    (k) costs of reletting, if Tenant is in default;
    (l) attorney fees and costs of court incurred in any proceeding against Tenant;
    (m) any fee due for early removal of an authorized keybox; and
    (n) other items tenant is responsible to pay under this Lease.

    (2) If deductions exceed the security deposit, Tenant will pay to Landlord the excess within ten (10) days after Landlord makes written demand. The security deposit will be applied first to any non-rent items, including late charges, returned check charges, repairs, brokerage fees, and periodic utilities, then to any unpaid rent.

12. UTILITIES: Tenant will pay all connection fees, service fees, usage fees, and all other costs and fees for all utilities to the Property (for example, electricity, gas, water, wastewater, garbage, telephone, alarm monitoring systems, and cable television) except the following which will be paid by Landlord:_____
_____. Unless provided by Landlord, Tenant must, at a minimum, keep the following utilities on (if available) at all times this Lease is in effect: gas; electricity; water; wastewater; and garbage services. If Tenant fails to do so, Tenant will be in default.

13. USE AND OCCUPANCY:

    A. <u>Occupant</u>: Tenant may use the Property as a private dwelling only. If Tenant fails to occupy and take possession of the Property within five (5) days of the Commencement Date, Tenant will be in default. The only persons Tenant may permit to reside in the Property during the term of this Lease will be (*include names of all occupants*): _____
_____. Tenant must promptly inform Landlord of any changes in Tenant's phone numbers (home or work) no later than five (5) days of any change. Tenant must comply with any owners' association rules or restrictive covenants affecting the Property. Tenant will pay any fines or other charges assessed against Tenant or Landlord for violations by Tenant of any owners' association rule or restrictive covenant.

    B. <u>Prohibitions</u>: Tenant may not permit any part of the Property to be used for:

        (1) any activity which is a nuisance, offensive, noisy, or dangerous;
        (2) the repair of any vehicle;
        (3) any business of any type, including child care;
        (4) any activity which violates any applicable owners' association rule or restrictive covenant;
        (5) any illegal or unlawful activity; or
        (6) other activity which will obstruct, interfere with, or infringe on the rights of other persons near the Property.

    C. <u>Guests</u>: Tenant may not permit any guest to stay on or in the Property longer than the lesser of:

        (1) the amount of time permitted by any owners' association rule or restrictive covenant; or
        (2) _____ days without Landlord's written permission.

14. VEHICLES: Tenant may not permit more than _____ vehicles (including but not limited to automobiles, trucks, recreational vehicles, trailers, motorcycles, and boats) on the Property unless authorized by Landlord in writing. Tenant may not park any vehicles in the yard. Tenant may not store any vehicles on or adjacent to the Property or on the street in front of the Property. Landlord may tow, at Tenant's expense, any improperly parked or inoperative vehicle on or adjacent to the Property in accordance with applicable state and local laws.

15. ACCESS BY LANDLORD: Landlord may prominently display a "For Sale" or "For Lease" or similarly worded sign on the Property during the term of this Lease or any renewal period. If Tenant fails to permit reasonable access under this paragraph, Tenant will be in default. Landlord or anyone authorized by Landlord may enter the Property by reasonable means at reasonable times without notice to:

    A. inspect the Property for condition;
    B. make repairs;

(TAR-2001) 10-01-97   Initialed for Identification by Tenants: ____, ____, ____, ____ and Landlord ____, ____   Page 3 of 8

Figure 21.1   Residential Lease Agreement (Continued)

Residential Lease concerning_____

   C. show the Property to prospective tenants, prospective purchasers, inspectors, fire marshals, lenders, appraisers, or insurance agents;

   D. exercise a contractual or statutory lien;

   E. leave written notices; or

   F. seize nonexempt property after default.

16. KEYBOX AUTHORIZATION:

   A. NOTICE: A keybox is a locked container in which a key to the Property is placed. The keybox may be placed on the Property and opened with a special key, combination, or electronic card. Keyboxes make it more convenient for the Property to be shown or repaired. All persons who have the special keys, combinations, or cards may have access to the Property. The use of a keybox involves risk (such as unauthorized entry, property damage, or personal injury). If a keybox is authorized Tenant should: (i) safeguard and/or remove all jewelry and valuables; (ii) discuss advantages and disadvantages of the keybox with real estate professionals, insurance agents, or attorneys; and (iii) obtain personal property insurance. *Check one*:

      ☐ (1) Tenant authorizes Landlord, Landlord's property manager, and Landlord's broker to place a keybox with a key on the Property during the last _____ days of this Lease or any renewal.

      ☐ (2) Tenant does not authorize a keybox to be placed on the Property.

   B. If a keybox is authorized, Tenant may withdraw Tenant's authorization to place a keybox on the Property by providing written notice to Landlord and paying Landlord a fee of_____ as consideration for the withdrawal. Landlord will remove the keybox within a reasonable time after receipt of the notice of withdrawal and the required fee.

   C. Landlord, Landlord's property manager, and Landlord's broker are not responsible to Tenant, Tenant's guests, family, or occupants for any damages, injuries, or losses arising from use of the keybox unless caused by the negligence of Landlord, Landlord's property manager, or Landlord's broker. Tenant assumes all risk of any loss, damage, or injury.

17. MOVE-IN CONDITION: Tenant has inspected and accepts the Property AS IS except for conditions materially affecting the safety or health of ordinary persons or unless expressly noted otherwise in this Lease. Landlord has made no express or implied warranties as to the condition of the Property and no agreements have been made regarding future repairs unless specified in this Lease. Tenant will complete an Inventory and Condition Form, noting any defects or damages to the Property, and deliver it to Landlord within 48 hours after the Commencement Date. Tenant's failure to timely deliver the Inventory and Condition Form will be deemed as Tenant's acceptance of the Property in a clean and good condition. **The Inventory and Condition Form is not a request for maintenance or repairs. Tenant must direct all requests for repairs in compliance with paragraph 20.**

18. MOVE-OUT CONDITION AND FORFEITURE OF TENANT'S PERSONAL PROPERTY: Tenant will surrender the Property in the same condition as when received, normal wear and tear excepted. "Normal wear and tear" means deterioration that occurs without negligence, carelessness, accident, or abuse. Tenant will leave the Property in a clean condition free of all trash, debris, and any personal property or belongings. If Tenant leaves any personal property or belongings in the Property after Tenant surrenders possession of the Property, all such personal property or belongings will be forfeited to and become the property of Landlord. "Surrender" means vacating the Property and returning all keys and access devices to Landlord.

19. PROPERTY MAINTENANCE:

   A. <u>Tenant's General Responsibilities</u>: Tenant, at Tenant's expense must:

      (1) keep the Property clean and sanitary;

      (2) promptly dispose of all garbage in appropriate receptacles;

      (3) supply and change heating and air conditioning filters at least once a month;

      (4) supply and replace light bulbs and smoke detector batteries;

      (5) promptly eliminate any dangerous condition on the Property caused by Tenant or Tenant's guests;

      (6) take precautions to prevent broken water pipes due to freezing;

      (7) replace any lost or misplaced keys;

      (8) pay any periodic, preventive, or additional extermination costs desired by Tenant; and

      (9) promptly notify Landlord of all needed repairs.

   B. <u>Yard Maintenance</u>: ☐ Landlord ☐ Tenant is responsible for all yard maintenance and will use reasonable diligence in maintaining the yard. "Yard" means all lawns, shrubbery, bushes, flowers, gardens, trees, rock or other landscaping, and other foliage on or encroaching on the Property or on any easement appurtenant to the Property, and does not include common areas maintained by an owners' association. "Yard maintenance" means such things as, but is not limited to, mowing, fertilizing, trimming, and control of yard pests. Landlord, at Landlord's discretion, will be responsible for treatment for

Figure 21.1   Residential Lease Agreement (Continued)

Residential Lease concerning_____

wood-destroying insects, if any. If Landlord maintains the yard, Tenant will permit Landlord and Landlord's contractors reasonable access to all parts of the yard and will remove any pet from the yard at appropriate times. Tenant will water the yard at reasonable and appropriate times.

C. Pool or Spa Maintenance: ☐ Landlord   ☐ Tenant   is responsible for all pool or spa maintenance and will use reasonable diligence in maintaining the pool or spa. "Pool or spa maintenance" means cleaning, sweeping, and applying appropriate chemicals. Tenant will maintain proper water heights in the pool or spa. If Landlord maintains the pool or spa, Tenant will permit Landlord and Landlord's contractors reasonable access to the pool or spa and will remove any pet in the yard in which the pool or spa is located at appropriate times.

D. Prohibitions: If Tenant installs any fixtures on the Property, authorized or unauthorized, such as additional smoke detectors, locks, alarm systems, cables, or other fixtures, such fixtures will become the property of the Landlord. Except as otherwise permitted by law, this Lease, or in writing by Landlord, Tenant may NOT:

(1) remove any part of the Property or any of Landlord's personal property from the Property;
(2) remove, change, or rekey any lock;
(3) make holes in the woodwork, floors, or walls, except that a reasonable number of small nails may be used to hang pictures in sheetrock and grooves in paneling;
(4) permit any water furniture on the Property;
(5) install new or additional telephone or television cables, outlets, antennas, satellite receivers, or alarm systems;
(6) replace or remove carpet, paint, or wallpaper;
(7) install or change any fixture;
(8) keep or permit any hazardous material on the Property such as flammable or explosive materials which might cause fire or extended insurance coverage to be suspended or canceled or any premiums to be increased;
(9) dispose of any environmentally detrimental substance (e.g., motor oil or radiator fluid) on the Property;
(10) cause or allow any mechanic's or materialman's lien to be filed against any portion of the Property or Tenant's interest in this Lease.

20. REPAIRS:

A. **Repairs to be Paid by Tenant:** Tenant will pay Landlord or any repairman Landlord directs Tenant to pay the cost to repair:

(1) a condition caused by Tenant, an occupant, a member of Tenant's family, or a guest or invitee of Tenant;
(2) damage from wastewater stoppages caused by foreign or improper objects in lines that exclusively service the property;
(3) damage to doors, windows, or screens; and
(4) damage from windows or doors left open.

B. **Repairs to be Paid by Landlord:** Landlord will pay the cost to repair:

(1) a condition caused by the Landlord or the negligence of the Landlord;
(2) wastewater stoppages or backups caused by deterioration, breakage, roots, ground condition, faulty construction, or malfunctioning equipment; and
(3) a condition that is not Tenant's obligation to pay under paragraph 20A and that adversely affects the health or safety of an ordinary tenant.

C. **Items Not to be Repaired:**   Landlord does not warrant and will not repair or replace the following:

_____.

D. **All other repairs: Except for repairs under paragraphs 20A, 20B, and 20C, Tenant will pay Landlord or any repairman Landlord directs Tenant to pay, the first _____ of the cost to repair any condition in need of repair, and Landlord will pay the remainder.**

E. **Repair Requests and Completion of Repairs: Subchapter B of Chapter 92 of the Texas Property Code governs the rights and obligations of the parties regarding repairs. All requests for repairs must be in writing and delivered to Landlord. Tenant may not repair or cause to be repaired any condition, regardless of the cause, without Landlord's permission. All decisions regarding repairs, including the completion of any repair, whether to repair or replace the item, and the selection of repairmen, will be at Landlord's sole discretion. Landlord is not obligated to complete a repair on a day other than a business day unless required to do so by the Property Code. Landlord may require advance payment of repairs for which Tenant is liable. If Tenant fails to promptly reimburse Landlord any repair costs that Tenant is obligated to pay, Tenant will be in default. If Tenant is delinquent in rent at the time the repair notices are given, Landlord is not obligated to make the repairs.**

(TAR-2001) 10-01-97   Initialed for Identification by Tenants: ____, ____, ____, ____ and Landlord ____, ____   Page 5 of 8

Figure 21.1   Residential Lease Agreement (Continued)

Residential Lease concerning_____

    F.   **Trip Charges:** If Landlord or a repair person is unable to access the Property after making arrangements with Tenant to complete the repair, Tenant shall pay any trip charges incurred.

21. SECURITY DEVICES AND EXTERIOR DOOR LOCKS:

    A.   Subchapter D of Chapter 92 of the Texas Property Code requires the Property to be equipped with certain types of locks and security devices and will govern the rights and obligations of the parties regarding security devices. "Security device" has the meaning assigned to that term in §92.151 of the Texas Property Code. **All notices or requests by Tenant for rekeying, changing, installing, repairing, or replacing security devices must be in writing. Installation of additional security devices or additional rekeying or replacement of security devices desired by Tenant will be paid by Tenant in advance and may only be installed by Landlord or Landlord's contractors after receiving a written request from Tenant.**

    B.   If required by Subchapter D of Chapter 92 of the Texas Property Code, Landlord has rekeyed the security devices on the Property since the date the last tenant vacated the Property or will rekey the security devices no later than seven (7) days after Tenant moves into the Property.

22. SMOKE DETECTORS: Subchapter F of Chapter 92 of the Texas Property Code requires the Property to be equipped with smoke detectors in certain locations and will govern the rights and obligations of the parties regarding smoke detectors. Requests for additional installation, inspection, or repair of smoke detectors must be in writing. Disconnecting or intentionally damaging a smoke detector or removing a battery without immediately replacing it with a working battery may subject Tenant to civil penalties and liability for damages and attorney fees under §92.2611 of the Texas Property Code.

23. LIABILITY: Unless caused by Landlord's negligence, Landlord is NOT responsible to Tenant, Tenant's guests, family, or occupants for any damages, injuries, or losses to person or property caused by fire, flood, water leaks, ice, snow, hail, winds, explosion, smoke, interruption of utilities, theft, burglary, robbery, assault, vandalism, other persons, condition of the Property, environmental contaminants (e.g., carbon monoxide, asbestos, radon, lead-based paint, etc.), or other occurrences or casualty losses. Tenant will promptly reimburse Landlord for any loss, property damage, or cost of repairs or service to the Property caused by the negligence or by the improper use by Tenant, Tenant's guests, family, or occupants. **NOTICE: Tenant should secure Tenant's own insurance coverage for protection against such liabilities and losses.**

24. DEFAULT AND ACCELERATION OF RENTS: If Landlord breaches this Lease, Tenant may seek any relief provided by law. If Tenant fails to timely pay all rents due under this Lease or otherwise fails to comply with this Lease, for any reason, Tenant will be in default and Landlord may terminate Tenant's right to occupy the Property by providing Tenant with at least three (3) days written notice. Notice may be by any means permitted by §24.005 of the Texas Property Code (such as mail, personal delivery, affixing notice to inside of main door). If Tenant breaches this Lease, all rents which are payable during the remainder of this Lease or any renewal period will be accelerated without notice or demand. Landlord will attempt to mitigate any damage or loss caused by Tenant's breach by attempting to relet the Property to acceptable tenants and reducing Tenant's liability accordingly. Unpaid rent and unpaid damages are reportable to credit reporting agencies. If Tenant breaches this Lease, Tenant will be liable for:

    A.   any lost rent;
    B.   Landlord's cost of reletting the Property including brokerage fees, advertising fees, and other fees necessary to relet the Property;
    C.   repairs to the Property for use beyond normal wear and tear;
    D.   all Landlord's costs associated with eviction of Tenant, such as attorney's fees, court costs, and prejudgment interest;
    E.   all Landlord's costs associated with collection of rent such as collection fees, late charges, and returned check charges; and
    F.   any other recovery to which Landlord may be entitled by law.

25. ABANDONMENT: If Tenant abandons the Property, Tenant will be in default. "Abandon" means Tenant fails to comply with any provision of this Lease and is absent from the Property for five (5) consecutive days.

26. HOLDOVER: If Tenant fails to vacate the Property on or before the Termination Date of this Lease or at the end of any renewal period, Tenant will pay rent for the holdover period and indemnify Landlord and/or prospective tenants for damages, including lost rent, lodging expenses, and attorneys' fees. In the event of holdover, Landlord at Landlord's option may extend this Lease up to one month by notifying Tenant, in writing. Rent for any holdover period will be two (2) times the monthly rent calculated on a daily basis and will be immediately due and payable daily without notice or demand.

27. RESIDENTIAL LANDLORD'S LIEN: Landlord will have a lien for unpaid rent against all of Tenant's nonexempt personal property that is in the Property and may seize such nonexempt property if Tenant fails to pay rent. Subchapter C of Chapter 54 of the Property Code governs the rights and obligations of the parties regarding Landlord's lien. Landlord may collect a charge for

Figure 21.1   Residential Lease Agreement (Continued)

Residential Lease concerning_____

packing, removing, or storing property seized in addition to any other amounts Landlord is entitled to receive. Landlord may sell or dispose of any seized property in accordance with the provisions of §54.045 of the Texas Property Code.

28. ASSIGNMENT AND SUBLETTING: Tenant may not assign or sublet the Property without Landlord's written consent.   An assignment or subletting of the Property without Landlord's written consent is voidable by Landlord.   Under no circumstances will Tenant be released from Tenant's obligations in this Lease by virtue of an assignment or sublease.

29. SUBORDINATION: This Lease and Tenant's leasehold interest are and will be subject, subordinate, and inferior to:

A.   any lien or encumbrance now or hereafter placed on the Property by Landlord;
B.   all advances made under any such lien or encumbrance;
C.   the interest payable on any such lien or encumbrance;
D.   any and all renewals and extensions of any such lien or encumbrance;
E.   any restrictive covenant; and
F.   the rights of any owners' association affecting the Property.

   NOTICE: Landlord's broker or any other broker to this transaction has **NOT** received any notice nor has any knowledge that Landlord is delinquent in payment of any lien against the Property or that the Property is posted for foreclosure.

30. CASUALTY LOSS OR CONDEMNATION: Section 92.054 of the Texas Property Code governs the rights and obligations of the parties regarding any casualty loss to the Property.   Any proceeds, payment for damages, settlements, awards, or other sums paid because of a casualty loss to the Property will be the sole property of Landlord. For the purpose of this Lease, any condemnation of all or a part of the Property is a casualty loss.

31. MILITARY: If Tenant is or becomes a member of the Armed Forces on active duty and receives change of station orders to leave the county in which the Property is located and Tenant is not in default of this Lease, Tenant may terminate this Lease by giving Landlord thirty (30) days written notice and a certified copy of the military orders.   Military orders authorizing base housing do not constitute grounds for termination unless specifically waived.

32. SPECIAL PROVISIONS:

33. ATTORNEY'S FEES: Any person who is a prevailing party in any legal proceeding brought under or related to the transaction described in this Lease is entitled to recover prejudgment interest, attorney's fees, and all other costs of litigation from the nonprevailing party.

34. REPRESENTATIONS: Tenant's statements in this Lease and any Application for Rental are material representations relied upon by Landlord. Each party signing this Lease states that he or she is of legal age to enter into a binding contract. If Tenant makes any misrepresentation in this Lease or in any Application for Rental, Tenant is in default.

35. ADDENDA: Incorporated   into this Lease   are   the following   addenda or other information:

❑ A.   Addendum Regarding Lead-Based Paint;
❑ B.   Landlord's Rules and Regulations or Instructions;
❑ C.   Owners' Association Rules;
❑ D.   Pet Agreement;
❑ E.   Application for Rental;
❑ F.   Lease Guaranty;
❑ G.   Agreement Between Brokers;
❑ H.   Inventory and Condition Form;
❑ I.   (Other)_____

(TAR-2001) 10-01-97   Initialed for Identification by Tenants: _____, _____, _____, _____ and Landlord _____, _____   Page 7 of 8

Figure 21.1   Residential Lease Agreement (Continued)

Residential Lease concerning_____

36. AGREEMENT OF PARTIES:

A. <u>Entire Agreement</u>: This Lease contains the entire agreement between Landlord and Tenant and may not be changed except by written agreement.

B. <u>Binding Effect</u>: This Lease is binding upon and inures to the benefit of the parties to this Lease and their respective heirs, executors, administrators, successors, and permitted assigns.

C. <u>Joint and Several</u>: All Tenants are jointly and severally liable for all provisions of this Lease. Any act or notice to, or refund to, or signature of, any one or more of the Tenants regarding any term of this Lease, its renewal, or its termination is binding on all Tenants executing this Lease.

D. <u>Controlling Law</u>: The laws of the State of Texas govern the interpretation, validity, performance, and enforcement of this Lease.

E. <u>Severable Clauses</u>: Should any clause in this Lease be found invalid or unenforceable by a court of law, the remainder of this Lease will not be affected and all other provisions of this Lease will remain valid and enforceable.

F. <u>Waiver</u>: Landlord's past delay, waiver, or non-enforcement of acceleration, contractual or statutory lien, rental due date, or any other right will not be deemed to be a waiver of any other breach by Tenant or any other term, condition, or covenant in this Lease.

37. NOTICES: All notices under this Lease must be delivered to Tenant at the Property address and to Landlord or Landlord's representative at:

❏ A.   the address specified in paragraph 5(2);
❏ B.   _____

The terms of this Lease are negotiable among the parties. This is intended to be a legal agreement binding upon final acceptance. READ IT CAREFULLY. If you do not understand the effect of this Lease, consult your attorney BEFORE signing.

_____   _____
Landlord   Date   Tenant   Date

_____   _____
Landlord   Date   Tenant   Date

By_____   _____
as_____ for Landlord   Tenant   Date

                                         _____
                                         Tenant   Date

Term of Lease The term of a lease is the period for which the lease will run. It should be stated precisely, including the beginning and ending dates, together with a statement of the total period of the lease. For instance, a lease might run "for a term of thirty years beginning June 1, 2000, and ending May 31, 2030." A perpetual lease for an inordinate amount of time or an indefinite term might be ruled invalid unless the language of the lease and the surrounding circumstances clearly indicate that the parties intended such a term.

Security Deposits Most leases require that the tenant provide some form of **security deposit,** to be held by the landlord during the lease term. The security deposit, which primarily safeguards against a tenant's destruction of the premises, is frequently equivalent to one month's rent. As a practical matter, it induces tenants to honor their lease agreement, maintain the premises more carefully during occupancy, and clean the premises thoroughly on leaving.

Under Texas law, within 30 days of the tenant's surrender of the premises, either a security deposit must be refunded to the tenant or the tenant must be provided with an explanation and accounting of damages and other charges being deducted from the deposit and for which the tenant is liable. However, the landlord is not obligated to return the security deposit until and unless the tenant has furnished the landlord with a written statement of the tenant's forwarding address. A landlord also must return a security deposit or rent prepayment when a tenant fails to occupy the premises under a lease and another tenant is secured.

H.B. 2803 (2001) creates an obligation for the landlord in a commercial lease to refund or account for a security deposit in a manner similar to that required in a residential lease.

A landlord may retain a security deposit for failure to give a move-out notice only if the notice requirement is underlined or printed in conspicuous bold print in the lease (see the TAR lease, Figure 21.1, paragraph 11(B)). Note, however, that under a Texas Apartment Association (TAA) lease, a security deposit would not be forfeited for failure to give a move-out notice. Instead, the tenant would be charged an agreed *reletting fee* to cover the owner's costs and efforts in attempting to relet. A landlord who in bad faith retains a security deposit or fails to furnish an itemized list of deductions may be held liable for three times the amount of the deposit wrongfully withheld plus $100 and attorney fees.

In Practice A lease should be clear as to whether a monetary deposit is to secure performance of the lease or merely serve to repair any damage caused by the tenant. A lease also should specify whether a payment is a security deposit, an advance rental, or an application deposit. If it is an application deposit and the applicant is rejected as a tenant, the deposit must be refunded. If it is a security deposit, the tenant generally is not entitled to apply it to the final month's rent. If it is an advance rental, the landlord must treat it as income for tax purposes. In addition, when a lessor sells a rental property, the sales contract should account for the transfer of all security deposit funds to the new owner. Security deposits are not prorated as are rents when the property sells.

LANDLORD AND TENANT ACT

Historically, leases were drawn up primarily for the benefit of the landlord. However, consumer awareness has fostered the belief that a valid lease is dependent on both parties' fulfillment of certain obligations. To provide laws outlining such obligations, Texas has passed statutes found in Section 92, Texas Property Code, known as the *Landlord and Tenant Act.* This law addresses such issues as the landlord's right of entry, maintenance of premises, the tenant's protection against landlord retaliation for complaints, installation of smoke detectors, the landlord's duty to install or rekey a security device, and the disclosure of the property owners' names and addresses to the tenants. The act further sets down specific remedies available to both the landlord and the tenant if a breach of the lease agreement occurs.

In Texas, a lease for more than one year must be in writing and may be recorded if signed and acknowledged before a notary public or other officer. Recording will take place in the county in which the property is located. Unless the lease is for three years or longer, it *usually is not recorded.* However, if the lessee intends to mortgage his or her leasehold interest, recordation is required. If the parties do not want the terms of the lease disclosed to the public, a *memorandum of lease* may be filed with the county clerk. Possession of the property by the lessee provides *constructive notice* to the world of a lessee's rights, and an inspection of the property will result in *actual notice* of the lessee's leasehold interest.

Possession of Leased Premises

Leases carry the implied covenant that the landlord will give the tenant exclusive possession of the premises. In Texas the landlord must give the tenant *actual* occupancy, or possession, of the leased premises. Thus, if the premises are occupied by a holdover tenant, or adverse claimant, at the beginning of the new lease period, it is the landlord's duty to bring whatever action is necessary to recover possession and to bear the expense of this action.

Improvements

Neither the landlord nor the tenant is required to make improvements to the leased property. In the absence of an agreement to the contrary, the tenant may make improvements with the landlord's permission. Any such alterations generally become the property of the landlord; that is, they become fixtures. However, as discussed in Chapter 2, a tenant may be given the right to install trade fixtures or chattel fixtures by the terms of the lease. Such trade fixtures customarily may be removed by the tenant before the lease expires, provided the tenant restores the premises to the condition they were in when he or she took possession.

Maintenance of Premises

Historically, under the principle of caveat emptor, a landlord was not obligated to make repairs to leased premises. However, many states—including Texas—now require that a residential lessor maintain dwelling units in a habitable condition and make any necessary repairs to common elements such as hallways, stairs, or elevators. The tenant does not have to make any repairs, but on vacating the premises, he or she must return the premises in the same condition they were received, with allowances for *ordinary wear and tear.*

The Habitability Statute (Section 92.052, Texas Property Code) states that the landlord has a duty to repair or remedy any condition that materially affects the physical health or safety of an ordinary tenant if the condition arises from normal wear and tear. For this obligation to be enforced, the tenant must give notice to the person to whom he or she pays rent and must be current in rent payments at the time of notification. If a landlord fails to make repairs within a reasonable time after receiving notice from the tenant, the tenant must send a second notice stating his intention to (1) terminate the lease, (2) repair the property and deduct the cost of such repairs from the rent (up to one month's rent or $500, whichever is greater), or (3) pursue available judicial remedies.

Smoke Detectors

Subchapter F, Texas Property Code, requires that landlords install smoke detectors in all residential rental property regardless of the term of the lease; however, temporary residential tenancies (not to exceed 90 days) created by a contract of sale are an exception. The statute specifies the number and placement of the detectors. They must be in good working order at the time the tenant takes possession and are presumed to be in good working order until the tenant requests repair. Replacement of batteries in a smoke detector is the tenant's responsibility. If a rental property does not have smoke detectors, it is the tenant's responsibility to request compliance from the landlord.

Security Devices

Residential rental dwellings must be equipped at the landlord's expense with specified security devices, including window latches, doorknob locks, sliding door handle latches, sliding door pinlocks, keyless deadbolts, and door viewers on each exterior door. The specific devices required for a particular property are based on the year the property was built. Regardless of the property construction date, all security devices operated by a key, card, or combination shall be rekeyed by the landlord at the landlord's expense not later than the seventh day after each tenant turnover date. The tenant turnover date was established by a 1999 statute as the date a new tenant moves in. If a tenant installs a new lock, it must be with the owner's permission and the owner must be given a key.

Occupancy Limits

Current HUD regulations limit occupancy in a rental dwelling to two people per living/sleeping room. The Texas Commission on Human Rights has the following occupancy standard: "A family may occupy an owner's dwelling if the family does not exceed two persons per bedroom *plus* a child who is less than 6 months old and who sleeps in the same bedroom with the child's parent, guardian, legal custodian, or person applying for that status."

Cash Payment

A residential landlord must accept a tenant's timely cash rental payment unless a written lease requires that a tenant pay rent by check or other traceable or negotiable instrument.

Assignment and Subleasing

The lessee may not assign the lease and may not **sublease** unless the lease terms permit it. A tenant who transfers all of his or her leasehold interests assigns the lease. One who transfers less than all leasehold interests by leasing them to a new tenant *subleases* (see Figure 21.2). For example, a transfer of a tenant's interest in a lease wherein the tenant retains a reversionary interest is a sublease, not an assignment.

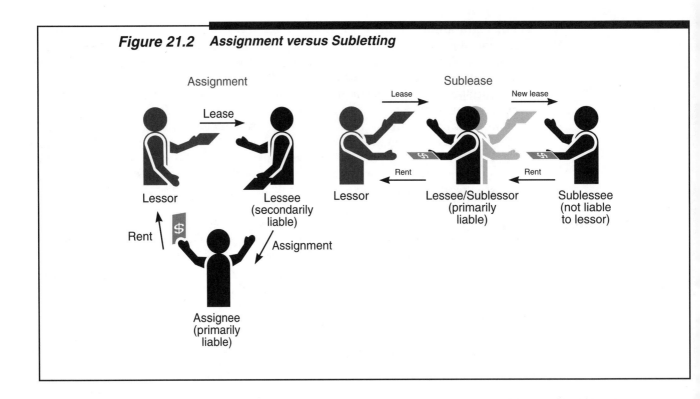

Figure 21.2   Assignment versus Subletting

In most cases the sublease or assignment does not relieve the original lessee of the obligation to make rental payments unless the landlord agrees to waive such liability. Texas law prohibits assignment or subleasing without the lessor's consent. This allows the lessor to retain control over the occupancy of the leased premises.

Options

Many leases contain an *option* that grants the lessee the privilege of *renewing* the lease but requires that the lessee give *notice* on or before a specific date of his or her intention to exercise the option. Some leases grant the lessee the option of purchasing the leased premises. Leases for the option to purchase vary widely; competent legal advice regarding the lease, note, and deed of trust would help avoid accidental violation of a due-on-sale clause, which could damage the lessor.

Termination of Lease

A written lease for a definite period of time expires at the end of that time period; no separate notice is required. Oral and written leases that do not specify a definite expiration date (such as a periodic estate or a tenancy at will) may be terminated by giving proper notice in advance. In Texas, unless otherwise provided by contract, tenancy from month to month may be terminated by one month's notice. Tenancy for a shorter period may be terminated by notice equal to such period.

When the conditions of a lease are breached, or broken, by a tenant, a landlord may terminate the lease and evict the tenant. This action must be handled through a Justice of the Peace court. In Texas, a landlord also may terminate a lease if the property is used for prostitution, obscene actions, or sexual performance by a child.

It is possible that the parties to a lease will mutually agree to cancel the lease. For example, the tenant's offer to surrender the lease and the landlord's acceptance will result in termination. A tenant who abandons leased property, however, remains liable for the terms of the lease—including the rent. By law, however, the landlord has a duty to *mitigate* damages by exercising reasonable care to find another tenant. The vacating tenant remains responsible under the terms of the lease only until another tenant begins rent payments.

When the owner of leased property dies or the property is sold, *the lease does not terminate.* The heirs of a deceased landlord are bound by the terms of existing valid leases. In addition, if a landlord conveys leased real estate, the new landlord takes the property subject to the rights of the tenants.

Breach of Lease

When a tenant breaches any lease provision, the landlord may attempt a lockout or interruption of utilities or may sue the tenant to obtain a judgment to cover past-due rent, damages to the premises, or other defaults. Likewise, when a landlord breaches any lease provision, the tenant is entitled to remedies against the landlord.

Landlord's lockout remedy. A landlord may attempt to collect rent on a residence by changing the locks of a tenant who is delinquent in paying all or a part of the rent. The landlord must first give the tenant written notice, three to five days in advance, that the locks are going to be changed for nonpayment of rent; the time frame is dependent on the method for giving notice. Then if the landlord or the real estate agent changes the door lock, the landlord or the agent must place a written notice on the tenant's front door giving the amount of rent and other charges due and a 24-hour address or phone number for the tenant to obtain a key to get into the property. In many cases, the tenant will pay the delinquent rent as a result of this forced personal contact. However, the new key must be given to the tenant whether or not the delinquent rent is paid. A landlord should seek legal advice to ensure that all legal requirements for tenant notice are followed.

Utilities interruption remedy. The landlord may interrupt or cause the interruption of electrical service furnished to a tenant in a residential dwelling if a tenant is at least seven days late in paying the rent, provided the tenant gets the required notice. By delivering to the tenant at least five days prior to the interruption of service a notice that states the amount of rent the tenant must pay to avoid the interruption, the landlord attempts to collect unpaid rent and avoid filing a suit for possession.

Suit for possession—actual eviction. When a tenant breaches a lease or improperly retains possession of leased premises, the landlord may regain possession through a **suit for possession,** known as **forcible entry and detainer.** This process is known as **actual eviction.** The law requires that the landlord serve *notice* on the tenant before commencing the suit. In Texas only a three-day notice must be given before filing a suit for possession based on a default in payment of rent; the lawsuit must be heard within ten days after the filing. When a court issues a judgment for possession to a landlord, the tenant has five days in which to file an appeal, after which the court may issue a *writ of possession* to the lessor. Within 48 hours after receiving the writ of possession, the landlord must deliver written notice that the writ will be enforced on or after a specific date and time, but not sooner than 24 hours after the warning is posted. The tenant must peaceably remove himself or herself and all belongings, or the landlord can have the judgment enforced by a *bailiff* or other court officer, who will oversee the forcible removal of the tenant and his or her possessions. As in other legal processes, additional stipulations in the laws could provide a lengthy tenancy while eviction proceedings are taking place.

Tenants' remedies—constructive eviction. If a landlord breaches any clause of a lease agreement, the tenant has the right to sue, claiming a judgment for damages against the landlord. If an action or omission on the landlord's part results in the leased premises becoming uninhabitable for the purpose intended in the lease, the tenant has the right to abandon the premises after giving written notice to the landlord. This action, called **constructive eviction,** terminates the lease agreement if the tenant can prove that the premises have become uninhabitable because of the conscious neglect of the landlord. To claim constructive eviction, the tenant must actually remove himself or herself from the premises while the uninhabitable condition exists. In Texas, the tenant also is entitled to receive a pro rata refund of rent paid or seek a court order requiring repairs to be made and awarding damages to the tenant.

For example, a lease requires the landlord to furnish central heat. If the landlord fails to repair a defective heating system and the leased premises subsequently become uninhabitable, the tenant may abandon them. (*Note:* Some leases provide that if failure to furnish heat is accidental and not the landlord's fault, the breach is not grounds for constructive eviction.)

FAIR CREDIT REPORTING ACT

The federal Fair Credit Reporting Act is designed to promote accuracy, fairness, and privacy of information in the files of consumer reporting agencies. Recent changes in the law affect property managers. If a property owner or his representative rejects an application for the rental of a property on the basis of the applicant's credit report, the applicant must be given the name of the credit reporting agency and must be told that he or she has a right to get a copy of the credit report. The applicant must also be told that the credit agency did not make the decision to reject the applicant. If a property owner or his representative rejects an applicant based upon information *other than a credit report,* the owner or the owner's representative must either disclose the reason or tell the applicant that he or she has the right to submit a request for disclosure of the reason for rejection.

TYPES OF LEASES

The manner in which rent is determined indicates the type of lease that is in force. The three primary types of leases are (1) the gross lease, (2) the net lease, and (3) the percentage lease (see Table 21.1).

Gross Lease

In a **gross lease** the tenant's obligation is to pay a *fixed rental* and the landlord pays all taxes, insurance, mortgage payments, repairs, and the like connected with the property (usually called *property charges*). This type of lease is used most often for residential apartment rentals. Tenants usually pay for utilities.

Table 21.1	Types of Leases	
Type of Lease	**Lessee**	**Lessor**
Gross Lease (residential)	Pays basic rent	Pays property charges (taxes, repairs, insurance)
Net lease (commercial/industrial)	Pays basic rent plus all or most property charges	May pay some property charges
Percentage Lease (commercial/industrial)	Pays basic rent plus percent of gross sales (may pay property costs)	May pay some or all property charges

Net Lease

The **net lease** provides that in addition to rent the *tenant pays most or all of the property charges.* The monthly rental paid to the landlord is in addition to these charges and, therefore, is net income for the landlord after operating costs have been paid. Leases for entire commercial or industrial buildings and the land on which they are located, ground leases, and long-term leases are usually net leases.

In a *triple net lease,* or *net-net-net lease,* the tenant pays all operating and other expenses, such as taxes, insurance, assessments, maintenance, and other charges.

Percentage Lease

Either a gross lease or a net lease may be a **percentage lease.** A percentage lease generally provides that the rental is based on a *percentage of the gross sales* made by the tenant doing business on the leased property. This type of lease usually is used in the rental of retail business locations.

The percentage lease usually provides for a minimum fixed rental fee plus a percentage of that portion of the tenant's business income that exceeds a stated minimum. The percentage charged in such leases varies widely with the nature of the business and is negotiable between landlord and tenant. A tenant's bargaining power is determined by his or her volume of business. Of course, percentages vary with the location of the property and general economic conditions.

Calculating Percentage Lease Rents.
A lease requires a minimum monthly rental of $1,300 per month plus 5 percent of the business's gross sales exceeding $160,000. On an annual sales volume of $250,000, the annual rent would be calculated as follows:

$1,300 per month x 12 months = $15,600
$250,000 – $160,000 = $90,000
$90,000 x .05 (5%) = $4,500
$15,600 base rent + $4,500 percentage rent = $20,100 total rent

Other Lease Types

Variable leases. Several types of leases allow for increases in the fixed rental charge during the lease period. Two of the more common ones are the *graduated lease,* which provides for increases in rent at set future dates, and the *index lease,* which allows rent to be increased or decreased periodically based on changes in the government cost-of-living index or some other index.

1. C
2.
3.
4.
5. D
6.
7. C
8.
9. A
10.
11. C
12.
13. D
14.
15. A
16.

Ground leases. When a landowner leases land to a tenant who agrees to *erect a building* on it, the lease usually is referred to as a **ground lease.** Such a lease must be for a long enough term to make the transaction desirable to the tenant making the investment in the building. These leases are generally *net leases* that require the lessee to pay rent as well as real estate taxes, insurance, upkeep, and repairs. Such leases often run for terms of 50 years or longer. Under Texas law a ground leasehold is considered to be an estate in land subject to the rights of a landlord.

Oil and gas leases. When oil companies lease land to explore for oil and gas, a special lease agreement must be negotiated. Usually the owner of the minerals receives a cash payment, called a *bonus*, for executing the lease. The mineral owner is frequently the landowner. If no well is drilled within a year or other period stated in the lease, the lease expires; however, most oil and gas leases provide that the oil company may continue its rights for another year by paying another flat fee, called a *delay rent*. Such rentals may be paid annually until a well is produced. If oil and/or gas is found, the landowner usually receives one-eighth or more of its value as a royalty. In this case, the lease will continue for as long as oil or gas is obtained in significant quantities. These royalty payments perpetuate the lease so long as production continues.

In Practice   Because of its long-term nature, as compared with a real estate sales contract, a lease is far more detailed and complicated. The lease document must anticipate and "presolve" many potential problems with the property as well as possible disagreements between the landlord and the tenant. Great care should be taken as to the form of lease to be used. For the protection of the landlord and tenant as well as the broker, each should seek competent legal counsel in a lease transaction.

Summary

A lease is an agreement that grants one person the right to use the property of another for a certain period in return for consideration. The lease agreement is a combination of a conveyance creating a leasehold interest in the property and a contract outlining the rights and obligations of the landlord and the tenant. A leasehold estate that runs for a specific length of time creates an estate for years, whereas one that runs for an indefinite period creates a periodic tenancy (year to year, month to month) or a tenancy at will. A leasehold estate generally is classified as personal property.

The requirements of a valid lease include offer and acceptance, consideration, capacity to contract, legal objectives, and a legal description. In addition, the Texas Statute of Frauds requires that any lease longer than one year must be in writing. Leases also generally include clauses relating to such rights and obligations of the landlord and tenant as the use of the premises, subletting, security deposits, maintenance of the premises, and termination of the lease period. Landlord/tenant laws cover requirements for installing smoke detectors and security devices.

Leases may be terminated by the expiration of the lease period, the mutual agreement of the parties, or a breach of the lease by either landlord or tenant. *Note:* Neither death of the tenant nor landlord's sale of the rental property terminates a lease. The lease "runs with the land," similar to an easement.

Upon a tenant's default on any of the lease provisions, a landlord may, following specific guidelines, utilize the lockout remedy, the utilities interruption remedy, or sue for a money judgment or for actual eviction. If the premises have become uninhabitable due to the landlord's negligence, the tenant may have the right of constructive eviction, that is, the right to abandon the premises and refuse to pay rent until the premises are repaired.

Basic lease types include net leases, gross leases, and percentage leases. These leases are classified according to the method used in determining the rental rate of the property.

1. Paul's estate for years lease will expire in two weeks. At that time, he will move to a larger apartment across town. What must Paul do to terminate this lease agreement?
   a. Paul must give the landlord one week's prior notice.
   b. Paul must give the landlord two weeks' prior notice.
   c. Paul needs to do nothing; the agreement will terminate automatically.
   d. The agreement will terminate only after Paul signs a lease for the new apartment.

2. A tenant's right to occupy, or take possession of, leased premises is a(n)
   a. reversionary interest.
   b. equitable title interest.
   c. leasehold interest.
   d. freehold estate.

3. A ground lease is usually
   a. short term.
   b. for 100 years or longer.
   c. long term.
   d. a gross lease.

4. A percentage lease is a lease that provides for
   a. rental of a percentage of a building's value.
   b. definite periodic rent not exceeding a stated percentage.
   c. definite monthly rent plus a percentage of the tenant's gross or net receipts in excess of a certain amount.
   d. a graduated amount due monthly and not exceeding a stated percentage.

5. If a store building collapsed because of conscious landlord neglect and the tenants moved out,
   a. the tenants would be liable for the rent until the expiration date of their leases.
   b. the landlord would not be responsible for any refund of rent.
   c. this would be an actual eviction.
   d. this would be a constructive eviction.

6. Which of the following statements describes a net lease?
   a. An agreement in which the tenant pays a fixed rent and the landlord pays all taxes, insurance, and related expenses on the property
   b. A lease in which the tenant pays rent plus maintenance and property charges
   c. A lease in which the tenant pays the landlord a percentage of the monthly income derived from the property
   d. An agreement granting an individual a leasehold interest in fishing rights for shoreline properties

7. A lease for more than one year must be in writing because
   a. the landlord or tenant may forget the terms.
   b. the tenant must sign the agreement to pay rent.
   c. the statute of frauds requires it.
   d. it is the customary procedure to protect the tenant.

8. A lease calls for a minimum rent of $1,200 per month plus 4 percent of the annual gross business over $150,000. If the total rent paid at the end of the year was $19,200, how much business did the tenant do during the year?
   a. $159,800　　c. $270,000
   b. $250,200　　d. $279,200

9. Paul Robinson occupies a building under a written lease for a five-year term with monthly rental payments. The lease expired last month, but Robinson has remained in possession and the landlord has accepted his most recent rent payment without comment. At this point
   a. Robinson is a holdover tenant.
   b. Robinson's lease has been renewed for another five years.
   c. Robinson's lease has been renewed for another month.
   d. Robinson is a tenant at sufferance.

10. The leasehold interest that automatically renews itself at each expiration is the
    a. tenancy for years.
    b. tenancy from period to period.
    c. tenancy at will.
    d. tenancy at sufferance.

11. Which term refers to a tenant's legal right to possession of leased property against the ownership claims of third parties?
    a. Tenancy at will
    b. Cognovit
    c. Covenant of quiet possession
    d. Constructive eviction

12. A tenant's lease has expired, the tenant has neither vacated nor negotiated a renewal lease, and the landlord has declared that she does not want the tenant to remain in the building. The form of possession is called a(n)
    a. estate for years.
    b. periodic estate.
    c. tenancy at will.
    d. tenancy at sufferance.

13. The requirements of a valid lease include all **EXCEPT** which of the following?
    a. Offer and acceptance
    b. Valuable consideration
    c. Capacity to contract
    d. Recordation in county clerk's office

14. If no special provision is included in the lease regarding permanent improvements made by a tenant, such improvements
    a. are fixtures.
    b. remain the property of the tenant after the lease expires.
    c. are adaptations of space to suit tenants' needs.
    d. are reimbursed to the tenant by the landlord.

15. Adams leased space in her new shopping center to Baker for his dress store. However, Baker's business fails and he sublets the space to Davis. If Davis fails to make rental payments when due,
    a. Adams would have recourse against Baker only.
    b. Adams would have recourse against Davis only.
    c. Adams would have recourse against both Baker and Davis.
    d. Davis would have recourse against Baker.

16. In June, Valerie signed a TAR lease for one year and moved into an apartment. She deposited the required security deposit with the landlord. Six months later, she paid the January rent and mysteriously moved out. Valerie did not arrange for a sublease or an assignment and made no further rent payments. She left the apartment in good condition. What is Valerie's liability to the landlord under these circumstances?
    a. Because half the rental amount has been paid and the apartment is in good condition, she has no further liability.
    b. She is liable for one month's additional rent only.
    c. She is liable for the balance of the rent only.
    d. She is liable for the balance of the rent plus forfeiture of the security deposit.

22 Property Management

Key Terms

business interruption
  insurance
casualty insurance
contents and personal
  property insurance
depreciated cost

fire and extended
  coverage insurance
liability insurance
management
  agreement
multiperil policies

property manager
replacement cost
risk management
surety bond
workers'
  compensation acts

OVERVIEW

A real estate owner who rents out the upstairs apartment in the building where he or she resides generally has no problem with property management—setting and collecting rents, maintenance, and repairs are easy enough with only one tenant. But the owners of large, multiunit developments often lack the time and/or expertise to manage their properties successfully. Enter the *property manager*, a real estate professional hired to maintain the property and ensure profitability of the owner's investment.

This chapter examines the growing property management profession and includes discussions of the types of property insurance available to further protect an owner's real estate investment.

PROPERTY MANAGEMENT

Property management involves leasing, managing, marketing, and overall maintenance of real estate owned by others. The increased size of buildings; the technical complexities of construction, maintenance, and repair; and the trend toward absentee ownership by individual investors and investment groups have led to the expanded use of professional property managers for both residential and commercial properties. Property management has become so important that many brokerage firms maintain separate management departments staffed by carefully selected, well-trained people. Some corporate and institutional owners of real estate also have established property management departments. A real estate license is required when a person, for a fee, rents or leases or procures tenants for a property, unless he or she is an on-site apartment manager or an employee (not an agent) of the owner.

The Property Manager

A **property manager** is someone who *preserves the value of an investment property while generating income as an agent for the owners.* More specifically, a property manager is expected to merchandise the property and control operating expenses to maximize income. In addition, a manager should maintain and modernize the property to preserve and enhance the owner's capital investment. The three areas of activities performed by the property manager can be summarized as administration, marketing, and physical management. The manager carries out these duties by (1) securing suitable tenants, (2) collecting the rents, (3) caring for the premises, (4) budgeting and controlling expenses, (5) hiring and supervising employees, and (6) keeping proper accounts and making periodic reports to the owner.

> A *property manager*
>
> - maintains the owner's investment and
> - ensures that the property produces income.

Securing Management Business

In today's market, property managers may look to corporate owners, apartments and condominiums, investment syndicates, trusts, and absentee owners as possible sources of management business. In securing business from any of these sources, word of mouth is often the best advertising. A manager who consistently demonstrates that he or she can increase property income over previous levels should have no difficulty finding new business.

Before contracting to manage any property, the professional property manager should be certain that the building owner has realistic income expectations and is willing to spend money on necessary maintenance. Attempting to meet impossible owner demands by dubious methods can endanger the manager's reputation and prove detrimental to obtaining future business.

The Management Agreement

The first step in taking over the management of any property is to enter into a **management agreement** with the owner. This agreement creates an agency relationship between the owner and the property manager. A property manager is usually considered a *general agent.* This means that the property manager has a much broader scope of responsibility and, therefore, greater liability than does a listing broker. As an agent for the property owner, the property manager is charged with the same basic fiduciary duties as the listing broker—care, obedience, accounting, loyalty, and disclosure (see Chapter 5 for a review of agency responsibilities).

The management agreement should be in writing and should cover the following eight points:

1. *Description* of the property.
2. *Time period* the agreement will cover.
3. *Definition of management's responsibilities:* All of the manager's duties should be stated in the contract; exceptions should be noted.
4. *Statement of owner's purpose:* This statement should indicate what the owner desires the manager to accomplish with the property. One owner may wish to maximize net income and therefore instruct the manager to cut expenses and minimize reinvestment. Another owner may want to increase the capital value of the investment, in which case the manager should initiate a program for improving the property's physical condition.

5. *Extent of manager's authority:* This provision should state what authority the manager is to have in such matters as hiring, firing, and supervising employees; fixing rental rates for space; making expenditures; and authorizing repairs within the limits established previously with the owner. (Repairs that exceed a certain expense limit may require the owner's written approval.)
6. *Reporting:* Agreement should be reached on the frequency and detail of the manager's periodic reports on operations and financial position. These reports serve as a means for the owner to monitor the manager's work and as a basis for both the owner and the manager to assess trends that can be used in shaping future management policy.
7. *Management fee:* The fee can be based on a percentage of gross or net income, a commission on new rentals, a fixed fee, or a combination of these.
8. *Allocation of costs:* The agreement should state which of the property manager's expenses, such as office rent, office help, telephone, advertising, association fees, and Social Security, will be paid by the manager and which will be charged to the property's expenses and paid by the owner.

> Management fees must be negotiated between the agent and the principal. Standardization of rates would be viewed as price fixing.

After entering into an agreement with a property owner, a manager must handle the property as if it were his or her own. In all activities, the manager must be aware that his or her responsibility is to *realize the highest return on the property that is consistent with the owner's instructions.*

MANAGEMENT CONSIDERATIONS

A property manager must protect the interest of the property owner by (1) constantly *improving the reputation* as well as the *physical condition* of the property, (2) protecting the owner from *insurable losses*, (3) protecting the owner by helping the neighborhood and the community to offer the best possible *residential and business environments*, (4) keeping a constant *check on all expenditures* to be sure that costs are kept as low as possible for the results that must be accomplished, and (5) *adjusting the rental rate* as necessary to produce the highest total income.

A property manager must live up to his or her end of the management agreement in both the letter and the spirit of the contract. The owner must be kept well informed on all matters of policy as well as on the financial condition of the property and its operation. Finally, a manager must keep in contact with others in the field, improving his or her knowledge of the subject and staying informed on current policies pertaining to the profession.

Budgeting Expenses   Before attempting to rent any property, a property manager should develop an operating budget based on anticipated revenues and expenses and reflecting the long-term goals of the owner. In preparing a budget, a manager should begin by allocating money for such continuous, fixed expenses as employees' salaries, real estate taxes, property taxes, and insurance premiums.

Next the manager should establish a cash reserve fund for such variable expenses as repairs, decorating, and supplies. The amount allocated for the reserve funds can be computed from the previous yearly costs of the variable expenses.

Capital expenditures. If an owner and a property manager decide that modernization or renovation of the property will enhance its value, the manager should budget money to cover the costs of remodeling. In the case of large-scale construction, the expenses charged against the property's income should be spread over several years. Although budgets should be as accurate an estimate of cost as possible, adjustments sometimes may be necessary, especially in the case of new properties.

Renting the Property

Effective rental of the property is essential to the success of a property manager. However, the role of the manager should not be confused with that of a broker or rental agency concerned solely with renting space. The property manager may use the services of a rental agency to solicit prospective tenants or collect rents, but the rental agency does not undertake the full responsibility of maintenance and management of the property.

Setting rental rates. In establishing rental rates for a property a basic concern must be that, in the long term, the income from the rentable space covers the fixed charges and operating expenses and also provides a fair return on the investment. However, consideration also must be given to the prevailing rates in comparable buildings and the current level of vacancy in the property to be rented. In the short term, rental rates are primarily a result of supply and demand. Decisions about rental rates should start with a detailed survey of the competitive space available in the neighborhood. Prices should be noted, and judgment should be applied to adjust for differences between neighboring properties and the property the manager will manage.

Apartment rental rates are stated in monthly amounts on a unit basis. However, office and commercial space rentals are usually stated according to either the annual or the monthly rate per square foot of space.

If a high vacancy level exists, an immediate effort should be made to determine what is wrong with the property or what is out of line in the rental rates. *A high level of vacancy does not necessarily indicate that rents are too high.* The trouble may be inept management or defects in the property. The manager should attempt to identify and correct the problems rather than lower the rent. Conversely, *although a high percentage of occupancy may appear to indicate an effective rental program, it also could mean that rental rates are too low.* Any time the occupancy level exceeds 95 percent, serious consideration should be given to raising the rents in an apartment house or office building.

Tenant selection. Generally, the highest rents can be secured from satisfied tenants. A broker may sell a property and then have no further dealings with the purchaser, but a building manager must continue to deal with each tenant, and the manager's success is greatly dependent on retaining sound, long-term relationships. In selecting prospective commercial or industrial tenants, a manager should be sure that each person will "fit the space." The manager should be certain that (1) the *size of the space* meets the tenant's requirements, (2) the tenant will have the *ability to pay* for the space for which he or she contracts, (3) the *tenant's business will be compatible* with the building and the other tenants, and (4) if the tenant is likely to expand in the future, *expansion space* will be available. After a prospect becomes a tenant, *the manager must be sure that the tenant remains satisfied in all respects commensurate with fair business dealing.* (*Note:* In selecting residential tenants, the property manager must comply with all federal and local fair housing laws, as discussed in Chapter 6.)

FTC privacy rule. Whether a property manager is selecting a tenant or giving a reference for a tenant who is moving, it is important to understand the applicability of the FTC privacy rule to a landlord's actions. Under the privacy rule, which went into effect on July 1, 2001, companies that are significantly engaged in certain financial activities must make specific disclosures to a consumer before they may pass the consumer's personal information on to unaffiliated third parties. If a property manager is asked to provide a tenant history and rental reference to another property manager, it would be prudent practice to obtain a written statement from the manager that the information provided will not be used for "credit granting" purposes. Before disclosing any information about a tenant to someone other than another rental housing owner or manager, a law enforcement officer, a consumer reporting agency, or a prospective employer of the tenant, the property manager must have written permission from the tenant.

Collecting rents. A building will not be a profitable operation unless the property manager can collect all rents when they are due. Any substantial loss resulting from nonpayment of rent will quickly eliminate the margin of profitability in an operation.

Careful selection of tenants simplifies the collection of rents.

The best way to minimize problems with rent collection is to make a *careful selection* of tenants in the first place. A property manager's desire to have a high level of occupancy should not override good judgment in accepting only those tenants who can be expected to meet their financial obligations to the property owner. A property manager should investigate financial references given by the prospect, local credit bureaus, and, when possible, the prospective tenant's former landlord.

The terms of rental payment should be spelled out in detail in the lease agreement. These details include the time and place of payment, provisions and penalties for late payment, and provisions for cancellation and damages in case of nonpayment. A *firm and consistent collection plan* with a sufficient system of notices and records should be established by the property manager. In cases of delinquency, every attempt must be made to make collections without resorting to legal action. However, for those cases in which it is required, a property manager must be prepared to initiate and follow through with the necessary steps in conjunction with the property owner's or management firm's legal counsel.

Maintaining the Property

One of the most important functions of a property manager is the supervision of property maintenance. A manager must learn to balance services provided with the costs they entail to satisfy the tenants' needs while minimizing operating expenses.

The broad term *maintenance* actually covers several types of activities. First, the manager must *protect the physical integrity of the property* to ensure that the condition of the building and its grounds are kept at present levels.

Preventive maintenance helps prevent problems and expenses.

Corrective maintenance corrects problems after they have occurred.

Routine maintenance keeps up with everyday wear and tear (housekeeping, pool maintenance, etc.).

Over the long term, preserving the property by repainting the exterior or replacing the heating plant will help to keep the building functional and decrease routine maintenance costs.

A property manager also must *supervise routine cleaning and repairs* of the building. Such day-to-day duties as cleaning common areas, minor carpentry and plumbing, and regularly scheduled upkeep of heating, air-conditioning, and landscaping generally are handled by regular building employees or by outside firms that have contracted with the manager to provide certain services.

In addition, especially when dealing with commercial or industrial space, a property manager will be called on to *alter the interior of the building to meet the functional demands of the tenant.* These alterations range from repainting to completely gutting the interior and redesigning the space.

Designing interior space is especially important when renting new buildings because the interior is usually left incomplete so that it can be adapted to the needs of the individual tenants. Another portion of a manager's responsibility is the supervision of modernization or renovation of buildings that have become functionally obsolete and thus unsuited to today's building needs. (See Chapter 14 for a definition of *functional obsolescence.*) The renovation of a building often increases the building's marketability and thus its potential income.

Employees versus contracted services. One of the major decisions a property manager faces is whether to contract for maintenance services from an outside firm or to hire on-site employees to perform such tasks. This decision should be based on a number of factors, including size of the building, complexity of tenants' requirements, and availability of suitable labor. In a large building or one where the tenants have sophisticated needs, a property manager may find that a large on-site crew is needed to deal with the day-to-day operations of the property; in a small apartment building, one full-time janitor can handle most of the everyday problems.

Handling Environmental Concerns

The property manager must be able to respond to a variety of environmental problems. Tenant concerns, as well as federal, state, and local regulations, determine the extent of the manager's environmental responsibilities. He or she may manage structures containing asbestos or radon or be called on to arrange an environmental audit of a property. Managers must see that any hazardous wastes produced by their employers or tenants are disposed of. Even the normally nonhazardous waste of an office building must be controlled to avoid violation of laws requiring segregation and recycling of types of wastes. Environmental issues are discussed in detail in Chapter 23.

The Americans with Disabilities Act

The *Americans with Disabilities Act (ADA)* has had a significant impact on the responsibilities of the property manager (operator), both in building amenities and in employment issues.

Title I of the ADA provides for the employment of qualified job applicants regardless of their disability. Any employer with 15 or more employees must adopt nondiscriminatory employment procedures. In addition, employers must make reasonable accommodations to enable individuals with disabilities to perform essential job functions.

Property managers also must be familiar with Title III of the ADA, which prohibits discrimination in commercial properties. The ADA requires that managers ensure that people with disabilities have full and equal access to facilities and services. The property manager typically is responsible for determining whether a building meets the ADA's accessibility requirements. The property manager must also prepare and execute a plan for restructuring or retrofitting a building that is not in compliance. ADA experts may be consulted, as may architectural designers who specialize in accessibility issues.

To protect owners of existing structures from the massive expense of extensive remodeling, the ADA recommends *reasonably achievable accommodations* to provide access to the facilities and services (see Figure 22.1).

The following are typical examples of readily achievable modifications—those that can be accomplished with little difficulty and at low cost.

- Ramping or removing an obstacle from an otherwise accessible entrance
- Lowering wall-mounted public telephones
- Adding raised letters and braille markings on elevator buttons
- Installing auditory signals in elevators
- Reversing the direction in which doors open

Alternative methods can be used to provide reasonable accommodations if extensive restructuring is impractical or if retrofitting is unduly expensive. For instance, installing a cup dispenser at a water fountain that is too high for an individual in a wheelchair may be more practical than installing a lower unit.

New construction and remodeling, however, must meet higher standards of accessibility and usability because it costs less to incorporate accessible features in the design than to retrofit. Though the law intends to provide for people with disabilities, many of the accessible design features and accommodations benefit everyone.

In Practice   The U.S. Department of Justice has ADA specialists available to answer general information questions about compliance issues. The ADA Information Line is at 1-800-514-0301.

RISK MANAGEMENT

Because enormous monetary losses can result from certain occurrences, one of the most critical areas of responsibility for a property manager is to protect the property owner against all major insurable risks. Awareness of the purposes of insurance coverage and how to make best use of the many types of insurance available is part of what is called **risk management.**

Risk management involves answering the question "What will happen if something goes wrong?" The perils of any risk must be evaluated in terms of

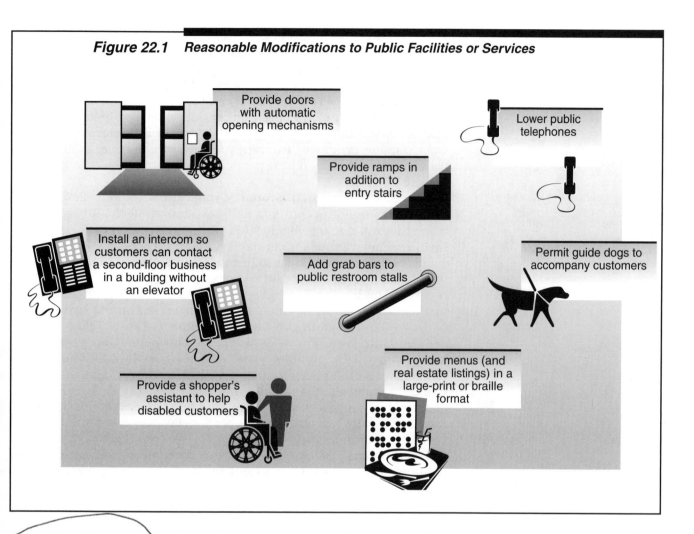

Figure 22.1   Reasonable Modifications to Public Facilities or Services

Provide doors with automatic opening mechanisms

Lower public telephones

Provide ramps in addition to entry stairs

Install an intercom so customers can contact a second-floor business in a building without an elevator

Add grab bars to public restroom stalls

Permit guide dogs to accompany customers

Provide a shopper's assistant to help disabled customers

Provide menus (and real estate listings) in a large-print or braille format

The four alternative risk management techniques may be remembered by the acronym *ACTOR:* *A*void, *C*ontrol, *T*ransfer or *R*etain.

options. In considering the possibility of a loss, the property manager must decide whether it is better to

- *avoid it,* by removing the source of risk, such as a swimming pool;
- *control it,* by installing sprinklers, fire doors, and other preventive measures;
- *transfer it,* by taking out an insurance policy—perhaps even *share it,* by insuring with a large deductible; or
- *retain it,* by deciding that the chances of the event's occurring are too small to justify the expense of any other response.

When insurance is considered, a competent, reliable insurance agent who is well versed in all areas of insurance pertaining to property should be selected to survey the property and make recommendations. If the manager is not completely satisfied with these recommendations, additional insurance surveys should be obtained. Final decisions, however, must be made by the property owner.

Types of Coverage   To manage the risks, many kinds of insurance coverage are available to owners and managers of income property. Six of the more common types are listed below:

1. **Fire and extended coverage insurance:** Fire insurance policies provide coverage against direct loss or damage to property from a fire on the premises. Extended coverage provides insurance to cover hazards such as windstorm, hurricanes, hail, explosion, riot, civil commotion, smoke, aircraft, and land vehicles.

2. **Business interruption insurance:** Most hazard policies insure against the actual loss of property but do not cover loss of revenues from income property. Interruption insurance covers the loss of income that occurs if the property cannot be used to produce income.

3. **Contents and personal property insurance:** *Inland marine insurance* covers building contents and personal property during periods when they are not actually located on the business premises.

4. **Liability insurance:** Public liability insurance covers the risks an owner assumes when the public enters the building. Claims are used to pay medical expenses for a person injured in the building as a result of the landlord's negligence. Another liability risk is that of medical or hospital payments for injuries sustained by building employees in the course of their employment. These claims are covered by state laws known as **workers' compensation acts.** These laws require that a building owner who is an employer obtain a workers' compensation policy from a private insurance company.

5. **Casualty insurance:** Casualty insurance policies include coverage against theft, burglary, vandalism, and machinery damage. Casualty policies usually are written on specific risks, such as theft, rather than being all-inclusive.

6. **Surety bonds:** Surety bonds cover an owner against financial losses resulting from an employee's criminal acts or negligence while carrying out his or her duties.

Today, many insurance companies offer **multiperil policies** for apartment and business buildings. These policies offer the property manager an insurance package that includes such standard types of commercial coverage as fire, hazard, public liability, and casualty.

Claims   When a claim is made under a policy insuring a building or another physical object, there are two possible methods of determining the amount of the claim. One is the **depreciated cost,** or actual cash value of the damaged property, and the other is **replacement cost.** If a 30-year-old building is damaged, the timbers and materials are 30 years old and therefore do not have the same value as new material. Thus, in determining the amount of the loss under what is called *actual cash value,* the cost of new material would be reduced by the estimated depreciation the item had suffered during the time it was in the building.

The alternate method is to cover *replacement cost.* This represents the actual amount a builder would charge to replace the damaged property, including materials, at the time of the loss.

When purchasing insurance, a manager must assess whether the property should be insured at full replacement cost or at a depreciated cost. As with the homeowners' policies discussed in Chapter 4, commercial policies include *coinsurance clauses* that require that the insured carry fire coverage, usually in an amount equal to 80 percent of the building's replacement value.

In Practice   Often a property owner pays for small casualty losses out of pocket and attempts to deduct the cost on his or her tax return instead of filing a claim with the company that insures the building. This is done to avoid rate increases or cancellation of a policy. However, the IRS does not allow such deductions because the taxpayer voluntarily elected not to claim reimbursement from the insurance company. Because the IRS allows a property owner to deduct all losses suffered up to the deductible portion of the insurance policy, some owners/managers might consider obtaining policies with a higher deductible, which also should result in a lower insurance premium.

THE MANAGEMENT PROFESSION

Most large cities have local associations of building and property owners and managers that are affiliates of regional and national associations. The Institute of Real Estate Management is one of the affiliates of the National Association of REALTORS®. It awards the designations of *Certified Property Manager* (CPM) and *Accredited Residential Manager* (ARM) to persons who have met certain requirements. The Building Owners and Managers Association International (BOMA International) is a federation of local associations of owners and managers, primarily of office buildings. The Building Owners and Managers Institute (BOMI) International, an independent institute affiliated with BOMA, offers training courses leading to several designations: *Real Property Administrator* (RPA), *Systems Maintenance Administrator* (SMA), and *Facilities Management Administrator* (FMA).

Within Texas, the Texas Apartment Association (TAA) has more than 10,000 members who manage more than 1.5 million rental housing units statewide. Participation in groups like these allows property managers to gain valuable professional knowledge and to discuss their problems with other managers facing similar issues. For the latest information on issues affecting property managers in Texas, visit the TAA web site at www.taa.org.

Summary

Property management is a specialized service to owners of income-producing properties in which the managerial function may be delegated to an individual or a firm with particular expertise in the field. The manager, as agent of the owner, becomes the administrator of the project and assumes the executive functions required for the care and operation of the property. The three areas of activities for the property manager are administration, marketing, and physical management.

A management agreement defines and authorizes the manager's duties and responsibilities. Additionally, it establishes the agency relationship between owner and manager.

After the management agreement is signed, the first step a property manager should take is to draw up a budget of estimated variable and fixed

1. B
2. B
3. D
4. C
5. C
6. D
7. D
8. C
9. A
10. A
11. C
12. B
13. D
14. C
15. B
16. C

expenses. The budget also should allow for any proposed expenditures for major renovation or modernization agreed on by the manager and the owner. These projected expenses, combined with the manager's analysis of the condition of the building and the rent patterns in the neighborhood, will form the basis on which rental rates are determined.

After a rent schedule is established, the property manager is responsible for soliciting tenants whose needs are suited to the available space and who are financially capable of meeting the proposed rents. The manager generally is obligated to collect rents, maintain the building, hire necessary employees, pay taxes for the building, and deal with tenant problems.

Once the property is rented, one of the manager's primary responsibilities is supervising its maintenance. Maintenance includes safeguarding the physical integrity of the property and performing routine cleaning and repairs as well as adapting the interior space and overall design of the property to suit the tenants' needs and meet the demands of the market.

In addition, the manager is expected to protect the owner's interests through effective risk management by securing adequate insurance coverage for the premises. The basic types of coverage applicable to commercial structures include fire and extended coverage insurance on the property and fixtures, business interruption insurance to protect the owner against income losses, and casualty insurance to provide coverage against such losses as theft, vandalism, and destruction of machinery. The manager also should secure public liability insurance to insure the owner against claims made by people injured on the premises and workers' compensation policies to cover the claims of employees injured on the job.

The Texas property manager must be a licensed real estate broker, unless exempt by the provisions of the Texas Real Estate License Act.

Questions

1. Which of the following types of insurance coverage insures the property owner against the claims of employees injured while on the job?
   a. Business interruption
   b. Workers' compensation
   c. Casualty
   d. Surety bond

2. Repairing a boiler is classified as which type of maintenance?
   a. Preventive
   b. Corrective
   c. Routine
   d. Construction

3. From a management point of view, apartment building occupancy that reaches as high as 98 percent might indicate that
   a. the building is poorly managed.
   b. the building is well managed.
   c. the building is a desirable place to live.
   d. rents should be raised.

4. A deliveryman slips on a defective stair in an apartment building and is hospitalized. A claim against the building owner for medical expenses will be made under which of the following policies held by the owner?
   a. Workers' compensation
   b. Casualty
   c. Liability
   d. Fire and hazard coverage

5. Which of the following should **NOT** be a consideration in selecting a tenant?
   a. The size of the space versus the tenant's requirements
   b. The tenant's ability to pay
   c. The racial and ethnic background of the tenant
   d. The compatibility of the tenant's business with other tenants' businesses

6. Contaminated groundwater, toxic fumes from paint and carpeting, and lack of proper ventilation are all examples of
   a. issues beyond the scope of a property manager's job description.
   b. problems faced only on newly constructed properties.
   c. issues that arise under the ADA.
   d. environmental concerns that a property manager may have to address.

7. An owner-manager agreement should include all of the following **EXCEPT**
   a. a statement of the owner's purpose for the building.
   b. a clear definition of the manager's authority.
   c. that portion of the property manager's personal operating expenses that will be paid by the owner.
   d. a listing of previous owners of the property.

8. A highrise apartment building burns to the ground. What type of insurance covers the landlord against the resulting loss of rent?
   a. Fire and hazard
   b. Liability
   c. Business interruption
   d. Casualty

9. Apartment rental rates are usually expressed
   a. in monthly amounts.
   b. on a per-room basis.
   c. in square feet per month.
   d. on a prorated yearly basis.

10. Rents should be determined by
    a. supply and demand factors.
    b. the local apartment owners' association.
    c. HUD.
    d. a tenants' union.

11. Property manager Freida Jacobs hires Albert Weston as the full-time janitor for one of the buildings she manages. While repairing a faucet in one of the apartments, Weston steals a television set. Jacobs could protect the owner against liability for this type of loss by purchasing
   a. liability insurance.
   b. workers' compensation insurance.
   c. a surety bond.
   d. casualty insurance.

12. A property manager is offered a choice of three insurance policies: one has a $500 deductible, one has a $1,000 deductible, and the third has a $5,000 deductible. If the property manager selects the policy with the highest deductible, which risk management technique is he or she using?
   a. Avoiding   c. Controlling
   b. Sharing   d. Transferring

13. The manager's responsibility for the maintenance of a property includes all of the following **EXCEPT**
   a. adapting the interior space of the building to meet the requirements of individual tenants.
   b. modernizing buildings.
   c. maintaining the present condition of the building and grounds.
   d. meeting the needs of tenants regardless of the expense to the owner.

14. The payment of workers' compensation to a repairman injured in the building you manage is controlled by
   a. the contract between the owner and each repairperson.
   b. the city council.
   c. state law.
   d. federal law.

15. A property manager who enters into a management agreement with an owner is usually a
   a. special agent.
   b. general agent.
   c. universal agent.
   d. designated agent.

16. In preparing a budget, a property manager should set up which of the following for variable expenses?
   a. Control account
   b. Floating allocation
   c. Cash reserve fund
   d. Asset account

Control of Land Use

Key Terms

buffer zone	extraterritorial	property report
building code	jurisdiction	public ownership
building permit	Interstate Land Sales	spot zoning
comprehensive plan	Full Disclosure Act	subdivision regulations
conditional use permit	laches	variance
covenant	municipal utility district	zoning board of
deed restriction	nonconforming use	adjustment
developer	planned unit	zoning ordinance
	development	

OVERVIEW

The various ownership rights a person possesses in a parcel of real estate are subject to certain public land-use controls (such as zoning ordinances, subdivision regulations, and building codes) and private controls (such as deed restrictions). The purpose of these controls is to ensure that our limited supply of land is being put to its highest and best use for the benefit of the general public as well as private owners.

This chapter discusses the three types of land-use controls and how they help shape and preserve the physical surface of our nation.

LAND-USE CONTROLS

The control and regulation of land use is accomplished in both the public and private sectors through three means. These are (1) public land-use controls, (2) private land-use controls through deed restrictions, and (3) public ownership of land—including parks, schools, and expressways—by the federal, state, and local governments.

Public Controls   Under the *police powers* granted by the Fourteenth Amendment to the U.S. Constitution, each state, and in turn its counties and municipalities, has the inherent authority to adopt regulations necessary to protect the public

453

health, safety, and general welfare. This includes limitations, or controls, on the use of privately owned real estate. The largely urban population and the increasing demands placed on finite natural resources have made it necessary for cities, towns, and villages to establish controls over the private use of real estate. Police power in many areas includes controls over noise, air, and water pollution as well as population density.

Privately owned real estate is regulated through

- zoning;
- subdivision regulations;
- codes that regulate building construction, safety, and public health; and
- environmental protection legislation.

The comprehensive plan. In the late 19th and early 20th centuries, some concerned individuals were dissatisfied with the haphazard manner in which metropolitan areas were developing. During this period, unofficial citizens' groups in cities like New York, Boston, and Chicago adopted city plans. One of the first such plans was the McMillan Improvement Plan for Washington, D.C. Adopted in 1901, it set forth the overall strategy for the development of the famous park system of our nation's capital.

A few years later, the Burnham Plan for the city of Chicago was published. The Burnham Plan was probably the most influential force in urban planning throughout the country. The subject matter of this plan encompassed rapid transit and suburban growth, a comprehensive park system, forest preserves, transportation and terminals, streets and subdivision control, and problems of the central city.

Today, the country is witnessing a much broader approach to urban planning and development. Local governments recognize development goals primarily through the formulation of a **comprehensive plan** (sometimes called a *master plan*). Cities and counties develop comprehensive plans to ensure that social and economic needs are balanced against environmental and aesthetic concerns. In most cases a city, county, or regional *planning commission* is created for these purposes. A comprehensive plan encompasses all geographic parts of the community and all elements that affect its physical development over a 20- to 30-year period. As a long-range, general framework for making development decisions, the comprehensive plan

- expresses community goals and objectives;
- designates areas for residential, commercial, and industrial development;
- indicates preferred locations for utility systems and for parks, golf courses, cemeteries, schools and libraries, fire stations, and other public facilities;
- proposes means for transporting people and products (roads, airports, railways);
- recommends treatment for such special problems as historic preservation, downtown renewal, flood control and drainage, noise mitigation, and other environmental concerns; and
- lists actions needed to carry out the plan.

Table 23.1	*Special Types of Zoning*
Type of Zoning	**Primary Purpose**
Bulk zoning	To control density and prevent overcrowding through restrictions on setback, building height, and percentage of open areas
Aesthetic zoning	To require that new buildings conform to specific types of architecture
Incentive zoning	To require that street floors of office buildings be used for retail establishments
Directive zoning	To use zoning as a planning tool to encourage use of land for its highest and best use

Economic and physical surveys are essential in preparing a comprehensive plan. Countywide or regional plans also must include the coordination of numerous civic plans and developments to ensure orderly city growth with stabilized property values.

Zoning

The **zoning ordinance** is a police power measure in which the community is divided into districts or zones for various classes of land use for the purpose of regulating the use of private land. Zoning is a tool for implementing a local comprehensive plan to *prevent* incompatible adjacent land uses, overcrowding, and traffic congestion; restrict height and size/bulk of buildings; provide setbacks to lessen fire hazards; and promote aesthetic value. Municipal zoning ordinances may be enacted to regulate the use of land, specify lot sizes or types of structures permitted, establish setbacks (the minimum distance away from streets and the side and rear property lines that structures may be built), and control density (the ratio of land area to structure area or population).

Typical land-use classifications are agricultural, residential, commercial, and industrial. A special zoning classification, **Planned Unit Development** (PUD), is used by many communities for *cluster zoning, multiple-use zoning,* or *special-purpose zoning.* To ensure adequate control, land-use areas are further divided into subclasses. For example, residential areas may be subdivided to provide for detached single-family dwellings, semidetached structures containing not more than four dwelling units, walkup apartments, highrise apartments, and so forth. In addition, some communities require the use of buffers (such as landscaped parks and playgrounds) or **buffer zones** (zoning districts that gradually change from a higher-intensity use to a lower-intensity use) to separate and screen residential areas from nonresidential areas. Some special types of zoning are listed in Table 23.1.

Zoning powers are conferred by state *enabling acts.* Texas adopted its version of the Standard Zoning Enabling Act in 1927 and delegated zoning powers to municipalities, but not to counties. There are no nationwide zoning regulations; and with the exception of Hawaii, no states have statewide zoning regulations. State and federal governments may, however, regulate land use through special legislation such as scenic easement and coastal management laws.

Adoption of zoning ordinances. Zoning ordinances are recommended by the Planning and Zoning Commission to the City Council for final approval. Zoning ordinances must not violate the rights of individuals and property holders (as provided under the due process provisions of the Fourteenth Amendment of the U.S. Constitution) or the various provisions of the state constitution of the state in which the real estate is located. If the means used to regulate the use of property are destructive, unreasonable, arbitrary, or confiscatory, the ordinances usually are considered void. Tests usually applied in determining the validity of ordinances require that

- power be exercised in a reasonable manner;
- provisions be clear and specific;
- ordinances be free from discrimination;
- ordinances promote public health, safety, and general welfare under the police power concept; and
- ordinances apply to all property in a similar manner.

Requests for an *amendment* to the official *zoning map* may be initiated by a property developer or by the city planning staff in response to the municipality's comprehensive plan. In Texas, each municipal governing body establishes procedures for zoning adoption and enforcement. There is a notification requirement for property owners within 200 feet of any proposed zoning change. Additionally, a 15-day notice published in a local newspaper must be given prior to a public hearing. The proposed amendment must be heard in a public hearing on the matter and approved by the governing body of the community. If 20 percent of the owners protest the zoning change, the governing body must approve the change by at least three-fourths vote.

Zoning variations that result in small areas that differ significantly from adjoining parcels in a way that is not in harmony with the general plan for the area might be considered spot zoning. An example would be a zoning map amendment that allows a convenience store in the middle of a residential area. If a court determines that changing the zoning was to the excessive benefit of a single property owner, it will not be permitted.

Zoning laws generally are enforced through local requirements that building permits be obtained before property owners can build on their land. A permit will not be issued unless a proposed structure conforms to the permitted zoning, among other regulations. Zoning helps protect private property values because property owners can comfortably invest in a site with reasonable expectation of the type of development that will occur in the adjacent areas.

Conditional use permits. In some instances, a use is only marginally acceptable in a specific zone. For example, a bar may be a general retail use; but when it is on the edge of a retail zone adjacent to a residential area, the externalities associated with a bar impose additional burdens that most retail uses do not. Therefore, a **conditional use permit** (sometimes referred to as a *special use permit* or *specific use permit*) might be issued with "conditions" such as a screening fence between the bar and the adjacent neighborhood, increased setback from the adjacent property, decibel limitations, and daily trash removal. A conditional use permit may be issued to either run with the land or run with the ownership. A conditional use permit is not rezoning and it is not a legislative action.

Conditional use permits allow a special use with certain stipulations.

Nonconforming use. After a rezoning process, sometimes the use of an existing building or the building itself no longer conforms to the new zoning classification; such use or property is referred to as a **nonconforming use** (sometimes referred to as being *"grandfathered" in*). Nonconforming status generally will result either from annexation (bringing land into city limits) or amending current regulations. In some instances, the nonconforming uses or properties may even predate the adoption of zoning ordinances for a particular district. Communities have different ways of dealing with these special cases. For example, the use may be allowed to continue until (1) the current use is discontinued, (2) the improvements are destroyed or torn down, or (3) the ownership of the property is transferred. In other cases nonconforming uses will be amortized over a specified period, allowing for a return on the owner's investment but setting a definite sunset period on out-of-place uses (common with sexually oriented businesses). Subsequent property use would be required to be in conformance with the current zoning ordinance.

> A *non-conforming use* is a use that predates the zoning ordinance or its amendments.

Zoning Boards of Adjustment (ZBA). **Zoning boards of adjustment** have been established in most communities to hear complaints about the effects of zoning ordinances on specific parcels of property. It is important to the community that members of the board be free of personal or political influence. Petitions may be presented to the ZBA for variances, or exceptions, to the zoning law. If the property owner is not satisfied with the decision of the ZBA, the decision may be appealed to a court of record.

> In contrast to most municipality issues, zoning variances are not heard by the city council.

A **variance** may be sought by a property owner when strict enforcement of a zoning ordinance would cause an undue hardship to the property owner because of special circumstances and through no fault of the owner. For example, if an owner's lot is level next to the road but slopes steeply 30 feet away from the road, the ZBA may be willing to allow a variance so the owner can build closer to the road than normally would be allowed. However, the board might refuse to allow a change if there were another possible building site on the same parcel and the only hardship that would result from using the alternate site was a longer driveway that would cost more money. Variances are not used to help owners cut development costs.

> *Variances* permit relief from certain zoning ordinance regulations to avoid undue hardship to the property owner.

In Practice   Purchasers of property must be aware of zoning requirements. Licensees should determine whether a buyer's proposed use for the property conforms to existing zoning ordinances. If either the seller or a licensee misrepresents the actual permitted zoning use, the buyer may be able to rescind the transaction on the basis of the misrepresentation.

Subdivision Regulations   The process of land development generally involves three distinct stages. These are (1) the initial planning stage, (2) the final planning stage, and (3) disposition, or start-up.

During the *initial planning stage*, the **developer** seeks out raw land in a suitable area that can be profitably subdivided. After the land is located, the property is analyzed for highest and best use, and a preliminary subdivision plat is drawn up by a licensed surveyor, as discussed in Chapter 10. The preliminary subdivision plat is then submitted to the city planning staff,

A *developer* buys undeveloped acreage; subdivides it; puts in utilities, curbs, and gutters; paves the streets; and then either builds and sells homes on the land or sells the lots.

and close contact is initiated between the developer and local planning and zoning officials. If the project requires an amendment to the zoning map or a zoning variance, negotiations begin along these lines. Surrounding property owners may need to be notified, and public hearings may be required. The developer also locates financial backers and initiates marketing strategies at this point in the process.

The city planning staff evaluate the preliminary subdivision plat to see that it is consistent with the city's comprehensive plan. **Subdivision regulations** are among the tools for implementing the comprehensive plan. They generally provide for

- location, grading, alignment, surfacing, and widths of streets, highways, and other rights-of-way;
- installation of sewers and water mains;
- dimensions of lots and length of blocks;
- areas to be reserved or dedicated for public use, such as parks or schools; and
- easements for public utilities.

FOR EXAMPLE: A subdivision with zero-lot-line homes illustrates the application of a regulation to a subdivision plat. One side of the home is built on the lot line; the other side has a 10-foot or more side setback. The plat notes which side has the zero lot line.

In the *final planning stage,* the final engineering plans and the final subdivision plat are prepared, and approval is sought from the appropriate local officials, usually the Planning and Zoning Commission and/or the City Council. Once the plat is approved, it is recorded in the county clerk's office, and the city issues a certificate to the developer. Permanent financing is obtained and the land is purchased. Also, final budgets are prepared and marketing programs are designed.

A property developer must receive credit toward capital improvement expenses (streets, curbs, gutters, sewers, etc.) for a portion of the ad valorem tax and utility service revenues that will be generated by the development (S.B. 243, 2001).

The *disposition* or *start-up stage* carries the development process to a conclusion. Streets, curbs, gutters, sanitary and storm sewers, and utilities are installed. Open parks and recreational areas are constructed and landscaped if they are part of the subdivision plan. Marketing programs are initiated, and title to the individual parcels of subdivided land is transferred as the lots are sold for home construction.

Extraterritorial jurisdiction. Many states, including Texas, have enacted legislation that provides that the subdivision of land located within one to five miles of an incorporated area (depending on the population size of the municipality) must be approved by the incorporated area, even if the property is not contiguous to the village, town, or city. This is known as **extraterritorial jurisdiction** (ETJ). During the 1999 Texas legislative session, municipal annexation procedures were revised extensively. A purchaser of property outside the city limits must be notified prior to executing a sales contract that the property might in the future be annexed by the city (S.B. 167, 1999). The purchaser is charged with contacting all municipalities in the general proximity of the property to determine if the property is located within, or is likely to be added to, a city's extraterritorial jurisdiction (see Chapter 13). The disclosures are given to put purchasers on notice that municipalities have no rights to control land use in the extraterritorial jurisdiction; however, if their land is annexed into the city, the city would have that right. Unless an annexation is voluntary or within one of the statute's exceptions, a municipality is required to give a minimum of three years' notice prior to an annexation, and any land acquired must be contiguous to the city's existing boundaries.

Building Codes

Most cities and towns have enacted ordinances to *specify construction standards* that must be met when repairing or erecting buildings. These are called **building codes,** and they set the requirements for kinds of materials, sanitary equipment, electrical wiring, fire prevention standards, and the like.

Most communities require the issuance of a **building permit** by the city building official or other official before a person can build a structure or alter or repair an existing building on property within the corporate limits of the municipality. Through the permit process, city officials are made aware of new construction or alterations and can verify compliance with building codes and zoning ordinances by examining the plans and inspecting the work. If the construction of a building or an alteration violates a deed restriction (discussed later in this chapter), the issuance of a building permit will *not* cure this violation. A building permit is merely evidence of the applicant's compliance with municipal regulations.

Under the provisions of House Bill 1704 (1999), commonly referred to as the "vested rights" or "freeze bill," builders and developers who have filed a development permit with a city need meet only those ordinances applicable at the time the application was filed. This legislation prevents governmental entities from imposing retroactive requirements once the permit application process has begun. After the completed structure has been inspected and found satisfactory, the city inspector issues a *certificate of occupancy.*

If a municipality can provide evidence that new residential construction in a particular area will result in a shortage of public facilities or prove detrimental to public health, safety, and welfare, a 120-day moratorium on the issuance of building permits may be adopted (S.B. 980, 2001).

The subject of city planning, zoning and restrictions on the use of real estate is extremely technical, and interpretation of the law is not altogether clear. Questions concerning any of these subjects in relation to real estate transactions should be referred to competent legal counsel.

Environmental Protection Legislation

Federal and state legislators have passed a number of environmental protection laws in an attempt to respond to the growing public concern over the improvement and preservation of America's natural resources. Table 23.2 contains a brief summary of significant federal environmental legislation; Table 23.3, of Texas environmental legislation. In addition to the states and the federal government, cities and counties may also pass environmental regulations or ordinances of their own. Understanding environmental issues that affect an agent's market area is essential. Environmental concerns abound—and solutions are forthcoming:

- Four Texas regions are in "nonattainment for ozone," a failure to meet the standards of the federal Clean Air Act—Houston-Galveston-Brazoria, Beaumont-Port Arthur, El Paso, and Dallas-Fort Worth. The areas

Table 23.2	**Federal Environmental Legislation**
Date	**Legislation**
1969	Presidential Order creates Federal Environmental Protection Agency (EPA).
1971	EPA adopts Federal Ambient Air Quality Standards.
1972	Congress adopts the Federal Clean Water Act.
1973	Congress passes the Endangered Species Act.
1974	Congress adopts the Federal Safe Drinking Water Act.
1976	Congress adopts the Resource Conservation and Recovery Act (RCRA), controlling the treatment, storage, and disposal of hazardous and solid waste.
1977	Congress adopts the Federal Clean Air Act.
1980	Congress enacts the Comprehensive Environmental Response, Compensation, and Liability Act (CERCLA), popularly known as the Superfund Law. Law authorizes cleanups of hazardous waste sites.
1984	Hazardous and Solid Waste Amendments (HSWA) pass, creating major amendments to RCRA.
1986	Congress adopts the Superfund Amendments and Reauthorization Act (SARA), reauthorizes CERCLA, and creates the Toxic Release Inventory (TRI).
1986	Congress amends the Federal Safe Drinking Water Act.
1990	Federal Clean Air Act Amendments increase the responsibilities of the Texas Air Control Board.

must make substantive air quality improvements by 2007 or face the loss of federal highway funds.

The Private Real Property Preservation Act (1995) requires the state government to reimburse land owners when their property values are reduced by 25 percent or more because of a statutory regulation.

- 238 water segments (46 percent of the water bodies in Texas) in five water basin groups have been identified as "impaired" (too polluted to support their designated use) under the Clean Water Act. To avoid environmental lawsuits, the Texas Natural Resource Conservation Commission (TNRCC) has a plan for cleaning up Texas' waters by 2010.
- Almost 250 Texas community water systems were on the TNRCC's "drought watch list" for summer 2000, meaning they were at some stage of water rationing to conserve supply and prevent customer overuse. Drought-readiness programs have been developed and legislation was enacted in both 1999 and 2001 to develop and implement plans for long-range water management.
- 450,000 brownfields sites exist nationwide, ranging in size from less than one acre to several thousand acres. *Brownfields* are land that has been used previously for industrial and/or manufacturing activities that may have residual contamination. Recent legislation is encouraging brownfields cleanup by removing barriers to redevelopment and alleviating liability concerns among developers.
- Texas has 7 million acres of wetlands protected by the federal Clean Water Act. Wetlands are areas saturated by water, including swamps, marshes, bogs, and similar areas, that often provide a critical habitat for plants, fish, insects, birds, and mammals.
- Texas has 63 animals and 28 plants on the endangered species list—animals ranging from the Mexican Spotted Owl and the Houston Toad to the San Marcos Texas Blind Salamander and the Woodpecker. Endangered plants include the Terlingua Creek Cat's Eye and Texas Snowbells.

Table 23.3 **Texas Environmental Legislation**

Date	Legislation
1913	The legislature creates the State Board of Water Engineers to establish procedures for defnining and administering the rights of surface water users.
1953	The legislature creates the Texas Water Pollution Advisory Council, the first state body charged with dealing with pollution-related issues.
1956	Texas' first air quality initiative is established; the State Department of Health, Division of Occupational Health and Radiation Control begins air sampling in the state.
1957	The legislature creates the Texas Water Development Board to forecast state water supply needs and to provide funding for water supply and water conservation projects.
1961	The legislature creates the Texas Water Pollution Board and eliminates the Water Pollution Advisory Council, creating the state's first true pollution control agency.
1962	Texas Board of Water Engineers is renamed the Texas Water Commission, with responsibility for surface water rights, water conservation, and pollution control.
1965	The legislature reorganizes the Texas Water Commission as the Texas Water Rights Commission, and transfers non-water rights functions to the Texas Water Development Board.
1965	The Texas Clean Air Act establishes the Texas Air Control Board.
1967	The legislature creates the Texas Water Quality Board, assuming all the functions of the Texas Water Pollution Board.
1969	The legislature adopts the Texas Solid Waste Disposal Act.
1971	The legislature creates a preconstruction permit review system.
1977	The legislature creates the Texas Department of Water Resources by combining the Water Rights Commission, Water Quality Board, and Water Development Board.
1985	The legislature transfers most regulatory and water rights duties to the re-created Texas Water Commission and most planning and finance responsibilities to the re-created Texas Department of Water Resources.
1992	The legislature transfers the Water Hygiene Division, Solid Waste Bureau, and Radioactive Waste Disposal Bureau from the Texas Department of Health to the Texas Water Commission.
1992	The Texas Water Commission and Texas Air Control Board are consolidated by S.B. 2 to create the Texas Natural Resource Conservation Commission, a comprehensive environmental protection agency with responsibilities for air, water, and land resource protection.
1997	TNRCC concludes a Performance Partnership Agreement with U.S. Environmental Protection Agency to allocate resources most appropriately throughout Texas on a regional basis.
1997	The legislature adopts S.B. 1, mandating water conservation planning for large water users and requiring development of drought contingency plans by public water suppliers.
1997	The legislature returns uranium mining, processing, and by-product disposal oversight functions to Texas Department of Health.
1999	The legislature transfers the functions of the Texas Low-Level Radioactive Waste Disposal Authority to the TNRCC.
2001	The legislature establishes the Texas Emissions Reduction Plan to bring many Texas cities into EPA compliance by 2007.
2001	The legislature adopts S.B. 2 to implement water strategies and recommendations developed as a result of S.B. 1.

- Texas has 87 active Superfund sites, areas requiring cleanup because contamination is a threat to human health or the environment. New cleanup standards were put in place in 1999 with the Texas Risk Reduction Program which establishes consistent corrective action requirements for all sites in Texas.

Increased public awareness of and concern about pollution problems and their effects on health and economics have had significant consequences on real estate sales and values. From an economic perspective, the actual dollar value of real property can be affected by both real and perceived pollution; the desirability and salability of land and buildings may change drastically. Also, the cost of cleaning up and removing pollution may be much greater than the dollar value of the property prior to pollution.

Disclosure and discovery of environmental hazards. In Texas, a property owner must disclose the presence of specific environmental hazards as well as "any condition on the Property which materially affects the physical health or safety of an individual." As discussed in Chapter 13, the *Seller's Disclosure of Property Condition* is the appropriate form for most disclosures. If the property was constructed prior to 1978, a purchaser must also be given a *Lead-Based Paint* disclosure form. For unimproved property, the disclosure for *Conditions under the Surface* might be required. It is the agent's duty to know which disclosures must be given in each transaction and to ensure that the seller has given them to the purchaser prior to the execution of a contract.

If there is any question about the environmental condition of the property, an environmental assessment addendum promulgated by TREC in 1993 creates a contract contingency allowing a buyer to get an environmental inspection in a residential transaction. The addendum permits a buyer to terminate a contract if environmental research or reports indicate conditions that adversely affect the use of the property. Real estate licensees are not expected to have the technical expertise necessary to discover the presence of environmental hazards. However, because they are presumed by the public to have special knowledge about real estate, licensees must be aware both of possible hazards and of sources for professional help. Some of the pollution and environmental risks in real estate transactions are listed in Table 23.4.

The first step for a licensee is to ask the owner about environmental hazards. The owner may be aware of a potential hazardous condition. Or he or she may already have conducted tests for carbon monoxide, radon or other hazards. If the owner has already done the detection and abatement work, an environmental hazard can actually be turned into a marketing plus. Potential buyers can be assured that an older home is no longer a lead paint or an asbestos risk.

The most appropriate people on whom a licensee can rely for sound environmental information are scientific or technical experts. *Environmental auditors* can provide the most comprehensive studies. Their services are usually relied on by developers and purchasers of commercial and industrial properties. An environmental audit includes the property's history of use and the results of extensive and complex tests of the soil, water, air, and structures. Trained inspectors conduct air-sampling tests to detect radon, asbestos, or electromagnetic fields. They can test soil and water quality and can inspect

Table 23.4 *Environmental Risks*

Environmental Risk	Description/Effect(s)
Asbestos	A mineral that has been used for many years as insulation; it has also been used in floor tile and in roofing material. Although it remains relatively harmless if not disturbed, it can become life-threatening when removed because of the accompanying dust—usually created through remodeling efforts or disintegration of materials.
Carbon monoxide	Colorless, odorless gas that occurs as a by-product due to incomplete combustion when burning such fuels as wood, oil, and natural gas.
Electromagnetic fields (EmFs)	Generated by the movement of electrical current through any electrical appliance. The major concern involves high-tension power lines. EmFs are suspected of causing cancer, hormonal changes, and behavioral abnormalities—although to date there is no proof.
Groundwater contamination	Not only the runoff at ground level but also the underground water systems that are sources for public and private wells. Contamination occurs from a number of sources, including waste disposal sites, underground storage tanks, pesticides, and herbicides.
Lead	A mineral that has been used in paint to protect wood from damage by water; it also has been used in the installation of water pipes. Lead becomes a health hazard when ingested (usually by peeling or flaking paint put into the mouths of small children or contamination through the water supply.) Disclosure notice required on properties built before 1978.
Mold	Molds make up 25 percent of the earth's biomass and are found in all nonsterile environments. Mold growth is generally associated with flooding or a building defect that has allowed water penetration. To date, no federal or state regulations establish exposure levels for molds as they affect air quality.
Polychlorinated biphenyl	A carcinogenic substance found in about 70 percent of utility company transformers and capacitors. Prior to the late 1970s, these PCB-contaminated transformers were buried; once in the ground the PCB will leach into underground water supplies.
Radon gas	An odorless, radioactive gas produced by the decay of other radioactive materials in rocks under the surface of the earth that generally enters a house through cracks in the foundation or through the floor drains. Long-term exposure to radon gas is said to cause lung cancer.
Underground storage tanks	Used in both residential and commercial settings. More than 3 million underground storage tanks in the United States contain hazardous substances such as gasoline or home heating oil. When the containers become old and rust and start to leak, the material can enter the groundwater and contaminate wells and pollute the soil.
Urea formaldehyde foam insulation (UFFI)	A man-made insulation material that becomes dangerous because of the gases released from the material after it hardens.
Waste disposal sites	Waste disposal sites for landfill operations or radioactive material disposal that can affect property values in surrounding areas. Landfills constructed on the wrong type of soil will leak waste into nearby wells. Emissions from radioactive waste can sometimes cause cancer or death.

for lead-based paints. (Lead inspections required by the *Residential Lead-Based Paint Hazard Reduction Act* must be conducted by certified inspectors.) While environmental auditors may be called on at any stage in a transaction, they are most frequently brought in as a condition of closing. Not only can such experts detect environmental problems, they can usually offer guidance about how best to resolve the conditions.

The landowner.　When the *Comprehensive Environmental Response, Compensation, and Liability Act* (CERCLA) was passed in 1980, it established a $9 billion *Superfund* to clean up uncontrolled hazardous waste sites and to respond to spills. It created a process for identifying potential responsible parties and ordering them to take responsibility for the cleanup action. Under CERCLA, a landowner is liable for cleanup when contamination exists—regardless of whether the contamination is the result of the landowner's actions or those of others. This liability includes the cleanup not only of the landowner's property but also of any neighboring property that has been contaminated. A landowner who is not responsible for the contamination can seek reimbursement for the cleanup cost from previous landowners, any other responsible party, or the Superfund. However, if other parties are not available, even a landowner who did not cause the problem could be solely responsible for the costs.

The *Superfund Amendments and Reauthorization Act* passed in 1985 created an *innocent landowner immunity*, stipulating that a landowner in the chain of ownership who was completely innocent of all wrongdoing should not be held liable. However, an innocent landowner seeking to be exempted from liability must have no actual or constructive knowledge of the damage. In addition, the landowner must have exercised due care when the property was purchased, making a reasonable search (an environmental Phase I site assessment) to determine that no damage to the property existed.

The real estate professionals.　Sellers and purchasers carry the most exposure to environmental liability, but real estate professionals may also be held liable under certain circumstances. Real estate licensees could be held liable for improper disclosure. Therefore, it is essential that licensees be aware of potential environmental risks from neighboring properties such as gas stations, manufacturing plants, or even funeral homes. Also the agent must ensure that the seller makes the required property disclosures to the purchaser.

> Banker's environmental risk insurance insures lenders when a loan goes into default and there is contamination on the property. It covers either the cost of cleaning up the property or paying off the loan balance.

Additional exposure is created for individuals involved in other aspects of real estate transactions. Lenders may end up owning worthless assets if owners default on the loans rather than undertaking expensive cleanup efforts. Real estate appraisers must identify and adjust for environmental problems. Adjustments to market value typically reflect the cleanup cost plus a factor of the degree of panic and suspicion that exist in the current market. The real estate appraiser's greatest responsibility is to the lender, who depends on the appraiser to identify environmental hazards. Although the lender may be protected under certain conditions through the 1986 amendments to the Superfund Act, the lender must be aware of potential problems and may require additional environmental reports. Insurance carriers also might be affected in the transactions. Mortgage insurance companies protect lenders' mortgage investments and might be required to carry part of the ultimate responsibility in cases of loss. More important, hazard insurance carriers might be directly responsible for damages if such coverage was included in the initial policy. An early and careful analysis of the potential environmental risks for each transaction will more likely ensure a positive result for all parties.

PRIVATE LAND-USE CONTROLS

A real estate owner can create a **deed restriction** (or restrictive covenant) by including a provision for it in the deed when the property is conveyed. It is usually placed on the property by a property developer.

Deed Restrictions

There is a distinction between restrictions on the owner's right to *sell* and restrictions on his or her right to *use*. In general, a deed conveying a fee simple estate may not restrict the owner's right to sell, mortgage, or convey it. Such restrictions attempt to limit the basic principle of the *free alienation (transfer) of property;* the courts usually consider them against public policy and therefore unenforceable. Deed restrictions in violation of fair housing laws, such as restricting the sale of property to a particular color or race, are void.

A developer may establish restrictions on the right to *use* land through a **covenant** in a deed or by a separate recorded declaration. When a lot in a subdivision is conveyed by an owner's deed, the deed refers to the plat or declaration of restrictions and incorporates these restrictions as limitations on the title conveyed by the deed. In this manner, the restrictive covenants are included in the deed by reference and become binding on all grantees. Such covenants or restrictions usually relate to (1) type of building; (2) use to which the land may be put; (3) type of construction, height, setbacks, and square footage; and (4) cost. For example, the restrictions in one subdevelopment might specify that the home be at least 80 percent brick with at least 2,000 square feet and that no boat or recreational vehicle may be kept on the street, driveway, or lot.

Most restrictions have a *time limitation;* for example, "effective for a period of 25 years from this date." After that time, the restrictions become inoperative unless they are extended by majority agreement of the people who then own the property. Frequently it also is provided that the effective term of the restrictions may be extended with the consent of a majority (or sometimes two-thirds) of the owners in a subdivision. In Texas, a lot owner has the right to opt out of the renewal or extension.

Deed restrictions usually are considered valid if they are reasonable restraints and are for the benefit of all property owners in the subdivision. If, however, such restrictions are too broad in their terms, they prevent the free transfer of property. If they are "repugnant" to the estate granted, such restrictions probably will not be enforceable. Any restrictive covenant or condition that is considered void by a court does not affect the validity of the deed or divest the grantee of his or her estate. The estate then stands free from the invalid covenant or condition.

In Practice

> In Texas, if a municipality uses zoning as a land-use control tool, the municipality cannot enforce deed restrictions. A deed restriction is a private contract between the developer and the property owner and the city does not get involved in this private contract—unless the city has no zoning ordinances.

Enforcement of deed restrictions. Subdividers usually place restrictions on the use of all lots in a subdivision as a *general plan* for the benefit of all lot owners. Such restrictions give each lot owner the right to apply to the court for an *injunction* to prevent a neighboring lot owner from violating the recorded restrictions. If granted, the court injunction directs the violator to stop or remove the violation upon penalty of being deemed in contempt of court. The court retains the power to punish the violator for failure to obey the court order. If adjoining lot owners stand idly by while a violation is being committed, they can *lose the right* to the court's injunction by their inaction; the court might claim their right was lost through **laches,** the loss of a right through undue delay or failure to assert it. Where extensive and continuing violations of deed restrictions are evident, Texas courts may refuse to enforce them because such violations indicate the lot owners have abandoned the original scheme or plan.

> A property owner may apply to a *justice of the peace (JP) court* for an injunction to enforce a deed restriction.

doctrine of laches

Altering deed restrictions. It may be necessary to obtain an alteration of the deed restrictions to use a certain property for a specific purpose. This may or may not be possible, depending on the circumstances. There are two methods of changing deed restrictions: *waiver* and *judicial.* To effect a waiver, a notarized document must be obtained from every property owner, mortgage lender (regardless of lien classification), and the original subdivider or his or her estate. Clearly this method is quite impractical for a large subdivision. In such a situation, judicial recourse is more practical. This involves filing a lawsuit to obtain a favorable ruling that declares the offending deed restriction to be void.

Conditions. *Conditions* in a deed are different from restrictions or covenants. A grantor's deed of conveyance can be subject to certain stated conditions whereby the buyer's title may *revert* (go back) to the seller. (This was discussed in Chapter 8 as a defeasible fee estate.)

FOR EXAMPLE Bill Potter conveys a lot to Jane Knish by a deed that includes a condition forbidding the sale, manufacture, or giving away of intoxicating liquor on the lot and provides that in case of violation the title (ownership) reverts to Potter. If Knish operates a tavern on the lot, Potter can file suit and obtain title to the property. Such a condition in the title is enforced by a *reverter,* or *reversion,* clause.

PUBLIC OWNERSHIP

Over the years, the government's general policy has been to encourage private ownership of land. However, a certain amount of land must be controlled by **public ownership** for such uses as municipal buildings, state legislative houses, schools, and military stations.

Other examples of necessary public ownership exist. Publicly owned streets and highways serve a necessary function for the entire population. In addition, public land often is used for such recreational purposes as parks. Not only do national and state parks and forest preserves create areas for public use and enjoyment, they help conserve our natural resources.

Texas ranks 44th among the 50 states in percentage of land owned by the public (both the federal and state governments). Within Texas, federal land holdings exceed 7 million acres—about 4 percent of the State of Texas. The State owns 825,000 acres—less than 1 percent of Texas. Although only 4 percent of the land in Texas is owned by the federal government, approximately one-third of the total area of the United States is owned by the federal government.

Floodplains

Flood-prone areas must be considered and dealt with accordingly. Floodplains and the required insurance for federally related loans were discussed in Chapter 4. In addition, certain statutory water authorities—such as the Brazos River Authority, Trinity River Authority, and Tarrant Water District—control the construction of structures to be located within the floodway. This is intended to permit floodwaters to flow through unimpeded by structures. In land planning, low-lying areas must be considered because control over these areas is exercised by others.

Municipal Utility Districts (MUDs)

A **municipal utility district** (MUD) is a defined geographic area created by a developer and located outside a municipality. It has some limited municipal characteristics, however, such as furnishing water and sewer utilities to its inhabitants and levying taxes to pay for the installation of those utilities. Section 50.301, Texas Water Code, requires that sellers of property situated in one of these MUDs sign, acknowledge, and deliver a statutory notice to the buyer, disclosing the bonded indebtedness of the MUD, its tax rate, and any standby fees. This notice must be signed by the buyer prior to final execution of the earnest money contract. The disclosure may be based on figures current on January 1. Information provided by the MUD is deemed conclusive, eliminating potential liability for a real estate licensee if the information provided proves to be inaccurate.

INTERSTATE LAND SALES FULL DISCLOSURE ACT

To protect consumers from "overenthusiastic sales promotions" by developers involved in interstate land sales, Congress passed a federal law, the **Interstate Land Sales Full Disclosure Act.** Basically a consumer protection act, the law requires those engaged in the interstate sale or leasing of 25 or more lots to file a *statement of record* and register the subdivision with HUD.

The seller is also required to furnish prospective buyers, prior to execution of a contract, a **property report** containing all essential information about the property, such as distance over paved roads to nearby communities, number of homes currently occupied, soil conditions affecting foundations and septic systems, type of title a buyer will receive, and existence of liens.

Any contract to purchase a lot covered by this act may be revoked at the purchaser's option before midnight of the seventh day following the signing of the contract. If the seller misrepresents the property in any sales promotion, a buyer induced by such a promotion is entitled to sue the seller for civil damages under federal law. Failure to comply with the law may also subject a seller to criminal penalties of fines and imprisonment. There is a three-year statute of limitations for fraud that does not begin until discovery of the fraud is made.

Summary

The control of land use is exercised in two ways: through public controls and private (or nongovernment) controls. Public controls are ordinances based on the state's police power to protect the public health, safety, and welfare. Through power conferred by state enabling acts, local governments enact comprehensive plans and use tools such as zoning, subdivision regulations, and capital improvement programming to implement the plans.

Zoning ordinances carrying out the provisions of the comprehensive plan segregate residential areas from business and industrial zones and manage not only land use but also height and bulk of buildings and density of populations. Zoning enforcement involves the city planning staff in issuing conditional use permits, working to resolve nonconforming uses. The zoning board of adjustment hears complaints on zoning administration issues and may issue variances for exceptions to the zoning ordinances. Subdivision regulations are required to maintain control of the development of expanding community areas so that growth will be harmonious with community standards.

Building codes control construction of buildings by specifying standards for construction, plumbing, sewers, electrical wiring, and equipment. Building permits allow construction, alteration, or repair of a building.

In addition to land-use control on the local level, the state and federal governments occasionally have intervened when necessary to preserve natural resources through environmental legislation. Concern about environmental risks from asbestos, carbon monoxide, electromagnetic fields, groundwater contamination, lead, mold, polychlorinated biphenyl, radon gas, underground storage tanks, urea formaldehyde foam insulation, and waste disposal sites is a responsibility of all real estate professionals. Sellers, buyers, real estate agents, appraisers, lenders, and insurance companies all have potential liability related to environmental hazards and to their disclosure.

Private controls are exercised by owners, generally developers, who control use of subdivision lots through carefully planned deed restrictions that apply to all lot owners. The usual recorded restrictions may be enforced by adjoining lot owners' obtaining a court injunction to stop a violator. Conditions are imposed by grantors, and violations may allow the grantors or their heirs a reversionary interest in the property.

Public ownership of land provides for such public benefits as parks, highways, schools, and municipal buildings.

Municipal utility districts or other districts for drainage or flood control must be disclosed to prospective purchasers of property that is situated

Municipal utility districts or other districts for drainage or flood control must be disclosed to prospective purchasers of property that is situated within these districts. Sellers and real estate licensees are liable for failure to make the required disclosures on the proper forms.

Questions

1. A covenant in a deed that limits the use of property is known as a
   a. zoning ordinance.
   b. deed restriction.
   c. laches.
   d. conditional-use clause.

2. If a landowner wants to use his or her property in a manner that is prohibited by a local zoning ordinance but the use would be acceptable if certain stipulations are met, this describes
   a. a variance.
   b. downzoning.
   c. a conditional use permit.
   d. an occupancy permit.

3. Public land-use controls include all of the following **EXCEPT**
   a. subdivision regulations.
   b. deed restrictions.
   c. environmental protection laws.
   d. zoning ordinances.

4. The purpose of a building permit is to
   a. override a deed restriction.
   b. maintain municipal control over the volume of building.
   c. provide evidence of compliance with municipal regulations.
   d. show compliance with restrictive covenants.

5. All of the following would properly be included in a list of deed restrictions **EXCEPT**
   a. types of buildings that may be constructed.
   b. activities that are not to be conducted at the site.
   c. allowable ethnic origins of purchasers.
   d. minimum size of buildings to be constructed.

6. Zoning powers are conferred on municipal governments
   a. by state enabling acts.
   b. through the comprehensive plan.
   c. by eminent domain.
   d. through escheat.

7. Zoning ordinances control the use of privately owned land by establishing land-use districts. Which one of the following is **NOT** a usual zoning district?
   a. Residential   c. Industrial
   b. Commercial   d. Rental

8. Zoning laws are generally enforced by
   a. zoning boards of adjustment.
   b. ordinances stipulating that building permits will not be issued unless the proposed structure conforms to the zoning ordinance.
   c. deed restrictions.
   d. federal legislation.

9. Zoning boards of adjustment are established to hear complaints about the effects of
   a. restrictive covenants.
   b. a zoning ordinance.
   c. building codes.
   d. laches.

10. Police power allows regulation of all of the following **EXCEPT**
    a. the number of buildings.
    b. the size of buildings.
    c. building ownership.
    d. building use.

11. A building that is permitted to continue in its former use even though that use does not conform to a newly enacted zoning ordinance is an example of
    a. a nonconforming use.
    b. a variance.
    c. a special use.
    d. inverse condemnation.

12. A restriction in a seller's deed may be enforced by which of the following?
    a. Court injunction
    b. Zoning board of adjustment
    c. City council
    d. State legislature

13. A subdivision declaration reads, "No property within this subdivision may be further subdivided for sale or otherwise, and no property may be used for other than single-family housing." This is an example of
    a. a restrictive covenant.
    b. an illegal reverter clause.
    c. R-1 zoning.
    d. a conditional use clause.

14. Gayle owns a large tract of land. After an adequate study of all the relevant facts, he legally divides the land into 30 lots suitable for the construction of residences; puts in utilities, curbs, and gutters; and paves the streets. Gayle is a(n)
    a. builder.   c. land planner.
    b. developer.   d. urban planner.

15. To protect the public from fraudulent interstate land sales, a developer involved in interstate land sales of 25 or more lots must
    a. provide each prospective purchaser with a printed report disclosing details of the property.
    b. pay the prospective buyer's expenses to see the property involved.
    c. provide preferential financing.
    d. allow a 30-day cancellation period.

16. Asbestos is most dangerous when it
    a. is used as insulation.
    b. crumbles and becomes airborne.
    c. gets wet.
    d. is wrapped around heating and water pipes.

17. Jason is a real estate salesperson. He shows a pre-World War II house on city water and sewer to Terri, a prospective buyer. Terri has two toddlers and is worried about potential health hazards. Which of the following is **TRUE?**
    a. There is a risk that urea-foam insulation was used in the original construction.
    b. Because the house is approximately 60 years old, Terri should have the water tested for polychlorinated biphenyl.
    c. Because the house was built before 1978, there is a good likelihood of the presence of lead-based paint.
    d. There is very little risk of asbestos insulation in the home.

18. All of the following are true of electromagnetic fields **EXCEPT** that EmFs are
    a. a suspected but unproven cause of cancer, hormonal abnormalities, and behavioral disorders.
    b. generated by all electrical appliances.
    c. present only near high-tension wires or large electrical transformers.
    d. caused by the movement of electricity.

24 Real Estate Investment

OVERVIEW

The market for real estate investment can be one of the most active in the country. Besides generating income and building up equity, real estate investment can aid in sheltering an owner's income against increasing taxes and the effects of inflation and deflation.

This chapter presents a basic introduction to real estate investment. Major emphasis is placed on investment opportunities open to small or beginning investors as well as the various tax shelters available to all real estate investors.

Note: The examples and computations given in this chapter are for *illustrative purposes only,* to explain a particular feature or concept of investment, *not to teach the reader how, when, or what amount of money to invest.*Competent legal and tax counsel must be obtained by the investor who desires maximum protection in a very complicated market. Because of this complexity, the practice of brokering investment real estate, although quite alluring, must be restricted to those brokers who are knowledgeable in this specialized field.

INVESTING IN REAL ESTATE

Often customers ask a real estate broker or salesperson to act as an investment counselor; too often, the licensee is placed in that role by eager, inexperienced investors with high hopes for quick profits. Although it may be the responsibility of real estate licensees to analyze and discuss with a potential investor his or her financial status, future goals, and investment motivations, brokers or salespersons should always *refer a potential real estate investor to a competent tax accountant, attorney, or investment specialist* who can give expert, specific advice.

Real estate practitioners should learn the essentials of real estate investment so they can counsel customers on a basic level. Any such discussion should begin with an examination of the traditional advantages and disadvantages of investing in real estate as opposed to other commodities.

Considerations for Prospective Real Estate Investors

In recent years, real estate values have fluctuated widely in various regions of the country. As a result, the ability of investments to produce a return greater than the inflation rate (to serve as an "inflation hedge") has been impaired. This lack of potential profitability has made some real estate investments very unattractive to potential investors.

Still, real estate investments have shown an above-average *rate of return,* generally higher than the prevailing interest rate charged by mortgage lenders. Theoretically, this means that an investor can use borrowed money to finance a real estate purchase and feel relatively sure that, if held long enough, the asset will yield more money than it costs to finance the purchase.

In addition, real estate entrepreneurs enjoy many **tax shelters** that are unavailable to investors in other moneymaking activities. These shelters may allow an investor to reduce or defer payment of large portions of his or her federal and state income taxes; however, the Tax Reform Act of 1986 decreased the attractiveness of many former tax shelters. The result is that investments now must be analyzed on their *investment* merit rather than as tax shelters for making a good investment out of a poor one. Some of the basic investment tax benefits will be discussed later in this chapter.

Finally, a distinct advantage of real estate investment is that an investor can use borrowed money to finance his or her assets, which significantly increases the investor's buying power. (This concept of *leverage* will be discussed later.) In addition to the advantage of using borrowed money, the portion of an investor's mortgage payments applied to the principal represents *equity buildup* and increases the value of the investor's ownership interest in the asset with each remittance. Careless use of leverage, however, can be disastrous in a declining market.

Unlike stocks and bonds, *real estate is not highly liquid* over a short period of time. An investor usually cannot sell real estate quickly without taking some loss. In contrast, an investor in listed stocks need only call a stockbroker to liquidate a portion of the assets when funds are needed quickly. Even if a real estate investor can raise a limited amount of cash by refinancing the property, it may have to be sold at a substantially lower price than its market value to facilitate a quick sale.

Investment decisions must be based on a careful study of all the facts, reinforced by a broad and thorough knowledge of real estate and how it is affected by the marketplace. As mentioned earlier, *all investors should seek legal and tax counsel before making any real estate investments or investment decisions.*

Rarely can a real estate investor sit idly by and watch his or her money grow; *management decisions must be made.* For example: Can the investor effectively manage the property personally, or is it preferable to hire a professional property manager? How much rent should be charged? How should repairs and tenant grievances be handled? Physical and mental energy usually must be invested to make the asset potentially profitable.

Finally, and most important, *a moderately high degree of risk* often is involved in real estate investment. An investor's property may decrease in value or may not generate an income sufficient to make it profitable. The investment may have *negative cash flow* if the income is insufficient to service the debt and pay the operating expenses.

THE INVESTMENT

The most important form of real estate investment is *direct ownership.* Individuals, partnerships, and corporations may own real estate directly and manage it for appreciation, cash flow (income) and tax shelter purposes.

Appreciation   Property held for **appreciation** generally is expected to increase in value and show a profit when sold at some future date. Income property is just that—property held for current income and an anticipated profit on its sale. Two main factors affect appreciation: inflation and intrinsic value.

Inflation. Historically, inflation has been a dominant factor in the growth of our economy. **Inflation** is defined as the *increase in the amount of money in circulation, which results in a decline in its value coupled with a rise in wholesale and retail prices.*

Intrinsic value. *The result of individual choice and preference for a given geographic area, based on features and amenities,* is what defines **intrinsic value.** For example, property located in a well-kept suburb near a shopping center has a greater intrinsic value to most people than similar property located near a sewage treatment plant. As a rule, the greater the intrinsic value, the more money a property can command upon its sale.

Agricultural and undeveloped land. Quite often, an investor speculates in purchases of either agricultural (farm) land or undeveloped (raw) land located in what he or she expects will be a major path of growth. In these cases, however, the property's intrinsic value and potential for appreciation are not easy to determine; therefore, this type of investment carries with it many inherent risks. The investor must consider these questions: How fast will the area develop? Will it grow sufficiently to make a good profit? Will the expected growth even occur? More important, will the profits eventually realized from the property be enough to offset the costs of holding the land?

Because technically land cannot wear out, the Internal Revenue Service does not allow the tax shelter of depreciation (cost recovery). Also, such land may not be liquid at certain times under certain circumstances; few people are willing to purchase raw or agricultural land on short notice. Despite all the risks, land is traditionally a good inflation hedge if held for the long term. It can also generate income to offset some of the holding costs. For example, agricultural land can be leased to tenant farmers for crops, timber production, or grazing. In certain areas of Texas, substantial income can be derived from leasing for recreational uses such as hunting or fishing.

The value of land purchased for appreciation must appreciate at a rate great enough to compensate the owner for the cost of holding it. For example, imagine that an investor purchased raw land for $2,000 per acre with annual real estate taxes of $80 per acre and miscellaneous expenses of approximately 10 percent per year. For the investor just to break even, the land must appreciate by an average of $280 per acre each year the investor holds the property—an appreciation rate of *14 percent per year* (10% × $2,000 = $200 + $80 = $280 ÷ $2,000 = 14%).

Most land speculation is based on the principle of present versus future intrinsic value. What was farmland a few years ago could very well be a booming community today. The wise investor knows how to identify, buy, and sell such speculative properties.

Income Generally speaking, rental income property is the wisest initial investment for someone who wishes to buy and personally manage real estate. An owner-occupied one-family to four-family building is an example.

Cash flow. The object of an investor's directing funds into income property is to generate spendable income, usually called *cash flow*. The **cash flow** is the total amount of money remaining after all expenditures have been paid, including taxes, operating costs, and mortgage payments. The cash flow produced by any given parcel of real estate is determined by at least three factors: (1) amount of rent received, (2) operating expenses, and (3) method of debt repayment.

Generally, the amount of *rent* (income) that a property can command depends on a number of factors, including location, physical appearance, and amenities. If the cash flow from rents is not enough to cover all expenses, *a negative cash flow* will result.

To keep cash flow high, an investor should *keep operating expenses reasonably low*. Operating expenses include general maintenance of the building, repairs, utilities, taxes, and tenant services (such as security systems). Like inadequate rental income, poor or overly expensive management can result in negative cash flow.

An investor often stands to make more money by investing borrowed money, usually obtained through a mortgage loan or deed of trust loan. *Low mortgage payments* spread over a long period of time result in a higher cash flow because they allow the investor to retain more income each month; conversely, higher mortgage payments contribute to a lower cash flow.

Cash-flow management. Cash flow may be manipulated as a means of either enhancing the attractiveness of a particular investment to command a higher selling price or producing higher or lower income levels to take advantage of high-income and low-income years for tax purposes. Cash flow may be controlled through the use of various management techniques, such as obtaining high temporary rents through short-term leases or postponing minor repairs to generate a higher cash flow for any given period of time.

Investment opportunities. Traditional income-producing property includes apartment buildings, hotels, motels, commercial properties, shopping centers, office buildings, and industrial properties. However, in recent years many communities have seen severe overbuilding of office space and shopping centers, with resulting high vacancy rates. Investors have historically found well-located one-family to four-family dwellings to be favorable investments. Investors must be realistic and objective to succeed.

LEVERAGE

Leverage is the use of *borrowed money to finance the bulk of an investment.* As a rule, an investor can receive a maximum return from his or her initial investment (the down payment) by making a small down payment, paying low interest rates, and spreading mortgage payments over as long a period as possible.

The effect of leveraging is to provide, on sale of the asset, a return that reflects the effect of market forces on the entire amount of the original purchase price but is measured against only the actual cash invested. For example, assume an investor purchases a single-family property with a selling price of $100,000 with $20,000 down, then sells that property five years later for $125,000; the return over five years is $25,000. Disregarding ownership expenses, the return is not 25 percent ($25,000 compared with $100,000), but 125 percent of the original amount invested ($25,000 compared with $20,000).

Risks generally are directly proportional to leverage. A high degree of leverage presents the investor and lender with a high degree of risk; lower leverage results in a lower risk. When values drop in an area or vacancy rates rise, the highly leveraged investor may be unable to pay even the financing costs of the property.

Equity buildup. Equity buildup is that portion of the payment directed toward the principal rather than the interest, *plus* any gain in property value due to appreciation. In a sense, equity buildup is like money in the bank to the investor. Although this accumulated equity is not as liquid as money in the bank, it may be sold, exchanged, or even refinanced to be used as leverage for other investments.

In Practice   This equity is not physically available to the investor until the property is sold. If the property decreases in value, equity may never be realized. In addition, that portion of the buildup that is due to appreciation will be subject to capital gains taxes at the time of sale. Any appreciation can be due mainly to inflation, which tends to erode the real profit.

Pyramiding through refinancing. By holding and refinancing using equity and appreciation buildup, rather than selling or exchanging properties already owned, an investor can increase holdings substantially without investing any additional capital. This practice is known as **pyramiding.** By reinvesting and doubling his or her holdings periodically, an investor who started out with a small initial cash down payment could own (heavily mortgaged) properties worth hundreds of thousands—even millions—of dollars. Eventually the income derived from such assets could possibly pay off the various mortgage debts and show a handsome profit.

TAX BENEFITS

One of the main reasons real estate investments are popular and profitable is that federal law allows investors to use losses generated by such investments to shelter certain portions of their incomes from taxation. Although tax laws change and some tax advantages of owning investment real estate are altered periodically by Congress, with professional tax advice the investor can make a wise real estate purchase.

The discussions and examples used in this section are designed to introduce the reader to general tax concepts. A tax attorney or CPA should be consulted for further details on specific regulations.

Capital Gains   The tax law no longer favors long-term investments by reducing taxable gain (profit) on their sale or exchange. *Capital gain* is defined as the difference between the adjusted basis of property and its net selling price. At various times, tax law has excluded a portion of capital gains from income tax, in percentages ranging from zero to 50 percent.

Basis.   A property's cost basis will determine the amount of gain to be taxed. The **basis** of the property is the investor's initial cost for the real estate. To derive the property's **adjusted basis,** the investor adds to the basis the cost of any physical improvements subsequently made to the property and subtracts from the basis the amount of any depreciation claimed as a tax deduction. When the property is sold by the investor, the amount by which the sales price exceeds the property's adjusted basis is the capital gain.

 An investor purchased for $45,000 a single-family dwelling for use as a rental property. The investor is now selling the property for $100,000. Shortly before the sale date, the investor made $3,000 worth of capital improvements to the home. Depreciation of $10,000 on the property improvements has been taken during the term of the investor's ownership. The investor will pay a broker's commission of 7 percent of the sales price and will also pay closing costs of $600. The investor's capital gain is computed as follows:

Selling price:			$100,000
Less:			
7% commission		$ 7,000	
Closing costs	+	600	
		$ 7,600	− 7,600
Net sales price			$ 92,400

Basis:

Original cost	$45,000	
Improvements	+ 3,000	
	$48,000	

Less:

Depreciation	− 10,000	
Adjusted basis:	$38,000	− 38,000
Total capital gain:		$ 54,400

Although currently all capital gains on investment real estate are considered taxable, the Taxpayer Relief Act of 1997 reduced the tax rate to 20 percent (10 percent for individuals in the 15 percent tax bracket) for investments held 12 months or longer. Under certain circumstances for purchases closed after December 31, 2000, a lower rate of 18 percent (8 percent for taxpayers in the 15 percent tax bracket) applies to transactions in which the asset was held more than five years.

Exchanges   By **exchanging** one property for another, a real estate investor can further reduce or defer the tax on the gain. Tax laws generally provide that gains are not taxed when the investor exchanges investment or income-producing properties of like kind. *Note:* The tax is *deferred, not eliminated.* On selling the property, the investor will be required to pay tax on the total capital gain. Or an investor can keep exchanging upward in value, adding to assets for as long as he or she lives without ever personally having to pay any tax on the profits.

To qualify as a tax-deferred exchange, the properties involved must be of *like kind*—for example, investment real estate for investment real estate. Any additional capital or personal property included with the transaction to even out the exchange is considered **boot,** and the party receiving it is taxed at the time of the exchange. The value of the boot is added to the basis of the property with which it is given. To the extent that liabilities are given up in excess of liabilities assumed (referred to as *net debt relief*), the difference, or boot, is taxed at the time of the exchange and the basis is increased by the gain.

 MATH CONCEPTS   Investor Smith owns an apartment building with a market value of $200,000 and an adjusted basis of $90,000. He wants to exchange it for a different apartment building, which has a market value of $250,000 and an adjusted basis of $150,000 and is owned by investor Jones.

	Investor Smith	**Investor Jones**
Market Value	$200,000	$250,000
Debt	0	0
Equity	$200,000	$250,000
To balance equities	$ 50,000	

Investor Smith must pay investor Jones $50,000 (boot) to balance the equities. After the exchange, the basis in investor Smith's new apartment building is $140,000, computed as follows:

Adjusted cost basis of old apartment building	$ 90,000
Boot given in the exchange	50,000
Adjusted cost basis of new apartment building	$140,000

Investor Jones, on the other hand, exchanged a building worth $250,000 with an adjusted cost basis of $150,000 for a building worth only $200,000 plus $50,000 cash. She must pay capital gains tax on the $50,000 boot, but her basis in the new building remains the same as for the building she exchanged ($150,000).

Market value of old apartment building	$250,000
Adjusted cost basis of old apartment building	150,000
Potential gain	$100,000

If investor Jones had received all cash, her capital gain would have been $100,000. Because she received only $50,000 in cash, she will pay capital gains tax only on the $50,000 cash received. The adjusted cost basis of her new apartment building is computed as follows:

Adjusted cost basis of old apartment building	$150,000
Gain recognized	50,000
Cash received	− 50,000
Adjusted cost basis of new apartment building	$150,000

Like-kind exchanges need not be simultaneous to be tax deferred. Under regulations enacted by Congress, a person may elect to have a delayed exchange. Using a delayed exchange, a person can relinquish his or her property and must identify the property to be received in the exchange within 45 days. The person then must take actual title to the property to be received within 180 days of relinquishing the original property. *Delayed exchanges require that exact steps be followed; they should not be entered into without professional assistance.*

Depreciation

Depreciation is an accounting concept that allows an investor to recover the cost of an income-producing asset by way of tax deductions over the period of the asset's useful life as determined by the IRS. Although investors rarely purchase property without the expectation that it will appreciate over time, the view of the IRS is that all physical structures will deteriorate and hence lose value over time. Depreciation may have very little relationship to the actual physical deterioration of the asset. Depreciation deductions may be taken only on personal property and improvements to land and only if they are used in a trade or business or for the production of income. Thus an individual cannot claim a depreciation deduction on his or her own personal residence. *Land cannot be depreciated*—technically it never wears out or becomes obsolete.

If depreciation is taken in equal amounts over an asset's useful life, the method used is called *straight-line depreciation.* For property placed in service as of January 1, 1987, the Tax Reform Act of 1986 (TRA '86) set the recovery period for residential rental property at 27.5 years and for nonresidential property at 31.5 years. For nonresidential property placed in service on or after May 13, 1993, the recovery period is increased to 39 years.

Normally, in the initial years of a real estate investment, the taxable loss may exceed cash outlays. This happens because depreciation may exceed the gross income generated by the investment. Thus an investor can have a positive cash flow from an investment and still report a loss on his or her tax return.

Installment Sales

An investor may defer federal income tax on a gain, provided he or she does not receive all cash for the asset at the time of sale but instead receives payments in two or more periods in what is called an **installment sale.** As the name implies, the seller receives payment in installments and pays income tax each year based on the amount received during that year. The installment method often saves an investor money by spreading out the gain over a number of years. The gain may be subject to a lower tax rate than if it were received in one lump-sum payment.

In Practice

Because the seller under an installment sale can defer part of his or her tax on the gain, the seller can accept a small cash down payment and thus expand the market of potential buyers. This also may put the seller in a position to negotiate for a higher sales price. Note, however, that IRS regulations prohibit a seller from reporting a loss for tax purposes when selling by means of an installment sale.

Deductions and TRA '86

The Tax Reform Act of 1986 limits the deductibility of losses from rental property. The first $25,000 of loss can be used to offset income from any source, provided the investor *actively participates* in the management and operation of the property and has taxable income of no more than $100,000 before the deduction is made. The deduction is reduced by $.50 for every dollar of income over $100,000 and is thus eliminated completely when income reaches $150,000. Two examples help illustrate the impact of this law.

1. Harvey has adjusted gross income of $130,000 and losses of $20,000 from three apartment buildings that he owns and personally manages. Harvey is entitled to a deduction of only $10,000 (because the $25,000 maximum is reduced by $.50 for every dollar of the $30,000 Harvey earned over $100,000), reducing his taxable income to $120,000.
2. Helen has adjusted gross income of $100,000 and losses of $20,000 from rental property that she actively manages. Helen is entitled to a deduction of the full $20,000 (her income does not exceed $100,000), reducing her taxable income to $80,000.

Active participation in management may range from personally managing the day-to-day operation of the rental property with no outside assistance to simply making management decisions (for example, approving new tenants and lease terms) while hiring others to provide services. *Passive* participation includes acting as a limited partner, that is, contributing investment monies but having no voice in management operations.

TRA '86 prevents an investor from using a loss from a passive activity to shelter active income (such as wages) or portfolio income (such as stock dividends, bank interest, and capital gains). Generally a passive investor can offset investment losses only against investment income. If the passive investor has no other current investment income, the loss may be carried over to offset investment income in future years. If the investment is sold before the loss is used, it may offset what otherwise would be a taxable gain on the sale.

Subsequent to the passing of the Tax Reform Act of 1986, certain passive loss rules have been relaxed with respect to real estate professionals. If a person (1) materially participates in the activities, (2) spends at least 750 hours in real property businesses, and (3) performs more than 50 percent of his or her personal services for the year in the real property businesses, then the person would be considered a real estate professional and would not be subject to the above passive loss limitations. The requirements must be met on a yearly basis. In one year, a person might be a real estate professional not subject to the passive loss limitations, and in the next year the person might be an active investor subject to the passive loss rules.

Tax credits. A **tax credit** is a direct reduction in tax due, rather than a deduction from income on which tax is computed. A tax credit is therefore of far greater value than a tax deduction.

Investors in older building renovations and low-income housing projects may use designated tax credits to offset tax on up to $25,000 of other income. This is a major exception to the rule requiring active participation in the project; even passive investors can take advantage of tax credits. The maximum income level at which the credits can be taken is also higher. Investors with adjusted gross income of up to $200,000 are entitled to the full $25,000 offset, which is reduced by $.50 for every additional dollar of income and eliminated entirely for incomes above $250,000.

Since 1976, tax credits have been provided for taxpayers who renovate historic property. Historic property is property so designated by the Department of the Interior and listed in the *National Register of Historic Landmarks* or property of historic significance that is located in an area certified by a state as a historic district. The allowable credit is 20 percent of the money spent on renovation of historic property. The property can be depreciated, but the full amount of the tax credit must be subtracted from the basis derived by adding purchase cost and renovation expenses.

The work must be accomplished in accordance with federal historic property guidelines and certified by the Department of the Interior. After renovation, the property must be used as a place of business or rented—it cannot be used as the personal residence of the person taking the tax credit.

REAL ESTATE INVESTMENT SYNDICATES

A *real estate investment syndicate* is a form of business venture in which a group of people pool their resources to own and/or develop a particular piece of property. In this manner, people with only modest capital can invest in large-scale, high-profit, high-risk operations such as high-rise apartment buildings and shopping centers. A certain amount of profit is realized from rents collected on the investment, but the main return usually comes when the syndicate sells the property after sufficient appreciation.

A syndicate investor enjoys the same federal income tax advantages as a direct ownership real estate investor because no matter how small his or her interest in the syndicate properties, the investor owns a certain percentage of a particular parcel of real estate. As a real estate owner, the syndicate investor is as much entitled to preferential tax treatment as is a sole owner of a similar property. However, syndicate interests may be more difficult to sell on the open market than real estate. In addition, approval by the syndicate's management may be required before an investor can sell his or her interest in the project. Some partnership agreements may require that such interest be sold only to another member of the syndicate.

Syndicate participation can take many different legal forms, from tenancy in common to various kinds of partnerships, corporations, and trusts. *Private syndication,* which generally involves a small group of closely associated and/or widely experienced investors, is distinguished from *public syndication,* which generally involves a much larger group of investors who may or may not be knowledgeable about real estate as an investment. The distinction between the two, however, usually is based on the nature of the arrangement between syndicator and investors, not on the type of syndicate. For this reason, any pooling of funds raises questions of registration of securities under federal and state securities laws, commonly referred to as *blue-sky laws.*

Securities laws include provisions to control and regulate the offering and sale of securities to protect members of the public who are not sophisticated investors. Real estate securities must be registered with state officials and/or with the federal Securities & Exchange Commission (SEC) when they meet the defined conditions of a public offering. The number of prospects solicited, the total number of investors or participants, the financial background and sophistication of the investors, and the value or price per unit of investment are pertinent facts. Salespeople of such real estate securities may be required to obtain special licenses and state registration.

Forms of Syndicates

Real estate investment syndicates usually are organized as general, limited, or limited liability partnerships. These partnership forms were described in Chapter 9 but are recapped here.

A *general partnership* is organized so that all members of the group share equally in the managerial decisions, profits, and losses involved with the investment. A certain member (or members) of the syndicate is designated to act as trustee for the group and holds title to the property and maintains it in the syndicate's name.

Under a *limited partnership* agreement, one party (or parties), usually a property developer or real estate broker, organizes, operates, and is responsible for the entire syndicate. This person is called the *general partner.* The other members of the partnership are passive investors with no voice in the organization and direction of the operation; they are called *limited partners.* The limited partners share in the profits, and out of such profits they compensate the general partner for his or her efforts. Unlike a general partnership, in which each member is responsible for the total losses (if any) of the syndicate, each limited partner stands to lose only as much as he or she invests—nothing more. The general partner(s) is (are) totally responsible for any excess losses incurred by the investment.

The sale of a limited partnership interest involves the sale of an investment security, as defined by the SEC. Therefore, such sales are subject to state and federal laws concerning the sale of securities. Unless exempt, the securities must be registered with the SEC and the appropriate state authorities. Texas regulates this activity with its blue-sky laws, which provide that if the offers to sell interests or shares are made to fewer than 35 people, it is a "private offering" and as such is exempt from registration.

The *limited liability partnership* protects individual partners from liability for debts and obligations of the partnership arising from errors, omissions, negligence, and incompetence on the part of one partner—unless there is knowledge of the misconduct at the time of the occurrence.

REAL ESTATE INVESTMENT TRUSTS

By directing their funds into **real estate investment trusts (REITs),** real estate investors can take advantage of the same tax benefits as mutual fund investors. A REIT does not have to pay corporate income tax as long as 90 percent of its income is distributed to its shareholders and certain other conditions are met. Among the conditions for qualifying as a REIT are the requirements that 100 or more members must hold shares in the trust and that 75 percent of the REIT's assets must be invested in real estate, other REITs, securities, or cash. The three types of investment trusts are equity trusts, mortgage trusts, and combination trusts.

Equity trusts. Much like mutual fund operations, equity REITs pool an assortment of large-scale income properties and sell shares to investors. This is in contrast to a real estate syndicate, through which several investors pool their funds to purchase *one* particular property. An equity trust also differs from a syndicate in that the trust realizes and directs its main profits through the *income* derived from the various properties it owns rather than from the sale of those properties.

Mortgage trusts. Mortgage trusts operate similarly to equity trusts, except that mortgage trusts buy and sell real estate mortgages (usually short-term junior instruments) rather than real property. A mortgage trust's major sources of income are mortgage interest and origination fees. Mortgage trusts also may make construction loans and finance land acquisitions.

Combination trusts. Combination trusts invest shareholders' funds in both real estate assets and mortgage loans. These types of trusts are felt by some to be best able to withstand economic slumps because they can balance their investments and liabilities more efficiently than the other types of trusts.

REAL ESTATE MORTGAGE INVESTMENT CONDUITS

The Tax Reform Act of 1986 created a new tax entity, the **real estate mortgage investment conduit (REMIC).** A REMIC is a tax device that allows cash flows from an underlying block of mortgages to be passed through to security holders without being subject to income taxes at the level of the trustee or agent. Complex rules have been established to create a REMIC, and reports on its activities must be made to the IRS.

Summary

Traditionally, real estate investments command a high rate of return, while at the same time allowing an investor to take advantage of many tax shelters unavailable to other types of investors. In addition, real estate is an effective inflation hedge, and an investor can make use of other people's money to make investments through leverage. On the other hand, real estate is *not* a highly liquid investment and often carries with it a high degree of risk. Also, investing in real estate is difficult without expert advice, and a certain amount of mental and physical effort is required to establish and maintain the investment.

Investment property held for appreciation purposes generally is expected to increase in value to a point where its selling price is enough to cover holding costs and show a profit as well. The two main factors affecting appreciation are inflation and the property's present and future intrinsic value. Real estate held for income purposes generally is expected to generate a steady flow of income, usually called *cash flow,* and to show a profit upon its sale.

For an investor to take advantage of maximum leverage in financing an investment, he or she should attempt to make a small down payment, pay low interest rates, and spread mortgage payments over as long a period as possible. By holding and refinancing properties, known as *pyramiding,* an investor can substantially increase holdings without investing additional capital.

By exchanging one property for another with an equal or greater selling value, an investor can defer paying tax on the gain realized until a sale is made. A total tax deferment is possible only if the investor receives no cash or other incentive (boot) to even out the exchange. Any cash or property received as boot is taxed.

Depreciation is a concept that allows an investor to recover in tax deductions the basis of an asset over the period of its useful life. Only costs of improvements to land may be recovered, not costs for the land itself.

Under certain conditions, an investor may be able to defer federal income taxes on gain realized from the sale of an investment property through an installment sale. In this situation, the investor pays income tax only on the adjusted portion of the total gain he or she receives in any year.

Individuals also may invest in real estate through an investment syndicate. Syndicates generally include general, limited, and limited liability partnerships. Two additional forms of real estate investment are the real estate investment trust (REIT) and the real estate mortgage investment conduit (REMIC). REITs can be equity trusts, real estate mortgage trusts, or combination trusts.

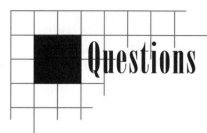

Questions

1. When an investor purchases a parcel of real estate through the use of borrowed funds, he or she is taking advantage of
   a. leverage.
   c. capital gains.
   b. depreciation.
   d. exchanging.

2. An investment syndicate in which all members share equally in the managerial decisions, profits, and losses involved in the venture is an example of which of the following?
   a. Real estate investment trust
   b. Limited partnership
   c. Real estate mortgage trust
   d. General partnership

3. The increase of money in circulation coupled with a rise in prices, resulting in a decline in the value of money, is called
   a. appreciation.
   b. inflation.
   c. deflation.
   d. recapture.

4. For both income and appreciation purposes, investor Mary Clark is contemplating purchasing an apartment building at a price of $150,000. All else being equal, which of the following choices should yield Clark the largest percentage of return on her initial investment after the first year?
   a. Clark pays $150,000 cash for the property.
   b. Clark gives the seller a $75,000 down payment and a 15-year purchase-money mortgage for the balance at 11.5 percent interest.
   c. Clark gives the seller $15,000 down and obtains a 30-year mortgage for the balance at 12 percent interest.
   d. Clark gives the seller $20,000 down and agrees to pay the seller 10 percent of the unpaid balance each year for ten years, plus 11 percent interest.

5. For tax purposes, the initial cost of an investment property, plus the cost of any subsequent improvements to the property, less recovery deductions, represents the investment's
   a. adjusted basis.
   c. basis.
   b. gains.
   d. salvage value.

6. Julia Kinder is exchanging her apartment building for an apartment building of greater market value and must include a $10,000 boot to even out the exchange. Which of the following may she use as a boot?
   a. $10,000 cash
   b. Common stock with a current market value of $10,000
   c. An automobile with a current market value of $10,000
   d. Any of the above if acceptable to the exchangers

7. A property's equity represents its current value less
   a. depreciation deductions.
   b. mortgage indebtedness.
   c. physical improvements.
   d. selling costs and depreciation deductions.

8. Barney Rudolph is exchanging his four-unit apartment building for a six-unit building of the same market value. His gain on the transaction is $28,000. This gain
   a. will not be taxed, because Rudolph exchanged properties.
   b. will be taxed.
   c. represents the exchange's cash boot.
   d. is referred to as *net debt relief.*

9. In an installment sale, taxable gain is received and must be reported as income by the seller
   a. in the year the sale is initiated.
   b. in the year the final installment payment is made.
   c. in each year that installment payments are received.
   d. at any one time during the period installment payments are received.

10. When an investor holds and refinances investment properties, using their equities as leverage, he or she is taking advantage of which of the following concepts?
    a. Pyramiding
    b. Tax sheltered income
    c. Recapture
    d. Useful life

11. A small multifamily property generates $50,000 in rental income with expenses of $45,000 annually, including $35,000 in debt service. The property appreciates about $25,000 a year. On this property the cash flow is
    a. $5,000.   c. $25,000.
    b. $15,000.   d. $30,000.

12. Shareholders in a real estate investment trust generally
    a. receive most of the trust's income each year.
    b. take an active part in management.
    c. find it difficult to sell their shares.
    d. realize their main profit through sales of property.

Sample Texas Real Estate Licensing Examination

Modern Real Estate Practice in Texas, 11th Edition, is designed to prepare you for a career in real estate. However, before you can become a broker or salesperson, you must obtain a license. Passing the real estate licensing examination plays a large part in determining your eligibility to become licensed. The exam is designed to test your knowledge of real estate laws, principles, and practices.

APPLYING TO TAKE THE EXAM

To be eligible for a license, an individual must be a citizen of the United States or a lawfully admitted alien, be at least 18 years of age, and be a legal resident of Texas at the time of filing the application. An applicant must satisfy the commission as to his or her honesty, trustworthiness, integrity, and competency. Competency is judged solely on the basis of an examination.

Getting approval to take the exam. To be eligible to apply for a real estate Salesperson License, you must first obtain a letter from the Texas Real Estate Commission (TREC) attesting to your completion of all education requirements. Send TREC a signed copy of the *Request for Evaluation of Education Documents* form (which can be downloaded from the web site at www.trec.state.tx.us), a *copy* of transcripts or course certificates reflecting the required real estate courses and/or related courses, a photograph, and a check or money order for $20. The transcript evaluation fee is good for one year.

Once you have the eligibility letter from TREC you may apply to take the examination. Effective September 1, 2001, you can apply to take the examination without initially being sponsored by a broker. Just complete the *Application for Inactive Salesperson License* form and send it to TREC, along with a check or money order for $77.50 (which includes $50 for the application fee, $17.50 for the Real Estate Center and $10 for the Recovery Fund), or apply online at the TREC web site. The Commission will send you a *Candidate Information Brochure* (CIB), which is essentially a permit to take the examination; you take the exam; and once you have successfully passed it, TREC will send you an *inactive* salesperson license. Before you will be eligible to practice real estate brokerage, however, you must be sponsored by an active real estate broker. You submit to TREC a *Request To Sponsor Salesperson Applicant* form and a $20 fee for transferring your license to your sponsoring broker. You will then receive from TREC an *active* salesperson license. If you have already chosen a sponsoring broker at the time you apply to take the examination and want to expedite the process for getting an *active* license, you may submit both forms at the same time—along with all fees associated with both forms.

Selecting a broker. You must have a broker-sponsor before you can begin the practice of real estate, as described above. Your license will be mailed to that broker and you will be working under that broker's license and supervision. Because selection of a broker-sponsor is crucial to your success in real estate, several suggestions for that process are listed below:

- Select four or five different brokers to interview:
  - Watch real estate ads in the paper.
  - Visit open houses and talk to REALTORS® in each office.
  - Ask friends and relatives about past dealings with REALTORS®.
  - Select an area you want to work in; see who is most active there.
  - Think through what you'll ask during an interview, and anticipate their questions.
- Consider your appointment interview as both the broker considering you and you considering the broker. Tell the broker what you have to offer the firm.
- Ask questions during the interview. Possible questions include the following:
  - What opportunities are there for floor duty? How often? How long?
  - What are the open house opportunities (to sit in for someone else)?
  - What type of training program do you have? What is covered? Who does it?
  - What types of promotional literature are available for marketing?
  - Are you (the broker) in the office to help me most of the time—or are you currently active in sales?
  - What is the commission split?
  - Who pays what expenses—business cards, stationery, signs, sign riders, phone expenses, desk space rental, MLS computer fees? (Realize that, as an agent, you are paid on commission only and need 3 to 6 months' living expenses set aside before you begin. As an independent contractor, you furnish your own car, gas, and insurance.)
  - Is secretarial help provided? Does the secretary enter listings on the computer?
  - What is the company policy about personal assistants?
  - Do I owe the company a commission if I buy a FSBO or sell my own home?
  - Is a franchise fee charged for each sale or listing?
  - Is a minimum number of transactions expected each month?
  - What is the firm's image? Years in business? Overall sales volume? Average sales per agent? Agent turnover?
  - May I have a copy of the policy manual before I make a decision? (Pay close attention to the policy regarding "pending sales" should you later decide to leave the firm.)
- Think about your personality, preferred market area, and the office atmosphere. Meet other agents in the office and talk with them about the real estate business. Do they have a positive attitude about the firm

and real estate in general? Then select the office you think you will "fit into" the best.

Candidate Information Brochure.   The Candidate Information Brochure (CIB), which is sent from TREC after you apply to take the exam, includes important information to assist you in scheduling and taking your examination. For instance, the Candidate Information Brochure includes

- test center locations;
- how to make an appointment to take the examination;
- what to expect at the testing site on the day of your examination;
- check-in procedures at the examination, what to bring and what not to bring;
- how the examination is administered (computerized testing procedures);
- methods of paying your examination fee;
- how to schedule a retake if you fail one or more parts of the exam;
- detailed content outline, references for study, and sample questions; and
- format of questions.

Making an appointment to take the examination.   *After* you have received approval from TREC to take the examination, you can schedule an appointment to take the exam. In the CIB, you will be provided with a toll-free 800 number to call to make an appointment to take your examination. You will have your choice of testing at one of the many Prometric Testing Centers located throughout the State of Texas. Do not call to make an appointment until *after* you have received the CIB.

What To Expect from the Exam

The Texas Real Estate Licensing Examination is currently prepared and administered by Experior, an independent testing company.

Salesperson and broker candidates are given separate examinations. The salesperson exam consists of 93 questions in two parts: Real Estate General Theory (70 questions) and Texas State-Specific Law and Regulations (23 questions). There are seven "pretest" questions included on the exam, but those answers are not scored. They are used by Experior as a means of testing those questions for future use.

The broker exam has 115 questions with 80 in the theory section and 35 in the Texas law and regulations section. There are eight "pretest" questions on the broker's examination. The items on the broker exam cover the same topics as the sales exam but are more difficult. Approximately 8 to 12 percent of the "theory" questions on both exams involve some mathematical calculations.

The questions are entirely multiple-choice in format, with four alternative answer choices for each question. Battery-operated, hand-held, paperless calculators are permitted while taking the exam, and scratch paper is provided. The exam must be completed within the allotted time, but ample time is provided if the test taker is prepared adequately (two hours for the salesperson exam and three hours for the broker exam).

You must pass both parts of the exam to qualify for your real estate license. Candidates who fail one part of the exam have to retake only the section they failed. If both parts of the examination are not passed within six months after the date on which the application for a license was filed, the candidate must make a new application to TREC, including the payment of all fees.

TAKING THE EXAMINATION

You will take your examination on a computer. Answers are recorded using either a "mouse" or keyboard. This system is very simple to use, even for candidates with no previous typing or computer experience. You have an opportunity to practice using the system before beginning your exam. The time used for practice is not counted in the time available for the actual exam.

All exams are "closed book." No study materials, notes, purses, backpacks, briefcases, or similar materials are allowed to be carried into the examination room. You will be provided with "scratch paper" to use during the examination.

Items on the examinations are confidential and copyrighted material. If a school or another applicant asks you to reveal examination material, you should refuse. Any disclosure of test questions is prohibited and can result in denial of licensure and/or civil or criminal prosecution.

As soon as you complete your test, you will receive a score report indicating your score, whether you passed or failed, and your strengths and weaknesses in various content areas of the exam. When taking the combined examination, you should always receive two separate score reports. You should keep your printed score reports as confirmation of having completed the examinations. Examination results are transmitted electronically to TREC every night. If the examination is passed and all other requirements for licensure are satisfied, the applicant can expect TREC to print a license the next business day. Passing the examination, however, does not authorize the applicant to act as a licensee. For the salesperson license, you must first apply for an *active* license under the sponsorship of an *active* real estate broker. For either the salesperson or broker license, you may not begin your practice until the license certificate is received.

If you fail one or more parts of your exam, you will receive instructions for retaking the examination. The exam may be taken more than once in the same day if space is available; however, this is not recommended. Before retaking the test, applicants are advised to study—based on the information contained in the examination analysis given at the examination site.

Just about anything you have studied in this book, in Law of Agency, and in Law of Contracts may be included on the exam; and all real estate subject matter is "fair game." The following section reflects the most recent "Examination Outline" for the Texas exam.

EXAMINATION OUTLINE

Part I—Real Estate
General Theory

Topic Headings	Number of Questions	
	Sales	Broker
I. Business Practices and Ethics	10	12

    A.   Professional ethics

         1.   Public and fiduciary responsibility
         2.   Unlawful practice of law

    B.   Federal requirements for real estate activities

         1.   Fair housing and antidiscrimination
         2.   Violations of Sherman Antitrust Act
         3.   Advertising

    C.   Record keeping and document handling

II. Agency and Listing	10	12

    A.   Principles of agency

         1.   Creating agency
         2.   Liabilities
         3.   Types and functions of agency
         4.   Roles and responsibilities of licensees
         5.   Terminating agency

    B.   Types of listing

    C.   Listing procedures

         1.   Disclosing agency relationships
         2.   Evaluating property
         3.   Disclosure of property conditions
         4.   Fraud and misrepresentation

    D.   Listing agreement

         1.   Legal requirements
         2.   Fiduciary duties and representations
         3.   Terminating listing

III. Property Characteristics, Descriptions, Ownership, Interests, and Restrictions*	11	12

    A.   Characteristics of property

         1.   Legal description of property
         2.   Interpreting physical and economic characteristics of property
         3.   Real and personal property

    B.   Ownership and estates in land

         1.   Title
         2.   Types of ownership
         3.   Types of estates

C.   Government restrictions

    1.   The four governmental powers (police power, eminent domain, escheat, taxation)
    2.   Environmental regulations and disclosures
    3.   Water rights

D.   Private restrictions

    1.   Voluntary and involuntary liens
    2.   Covenants, conditions, and restrictions
    3.   Other encumbrances

IV.   Property Valuation and the Appraisal Process[*]   7   8

A.   Principles of valuation

    1.   Value, price, and cost
    2.   Characteristics of property that affect value
    3.   Principles of value

B.   Determining value

    1.   Direct sales comparison (market data) approach
    2.   Cost approach
    3.   Income approach

C.   Appraisal

    1.   Purpose and use of appraisal
    2.   Role of appraiser
    3.   Role of licensee in property valuation

V.   Real Estate Contracts   11   12

A.   Purpose, scope, and elements of real estate sales contracts

B.   Offers and counteroffers

    1.   Purpose of offer and counteroffer
    2.   Valid methods of communicating offers

C.   Earnest money

D.   Completion, termination, breach

VI.   Financing Sources[*]   7   8

A.   Essentials of financing

    1.   Mortgages, deeds of trust, and their provisions

B.   Qualifying buyer for financing

    1.   Prequalifying considerations
    2.   Loan repayment

C.   Types of financing

    1.   Loan programs, their benefits and requirements
    2.   Financing methods

D.   Foreclosure and alternatives

    E.   Pertinent laws and regulations

        1.   *Truth-in-Lending Act* and Regulation Z
        2.   *Equal Credit Opportunity Act*
        3.   *Fair Credit Reporting Act*

VII. Closing/Settlement and Transferring Title*   **10**   **12**

    A.   Settlement statement and other critical documents

    B.   Closing/settlement

        1.   Purpose of closing/settlement
        2.   Legal requirements (includes RESPA)

    C.   Transferring title

        1.   Methods of transfer (includes deeds)
        2.   Recording title

    D.   Title insurance

        1.   Purpose and scope of title insurance
        2.   Essentials of title insurance

VIII.   Property Management*   **4**   **4**

    A.   Leases, estates, tenancies

    B.   Property manager and owner relationship

    C.   Laws affecting property management

Total   **70**   **80**

(*Topic includes math items, 8 to 12 percent of total items on exam)

Part 2—Texas State-Specific Law and Regulations

Topic Headings	Number of Questions	
	Sales	Broker
I. Commission Duties and Powers	**2**	**4**

    A.   General Powers

        1.   Composition, Duties, and Powers [TRELA Sections 5, 7(f), Rule 535.42]
        2.   Real Estate Broker-Lawyer Committee [TRELA Section 16(c)-(e)]

    B.   Investigations and Subpoena Power

        1.   Investigations [TRELA Sections 15, 15B, Rule 535.141]
        2.   Subpoena Power Investigations [TRELA Section 15(e)]
        3.   Subpoena Power Hearings [TRELA Sections 17, 19A(h-1)]

    C.   Hearings and Appeals

        1.   Hearings [TRELA Sections 17, 19A(h-1)]
        2.   Appeals [TRELA Sections 10, 18, Rule 535.94]

D. Penalties for Violation

   1. Unlicensed Activity [TRELA Section 19]
   2. Penalties [TRELA Section 19A(a-b), Rule 535.181]
   3. Recovery Fund [TRELA Section 8]

II. Licensing   **3**   **4**

A. Activities Requiring License

   1. Scope of Practice [TRELA Sections 2, 4, Rules 535.1-535.21]
   2. Exemptions [TRELA Sections 3, 24]
   3. Corporations/Limited Liability Companies [TRELA Section 6(c)]
   4. Nonresident broker [TRELA Section 14 Rules 535.131-535.133]
   5. Inspectors and Appraisers [TX CIV, STAT. Art. 6573a.1, TRELA Section 23, Rules 535.201-535.228]

B. Licensing Process

   1. General Requirements (age, moral character, residency, sponsor, etc.) [TRELA Sections 6, 6A, 14]
   2. Education [TRELA Section 7]
      a. Salesperson
      b. Broker
   3. Examination [TRELA Sections 6, 7]
   4. Disapproval of Application and Appeals [TRELA Section 10, Rule 535.94]

C. License Renewal [TRELA Sections 9(c-e) Rules 535.91-535.93, 535.95]

   1. Continuing Education [TRELA Section 7A, Rule 535.93]
   2. Place of Business [TRELA Section 12, Rules 535.111-535.113]
   3. Change of Salesperson Sponsorship [TRELA Section 13 Rules 535.121-535.122]
   4. Inactive Status [TRELA Section 13A, Rules 535.121-535.123]

III. Standards of Conduct   **9**   **15**

A. Professional Ethics and Conduct [Rule 531]

B. Single Act [TRELA Section 4]

C. Disciplinary Actions

   1. Power/Authority [TRELA Sections 15, 15B]
   2. Grounds for Suspension and Revocation [TRELA Sections l(b-e), 9(b), 15(a-c), 15(C), Rules 535.3, 535.141-535.164, 541.1, TX CIV STAT. 6252-13c]

D. Unlawful Practice of Law [TRELA Section 16]

E. Responsibilities of Brokers [TRELA Section 1, Rule 535.2]

F. Splitting Fees [TRELA Section 14(a), Rule 535.131]

G. Use of Standard Forms [Rule 537.11-537.42, Standard Forms]

    1. Contracts

    2. Deed of Trust

IV.   Agency/Brokerage   5   7

A. Disclosure

B. Intermediary Practice [TRELA Section 15(C)]

C. Enforcing Compensation Agreements [TRELA Sections 15C, 20 Rules 535.191-535.192]

D. Liability for Another's Acts [TRELA Sections 1(c), 15(F)]

V.   Special Topics   4   5

A. Community Property [TX Constitution, Art. 16, Section 15, Family Code Section 5.01 et seq.]

B. Homestead [TX Constitution Art.16, Sections 50-51, Family Code Section 5.81 et seq., Tax Code Sections 11.3, 11.41, 34.21]

C. Deceptive Trade Practices Act [Business and Commerce Code, Sections 17.42-17.50]

D. Assumed Names [Business and Commerce Code, Section 36.01 et seq.]

E. Descent and Distribution [TX Constitution, Art. 16, Section 52 Probate Code, Section 37]

F. Intestate Succession [TX Probate Code, Sections 37-38]

G. Seller Disclosure Requirements [Property Code, Section 5.008 Natural Resources Code, Sections 33.135, 61.025, Water Code, Section 49.452]

H. Property Tax Consulting [TX CIV STAT. Art. 8886]

I. Landlord-Tenant Issues [Property Code, Sections 24.001 et seq. 54.041 et seq., 92.001 et seq.]

J. Statute of Frauds [Business and Commerce Code, Section 26.01]

K. Foreclosures [Property Code, Sections 51.002, 51.004]

L. Recording Statutes [Property Code, Section 13.001 et seq.]

M. Mechanic's and Materialman's Liens [Property Code, Section 53.001 et seq.]

Total   23   35

MULTIPLE-CHOICE QUESTIONS: TEST-TAKING STRATEGIES

There are as many different ways to prepare for and take multiple-choice examinations as there are test takers. Before you try the following sample exams, take some time to read this brief overview of test-taking strategies.

While no one can tell you which method will work best for you, it is always a good idea to think about what you are going to do before you do it.

One of the most important things to remember about multiple-choice test questions is this: they always give you the correct answer. You don't have to remember how things are spelled, and you don't have to try to guess what the question is about. The answer is always there, right in front of you.

Of course, if it were as easy as that, it wouldn't be much of a test. The key to success in taking multiple-choice examinations is actually two keys: first, *know the correct answer.* You do that by going to class, paying attention, taking good notes, and studying the material. Then, if you don't know the answer, you can analyze the questions and answers effectively, and you can apply the second key: *be able to make a reasonable guess.* Even if you don't know the answer, you will probably know which answers are clearly wrong and which ones are more likely than the others to be right.

If you can eliminate one answer as wrong, you have improved your odds in "guessing correctly" by 25 percent, from 4-to-1 to 3-to-1. If you can eliminate two wrong answers, you have a 50/50 shot at a correct guess. Of course, if you can eliminate *three* wrong answers, your chance of a correct response is 100 percent. In any case, there is no secret formula. *The only sure way to improve your odds of a correct answer is to study and learn the material.*

Structure of the question. A multiple-choice question has a basic structure. It starts with what test writers call the *stem.* That's the text of the question that sets up the need for an answer. The stem may be an incomplete statement that is finished by the correct answer; it may be a story problem or hypothetical example (called a *fact-pattern*) about which you will be asked a question. Or it may be a math problem, in which you are given basic information and asked to solve a mathematical issue, such as the amount of a commission or capital gain.

The stem is always followed by *options:* four possible answers to the question presented by the stem. Depending on the structure and content of the stem, the options may be single words or numbers, phrases, or complete sentences. Three of the options are *distractors:* incorrect answers intended to "distract" you from the correct choice. One of the options is the correct answer, called the *key.*

Reading a multiple-choice question. Here are three methods for approaching a multiple-choice test question:

1. *The Traditional Method.* Read the question through from start to finish; then, read the options. When you get to the correct answer, mark it and move on. This method works best for short questions, such as those that require completion or simply define a term. For long, more complicated questions or those that are not quite clear, however, you may miss important information.
2. *The Focus Method.* As we've seen, multiple-choice questions have different parts. In longer math or story-type questions, the last line of the stem will contain the question's *focus:* the basic issue the item asks you to address. That is, *the question is always in the last line of*

the stem. In the focus method, when you come to a longer item, read the last line of the stem first. This will clue you in to what the question is about. Then go back and read the stem from beginning to end. The advantage is this: while you are reading complicated facts or math elements, you know what to look for. You can watch for important items and disregard unnecessary information.

3. *The Upside-Down Method.* This technique takes the focus method one step farther. Here, you do just what the name implies: you start reading the question from the bottom up. By reading the four options first, you can learn exactly what the test writer wants you to focus on. For instance, a fact-pattern problem might include several dollar values in the stem, leading you to believe you're going to have to do a math calculation. You'll be trying to recall all the equations you've memorized, only to find at the end of the stem that you're only expected to define a term. If you've read the options first, you know what to look for.

TAKING THE SAMPLE EXAMINATION

The following sample examination has been designed to help you prepare for the actual licensing exam. It matches the salesperson exam in topic structure. You should take no longer than two hours to answer the 100 questions—90 minutes for the theory section and 30 minutes for the state-specific section. If any of your answers is incorrect, restudy the related sections of this text. The questions in this exam are ordered according to the "examination content outline" included previously, to make it easier for you to determine which topics need review.

Sample Examination—Part One
Real Estate General Theory

1. Which Canon of Professional Ethics requires that the broker or salesperson employ prudence and caution in the discharge of his or her duties to avoid misrepresentation?
   a. Fidelity
   b. Integrity
   c. Competency
   d. Accounting

2. A person licensed as a salesperson
   a. can work independently, without a broker, if he or she is properly licensed.
   b. can work independently, without a broker, if he or she cannot find a broker-sponsor.
   c. can work independently, without a broker, if his or her broker ceases to be licensed.
   d. cannot work independently, without a broker.

3. It is unlawful for a real estate licensee to prepare a deed unless the licensee is
   a. directed to do so by the seller.
   b. directed to do so by the buyer.
   c. a broker.
   d. an attorney.

4. Under the federal Fair Housing Act, it is illegal to discriminate because a person
   a. has a history of dangerous behavior.
   b. is single.
   c. has AIDS.
   d. has been convicted of distributing a controlled substance.

5. Which of the following would most likely be legal under the provisions of the Civil Rights Act of 1968?
   a. A lender refuses to make loans in areas where more than 25 percent of the population is Hispanic.
   b. A private country club development ties home ownership to club membership but due to local demographics, all club members are white.
   c. A church excludes African Americans from membership and rents its nonprofit housing to church members only.
   d. A licensee directs prospective buyers away from areas where they are likely to feel uncomfortable because of their race.

6. Which person or family would **NOT** be protected under the "familial status" provision of the Fair Housing Act?
   a. An adult with children under 18
   b. Someone who is under age 18 and pregnant
   c. Someone who is in the process of securing legal custody of a child under 18
   d. Two single females

7. The practice of blockbusting means
   a. making a profit by inducing owners to sell or rent because of the prospective entry of minority persons into the neighborhood.
   b. channeling homeseekers to particular areas to maintain the homogeneity of an area.
   c. denying people membership in a service organization as a means of discrimination.
   d. representing to any person, as a means of discrimination, that a dwelling is not available for sale or rental.

8. There is a spectacular house that a salesperson from Firm A has been trying for several weeks to list for sale. The owners have been interviewing salespeople from different firms. They tell A's salesperson that Firm B will charge 2 percent less commission for selling the house. What should A's salesperson say to the owner to get the listing?
   a. Most brokers in the area charge a standard rate of commission, including Firm A.
   b. Firm B cannot provide good services because they charge less.
   c. Firm A provides excellent services to market their sellers' properties.
   d. Your broker believes his fee structure is in line with those of other brokers in the area.

9. Elmer and Warren were found guilty of conspiring with each other to allocate real estate brokerage markets. Paul suffered a $90,000 loss because of the illegal activities. If Paul brings a civil suit against Elmer and Warren, what can he expect to recover?
   a. Nothing; a civil suit cannot be brought for damages resulting from antitrust activities
   b. Only $90,000—the amount of actual damages suffered
   c. Actual damages plus attorney's fees and costs
   d. $270,000 plus attorney's fees and costs

10. Mary and Natalie are real estate brokers. Mary places a newspaper ad for a property that says, "Features a lovely bay window perfect for a piano or the Christmas tree." Natalie's ad on the Internet says, "Male roommate sought for walkup apartment in good neighborhood." Which of these brokers have violated HUD's advertising guidelines?
    a. Mary and Natalie have both violated the guidelines.
    b. Mary only; Mary's ad violates the rule against stating a religious preference.
    c. Natalie only; Natalie's ad violates the rule against stating an explicit preference based on sex.
    d. Neither Mary nor Natalie has violated the guidelines.

11. Henry is a real estate broker. Stan signs a buyer's brokerage agreement under which Henry will help Stan find a three-bedroom house in the $85,000 to $100,000 price range. James comes into Henry's office and signs a listing agreement to sell James's two-bedroom condominium for $70,000. Based on these facts, which of the following is true?
    a. Stan is Henry's client; James is Henry's customer.
    b. Stan is Henry's customer; James is Henry's client.
    c. While both Stan and James are clients, Henry owes the fiduciary duties of an agent to James.
    d. Because both Stan and James are Henry's clients, Henry owes the fiduciary duties of an agent to both.

12. Janet enters into an exclusive-agency buyer agency agreement with a real estate broker. Based on this fact, which of the following statements is true?
    a. Janet is obligated to pay the broker regardless of who finds a suitable property.
    b. If Janet finds a suitable property without the broker's assistance, she is under no obligation to pay the broker.
    c. Janet may enter into other, similar agreements with other brokers.
    d. If Janet finds a suitable property without the broker's assistance, Janet will have to pay the broker.

13. In an intermediary transaction involving an appointed licensee,
    a. the broker may work with the buyer and the listing salesperson may continue to work with the seller.
    b. a licensed sales associate may be appointed to work with either the buyer or the seller; the broker would work with the other party.
    c. a licensed sales associate must be appointed to work with the buyer and another to work with the seller.
    d. the broker may work with both parties as an appointed licensee.

14. Kent signs a listing agreement with broker Ernie. Broker Nancy obtains a buyer for the house, and Ernie does not receive a commission. Ernie does not sue Kent. The listing agreement between Kent and Ernie was probably which of the following?
    a. Exclusive-right-to-sell
    b. Open
    c. Exclusive-agency
    d. Dual-agency

15. The statutory "Information about Brokerage Services" notice must be presented to prospects
    a. prior to signing a purchase agreement.
    b. sometime prior to closing.
    c. at the first contact.
    d. at the first face-to-face meeting between licensee and prospect.

16. After an offer is accepted, the seller finds that his listing broker was also the undisclosed agent for the buyer. The seller may
    a. withdraw without obligation to broker or buyer.
    b. withdraw but would be subject to liquidated damages.
    c. withdraw but only with the concurrence of the buyer.
    d. refuse to sell but would be subject to a suit for specific performance.

17. Rebecca listed her home with broker Kent for $90,000. Rebecca told Kent, "I have to sell quickly because of a job transfer. If necessary, I can accept a price as low as $75,000." Kent tells a prospective buyer to offer $80,000 "because Rebecca is desperate to sell." Rebecca accepts the buyer's offer. In this situation, which of the following is true?
    a. Kent's action did not violate his agency relationship with Rebecca because Kent did not reveal Rebecca's lowest acceptable price.
    b. Kent violated his agency relationship with Rebecca.
    c. Kent acted properly to obtain a quick offer on Rebecca's property, in accordance with Rebecca's instructions.
    d. Kent violated his common-law duties toward the buyer by failing to disclose that Rebecca would accept a lower price than the buyer offered.

18. A broker took a listing and later discovered that the client had been declared incompetent by a court. What is the current status of the listing?
    a. The listing is unaffected because the broker acted in good faith as the owner's agent.
    b. The listing is of no value to the broker because the listing contract is void.
    c. The listing is the basis for recovery of a commission from the client's guardian or trustee if the broker produces a buyer.
    d. The listing may be renegotiated between the broker and the client, based on the new information.

19. The listing and selling brokers agree to split a 7 percent commission 50-50 on a $95,900 sale. The listing broker gives the listing salesperson 30 percent of his commission, and the selling broker gives the selling salesperson 35 percent of his commission. How much does the selling salesperson earn from the sale after deducting expenses of $35?
    a. $1,139.78
    b. $1,174.78
    c. $1,183.95
    d. $1,971.95

20. A metes-and-bounds legal description
    a. can be made only in areas excluded from the rectangular survey system.
    b. is not acceptable in court in most jurisdictions.
    c. must commence and finish at the same identifiable point.
    d. is used to complete areas omitted from recorded subdivision plats.

21. Which physical or economic characteristic is the basis for the statement, "Land is not insurable"?
    a. Nonhomogeneity
    b. Relative scarcity
    c. Permanence of investment
    d. Indestructibility

22. Kevin moved into an abandoned home and installed new cabinets in the kitchen. When the owner discovered the occupancy, the owner had Kevin evicted. What is the status of the kitchen cabinets?
    a. Kevin has no right to the cabinets.
    b. The cabinets remain because they are trade fixtures.
    c. Although the cabinets stay, Kevin is entitled to the value of the improvements.
    d. Kevin can keep the cabinets if they can be removed without damaging the real estate.

23. Sally and Ted, who are not married, own a parcel of real estate. Each owns an undivided interest, with Sally owning one-third and Ted owning two-thirds. The form of ownership under which Sally and Ted own their property is
    a. severalty.
    b. joint tenancy.
    c. tenancy at will.
    d. tenancy in common.

24. Under community property laws
    a. income from separate property is considered separate property.
    b. the property that a person received as a gift during marriage is considered community property.
    c. all property owned by a married person is considered community property.
    d. the property that a person accumulated prior to marriage is considered separate property.

25. Maria conveys the ownership of an office building to a nursing home. The nursing home agrees that the rental income will pay for the expenses of caring for Maria's parents. When Maria's parents die, ownership of the office building will revert to Maria. The estate held by the nursing home is a
    a. remainder life estate.
    b. legal life estate.
    c. life estate pur autre vie.
    d. temporary leasehold estate.

26. Grant owns two properties: Redacre and Brownacre. He conveys Redacre to Sharon with no restrictions; Sharon holds all rights to Redacre forever. Grant then conveys Brownacre to Tim "so long as no real estate broker or salesperson sets foot on the property." If a broker or salesperson visits Brownacre, ownership will revert to Grant. Based on these two conveyances, which of the following is true?
    a. Sharon holds Redacre in fee simple; Tim holds Brownacre in fee simple determinable.
    b. Sharon holes Redacre in fee simple; Tim holds Brownacre in fee simple defeasible, subject to a condition subsequent.
    c. Tim may not transfer ownership of Brownacre without Grant's permission.
    d. Grant has retained a right of reentry with regard to Brownacre.

27. A homestead is protected against judgments that result from
    a. unsecured creditors.
    b. unpaid taxes.
    c. foreclosure of a mortgage.
    d. home improvement liens.

28. Ric bought a home in 1998 for $74,800. Three years later, he sold the home for $103,600 and moved into an apartment. In computing Ric's income tax, what amount of this transaction is taxable?
    a. $9,600
    b. $16,980
    c. $28,800
    d. Nothing is taxable; Ric's capital gain is within the exclusion guidelines.

29. The state wants to acquire a strip of farmland to build a highway. Does the state have the right to acquire privately owned land for public use?
    a. Yes; the state's right is called *condemnation.*
    b. Yes; the state's right is called *eminent domain.*
    c. Yes; the state's right is called *escheat.*
    d. No; under the U.S. Constitution, private property may never be taken by state governments or the federal government.

30. What is the difference between a general lien and a specific lien?
    a. A general lien cannot be enforced in court, while a specific lien can.
    b. A specific lien is held by only one person, while a general lien must be held by two or more.
    c. A general lien is a lien against personal property, while a specific lien is a lien against real estate.
    d. A specific lien is a lien against a certain parcel of real estate, while a general lien covers all of a debtor's property.

31. Vicki buys 348,480 square feet of land at $0.75 per square foot. She divides the land into ½-acre lots. If she keeps three lots for herself and sells the others for $24,125 each, what percent of profit does she realize?
    a. 47.4%
    b. 32.3%
    c. 20%
    d. 16.7%

32. Barry's home is the smallest in a neighborhood of large, expensive houses. The effect of the other houses on the value of his home is known as
    a. increasing and diminishing returns.
    b. conformity.
    c. substitution.
    d. contribution.

33. Quinn, an appraiser, estimates the value of a property using the cost approach. Which of the following describes what Quinn should do?
    a. Estimate the replacement cost of the improvements.
    b. Deduct the depreciation of the land and buildings.
    c. Determine the original cost and adjust for depreciation.
    d. Review the sales prices of comparable properties.

34. Which of the following is an example of external obsolescence?
    a. Numerous pillars supporting the ceiling in a store
    b. Leaks in the roof of a warehouse, making the premises unusable and therefore unrentable
    c. Coal cellar in a house with central heating
    d. Vacant, abandoned and run-down building in an area

35. Which of the following **BEST** describes the capitalization rate under the income approach to estimating the value of real estate?
    a. Rate at which a property increases in value
    b. Rate of return a property earns as an investment
    c. Rate of capital required to keep a property operating most efficiently
    d. Maximum rate of return allowed by law on an investment

36. In one commercial building, the tenant intends to start a health food shop using her life savings. In an identical adjacent building is a showroom leased to a major national retailing chain. Both tenants have long-term leases with identical rents. Which of the following statements is correct?
    a. If the values of the buildings were the same before the leases, the values will be the same after the leases.
    b. An appraiser would most likely use a higher capitalization rate for the store leased to the national retailing chain.
    c. The most accurate appraisal method would be the sales comparison approach to value.
    d. The building with the health food shop will probably appraise for less than the other building.

37. An owner is concerned about how much money she can get when she sells her home. A competitive market analysis may help her determine a realistic listing price. Which of the following is true of a CMA?
   a. A competitive market analysis is the same as an appraisal.
   b. A broker, not a salesperson, is permitted to prepare a competitive market analysis.
   c. A competitive market analysis is prepared by a certified real estate appraiser.
   d. A competitive market analysis contains a compilation of other, similar properties that have sold.

38. An income-producing property has $62,500 annual gross income and monthly expenses of $1,530. What is the appraised value if the appraiser uses a 10 percent capitalization rate?
   a. $183,600
   b. $441,400
   c. $609,700
   d. $625,000

39. Broker Kathy arrives to present a purchase offer to Dan, who is seriously ill, and finds Dan's son and daughter-in-law also present. The son and daughter-in-law angrily urge Dan to accept the offer, even though it is much less than the asking price for the property. If Dan accepts the offer, he may later claim that
   a. Kathy improperly presented an offer that was less than the asking price.
   b. Kathy's failure to protect Dan from the son and daughter-in-law constituted a violation of Kathy's fiduciary duties.
   c. Dan's rights under the ADA have been violated by the son and daughter-in-law.
   d. Dan was under influence from the son and daughter-in-law, so the contract is voidable.

40. Grace purchases a home under a land contract. Until the contract is paid in full, what is the status of her interest in the property?
   a. Grace holds legal title to the premises.
   b. Grace has no legal interest in the property.
   c. Grace possess a legal life estate in the premises.
   d. Grace has equitable title in the property.

41. In an option to purchase real estate, which of the following statements is **TRUE** of the optionee?
   a. The optionee must purchase the property, but may do so at any time within the option period.
   b. The optionee is limited to a refund of the option consideration if the option is exercised.
   c. The optionee cannot obtain third-party financing on the property until after the option has expired.
   d. The optionee has no obligation to purchase the property during the option period.

42. Which of the following is **NOT** an essential element of a contract?
   a. Date
   b. Consideration
   c. Meeting of the minds
   d. Signatures of the parties authorized to perform

43. On Monday, Tom offers to sell his vacant lot to Kay for $12,000. On Tuesday, Kay counteroffers to buy the lot for $10,500. On Friday, Kay withdraws her counteroffer and accepts Tom's original price of $12,000. Under these circumstances
   a. a valid agreement exists because Kay accepted Tom's offer exactly as it was made, regardless of the fact that it was not accepted immediately.
   b. a valid agreement exists because Kay accepted before Tom advised her that the offer was withdrawn.
   c. no valid agreement exists because Tom's offer was not accepted within 72 hours of its having been made.
   d. no valid agreement exists because Kay's counteroffer was a rejection of Tom's offer, and once rejected, it cannot be accepted later.

44. A broker receives a check for earnest money from a buyer and deposits the money in the broker's personal interest-bearing checking account over the weekend. This action exposes the broker to a charge of
   a. commingling.
   b. novation.
   c. subrogation.
   d. accretion.

45. An offer would be terminated by all of the following events **EXCEPT**
    a. Wayne signed a written offer to buy a house, but called the seller and revoked the offer just after his agent presented it and before it was formally signed.
    b. Sharon signed a written offer to buy a house and then died.
    c. Paul signed a written offer to buy a house, and the seller made a counteroffer.
    d. listing salesperson Jeff died before an offer was accepted by both parties.

46. A broker received a deposit along with a written offer from a buyer. The offer stated: "The offeror will leave this offer open for the seller's acceptance for a period of ten days." On the fifth day, and before acceptance by the seller, the offeror notified the broker that the offer was withdrawn and demanded the return of the deposit. Which of the following statements is true in this situation?
    a. The offeror cannot withdraw the offer; it must be held open for the full ten-day period, as promised.
    b. The offeror has the right to withdraw the offer and secure the return of the deposit any time before being notified of the seller's acceptance.
    c. The offeror can withdraw the offer, and the seller and the broker will each retain one-half of the forfeited deposit.
    d. While the offeror can withdraw the offer, the broker is legally entitled to declare the deposit forfeited and retain all of it in lieu of the lost commission.

47. Carol has a contract to paint Otto's garage door for $200. Before starting the project, Carol has a skiing accident and breaks both arms. Carol asks another painter, Jamie, to take over the job. Jamie paints Otto's garage door, and Otto pays Jamie $200 for the work. This scenario is an example of
    a. assignment.   c. acceptance.
    b. novation.   d. revocation.

48. To be considered *effective*, the notice of contract acceptance
    a. must be communicated directly to the buyer if a transaction involves subagency.
    b. must be communicated to the agent who wrote the buyer's contract if the transaction involves subagency.
    c. must be communicated to the seller if the transaction involves subagency.
    d. must be communicated by telephone to the seller if the transaction involves buyer representation.

49. The section of a purchase contract that provides for the buyer to forfeit any earnest money if the buyer fails to complete the purchase is known as the provision for
    a. liquidated damages.
    b. punitive damages.
    c. hypothecation.
    d. subordination.

50. Wilson is purchasing a condominium unit in a subdivision and obtains financing from a local savings association. In this situation, which of the following **BEST** describes Wilson?
    a. Vendor   c. Grantor
    b. Mortgagor   d. Lessor

51. A clause in a mortgage instrument that would prevent the assumption of the mortgage by a new purchaser is a(n)
    a. due-on-sale clause.
    b. power-of-sale clause.
    c. defeasance clause.
    d. acceleration clause.

52. A borrower takes out a mortgage loan that requires monthly payments of $875.70 for 20 years and a final payment of $24,095. This is what type of loan?
    a. Wraparound   c. Balloon
    b. Accelerated   d. Variable

53. A veteran wishes to finance his home with a VA-guaranteed loan. The lender is willing, but insists on 3½ discount points. In this situation, the veteran can
    a. finance with a VA loan, provided the lender charges no discount points.
    b. finance with a VA loan, provided the lender charges no more than two discount points.
    c. be required to pay a maximum of 1 percent of the loan as an origination fee.
    d. proceed with the refinance loan and pay the discount points.

54. A first-time homebuyer finds that he is unlikely to qualify for a mortgage under current interest rates. His parents agree to pay a lump sum in cash to the lender at closing to offset the high rate. What type of loan is this?
    a. Equity
    b. Participation
    c. Open-end
    d. Buydown

55. A borrower defaulted on his home mortgage loan payments, and the lender obtained a court order to foreclose on the property. At the foreclosure sale, the property sold for $64,000; the unpaid balance on the loan at the time of foreclosure was $78,000. What must the lender do to recover the $14,000 that the borrower still owes?
    a. Sue for specific performance
    b. Sue for damages
    c. Seek a deficiency judgment
    d. Seek a judgment by default

56. The rescission provisions of the Truth-in-Lending Act apply to which of the following transactions?
    a. Home purchase loans
    b. Construction lending
    c. Business financing
    d. Consumer credit

57. The Equal Credit Opportunity Act makes it illegal for lenders to refuse credit to or otherwise discriminate against which of the following applicants?
    a. Parent of twins who receives public assistance and who cannot afford the monthly mortgage payments
    b. New homebuyer who does not have a credit history
    c. Single person who receives public assistance
    d. Unemployed person with no job prospects and no identifiable source of income

58. If a buyer makes a down payment of $18,750, what is the loan-to-value ratio for a property that sold for $128,000 and appraised at $125,000?
    a. 97.7%
    b. 87.7%
    c. 85.0%
    d. 13.0%

59. Sue earns $20,000 per year and can qualify for a monthly PITI payment equal to 25 percent of her monthly salary. If the annual tax and insurance is $678.24, what is the loan amount she will qualify for if the monthly PI payment factor is $10.29 per $1,000 of loan amount?
    a. $35,000
    b. $40,500
    c. $43,000
    d. $66,000

60. On a settlement statement, prorations for real estate taxes paid in arrears are shown as a
    a. credit to the seller and a debit to the buyer.
    b. debit to the seller and a credit to the buyer.
    c. credit to both the seller and the buyer.
    d. debit to both the seller and the buyer.

61. A buyer's earnest money deposit would be entered on the HUD-1 form as a
    a. credit to buyer only.
    b. credit to seller, debit to buyer.
    c. credit to buyer and seller.
    d. debit to buyer only.

62. If a property has encumbrances, it
    a. cannot be sold.
    b. can be sold only if title insurance is provided.
    c. cannot have a deed recorded without a survey.
    d. can still be sold if a buyer agrees to take it subject to the encumbrances.

63. All of the following are violations of the Real Estate Settlement Procedures Act (RESPA) **EXCEPT**
    a. providing a completed HUD-1 Uniform Settlement Statement to a borrower one day before the closing.
    b. accepting a kickback on a loan subject to RESPA requirements.
    c. requiring a particular title insurance company.
    d. accepting a fee or charging for services that were not performed.

64. For a deed to be valid, the
    a. grantor must be legally competent.
    b. signature of the grantor must be witnessed.
    c. deed must be recorded.
    d. grantee must sign the deed.

65. Terrence conveys property to Natalie by delivering a deed. The deed contains two covenants. This is most likely a
    a. general warranty deed.
    b. quitclaim deed.
    c. bargain and sale deed.
    d. special warranty deed.

66. The seller conveyed a quitclaim deed to the buyer. On receipt of the deed, the buyer may be certain that
    a. the seller owned the property.
    b. there are no encumbrances against the property.
    c. the buyer now owns the property subject to certain claims of the seller.
    d. all of the seller's interests in the property at the time of conveyance belong to the buyer.

67. Jacob, a resident of Iowa, plans to retire in Texas and purchased two sections of land in Bailey County, Texas, in 1988. He has not yet moved to Texas, although he has visited the area twice since purchasing the land. In January 1990, the Morris family moved a manufactured home onto the land, drilled a well, and began farming 50 acres. What would be the status of the Morris family's ability to assert a claim for adverse possession?
    a. The adverse possession requirements under the 3-year statute have been met.
    b. The adverse possession requirements under the 5-year statute have been met.
    c. The adverse possession requirements under the 10-year statute have been met.
    d. The adverse possession requirements under the 3-, 5-, and 10-year statutes have been met.

68. Against a recorded deed from the owner of record, the party with the weakest position is a
    a. person with a prior unrecorded deed who is not in possession.
    b. person in possession with a prior unrecorded deed.
    c. tenant in possession with nine months remaining on the lease.
    d. painter who is half-finished painting the house at the time of the sale and who has not yet been paid.

69. A title insurance policy is a guarantee
    a. that the owner's title will be marketable.
    b. that the loan company will be reimbursed for potential losses in the event of mortgage foreclosure.
    c. that the owner will be reimbursed for any losses sustained as a result of defects in the title.
    d. of continued ownership of the property if a title defect is later discovered.

70. A buyer is assuming the balance of a seller's loan. The interest rate is 8 percent and the last monthly payment of $578.16 was paid on April 1, leaving an outstanding balance of $18,450. Compute the interest to be paid by the seller if the sale is to be closed on April 19. Use a banker's year and prorate through the day of closing.
    a. $77.90
    b. $82.00
    c. $110.83
    d. $123.00

71. Dennis's landlord has sold the building in which Dennis lives to the state so that a freeway can be built. Dennis's lease has expired, but the landlord permits him to stay in the apartment until the building is torn down. Dennis continues to pay the rent as prescribed in the lease. What kind of tenancy does Dennis have?
    a. Holdover tenancy
    b. Month-to-month tenancy
    c. Tenancy at sufferance
    d. Tenancy at will

72. Steve and Wally orally enter into a six-month lease. If Wally defaults, which of the following statements is **TRUE**?
    a. Steve may not bring a court action because six-month leases must be in writing under the parol evidence rule.
    b. Steve may not bring a court action because the statute of frauds governs six-month leases.
    c. Steve may bring a court action because six-month leases need not be in writing to be enforceable.
    d. Steve may bring a court action because the statute of limitations does not apply to oral leases, regardless of their term.

73. An apartment manager decides not to purchase flood insurance. Instead, the manager installs raised platforms in the basement storage areas and has the furnace placed on eight-inch legs. This form of risk management is known as
    a. avoiding the risk.
    b. controlling the risk.
    c. retaining the risk.
    d. transferring the risk.

74. An owner sells his fourplex, in which all four units are leased. What is the status of the leases after the sale is closed?
    a. The tenants may void their leases.
    b. The lender may void the leases.
    c. The current leases must be honored by the new landlord.
    d. The current leases may be discharged by the previous landlord.

75. A lease calls for $1,000 per month minimum plus 2 percent of annual sales in excess of $100,000. What is the annual rent if the annual sales were $150,000?
    a. $12,000
    b. $13,000
    c. $14,000
    d. $15,000

Sample Examination—Part Two
Texas State-Specific Law and Regulations

1. The Texas Real Estate Commission is composed of
   a. 9 members—6 broker members and 3 public members.
   b. 9 members—6 public members and 3 broker members.
   c. 9 members—6 appointed by the Governor and 3 appointed by the State Bar.
   d. 12 members—6 appointed by the Governor and 6 appointed by the State Bar.

2. The penalty for a Class A misdemeanor for acting as a real estate broker or salesperson without a license is
   a. $1,000 or six month imprisonment or both.
   b. $2,000 or six month imprisonment or both.
   c. $3,000 or 1 year imprisonment or both.
   d. $4,000 or 1 year imprisonment or both.

3. Under the provisions of the Texas Real Estate License Act, a licensee must inquire about and make disclosures related to whether a
   a. previous or current occupant of a property has or may have AIDS or an HIV-related illness.
   b. death occurred on a property by suicide.
   c. death occurred on a property by natural causes.
   d. death occurred on a property by accident related to the condition of the property.

4. The License Act provisions for the real estate recovery fund allow for the Commission to
   a. collect $25 on each original application for license or registration to deposit into the recovery fund.
   b. assess an additional fee to each broker and salesperson if the recovery fund balance is less than $1 million at the end of any year.
   c. hear consumer complaints against licensees and award settlements from the recovery fund.
   d. make payments from the recovery fund not to exceed $100,000 for claims arising out of one transaction.

5. For which person or entity would a real estate license **NOT** be required?
   a. An auctioneer who both calls the auction and negotiates the contract for

6. Regarding nonresident brokers and business conducted from another state, the Texas Real Estate License Act (TRELA) provides that
   a. all real estate transactions conducted within the state will be regulated by the TRELA, regardless of the location of the real estate.
   b. Texas-licensed brokers may not share commissions with persons licensed as brokers in other states.
   c. Business conducted from another state by mail, telephone, the Internet, e-mail, or other electronic medium is not regulated by the TRELA.
   d. a nonresident licensee must maintain an office within Texas.

7. A Texas-licensed real estate inspector may
   a. establish a fee based on the number of repairs recommended for a subject property.
   b. act as the inspector on a property for which the inspector is also the listing agent.
   c. perform repairs reported as a part of the real estate inspection.
   d. perform environmental testing on a home that has been inspected if licensed or certified to do so.

8. All of the following are requirements for obtaining a Texas broker's license **EXCEPT**
   a. being a resident of Texas for at least 30 days at the time of application.
   b. being of good moral character.
   c. having successfully completed 60 semester hours or 900 clock hours of approved courses.
   d. having been actively engaged as a licensed salesperson for at least two of the three years prior to broker application.

9. The Mandatory Continuing Education (MCE) requirement for licensees who have completed Salesperson Annual Education (SAE) requirements is
   a. six clock hours each year.
   b. eight clock hours each year.
   c. twelve clock hours in each of two years.
   d. fifteen clock hours in each of two years.

10. If a broker applies for inactive status, the broker,
    a. must have given 30 days' notice to any salesperson sponsored by the broker.
    b. may do so up to 30 days after the license renewal date.
    c. must continue to meet MCE education requirements.
    d. will not have to pay annual fees during the inactive period.

11. The Texas Real Estate Commission may suspend or revoke a real estate license for all causes **EXCEPT**
    a. receiving an undisclosed commission from the buyer.
    b. offering real estate for sale through a lottery.
    c. failing to specify a definite termination date in a lease.
    d. placing a sign on real estate without written consent of the owner.

12. Under which circumstance would a licensee be required to use a contract form that has been promulgated by the Texas Real Estate Commission?
    a. A transaction in which the licensee is functioning solely as a principal, not as an agent
    b. A transaction in which the licensee is working with a relocation company
    c. A transaction in which an agency of the government requires a different form
    d. A transaction in which a property owner would prefer to use a form drawn by his or her attorney

13. Which of the following would be considered to be acting in a lawful position as an intermediary?
    a. A broker acting as an appointed licensee for both the buyer and the seller
    b. A broker obtaining verbal permission to act as an intermediary
    c. A broker appointing licensees to each party, calling them to deliver the notice of appointments
    d. A broker communicating with and carrying out the instructions of different principals in one transaction

14. To receive compensation for performing brokerage services in Texas, all the following requirements must be met **EXCEPT**
   a. the person claiming compensation must be licensed as a real estate broker, salesperson or attorney.
   b. there must be a written agreement for compensation, signed by the principal.
   c. there must have been a separate earnest money escrow account established for the transaction.
   d. the real estate agent must have given appropriate title notices to the buyer.

15. Gayle and Sam have just been married. Which property is separate property after the marriage?
   a. Gayle's next paycheck
   b. Gayle's inheritance from her grandmother's estate
   c. Interest income from Sam's savings account
   d. Net rental proceeds from separate real property owned by Sam prior to marriage

16. In Texas, the amount of property protected under homestead laws is
   a. a lot or lots not to exceed 1 acre for an urban homestead.
   b. a lot or lots not to exceed 10 acres for an urban homestead.
   c. one or more parcels not to exceed 10 acres for a rural homestead.
   d. one or more parcels not to exceed 100 acres for a rural homestead.

17. A salesperson who represents the seller is showing a house to a prospective buyer. The salesperson knows that the house has a wet basement. Which of the following is true?
   a. Withholding the information protects the confidence of the seller.
   b. Disclosing the information could create a fiduciary relationship with the buyer.
   c. Withholding the information violates the provisions of the Texas Deceptive Trade Practices—Consumer Protection Act.
   d. Disclosing the information violates the fiduciary duty to the seller.

18. An assumed name certificate would be filed
   a. in the city tax office where the business is located.
   b. in the county clerk's office where the business is located.
   c. with the Texas Secretary of State in Austin.
   d. with the U.S. Treasury Department.

19. In Texas the laws of intestate succession provide that
   a. all community property passes to the surviving spouse if the children of the deceased are also the children of the surviving spouse.
   b. one-half of the community property passes to the surviving spouse and one-half to the children of the deceased.
   c. all separate property of the deceased passes to the surviving spouse.
   d. one-half of the separate property passes to the surviving spouse and one-half is shared equally by all the children of the deceased.

20. Which of the following disclosures is wholly included within the TREC promulgated residential sales contract forms?
   a. The Seller's Disclosure Notice
   b. The Seller's Disclosure of Lead-Based Paint
   c. The statutory notice relating to the bonded indebtedness of a water district
   d. The broker's notice to the buyer to have an abstract examined by the buyer's attorney or to get a title policy

21. Which statement **BEST** reflects the Texas Property Code requirements for smoke detectors in rental property?
   a. Smoke detectors are required in all rental properties, including those under a buyer's temporary lease resulting from a contract of sale.
   b. Smoke detectors must be in working order at the time the tenant takes possession.
   c. Replacement of batteries in a smoke detector is the responsibility of the landlord.
   d. Ensuring that a rental property has a smoke detector is the responsibility of the landlord.

22. The Texas Statute of Frauds provides that
    a. no action can be brought in a Texas court for the recovery of a commission unless the agreement is in writing and signed by the party to be charged.
    b. the signature of one spouse is sufficient to transfer title to community property.
    c. a lease for a term of more than six months must be in writing to be enforceable.
    d. only the tenant is required to sign a lease agreement for it to be enforceable.

23. When a debtor's residence is foreclosed on in Texas,
    a. nonjudicial foreclosure is permitted through the *acceleration clause* in the deed of trust.
    b. the debtor must be given 60 days' notice to cure the default before notice of sale is given.
    c. written notice of the proposed sale must be posted at the county courthouse at least 30 days before the date of sale.
    d. the notice of proposed sale must state at which courthouse entrance the sale will take place.

24. Under the provisions of the Texas recording statutes,
    a. all deeds must be acknowledged and filed of record to be valid.
    b. acknowledgment is not required for a deed to be valid.
    c. filing a document will provide actual notice to parties interested in the title to a property.
    d. possession of a property by the owner will provide actual notice to parties interested in its title.

25. In Texas, a mechanic's lien
    a. is a *general, voluntary lien*, giving security to persons or companies that perform labor or furnish material to improve real property.
    b. is available to owners as a protection against contractors who do not pay subcontractors.
    c. can force sale of homestead property if there was a contract signed by both spouses and acknowledged prior to the time the work was begun or the materials delivered.
    d. can force sale of homestead property, with a statutory right of redemption after the sale.

Glossary of Real Estate Terms

abandonment The voluntary surrender or relinquishment of possession of real property with the intention of terminating one's possession or interest but without the vesting of this interest in any other person, such as when a person moves and abandons leased property before the lease term has expired.

abatement Elimination or reduction of real estate taxes to attract new business to an area.

abstract of title The condensed history of a title to a particular parcel of real estate, consisting of a summary of the original grant and all subsequent conveyances and encumbrances affecting the property and a certification by the abstractor that the history is complete and accurate.

abstract of title with lawyer's opinion An abstract of title that a lawyer has examined and has certified to be, in his or her opinion, an accurate statement of fact.

acceleration clause The clause in a mortgage or trust deed or note that can be enforced to make the entire amount of principal and interest due immediately if the mortgagor defaults on an installment payment or other covenant.

accession Acquiring title to additions or improvements to real property as a result of the annexation of fixtures or the accretion of alluvial deposits along the banks of streams.

accretion The increase or addition of land by the deposit of sand or soil washed up naturally from a river, lake, or sea.

accrued items On a closing statement, items of expense that are incurred but not yet payable, such as interest on a mortgage loan or taxes on real property.

acknowledgment A formal declaration made before a duly authorized officer, usually a notary public, by a person who has signed a document attesting that the instrument was executed by him and that it was his free and voluntary act.

acre A measure of land equal to 43,560 square feet, 4,840 square yards, 4,047 square meters, 160 square rods, or 0.4047 hectare.

actual eviction The result of legal action, originated by a lessor, whereby a defaulted tenant is physically ousted from the rented property pursuant to a court order. *See also* eviction.

actual notice Express information or fact; that which is known; direct knowledge.

adjustable-rate mortgage (ARM) A mortgage loan in which the interest rate may increase or decrease at specified intervals over the life of the loan.

adjusted basis *See* basis.

adjusted sales price For income tax purposes, the actual sales price reduced by allowable sales expenses.

administrator/administratrix A man/woman appointed by a court to settle the estate of a deceased person when there is no will; *contrast with* executor/executrix.

ad valorem tax A tax levied according to value; generally used to refer to real estate tax; also called the *general tax.*

adverse possession The actual, visible, hostile, notorious, exclusive, and continuous possession of another's land under a claim of title. Possession for a statutory period may be a means of acquiring title.

affidavit of title A written statement, made under oath by a seller or grantor of real property and acknowledged by a notary public, in which the grantor (1) identifies himself or herself and indicates marital status, (2) certifies that since the examination of the title on the date of the contract no defects have occurred in the title, and (3) certifies that he or she is in possession of the property (if applicable); not used in Texas.

agency The relationship existing between a principal and an agent who acts for the principal within the specified authority granted by the principal. The principal is entitled to rely on the agent, who places the principal's interests above those of his own.

agency by ratification An agency relationship that is established after the fact.

agent One who acts or has the power to act for another. A fiduciary relationship is created under the *law of agency* when a property owner, as the principal, executes a listing agreement or management contract authorizing a licensed real estate broker to be his or her agent.

air lot A designated airspace over a piece of land. An air lot, like surface property, may be transferred.

air rights The right to use the open space above a property, generally allowing the surface to be used for another purpose.

alienation The act of transferring property to another. Alienation may be voluntary, such as by gift or sale, or involuntary, as through eminent domain or adverse possession.

alienation clause The clause in a mortgage or deed of trust that states that the balance of the secured debt becomes immediately due and payable at the mortgagee's option if the property is sold by the mortgagor. In effect this clause prevents the mortgagor from assigning the debt without the mortgagee's approval; also called a *due-on-sale clause.*

allodial system A system of land ownership in which land is held free and clear of any rent or service due to the government; commonly contrasted to the feudal system. In the United States, land is held under the allodial system.

Americans with Disabilities Act A federal law to eliminate discrimination against individuals with disabilities by mandating equal access to jobs, public accommodations, government services, public transportation, and telecommunications.

amortization A loan in which the principal as well as the interest is payable in monthly or other periodic installments over the term of the loan.

amount realized on sale The amount of gain, or profit, subject to the income tax.

antitrust laws Laws designed to preserve the free enterprise of the open marketplace by making illegal certain private conspiracies and combinations formed to minimize competition. Violations of antitrust laws in the real estate business generally involve *price-fixing* (brokers conspiring to set fixed compensation rates), *allocation of customers or markets* (brokers agreeing to limit their areas of trade or dealing to certain areas or properties), or agreement to boycott competitors.

appointed licensee A licensee associated with and appointed by an intermediary broker to communicate with, carry out instructions of, and provide opinions and advice to the parties to whom the licensee is appointed.

appraisal An estimate of the quantity, quality, or value of something. The process through which conclusions of property value are obtained; also refers to the report that sets forth the process of estimation and conclusion of value.

appraisal review board A group of people who hear appeals concerning assessed valuations for tax purposes and recommend or deny changes in values shown of record.

appraised value An estimate of the present worth of a property.

appreciation An increase in the worth or value of a property due to economic or related causes, which may prove to be either temporary or permanent; opposite of depreciation.

appurtenances Those rights, privileges, and improvements that belong to and pass with the transfer of real property but are not necessarily a part of the property, such as rights-of-way, easements, water rights, and property improvements.

area The size in square units (square inches, etc.) of a two-dimensional figure such as a triangle or rectangle.

ARELLO The Association of Real Estate License Law Officials.

assemblage The combining of two or more adjoining lots into one larger tract to increase their total value.

assessed value The value set upon property for taxation purposes.

assessment The imposition of a tax, charge, or levy, usually according to established rates.

assessment roll The public record of the assessed values of all lands and buildings within a specific area.

assignment The transfer in writing of interest in a bond, mortgage, lease, or other instrument.

assumption of mortgage Acquiring title to property on which there is an existing mortgage and agreeing to be personally liable for the terms and conditions of the mortgage, including payments; *contrast with* subject to mortgage.

attachment 1. The act of taking a person's property into legal custody by writ or other judicial order to hold it available for application to that person's debt to a creditor. 2. A process of converting personal property to real estate.

attorney One who acts for or represents another. Must be licensed as such to give legal advice. No license is required to act under a power of attorney (an attorney-in-fact).

attorney's opinion of title A writing based on a lawyer's reading of an abstract of title that specifies any title defects and names the legal titleholder as the lawyer interprets it; states whether a seller may convey good title.

automatic extension A clause in a listing agreement that states that the agreement will continue automatically for a certain period of time after its expiration date; illegal in Texas.

avulsion The sudden tearing away of land, as by earthquake, flood, volcanic action, or a sudden change in the course of a stream.

balloon payment A final payment of a mortgage loan that is considerably larger than the required periodic payments because the loan amount was not fully amortized.

bargain and sale deed A deed that carries with it no warranties against liens or other encumbrances but that does imply that the grantor has the right to convey title. The grantor may add warranties to the deed at his or her discretion.

base line One of a set of imaginary lines running east and west and crossing a principal meridian at a definite point, used by surveyors for reference in locating and describing land under the rectangular survey (or government survey) system of property description.

basis The financial interest that the Internal Revenue Service attributes to an owner of an investment property for the purpose of determining annual depreciation and gain or loss on the sale of the asset. If a property was acquired by purchase, the owner's basis is the cost of the property, plus the value of any capital expenditures for improvements to the property, minus any depreciation allowable or actually taken. This new basis is called the *adjusted basis.*

bench mark A permanent reference mark or point established for use by surveyors in measuring differences in elevation.

beneficiary 1. The person for whom a trust operates or in whose behalf the income from a trust estate is drawn. 2. A lender who lends money on real estate and takes back a note and trust deed from the borrower.

bequest The transfer of personal property to a legatee in accordance with a will.

bilateral contract *See* contract.

bill of sale A written instrument given to pass title to personal property.

biweekly payment plan A loan that calls for 26 half-month payments a year, resulting in an earlier loan retirement date and lower total interest costs than with a typical fully amortized loan.

blanket mortgage A mortgage covering more than one parcel of real estate, providing for each parcel's partial release from the mortgage lien on repayment of a definite portion of the debt.

blockbusting The illegal practice of inducing homeowners to sell their properties by making representations regarding the entry or prospective entry of minority persons into the neighborhood.

blue-sky laws Common name for state and federal laws that regulate the registration and sale of investment securities.

boot Money or property given to make up any difference in value or equity between two properties in an *exchange.*

branch office A secondary place of business apart from the principal or main office from which real estate business is conducted. A branch office generally must be run by a licensed real estate broker working on behalf of the broker who operates the principal office.

breach of contract Violation of any terms or conditions in a contract without legal excuse; for example, failure to make a payment when it is due.

broker One who buys and sells for another for a commission. *See also* real estate broker.

brokerage For a commission or fee, bringing together parties interested in buying, selling, exchanging, or leasing real property.

broker-salesperson A person who has passed the broker's licensing examination but works on behalf of another licensed broker.

buffer zone Zoning districts that gradually change from a higher-intensity use to a lower-intensity use.

building code An ordinance that specifies minimum standards of construction for buildings to protect public safety and health.

building line A line fixed at a certain distance from the front and/or sides of a lot beyond which no structure can project. *See* setback.

building permit A permission issued by a city for the construction of a building to ensure compliance with building codes.

bundle of legal rights The concept of land ownership that means *ownership of all legal rights to the land*—for example, possession, control within the law, and enjoyment—rather than ownership of the land itself.

business cycle Upward and downward fluctuations in business activity through the stages of expansion, recession, depression, and revival.

business interruption insurance A form of coverage that provides income to a business in the event the premises become untenable.

buydown A cash payment, usually measured in points, to a lender to reduce the interest rate a borrower must pay.

buydown mortgage A mortgage on which a cash payment has been made to the lender to reduce the interest rate a borrower must pay; usually "bought down" for the first two or three years of the loan.

buyer agency An agency relationship between the broker and the buyer, with fiduciary duties owed to the buyer.

buyer representation agreement A contract that establishes a broker-buyer agency relationship.

buyer's broker A licensee who has declared to represent only the buyer in a transaction, regardless of whether compensation is paid by the buyer or the listing broker through a commission split.

Canons of Professional Ethics and Conduct A code of ethics established by the Texas Real Estate Commission and published in its Rules.

capital gain Income earned from the sale of an asset.

capital investment The initial capital and the long-term expenditures made to establish and maintain a business or investment property.

capitalization A mathematical process for estimating the value of an income-producing property by dividing the annual net operating income by the capitalization rate. The formula is expressed as

$$\frac{\text{Income}}{\text{Rate}} = \text{Value}$$

capitalization rate The rate of return a property will produce on the owner's investment.

cash flow The net spendable income from an investment, determined by deducting all operating and fixed expenses from the gross income. If expenses exceed income, a *negative cash flow* is the result.

casualty insurance A type of policy that protects a property owner or other person from loss or injury sustained as a result of theft, vandalism, or similar occurrences.

caveat emptor A Latin phrase meaning "Let the buyer beware."

certificate of sale The document generally given to a purchaser at a tax foreclosure sale. A certificate of sale does not convey title; generally it is an instrument certifying that the holder received title to the property after the redemption period had passed and that the holder paid the property taxes for that interim period.

certificate of title A statement of opinion on the status of the title to a parcel of real property based on an examination of specified public records.

chain of title The succession of conveyances from some accepted starting point, whereby the present holder of real property derives his or her title.

channeling The illegal practice of directing people to, or away from, certain areas or neighborhoods because of minority status. *See also* steering.

chattel Personal property; personalty.

Civil Rights Act of 1866 The first and primary law guaranteeing equal rights to all U.S. citizens; prohibits all discrimination based on race.

client The person who employs an agent to perform a service for a fee.

closing The consummation of a real estate transaction, when the seller delivers title to the buyer in exchange for payment by the buyer of the purchase price.

closing agent The person responsible for conducting the settlement of a real estate sale.

closing statement A detailed cash accounting of a real estate transaction showing all cash received, all charges and credits made, and all cash paid out in the transaction. *See also* HUD -1.

cloud on the title Any document, claim, unreleased lien, or encumbrance that may impair the title to real property or make the title doubtful; usually revealed by a title search and removed by either a quitclaim deed or suit to quiet title.

Code of Ethics An agreement to which all REAL-TORS® must subscribe and that holds the members to high standards of conduct.

codicil A supplement or an addition to a will, executed with the same formalities as a will, that normally does not revoke the entire will.

coinsurance clause A provision in insurance policies covering real property that requires that the policyholder maintain fire insurance coverage generally equal to at least 80 percent of the property's actual replacement cost.

collateral Something of value deposited with a lender as a pledge to secure repayment of a loan.

commingle The illegal act of a real estate broker who mixes the money of other people with his or her own money. By law brokers are required to maintain a separate *trust account* for other parties' funds held temporarily by the broker.

commission Payment to a broker for services rendered such as in the sale or purchase of real property; usually a percentage of the selling price of the property.

common elements Parts of a property that are necessary or convenient to the existence, maintenance, and safety of a condominium or are normally in common use by all of the condominium residents. Each condominium owner has an undivided ownership interest in the general and limited common elements.

common law The body of law based on custom, usage, and court decisions.

community property A system of property ownership based on the theory that each spouse has an equal interest in the property acquired by the efforts of either spouse during marriage.

community property right of survivorship A declaration made by husband and wife that community property will go to the survivor upon the death of one party; eliminates probate.

Community Reinvestment Act The federal law that requires that federally regulated lenders describe the geographic market area they serve. Deposits from that area are to be reinvested in that area whenever practical.

comparables Properties listed in an appraisal report that are substantially equivalent to the subject property and are used to compare and establish a value of the subject property.

competent parties People who are recognized by law as being able to contract with others; usually those of legal age and sound mind.

competitive market analysis (CMA) A comparison of the prices of recently sold homes that are similar to the subject home in terms of location, style, and amenities. Based on this analysis, a broker or salesperson can help the seller determine a listing price.

comprehensive plan A master plan to guide the long-term physical development of a particular area.

computerized loan origination (CLO) A computer network tied into a major lender that allows agents across the country to initiate mortgage loan applications in their own offices.

condemnation A judicial or an administrative proceeding to exercise the power of eminent domain, through which a government agency takes private property for public use and compensates the owner.

condition A contingency, qualification, or occurrence on which an estate or property right is gained or lost.

conditional use permit A grant approved by a zoning ordinance allowing, with conditions, a special use of property that is in the public interest.

condominium The absolute ownership of an apartment or a unit (generally in a multiunit building) based on a legal description of the airspace the unit actually occupies, plus an undivided interest in the ownership of the common elements, which are owned jointly with the other condominium unit owners.

consideration Something of value that induces a person to enter into a contract. Consideration may be "valuable" (money) or "good" (love and affection).

construction loan *See* interim financing.

constructive eviction Actions of the landlord that so materially disturb or impair the tenant's enjoyment of the leased premises that the tenant is effectively forced to move out and terminate the lease without liability for any further rent.

constructive notice Notice given to the world by recorded documents. All people are charged with knowledge of such documents and their contents, whether or not they actually have examined them. Possession of property also is considered constructive notice that the person in possession has an interest in the property.

contents insurance *See* renters' (tenants') insurance.

contract An agreement entered into by two or more legally competent parties by the terms of which one or more of the parties, for a consideration, undertake to do or refrain from doing some legal act or acts. A contract may be either *unilateral*, where only one party is bound to act, or *bilateral*, where all parties to the instrument are legally bound to act as prescribed.

contract for deed A contract for the sale of real estate wherein the purchase price is paid in periodic installments by the purchaser, who is in possession of the property even though title is retained by the seller until final payment. Also called an *installment contract, a land contract, a contract of sale,* or *articles of agreement for warranty deed.*

conventional loan A loan that is not insured by the FHA or guaranteed by the VA.

conveyance Written instrument, such as a deed or lease, that evidences transfer of some ownership interest in real property from one person to another.

cooperative A residential multiunit building whose title is held by a trust or corporation that is owned by and operated for the benefit of persons living within the building, who are the beneficial owners of the trust or stockholders of the corporation, each possessing a proprietary lease.

co-ownership A broad category of ownership by more than one person. Examples are tenants in common and joint tenants.

core real estate course A real estate course included in the statute or approved by the Texas Real Estate Commission as fulfilling part of the core requirements for licensure. Permitted by statute or Rule: Principles of Real Estate, Real Estate Appraisal, Real Estate Law, Real Estate Finance, Real Estate Marketing, Real Estate Mathematics, Real Estate Brokerage, Property Management, Real Estate Investments, Law of Agency, Law of Contracts, Promulgated Contract Forms, and Residential Inspection for Real Estate Agents.

corporation An entity or organization, created by operation of law, whose rights of doing business are essentially the same as those of an individual. The entity has continuous existence until it is dissolved according to legal procedures.

corporeal right A tangible interest in real estate.

cost The capital outlay for land, labor, materials, and profits necessary to bring a property into existence.

cost approach to value An estimate of value based on current construction costs, less depreciation, plus land value. *Contrast with* the income approach to value and the sales comparison approach to value.

cost recovery An Internal Revenue Service term for *depreciation.* An accounting deduction for tax purposes by which a business can recover the cost of personal and some real property over a specified time period. This technique replaces depreciation for property placed in service after 1980. It is essentially the same as depreciation except that costs are recovered without regard to the actual condition or useful life of the property.

counseling The business of providing people with expert advice on a subject, based on the counselor's extensive, expert knowledge of the subject.

counteroffer A new offer made as a reply to an offer received. It has the effect of rejecting the original offer, which cannot be accepted thereafter unless revived by the offeror's repeating it.

covenant A written agreement between two or more parties in which a pledge is made to perform specified acts with regard to property; usually found in such real estate documents as deeds, mortgages, leases, and contracts for deed.

credit On a closing statement, an amount entered in a person's favor—either an amount the party has paid or an amount for which the party must be reimbursed.

curtesy A life estate, usually a fractional interest, given by some states to the surviving husband in real estate owned by his deceased wife. Most states, including Texas, have abolished curtesy.

customer One who purchases or sells property without being represented by an agent.

cycle A recurring sequence of events that regularly follow one another, generally within a fixed interval of time.

datum A horizontal plane from which heights and depths are measured.

debit On a closing statement, an amount charged, that is, an amount that the debited party must pay.

decedent A person who has died.

Deceptive Trade Practices Act (DTPA) Part of the federal Consumer Protection Act originally passed in 1973 and made specifically applicable to real estate in 1975 prohibiting a number of false, misleading, or deceptive acts or practices.

dedication The voluntary transfer of private property by its owner to the public for some public use, such as for streets or schools.

deductible clause A clause in an insurance policy that limits the exposure to loss for an insured homeowner.

deed A written instrument that, when executed and delivered, conveys title to or an interest in real estate.

deed in lieu of foreclosure A deed to a lender given by an owner conveying mortgaged property on which the mortgage is in default.

deed in trust A form of deed by which real estate is conveyed to a trustee.

deed of reconveyance The instrument used to reconvey title to a trustor under a trust deed after the debt has been satisfied.

deed of trust An instrument used to create a mortgage lien by which the mortgagor (trustor) conveys his or her title to a trustee, who holds it as security for the benefit of the lender (beneficiary); also called a *trust deed*.

deed restrictions Clauses in a deed limiting the future uses of the property.

default The nonperformance of a duty, whether arising under a contract or otherwise; failure to meet an obligation when due.

defeasance clause A provision in leases and mortgages that cancels a specified right on the occurrence of a certain condition, such as cancellation of a mortgage on repayment of the mortgage loan.

defeasible fee estate An estate in which the holder has a fee simple title that may be divested on the occurrence or nonoccurrence of a specified event. The two categories of defeasible fee estates are fee simple determinable and fee simple subject to a condition subsequent.

deficiency judgment A personal judgment levied against the mortgagor when a foreclosure sale does not produce sufficient funds to pay the mortgage debt in full.

delinquent taxes Unpaid taxes that are past due.

delivery and acceptance The actual transfer of the deed, or an act of a seller showing intent to make a deed effective, without which there is no transfer of title to the property.

demand The amount of goods people are willing and able to buy at a given price; often coupled with *supply*.

demographics The characteristics of human populations, such as size, growth, density, distribution, and vital statistics.

density zoning Zoning ordinances that restrict the maximum average number of houses per acre that may be built within a particular area, generally a subdivision.

Department of Housing and Urban Development (HUD) Federal agency that administers the Fair Housing Act of 1968.

depreciated cost The value of a property after deducting an allowance for depreciation.

depreciation 1. In appraisal, a loss of value in property due to any cause, including *physical deterioration, functional obsolescence,* and *external obsolescence.* 2. In real estate investment, an expense deduction for tax purposes taken over the period of ownership of income property. *See also* cost recovery.

descent Acquisition of property through inheritance laws when there is no will.

determinable fee estate A fee simple estate in which the property automatically reverts to the grantor upon the occurrence of a specified event or condition.

developer One who converts raw land into a platted subdivision, installs utilities, builds streets, and so forth, and who also may construct buildings on lots and sells them.

devise A gift of real property by will. The donor is the devisor and the recipient is the devisee.

discount points An added loan fee charged by a lender to make the yield on a lower-than-market-value loan competitive with higher-interest-rate loans.

discount rate 1. The interest rate charged member banks that borrow from the Federal Reserve System. 2. The rate used to convert future income into present value.

doctrine of relation back Irrevocable deposit of the executed deed, purchase money, and instructions into escrow pending performance of escrow conditions.

dominant tenement A property that includes in its ownership the appurtenant right to use an easement over another person's property for a specific purpose.

dower The legal right or interest, recognized in some states, that a wife acquires in the property her husband held or acquired during their marriage. During the husband's lifetime the right is only a possibility of an interest; on his death it can become an interest in land. Dower is not recognized in Texas.

duress Unlawful constraint or action exercised on a person whereby the person is forced to perform an act against his or her will. A contract entered into under duress is considered voidable.

earnest money deposit An amount of money, deposited by a prospective buyer as evidence of good faith under the terms of a contract, that is to be forfeited if the buyer defaults but applied to the purchase price if the sale is closed.

easement A right to use the land of another for a specific purpose, such as for a right-of-way or utilities; an incorporeal interest in land.

easement appurtenant An easement that passes with the land on conveyance.

easement by implication An easement that arises when the parties' actions imply that they intend to create an easement.

easement by necessity An easement allowed by law as necessary for the full enjoyment of a parcel of real estate; for example, a right of ingress and egress over a grantor's land.

easement by prescription An easement acquired by continuous, open, uninterrupted, exclusive, and adverse use of the property for the period of time prescribed by state law.

easement in gross An easement that is not created for the benefit of any *land* owned by the owner of the easement but that attaches *personally to the easement owner.* For example, a utility easement.

economic life The period of time during which a structure may reasonably be expected to perform the function for which it was designed or intended.

economic obsolescence *See* external obsolescence.

emblements Growing crops, such as grapes and corn, that are produced annually through labor and industry; deemed to be personal property.

eminent domain The right of a government or municipal quasi-public body to acquire property for public use through a court action called *condemnation,* in which the court decides that the use is a public use and determines the price or compensation to be paid to the owner.

employee Someone who works as a direct employee of an employer and has employee status. The employer is obligated to withhold income taxes and Social Security taxes from the compensation of his or her employees. *See also* independent contractor.

employment contract A document evidencing formal employment between employer and employee or between principal and agent. In the real estate business, this generally takes the form of a listing agreement or management agreement.

enabling acts State legislation that confers certain powers, such as municipal zoning ordinances.

encroachment A building or some portion of it—a wall or fence, for instance—that extends beyond the land of the owner and illegally intrudes on some land of an adjoining owner or a street or alley.

encumbrance Any lien (such as a mortgage, tax, or judgment lien or an easement or a restriction on the use of the land) that may diminish the value of a property; a cloud against clear, free title to property.

endorsement 1. An additional document attached to an original insurance policy that amends the original; a rider. 2. Writing one's name, with or without additional words, on a negotiable instrument.

Equal Credit Opportunity Act A federal law to ensure that funds are available to qualified loan applicants without discrimination on the basis of race, color, religion, sex, national origin, age, marital status, or receipt of public assistance.

equal opportunity in housing A federal code that ensures that all U.S. citizens have access to housing without discrimination.

equitable lien A lien arising out of common law. *See* statutory lien.

equitable right of redemption The right to redeem a property *before* a foreclosure sale by paying the full debt plus interest and accrued charges.

equitable title The interest held by a vendee under a contract for deed or an installment contract; the equitable right to obtain absolute ownership to property when legal title is held in another's name.

equity The interest or value that an owner has in his or her property over and above any mortgage indebtedness.

equity loan A line of credit made against the equity in the borrower's home.

erosion The gradual wearing away of land by water, wind, and general weather conditions; the diminishing of property caused by the elements.

escheat The reversion of property to the state or county, as provided by state law, in the event the property is abandoned or the owner dies without leaving a will and has no heirs to whom the property may pass.

escrow The closing of a transaction through a third party called an *escrow agent,* or *escrowee,* who receives certain funds and documents to be delivered on the performance of certain conditions outlined in the escrow agreement.

escrow agreement A contract, used when a transaction is closed through an escrow, that sets forth the duties of the escrow agent as well as the requirements and obligations of the parties to the transaction.

estate for years A leased interest in property for a certain, exact period of time and for a specified consideration.

estate from period to period *See* periodic estate.

estate in land The degree, quantity, nature, and extent of interest that a person has in real property.

estate taxes Federal taxes on a decedent's real and personal property.

estimate of value An appraisal; the appraised value.

estoppel certificate A document in which a borrower certifies the amount he or she owes on a mortgage loan and the rate of interest.

eviction A legal process to oust a person from possession of real estate. *See* forcible entry and detainer.

evidence of title Proof of ownership of property, commonly a title insurance policy or an abstract of title with lawyer's opinion.

exception As used in the conveyance of real estate, the exclusion of some part of the property conveyed, with the title of that excepted part remaining with the grantor; *contrast with* reservation.

exchange A transaction in which all or part of the consideration is the transfer of like-kind property (such as investment real estate for investment real estate).

exclusive agency A listing contract under which an owner appoints a real estate broker as his or her exclusive agent for a designated period of time to sell a property, on the owner's stated terms, for a commission. The owner reserves the right to sell without paying anyone a commission if he or she sells to a prospect who has not been introduced or claimed by the broker.

exclusive right to sell A listing contract under which an owner appoints a real estate broker as his or her exclusive agent for a designated period of time to sell a property on the owner's stated terms and agrees to pay the broker a commission when the property is sold, whether by the broker, the owner, or another broker.

executed contract A contract in which all parties have fulfilled their promises and thus performed the contract.

execution The signing and delivery of an instrument. Also, a legal order directing an official to enforce a judgment against the property of a debtor.

executor/executrix The man/woman appointed in a will to carry out the requests of the will; *contrast with* administrator/administratrix.

executory contract A contract under which something remains to be done by one or more of the parties.

expenses Short-term costs, such as minor repairs, regular maintenance, and renting costs, that are deducted from an investment property's income.

express agency An agency created by specific agreement, whether written or oral, of principal and agent.

express contract An oral or a written contract in which the parties state the contract's terms and express their intentions in words.

external obsolescence Reduction in property's value caused by factors outside the subject property, such as social or environmental forces; also called *economic* (or *locational*) *obsolescence.*

extraterritorial jurisdiction A one- to five-mile area surrounding an incorporated area over which the municipality has the right of subdivision approval and the potential for annexation.

Fair Housing Act of 1968 A sweeping update of the federal laws to prevent discrimination in housing because of race, color, religion, or national origin, in the selling or renting of homes or apartments and in other specified transactions; amended in 1974 to include sex and in 1988 to include handicap and familial status in the categories covered by the act.

Fannie Mae A privately owned corporation that participates in the secondary market by buying conventional, FHA and VA loans. Formerly the *Federal National Mortgage Association (FNMA).*

Farm Service Agency (FSA) An agency of the United States Department of Agriculture that makes and guarantees loans and provides credit counseling and supervision to farmers and ranchers who are temporarily unable to obtain private, commercial credit.

Federal Agricultural Mortgage Corporation A secondary market for farm real estate loans; known as *Farmer Mac.*

Federal Home Loan Mortgage Corporation (FHLMC). *See* Freddie Mac.

Federal National Mortgage Association (FNMA). *See* Fannie Mae.

federal judgment lien Lien obtained by the United States or an agency, department, commission, board, or other U.S. entity that affects all real and personal property of the judgment debtor.

Federal Reserve System A central banking system designed to manage the nation's economy; "the Fed."

fee simple estate The maximum possible estate or right of ownership of real property, continuing forever. Sometimes called a *fee* or *fee simple absolute.*

fee simple subject to a condition subsequent An estate conveyed "provided that" or "if" it is used for a specific purpose. If it is no longer used for that purpose, it reverts to the original grantor or his heirs by their exercise of the right of reentry.

feudal system A system of ownership usually associated with precolonial England in which the king or other sovereign was the source of all rights. The right to possess real property was granted by the sovereign to an individual as a life estate only. On the death of the individual, title passed back to the sovereign, not to the decedent's heirs.

FHA loan A loan insured by the Federal Housing Administration and made by an approved lender in accordance with FHA regulations.

fiduciary relationship A relationship of trust and confidence, as between trustee and beneficiary, attorney and client, or principal and agent.

financing statement *See* Uniform Commercial Code.

fire and extended coverage insurance A type of policy to protect against fire, hail, windstorm, and other such damage.

first mortgage A mortgage that creates a superior lien on the property mortgaged relative to other charges or encumbrances against same.

fiscal policy The government's policy in regard to taxation and spending programs. The balance between these two areas determines the amount of money the government will withdraw from or feed into the economy, which can counter economic peaks and slumps.

fixture An item of personal property that has been converted to real property by being permanently affixed to the realty.

flexible-payment loan A payment plan in which a mortgagor makes lower monthly payments for the first few years of a loan and larger payments for the remainder of the term.

forcible entry and detainer A court suit initiated by a landlord to evict a tenant from leased premises after the tenant has breached one of the terms of the lease or has held possession of the property after the lease's expiration.

foreclosure A legal procedure whereby property used as security for a debt is sold to satisfy the debt in the event of default in payment of the mortgage note or default of other terms in the mortgage document. The foreclosure procedure brings the rights of all parties to a conclusion and passes the title in the mortgaged property to either the holder of the mortgage or a third party who may purchase the realty at the foreclosure sale, free of all encumbrances affecting the property subsequent to the mortgage.

formal will A written instrument disposing of property on the death of the maker. The testator must be of legal age and sound mind, and not subject to undue influence. The document must be signed and witnessed; also known as a *witnessed will.*

franchise tax A state tax on corporations that permits them to do business in Texas.

fraud A misstatement of a material fact made with intent to deceive or made with reckless disregard of the truth, and that actually does deceive.

Freddie Mac A corporation established to purchase primarily conventional mortgage loans in the secondary mortgage market. Chartered as the *Federal Home Loan Mortgage Corporation (FHLMC).*

freehold estate An estate in land in which ownership is for an indeterminate length of time, in contrast to a leasehold estate.

fully amortized loan A loan in which the principal and interest are payable in monthly or other installments to reduce the loan balance to zero at the end of the loan term.

functional obsolescence A loss of value of an improvement to real estate arising from functional problems, often caused by age or poor design.

future interest A person's present right to an interest in real property that will not result in possession or enjoyment until some time in the future, such as a reversion or right of reentry.

gap A defect in the chain of title of a particular parcel of real estate; a missing document or conveyance that raises doubt as to the present ownership of the land.

general agent One authorized by his or her principal to represent the principal in a broad range of matters, for example, a property manager.

general contractor A construction specialist who enters into a formal construction contract with a landowner or master lessee to construct a real estate building or project. The general contractor often contracts with several subcontractors specializing in various aspects of the building process to perform individual jobs.

general lien The right of a creditor to have all of a debtor's property—both real and personal—sold to satisfy a debt.

general partnership *See* partnership.

general tax *See* ad valorem tax.

general warranty deed *See* warranty deed.

Ginnie Mae A corporation within HUD that participates in the secondary market. It sells mortgage-backed securities that are backed by pools of FHA and VA loans. Chartered as the *Government National Mortgage Association (GNMA)*.

good and indefeasible title Title that cannot be defeated by a superior claim, set aside, or made void.

Government National Mortgage Association (GNMA) *See* Ginnie Mae.

government survey system *See* rectangular survey system.

graduated-payment method A payment plan that allows a mortgagor to make lower monthly payments for the first few years of the loan; usually based on an artificially low payment schedule, resulting in negative amortization or deferred interest.

grantee A person who receives a conveyance of real property from the grantor.

granting clause Words in a deed of conveyance that state the grantor's intention to convey the property at the present time. This clause generally is worded as "convey and warrant," "grant," "grant, bargain and sell," or the like.

grantor The person transferring title to or an interest in real property to a grantee.

gross income multiplier The ratio used to convert annual income into market value in appraising industrial and commercial properties.

gross lease A lease of property under which a landlord pays all property charges regularly incurred through ownership, such as repairs, taxes, insurance, and operating expenses. Most residential leases are gross leases.

gross rent multiplier A figure used as a multiplier of the gross monthly rental income of a property to produce an estimate of the property's value.

ground lease A lease of land only, on which the tenant usually owns a building or is required to build his or her own building as specified in the lease. Such leases are usually long-term net leases; the tenant's rights and obligations continue until the lease expires or is terminated through default.

groundwater rights Water under the earth's surface below the saturation point and used by a property owner through the rule of capture.

habendum clause That part of a deed beginning with the words "to have and to hold," following the granting clause and defining the extent of ownership the grantor is conveying.

hereditaments Every kind of inheritable property, including real, personal, corporeal, and incorporeal property.

heir One who might inherit or succeed to an interest in land under the state law of descent when the owner dies without leaving a valid will.

heterogeneity *See* nonhomogeneity.

highest and best use That possible use of land that would produce the greatest return and thereby develop the highest land value. The optimum use of a site, as used in appraisal.

holdover tenancy A tenancy whereby a lessee retains possession of leased property after his or her lease has expired and the landlord, by continuing to accept rent, agrees to the tenant's continued occupancy, as defined by state law.

holographic will A will that is written, dated, and signed in the testator's handwriting but is not witnessed.

Home Mortgage Disclosure Act A federal law that prevents "redlining" or denial of funds to certain areas; requires that public notices be posted by housing lenders.

homeowner's insurance policy A standardized package insurance policy that covers a residential real estate owner against financial loss from fire, theft, public liability, and other common risks.

homestead Land that is owned and occupied as the family home. In Texas, a portion of the area or value of this land is protected or exempt from forced sale by creditors for judgments for debts with several exceptions.

HUD-1 *See* Uniform Settlement Statement.

hypothecation The pledge of specific real or personal property as security for an obligation without surrendering possession of it.

implied agency An agency created by acts or words of principal and agent; an agency inferred by circumstances.

implied contract A contract under which the agreement of the parties is demonstrated by their acts and conduct.

improvement 1. An improvement *on* land is any structure, usually privately owned, erected on a site to enhance the value of the property; for example, buildings, fences, and driveways. 2. An improvement *to* land is usually a publicly owned structure, such as a curb, sidewalk, street, or sewer.

income approach The process of estimating the value of an income-producing property by capitalization of the annual net income expected to be produced by the property during its remaining useful life.

incorporeal right A nonpossessory right in real estate, for example, an easement or right-of-way.

independent contractor Someone retained to perform a certain act but who is subject to the control and direction of another only as to the end result and not as to the way in which he or she performs the act. Unlike an employee, an independent contractor pays for all his or her expenses and Social Security and income taxes and receives no employee benefits. Most real estate salespeople are independent contractors.

infant A person who has not reached the legal age of majority; a minor.

inflation An increase in the volume of money and credit relative to available goods resulting in a substantial and continuing rise in the general price level.

inheritance taxes State-imposed taxes on a decedent's real and personal property.

inspector *See* real estate inspector.

installment contract *See* contract for deed.

installment sale A transaction in which the sales price is paid in two or more installments over two or more years. If the sale meets certain requirements, a taxpayer can postpone reporting such income to future years by paying tax each year only on the proceeds received that year.

insurable title A title that a title company will insure.

interest 1. A charge made by a lender for the use of money. 2. The type and extent of ownership in property.

interim financing A short-term loan usually made during the construction phase of a building project (in this case, often referred to as a *construction loan*).

intermediary broker A broker who is employed to negotiate a transaction between both parties and who for that purpose may be an agent of both parties to the transaction, acting fairly so as not to favor one party over the other.

Internal Revenue Service tax lien A general lien imposed by the IRS for the nonpayment of income taxes.

Interstate Land Sales Full Disclosure Act A federal law requiring that a property report be furnished to prospective buyers of certain types of real estate.

intestate The condition of a property owner who dies without leaving a valid will. Title to the property will pass to his or her heirs as provided in the state law of descent.

intimidation As defined in the fair housing laws, the illegal act of coercing, threatening, or interfering with a person for exercising or enjoying any right granted or protected by federal, state, or local fair housing laws.

intrinsic value An appraisal term meaning the result of a person's individual choices and preferences.

investment Money directed toward the purchase, improvement, and development of an asset in expectation of income or profits.

involuntary alienation *See* alienation.

involuntary lien A lien that arises by the action of another, such as a judgment lien.

joint tenancy Ownership of real estate between two or more parties who have been named in one conveyance as joint tenants. Upon the death of one joint tenant, his or her interest passes to the surviving joint tenant or tenants by the *right of survivorship*. Not automatically created in Texas.

joint venture The joining of two or more people to conduct a specific business enterprise. A joint venture is similar to a partnership in that it must be created by agreement between the parties to share in the losses and profits of the venture. It is *unlike* a partnership in that the venture is for one specific project only, rather than for a continuing business relationship.

judgment The formal decision of a court on the respective rights and claims of the parties to an action or suit. After a judgment has been entered and recorded with the county recorder, it usually becomes a general lien on the property of the defendant.

junior lien An obligation, such as a second mortgage, that is subordinate in right or lien priority to an existing lien on the same realty.

laches An equitable doctrine used by courts to bar a legal claim or prevent the assertion of a right because of undue delay or failure to assert the claim or right.

land The earth's surface, extending downward to the center of the earth and upward infinitely into space.

land contract *See* contract for deed.

last will and testament *See* will.

latent defect A hidden structural defect presumably resulting from faulty construction, known to the seller but not to the purchaser and not readily discoverable by inspection.

law of agency *See* agent.

league In Texas, a tract of land that was granted to a settler by the Mexican government; a league consists of 6.919 square miles.

lease A written or oral contract between a landlord (the lessor) and a tenant (the lessee) that transfers the right to exclusive possession and use of the landlord's real property to the lessee for a specified period of time and for a stated consideration (rent). By state law, leases for longer than one year must be in writing to be enforceable.

leasehold estate A tenant's right to occupy real estate during the term of a lease; generally considered to be a personal property interest.

legacy A disposition of money or personal property by will.

legal description A description of a specific parcel of real estate complete enough for an independent surveyor to locate and identify it.

legality of object An essential component of a valid contract; a contract must be for a legal purpose and in compliance with public policy.

lessee *See* lease.

less favorable treatment Any time a person is treated differently on the basis of race, sex, religion, color, national origin, handicap, or familial status, either by act or inaction, in the selling or leasing of real property it is a violation of the fair housing laws. Also known as *unequal treatment* or *different treatment*.

lessor *See* lease.

leverage The use of borrowed money to finance the bulk of an investment and to magnify the rate of return.

levy 1. To assess; to levy a tax is to assess a property and set the rate of taxation. 2. To seize or collect; to levy an execution is to officially seize an owner's property to satisfy an obligation.

liability coverage Insurance that protects against risks that could render the property owner responsible for certain damages to the property or persons of others.

license 1. A privilege or right granted to a person by a state to operate as a real estate broker or salesperson. 2. The revocable permission for a temporary use of land—a personal right that cannot be sold.

lien A right given by law to certain creditors to have debts paid out of the property of a defaulting debtor, usually by means of a court sale.

lien theory Some states' interpretation of a mortgage as being purely a lien on real property. The mortgagee thus has no right of possession but must foreclose the lien and sell the property if the mortgagor defaults. Texas is a lien theory state.

life estate An interest in real or personal property that is limited in duration to the lifetime of its owner or some other designated person.

life tenant A person in possession of a life estate.

like-kind property *See* exchange.

limited liability company A business organization in which a member or manager is not generally held liable for debts, obligations, or liabilities of the company.

limited partnership *See* partnership.

linear measure A measurement made on a line. The linear measure of a 4-foot square is 16 feet; also called *lineal measure.*

liquidity The ability to sell an asset and convert it into cash at a price close to its true value in a short period of time.

lis pendens A recorded legal document giving constructive notice that an action affecting a particular property has been filed in either a state or a federal court.

listing agreement A contract between a landowner (as principal) and a licensed real estate broker (as agent) by which the broker is employed to sell real estate on the owner's terms within a given time, for which service the landowner agrees to pay a commission.

listing broker The broker in a multiple-listing situation from whose office a listing agreement is initiated, as opposed to the *selling broker,* from whose office negotiations leading up to a sale are initiated. The listing broker and the selling broker may be the same person if disclosed to all parties. *See also* multiple listing.

littoral rights 1. A landowner's claim to use water in large navigable lakes and oceans that are adjacent to his or her property. 2. The ownership rights to land bordering these bodies of water up to the high-water mark.

loan discount *See* discount points.

loan origination fee The finance fee charged by a lender, in addition to interest, for services in connection with granting a loan; usually a percentage of the face amount of the loan.

locational obsolescence *See* external obsolescence.

loss The difference between the purchase price and the selling price of a property if the purchase price exceeded the selling price.

lot-and-block description A description of real property that identifies a parcel of land by reference to lot and block numbers within a subdivision, as specified on a plat of subdivision duly recorded in the county recorder's office.

management agreement A contract between the owner of income property and a management firm or an individual property manager that outlines the scope of the manager's authority to manage the property.

Mandatory Continuing Education (MCE) A requirement for most brokers and all salespersons to complete 15 classroom hours of education once every two years in order to renew a real estate license; becomes effective after the completion of salesperson annual education (SAE) requirements are met.

market A place where goods can be bought and sold and a price established.

marketable title Good or clear title, reasonably free from the risk of litigation over possible defects.

market data approach to value *See* sales comparison approach.

market price The actual selling price of a property.

market value The highest price a ready, willing, and able buyer would pay and the lowest price a ready, willing, and able seller would accept, neither being under any pressure to act.

mechanic's lien A statutory lien created in favor of contractors, laborers, materialmen, and others (including architects, engineers, or surveyors) who have performed work or furnished materials in the erection or repair of a building.

metes-and-bounds description A legal description of a parcel of land that begins at a well-marked point and follows the boundaries, using direction and distances around the tract back to the place of beginning. *See also* point (place) of beginning.

minority As defined in the Civil Rights Act of 1968 as part of the Fair Housing Law, "'minority' means any group, or any member of a group, that can be identified either: (1) by race, color, religion, sex, or national origin; or (2) by any other characteristic on the basis of which discrimination is prohibited by a federal, state, or local fair housing law." (As of 1988, includes handicap and familial status.)

misrepresentation A false statement, or concealment, of material fact with the intention of inducing action of another.

monetary policy Governmental regulation of the amount of money in circulation through such institutions as the Federal Reserve Board.

money judgment A court judgment ordering payment of money rather than specific performance of a certain action. *See also* judgment.

month-to-month tenancy A periodic tenancy under which the tenant rents for one month at a time. In the absence of a rental agreement (oral or written), a tenancy is generally considered to be month to month.

monument A fixed natural or artificial object used to establish real estate boundaries for a metes-and-bounds description.

mortgage A conditional transfer or pledge of real estate as security for the payment of a debt. Also, the document creating a mortgage lien.

mortgage-backed securities Securities that are secured by pools of mortgages and are used to channel funds from securities markets to housing markets; Fannie Mae, Freddie Mac, and Ginnie Mae have mortgage-backed securities programs.

mortgage banker A person or firm that originates, sells, and then services mortgage loans; *contrast with* mortgage broker.

mortgage broker A person who, for a fee, brings borrowers and lenders together but does not service the loans that have been arranged; contrast with mortgage banker.

mortgage (purchase-money) lien A lien or charge on the property of a mortgagor that secures the underlying debt obligations.

mortgagee A lender in a mortgage loan transaction.

mortgagor A borrower who conveys his or her property as security for a loan.

multiperil policies A type of insurance that packages several types of coverage into one policy.

multiple listing An exclusive listing (generally an exclusive right to sell) with the additional authority and obligation on the part of the listing broker to distribute the listing to other brokers in a *multiple-listing service*. Not a separate type of listing.

municipal utility district A defined geographic area created by a developer that levies taxes to pay for providing water and sewer utilities to its inhabitants (usually outside a municipality).

National Association of REALTORS® (NAR) The largest real estate professional organization in the world, representing all branches of the real estate industry. Active members are allowed to use the trademark REALTOR®.

negative cash flow *See* cash flow.

negotiable instrument A written instrument, such as a note, that may be transferred by endorsement or delivery. The holder, or payee, may sign the instrument over to another person or, in certain cases, merely deliver it to him or her. The transferee then has the original payee's right to payment.

net lease A lease requiring that the tenant pay not only rent but also all costs incurred in maintaining the property, including taxes, insurance, utilities, and repairs.

net listing A listing based on the net price the seller will receive if the property is sold. Under a net listing, the broker is free to offer the property for sale at the highest price he or she can get in order to increase the commission. This type of listing is outlawed in many states; it is not recommended in Texas.

nonconforming use A use of property that is permitted to continue after a zoning ordinance prohibiting it has been established for the area.

nonhomogeneity A lack of uniformity; dissimilarity. Because no two parcels of land are exactly alike, real estate is said to be *nonhomogeneous;* also known as *heterogeneity.*

nonresident licensee A resident broker of another state also licensed in Texas but not a Texas resident.

note An instrument of credit attesting to a debt and promising to pay.

novation Substituting a new obligation for an old one or substituting new parties to an existing obligation, as when the parties to an agreement accept a new debtor in place of the former one.

nuncupative will An oral will declared by the testator in his or her final illness, made before witnesses and afterward reduced to writing.

objective value The actual value measured in dollars of an aspect of construction or location.

offer and acceptance Two essential components of a valid contract; a "meeting of the minds."

open-end mortgage A mortgage loan that is expandable by increments up to a maximum dollar amount, the full loan being secured by the same original mortgage.

open listing A listing contract under which the broker's commission is contingent on the broker's producing a ready, willing, and able buyer before the property is sold by the seller or another broker.

open market An economic model that allows the price of a commodity to respond freely to the forces of supply and demand.

option The right to purchase property within a definite time at a specified price. There is no obligation to purchase, but the seller is obligated to sell if the option holder exercises the right to purchase.

origination fee *See* loan origination fee.

ostensible agency A form of implied agency relationship created by the actions of the parties involved rather than by written agreement or document.

owelty The difference paid or secured by one cotenant to another for the purpose of equalizing a partition of assets.

package mortgage A method of financing in which the loan that finances the purchase of a home also finances the purchase of certain items of personal property such as a washer, dryer, refrigerator, stove, and other specified appliances.

panic peddling The illegal practice of inducing panic selling in a neighborhood by making representations of the entry, or prospective entry, of members of a minority group; also called *blockbusting.*

parcel A specific portion of a large tract of real estate; a lot.

partition The division of cotenants' interests in real property when the parties do not agree to terminate the co-ownership voluntarily; takes place through court procedures.

partnership An association of two or more individuals who carry on a continuing business for profit as co-owners. In a *general partnership* each general partner shares in the administration, profits, and losses of the operation. A *limited partnership* is a business arrangement whereby the operation is administered by one or more general partners and funded, by and large, by limited or silent partners, who are by law responsible for losses only to the extent of their investments. A *limited liability partnership* limits an individual partner's liability arising from negligence on the part of another partner.

party wall A wall that is located on or at a boundary line between two adjoining parcels of land and is used or is intended to be used by the owners of both properties.

patent A grant or franchise of land from the U.S. government.

percent By the hundred.

percentage lease A lease, commonly used for commercial property, whose rental is based on the tenant's gross sales at the premises; it generally stipulates a base monthly rental plus a percentage of any gross sales above a certain amount.

periodic estate An interest in leased property that continues from period to period—week to week, month to month, or year to year.

personal property Items, called *chattels*, that do not fit into the definition of real property; movable objects; personalty.

personalty Items of personal property, chattel.

physical deterioration A reduction in a property's value resulting from a decline in physical condition; can be caused by action of the elements or by ordinary wear and tear.

PITI Principal, interest, taxes, and insurance.

planned unit development A planned combination of diverse land uses, such as housing, recreation, and shopping, in one contained development or subdivision.

plat A map of a town, section, or subdivision indicating the location and boundaries of individual properties.

plottage value The increase in value or utility resulting from the consolidation (*assemblage*) of two or more adjacent lots into one larger lot.

point A unit of measurement used for various loan charges; one point equals 1 percent of the amount of the loan. *See also* discount points.

point (place) of beginning In a metes-and-bounds legal description, the starting point of the survey, situated in one corner of the parcel; all *metes-and-bounds descriptions* must follow the boundaries of the parcel back to the point of beginning.

police power The government's right to impose laws, statutes, and ordinances, including zoning ordinances and building codes, to protect the public health, safety, and welfare.

power of attorney A written instrument authorizing a person, the *attorney-in-fact,* to act as agent on behalf of another person to the extent indicated in the instrument.

power-of-sale clause A provision in a deed of trust authorizing the trustee to sell a property in the event of the borrower's default.

precedent In law, the requirements established by prior court decisions.

prepaid item Item on a closing statement that has been paid in advance by the seller, such as insurance premiums, for which he or she must be reimbursed by the buyer.

prepayment penalty A charge imposed on a borrower who pays off the loan principal early. This penalty compensates the lender for interest and other charges that otherwise are lost.

price The amount of money paid for an item.

price-fixing *See* antitrust laws.

primary mortgage market *See* secondary mortgage market.

prime rate The interest or discount rate charged by a commercial bank to its largest and strongest customers.

principal 1. A sum lent or employed as a fund or investment, as distinguished from its income or profits. 2. The amount of the note due and payable. 3. A main party to a transaction—the person for whom the agent works.

principal meridian One of 35 north and south survey lines established and defined as part of the rectangular survey (government survey) system.

principle of conformity An appraisal principle holding that the maximum value is realized when a reasonable degree of homogeneity (sameness) exists in a neighborhood.

prior appropriation A concept of water ownership in which the landowner's right to use available water is based on a government-administered permit system.

priority The order of position of time. The priority of liens generally is determined by the chronological order in which the lien documents are recorded. Tax liens, however, have priority even over previously recorded liens.

private mortgage insurance (PMI) Default insurance on conventional loans, normally insuring the top 20 percent to 25 percent of the loan and not the whole loan.

probate A legal process by which a court determines who will inherit a decedent's property and what the estate's assets are; literally means "to prove."

procuring cause The effort that brings about the desired result. Under an open listing, the broker who is the procuring cause of the sale receives the commission.

profit The increase in value when the selling price exceeds the purchase price.

promissory note An unconditional written promise of one person to pay a certain sum of money to another at a future specified time.

promulgated contracts Various standard contracts prepared and authorized by the Texas Real Estate Commission that must be used by all licensees when acting as agents in real estate transactions, with limited specific exceptions.

property manager Someone who manages real estate for another person for compensation.

Duties include collecting rents, maintaining the property, and keeping up all accounting.

prorate To divide or distribute expenses, either prepaid or paid in arrears, between buyer and seller at the closing (such as taxes, interest, and rents).

public ownership Ownership of land by a government entity.

puffing Exaggerated or superlative comments or opinions not made as representations of fact and thus not grounds for misrepresentation.

pur autre vie For the life of another. A *life estate pur autre vie* is a life estate that is measured by the life of a person other than the grantee.

purchase-money mortgage A note secured by a mortgage or trust deed given by a buyer, as mortgagor, to a seller, as mortgagee, as part of the purchase price of the real estate.

pyramiding A process of acquiring additional properties through refinancing properties already owned and then reinvesting the loan proceeds in additional property.

quiet title suit *See* suit to quiet title.

quitclaim deed A conveyance by which the grantor transfers whatever interest he or she has in the real estate, without warranties or obligations.

range A strip of land six miles wide, extending north and south, and numbered east and west according to its distance from the principal meridian in the rectangular (government) survey system of land description.

ready, willing, and able buyer One who is prepared to buy property on the seller's terms and is ready to take positive steps to consummate the transaction.

real estate Land; a portion of the earth's surface extending downward to the center of the earth and upward infinitely into space, including all things permanently attached thereto, whether by nature or by a person; any and every interest in land.

real estate broker Any person or corporation who sells (or offers to sell), buys (or offers to buy), or negotiates the purchase, sale, or exchange of real estate or who leases (or offers to lease) or rents (or offers to rent) any real estate or the improvements thereon for others and for a compensation or valuable consideration. A real estate broker may not conduct business without a real estate broker's license.

Real Estate Center A real estate research center located at Texas A&M University; broker and salesperson licensees pay fees to the Center

with each renewal. Also known as the *Texas Real Estate Research Center.*

real estate inspector A person who accepts employment for the purpose of performing a real property inspection for a buyer or seller.

real estate investment syndicate *See* syndicate.

real estate investment trust (REIT) Trust ownership of real estate by a group of at least 100 individuals who purchase certificates of ownership in the trust, which in turn invests the money in real property and distributes the profits back to the investors free of corporate income tax.

real estate license law State laws enacted to protect the public from fraud, dishonesty, and incompetence in the purchase and sale of real estate.

real estate mortgage investment conduit (REMIC) A tax device that allows cash flows from an underlying block of mortgages to be passed through to security holders without being subject to income taxes at the level of trustee or agent.

real estate recovery fund A fund established by Texas law to reimburse persons damaged by the actions of a broker or salesperson.

real property The earth's surface extending downward to the center of the earth and upward into space, including all things permanently attached to it by nature or by people, as well as the interests, benefits, and rights inherent in real estate ownership.

Realtist A person who is a member of the National Association of Real Estate Boards.

REALTOR® A registered trademark term reserved for the sole use of active members of local associations affiliated with the National Association of REALTORS®.

reconciliation The final step in the appraisal process, in which the appraiser weighs the estimates of value received from the sales comparison, cost, and income approaches to arrive at a final estimate of market value for the subject property.

recorded plat A subdivision map filed in the county recorder's office that shows the location and boundaries (lot and block number) of individual parcels of land; *contrast with* rectangular survey system *and with* metes-and-bounds description.

recording The act of entering documents affecting or conveying interests in real estate in the recorder's office established in each county. Until it is recorded, a deed or mortgage generally is not effective against subsequent purchasers or mortgages.

recovery fund A fund established from real estate license revenues to cover claims of aggrieved parties who have suffered monetary damage through the illegal actions of a real estate or property inspection licensee.

rectangular survey system A system established in 1785 by the federal government providing for surveying and describing land by reference to principal meridians and base lines. Also called the *government survey system.*

redemption Buying back real estate sold in a tax sale. The defaulted owner is said to have the right of redemption. Also applies to certain rights of defaulted owners after a foreclosure sale.

redemption period A period established by state law during which a property owner has the right to redeem his or her real estate from a foreclosure or tax sale by paying the sales price, interest, and costs. Texas law does not permit redemption after a deed of trust foreclosure.

redlining The illegal practice of a lending institution's denying loans or restricting their number for certain areas of a community.

Regulation Z Law requiring credit institutions to inform borrowers of the true cost of obtaining credit; commonly called the *Truth-in-Lending Act.*

release deed A document that transfers all rights given a trustee under a trust deed loan back to the grantor after the loan has been fully repaid; also known as a *deed of reconveyance.*

release of lien An instrument indicating that a previously existing lien has been released and is no longer enforceable.

remainder interest The future interest in an estate that takes effect after the termination of another estate, such as a life estate; what is left at the termination of a life estate.

rent A fixed, periodic payment made by a tenant of a property to the owner for possession and use, usually by prior agreement of the parties.

renters' insurance The type of insurance that covers the personal property and household goods of renters or condominium owners but does not cover the structure.

rent schedule A statement of proposed rental rates, determined by the owner or the property manager or both, based on a building's estimated expenses, market supply and demand, and the owner's long-range goals for the property.

replacement cost The construction cost at current prices of a property that is not necessarily an exact duplicate of the subject property but serves the same purpose or function as the original.

reproduction cost The construction cost at current prices of an exact duplicate of the subject property.

reservation Something retained by the seller; for example, minerals or life estate.

residential rental locator A person, other than the owner of the property or an on-site manager, who offers, for consideration, to locate a unit in an apartment complex for lease to a prospective tenant.

RESPA The Real Estate Settlement Procedures Act.

restriction A limitation on the use of real property, generally originated by the owner or subdivider in a deed. *See also* deed restrictions.

reverse annuity mortgage A form of mortgage that enables homeowners age 62 and older to borrow against the equity in their homes, receiving monthly payments to help meet living costs.

reversion The remnant of an estate that the grantor holds after he or she has granted a life estate to another person—the estate will return, or revert, to the grantor; also called a *reverter.*

reversionary interest *See* reversion.

reversionary right An owner's right to regain possession of leased property on termination of the lease agreement.

revocation Termination of licensure privileges for cause.

rider *See* endorsement.

right of survivorship *See* joint tenancy.

right-of-way The right or privilege, acquired through accepted usage or contract, to pass over a designated portion of the property of another.

riparian rights An owner's rights in land that borders on or includes a stream, river, or lake. These rights include access to and use of the water for domestic purposes.

risk management Evaluation and selection of appropriate property and other insurance.

rules and regulations As used in this text, those actions taken by the Texas Real Estate Commission that have the net effect of law on licensees. These rules interpret the license act.

sale and leaseback A transaction in which an owner sells his or her improved property and, as part of the same transaction, signs a long-term lease to remain in possession of the premises.

sales comparison approach The process of estimating the value of a property by examining and comparing actual sales of comparable properties.

sales contract A contract containing the complete terms of the agreement between buyer and seller for the sale of a particular parcel or parcels of real estate.

salesperson A person who performs real estate activities while employed by or associated with a licensed real estate broker.

salesperson annual education (SAE) A requirement for education beyond that needed to obtain a real estate salesperson license; 6 semester hours or 90 classroom hours within the first three years of licensure.

satisfaction of mortgage A document acknowledging the payment of a debt.

secondary mortgage market A market for the purchase and sale of existing mortgages, designed to provide greater liquidity for mortgages; also called the *secondary money market*. Mortgages are first originated in the *primary mortgage market*.

section A portion of a township under the rectangular survey (government survey) system. A township is divided into 36 sections, numbered 1 to 36. A section is a square with mile-long sides and an area of one square mile, or 640 acres.

security agreement *See* Uniform Commercial Code.

security deposit A payment by a tenant, held by the landlord during the lease term and kept (wholly or partially) on default or destruction of the premises by the tenant.

seller's broker A real estate broker, also called the *listing broker*, who is employed by and represents only the seller in a real estate transaction. Not to be confused with the *selling broker*.

Seller's Disclosure Notice A notice required of most sellers of real property; must state latent structural defects or any other known structural defects.

selling broker The broker working with or representing a buyer in the purchase of a listed property.

separate property Under community property law, property owned solely by either spouse before the marriage, or acquired by gift or inheritance during the marriage, or purchased with separate funds during the marriage, or separated by written agreement during the marriage.

servient tenement Land on which an easement exists in favor of an adjacent property (called the *dominant tenement*); also called *servient estate*.

setback The amount of space local zoning regulations require between a lot line and a building line.

severalty Ownership of real property by one person or one legal entity only; also called *sole ownership*.

severance Changing an item of real estate to personal property by detaching it from the land; for example, cutting down a tree.

shared-appreciation mortgage A mortgage loan in which the lender, in exchange for a loan with a favorable interest rate, participates in the profits (if any) the mortgagor receives when the property is eventually sold.

situs The personal preference of people for one area over another, not necessarily based on objective facts and knowledge.

sole ownership *See* severalty.

special agent One authorized by a principal to perform a single act or transaction; a real estate broker is usually a special agent for a seller, authorized to find a ready, willing, and able buyer for a particular property.

special assessment A tax or levy customarily imposed against only those specific parcels of real estate that will benefit from a proposed public improvement like a street or sewer.

special warranty deed A deed in which the grantor warrants, or guarantees, the title only against defects arising during the period of his or her tenure and ownership of the property and not against defects existing before that time, generally using the language, "by, through or under the grantor but not otherwise."

specific lien A lien affecting or attaching only to a certain, specific parcel of land or piece of property.

specific performance A legal action brought in a court of equity in special cases to compel a party to carry out the terms of a contract. The basis for an equity court's jurisdiction in breach of a real estate contract is the fact that land is unique and therefore mere legal damages would not adequately compensate the buyer for the seller's breach.

spot zoning A change in a local zoning ordinance to permit a particular use that is inconsistent with the area's zoning classification. Spot zoning is not favored in the law.

statute of frauds That part of state law that requires certain instruments, such as deeds, real estate sales contracts, and certain leases, to be in writing to be legally enforceable.

statute of limitations That law pertaining to the period of time within which certain actions must be brought to court.

statutory lien A lien imposed on property by statute—a tax lien, for example—in contrast to an equitable lien, which arises out of common law.

statutory right of redemption The right of a defaulted property owner to recover the property after its sale by paying the appropriate fees and charges; available in Texas for tax foreclosures and homeowner's association assessment liens; not available for a deed of trust foreclosure.

statutory year A year composed of 12 months, each with 30 days, for a total of 360 days in a statutory year. Also known as a *banker's year; contrast with* a calendar year, which has 365 days, or 366 in a leap year.

steering The illegal practice of channeling home seekers to particular areas, either to maintain the homogeneity of an area or to change the character of an area to create a speculative situation. *See also* channeling.

straight-line method A method of calculating depreciation for tax purposes, computed by dividing the adjusted basis of a property by the estimated number of years of remaining useful life.

straight (term) loan A loan in which only interest is paid during the term of the loan, with the entire principal amount due with the final interest payment.

subagent A licensee who represents a principal through cooperation with and consent of a broker representing the principal and who is not sponsored by or associated with the principal's broker.

subcontractor *See* general contractor.

subdivider One who buys undeveloped land; divides it into smaller, usable lots; and sells the lots to potential users (often *developers*).

subdivision A tract of land divided by the owner, known as the *subdivider,* into blocks, building lots, and streets according to a recorded subdivision plat, which must comply with local ordinances and regulations.

subjective value The perceived value of an item based on the relative benefits expected to be derived from its use.

"subject to" clause A provision in a deed specifying exceptions and reservations affecting the title.

subject to mortgage The buyer of an already mortgaged property makes the payments but does not take personal responsibility for the loan.

Should the mortgage be foreclosed and the property sold for a lesser amount than is owed, the grantee-buyer is not personally liable for the deficiency, but the grantor-seller is; *contrast with* assumption of mortgage.

sublease The leasing of premises by a lessee to a third party for part of the lessee's remaining term. *See also* assignment.

subordination Relegation to a lesser position, usually in respect to a right or security.

subordination agreement A written agreement between holders of liens on a property that changes the priority of mortgage, judgment, and other liens under certain circumstances.

subpoena A legal process ordering a witness to appear and give testimony or to present documents under penalty of law. TREC has subpoena powers.

subrogation The substitution of one creditor for another, with the substituted person succeeding to the legal rights and claims of the original claimant. Subrogation is used by title insurers to acquire from the injured party rights to sue to recover any claims they have paid.

substitution An appraisal principle that states that the maximum value of a property tends to be set by the cost of purchasing an equally desirable and valuable substitute property, assuming that no costly delay is encountered in making the substitution.

subsurface rights Ownership rights in a parcel of real estate to the water, minerals, gas, oil, and so forth that lie beneath the surface of the property.

suit for possession *See* forcible entry and detainer.

suit to quiet title A court action intended to establish or settle the title to a particular property, especially when a cloud on the title exists.

supply The amount of goods available in the market to be sold at a given price. The term often is coupled with *demand.*

surety bail bond A pledge of real estate instead of cash as security for bail.

surety bond An agreement by an insurance or bonding company to be responsible for certain possible defaults, debts, or obligations contracted for by an insured party; in essence, a policy insuring one's personal and/or financial integrity. In the real estate business a surety bond generally is used to ensure that a particular project will be completed at a certain date or that a contract will be performed as stated.

surface rights Ownership rights in a parcel of real estate that are limited to the surface of the property and do not include the air above it (*air rights*) or the minerals below the surface (*subsurface rights*).

survey The process by which boundaries are measured and land areas are determined; the onsite measurement of lot lines, dimensions, and position of a house on a lot, including the determination of any existing encroachments or easements.

syndicate A combination of people or firms formed to accomplish a business venture of mutual interest by pooling resources. In a *real estate investment syndicate*, the parties own and/or develop property with the main profit generally arising from the sale of the property.

tacking Adding or combining successive periods of continuous occupation of real property by adverse possessors. This strategy enables someone who has not been in possession for the entire statutory period to establish a claim of adverse possession.

taxation The process by which a government or municipal quasi-public body raises monies to fund its operation.

tax basis The amount on which future gain is measured. Also the amount of remaining depreciation.

tax credit An amount by which tax owed is reduced directly.

tax deed An instrument, similar to a certificate of sale, given to a purchaser at a tax sale. *See also* certificate of sale.

tax levy *See* levy.

tax lien A charge against property created by operation of law. Tax liens and assessments take priority over all other liens.

tax rate The rate at which real property is taxed in a tax district or county. For example, in a certain county, real property may be taxed at a rate of .056 cents per $1 of assessed valuation.

tax sale A court-ordered sale of real property to raise money to cover delinquent taxes.

tax shelter A (legal) means by which an investor may reduce or defer payment of part of his or her federal income tax.

tenancy at sufferance The tenancy of a lessee who lawfully comes into possession of a landlord's real estate but who continues to occupy the premises improperly after his or her lease rights have expired.

tenancy at will An estate that gives the lessee the right to possession until the estate is terminated by either party; the term of this estate is indefinite.

tenancy in common A form of co-ownership by which each owner holds an undivided interest in real property as if he or she were sole owner. Each individual owner has the right to partition. Unlike joint tenants, tenants in common have no right of survivorship.

tenant One who holds or possesses lands or tenements by any kind of right or title.

testate Having made and left a valid will.

testator A person who makes a last will and testament.

Texas Commission on Human Rights The organization authorized to receive, investigate, and seek to conciliate complaints of violations of the Texas Fair Housing Act.

Texas Deceptive Trade Practices—Consumer Protection Act (DTPA) Makes it illegal to use false, misleading, or deceptive acts or practices in the advertising, offering for sale, selling, or leasing of any real or personal property. The act provides for civil penalties and, in some cases, for mandatory triple damages and attorney fees for the aggrieved party.

Texas Department of Housing and Community Affairs A Texas governmental agency that has financing programs to help low-income and moderate-income families acquire housing.

Texas Fair Housing Act A "substantially equivalent" fair housing law that allows complaints to be heard by the Texas Commission on Human Rights or in state courts.

Texas Real Estate Broker-Lawyer Committee A committee that drafts and revises standard contract forms to be used by real estate licensees.

Texas Real Estate Commission (TREC) A group of people appointed by the governor to set policy in implementing the license act.

Texas Real Estate License Act The statute that controls the licensing of persons permitted to practice real estate brokerage in Texas.

Texas Veterans Home Improvement Program This program assists Texas veterans in the repair and improvement of their principal residence by providing low-interest home improvement loans.

Texas Veterans Housing Assistance Program (VHAP) Established by a constitutional amendment in 1984, the VHAP assists Texas veterans in the purchase of a principal residence.

Texas Veterans Land Program Established to assist Texas veterans to buy land with a small down payment and with long-term mortgages with low interest rates.

time is of the essence A phrase in a contract that requires the strict performance of a certain act within a stated time frame.

time-sharing A form of ownership where permission is given to use certain property for certain intervals of time. Variations can create an additional interest in title.

title 1. The right to or ownership of land. 2. The evidence of ownership of land.

title insurance A policy insuring the owner or mortgagee against loss by reason of defects in the title to a parcel of real estate, other than encumbrances, defects, and matters specifically excluded by the policy.

title search An examination of the public records to determine what, if any, defects there are in the chain of title; usually performed by a title company or abstracter.

title theory Some states' interpretation of a mortgage to mean that the lender is the owner of mortgaged land. On full payment of the mortgage debt, the borrower becomes the landowner; not recognized in Texas.

township line Lines running at six-mile intervals parallel to the base lines in the rectangular survey (government survey) system.

township square The principal unit of the rectangular survey (government survey) system. A township is a square with six-mile sides and an area of 36 square miles.

township tier A strip of land running east and west in the government (rectangular) survey system.

trade fixture Article installed by a tenant under the terms of a lease and removable by the tenant before the lease expires. These remain personal property and are not true fixtures.

TREC Texas Real Estate Commission.

trust A fiduciary arrangement whereby property is conveyed by a *trustor* to a person or institution, called a *trustee*, to be held and administered on behalf of another person, called a *beneficiary*.

trust account *See* commingle.

trust deed A deed of trust.

trustee *See* trust.

trustee's deed A deed executed by a trustee conveying land held in a trust.

trustor *See* trust.

undivided interest *See* tenancy in common.

unenforceable contract A contract that has all the elements of a valid contract, yet neither party can sue the other to force performance of it. For example, an unsigned contract is generally unenforceable.

Uniform Commercial Code A codification of commercial law, adopted in most states, that attempts to make uniform all laws relating to commercial transactions, including chattel mortgages and bulk transfers. Security interests in chattels are created by an instrument known as a *security agreement.* To give notice of the security interest, a *financing statement* must be recorded. Article 6 of the code regulates *bulk transfers*—the sale of a business as a whole, including all fixtures, chattels, and merchandise.

Uniform Settlement Statement A form required by RESPA for the closing of certain real estate transactions; the "HUD-1" form.

unilateral contract A one-sided contract wherein one party makes a promise in order to induce a second party to do something. The second party is not legally bound to perform; however, if the second party does comply, the first party is obligated to keep the promise.

unity of ownership The four unities that traditionally are needed to create a joint tenancy—unity of title, time, interest, and possession.

urban renewal The acquisition of rundown city areas for purposes of redevelopment.

useful life In real estate investment, the number of years a property will be useful to the investors.

usury Charging interest at a rate higher than the maximum rate established by state law.

valid contract A contract that complies with all the essentials of a contract and is binding and enforceable on all parties to it.

VA loan A mortgage loan on approved property made to a qualified veteran by an authorized lender and guaranteed by the Department of Veterans Affairs to limit the lender's possible loss.

value The power of a good or service to command other goods in exchange for the present worth of future rights to its income or amenities.

vara In Texas, a measurement of length; one vara equals 33⅓ inches.

variable-rate mortgage A mortgage loan in which the interest rate may increase or decrease at specified intervals within certain limits, based on an economic indicator.

variance Permission obtained from zoning authorities to build a structure or conduct a use that is expressly prohibited by the current zoning laws; an exception to the zoning ordinances.

vendee A buyer.

vendee's lien A buyer's claim against a seller's property when the seller has not delivered title to the buyer, as in an installment contract or contract for deed.

vendor A seller.

vendor's lien The equitable lien of the grantor upon the land conveyed, in the amount of the unpaid purchase price.

voidable contract A contract that seems to be valid on the surface but may be rejected or disaffirmed by one or both parties.

void contract A "contract" that has no legal force or effect because it does not meet the essential elements of a contract and therefore is not a contract.

volume The size in cubic units (cubic inches, etc.) of a three-dimensional figure such as a cube.

voluntary alienation *See* alienation.

voluntary lien A lien that arises because of actions permitted by a person, such as when signing a deed of trust or mortgage.

warehousing agency An agency that purchases a number of mortgage loans and assembles them into one or more packages of loans for resale to investors; Fannie Mae, Freddie Mac, and Ginnie Mae are warehousing agencies.

warranty clause The part of a deed in which the seller warrants the title conveyed to the buyer.

warranty deed A deed in which the grantor fully warrants good clear title to the premises. Used in most real estate deed transfers, a warranty deed offers the greatest protection of any deed.

waste An improper use or an abuse of a property by a possessor who holds less than fee ownership, such as a tenant, life tenant, mortgagor, or vendee. Such waste generally impairs the value of the land or the interest of the person holding the title or the reversionary rights.

will A document providing for the transfer of title to property owned by the deceased, called the *testator*. *See* formal will and holographic will.

workers' compensation acts State legislation requiring a fund to provide income to a worker who is hurt on the job.

wraparound mortgage A method of refinancing in which the new mortgage is placed in a secondary, or subordinate, position; the new mortgage includes both the unpaid principal balance of the first mortgage and whatever additional sums are advanced by the lender. If the lender is the seller, such sum is not "advanced" but rather carried back as a part of the purchase money. In essence, it is an additional mortgage in which another lender refinances a borrower by lending an amount over the existing first mortgage amount without disturbing the existence of the first mortgage.

writ of execution A court order that authorizes and directs a designated officer of the court (usually the sheriff) to carry into effect the judgment or decree of the court.

year-to-year tenancy A periodic tenancy in which rent is collected yearly.

zero lot line A term generally used to describe the positioning of a structure on a lot so that one side rests directly on the lot's boundary line (no setback). Where allowed by zoning, a zero lot line is used for "garden homes."

zoning board of adjustment Group established to hear complaints about the effects of zoning ordinances on specific parcels of property.

zoning ordinance An exercise of police power by a municipality to regulate and control the character and use of property.

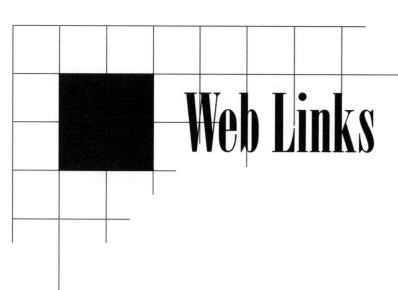

Web Links

WEB LINKS BY CHAPTER

Chapter 1
www.nar.realtor.com
   National Association of REALTORS®

Chapter 2
www.hud.gov
   Department of Housing and Urban
   Development (HUD)

Chapter 4
www.fema.gov
   Federal Emergency Management Agency
   (FEMA)
http://recenter.tamu.edu
   Real Estate Center

Housing affordability sites:
www.homeadvisor.com
www.homepath.com
www.mbaa.org/consumer
http://realestate.yahoo.com
www.realtor.com

Chapter 6
www.hud.gov
www.usdoj.gov/crt/housing
   Fair Housing (administered by HUD)

Chapter 7
www.trec.state.tx.us
   Texas Real Estate Commission (TREC)

Chapter 8
www.capitol.state.tx.us
   Texas Legislature (bills)

Chapter 13
www.hud.gov/offices/lead
   HUD lead-based paint
www.txdps.state.tx.us
   Texas Department of Public Safety

Chapter 14
www.talcb.state.tx.us

Chapter 16
www.fanniemae.com
   Fannie Mae
www.fsa.usda.gov
   Farm Service Agency (FSA)
www.freddiemac.com
   Freddie Mac
www.ginniemae.gov
   Ginnie Mae
www.tdhca.state.tx.us
   Texas Department of Housing and Community
   Affairs
www.glo.state.tx.us
   Texas Veterans Land Board

Loan qualifying sites:
www.homeloans.va.gov (VA loans)
www.homepath.com (Fannie Mae loans)
www.hud.gov/qualify.cfm (FHA loans)
www.mortgagequotes.lycos.com/calc.html

Chapter 20
www.hud.gov/fha/sfh/res/respa_hm.html
   Real Estate Settlement Procedures Act

Chapter 21
www.taa.org
   Texas Apartment Association

Chapter 23
www.epa.gov
   Environmental Protection Agency (EPA)
www.tnrcc.state.tx.us
   Texas Natural Resource Conservation Commission

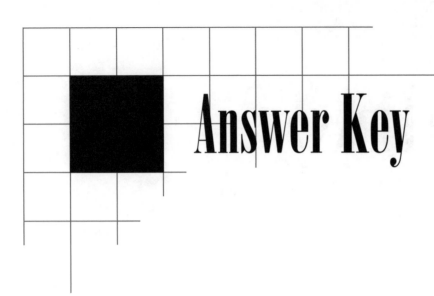

Answer Key

**Chapter 1
Introduction to
Modern Real Estate
Practice**

1. d
2. d
3. c
4. c
5. a
6. c
7. c
8. c
9. c
10. d
11. a
12. a

**Chapter 2
Real Property**

1. d
2. b
3. c
4. b
5. b
6. d
7. b
8. b
9. c
10. c
11. b
12. b

13. d
14. c
15. a
16. b
17. b
18. a

**Chapter 3
The Real Estate
Market**

1. c
2. a
3. c
4. a
5. c
6. c
7. d
8. c
9. a
10. c
11. d
12. d
13. c
14. b

**Chapter 4
Concepts of Home
Ownership**

1. d
2. d
3. b

4. d
5. d
6. a
7. b
8. a
9. c
10. d
11. a
12. c
13. b
14. d
15. a
16. b

**Chapter 5
Real Estate
Brokerage and the
Law of Agency**

1. a
2. b
3. b
4. c
5. b
6. c
7. b
8. b
9. b

10. a
11. c
12. c
13. a
14. b

**Chapter 6
Fair Housing Laws
and Ethical
Practices**

1. b
2. a
3. c
4. c
5. c
6. b
7. a
8. d
9. c
10. b
11. c
12. d
13. a
14. c
15. c
16. a
17. b

Chapter 7
Texas Real Estate License Act

Analysis Form

1. 1949

2. 2001

3.

Broker	**Salesperson**
a. 18 years	18 years
b. day of filing	day of filing
c. two years as licensed salesperson	—
d. 900 classroom hours	180 classroom hours
e. yes	yes
f. $10	$10

4. Auction, sell, exchange, purchase, rent, assist in procuring prospects, assist in finding listings, appraise, collect rents, subdivide, trade, lease, buy, buy easements, inspect property condition, locate renters

5. A real estate broker includes any person or corporation who for another person and in expectation of receiving a compensation does any action listed in Question 4, as checked.

6. Any person employed by or engaged by a licensed real estate broker to do any of the actions that a broker is licensed to perform

7. a. Any person who does not engage in the activities of a real estate broker as an occupation
    b. An owner and his or her regular employees who do not conduct or appear to conduct a real estate brokerage business
    c. An attorney-in-fact authorized to finally consummate an owner's transaction
    d. An attorney at law
    e. An escrow holder, receiver, trustee in bankruptcy, administrator, executor, person acting under order of court, trustee under trust agreement, deed of trust or will or the regular salaried employee thereof, or public officer or employee while performing duties as such
    f. On-site manager of an apartment complex
    g. Sale of cemetery lots
    h. Transactions involving mining and mineral interests
    i. A person who conducts a real estate auction
    j. Transactions involving renting, leasing, or managing a hotel or motel
    k. A partnership or limited liability partnership acting as a broker through a partner who is licensed

9.

Broker	**Salesperson**
a. $100*	$50
b. $100	$100
c. $100*	$50
d. $20	—
e. $20	$20
f. $20	$20
g. $20	$17.50
h. $20	$20

Increased by a $200 tax under Section 11A.

9. a. Two years from date of issue after postlicensing requirements have been satisfied.
    b. The expiration date on the license

10. List any seven reasons cited in Sections 15 and 16; among those:
    a. Accepting an undisclosed rebate or profit on an expenditure for a principal
    b. Acting in the dual capacity of broker and an undisclosed principal in any transaction
    c. Pursuing a continued and flagrant course of misrepresentation
    d. Making false promises through salespersons, advertising, and so on
    e. Acting for more than one party without the approval of all parties
    f. Failing to remit or account for funds belonging to others
    g. Using misleading advertising or an ad without the broker's name
    h. Misusing the term REALTOR® or other insignia of membership
    i. Procuring license by fraud; filing a fraudulent application
    j. Willfully disregarding or violating any provisions of the act
    k. Paying a commission to any unlicensed person in violation of the act
    l. Inducing a party to break a sales contract or lease to substitute a new one
    m. Being convicted of a felony
    n. Displaying a "for sale" sign without the seller's proper written authority
    o. Knowingly preparing an inaccurate statement or invoice
    p. Dishonest dealings, bad faith, untrustworthiness, or incompetency in conduct
    q. Employing unlicensed salespersons by any means or methods
    r. Discrimination on the basis of race, color, religion, sex, handicap, familial status, or national origin
    s. Unlawfully practicing law
    t. Commingling funds of others with his or her own
    u. Failing to deposit the money of others in an escrow or trustee account within a reasonable time
    v. Failing to advise a purchaser in writing to have the abstract examined or to obtain a title insurance policy

11. **Class A misdemeanor:**
    Punishable by a fine up to $4,000 or imprisonment for up to one year or both

12. Nine members; staggered term of six years

13. Section 12 of the act requires that every licensed real estate broker maintain a definite place of business in this state and to display therein his or her license and those of the salespeople.

14. Section 13 provides that the broker shall immediately return the salesperson's license to the commission. Notice of termination of sponsorship must be in writing—from the broker or from the salesperson. It may be activated for a new sponsoring broker upon payment of the transfer fee of $20.

15. Section 16 defines the unauthorized practice of law: For consideration, reward, or monetary benefit, a licensee drew a deed, note, deed of trust, or other written instrument that may transfer or affect title to real estate; does not include completion of promulgated contract forms.

16. The Recovery Fund (Section 8) is established by a $10 deposit from each broker and salesperson licensee to reimburse aggrieved persons who suffer actual damages by reason of acts committed by a licensed broker or salesperson, provided recovery is ordered by a court of competent jurisdiction. Limits are $50,000 for claims arising out of the same transaction and $100,000 for claims against any one licensee.

    When recovery is ordered by a court against a licensed broker or salesperson and the licensee cannot pay the full amount of the judgment ordered by the court, the aggrieved person may apply to the court in which the judgment was entered for an order directing payment out of the real estate recovery fund of the amount unpaid on the judgment.

17. Apprentice Inspector: none

Real Estate Inspector: not less than 90 classroom hours of core real estate inspection courses Professional Inspector: not less than 120 classroom hours of core real estate inspection courses, plus 8 classroom hours related to standards of professional practice.

The commission may suspend or revoke a registration or license if an inspector: accepts an assignment on which the fee is contingent upon specific findings by the inspector; acts in a dishonest or fraudulent manner; performs an inspection in a negligent manner; acts in the dual capacity of inspector and undisclosed principal; acts in the dual capacity of inspector and real estate broker or salesperson; performs or agrees to perform repairs for a property inspected; or violates the rules of the commission or the TRELA.

18. The Broker-Lawyer Committee has 12 members: 6 appointed by the Texas Real Estate Commission and 6 appointed by the President of the State Bar of Texas. The primary function of the committee is to prepare contract forms, including special addenda, which are presented to the Commission for possible approval or promulgation. (Section 16)

19. As a condition for the first, second, and third renewals of a salesperson license (SAE requirement), the applicant shall furnish proof of completing at least 2 additional semester hours (30 classroom hours) each year. Real estate core requirements are 10 total hours of core by the first renewal, 12 hours by the second renewal, and 14 hours by the third renewal.

Persons who have completed SAE requirements must furnish proof of completing at least 15 classroom hours of Mandatory Continuing Education (MCE) during the two-year period preceding license renewal; at least 6 hours must be on legal topics approved by the commission. Some exemptions apply to the MCE requirements. They apply to persons holding a broker's license for at least ten years as of September 1, 1991, whose principal place of business on June 1, 1991, was located in a county with a population of 225,000 or less, and who paid a fee to opt out by October 30, 1991.

Chapter 7 Questions (continued)

1. c
2. b
3. a
4. d
5. b
6. d
7. b
8. a
9. b
10. c
11. b
12. a
13. b
14. a
15. c
16. d
17. b

Chapter 8 Interests in Real Estate

1. b
2. b
3. b
4. a
5. a
6. c
7. d
8. b
9. c
10. d
11. b
12. a
13. c
14. a
15. a
16. a
17. b
18. d

Chapter 9 How Ownership Is Held

1. a
2. b
3. d
4. d
5. a
6. b

7. c
8. c
9. a
10. a
11. b
12. b
13. c
14. b
15. a
16. c
17. a
18. a
19. b
20. c
21. c
22. c

Chapter 10 Legal Descriptions

1. b
2. d
3. b
4. b
5. c
6. c

7. c
8. b
9. d
10. d
11. c
12. b
13. d
14. a
15. a
16. a
17. c
18. c
19. c
20. c
21. c
22. b
23. b

Chapter 11 Real Estate Taxes and Other Liens

1. c
2. c
3. c
4. c

5. b
6. b
7. b
8. c
9. c
10. c
11. b
12. d
13. b
14. b
15. d
16. c
17. b
18. b
19. b
20. a
21. d

Chapter 12
Real Estate
Contracts

1. c
2. c
3. a
4. d
5. d
6. b
7. c
8. b
9. b
10. a
11. b
12. d
13. b
14. d
15. b
16. c
17. a
18. b
19. a
20. d
21. b
22. d
23. b
24. a

Chapter 13
Listing Agreements

1. a
2. c
3. a
4. c
5. c

6. b
7. b
8. a
9. c
10. a
11. b
12. b
13. b
14. c
15. b

Chapter 14
Real Estate
Appraisal

1. b
2. b
3. b
4. a
5. d
6. a
7. b
8. b
9. a
10. c
11. b
12. c
13. a
14. b
15. c
16. d
17. a
18. d
19. b
20. a
21. c
22. b

Chapter 15
Real Estate
Financing:
Principles

1. a
2. d
3. b
4. c
5. b
6. b
7. b
8. b
9. a
10. d
11. d
12. b

13. a
14. b
15. c
16. a

Chapter 16
Real Estate
Financing: Practice

1. b
2. a
3. b
4. c
5. d
6. d
7. a
8. b
9. b
10. d
11. c
12. d
13. b
14. b
15. c
16. b
17. b
18. b
19. b
20. b
21. c

Chapter 17
Transfer of Title

1. c
2. a
3. d
4. a
5. c
6. b
7. a
8. b
9. b
10. a
11. a
12. b
13. c
14. b
15. d
16. d
17. b
18. b
19. a

Chapter 18
Title Records

1. b
2. b
3. c
4. a
5. d
6. b
7. c
8. b
9. d
10. a
11. b
12. a
13. d
14. a
15. a
16. c
17. a
18. a

Chapter 19
Real Estate Mathematics

1. c $4,350 due at closing

100% Total Value – 90% Loan = 10% Down Payment

Down Payment (Part) = ?	
$88,500 (Total)	10% = 0.1 (Rate)

$88,500 (Total) × 0.1 (Rate) = $8,850 Down Payment
$8,850 Down Payment – $4,500 Earnest Money = **$4,350 due at closing**

2. b $88,100 original cost

100% Total Original Cost + 12% Profit = 112% Sales Price

$98,672 Sales Price (Part)	
Original Cost (Total) = ?	112% = 1.12 (Rate)

$98,672 (Part) ÷ 1.12 (Rate) = **$88,100 (original cost)**

3. c 27 percent

$80,000 + $87,500 + $87,500 = $255,000 Invested by Three People
$350,000 – $255,000 = $95,000 Fourth Investor's Share

$95,000 (Part)	
$350,000 (Total)	Rate = ?

$95,000 (Part) ÷ $350,000 (Total) = 0.2714 = **27% fourth investor's share**

4. b $40,843.83 principal balance

$391.42 Monthly Interest × 12 = $4,697.04 Annual Interest

$4,697.04 Annual Interest (Part)		
Principal (Total) = ?	11½% = 0.115 (Rate)	1 Year (Time)

$4,697.04 (Part) ÷ [0.115 (Rate) × 1 (Time)] = **$40,843.83 principal balance**

5. d $135.38 monthly taxes

Annual Taxes (Part) = ?	
$95,000 (Total)	$1.71 ÷ 100 = 0.0171 (Rate)

$95,000 (Total) × $0.0171 (Rate) = $1,624.50 Annual Taxes
$1,624.50 ÷ 12 = **$135.38 monthly taxes**

6. c $1,194.00 total cost

Concrete:
4″ ÷ 12 = 0.333′
15′ × 40′ × 0.333′ = 199.8 Cubic Feet ÷ 27 = 7.4 Cubic Yards
7.4 Cubic Yards × $60/Cubic Yard = $444 Concrete Cost
Labor:
15′ × 40′ = 600 Square Feet × $1.25/Square Foot = $750 Labor Cost
$444 Concrete Cost + $750 Labor Cost = **$1,194.00 total cost**

7. d $51,000 sales price

$47,300 Net to Seller + $1,150 Closing Costs = $48,450 Net after Commission
100% (Total Rate) – 5% (Commission Rate) = 95% Net after Commission

$48,450 Net after Commission (Part)	
Sales Price (Total) = ?	95% = 0.95 (Rate)

$48,450 (Part) ÷ .95 (Rate) = **$51,000 sales price**

8. d $652.08 average monthly rent

$75,000 Gross Annual Sales - $50,000 = $25,000 Annual Sales Subject to 2.5%

Annual Percentage Rent (Part) = ?	
$25,000 (Total)	2.5% = 0.025 (Rate)

$25,000 (Total) × 0.025 (Rate) = $625 Annual Percentage Rent
$625 ÷ 12 = $52.08 Monthly Percentage Rent
$600 Monthly Minimum Rent + $52.08 Monthly Percentage Rent = **$652.08 average monthly rent**

9. a $657 commission to Janice

Total Commission (Part) = ?	
$73,000 Sales Price (Total)	6% = 0.06 (Rate)

$73,000 (Total) × .06 (Rate) = $4,380 Total Commission (Part)
$4,380 ÷ 2 = $2,190 Broker's Share of the Commission

Commission to Janice (Part) = ?	
$2,190 Broker's Commission (Total)	30% = 0.3 (Rate)

$2,190 (Total) × 0.3 (Rate) = $657 commission to Janice

10. a $127.11 interest proration (credit buyer; debit seller)

Step 1: Calculate the daily rate.
$43,580 (Total) × 10½% (Rate) × 1/12 (Time) = $381.325 Month's Interest
$381.325 ÷ 30 = $12.711 Day's Interest

Step 2: Calculate time.
August 1 through August 10 = 10 days

Step 3: Multiply the daily amount by the number of days.
$12.711 × 10 = **$127.11 interest proration**

11. c $5,512.50 for points

2.5 Points Loan Discount + 1 Point Origination Fee = 3.5 Points

Loan Amount (Part) = ?	
$175,000 Sales Price (Total)	90% = 0.9 (Rate)

$175,000 (Total) × 0.9 (Rate) = $157,500 Loan Amount (Part)

Points (Part) = ?	
$157,500 Loan Amount (Total)	3.5% = 0.035 (Rate)

$157,500 (Total) × 0.035 (Rate) = **$5,512.50 for points**

12. b $316.67 interest

Interest (Part) = ?		
$5,000 Loan (Total)	9½%= 0.095 (Rate)	⁸⁄₁₂ Time*

$5,000 (Total) × 0.095 (Rate) × 8 months ÷12 = **$316.67 interest**

*When the "time fraction" would convert to a "repeating decimal" (for example, 8 ÷ 12 = 0.6666666), don't convert the fraction to a decimal. Multiply the Total by the Rate and then by the fraction's numerator; then divide by the denominator.

13. b $502.22 tax proration
Step 1: Calculate monthly and daily rates.
$1,282 Annual Tax ÷ 365 = $3.512 Daily Tax

Step 2: Calculate time.
Seller owes the Buyer for January 1 through May 23 =
(J=31) + (F=28) + (M=31) + (A=30) + (M=23) = 143 days

Step 3: Multiply daily rates by the number of days.
$3.512 × 143 days = **$502.22 tax proration**

14. b $1,197.92 monthly net operating income

Annual Net Operating Income (Part) = ?	
$115,000 Investment (Total)	12½% = 0.125 (Rate)

$115,000 (Total) × 0.125 (Rate) = $14,375 Annual Net Operating Income
$14,375 ÷ 12 = **$1,197.92 monthly net operating income**

15. b 9% annual interest rate

$450 Semiannual Interest (Part)		
$10,000 Loan (Total)	Rate = ?	⁶⁄₁₂ = 0.5 (Time)

$450 (Part) ÷ [$10,000 (Total) × 0.5 (Time)] = 0.09 = **9% annual interest rate**

16. b $571,500 price

$68,580 Annual Net Operating Income (Part)	
Price (Total)	12% = 0.12 (Rate)

$68,580 (Part) ÷ 0.12 (Rate) = **$571,500 price**

17. b $80,000 sales price

$5,200 Commission (Part)	
Sales Price (Total)	6.5% = 0.065 (Rate)

$5,200 (Part) ÷ 0.065 = **$80,000 sales price**

18. a $2,072 monthly PITI payment
$60,000 Annual Salary ÷ 12 = $5,000 Bill's Monthly Salary + $2,400 Betty's Monthly Salary = $7,400 Total Monthly Salary

Monthly PITI Payment (Part)	
$7,400 Monthly Salary (Total)	28% = 0.28 (Rate)

$7,400 (Total) × .28 (Rate) = **$2,072 monthly PITI payment**

19. c 30% rate of profit

$10,500 + $93,000 = $103,500 Cost of the Home

$134,550 Sales Price – $103,500 Cost of the Home = $31,050 Profit

$$\frac{\$31{,}050 \text{ Profit (Part)}}{\$103{,}500 \text{ Cost (Total)*}} \quad \Big| \quad \text{Rate = ?}$$

$31,050 (Part) ÷ $103,500 (Total) = 0.3 = **30% rate of profit**

*Profit and loss are based on cost or a prior year's figure. For example, to calculate the increase in profit from year 2001 to 2002, Total will be the year 2001 figure.

20. c 940 running feet

125′ + 350′ + 125′ + 350′ – 10′ Gate = **940 running feet**

21. d 27,225 square feet per lot

⅛ = 0.125 for Streets

100 Acres × .125 = 12.5 Acres for Streets

100 Total Acres – 12.5 Acres for Streets = 87.5 Acres for Lots

87.5 Acres for Lots × 43,560 = 3,811,500 Square Feet

3,811,500 Square Feet ÷ 140 Lots = **27,225 square feet per lot**

Chapter 20
Closing the Real
Estate Transaction

1. c
2. a
3. d
4. c
5. b
6. c
7. a
8. c
9. b
10. b
11. c
12. b
13. d
14. a
15. b
16. c
17. d
18. a
19. c
20. a
21. b

Chapter 21
Leases

1. c
2. c
3. c
4. c
5. d
6. b
7. c
8. c
9. a
10. b
11. c
12. d
13. d
14. a
15. a
16. d

Chapter 22
Property
Management

1. b
2. b

3. d
4. c
5. c
6. d
7. d
8. c
9. a
10. a
11. c
12. b
13. d
14. c
15. b
16. c

Chapter 23
Control of Land Use

1. b
2. c
3. b
4. c
5. c
6. a
7. d
8. b

9. b
10. c
11. a
12. a
13. a
14. b
15. a
16. b
17. c
18. c

Chapter 24
Real Estate
Investment

1. a
2. d
3. b
4. c
5. a
6. d
7. b
8. b
9. c
10. a
11. a
12. a

Sample Texas Real Estate Licensing Examination
General Theory Section

1. b		53. d	
2. d		54. d	
3. d		55. c	
4. c		56. d	
5. b		57. c	
6. d		58. c	
7. a		59. a	
8. c		60. b	
9. d		61. a	
10. d		62. d	
11. d		63. a	
12. b		64. a	
13. c		65. a	
14. b		66. d	
15. d		67. c	
16. a		68. a	
17. b		69. c	
18. b		70. a	
19. a		71. d	
20. c		72. c	
21. d		73. b	
22. a		74. c	
23. d		75. b	
24. d			
25. c		**State-Specific**	
26. a		**Section**	
27. a			
28. d		1. a	
29. b		2. d	
30. d		3. d	
31. c		4. b	
32. b		5. c	
33. a		6. a	
34. d		7. d	
35. b		8. a	
36. d		9. d	
37. d		10. a	
38. b		11. c	
39. d		12. b	
40. d		13. d	
41. d		14. c	
42. a		15. b	
43. d		16. b	
44. a		17. c	
45. d		18. b	
46. b		19. a	
47. a		20. d	
48. a		21. b	
49. a		22. a	
50. b		23. d	
51. a		24. b	
52. c		25. c	

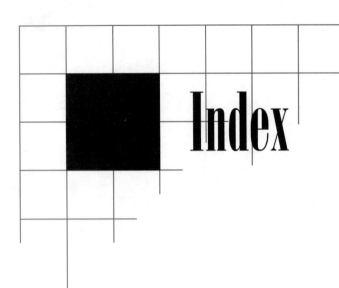

Index